# SELF-HELP THAT WORKS

# SELF-HELP THAT WORKS

Resources to Improve Emotional Health and Strengthen Relationships

FOURTH EDITION

John C. Norcross, PhD
Linda F. Campbell, PhD
John M. Grohol, PsyD
John W. Santrock, PhD
Florin Selagea, MS
Robert Sommer, PhD

Previous editions titled
AUTHORITATIVE GUIDE TO SELF-HELP
RESOURCES IN MENTAL HEALTH

OXFORD
UNIVERSITY PRESS

# OXFORD
UNIVERSITY PRESS

Oxford University Press is a department of the University of Oxford.
It furthers the University's objective of excellence in research, scholarship,
and education by publishing worldwide.

Oxford   New York
Auckland   Cape Town   Dar es Salaam   Hong Kong   Karachi
Kuala Lumpur   Madrid   Melbourne   Mexico City   Nairobi
New Delhi   Shanghai   Taipei   Toronto

With offices in
Argentina   Austria   Brazil   Chile   Czech Republic   France   Greece
Guatemala   Hungary   Italy   Japan   Poland   Portugal   Singapore
South Korea   Switzerland   Thailand   Turkey   Ukraine   Vietnam

Oxford is a registered trademark of Oxford University Press in the UK and certain other
countries.

Published in the United States of America by
Oxford University Press
198 Madison Avenue, New York, NY 10016

Library of Congress Cataloging-in-Publication Data
Self-help that works: resources to improve emotional health and
strengthen relationships / John C. Norcross ... [et al.]. – 4th. ed.
    p. cm.
Previously published under title: Authoritative guide to self-help resources in mental health.
Includes bibliographical references and index.
ISBN 978-0-19-991515-6
1. Mental health—United States—Indexes.   2. Mental illness—United States – Indexes.
3. Mental health services—United States—Directories.   I. Norcross, John C., 1957–
RA790.6.A94 2013
362.1968900973—dc23                              2012024744

ISBN 978-0-19-991515-6

9 8 7 6 5 4 3 2 1
Printed in the United States of America on acid-free paper

# CONTENTS

# PREFACE

A cordial welcome to *Self-Help That Works*. Designed for both the public and the professional, this extensive volume critically reviews self-help—books, autobiographies, films, online programs, support groups, and Internet sites—for 41 behavioral disorders and life challenges. Our admittedly ambitious goal is to guide laypersons in selecting effective self-help resources and to assist mental health professionals in recommending them to their clients. We separate the chaff from the wheat among the tens of thousands of self-help books and websites.

More than a staggering 95% of self-help resources in mental health possess no scientific research attesting to their success (or failure) as a self-help method. Some bestsellers and popular websites even contain advice contradicted by the available research. If FDA approval were required for the usefulness and safety of self-help resources, then we estimate that fewer than 5% would ever be published. Flip through a popular book off the shelf: you'll find lots of testimonials and "amazing stories," but almost never any hard numbers based on controlled research. Author boasts and client anecdotes don't constitute scientific research.

Therein lies our mission: to bring careful research and practitioner expertise to the task of selecting and recommending self-help resources. The popular term these days for that task is *evidence-based practice*, which integrates the best available research with clinical expertise in the context of patient characteristics, culture, and preferences (APA Task Force on Evidence-Based Practice, 2006; Norcross, Hogan, & Koocher, 2008). *Self-Help That Works* brings together, in plain language, scientific research and clinical consensus, secured through a dozen national studies, to publicize and enhance self-help that you can adapt to your goals, preferences, and culture.

## ■ WHAT'S NEW IN THIS EDITION

This edition features a new title, a new publisher, and of course, new and expanded content. After three editions under *Authoritative Guide to Self-Help Resources in Mental Health*, we simplified the title to emphasize our quest to determine what works. *Self-Help That Works* does just that.

We are delighted that this edition will be published by Oxford University Press, inarguably one of the world's largest, oldest, and most prestigious publishers. Oxford brings an unparalleled capacity to place the book in the hands of both laypersons and professionals. At the same time, this book joins their similarly titled, pioneering books *Treatments That*

*Work, Assessments That Work,* and *Psychotherapy Relationships That Work.* All favor balanced, evidence-based means to improve clinical practice and public health.

Since the last edition, the self-help movement has expanded mightily online. Accordingly, we now feature online self-help programs that can be accessed from any connected computer or mobile device. We include only those available to the public with research support for their effectiveness; more will certainly appear in our next edition.

As with each of our previous editions, this book updates the self-help resources launched in the intervening years and expands the content. New chapters focus on autism and Asperger's, bullying, chronic pain, GLB issues, and happiness. Because the earlier chapter on addiction was becoming so lengthy and comprehensive, we split it in half: one chapter is now devoted to substance abuse and another to nonchemical addictions (gambling, sex, Internet). We also divided our concluding chapter on strategies for selecting self-help resources into two: one for consumers evaluating self-help, the other for professionals integrating self-help into treatment. All told, this edition now features 44 chapters that evaluate more than 2,000 self-help books, autobiographies, films, and websites.

# ACKNOWLEDGMENTS

This massive project has required the generous contributions of a number of people over the years. First, we acknowledge the nearly 5,000 clinical and counseling psychologists who took the time from their busy schedules to complete the lengthy questionnaires associated with our dozen national studies. Second, we genuinely appreciate the diligent support of our research assistants at the University of Scranton who shepherded the national studies through their entire development—from gathering prodigious lists of books and films, creating the questionnaires, distributing the questionnaires, to conducting the data analyses. Kavita Shah, Victoria Alogna, and Brian Zaboski survived and thrived throughout the nine-month ordeal. Third, for our most recent studies, we used the email addresses of the National Register of Health Service Providers in Psychology (www.nationalregister.org). We gratefully acknowledge the assistance of Judy Hall and Andrew Boucher, in particular. Fourth, we extend a rousing thanks to the good folks at The Guilford Press, who published the earlier editions of this book. Seymour Weingarten and Kitty Moore translated their enthusiasm for the project into concrete suggestions that improved the product.

We reserve our final expression of collective gratitude to two co-authors on the previous editions: Thomas P. Smith, PsyD, and Edward L. Zuckerman, PhD. Many of your contributions are still reflected in the following pages, and your collaborations are missed, friends. Thank you for participating when you could.

We each would also like to acknowledge those individuals and organizations assisting us personally. John Norcross appreciates the continuing support of the University of Scranton, specifically the Department of Psychology, its award-winning Donna Rupp, the Faculty-Student Research Program, and the Distinguished University Fellowship. Linda Campbell expresses her appreciation to her husband for his continued support and to her departmental colleagues who pursue and value scholarship. John Grohol is thankful for the unwavering support of his wife, Nancy. John Santrock is grateful to his two co-authors on the first edition—Ann Minnett and Barbara Campbell—and to the many students who tracked down books, references, and reviews. Bob Sommer credits Sheila Layton for helping him collect information on many autobiographies. Florin Selagea expresses his deepest thanks to his wife, Rebeca, for her seemingly endless patience, and to John Norcross and Linda Campbell for inviting him to join in the project that produced this wonderful book.

# ABOUT THE AUTHORS

**John C. Norcross, PhD, ABPP,** is Professor of Psychology and Distinguished University Fellow at the University of Scranton, Adjunct Professor of Psychiatry at SUNY Upstate Medical University, and a board-certified clinical psychologist in a part-time practice. Author of more than 300 scholarly publications, Dr. Norcross has co-written or edited 20 books, including *Psychotherapy Relationships That Work, Clinician's Guide to Evidence-Based Practice in Mental Health, Changeology, Insider's Guide to Graduate Programs in Clinical & Counseling Psychology,* and *Systems of Psychotherapy: A Transtheoretical Analysis,* now in its 8th edition. He has served as president of the American Psychological Association (APA) Division of Clinical Psychology and the APA Division of Psychotherapy. Dr. Norcross is also editor of *Journal of Clinical Psychology: In Session* and has been on the editorial boards of a dozen journals. Among his awards are APA's Distinguished Career Contributions to Education & Training Award, Pennsylvania Professor of the Year from the Carnegie Foundation, and election to the National Academies of Practice.

**Linda F. Campbell, PhD,** is a professor and director of the training clinic in the Department of Counseling and Human Development at the University of Georgia. Dr. Campbell recently co-authored the *APA Ethics Code Commentary and Case Illustrations* text and other scholarly publications. She has chaired the APA Ethics Committee and the APA Board of Educational Affairs and served as president of the APA Division of Psychotherapy and the APA Division of State, Provincial, and Territorial State Associations. Dr. Campbell currently serves on the APA Council of Representatives, the APA Policy and Planning Board, and the Georgia State Board of Examiners of Psychologists. She has received multiple awards for her professional contributions, including an APA Presidential Citation for Distinguished Contributions, APA Educational Advocacy Award, Distinguished Psychologist Award from the Division of Psychotherapy, and the University of Georgia Outstanding Teacher Award.

**John M. Grohol, PsyD,** is an expert in online psychology, researcher, author, and CEO and founder of the leading mental health network online, PsychCentral.com. Beginning in 1995, he has developed, designed, and consulted with e-health companies on their mental health resources online, from former Surgeon General C. Everett Koop's drkoop.com to Steve Case's RevolutionHealth.com. In the late 1990s, Dr. Grohol wrote the comprehensive *Insider's Guide to Mental Health Resources Online.* He is a founding board member of the Society for Participatory Medicine and sits on the board of the International Foundation for Research and Education on Depression (iFred), as well as the editorial board of

*Cyberpsychology, Behavior & Social Networking.* In 2011 he received the APA Division 46's Distinguished Professional Contribution to Media Psychology award. Dr. Grohol's PsychCentral.com was recognized by TIME.com as one of the 50 Best Websites of 2008.

**John W. Santrock, PhD,** did his doctoral work at the University of Minnesota. He taught at the University of Charleston and the University of Georgia before joining the psychology department at the University of Texas at Dallas, where he is a professor and former department chair. Dr. Santrock is a leading author of psychology texts, including *Life-Span Development* (13th ed.), *Child Development* (13th ed.), and *Adolescence* (14th ed.). He is the co-author of *Your Guide to College Success.* He has been a member of the editorial boards of *Developmental Psychology* and *Child Development.* Among his honors are a Templeton Foundation Award for Outstanding Contribution to the Study of Psychology and Religion and the Effective Teaching Award from the University of Texas.

**Florin Selagea, MS,** is a doctoral student in counseling psychology at the University of Georgia. He holds a master's degree in professional counseling from Georgia State University and a bachelor's degree in psychology from Michigan State University. He currently chairs the Graduate Student Teaching Association in APA's Division 2, Society for the Teaching of Psychology. He and his wife live in the suburbs of Atlanta, Georgia, together with their two cats, Chairman Meow and Senator Whiskers.

**Robert Sommer, PhD,** is Distinguished Professor of Psychology Emeritus at the University of California, Davis, where he chaired four departments (Psychology, Environmental Design, Rhetoric and Communication, and Art), although not all at the same time. Author of 11 books and numerous articles, he has done research on autobiographies of mental health clients for more than four decades. He is a past president of the American Psychological Association's Division of Population and Environmental Psychology. Dr. Sommer received a Fulbright Fellowship to Estonia, a Career Research Award from the Environmental Design Research Association, a Research Award from the California Alliance for the Mentally Ill, the Kurt Lewin Award, and an honorary doctorate from Tallinn Pedagogical University.

# CHAPTER 1

# SELF-HELP IN MENTAL HEALTH

You have probably heard about or read several of these self-help books:

*Feeling Good* by David Burns
*The Secret* by Rhonda Byrne
*What Color Is Your Parachute?* by Robert Bolles
*Healthy Aging* by Andrew Weil
*Who Moved My Cheese?* by Spencer Johnson
*Dianetics* by L. Ron Hubbard
*Infants and Mothers* by T. Berry Brazelton
*The Courage to Heal* by Ellen Bass and Laura Davis
*Ageless Body, Timeless Mind* by Deepak Chopra
*Battle Hymn of the Tiger Mother* by Amy Chua
*When Bad Things Happen to Good People* by Harold Kushner
*Your Perfect Right* by Robert Alberti and Michael Emmons
*Our Bodies, Ourselves* by Boston Women's Health Collective
*How to Win Friends and Influence People* by Dale Carnegie
*Men Are from Mars, Women Are from Venus* by John Gray
*What to Expect When You're Expecting* by Arlene Eisenberg and others
*5 Love Languages* by Gary Chapman
*The Power of Positive Thinking* by Norman Vincent Peale
*The 7 Habits of Highly Effective People* by Steven Covey
*"Get Out of My Life but First Could You Drive Me and Cheryl to the Mall?"* by Anthony Wolf

You have probably also seen several of the following films on family relationships and mental health topics:

| | |
|---|---|
| *Juno* | *Black Swan* |
| *Slumdog Millionaire* | *Grumpy Old Men* |
| *The Color Purple* | *The Prince of Tides* |
| *Up in the Air* | *Days of Wine and Roses* |
| *The War of the Roses* | *As Good as It Gets* |
| *Last Tango in Paris* | *Brokeback Mountain* |
| *Ordinary People* | *Baby Boom* |
| *Rain Man* | *A Beautiful Mind* |
| *Dead Poets Society* | *The Soloist* |

Each of these books has been at or near the top of national bestseller lists, and each of the films has been seen by millions of people. Are they good self-help books and films? That is, do they provide accurate information? Do they help individuals cope effectively with problems? Are they useful as ancillary resources for psychotherapy? Do they foster personal growth and societal development? The consensus of mental health experts in the United States is that one-third of these books and films are *not* effective self-help resources; even though they were bestsellers and top-grossing films, most experts view them negatively. The other two-thirds of the books and movies on this list are excellent self-help materials. In *Self-Help That Works*, we tell which are the good ones and which are the bad ones, which ones will probably help and which ones are mostly hype.

## ■ SELF-HELP RESOURCES

A massive revolution is occurring in mental health: self-help with or without professional treatment. This self-help revolution entails diverse activities: changing behavior by oneself, reading and applying self-help books, attending support and 12-step groups, watching films and incorporating their cinematic lessons, surfing the Internet for advice and support, completing smartphone applications ("apps") to improve daily behavior, and participating in alternative health care. All these and many other examples compellingly indicate that people are making concerted efforts to change themselves on their own.

Self-help has become an indispensable source of psychological advice for millions of Americans. Whether we want to improve our relationships, control our anger, gain self-fulfillment, overcome depression, become better parents, cope with stress, recover from addictions, or tackle another problem, there is a self-help resource. The affordability, accessibility, anonymity, and efficacy of self-help have much to offer and the potential to reach millions more (Kazdin & Blase, 2011).

What do we mean by *self-help*? The concerted, self-directed attempt to improve behavior without (or with minimal) professional treatment. In a few cases, the definition of self-help is expanded to families, caregivers, and friends when a person (such as a child) is largely incapable of directing his or her own self-help attempt.

Even though *self-help* refers to self-administered efforts often unassisted by professionals, this book is also written for mental health professionals as an ancillary to the services they provide. In this book, our reviews of self-help books, films, and online programs describe their content and themes in ways that professionals can incorporate into treatment. Many of the reviews include sections written for practitioners offering suggestions on using the resource with their clients.

Self-help comes in many guises. In this book, we do not evaluate resources that are primarily religious in nature or medical in content. Our target is self-help for mental health topics: behavioral disorders (such as anxiety, depression, addictions, eating disorders), relationships (parenting, marriage, divorce, families, etc.), and life challenges (aging, career development, people skills, stress management). There are 41 self-help topics in all, traversing the lifespan from infancy to aging and death, and ranging from understanding severe disorders all the way to achieving happiness.

The preoccupation with self-improvement is nothing new; it's been around since the Bible. Benjamin Franklin dispensed self-improvement advice in *Poor Richard's Almanac*: "Early to bed, early to rise, makes a man healthy, wealthy, and wise." In the 19th century, homemakers read *Married Lady's Companion* for help in managing their houses and families. In the 1930s, Dale Carnegie's *How to Win Friends and Influence People* made him the aspiring businessman's guru. They turned out to be only the tip of the iceberg.

Call it (Ralph Waldo) Emersonian self-reliance, the do-it-yourself nation, or the Home Depot effect, but the self-help revolution is upon us. Although health professionals naturally focus on the treatments they provide, the fact of the matter is that self-help is the major pathway to behavior change. In other words, more people change their behavior on their own than with the assistance of treatment. This year, more people will read a self-help book, obtain psychological information on the Web, and attend a self-help group than consult all the mental health professionals (Kessler, Mickelson, & Zhao, 1997).

The advent of popular films, the information revolution, and the ascendancy of the Internet have given rise to a dizzying diversity of self-help resources. The urgent task, then, is to separate the wheat from the chaff. "The trick is knowing which one to read," as a "Dilbert" comic strip put it about the thousands of self-help books. The soaring volume of self-help materials makes the question of quality—which ones will work?—increasingly urgent. Which information and which sites should be trusted?

This book is designed to guide you through this morass of self-help information—and misinformation—by providing quality ratings and concise reviews of six types of self-help: books, autobiographies, films, online programs, Internet sites, and support groups.

## 1. Self-Help Books

The self-help book market has an overwhelming, bewildering array of choices. Self-help books (including parenting advice) appear at the rate of about 5,000 per year (Bogart, 2011), and they routinely occupy prominent places on bestseller lists. But more than 95% of self-help books are published without any research documenting their effectiveness (Rosen, 1987, 1993). Buyers hope that they will work, but we do not have any systematic evidence to indicate that most will.

So how do people select self-help books? Until this book—*Self-Help That Works*—people have largely relied on the opinions of friends, ministers, doctors, therapists, talk shows, or the promotional information on the book's cover. But even personal contact with professionals, such as physicians and psychologists, provides limited information about which book to purchase. Self-help books have been published at such an astonishing pace that even the well-intentioned professional has difficulty keeping up with them. The professional may be well informed about books in one or two areas, such as depression or anxiety, but may know little about books in other areas, such as eating disorders, women's issues, relaxation, and parenting.

With literally thousands of titles on the market, we wanted to know what the leading psychologists in the United States think are the best and the worst self-help books. After all, restaurant critics inform us which restaurants are superb and which ones to avoid; automobile guides educate us about the gems and the lemons; and consumer magazines dispense advice on buying refrigerators, computers, and smartphones. A guide to self-help resources based on professional expertise and the best research is sorely needed. ***This book is that guide.***

The good news from research is that self-help programs can be quite effective. Research reviews have determined that the effectiveness of self-help substantially exceeds that of no treatment and nearly reaches that of professional treatment (e.g., Anderson, Carlbring, & Grimlund, 2008; Menchola, Arkowitz, & Burke, 2007; Cuijpers et al., 2010). For example, in one analysis of the effectiveness of 40 self-help studies, effect sizes for self-help were nearly as large as for therapist-assisted treatments (Gould & Clum, 1993). Fears, depression, headaches, and sleep disturbances were especially amenable to self-help.

Similarly, *bibliotherapy*—a fancy way of describing the use of self-help books—has been shown to be valuable for many adults (Marrs, 1995). Comparable findings have been reported for the effectiveness of self-help books with specific disorders, such as sexual dysfunctions (van Lankveld, 1998), depression (Gregory et al., 2004), anxiety disorders (Weekes, 1996), problem drinking (Apodaca & Miller, 2003; Riper et al., 2011), panic disorder (Carlbring, Westling, & Andersson, 2000), and geriatric depression (Scogin, 1998).

Others have compiled personal recommendations of self-help books (for example, Fried & Schultis, 1995; Joshua & DiMenna, 2000; Zaccaria & Moses, 1968); however, our compilation is unique and, we believe, superior because our ratings are based on the collective wisdom of thousands of mental health experts. In 12 national studies, we asked mental health professionals to rate more than a thousand self-help books. We chose the books to be rated by the experts by examining the shelves of major national bookstore chains, by perusing the wares of large Internet book dealers (Amazon.com, bn.com), by discussing self-help books with psychologists, by consulting the bestseller lists, and by reading numerous articles.

## 2. Autobiographies

The story of a life has been one of the most durable and popular literary forms. What is Facebook (and most blogs) if not a slew of autobiographies in progress?

People love personal, compelling stories of self-transformation. Autobiographies provide an inside view of life's problems, drawing on the human capacity for self-description and self-analysis. Memoirs complement research and case studies performed from the outside looking in. Written in the person's own words, an autobiography emphasizes issues that the writer, as distinct from a psychotherapist or researcher, considers important. Autobiographies describe disorders in their family and environmental context, provide interesting narratives with strong storylines, and in the end typically reveal a successful outcome.

A recent tide of confessions and revelations dominate the bookshelves (and Kindles and Nooks). Borrowing from Freud, Joyce Carol Oates coined the term *pathography* for the profusion of biographies featuring psychopathology. Hundreds of autobiographies by mental health clients provide an inside view of facing life's problems. These memoirs cover virtually all diagnostic categories.

Autobiographical authors and their credentials vary tremendously. Some authors are celebrities, already the subject of public interest; others are writers, poets, and artists capable of portraying their inner worlds in words, songs, and drawings. Many accounts are written by ordinary people whose first contact with publishing is writing about their disorder. Some earlier accounts have become classics in mental health education; other books, by Kay Jamison (*An Unquiet Mind*), William Styron (*Darkness Visible*), and Mark Vonnegut (*The Eden Express*), are likely to become future classics. The books have been used in training mental health professionals and as part of therapy for mental health consumers (Sommer, Clifford, & Norcross, 1998).

The autobiographies listed and evaluated in this book were selected specifically for their availability. Our earlier research articles on autobiographies contained many historical accounts, often very difficult to obtain. For this book, we focused on first-person accounts still in print that covered mental health problems and life challenges. We visited bookstores and checked electronic booksellers to make sure that the book was still available. The date listed is that of the most recent edition, often in paperback. Even so, some books may no longer be available by the time this book is published. However, it is likely that an out-of-print title can be obtained on the used book market.

An autobiographical account presents a personal view of the disorder and its treatment. When an author says that a mood disorder was relieved by Prozac or blames a family member for some transgression, this represents the person's view of the situation. Most of the books listed were written by the person with the disorder, but in a few cases they were written by a family member, which provides yet another perspective on the disorder and its treatment.

The self-help industry is virtually unregulated. Those with the most influence on which autobiographies are published and marketed are the publishers, the owners of large bookstore chains, and a hodgepodge of authors with a vast range of credentials, knowledge, and competencies. We hope our studies and this book exert a corrective influence. Systematic research and informed mental health professionals are superior to the merchandisers.

## 3. Films

Films are a powerful and pervasive part of our culture. The widespread availability of movie theaters, laptop computers, videotapes, and DVDs allows most Americans ready access to movies. Gallup polls indicate that watching movies at home or in the theater is one of adults' favorite pastimes (along with reading, watching television, and participating in family activities). Domestic box-office revenues top, according to *Variety*, a staggering $20 billion for the 100 top-performing films.

Movies frequently touch us emotionally more than books. Psychologist Ken Gergen (1991) observes that movies have become one of the most influential rhetorical devices in the world: "Films can catapult us rapidly and effectively into states of fear, anger, sadness, romance, lust, and aesthetic ecstasy—often within the same two-hour period. It is undoubtedly true that for many people film relationships provide the most emotionally wrenching experiences of the average week" (pp. 56–57).

Films possess a number of advantages over books and computers as sources of information about mental health. Films are fun to watch, require only a small investment of time, appeal to more people than reading, and are already part of many clients' usual routines. Instead of spending days or weeks reading a book, people get the thrust in a few hours. As a result, people may be more interested in watching movies, which are more accessible, fun, and familiar than reading a book or a computer screen.

Watching movies for therapeutic benefit—call it *videotherapy, cinema treatment,* or *reel therapy*—is a hot prescription in mental health these days. The use of films for treatment purposes can be traced back to the 1930s, but more and more professionals recommend specific films to enhance the effects of treatment. The objectives of doing so are to educate, inspire, motivate, and promote growth.

We are not the first to recommend particular films to enhance self-help, but we may well be the most systematic. Several mental health professionals have penned fine compilations of popular movies to use in understanding psychopathology (Wedding, Boyd, & Niemiec, 2010), to use in psychotherapy (Hesley & Hesley, 2001), to help with life's problems (Solomon, 1995), and to illustrate how psychiatry is depicted in the American cinema (Gabbard & Gabbard, 1999). But all of their books essentially present the opinions of one or two individuals. By contrast, here in *Self-Help That Works* we present the consensus of nearly 5,000 mental health experts.

In preparation for our national studies, we compiled a large list of healing films by reviewing movie books (including those listed above), tracking the top-grossing films, examining earlier research (e.g., Lampropoulos et al., 2004), and throwing in some of our personal favorites. We also used the excellent Internet Movie Database (www.imdb.com)

and Amazon.com to search for reviews. We conducted small pilot studies of colleagues to identify films that a sizable proportion had actually seen. The result was a list of popular, commercially available films that have played in theaters or, in a few cases, only on television. These were then evaluated by thousands of psychologists.

A superb film does not necessarily translate into superb self-help. As one of our experts wrote, "Just because a film has a character who is mentally ill doesn't make it helpful to a client with a similar illness." *High Anxiety* and *What About Bob?* were hilarious movies about anxiety, and *First Wives' Club* and *The War of the Roses* about divorce, but the experts certainly do not recommend them for personal or relational growth. Keep in mind that the movies are rated for their effectiveness as self-help.

The movies portray healing stories. The best of them typically increase awareness about a disorder or treatment; *As Good as It Gets* comes immediately to mind for its accurate and humorous depiction of obsessive–compulsive disorder (OCD). *Slumdog Millionaire* portrays chronic poverty better than any book but also inspires with the boy's ability to transcend poverty and abuse. The best also show flawed yet effective role models struggling realistically with problems and ultimately resolving them; two cases in point are *The Color Purple* about overcoming childhood abuse and *On Golden Pond* about accepting the ravages of aging and healing family rifts. The favorably rated films typically generate hope and inspiration and perhaps give a new perspective on ourselves and our relationships.

### 4. Online Self-Help

Online apps and programs represent the newest additions to self-help. Most of these resources were developed in the past five years. Recent changes in technology—the improved capabilities of personal computers and the widespread availability of high-speed Internet connections—helped to overcome previous limitations. Newer computers and smartphones can handle the demands of multimedia presentations and interactive components. Quick Internet service means that we no longer require a CD-ROM or other program disk. Now, we can access most Web-based self-help from any connected laptop, tablet, or smartphone. This edition of *Self-Help That Works* features these online self-help programs.

Online or computerized self-help is available for many behavioral disorders and life challenges. Compared to a book with the same content, online self-help confers at least five advantages: greater interactivity, improved public access, more tailoring to the user's needs, quicker updates to the content, and ease of completing research studies on their use (Marks, Cavanagh, & Gega, 2007).

In the tradition of evidence-based practice, we decided to include only those online programs available to the public with research support for their effectiveness as self-help. That early research on the effectiveness of Internet-based self-help (sometimes with brief therapist contact) for anxiety, depression, and substance abuse is quite promising (e.g., Andersson & Cuijpers, 2009; Barak, Hen, Boniel-Nissim, & Shapira, 2008; Gallego & Emmelkamp, 2011; Richards & Richardson, 2012; Riper et al., 2011).

Locating these resources poses a challenge. There are still relatively few research-supported self-help resources; most Internet searches take you to online counseling, a treatment center, or informational website. Three sources that were especially helpful to us were *Self-help Resources in Mental Health* (Harwood & L'Abate, 2010), *Hands-on Help: Computer-aided Psychotherapy* (Marks, Cavanagh, & Gega, 2007), and Beacon (beacon.anu.edu.au). The books contain descriptions and research findings for a large number of computerized and Internet-based self-help programs. The Beacon website provides a peer-reviewed portal to online applications for mental disorders. A shout-out to our colleagues in the United Kingdom, particularly Australia, who are far more advanced than the United States in promoting research-supported online self-help.

Sadly, only a few online programs have moved from academic research to a commercial product available to the public. Of course, research trials are ongoing, and more programs are being developed as apps for smart phones. Smartphones are far more convenient than computers because they are small, portable, integral to our activities, and with many of us virtually all of the time. Future editions of this book will certainly include these rapidly evolving technologies.

If a website is largely for education, referral, and/or screening, then it falls under Internet Resources, as described in the next section. But many online programs and apps now offer a psychoeducational treatment or self-guided help. These belong in this new section of Online Self-Help. They typically fall into three categories: self-guided Web-based help; peer-mediated Web-based help; and professional-supported Web-based help (minimal therapist contact of, say, a maximum of two hours).

Our criteria for recommending Online Self-Help differ from those used in other book sections, which rely on professional expertise; here, we insist on demonstrated effectiveness in empirical research. Thus, we excluded online programs from the listings if they did not present any scientific research attesting to their effectiveness as standalone self-help. We also did not list online psychotherapy, distance coaching, or transparent commercials. There are thousands of untested commercial products designed to separate you from your money; *be cautious and careful.*

### 5. Internet Resources

The Internet has opened a whole new world for people seeking information and advice. Recent estimates put the number of webpages at between 40 and 50 billion (and growing), and there are online sites for every aspect of human life, emotional support, and psychological suffering. Researchers estimate that 80% of all Internet users have already sought health-care information online (pewinternet.org/Reports/2010/Generations-2010.aspx). And mental health topics are among the most frequently searched topics on the Internet (Davis & Miller, 1999).

The Internet has grown by leaps and bounds since publication of our last edition, and no place do we see this more than in the rise of social networking websites. While such websites are great for keeping in touch with friends and family, they offer limited information, so our focus remains on websites that offer informational and educational resources.

But which sites and which information should be trusted? Internet sites are notoriously unregulated, and their quality varies enormously. Credibility on the Web, unfortunately, is frequently a function of how cool and slick the site looks. Research studies suggest that the quality of mental health sites is variable, and many suffer from flaws in accuracy and specificity (Lissman & Boehnlein, 2001; Reavley & Jorm, 2011).

Gleaning trustworthy information on the Internet is akin to taking a 2-year-old on a walk: the toddler picks up a few attractive pebbles, but also lots of garbage and dirt (Skow, 1999). Professionals may know when inaccurate or misleading content can be dismissed with a click of the mouse, but the average person rarely does.

Although there are no set criteria for how a person should judge a health website, we are informed by the research conducted about finding reliable sources of information, including guides such as the HONCode (www.hon.ch/HONcode/Conduct.html). That means we are primarily looking for websites that are not only relevant to the topic but also show signs of being regularly updated, with dates and author attributions on articles clearly published on the website. We avoid listing websites that lack these features, as it becomes impossible to judge whether the information is updated, accurate, and written by someone with knowledge or personal experience on the subject.

A health professional should personally review the websites we cover in this book because their contents may be inappropriate for some clients, may conflict with a particular treatment plan, or may have changed since the evaluations described herein. Please note that if a URL is hyphenated in the text because it doesn't fit on a single line, you should remove the hyphen when typing the URL into your web browser. Alternatively, you can often find the URL by simply typing the name of the resource into your favorite search engine, such as Google.

In each chapter, Internet sites are listed under these headings:

*General Websites.* These are rich collections of evergreen, library-quality information, as well as links to other online materials on the topic. Laypersons might be overwhelmed by these websites because they may offer hundreds or even thousands of resources; however, for those needing specific help not available through a search engine, these sites may be of benefit.

*Psychoeducational Materials.* These sites offer more specific information to clients and their families. When there are large numbers of quality sites, subheadings have been added to simplify searching. Where an author's name does *not* appear, we could find no author.

*Online Support Groups.* We have placed online support groups into their own category for this edition of *Self-Help That Works.* This makes it easier to find them when seeking emotional support and information from others who've "been there." Research finds that individuals participating in these computer-mediated support groups typically experience increased social support, improved quality of life, and enhanced confidence to manage their health condition (Rains & Young, 2009).

Our compilation of online listings is not exhaustive. If you desire additional or different sites, we heartily recommend that you refer to other practical sources. Relying on a search engine alone virtually guarantees that you will be sent to commercial sites pushing a particular product. A comprehensive and excellent site is Psych Central (psychcentral. com), which is managed by one of this book's coauthors, Dr. John Grohol. Two other wonderfully rich sites are *HelpGuide* (www.helpguide.org) and Dr. Ladd's online book, *Psychological Self-Help* (www.psychologicalselfhelp.org). These three resources are often highlighted in the chapters for their high-quality informational resources.

## 6. Self-Help/Support Groups

A self-help group is a supportive, educational mutual-aid group that addresses a single life problem or condition shared by its members (Kurtz, 1997). Participation is voluntary, members serve as leaders, and professionals rarely play an active role in the group's activities. All forms of self-help groups have one thing in common: promotion of the member's inner strengths. The groups do so by imparting information, emphasizing self-determination, providing mutual support, and mobilizing the resources of the person, the group, and the community (Reissman & Caroll, 1995).

Millions of Americans have come to rely on self-help or support groups for assistance with virtually every human challenge. The most recognizable of these are the 12-step groups patterned after Alcoholics Anonymous (AA) that address a wide spectrum of addictive disorders, such as those to drugs, food, and sex. But self-help groups encompass much more than addictions. There are groups for dealing with death, Alzheimer's, attention-deficit disorder, difficult children, and abusive partners, as even a casual glance of the blue pages of a telephone directory will confirm.

The popularity of self-help groups is easy to understand: they are typically free, widely available, and surprisingly effective. Although research studies on these groups have not been frequent, they do generally show positive results. Sophisticated analyses (Kownacki & Shadish, 1999; Tonigan, Toscoova, & Miller, 1995) have found that participation in AA and reduction in drinking were positively related, especially in outpatient populations. Several large and well-controlled evaluations of 12-step programs for addictive disorders have shown that they generally perform as effectively as professional treatment, including at follow-up (Morgenstern, et al. 1997; Ouimette, Finney, & Moos, 1997; Project MATCH Research Group, 1997).

Research on other self-help mutual-aid groups also typically concludes that participation is beneficial. Attending self-help groups produces higher rates of patient improvement (Barlow, Burlingame, Nebeker, & Anderson, 1999). And participants frequently evaluate self-help groups as helpful as psychotherapy (Seligman, 1995).

At the end of most chapters of this book, we alphabetically list prominent self-help/ support groups for that particular challenge or disorder. These are listed without ratings— and for good reason. The effectiveness of self-help groups largely depends on the local members and leaders, so it is impossible to make general claims about the quality of any particular group. We provide contact numbers for the national office and online sites so that you can identify the mission of the organization and determine whether there is a local group in your locale.

The American Self-Help Clearinghouse's *Self-Help Sourcebook* at mentalhelp.net/self-help/ serves "as your starting point for exploring real-life support groups and networks that are available throughout the world and in your community." The similar National Mental Health Consumers' Self-Help Clearinghouse at www.mhselfhelp.org is a consumer-run association to connect mental health consumers with peer-run groups and to offer technical assistance with self-help groups. We strongly recommend that you visit these sites, especially if you are searching for a support group on a topic or disorder not covered in this guide.

## ▦ 12 NATIONAL STUDIES

We have conducted a series of national studies over the past two decades to determine the most useful self-help resources according to the experts. In each study, the methodology and the samples were very similar: a lengthy survey distributed to clinical and counseling psychologists residing throughout the United States. Across the 12 studies, nearly 5,000 psychologists contributed their expertise and judgment to evaluate self-help books, autobiographies, and movies. Appendix A presents the methodological details of these studies.

These mental health professionals are all members of the clinical or counseling divisions of the American Psychological Association and/or the National Register of Health Service Providers in Psychology. To be members, mental health professionals are required to have earned a doctorate in psychology from an accredited university and have been recommended for membership by their colleagues. Their ratings and comments on the books, autobiographies, and films are based on many years of experience in helping people with particular problems and are an invaluable resource for sorting through the confusing maze of self-help.

Our studies are probably the earliest and the most thorough to be conducted on a large-scale, national basis. A number of the mental health professionals who participated in the studies spontaneously commented about the virtual absence of information available to the public about how to select exemplary self-help materials. Their positive comments about the need for our studies and the extensiveness of the materials rated bolstered our motivation for writing this book.

The psychologists rated self-help resources with which they were sufficiently familiar on the same 5-point scale:

| | | |
|---|---|---|
| +2 | Extremely good | Outstanding; highly recommended book, best or among best in category |
| +1 | Moderately good | Provides good advice, can be helpful; worth purchasing |
| 0 | Average | An average self-help book |
| −1 | Moderately bad | Not a good self-help book; may provide misleading or inaccurate information |
| −2 | Extremely bad | This book exemplifies the worst of the self-help books; worst, or among worst in its category |

The wording was slightly modified for rating autobiographies and films—for example, "an average autobiographical account" and "outstanding; highly recommended film."

Mental health professionals rated self-help materials in the following 41 categories:

Abuse
Addictions
Adult Development
Aging
Anger
Anxiety Disorders
Assertiveness
Attention-Deficit/Hyperactivity Disorder
Autism and Asperger's
Bipolar Disorder (Manic-Depression)
Borderline & Narcissistic Disorders
Bullying
Career Development
Child Development and Parenting
Chronic Pain
Communication and People Skills
Death and Grieving
Dementia/Alzheimer's
Depression
Divorce

Eating Disorders
Families and Stepfamilies
Gay, Lesbian, and Bisexual Issues
Happiness
Infant Development and Parenting
Love and Intimacy
Marriage
Men's Issues
Obsessive–Compulsive Disorder
Posttraumatic Stress Disorder
Pregnancy
Schizophrenia
Self-Management and Self-Enhancement
Sexuality
Spiritual and Existential Concerns
Stress Management and Relaxation
Substance Abuse
Suicide
Teenagers and Parenting
Violent Youth
Women's Issues

## ■ ONE TO FIVE STARS AND A DAGGER

We analyzed the responses to our 12 national studies by computing how often the self-help resources were rated and how high or low the ratings were. All resources not listed at least 10 times were eliminated from the final ratings. Then, based on how often and high they were rated, books and films with positive ratings were accorded 1 to 5 stars. Self-help books and films receiving a negative rating were given a dagger. Specifically:

★★★★★　Average rating of 1.25 or higher and rated by 30 or more mental health professionals

★★★★　Average rating of 1.00 or higher and rated by 20 or more mental health professionals

★★★　Average rating of .50 through .99 and rated 10 or more times

★★　Average rating of .25 through .49 and rated 10 or more times

★　Average rating of .00 through .24 and rated 10 or more times

†　Average negative rating and rated by 10 or more mental health professionals

The sole exception to this rating system was the autobiographies. There, we used a cut-off of 8 or more ratings as opposed to 10, simply because fewer psychologists were sufficiently familiar with autobiographies compared to self-help books or films and because we had previously used 8 as the minimum number of raters. Thus, the rating system for autobiographies was:

★★★★★　Average rating of 1.25 or higher and rated by 24 or more mental health professionals

★★★★　Average rating of 1.00 or higher and rated by 16 or more mental health professionals

★★★　Average rating of .50 through .99 and rated 8 or more times

★★　Average rating of .25 through .49 and rated 8 or more times

★　Average rating .00 through .24 and rated 8 or more times

†　Average negative rating and rated by 8 or more mental health professionals

The online self-help programs and the Internet resources, as previously noted, were not part of the national studies. Instead, they were individually evaluated by a psychologist using a similar rating system to designate their quality and utility. For online self-help, we depended not on professional consensus but on scientific research on their demonstrated effectiveness:

★★★★★　The online program is supported by two or more scientific studies attesting to its efficacy and safety; the studies show the resource to be effective when delivered as online self-help and for both the population and problem advertised.

★★★★　The online program is supported by one scientific study attesting to its efficacy and safety; that study shows the resource to be effective when delivered as online self-help and for both the population and problem advertised.

★★★　The online program is promising but has not yet been verified with controlled research published in the scientific literature. The program may claim research support, but it has not yet been published or not published in a peer-reviewed publication. Alternatively, the online program may have been adapted from other formats, such as self-help books.

★★ The online program may be useful but is lacking research support; these resources have been excluded from this book.

★ The online program does not appear to be particularly beneficial or helpful; these programs have also been excluded from our book.

For the Internet resources, we focused on their quality and relevance:

★★★★★ Quality interactive materials and/or lots of readings with value for patient education; accessible, accurate, current, clearly presented, and pitched at a common reading level

★★★★ Some readings or other material of high quality

★★★ A limited number of readings that can help extend a client's understanding

★★ One small reading that was, however, all that is available on the Internet on that topic

★ Of limited value for self-help or patient education; sites with this rating have been excluded from the book

In this book, the 4-star and 5-star self-help resources are Strongly Recommended; the 3-star resources are Recommended; the 1-star and 2-star books are Not Recommended; and the daggered books are Strongly Not Recommended. In addition to these ratings, some self-help books, autobiographies, and films received high ratings but were rated infrequently, or they were released just as this book was going to press. These resources were designated as Diamonds in the Rough ( ♦ ). They have the potential to become 4-star or 5-star books if they become more widely known.

## ■ HOW THIS BOOK IS ORGANIZED

The following chapters present the self-help categories alphabetically, beginning with Abuse and ending with Women's Issues. Each chapter opens with a brief description of the life challenge or disorder and of the audiences to which the self-help resources are addressed. We then provide our Recommendation Highlights for that chapter, which include all 5-star resources, most 4-star resources, and select Diamonds in the Rough. Next, we present the expert ratings and our concise reviews of, in order, self-help books, autobiographies, films, online self-help, and Internet sites. The chapters conclude with brief descriptions and contact information for self-help/support groups. Not every chapter provides listings of all types of self-help, either because there were too many resources available for that disorder or, conversely, there were too few.

The final two chapters are intended for our dual audiences. Chapter 43, For Consumers, features strategies for evaluating and selecting self-help resources. Chapter 44, For Practitioners, offers practical suggestions for integrating self-help into formal treatment.

The four appendixes contain statistical and methodological data. Appendix A details the methodology of our dozen national studies. Appendix B presents the experts' average ratings for all the self-help books evaluated by five or more psychologists. Appendix C presents the average ratings for all the autobiographies evaluated by five or more respondents, and Appendix D does likewise for all the films.

**TABLE 1.1  Estimated Effect of Self-Help Resources Recommended by Psychologists**

| Effect | Self-Help Books (N = 760) | Auto-Biographies (N = 358) | Films (N = 530) | Internet Sites (N = 625) | Self-Help Groups (N = 685) | Online Programs (N = 326) |
|---|---|---|---|---|---|---|
| Very harmful | 2% | 0% | 0% | 2% | 2% | 1% |
| Somewhat harmful | 5% | 3% | 5% | 5% | 4% | 6% |
| No effect | 8% | 40% | 27% | 14% | 8% | 55% |
| Somewhat helpful | 58% | 47% | 57% | 60% | 63% | 34% |
| Very Helpful | 27% | 10% | 11% | 19% | 23% | 4% |

*Note:* The survey asked, "In general, what help do your patients/clients report from using the self-help resources that you recommended?"

## ▨ USING THIS BOOK EFFECTIVELY

*Self-Help That Works* is designed for both the general public and health professionals.

For laypersons, the self-help market resembles a Persian bazaar with proliferating choices and without clear directions: Should you nurture others or nurture your inner child; go fast or slow down; seek success or simplicity; just say no or just do it; confront your fears or honor them (Albom, 1997)? Sorely needed are trustworthy and scientific means to determine the quality of self-help resources. This book can help you become a knowledgeable consumer, appreciate the large volume of self-help resources, and navigate the bazaar to select the genuine articles and avoid the imitations. *This is a research-based self-help book on self-help.*

Mental health professionals increasingly recommend self-help to their clients. In our latest national studies, 85% of psychologists recommended self-help books, 79% self-help groups, 78% an Internet site, 28% autobiographies, and 23% an online self-help program in the past year. Moreover, practitioners are becoming convinced of the effectiveness of self-help resources in conjunction with psychotherapy. Table 1.1 presents the results of our 2011 studies; it clearly demonstrates that psychologists find self-help materials to be somewhat helpful or very helpful in 70% to 90% of psychotherapy cases.

Practitioners can use this professional resource to determine the quality of self-help resources on a wide-ranging set of behavioral disorders and life transitions. The evaluative ratings and concise reviews will increase their knowledge of thousands of resources that can be used with or without professional treatment. Since all this information is packed into this single volume, books, autobiographies, films, computer programs, and Internet resources can be quickly accessed and compared to determine their appropriateness.

Now that we have introduced self-help, our national studies, and the organization of this book, let's turn to the specific behavioral disorders and life challenges.

# CHAPTER 2

# ABUSE

Experiencing abuse can transform a person's life. Once victimized, many individuals never again feel quite as strong or trusting. Determining the scope of abuse is difficult because many abused individuals never reveal their experiences. Especially disturbing in the available data are the abuses perpetrated by close friends and family members. Acquaintances of the victim are implicated in almost 50% of child sexual assaults, romantic partners in 50% to 75% of sexual assaults reported by college-age and adult women. The burden of abuse falls on women unequally: more than 75% of the reported cases of child sexual abuse involve girls, and more than 90% of adult rape victims are women.

The more recent self-help resources focus on sexual abuse of girls and of boys as children, adults who were abused as children, and those who have a loved one who has been traumatized by abuse. Earlier entries in this chapter describe the false memory concerns that were prevalent in the 1990s. As you may recall, a professional and legal controversy erupted over the reality of childhood abuse uncovered during psychotherapy. On the one side were those mental health professionals who regularly encounter clients who report being physically or sexually abused as children but who have repressed these traumatic memories because they were too painful. On the other side are some mental health professionals, memory researchers, and accused parents who contend that the "recovered" memories of abuse can be fictitious accounts subtly prompted by suggestive and hypnotic therapy techniques and by social hysteria. The storm spilled over into the professional literature, into the nation's courtrooms, and, yes, into self-help materials.

Following is a summary of the self-help books, autobiographies, films, and Internet sites that our psychological experts recommend on the national epidemic of abuse. But first, our Recommendation Highlights (Box 2.1).

## ■ SELF-HELP BOOKS

### An Embattled Book

★★★★★ *The Courage to Heal* (3rd ed., 1994) by Ellen Bass and Laura Davis. New York: Harper Perennial.

This self-help book has become a bible for many women who were sexually abused as children. Originally published in 1988, a third edition appeared in 1994. Ellen Bass realized how little help was available to adult survivors of child sexual abuse when she was teaching creative writing workshops in the 1970s. Although not a mental health professional, she

## BOX 2.1
## RECOMMENDATION HIGHLIGHTS

**SELF-HELP BOOKS**

■ On adult women's recovery from child sexual abuse:

★★★★★ *Healing the Incest Wound* by Christine A. Courtois

■ On adult men's recovery from child sexual abuse:

★★★★ *Victims No Longer* by Michael Lew

■ For the partners of adult survivors of child sexual abuse:

★★★★ *Allies in Healing* by Laura Davis

■ On battered women who have been abused by their partners:

★★★★ *The Battered Woman* by Lenore Walker

★★★★ *Getting Free* by Ginny NiCarthy

■ For women who have endured verbal abuse:

★★★ *The Verbally Abusive Relationship* by Patricia Evans

★★★ *The Secret of Overcoming Verbal Abuse* by Albert Ellis and Marcia Powers

■ For parents of a child who has been molested:

★★★ *When Your Child Has Been Molested* by Kathryn B. Hagans and Joyce Case

**AUTOBIOGRAPHIES**

■ On sexual abuse and incest:

★★★ *Daddy's Girl* by Charlotte Vale Allen

♦ *Tiger, Tiger: A Memoir* by Margaux Fragoso

■ On physical and sexual abuse:

★★★★ *The Lost Boy* by Dave Pelzer

★★★ *Crazy Love* by Leslie Morgan Steiner

★★★ *Lucky: A Memoir* by Alice Sebold

■ On sexual obsessions following sexual molestation:

★★★ *Secret Life* by Michael Ryan

**FILMS**

♦ On domestic abuse and triumphant survival:

★★★★ *The Color Purple*

★★★★ *This Boy's Life*

★★★★ *Antwone Fisher*

★★★★ *Slumdog Millionaire*

■ On sexual abuse of children:

★★★★ *Mystic River*

★★★★ *A Thousand Acres*

■ On spousal abuse:

★★★ *What's Love Got to Do with It?*

**INTERNET RESOURCES**
- On domestic violence:
  - ★★★★★ *Domestic Violence and Abuse* www.helpguide.org/mental/domestic_violence_abuse_types_signs_causes_effects.htm
- On child abuse:
  - ★★★★★ *Childhelp* www.childhelp.org
- On abuse against women:
  - ★★★★★ Violence Against Women Office www.ovw.usdoj.gov
- On sexual assault:
  - ★★★★ *Pandora's Project* www.pandys.org

decided to offer groups for survivors and developed the "I Never Told Anyone" workshops, creating a safe context where women could face their own pain and anger and begin to heal. Laura Davis was sexually abused as a child and turned to Ellen Bass for help.

*The Courage to Heal* begins with a brief introduction about how healing is possible. Readers answer a series of 14 questions that help them determine whether they were victims of child sexual abuse. The bulk of the book is divided into five parts: Taking Stock, The Healing Process, Changing Patterns, For Supporters of Survivors, and Courageous Women. Two sections toward the end of the book focus on counseling and healing resources. Women who definitely know that they were sexually abused as children may benefit from this book. The writing is clear, the survivors' stories are artfully woven through the book, the writing exercises are valuable, and the authors' compassion and insight are apparent. Unlike some recovery books that dwell too extensively on the past, this resource moves on in positive ways to help women recover.

Although a visible and bestselling book on sexual abuse, *The Courage to Heal* is not without its significant cautions. Its laundry list of diagnostic questions is not supported by research and, according to critics, exaggerates the prevalence. The book's authors were also drawn into the repressed-versus-false-memory storm. The authors contend that women who strongly sense that they were sexually abused but do not have specific memories of it were probably abused. While this position fosters an acceptance toward women whose abuse may have been denied by others, it simultaneously may generate or perpetuate false "memories" of abuse that never occurred. Critics contend that specific memories of early childhood abuse are notoriously unreliable and that the authors' encouraging language can create false memories and thus false accusations against innocent family members. In that respect, the book has been involved in lawsuits and implicated in false memories.

*The Courage to Heal* is probably the most controversial and polarizing self-help book among psychologists in this entire volume. We have received congratulations from some colleagues for featuring this empowering book and for telling the awful truth about sexual abuse, as well as condemnation from other colleagues for even listing a book that has been identified as a probable source of false memories and false accusations. We have faithfully reported that mental health professionals evaluated *The Courage to Heal* as the top-rated book on abuse in our national studies, but immediately note that those ratings occurred in the 1990s, before the false memory controversy and other professional developments.

In the end, we decided to respect both the original ratings and the ensuing storm: we retain the listing, place it under the singular heading of "An Embattled Book," present both sides of that battle, detail its controversy, and, given the necessary cautions, remove it from the Recommendation list. Our position will probably not satisfy either side of the debate, but we believe it best reflects the emerging consensus and best serves the interests of clinicians and consumers alike.

*The Courage to Heal Workbook* (1990) was subsequently written by Laura Davis to provide in-depth exercises for both women and men who were sexually abused as children. The workbook includes a combination of checklists, open-ended questions, writing exercises, art projects, and activities that take the adult survivor through the healing process. This book is a companion to *The Courage to Heal* and is organized into four main sections: Survival Skills, Taking Stock, Aspects of Healing, and Guidelines for Healing Sexually.

**Strongly Recommended**

★★★★★ *Healing the Incest Wound: Adult Survivors in Therapy* (1996) by Christine A. Courtois. New York: Norton.

This sensitive guide to understanding and treating incest gives the reader a poignant view of the suffering of survivors and a hopeful view of recovery. The text is comprehensive in its range of information and could be used as a textbook, a practitioner's guide, a self-discovery book, or a training guide. The topics focus first on understanding incest by citation of demographics and characteristics (e.g., types of behavior, age and sex of victims and perpetrators, family structure), dynamics of incestuous families, and parent–child patterns. Then, symptoms and secondary elaborations are differentiated between young children, adolescents, and adults. Various theories of incest are reviewed, and an important chapter details how these individuals present in therapy and how assessment and diagnostic patterns often manifest. The third section attends to treatment goals, strategies, and techniques. Attention is given to group screening, ground rules, and process issues in group therapy. A highly rated self-help resource on a controversial topic, but a book that might be too academic for some patients.

★★★★ *The Battered Woman* (1979) by Lenore Walker. New York: Harper & Row.

This excellent self-help book is written for women who have been or continue to be abused by their husbands or romantic partners. Lenore Walker is widely recognized as a leading therapist who studies and counsels battered women. The book is divided into three main parts: Psychology of the Battered Woman includes valuable information about the myths and realities of abuse as well as psychological theories that help explain the victimization of the battered woman; Coercive Techniques in Battering Relationships provides vivid, heart-wrenching stories told by battered women themselves; and The Way Out examines not only the dark side of legal, medical, and psychological systems that tend to keep battered women as victims, but also the services battered women themselves say would be more helpful. Walker asserts that battered women undergo a process of victimization, acquiring a sense of learned helplessness that leaves them prey to abuse, unable to fault their abusers, and unwilling to leave them. The case studies present battering from a woman's perspective; indeed, Walker acknowledges that the book is written from a woman's point of view. *The Battered Woman* was written in 1979 and has not been revised.

**** *Allies in Healing* (1991) by Laura Davis. New York: Harper Perennial.

The partners of survivors are an overlooked group. This book, by one of the coauthors of *The Courage to Heal*, is written for partners who may not have been abused themselves but who are living with the effects of abuse. The question-and-answer format makes the book highly readable, with each question at the top of a page. Questions are organized under basic topics, including My Needs and Feelings, Dealing with Crisis, Intimacy, Family Issues, and Realistic Expectations. Sensitive and difficult questions are asked, and the answers are candid and informative. A significant part of the book describes the stories of eight partners and their struggles and triumphs.

**** *Victims No Longer: Men Recovering from Incest and Other Sexual Child Abuse* (1990) by Michael Lew. New York: Harper & Row.

This splendid self-help book was written for men who experienced childhood incest and other sexual abuse in their childhoods. The focus section lends special emphasis or specific experience to the chapter subject (e.g., defining victim and survivor, debt to the women's movement, myths that interfere with recovery). Personal accounts from survivors are sprinkled between chapters. Topics are clustered into myths and realities of abuse, messages about masculinity, surviving abuse, and recovery. This book provides an emotional journey for the reader and tells the story of courageous recoveries.

**** *Getting Free: You Can End Abuse and Take Back Your Life* (3rd ed., 1997) by Ginny NiCarthy. Seattle, WA: Seal.

This book is intended for women and is about battering. It is presented in six sections: Making the Decision to Leave or Stay, Getting Professional Help, Helping Yourself to Survival, After You Leave, The Ones Who Got Away, and New Directions. The final section examines topics that do not appear in the other books on battered women listed here and provides valuable analysis and recovery advice for abused teens and abused lesbians. *Getting Free* has an extensive number of exercises for readers and is thus virtually a combination of narrative and workbook.

### Recommended

*** *The Verbally Abusive Relationship* (1996) by Patricia Evans. Holbrook, MA: Adams.

The stories in this book were told by 40 women who were verbally abused. Their experiences serve as validation for abused women who have questioned the legitimacy and reality of their experiences. Verbal abuse is discussed from the perspective of power and dominance. The first part of the book presents a self-evaluation questionnaire, and the second part characterizes categories of verbal abuse (e.g., withholding, discounting, accusing, trivializing, denial), using illustrations of typical scenarios. A valuable aspect of the book is that it addresses how to respond effectively to verbal abuse. Examples provide clear ways to interpret and deal with abusive communication. This edition includes a chapter for psychotherapists that considers verbal abuse from a clinical standpoint, and chapters on children in abusive environments. The book received a stellar rating of 1.61 in one of our national studies but was rated by only 13 experts, thus leading to its 3-star rating and likely to an underestimation of its probable usefulness.

★★★  *I Never Called It Rape* (1994) by Robin Warshaw. New York: Harper Perennial.

A major study conducted by *Ms.* magazine and the National Institute of Mental Health as well as interviews of 150 women conducted by the author are cited throughout this book in describing acquaintance rape. Author Warshaw presents a road to recovery for those sexually assaulted by an acquaintance. The denial of acquaintance rape in our culture and the uphill battle of survivors are thoughtfully chronicled. The book focuses on acquaintance rape on the college campus, in the workplace, and in other settings. The intended audience is not only the survivors of acquaintance rape but also family, parents, educators, counselors, and those in the legal system. The book is not widely known among experts in our studies, but those who do know it accord it high ratings. Any female who has experienced date rape can benefit from Warshaw's portrayal of the healing process; any dating female can benefit from the book's detailed observations about how and why date rape happens; and males can benefit from the book's description of the devastating after-effects of date rape.

★★★  *The Sexual Healing Journey* (2001) by Wendy Maltz. New York: Harper Perennial.

The healing journey is intended to augment psychotherapy or to prepare for change at the reader's own pace. The reader is helped to understand how sexuality has been affected by sexual abuse, a realization that most survivors don't make on their own and that is often at the root of sexual difficulties. Types of sexual abuse, fears of acknowledgment, and the impact of abuse on sexuality are informatively described. Healing steps to take with one's partner are suggested, and techniques for relearning touch and solving specific sexual problems are explained. The text effectively includes exercises and exploratory questions. The interactive format in each chapter allows the reader to participate. A highly valued but infrequently rated book in our studies, thus designated as a 3-star resource.

★★★  *When Your Child Has Been Molested* (1998) by Kathryn B. Hagans and Joyce Case. San Francisco: Jossey-Bass.

This informative guide on child molestation provides a series of observations and recommendations called "reality checks" that will assist parents in making decisions and in attending to the needs of their child. Topics include believing your child's reality, understanding the child's continued fears, the grief process, dealing with guilt, healing the communication process in the family, the child's appearance in court, and what to say to others. The reality checks are helpful questions to ask or observations to make: ways to talk with your child, signs of possible molestation, how shock and denial are expressed in the grief process, questions to ask a potential therapist, and preparing your child for court. This book is unique in providing information about the court process and what to expect. A glossary of terms is helpful and covers legal and psychological expressions. A final checklist can determine whether the family is getting better and what to do about it. This is another book that would likely have merited more stars had it been more widely known and thus more frequently rated in our studies.

★★★  *The Secret Trauma* (1999) by Diana E.H. Russell. New York: Basic Books.

This book is based on an extensive study conducted by the author to investigate incestuous abuse, extrafamilial child sexual abuse, rape, and other types of sexual assault perpetrated against females. Personal interviews were conducted with 930 randomly chosen women. The methodology of the study and the extensive results are reported. The findings are clustered into initial descriptions of the problem of incest, including reporting trends, characteristics of incest abuse, and social factors. A major part of the book is devoted to understanding victims: who they are and how they cope, revictimization, long-term effects, and several case studies. Also, different than many other books on abuse, this book presents information on the perpetrators: who they are, father–daughter incest, biological father versus stepfather incest, and other familial incidences of incest. Myths versus realities of the findings are outlined in an attempt to more accurately portray incestuous abuse. This book was highly but infrequently rated, perhaps due to its more scholarly orientation.

★★★  *Healing the Trauma of Abuse: A Women's Workbook* (2000) by Mary Ellen Copeland and Maxine Harris. Oakland, CA: New Harbinger.

This book is a step-by-step guide for women who have been abused sexually, emotionally, or physically. The material is designed as a self-help book to be read sequentially. The format of each chapter entails a beginning and an ending ritual of identifying positive experiences in the person's current life, reading about and understanding the problem in question (e.g., emotional abuse, physical abuse), recommendations for coping, optional activities to be practiced, and things to remember about oneself (e.g., positive affirmations). Chapter subjects lend themselves to self-exploration and prepare the reader to conduct change activities. The latter chapters identify ways of making life changes through understanding family myths, making better decisions, and understanding blame and acceptance. The book closes with a self-inventory that was also done at the beginning of the book, with the goal of contrasting the perceptual changes the reader has made through these exercises. A highly valued book in our national studies; had it been more frequently rated, it would have probably reached 4-star or 5-star status.

★★★  *Battered Wives* (revised ed., 1989) by Del Martin. Volcano, CA: Volcano.

This book is intended for women who have been in an abusive relationship with a man or who continue to be abused in the relationship. While the book is titled *Battered Wives*, Martin says that her book applies equally to unmarried women who live with violent men; many of the examples she uses involve unmarried cohabitants. In Martin's view, the underlying problem that has led to the battering of so many women is found not in the husband–wife interaction or immediate triggering events but rather in the institution of marriage itself, historically negative attitudes toward women in society, the economy, and inadequacies in legal and social services. The book is at its best in its scathing feminist critiques of a society that discriminates against women and, in this respect, is a more sociological analysis of battered women than an in-depth psychological analysis. The textbook style of writing makes for difficult reading in many places. And even the 1989 revision of *Battered Wives* is dated.

★★★   *Breaking the Cycle of Abuse: How to Move Beyond Your Past to Create an Abuse Free Future* (2005) by Beverly Engel. Hoboken, NJ: Wiley.

The cycle of abuse is effectively described not as a cycle within a single relationship but across generations. Examples followed by explanations of the abuse cycle make clear the fact that individuals who were victimized, were abusers, or were observers have absorbed these patterns into their own development in ways that can be veiled for years, making them vulnerable to repeat the same patterns with their own children, partners, and others. The target readers for this narrative are those who see signs of an abuse factor within themselves, those who have been victimized, and those who were abused as children and are afraid of their own actions with their own children. A step-by-step guide takes the reader through short- and long-term strategies, identifying risk factors, and how to manage emotionality, shame, anger, and fear. The message is meant to reach individuals touched by abuse without engendering shame, anger, or another obstacle to change through exercises, questions, writing, and other active methods.

★★★   *Beginning to Heal: A First Book for Survivors of Child Sexual Abuse* (1993) by Ellen Bass and Laura Davis. New York: Harper Perennial.

*Beginning to Heal* is a condensed version of *The Courage to Heal*, reviewed above, and is designed for those who are just starting to face the abuse they experienced earlier in life. The approach offers an empathic and validating perspective that involves healing, believing it happened, grieving, anger, change, and moving on. Inserts, including quotes, and observations in boxed form contribute to clarity on such subjects as surviving the panic stage, how most people begin to remember, breaking the silence, and how to change. A significant section of the book recalls the stories of five women who were abused as children and how they moved through the healing process. This book serves as an invitation and introduction to recovery from child sexual abuse.

★★★   *The Secret of Overcoming Verbal Abuse* (2000) by Albert Ellis and Marcia Grad Powers. Hollywood, CA: Wilshire.

The story of verbal abuse is told from a woman's perspective—of sadness, of disrespect, of the personality change of Prince Charming, and of the loss of a relationship that was not to be. The abuse syndrome and accompanying dynamics are richly described for the reader who may feel unique and alone. The authors effectively present the typical feelings and thoughts of the abuse victim and signs that one is in an abusive relationship. Rational-Emotive Behavioral Therapy (REBT) is explained and applied to the verbal abuse syndrome, with attention given to the role of cognitive distortions and the importance of moving toward unconditional self-acceptance. The fears of aloneness, change, and the unknown are discussed as obstacles to change. Skill development, relaxation, and other techniques are presented as additional therapeutic interventions. Resolving the fears that keep individuals stuck is a focus of the therapeutic intervention.

★★★   *Wounded Boys, Heroic Men: A Man's Guide to Recovering from Child Abuse* (1992) by Daniel Jay Sonkin. Stamford, CT: Longmeadow.

The step-by-step material in this book is designed for men who were abused physically, sexually, or psychologically when they were boys as well as for their partners, friends, and family members. Special focus is given to the gender-based roadblocks that men face, including not seeking help, being expected to pull themselves up by their bootstraps, thinking and not feeling, and taking punishment like a real man. Topics are how to begin the journey, types of abuse, breaking the pattern of denial, and healing through attitude and behavior change. Bullet points highlight the message of each chapter (e.g., knowing you're on the right track, how abuse affects you today). This book provides a hopeful and demythologizing message about recovery.

★★★ *Healing the Shame That Binds You* (1988) by John Bradshaw. Deerfield Beach, FL: Health Communications.

This book appeared on the *New York Times* bestseller list and sold more than half a million copies. Bradshaw believes that people with a wide array of problems, including addictions and compulsions, developed their problems because of toxic shame. What is toxic shame? Bradshaw never gives a clear definition, but he does hint about its nature. He says toxic shame is present when people believe that things are hopeless and feel that they themselves are worthless. They feel defective, flawed, and inadequate as people. Individuals with toxic shame perceive that they lack power. How can people get rid of shame-based feelings? Bradshaw believes that the healing process involves getting the shame out of hiding and externalizing it. This involves liberating the lost inner child, integrating disowned parts, loving the self, healing memories, improving self-image, confronting and changing inner voices, coping with toxic shame relationships, and awakening spiritually. Bradshaw describes a number of therapy strategies that can be used to help individuals externalize their toxic shame. Although popular with the public, this book received tepid and mixed evaluations by the mental health experts in our national studies.

**Diamonds in the Rough**

♦ *Your Turn for Care: Surviving the Aging and Death of the Adults who Harmed You* (2012) by Laura S. Brown.

This valuable book was released in late 2012 and fills a gap in the self-help literature: How should survivors deal with the care and death of elders who abused them? Psychologist Brown lays out many of the reality issues and mixed feelings that arise in such a confounded circumstance. The book offers emotional support for adult survivors, advises them to listen to their inner wisdom, presents pragmatic guidelines, and enjoins them to take care of themselves first. A wise and compassionate book, informed by both survivor stories and research studies, for what often proves a time of turmoil.

♦ *You Are Not Alone: A Guide for Battered Women* (2000) by Linda P. Rouse. Holmes Beach, FL: Learning Publications.

This book is written for women who have experienced battering at the hands of a man who is not a stranger to them. Rouse provides a straightforward self-evaluation in order for women to determine where their relationships are. The profile of battering men is described, and the societal and familial roots of battering men are explored, including low self-esteem, traditional sex-role expectations, jealousy and control focus, abusive family background, and failure to acknowledge the need for change. The author provides valuable information regarding contacting a shelter, the importance of medical care, the centrality of psychological services, and a flowchart on navigating the legal system. Helpful resources in the appendices include worksheets on fears in leaving, secondary gains, and strength resilience. This book was infrequently rated in our national studies but was rated very highly by those who did read it.

### Not Recommended

* ★ *Reclaiming the Inner Child* (1990) edited by Jeremiah Abrams. Los Angeles: Jeremy P. Tarcher.
* ★ *It's My Life Now* (2006) by Meg Kennedy Dugan and Roger R. Hock. New York: Routledge.
* ★★ *From Child Sexual Abuse to Adult Sexual Risk* (2003) by Linda J. Koenig, Lynda S. Doll, Ann O'Leary, and Willo Pequegnat. Washington, DC: American Psychological Association.
* ★★ *Why Does He Do That?* (2003) by Lundy Bancroft. New York: Berkley.
* ★★ *Hush: Moving from Silence to Healing after Childhood Sexual Abuse* (2007) by Nicole Braddock Bradley. Chicago, IL: Moody.
* ★★ *Toxic Parents: Overcoming Their Hurtful Legacy and Reclaiming Your Life* (1989) by Susan Forward. New York: Bantam.
* ★★ *Abused No More: Recovery for Women from Abusive or Co-Dependent Relationships* (1989) by Robert Ackerman and Susan E. Pickering. Blue Ridge Summit, PA: T.A.B.

## ■ AUTOBIOGRAPHIES

### Strongly Recommended

* ★★★★ *A Man Named Dave: A Story of Triumph and Forgiveness* (2000) by Dave Pelzer. New York: Plume.

Pelzer's trilogy begins with his life in an abusive household, his 9 years in various foster homes, and now his life as an adult. This is a story of survival, resilience, willpower, coming to terms with a horrific past, incorporating that information in one's life, and moving on. Pelzer enlisted in the Air Force at age 18 and served in Operations Desert Shield and Desert Storm. While in the Air Force he worked with at-risk youth and since retiring has become a child advocate whose work received national and international recognition. Some readers may be put off by the graphic descriptions of abuse, but if they have gotten through the two earlier books, this one will provide a degree of closure, especially when the author describes his positive relationship with his young son and his reconciliation with his father. The lessons are clear—abuse can be survived and surmounted, and even gruesome experiences can lay the basis for a productive career and a satisfying life.

* ★★★★ *The Lost Boy: A Foster Child's Search for the Love of a Family* (1997) by Dave Pelzer. Deerfield Park, FL: Health Communications.

This is the second book of a trilogy, whose first volume, *A Child Called "It,"* describes the author's harrowing early life with an extremely abusive mother. This book covers the author's subsequent 9 years in the foster care system, moving from one home to another until he finally lands in a home that can give him the love he so desperately craves. Emotionally wrenching to read, not only because of the past abuse but also because of the shame, insecurity, and loneliness of kids moved from one household to another. On the positive side, the book underscores the fact that resilient kids can come through. An excellent book for foster parents interested in the inner worlds of their children and for foster children who want to know how others have survived the combination of abuse and foster care.

**Recommended**

★★★  *A Child Called "It": One Child's Courage to Survive* (1995) by Dave Pelzer. Deerfield Beach, FL: Health Communications.

This is the first book of a trilogy describing different periods in the author's life. It is a horrifying account of his abuse as a child by a sadistic and alcoholic mother who nearly killed him. She referred to him as "It" and starved and burned him. Eventually Dave was rescued by an alert schoolteacher. This bestselling book demonstrates how hope and love can overcome extreme adversity in childhood. The account of abuse is so horrifying as to shock sensitive readers, but the books contains underlying themes of hope and recovery.

★★★  *Daddy's Girl* (1995) by Charlotte Vale Allen. New York: Berkeley.

A professional writer struggles to free herself from memories of her father's incestuous demands, which started when she was 7 years old and continued until she was 17, and from her image of herself as ugly and unlovable. The author is now active on behalf of victims of child abuse and domestic violence. A compelling autobiography and a good discussion of the connection between childhood abuse and adult relationships.

★★★  *Sleepers* (1996) by Lorenzo Carcaterra. New York: Ballantine.

As a young man growing up in a poor neighborhood, the author and his friends engaged in petty crimes. When they were caught, the young men were sent to a juvenile home, where they were assaulted and raped by guards. Years later, the men took revenge against their tormenters. The book was made into a popular movie of the same name. There is some question about the authenticity of the author's account, which is sometimes described as fiction. (Also reviewed in Chapter 41 on Violent Youth.)

★★★  *Secret Life* (1996) by Michael Ryan. New York: Vintage.

Poet Michael Ryan attributes the sexual obsessions of his adult years to having been molested at age 5 by a neighbor and being physically abused by an alcoholic father. He bares his soul to the reader in this searing autobiography. Excellent and disturbing portrait of sex addiction, the compulsive drive for sex heedless of the consequences for self and others.

★★★  *Crazy Love* (2010) by Leslie Morgan Steiner. New York: St. Martin's Press.

Harrowing story of a young woman in her 20s with everything going for her falling for the wrong man. Leslie Steiner was attractive, came from an affluent family, and had degrees from Harvard and Chicago and a glamorous editorial position in Manhattan. She meets a Wall Street banker named Conor on the train; they start dating and become engaged. Even before their marriage, Conor hit Leslie. She doesn't take the hint and proceeds to marry him. The physical abuse continues up to the point when a particularly bad beating left her unconscious. This brought the realization that the relationship was potentially deadly. She concludes that Conor isn't going to change and she has to get out. The book attempts to understand why she remained in an abusive and dangerous relationship as long as she did. There was no explanation other than blind hope, crazy love, and denial of the obvious.

★★★  *All That Is Bitter and Sweet: A Memoir* (2011) by Ashley Judd and Maryanne Voller. New York: Random House.

Actress Ashley Judd's mother, the world-famous country-western singer Naomi Judd, pursued her spectacular career at the expense of her daughters. Ashley, in particular, felt neglected and abused. The story of her depression and confusion as a result of childhood abandonment occupy only a few chapters in a much longer account of her humanitarian work with impoverished women in Africa and Asia. In essence, her childhood scars gave purpose to her life and fueled her charitable work.

★★★  *Beyond the Tears: A True Survivor's Story* (2003) by Lynn C. Tolson. Bloomington, IN: Authorhouse.

The author tries to understand her attempted suicide at age 25 and subsequent anxiety and depression. She finds a caring therapist and together they embark on a journey back to her childhood in a dysfunctional family, her sexual molestation, the mental illness of a parent, adults around her whom she could not trust and who did not believe her, a teenage rape, and her attempts to find relief in drugs and alcohol. The therapist diagnoses her condition as posttraumatic stress disorder and views Lynn as a survivor who can have a productive life. The therapy was the first time Lynn could discuss her childhood trauma and abuse. Gradually came insight into the psychological prison in which she had been trapped. She regained her voice and took control of her life. A heart-wrenching but very positive book.

★★★  *Lucky: A Memoir* (2002) by Alice Sebold. New York: Little, Brown.

Harrowing story of sexual assault and its aftermaths in the form of self-destructive behaviors. Sebold was a university freshman walking home from a friend's apartment at night when she was raped. Like other rape victims, she felt the experience turned her into a freak, a Martian, damaged goods forever ruined. Family and friends did not know what to say, stared, left her on her own. It took a decade for her to begin healing. In the interim was a period of posttraumatic stress disorder and heroin addiction. A turning point was the capture and trial of the rapist. The trial was stressful but she toughs it out, still bearing today the emotional scars but able, finally, to break the silence. She concludes, "You save yourself or you remain unsaved." Sebold became a novelist, poet, and teacher, drawing strength from her interactions with her students.

### Diamond in the Rough

♦  *Tiger, Tiger: A Memoir* (2011). by Margaux Fragoso. New York: Farrar, Straus, and Giroux.

Margaux Fragoso was 8 years old when 15 years of sexual abuse by Peter, a 51-year-old man, started. Her parents had their own problems and either didn't notice or didn't care what was happening. She later learned that Peter was a convicted pedophile who had molested other children, and she was not his first or last victim. She describes in vivid detail his methods of seduction and how he kept the predator–prey relationship going for so many years. Similar to the Stockholm syndrome, she defended her abuser and tried to protect him. Friends and neighbors suspected something illicit was going on and reported Peter to Social Services, but no action was taken. Finally, overcome with guilt, Peter committed suicide at age 66. She emerged from the experience with a form of post-traumatic stress disorder. Writing this brave and sensitive memoir provided catharsis and probably an assist to others experiencing such horrific abuse. Listed as a Diamond in the Rough as it was published just prior to our latest national survey and thus was not yet well known.

## ■ FILMS

### Strongly Recommended

★★★★ *The Color Purple* (1986) directed by Steven Spielberg. PG-13 rating. 152 minutes.

This unforgettable movie depicts a magnificent triumph of the human spirit over endless and vile cruelties—physical and sexual—brought about by family separation, abuse, and ignorance. Despite her sufferings, Celie, a poor, unloved, unlovely, African-American woman in the turn-of-the-century South, discovers her beauty, her courage, and her potential. If she can do it, we all can. The movie is notable for its superb performances and the Oscars it won.

★★★★ *This Boy's Life* (1994) directed by Michael Caton-Jones. R rating. 115 minutes.

A mother takes her son and heads west after divorce to the little town of Concrete. Desperate for marriage, she weds a pathetic bully. The heart of the story is the war between a nice kid and his sadistic, lying, con-artist stepfather, who is perfectly portrayed as a sick adult child, always feeling cheated and misunderstood and blaming the boy. The film illustrates the boy's growth in confidence and hope to escape, the mother's passivity, and the loathsome man's character weaknesses. As such, it demonstrates hope and growth despite a terrible childhood.

★★★★ *Mystic River* (2003) directed by Clint Eastwood. R rating. 138 minutes.

This is the story of three young boys, one of whom was kidnapped while they were playing and then was raped over a period of several days but finally escaped. Fast-forward 25 years, the boys went their separate ways, but the disappearance and murder of one of their daughters brings them back together, for one of them who is a detective attempts to solve this horrific crime. The tangled and complex relationships among the men, their wives, and children gives testimony to the long-reaching effects of abuse—the isolation, suspicion, and invisible wall it creates. The course of action in solving the murder, the forced re-engagement by the three men and families, and the lessons learned about the healing power of love, friendship, and recommitment make this film a powerful statement about hope and resilience. The film conveys the message that abuse can be survived at an emotional cost to the victim, yet with the eventual realization of healthy relationships and regaining of one's life.

★★★★  *The Magdalene Sisters* (2002) directed by Peter Mullan. R rating. 119 minutes.

The Magdalene Asylums for young women operated in Catholic Ireland in the mid-1960s until the mid-1990s for "fallen women." The sadistic treatment by Sister Bridget, the oppression and humiliation, and the squalid living conditions made life at the asylum intolerable. The girls worked in hard labor conditions, earning substantial income for the asylum but not for themselves. The film tells of three young women who together suffered through physical, psychological, and emotional abuse. Each in time found ways to defy the domination of Sister Bridget, and two of them were able to escape and live in society. The Magdalene Asylums did exist, but the stories of these particular women are collectives of individual stories. The underlying message is one of resilience and strength in the face of sadistic treatment.

★★★★  *The Accused* (1988) directed by Jonathan Kaplan. R rating. 111 minutes.

The story of a working-class woman in a small town who is gang-raped at a local bar. The story within the story is that the circumstances leading up to the rape were seen by the community and the court as a not-guilty verdict for the perpetrators. The woman had dressed provocatively, had flirted with one of the men, and, as was brought out in court, had taken marijuana earlier in the evening. The gender stereotyping of blame, being held accountable for the actions of the men, and the disdain shown to the victim in the court and by the community are poignant reminders of failures in our judicial system and in moral treatment of each other. The onlookers to the rape were brought to justice, but the fair judgment of the perpetrators was never rendered. The emotional toll, humiliation, and abandonment of the victim are portrayed starkly and realistically by Jodie Foster. This film sends the message that, regardless of injustice, one's faith in self and strength to fight for justice is affirming. (Also reviewed in Chapter 31 on Posttraumatic Stress Disorder.)

★★★★  *Antwone Fisher* (2002) directed by Denzel Washington. PG-13 rating. 120 minutes.

A true story of a Navy sailor prone to fighting, angry outbursts, and impulsive behavior. Upon the likelihood of being released from the military, Antwone saw a naval psychiatrist, and although undisclosing at first, eventually embarked on a path of healing and recovery. His vivid account of physical, sexual, emotional, and psychological abuse is starkly realistic and honestly portrayed. An inspiring tale of overcoming horrific abuse and going on with life. Antwone went on to overcome his obstacles and become a writer and Hollywood producer. (Also reviewed in Chapter 29 on Men's Issues.)

★★★★  *Slumdog Millionaire* (2008) directed by Danny Boyle & Loveleen Tandan. R rating. 120 minutes.

The poverty and despair of an 18-year-old orphaned boy in Mumbai is told in retrospect as he is interrogated by police who accuse him of cheating on a game show. The boy correctly answers all of the questions, but because he hails from the slums and has no formal education, his knowing the answers is considered suspicious. The boy responds to the police interrogation by telling them of the events, both tragic and significant, he has experienced. He has the capacity to learn important meanings about life, people, values, tenacity, and resilience through these life-shaping experiences. Through these travails, he has shown loyalty when it was not reciprocated and love when it was turned on him. The cinematic theme, which has many viewers giving standing ovations, is abuse and maltreatment from which comes determination and hope.

★★★★ *Radio Flyer* (1992) directed by Richard Donner. PG-13 rating. 120 minutes.

This beautiful but painful film illustrates the denial patterns of a codependent wife and her physically and verbally abusive alcoholic husband. The two boys who are the focus of the story try to protect her and each other from his beatings. While the movie offers no usable guidance for coping with or overcoming the abuse or its denial, the nature of the pathology is clearly displayed.

★★★★ *A Thousand Acres* (1997) directed by Jocelyn Moorhouse. R rating. 105 minutes.

An aging farmer transfers ownership of the family farm to his grown daughters and their husbands. The film sensitively traces the generational struggle for control and power—*King Lear* set on an Iowa farm—but is riveting in gradually revealing the secrets of the father's physical and sexual abuse years ago. He beat the children and forced himself sexually on two daughters, who together protected their younger sibling from him. The discovery and confrontation of incest in a family of origin are frighteningly realistic and, in the end, only partially effective as minimization prevails. The father never expresses remorse or achieves understanding. An effective (and potentially painful) film for those who have been physically or sexually abused.

**Recommended**

★★★ *Dolores Claiborne* (1995) directed by Taylor Hackford. R rating. 132 minutes.

Dolores is a maid working in remote Maine who is accused of murdering her wealthy employer. Dolores' daughter, Selena, returns to her mother's side after 15 years of estrangement and anger. We discover that Dolores' alcoholic husband beat her and sexually molested Selena. Although initially idealizing her father and resenting her mother, Selena eventually realizes that her father molested her and that her mother protected her the best she could. A poignant and realistic film for women who were abused by spouses, for adults who were sexually abused as children, and for those wanting to understand the complicated dynamics of abusive relationships.

★★★ *Capturing the Friedmans* (2003) directed by Andrew Jarecki. 107 minutes.

The emotional trauma, the disbelief, and the outrage of pedophilia sweep us up into demands for justice, finding the perpetrators and ensuring punishment that fits the crime. In the case of the Friedmans, Arnold, the father, was caught in a sting operation of buying and distributing child pornography. As the case unfolded, his son Jesse was found also to be involved in child pornography. Further investigations led to the belief that Arnold and his son were sexually abusing children in the computer classes he conducted in his home. As Arnold and Jesse were further interviewed, Arnold admitted to sexually abusing his younger brother when they both were children, abusing several other children as an adult, and sexually abusing Jesse when he was young. Both Arnold and Jesse later claimed that they confessed only because their lawyers said it would be strategically advantageous for Jesse and for Arnold to confess, and would have helped Jesse in sentencing. Child sexual abuse is a tragedy for all involved, but not uncommonly confessions are recanted and defenses altered. This scenario leaves the family and the public wanting justice, but not injustice. This film unmasks the tragedy of sexual abuse in families and the conflicting feelings of loyalty, despair, shame, and betrayal.

★★★  *What's Love Got to Do with It?* (1994) directed by Brian Gibson. R rating. 119 minutes.

A true and completely believable story of a seductive, charming, abusive husband and his talented wife, who stays with him long beyond what reason or love would require. He beats her, flaunts his girlfriends, and abuses cocaine. She excuses him, believes his apologies, and gives him many more chances. The movie is an unflinching and honest look at how such patterns can exist in any family, even among rich, public, Hollywood families.

★★★  *Monster* (2003) directed by Patty Jenkins. R rating. 109 minutes.

The cruelties and abuses of childhood can set the trajectory for a lifetime of choices that bring even more tragedy and despair. This is the true story of Aileen Wuornos, who became a prostitute at the age of 13, became pregnant at the same age, and adopted a life of highway prostitution in soliciting truck drivers. This choice led to many attacks and beatings by men. Aileen began to murder these men for their money and at times for her self-defense. She met and partnered with another woman, for whom Aileen became responsible financially and emotionally. Her partner began to suspect that Aileen was the highway killer, and Aileen's life began to unravel. Aileen was now a victim and a perpetrator: a sexual abuse victim and a serial killer. This film depicts the thin line that separates the tragic victim and the predator and attempts to explain the complexities of Aileen's life.

★★★  *The Apostle* (1997) directed by Robert Duvall. PG-13 rating. 134 minutes.

A fundamentalist preacher in the South showers love and concern on his congregation but violence and infidelity on his marriage. Sonny (Robert Duvall) is a complex man—good and bad, loving and abusing, saintly and devilish—and an ambiguous apostle. Viewers with no experience in the southern Pentecostal culture might find the film confusing, but it is a strong story of a fatally flawed, religiously militant man who abuses his spouse.

★★★  *Sleeping with the Enemy* (1991) directed by Joseph Ruben. R rating. 98 minutes.

A battered trophy wife fakes her own death in order to break away from the total dominance and control of her husband. She runs away to start her life again; he finds her and threatens her again. That is all the film has to offer. It is best used to illustrate the characters and dynamics of the couple.

### Not Recommended

★★  *Thelma and Louise* (1992) directed by Ridley Scott. R rating. 129 minutes.
★★  *Mommie Dearest* (1981) directed by Frank Perry. PG rating. 129 minutes.
★★  *Matilda* (1996) directed by Danny DeVito. PG rating. 98 minutes.

**Strongly Not Recommended**

    †   *The Prince of Tides* (1992) directed by Barbra Streisand. R rating. 132 minutes.


## ■ INTERNET RESOURCES

There are an enormous number of resources available online about all kinds of abuse. The sites described here focus on sexual assault, domestic violence, child abuse, abused males, and abuse by professionals. Excluded are materials primarily about workplace violence; the legal side (prosecution, lawsuits, advocacy); sexual harassment; sex offenders; ritual abuse and torture; and sites that combine abuse with materials on dissociation. Reading some of the following sites may trigger memories in those who have experienced abuse; please exercise caution.


### General Websites

    ★★★★★   *MINCAVA Electronic Clearinghouse* www.mincava.umn.edu

    The Minnesota Center Against Violence and Abuse website offers a wealth of information on child abuse, domestic violence, and sexual violence.

    ★★★★★   *Domestic Violence and Abuse* www.helpguide.org/mental/domestic_violence_abuse_types_signs_causes_effects.htm

    This single-page article from the nonprofit HelpGuide offers help for victims, fact sheets, and information about what you can do if you're in an abusive relationship.

    ★★★★★   *Violence Against Women Office* www.ovw.usdoj.gov

    This federal government site offers links, hotlines, laws, toolkits, grants, and much more on all aspects of abuse, violence, stalking, and battering.


### Psychoeducational Materials

#### *Sexual Assault and Abuse*

    ★★★★   *Coercion, Rape, and Surviving*    www.student-affairs.buffalo.edu/shs/ccenter/violence.php

    A helpful guide to sexual violence from the University of Buffalo's Counseling Services.

    ★★★   *Sexual Abuse* soulselfhelp.on.ca/sexabusemain.html

    There are about 10 pages on definitions, effects, memory recovery, anger, obesity, and getting support. The section on Tools in Recovery is a good set of tips and advice on relapse prevention, helpful slogans, definitions, and so forth.

    ★★★★   *Sexual Violence* www.cmhc.utexas.edu/sexualviolence.html

    The site provides definitions and information on immediate responses, coping, recovering, and self-care, plus suggestions for family, from the University of Texas at Austin.

**★★★★**    *Rape, Abuse & Incest National Network (RAINN)* www.rainn.org

A large library of information and resources related to sexual violence, abuse, and incest from the nation's largest anti-sexual violence nonprofit.

**★★★★**    *Rape Victim Advocacy Program* www.uiowa.edu/~rvap

This is a counseling center in Iowa; its online readings for victims include Facts about Sexual Assault, If You Have Been Assaulted, What To Do If My Child Has Been Assaulted, and What to Say to a Rape Survivor.

**★★★★**    *Connecticut Sexual Assault Crisis Services* www.connsacs.org

A comprehensive and informative website that addresses legal and medical concerns as well as sexual assault issues.

**★★★★**    *"Friends" Raping Friends—Could It Happen to You?* by Jean O'Gorman Hughes and Bernice R. Sandler www.bernicesandler.com/id46.htm

A lengthy article discussing the phenomenon of date rape and acquaintance rape, including warning signs and what to do if it happens to you.

**★★★★**    *For Persons Who Have Been Sexually Assaulted: What You Should Know About Sexually Transmitted Diseases* www.health.state.mn.us/divs/idepc/ dtopics/stds

A helpful informational page from the Minnesota Department of Health.

**★★★**    *Pandora's Project* www.pandys.org

Pandora's Project is an interesting and valuable resource, offering a rich library of sexual assault articles (click on "Library, Articles" to find them). Topics that are well covered include sexual assault, rape, child sexual assault, relationship violence, recovering from trauma, and caring for yourself after sexual violence, among many more. The site also hosts an active and thriving online self-help support community.

**★★★**    *Help for Adult Victims of Child Abuse* www.havoca.org/HAVOCA_home.htm

This websites provides emotional support, information, and advice for anyone who's been affected by past childhood abuse. Lots of potentially helpful articles here, although sadly they don't carry authorship or dates.

**★★★★**    *Adult Survivors of Child Abuse* www.ascasupport.org

This group offers a helpful "Survivor to Thriver Manual" that is available online and as a PDF here: www.ascasupport.org/manual.php

★★★★ *Surviving Childhood Sexual Abuse* psychcentral.com/lib/2012/surviving-child-sexual-abuse

This article from the University of Illinois at Urbana-Champaign's counseling center covers the basics of child sexual abuse.

### Domestic Violence

★★★★★ *Domestic Abuse* www.police.Nashville.org/bureaus/investigative/domestic
A wealth of information about domestic violence, including downloadable brochures that cover topics such as stalking, threat assessment, devising a safety plan, and domestic violence in the workplace.

★★★★ *Trust Betrayed* www.wvdhhr.org/bph/trust/trust-to.htm

A superb booklet of about 20 pages teaches what are healthy and controlling relationships and ways of dealing with abusive relationships.

★★★★★ *Love: The Good, the Bad and the Ugly* lovegoodbadugly.com

A superb and stylish website that provides information on everything a person might need to know about both healthy and abusive relationships, as well as help in thinking about respect and the purpose of healthy relationships in our lives.

★★★ *Hope for Healing* www.hopeforhealing.org

Hope for Healing is a nonprofit organization devoted to helping people cope with abuse and rape and to finding resources to help them in their recovery. A good set of more than a dozen informational articles can be found on the site, as well as a blog and information about the organization's projects (such as the Hope Quilt).

★★★ *Domestic Violence Resources* by Daniel Jay Sonken, PhD www.daniel-sonkin.com

Under "Books, Articles and Presentations" you'll find a few articles for the public with solid information, techniques, and advice for abusers.

★★★ *AWARE: Arming Women Against Rape and Endangerment* www.aware.org

A fine introduction to self-defense and "effective self-protection for intelligent women who want help, not hype."

★★★★★ *Domestic Violence Resource Center Victoria* www.dvirc.org.au

An Australian website that offers a large amount of resources and informational articles about domestic violence.

★★★    *What is domestic violence?* au.reachout.com/What-is-domestic-violence

A good introduction to domestic violence topics from Reach Out.com, an Australian resource sponsored by the Inspire Foundation. While basic in its scope, it's easy to understand and links to additional resources.

★★★★    *Violence: "Domestic," Elder, Workplace, and School* www.clinicalsocialwork.com/violence.html

A good resource listing by clinical social worker Pat McClendon of hundreds of websites and other resources related to domestic violence and workplace and school violence too.

★★★    *Blain Nelson's Abuse Pages* blainn.com/abuse

Nelson offers two questionnaires that are designed to raise awareness about abuse. Not all abuse is simple or physical.

★★★    *Is Your Relationship Heading into Dangerous Territory?* cmhc.utexas.edu/booklets/relatvio/relaviol.html

Six pages of checklists raise awareness, comparing violent and nonviolent relationships, the cycle of domestic violence, and what to do.

★★★    *Know Excuses* www.csswashtenaw.org/ada/resources/community/poster_words.html

The site lists perhaps hundreds of short statements used by abusers as excuses. The seemingly endless list is powerful and thus valuable for confrontation of denial, but it can be overwhelming. It is also available as a poster.

### Child Abuse
★★★★★    *Childhelp* www.childhelp.org

This national nonprofit organization promotes education about child abuse and related issues such as domestic violence. The "Get Help" section offers articles specific to kids, parents, and professionals. "Statistics" provides useful data on the extent of the problem, while the "Stories" section gives people hope about seeking help.

★★★★    *Child Abuse and Neglect* helpguide.org/mental/child_abuse_physical_emotional_sexual_neglect.htm

This single-page article from the nonprofit HelpGuide offers valuable information on how to recognize the signs of child abuse and work to help prevent it.

★★★★    *Frequently Asked Questions: Child Abuse & Neglect* www.childwelfare.gov/can/faq.cfm

Frequently asked questions about child abuse and neglect from the U.S. Department of Health & Human Services.

### Abused Males
★★★★  *Male Survivor* www.malesurvivor.org

A comprehensive website offering information and resources about sexual victimization of boys and men.

### Self-Injury
★★★  *Self-Injury: You Are Not the Only One* users.palace.net/~llama/selfinjury

This is a high-quality, rich site that sadly hasn't been updated in years. The "Quick Primer" is very educational, as is the "Self-Help" section. There are a questionnaire, quotes, references, chat, and more. Much of it can be used with Linehan's Dialectical Behavior Therapy.

★★★  *Psyke.org* www.psyke.org

Although apparently not updated any longer, this website still offers valuable resources for people who self-injure, including personal stories, poetry, pictures, coping advice, and frequently asked questions.

### Abuse by Professionals
★★★★  *Sexual Exploitation by Helping Professionals* www.rainn.org/get-information/ types-of-sexual-assault/sexual-exploitation-by-helping-professional

A good introduction to this sensitive topic, offering an understanding to those who may have been abused by mental health professionals.

★★★★  *Survivors Network of Those Abused by Priests* www.snapnetwork.org

This is a self-help online support group with many resources listed. See also the support group SOSA: Survivors of Spiritual Abuse at www.sosa.org.

### Other Aspects of Abuse
★★★★★  *WHOA (Working to Halt Online Abuse)* www.haltabuse.org

This site provides articles, technical suggestions, how to do your own research into halting your own abuse, and support for those harassed or stalked in the online world.

★★★★★  *National Center on Elder Abuse* www.ncea.aoa.gov

From the U.S. Administration on Aging, a comprehensive government site offering a wealth of resources, definitions, and informational articles about elder abuse.

★★★★  *Emotional Abuse* www.counselingcenter.illinois.edu/?page_id=168

This article from the University of Illinois at Urbana-Champaign's counseling center offers a nice overview of recognizing and understanding emotional abuse.

# ■ SUPPORT GROUPS

### Batterers Anonymous

Phone: 909–355–1100
www.battersanonymous.com
For men who wish to control their anger and eliminate their abusive behavior.

### Child Help USA Hotline

Phone: 480–922–8212
www.childhelpusa.org
General information on child abuse and related issues and some crisis counseling. Referrals to local agencies for child abuse reporting.

### Domestic Violence Anonymous

Phone: 415–681–4850
www.BayLaw.com
Twelve-step spiritual support for men and women who are recovering from domestic violence.

### False Memory Syndrome Foundation

Phone: 215–940–1040
www.FMSFonline.org
Research-oriented organization for persons falsely accused of childhood sex abuse based on recovered or repressed memories.

### National Child Abuse Hotline

Phone: 800-422-4453 or 800-222-4453 (TDD)

### National Domestic Violence Hotline

Phone: 800-799-SAFE (7233) or 800-787-3224 (TDD)
www.ndvh.org
Information and referrals for victims of domestic violence.

### Network for Battered Lesbians and Bisexual Women

Phone: 617-742-4911 or 617-227-4911
www.thenetworklared.org

### Parents Anonymous

Phone: 909-621-6184
www.parentsanonymous.org

Professionally facilitated peer-led group for parents who would like to learn more effective ways of raising their children.

### RAINN (Rape Abuse and Incest National Network)

Phone: 800-656-4673
www.rainn.org
Offers a national hotline network for victims and survivors of sexual abuse who cannot get to a local rape crisis center.

### SAFE (Self-Abuse Finally Ends) Alternative Information Line

Phone: 800-DONT-CUT
www.selfinjury.com
Provides information on dealing with self-abuse and self-mutilation and the treatment options.

### SESAME (Stop Educator Sexual Abuse Misconduct and Exploitation)

Phone: 702-371-1290
www.sesamenet.org
Support and information network for families of children who have been sexually abused by a school staff member.

### S.I.A. (Survivors of Incest Anonymous) World Service Office

Phone: 410-893-3322
www.siawso.org
Twelve-step program for men and women who have been victims of child sexual abuse and want to be survivors.

### SNAP (Survivors Network of Those Abused by Priests)

Phone: 312-409-2720
www.survivorsnetwork.org
Support for men and women who were sexually abused by any clergy person.

### Violence Against Women Office

Phone: 202-307-6026
www.ovw.u3doj.gov
From the U.S. Department of Justice, this site offers lots of information on interventions, advocates, and resources concerning domestic violence.

**See also** Posttraumatic Stress Disorder (Chapter 31) and Violent Youth (Chapter 41).

# CHAPTER 3

# ADDICTIONS

Addiction occurs when the use of a substance or behavior persists despite adverse consequences. The hallmarks of addiction include preoccupation with the behavior, increasing tolerance to its effects (requiring more and more to experience the same effect), and withdrawal symptoms when reducing the behavior. Chapter 38 is devoted solely to substance abuse, whereas this chapter addresses other addictive disorders. We choose to focus on gambling, sex, pornography, and cyber addictions.

In addition to materials on nonchemical addictions, we consider a handful of self-help books devoted to the controversial concept of codependency. Although codependency originally referred to the problems of people married to alcoholics, it spread rapidly, perhaps indiscriminately, to include a host of other circumstances. Agreement on a precise definition of codependency has not been forthcoming, but those who write about the topic agree that the number of women who are codependent is significant. And they agree that women who are codependent often have low self-esteem, grew up in a dysfunctional family, and should focus more on their own inner feelings instead of catering to someone else's needs. In the language of codependency, many women stay with an unreliable partner, usually a male, because they are pathologically attracted (or addicted) to the relationship dynamics of being subservient to a male.

In this chapter, we present the experts' consensual ratings on self-help books, autobiographies, films, online self-help, and Internet resources on addictions and codependency (Box 3.1). The titles and contact information for prominent self-help organizations are included as well.

## ■ SELF-HELP BOOKS

### Recommended

★★★  *Beyond Codependency* (1989) by Melodie Beattie. New York: Harper & Row.

This sequel to Beattie's autobiographical *Codependent No More* elaborates the self-sabotaging behavior patterns of codependency in which a codependent person overcares for an unreliable, addictive person. Beattie addresses healthy recovery, the role of recycling (falling into old bad habits) in recovery, and how positive affirmations can counter negative messages. Testimonials from people who have used this method to break away from addictive relationships are liberally interspersed throughout the book. This book, like

## BOX 3.1
## RECOMMENDATION HIGHLIGHTS

**SELF-HELP BOOKS**
- On codependency across addictions:
    - *** *Beyond Codependency* by Melodie Beattie
- On sexual addiction:
    - *** *Out of the Shadows* by Patrick Carnes
- On Internet addiction:
    - *** *In the Shadows of the Net* by Patrick Carnes and associates

**AUTOBIOGRAPHIES**
- On codependency and substance abuse:
    - **** *Codependent No More* by Melodie Beattie
- On gambling addiction:
    - *** *Born to Lose: Memoirs of a Compulsive Gambler* by Bill Lee
- On cyber addiction:
    - *** *Cyber Junkie: Escape the Gaming and Internet Trap* by Kevin J. Roberts
- On sex addiction:
    - *** *Love Sick* by Sue William Silverman

**FILMS**
- On gambling addiction:
    - *** *The Gambler*
    - ♦ *Owning Mahowny*
- On sex addiction:
    - *** *Choke*

**ONLINE SELF-HELP**
- For objective evaluation and feedback on gambling risk:
    - **** *Check Your Gambling* www.checkyourgambling.net

**INTERNET RESOURCES**
- On Internet addiction:
    - **** *Internet Addiction* www.helpguide.org/mental/internet_cybersex_addiction
- For pornography addiction:
    - **** *CyberSexual Addiction* www.cybersexualaddiction.com
- For compulsive gambling:
    - **** *National Council on Problem Gambling* www.ncpgambling.org

Beattie's predecessor, received a 3-star rating in the national studies, and virtually the same plaudits and criticisms that characterize reviews of Beattie's earlier work apply to *Beyond Codependency*.

★★★ *In the Shadows of the Net* (2007) by Patrick Carnes, David Delmonico, Elizabeth Griffin, and Joseph Moriarity. Minneapolis: Hazelden Foundation.

Compulsive Internet sexual behavior is explained through how the behavior begins and then evolves in a way that becomes integrated into one's daily life, and the panic and fear that ensue when one realizes that the addiction is in control and not oneself. Many poignant stories are told of everyday people and the impact cybersex has had on their lives. The power of this addiction is often in the fact that individuals don't realize their compulsion until it has a strong hold. Means of identifying the problem, strategies to intervene, and methods to gain control over one's life again are explained. The perspective of the text is one of patience, acceptance, and support for those who decide to regain their lives.

★★★ *The Truth about Addiction and Recovery* (1992) by Stanton Peele, Archie Brodsky, and Mary Arnold. New York: Fireside.

Drawing on recent research and case studies, the authors conclude that addictions are not diseases and they are not necessarily lifelong problems. Instead of medical treatment or a 12-step program, Peele, Brodsky, and Arnold recommend a life process program that emphasizes coping with stress and achieving one's goals. The book is a calm and reasoned alternative to the disease model of addiction that can prove very helpful. While it does include a number of case studies, it is more like a textbook than the other books in this category. A number of research studies and academic sources are cited to support the author's interpretations and recommendations. The book is well documented but somewhat difficult to digest. It is particularly applicable to people seeking or valuing an alternative to the 12-step approach.

★★★ *Out of the Shadows: Understanding Sexual Addiction* (3rd ed., 2001) by Patrick Carnes. Minneapolis: Hazelden Foundation.

This book is a guide to understanding sexual addictions using a 12-step program as a means to recovery. Important milestones (for example, the moment that comes for every addict), the cycle and levels of the addictive process, and the family's relationship to the world of a person and his or her addiction are discussed. Charts and diagrams are used to explain the system's levels, beliefs, and the 12 steps of AA and their adaptation to sexual addiction. The author states that, like other addictions, sexual addiction is rooted in a complex web of family and marital relationships and that part of therapy is to discover the role of the previous generation in the addiction. The author examines the tangled web of love, addictive sex, hate, fear, and relationships. Ultimately, this book is about hope. If you are a sex addict or suspect you are and have the courage to face yourself, this book is intended for you.

★★★ *Healing the Wounds of Sexual Addiction* (2004) by Mark Laaser. Grand Rapids, MI: Zondervan.

Sexual addiction has represented a level of shame and personal failure beyond most other addictions, thereby making the search for help and healing often out of reach. Aspects of this addiction highlighted here include the impact of the Internet, the relatively recent acknowledgement of female addiction, and effective methods one can adopt to enhance healing. Internet access, affordability, and anonymity are powerful variables that are explored and encountered. Triggers are identified, and important suggestions are offered about how to choose a mental health professional who will understand and be able to help. Characteristics and types of addiction, "building block" behaviors that lead to addiction, and treatment issues are discussed. The book is written by a Christian minister who himself has suffered from this addiction (although the message is applicable to all who deal with this addiction) and offers spirituality as one healing factor.

### Diamond in the Rough

♦ *Sex, Drugs, Gambling, & Chocolate: A Workbook for Overcoming Addictions* (1998) by A. Thomas Horvath. San Luis Obispo, CA: Impact.

This notable workbook on addictions is distinguished by three features: it covers multiple addictions as a whole instead of a single one; it advances a cognitive-behavioral model instead of a medical or 12-step model; and it is based on scientifically supported methods of change. The book is replete with specific exercises and self-study questions and covers many topics ignored by competing self-help resources, such as the research on cue reactivity, natural recovery, relapse prevention, and harm reduction. The workbook format and easy reading make it attractive to consumers, although many adherents of 12-step models will find the book contrary to their established beliefs.

### Not Recommended

★★ *How to Break Your Addiction to a Person* (1982) by Howard Halpern. New York: McGraw-Hill.

★★ *The Sex Addiction Workbook* (2004) by Tamara Penix Sbraga, William T. O'Donohue, and John Bancroft. Center City, MN: Hazelden Foundation.

★★ *Real Solutions for Overcoming Internet Addictions* (2001) by Stephen O. Watters. Vine Books.

★ *Overcoming Your Pathological Gambling* (2006) by Robert Ladouceur and Stella Lachance. New York: Oxford University Press.

★ *Love Is a Choice* (1989) by Robert Helmfelt, Frank Minirth, and Paul Meier. Nashville, TN: Thomas Nelson.

★ *Co-Dependence: Healing the Human Condition* (1991) by Charles Whitfield. Deerfield Beach, FL: Health Communications.

## ■ AUTOBIOGRAPHIES

### Strongly Recommended

★★★★ *Codependent No More: How to Stop Controlling Others and Start Caring for Yourself* (2nd ed., 1996) by Melodie Beattie. Center City, MN: Hazelden.

This is Melodie Beattie's best-selling narrative about being addicted to a codependent relationship and how she recovered from it. This second edition updates Beattie's views on how to break away from destructive codependent relationships. She tried various self-help groups, including AA, Al-Anon, and Sex Addicts Anonymous, and she advocates their use for those in codependent relationships. Beattie describes her previous drinking problem, recovery, and work as an alcohol counselor. In an engaging writing style, she emphasizes the effects of addiction on family and friends.

In addition to describing her own struggles, she discusses the nature of codependency and how to recover from it. Beattie estimates that upwards of 80 million Americans are emotionally involved with an addict or are addicted themselves, not necessarily to alcohol or drugs but also to sex, work, food, or shopping. What characterizes codependents? Beattie says that they feel anxiety, pity, and guilt when other people have a problem and that they overcommit themselves.

This volume received a 4-star rating but a mixed reception in our national studies. Most respondents called it a great book, but some an awful book. Although *Codependent No More* was on the *New York Times* bestseller list for 115 weeks and has sold upwards of 4 million copies, mental health professionals are not uniformly enthusiastic about it.

## Recommended

★★★   *Love Sick: One Woman's Journey through Sexual Addiction* (2008) by Sue William Silverman. New York: Norton.

A childhood experience of sexual abuse by her father with a complicit mother left the author feeling unloved and probably played a role in her becoming a sex addict with obsessive shadowy liaisons with dangerous men. She looked for love in all the wrong places and went through 10 clinicians before entering a facility with a program for sex addicts, where she stayed for 28 days. In addition to writing two self-help books and another on memoir writing, Silverman is a professional speaker and college instructor.

★★★   *Cyber Junkie: Escape the Gaming and Internet Trap* (2010) by Kevin J. Roberts. Deerfield Beach, FL: Health Communications.

The author is a recovering videogame addict who runs support groups for people similarly afflicted and lectures on ADHD. This book is not anti-gaming or anti-social networking; it takes the position that cyber play can be useful and enjoyable, but for some it can become a compulsion leading to the exclusion of family, friends, school, and work relationships. Roberts describes his personal struggle with cyber addiction and how he successfully achieved step-by-step balance between cyber play and the real world. The book will be especially useful to parents trying to manage time budgets for teenagers obsessed with videogames.

★★★   *Born to Lose: Memoirs of a Compulsive Gambler* (2005) by Bill Lee. Center City, MN: Hazelden Publishing.

Candid insider account of the author's 40-year gambling addiction, including 15 years in Gambler's Anonymous. The book is divided into two sections, "My drug of choice" and "The road to recovery." The latter section describes the difficult transition from denial to control over his gaming habit. An interesting feature of the book is its setting in San Francisco's Chinatown, where there is a long tradition of serious and sometimes self-destructive gambling. In Bill Lee's case, his addiction wiped him out financially. Heavily into debt, Lee attends a Gambler's Anonymous meeting, which sets him on the road to recovery. A good book for individuals and families who are struggling with gambling problems as well as for the professionals who treat them.

## ■ FILMS

### Recommended

★★★ *The Gambler* (1997) directed by Károly Makk. R rating. 97 minutes.

Dostoyevsky is a gifted writer lost in his gambling addiction. In the course of his desperation, he made an agreement that his publisher would pay off all of his debts if he could deliver a manuscript within a month. If he failed, the publisher would be granted all of the rights to his future writings. To accomplish this feat, Dostoyevsky hires a young stenographer, Anna, who becomes more than a note taker. A spring-to-autumn love story develops in which Anna learns about herself and gains personal meaning, although caught up in the compulsion of gambling and the power of addiction. This film delivers the message that giftedness and intellect cannot resist the power of addiction.

★★★ *Choke* (2008) directed by Clark Gregg. R rating. 92 minutes.

Victor is a colonial re-enactment player during the day and a sex-addicted con-man during the evening, when he goes to expensive restaurants, pretends to choke on his food, and then latches on to the unfortunate patron who "saves his life" for the purpose of keeping his Alzheimer's-ridden mother in a care home. During a visit to his mother, she reveals that she has kept the identity of his biological father a secret all these years. Victor and his mother's beautiful physician, Paige, embark on discovering his father's identity. Eventually, the mother confesses that she stole Victor as a baby and has no idea who his parents are. Victor discovers in course that Paige is a voluntary patient in the care home who fell in love with Victor through the many stories his mother told. This film interweaves several side-bar plots that add unpredictability and distinctiveness, but Victor's struggle to control his sexual addiction and to find a way to bring his life back will resonate with those grappling with this addiction.

★★★ *Rounders* (1998) directed by John Dahl. R rating. 121 minutes.

Mike (Matt Damon) is a high-stakes poker player trying to earn enough money to play in the World Series of Poker. After losing his money to "the Russian" (John Malkovich), he goes straight and drives a truck for his friend while earning money to attend law school. His girlfriend supports his going to law school, and all is well until his childhood friend "Worm" (Edward Norton) gets out of prison and persuades Mike to play poker with him to settle a debt he owes to the same Russian. Mike gets caught up in the frenzy of playing, his girlfriend leaves him, and poker becomes his obsession. Worm cheats during a card game and loses it for them. Mike cuts ties with Worm and takes on an all-or-nothing game with the Russian. The pressure is on, but Mike prevails and wins. He pays off his and Worm's debt, and pays back his friend who lent him the money to play. The film ends with Mike driving to Las Vegas to enter the World Series of Poker. This film does not portray a success story against a gambling addiction, but does realistically and sympathetically reveal the intense influence of an addiction pulled back to it. The film includes, however, the potential for the positive influence of friends and mentors.

**Diamonds in the Rough**

- *Love Sick: Secrets of a Sex Addict* (2008) directed by Grant Harvey. PG rating. 89 minutes.

Sue is married to the hard-working Andrew, who expects Sue to hold a full-time job and to maintain the house and other responsibilities. This fact is presented as an impetus for Sue to have not affairs but random and frequent sexual encounters with strangers, Andrew's friends, and her friends' husbands. It is apparent that Sue has a sexual addiction she has not acknowledged. After many encounters and close calls, at a party given by her parents we find Sue's father talking to her in suggestive terms; it is revealed that Sue was molested by her father as a child. When Sue is later discovered at the party trying to seduce her best friend's husband, she realizes that she needs help. She attends an inpatient clinic directed by Dr. Gardner. After several weeks, Dr. Gardner arranges to meet Sue on the grounds of the clinic and suggests a tryst. Sue decides to resist the overture and walks away. The viewers do not actually know if this was part of the treatment in testing Sue or if Dr. Gardner was a predator. We do know that Sue walked away and that she had gained the internal resources and skills to stand for herself and begin a new life. Based on the memoir by Sue William Silverman (reviewed above) about her struggle with and triumph over sexual addiction.

- *Owning Mahowny* (2003) directed by Richard Kwietniowski. R rating. 104 minutes.

The story of Dan Mahowny is a true and tragic one. Dan has a good job and a rising position in the Canadian Imperial Bank, a girlfriend for whom he cares deeply, and many friends. The other side of Dan is that he is executing the largest bank fraud in Canadian history, stealing over $10 million. Dan is spending all of the stolen money on gambling, primarily horse races and sports. He created accounts and found ways to go undetected as he flew to Atlantic City and other gambling spots in his secret life. He feels little satisfaction in winning and keeps betting until he has no more money; gambling gives him no satisfaction and he inevitably feels lonely, isolated, and broke. Eventually, Dan was caught stealing the money and went to jail. Part of this film is a true story and ends without redemption or successful treatment; however, the viewer does see the portrayal of a man who was smart, likeable, and successful but did not get treatment that would have offered him alternative endings. This decision point is one that the viewer will take away.

## ■ ONLINE SELF-HELP

★★★★   *Check Your Gambling* www.checkyourgambling.net

This site provides a free questionnaire and feedback for people interested in examining their gambling behaviors and attitudes. After completing the anonymous test, users are given customized feedback. User responses are compared to research data to determine their level of gambling risk. This computer-delivered program provides accurate information regarding gambling and common gambling thinking mistakes.

## ▓ INTERNET RESOURCES

### General Websites

★★★    *Center for Internet Addiction* www.netaddiction.com

The Center for Internet Addiction is the clinical practice of Kimberly Young, PhD, the professional who coined the term "Internet addiction" in 1996. In addition to offering information about Internet addiction, she also offers resources that cover "cyberporn" (online pornography), online affairs, online gambling, online gaming, compulsive surfing, and "eBay addiction." The articles tend to be short, however, and push readers to Young's book or treatment services.

### *Internet Addiction*

★★★★    *Internet Addiction* psychcentral.com/netaddiction

A skeptical view of Internet addiction from Psych Central nonetheless offers an alternative way of looking at the issue, as well as self-help resources for those seeking help for this concern. Can be a bit academic as it discusses some of the theories behind this problem.

★★★★    *Internet Addiction* www.helpguide.org/mental/internet_cybersex_addiction.htm

This single article from the nonprofit HelpGuide offers a nice general overview of the problem, as well as simple tips for trying to cope with it.

★★★    *Internet Addiction* www.counseling.txstate.edu/resources/shoverview/bro/interadd.html

This single article from the Texas State University's counseling center gives a lengthy overview, appropriate for both students and laypeople who need a quick primer on Internet addiction.

### *Pornography Addiction*

★★★★    *CyberSexual Addiction* www.cybersexualaddiction.com

Robert Weiss, LCSW, and Jennifer Schneider, MD, PhD, created this generally helpful website devoted to either an online pornography or "cybersex" addiction, which features self-tests and FAQs in addition to articles. Doesn't appear to be updated too often.

★★★★    *Sex and Intimacy in the Digital Age* blogs.psychcentral.com/sex

This blog, also from Robert Weiss, LCSW, on Psych Central offers a more nuanced look at sexuality in an always-on, connected world. It's an engaging and active blog, with discussions following each blog entry.

### *Compulsive Gambling*

★★★★    *National Council on Problem Gambling* www.ncpgambling.org

Under the "Problem Gamblers" section, their publications are quite helpful. Includes information about how pathological gambling is diagnosed.

★★★ *Gambling Addiction and Problem Gambling* www.helpguide.org/mental/gambling_addiction.htm

This single page from the nonprofit HelpGuide offers a general overview of problem gambling and gambling addiction, as well as some ways to treat it and how to help a family member.

★★★★ *California Council on Problem Gambling* www.calproblemgambling.org

Many states offer their own government resources about problem gambling in their state, but this one, a California nonprofit organization, offers a wealth of resources and information (and is relevant to people in any state). Topics covered include the symptoms of problem gambling, types, phases, risk groups, and impact.

### Other Resources
★★★★ *Sex and Love Addicts Anonymous* www.slaafws.org

If it's true you can be addicted to anything, then sex and love seem to be good choices. This international group offers education, information, and support resources for those who are addicted to love or sex.

★★★ *Sexual Recovery Institute* www.sexualrecovery.com

Covering topics such as love addiction, sexual addiction, and pornography addiction, this website is primarily a way to advertise the institute's services (which include treatment, workshops, and courses). The site, however, does also offer good introductory articles on these topics, as well as FAQs, videos, and more.

## ▣ SUPPORT GROUPS

### Debtors Anonymous

Phone: 781-453-2743
www.debtorsanonymous.org
Follows the AA 12-step program for recovering from compulsive indebtedness.

### Gamblers Anonymous

Phone: 213-386-8789
www.gamblersanonymous.org

### Gam-Anon Family Groups

Phone: 718-352-1671
www.Gam-Anon.org
Twelve-step program of recovery for relatives and friends of compulsive gamblers.

**Sex Addicts Anonymous**

Phone: 713-869-4902
E-mail: info@saa-recovery.org
www.sexaa.org
A 12-step program of recovery from compulsive sexual behavior.

**Sexual Compulsives Anonymous**

Phone: 800-977-4325
E-mail: info@sca-recovery.org
www.sca-recovery.org

**See also** Substance Abuse (Chapter 38).

# CHAPTER 4

# ADULT DEVELOPMENT

For too long, psychologists believed that development was something that happens only to children. To be sure, growth and development are dramatic in the initial decades of life, but development goes on in the adult years, too. Midlife—those years between 30 and 70—is probably the least charted territory in human development, according to many psychologists. In this chapter, we consider self-help resources for people in the middle adult years.

Several topics tend to emerge repeatedly during the middle years in the self-help literature. Prominent among these are midlife crises, menopause, and retirement planning. Another topic of recent interest concerns enhancing communication with aging parents.

The adult years are important not only to the adults who are passing through them but also to their children, who often want to better understand their parents and improve their relationships with them. Changes in body, personality, and ability can be considerable during the adult years. Adults want to know how to adjust to these changes and how to make the transitions smoothly.

Here, then, are the evaluative ratings and reviews of self-help books, autobiographies, films, online self-help, and Internet sites devoted to adult development. We begin with a snapshot of our primary recommendations (Box 4.1).

## ■ SELF-HELP BOOKS

### Strongly Recommended

★★★★　*Necessary Losses* (reprint ed., 1998) by Judith Viorst. New York: Fireside.

This book, on bestseller lists for more than a year, describes how we can grow and change through the losses that are an inevitable part of our lives. When we think of loss, we often think of the death of people we love. But Viorst talks about loss as a far more encompassing theme of life. She says we lose not only through death but also by leaving and being left, by changing and letting go and moving on. Viorst also describes the losses we experience as a result of impossible expectations, illusions of freedom and power, illusions of safety, and the loss of our own younger self, the self we always thought would be unwrinkled, invulnerable, and immortal. Although most of us try to avoid loss, Viorst gives a positive tone to our emotional struggles. She believes that through the loss of our mother's protection, the loss of impossible expectations we bring to relationships, and the loss of loved ones through

## BOX 4.1
## RECOMMENDATION HIGHLIGHTS

**SELF-HELP BOOKS**
- For adults seeking to understand and improve relationship with their parents:
  - ★★★★ *Necessary Losses* by Judith Viorst
  - ★★★ *How to Deal with Your Parents When They Still Treat You Like a Child* by Lynn Osterkamp
- For men wanting to learn about stages of adult development:
  - ★★★★ *Seasons of a Man's Life* by Daniel J. Levinson
- For women wanting to learn about stages of adult development:
  - ★★★ *Passages* by Gail Sheehy
- For those seeking to understand menopause:
  - ★★★ *The Silent Passage* by Gail Sheehy
- For those considering retirement:
  - ★★★ *Retire Smart, Retire Happy* by Nancy K. Schlossberg

**AUTOBIOGRAPHIES**
- For a tutorial on life's (and death's) lessons:
  - ★★★★★ *Tuesdays with Morrie* by Mitch Albom
- For confronting and moving beyond middle age:
  - ★★★ *Forward from Here* by Reeve Lindbergh
  - ◆ *Whatever!* by Beverly Mahone
- For dealing with a midlife crisis:
  - ★★★ *Fly Fishing through the Midlife Crisis* by Howell Raines

**FILMS**
- For living with adult children while maintaining one's independence:
  - ★★★★★ *The Trip to Bountiful*
- For becoming a caring patient and partner:
  - ★★★★★ *The Doctor*
- For inspiring fables on life paths and second chances:
  - ★★★★ *It's a Wonderful Life*
  - ★★★★ *Mr. Holland's Opus*

**INTERNET RESOURCES**
- For valuable information on adult development:
  - ★★★★ *Men at Midlife* www.midlife-men.com
  - ★★★★ *Pick the Brain* www.pickthebrain.com
  - ★★★★ *Positively Aging blog* www.jannfreed.com/positively-aging

separation and death, we gain a deeper perspective, true maturity, and fuller wisdom about life. This splendid self-help book was the highest-rated book in the adult development category. Viorst writes very well and her sensitive voice comes through clearly. Most adults can benefit from reading *Necessary Losses* and will relate to its many examples.

**** *Seasons of a Man's Life* (reissue ed., 1986) by Daniel J. Levinson. New York: Ballantine.

This national bestseller is an adult development book that outlines the stages adults pass through, with a special emphasis on the midlife crisis. The book's title accurately reveals that *Seasons of a Man's Life* is more appropriate for men than for women. Levinson and his colleagues summarize the results of their extensive interviews with 40 middle-aged men. Conclusions are bolstered with biographies of famous men and memorable characters from literature. Although Levinson's main interest is midlife change, he describes a number of stages and transitions in the life cycle between ages 17 and 65. Levinson believes that successful adjustment requires mastering developmental tasks at each stage. He sees the 20s as a novice phase of adult development. People need to make a transition from dependence to independence. From about 28 to 33, people go through a transition period in which they must face the more serious question of determining their development. In the 30s, individuals enter the phase of "becoming one's own man." By age 40, they have reached a stable location in their careers and now must look forward to the kind of lives they will lead as middle-aged adults. Levinson reports that 70% to 80% of the men he interviewed found the midlife transition (ages 40 to 45) tumultuous and psychologically painful. This book is one of several that helped form the American public's image of a midlife crisis. The book is several decades old now and, given the increasing lifespan and societal changes, Levinson's expectations of life accomplishments cannot be as accurately categorized as in earlier years. However, this book remains a classic self-help resource.

**Recommended**

*** *Making Peace with Your Parents* (reissued 1996) by Harold Bloomfield. New York: Random House.

This book is about adults' relationships with their parents. According to Bloomfield, to become a fulfilled and competent person, you need to resolve the conflicts surrounding your relationship with your parents. Drawing on insights from his clinical practice, research in the area of adult children–parent relationships, and personal experiences in his own family, Bloomfield describes the problems many adults encounter in expressing love and anger toward their parents. *Making Peace with Your Parents* contains exercises and case studies that help adults improve their communication with their parents; cope effectively with difficult parents; unravel parental messages about love, sex, and marriage; and deal with parents' aging, dying, and death. The author especially believes that adults have to become their own best parent by nurturing themselves and engaging in self-responsibility instead of relying on their parents to satisfy important needs. This book just missed making the 4-star category. It is an excellent book for adults who have a great deal of anger toward their parents. The message of self-responsibility and the clear examples can help adults become aware of how their relationships with their parents have continued to shape their lives as adults.

★★★  *Retire Smart, Retire Happy* (2004) by Nancy K. Schlossberg. Washington, DC: American Psychological Association.

Will I find meaning? Will I feel excited about this next transition? The author of this book argues that we can say "yes" to these and related questions. The audiences for this book are those anticipating retirement and those already retired and feeling confused or anxious about what they should do now. Schlossberg interviewed 100 people from all walks of life regarding their transition into retirement. Emerging from these interviews were key elements for a successful transition, including (1) attending to role changes, (2) demystifying change, (3) looking inward at goals, (4) cultivating relationships, and (5) setting a path. Some of the toughest challenges are discussed directly, including changing routines, modifying the environment, and balancing old and new relationships.

★★★  *The Social Animal* (2011) by David Brooks. New York: Random House.

We sometimes seem to be observers of our own actions and feelings, wondering "Where did that reaction come from?" Our conscious, reasonable selves and our unconscious, emotional selves are portrayed in narratives about people. A commentary, not unlike the second-by-second reporting of a football game, takes us through couples meeting for the first time, people making important decisions, and major life events that are decided by a complex interaction of reason and emotion. These narratives are not rehashings of analytic beliefs about the unconscious, but rather a close look at the need for relationships and the role of emotionality, intuition, character, and social norms in determining our interpretations of life events. All of us have wondered why we like or dislike another person, why we made some of our professional choices, and how we arrive at life decisions when often they seem to go against the grain of what we would logically have chosen. Columnist David Brooks explains the wonder of our inner minds at work and reveal why we are not entirely predictable, even to ourselves.

★★★  *The Silent Passage* (rev. ed., 1998) by Gail Sheehy. New York: Random House.

This bestseller concerns menopause, the time in middle age—usually in the late 40s or early 50s—when a woman's menstrual periods and childbearing capability cease and production of estrogen drops considerably. Journalist Gail Sheehy is also the author of the widely read adult development book *Passages*, reviewed below. To better understand menopause, Sheehy interviewed many middle-aged women and talked with experts in a number of fields. Sheehy argues that the passage through menopause is seldom easy for women because of distracting symptoms, confusing medical advice, unsympathetic reactions from loved ones, and the scornful attitudes of society. For these reasons, menopause has been a lonely and emotionally draining experience for many women. Sheehy's goal is to erase the stigma of menopause and help women understand that it is a normal physical process. She describes her own difficult experiences and reports the frustrations of many women she interviewed. Sheehy's optimism comes through in her hope that menopause will come to be known as "the gateway to a second adulthood" for women. Sheehy is a masterful writer and the book is quick and easy reading (it's a small-format book, only about 150 pages long). Few self-help writers' books ring with the clear-toned prose that Sheehy's do.

★★★  *Passages: Predictable Crises of Adult Life* (1976) by Gail Sheehy.
New York: Dutton.

Like *Seasons of a Man's Life*, *Passages* is about the stages of adult development. In the mid-1970s Sheehy's book was so popular that it topped the *New York Times* bestseller list for 27 weeks. Sheehy argues that we all go through developmental stages roughly bound by chronological age. Each stage brings problems people must solve before they can progress to the next stage. The periods between the stages are called *passages*. Sheehy uses catchy phrases to describe each stage: "the trying 20s," "catch 30," "the deadline decade" (35 to 45 years of age), and "the age 40 crucible." Sheehy's advice never waivers: adults in transition may feel miserable, but those who face up to agonizing self-evaluation, who appraise their weaknesses as well as their strengths, who set goals for the future, and who try to be as independent as possible will find happiness more often than those who do not fully experience these trials. Sheehy believes that these passages earn people an authentic identity, one that is not based on the authority of one's parents or on cultural prescriptions. Not surprisingly, given its popularity with the public, this was one of the most frequently rated books in our national studies. But the experts' evaluations, while largely positive, were mixed. On the positive side, some mental health experts believe the book has given people in their 30s, 40s, and 50s new insights about the transitions in adult development. On the negative side, some experts believe that Sheehy's book describes midlife as too much of a crisis and does not adequately consider the many individual ways people go through midlife. Dilemmas in adult development do not spring forth neatly at 10-year intervals as Sheehy implies.

★★★  *When You and Your Mother Can't Be Friends* (1990) by Victoria Secunda.
New York: Delacorte.

As the title of this book suggests, Secunda writes about the problems that can unfold in mother–daughter relationships when daughters become adults—daughters who have not resolved unhappy childhood attachments to their mothers and who continue to have unhappy relationships with them. Secunda believes that many adult women won't admit or explore their emotional confusion about their mothers, yet honesty is exactly what is needed to go beyond mother–daughter bitterness, she says. One problem is that many adult daughters may not recognize how their relationships with their mothers have skewed their adulthood. Such women may play out their unresolved disaffection with husbands and lovers, coworkers and friends, and especially with their own children. Adult daughters can resolve unhappy relationships with their mothers and develop affectionate truces. Excerpts from 100 interviews with adult daughters are interspersed throughout the book to help adult daughters come to know, understand, and accept their mothers. This is an excellent book for adult daughters who have problematic relationships with their mothers. It is also easy to read, with an optimistic tone and many real-life examples. On the other hand, some mental health professionals marked down the book, citing it as stereotyping adult daughter–mother relationships and giving too little attention to individual variations.

★★★  *How to Deal with Your Parents When They Still Treat You Like a Child* (1992) by Lynn Osterkamp. New York: Berkley.

This book was written for adult children who want to understand and improve their relationships with their parents. Osterkamp helps the reader answer several important questions: Why are so many adults still worrying about what their parents think? Why can't I talk to my parents the way I talk to other people? Why do we keep having the same arguments? How can I stop feeling guilty? How can I change family gatherings and holidays? What role would I like for my parents to play in my life today? Osterkamp's analysis of adult children–parent relationships can especially benefit adults in their 20s and 30s who want to get along better with their parents. Osterkamp suggests ways to communicate more effectively with parents, and she motivates the reader to develop a step-by-step action plan to accomplish relationship goals. Well written and well researched, this book is full of helpful examples and wise advice.

### Diamonds in the Rough

◆   *Your Renaissance Years* (1991) by Robert Veninga. Boston: Little, Brown.

This volume, subtitled *Making Retirement the Best Years of Your Life*, begins by describing the secrets of successful retirement and urging the reader to consider early retirement. Subsequent parts of the book focus on the retirement concerns of money, housing, health, leisure, relationships, and spirituality. Case histories of 135 retirees are interspersed throughout. *Your Renaissance Years* was positively rated in our national studies, but by only five psychologists; few of the mental health professionals were familiar with it. Nonetheless, it is a valuable, well-written, and in-depth resource for coping effectively with retirement. (Also reviewed in Chapter 5 on Aging.)

### Not Recommended

★   *The 50+ Wellness Program* (1990) by Harris Mcllwain, Debra Fulghum, Robert Fulghum, and Robert Bruce. New York: Wiley.

### Strongly Not Recommended

†   *Bad Childhood—Good Life* (2009) by Laura Schlessinger. New York: HarperCollins.

## ■ AUTOBIOGRAPHIES

### Strongly Recommended

★★★★★   *Tuesdays with Morrie: An Old Man, a Young Man, and Life's Greatest Secrets* (1997) by Mitch Albom. New York: Doubleday.

Sportswriter Albom had been a student of sociology professor Morrie Schwartz 20 years earlier. Reunited after he saw Schwartz on *Nightline*, Albom finds that his former professor is dying from Lou Gehrig's disease. The book describes 14 Tuesday visits Albom made to his dying mentor and the content of their conversations. It is a moving bestseller (also reviewed in Chapter 5).

### Recommended

★★★   *Fly Fishing through the Midlife Crisis* (1994) by Howell Raines. New York: Doubleday.

Similar in approach to Robert Pirsig's *Zen and the Art of Motorcycle Maintenance*, Pulitzer Prize-winning journalist Raines uses fly fishing as a metaphor for midlife, reflecting on being a son, brother, and husband tutored by older men. He started as an acquisitive "Redneck Fisher," determined to catch and keep everything. From his Uncle Erskine he learned the higher order of fly fishing, which was more about attitude, contemplation, elegance, and friendship than catching fish. The book is about life, death, and what comes in between, at the borderline between sport and reflection. Fly fishing has been more than a release or therapy for the author, a way of coping with family problems, divorce, and death, but a metaphor for a reflective life. You don't have to be an angler to appreciate this book.

★★★   *Forward from Here: Leaving Middle Age—and Other Unexpected Adventures* (2009) by Reeve Lindbergh. New York: Simon & Schuster.

Author of children's books and the daughter of famous parents, Reeve Lindbergh philosophizes about nature, love, loss, and the move beyond middle age, the 60-plus period her mother called "the youth of old age." As long as she is making this journey, she wants to get the most out of it and share the trip with others. She sees herself moving forward but carrying her past with her—"As I journey on, I carry my lost loved ones with me: my sister, my mother, and all the others. I have learned over the years that I can do this, that love continues beyond loss." Lindbergh sensitively describes living in an aging body and the disappearance of the foolishness and vanities of youth—more specifically, "after a certain age there's only so good you can look." Writing about mundane aspects of her life in rural Vermont ("dailiness outlasts despair") was an important coping strategy. There is a chapter on her brain tumor (fortunately benign) with the expectation we will hear more about this examined life.

### Diamond in the Rough

♦   *Whatever! A Baby Boomer's Journey into Middle Age* (2006) by Beverly Mahone. Self-published.

A journalist and motivational speaker with 25 years of experience in TV and radio news reporting, the author of this memoir and a previous book, *Don't Ask and I Won't Have to Lie*, describes her transition to middle age in a lively, witty style. She discusses the changes associated with menopause (mood swings, hot flashes, and night sweats), weight gain, middle-age dating, and religious issues. The book should be useful for women, especially Baby Boomers, making this journey and the men in their lives. Not well known by psychologists, thus earning the designation of Diamond in the Rough.

## ▤ FILMS

### Strongly Recommended

★★★★★   *The Trip to Bountiful* (1985) directed by Peter Masterson. PG rating. 106 minutes.

A country woman forced by circumstances to live with her son and daughter-in-law in a small city apartment is surprised to discover how old she has become and decides to revisit her girlhood home in Bountiful, Texas. She stubbornly persists, evading her family's fears about this trip, and makes the journey to reminisce and imagine her parents in the old house. In a subplot, she relates with a young girl during the brief bus trip to Bountiful, and we see her learn to accept her life and choose to make the best of it. This film illustrates but does not resolve the conflicts between people of different generations and demonstrates what adult development is like.

★★★★★ *The Doctor* (1991) directed by Randa Haines. PG-13 rating. 125 minutes.

A pompous surgeon (played by William Hurt) develops throat cancer and experiences what it is like to be a patient in an uncaring and mechanical system. He discovers his disconcerting mortality and gets a reprieve to lead a life of caring and compassion. This uplifting film may prove useful for those lacking empathy, struggling with what the health-care system has become, or needing an example of how to communicate with a spouse made distant.

★★★★ *It's a Wonderful Life* (1946) directed by Frank Capra. G rating. 129 minutes.

A man who has done the right thing all his life, living by his values and those of his neighbors, is brought low by an uncle's accidental misplacement of bank funds and contemplates suicide. An angel appears and shows him how badly his town, its families, and its ordinary citizens would have suffered had he not been there to lend them funds and advice. The movie works as an inspiring fable encouraging people to examine their lives, gain perspective, and take a second chance.

★★★★ *Hr. Holland's Opus* (1996) directed by Stephen Herek. PG rating. 142 minutes.

Glen Holland is a composer who accepts a temporary teaching position to pay the rent while he composes a memorable piece of music to leave his mark on the world. However, his temporary job turns into a lifetime commitment to his students and music education. His definition of success grows over the course of his career to encompass assisting his students and his family. A powerful film for addressing the meaning of success, the midlife reevaluation of career choices, and the personal sacrifices made for family gains.

**Recommended**

★★★ *Field of Dreams* (1989) directed by Phil Alden Robinson. PG rating. 106 minutes.

A couple choose a simple farming lifestyle instead of the hectic modern world. The husband then hears a voice telling him to "build it and they will come." Despite his doubts, the threat of foreclosure, and family opposition, with his wife's support he builds a baseball diamond in a cornfield, and the legends of a simpler time in professional baseball emerge and toss a few around. This movie may inspire self-doubters to cling to their dreams and others to take the risk of supporting their loved one's dreams. At the same time, it is important to recognize the fantasy and insubstantiality of the plot.

★★★ *A Christmas Carol* (1938) directed by Edwin L. Marin. Not rated. 69 minutes.

Ideal for reminding those too focused on making money that family can provide enormous satisfaction. But this theme can be expanded to include examining any of one's values:

relationships, seeking fame, accepting invitations to become different, and generally looking at the future outcomes of current choices (the three ghosts' visits).

**Not Recommended**

★★  *17 Again* (2009) directed by Burr Steers. PG-13 rating. 102 minutes.

## ■ INTERNET RESOURCES

### General Websites

★★★★  *USA.gov Senior Citizens' Resources* www.usa.gov/Topics/Seniors.shtml

Although not about adult development per se, this comprehensive U.S. government resource provides links to hundreds of helpful resources for people who are aging.

### Psychoeducational Materials

★★★★★  *Social Gerontology* www.trinity.edu/~mkearl/geron.html

Written for the college-educated person, this page offers introductory context and connections for understanding aging from a social psychology perspective. The website helps the reader understand aging in a helpful lifespan context.

★★★★★  *Ageism* by Barrie Robinson www.oaltc.ku.edu/gerorich/reports/ageismandolderadult.pdf

Prepared as resources for college courses, the exercises in the appendices and the other contents can help anyone become more aware of this subtle prejudice, its crippling myths, and the liberating truths.

★★★★★  *Attitudes: Key to Health, Happiness & Longevity* www.attitudefactor.com

The 20-item questionnaire asks about feelings of well-being, happiness, and hopefulness. The site then scores and returns information on the longevity consequences of your answers. This could be useful feedback for unhappy persons who cannot commit to therapy or change. The site offers the empirical support citations for this relationship and many readings on this issue.

★★★★  *Men at Midlife* www.midlife-men.com

This website from Noel McNaughton offers not only his personal experience with making it through a midlife crisis but also a wealth of articles on spirituality, depression, stages of life, your life's mission, health, personal stories, and more. Although primarily aimed at a male audience, some of the articles and topics are relevant and valuable for women too.

★★★★  *Pick the Brain* www.pickthebrain.com

A handy self-improvement website that focuses on topics valuable to people in any stage of their life, from motivation and personal productivity, to psychology and self-education.

★★★★   *Positively Aging blog* www.jannfreed.com/category/positively-aging

Understanding that learning is a lifelong process that has the potential to result in wisdom, this blog by Jann Freed offers weekly tips and case stories.

★★★★   *Boomers on the Rise: Aging Well* blogs.psychcentral.com/aging

This blog by Tamara McClintock Greenberg, PsyD, focuses on the complicated landscape of modern-day aging.

★★★   *Awakenings* www.lessons4living.com

Offering "Lessons for Living," this website hosts an eclectic mix of articles from Daniel Johnston, PhD. Under article titles such as "Cycle of Change," "Midlife," and "Lessons for Life," you'll find helpful advice and tips for getting through middle life's bumps.

**See also** Aging (Chapter 5), Death and Grieving (Chapter 18), Men's Issues (Chapter 29), and Women's Issues (Chapter 42).

# AGING

M ore than a century ago, Oliver Wendell Holmes said, "To be seventy years young is sometimes far more cheerful and hopeful than to be forty years old." In Holmes's day, being 70 years young was unusual, as the average life expectancy was less than 45 years. In the ensuing century, we have gained an average of more than 30 years of life, mainly because of improvements in sanitation, nutrition, and medical knowledge. In fact, elderly people (those age 65 and older) now constitute a greater proportion of the population, about 13%, than at any other time.

For too long, the aging process was thought of as an inevitable, irreversible decline. Aging involves both decline and growth, loss and gain. The previous view of aging was that we should passively live out our final years. The new view stresses that, although we are in the evening of our lives, we are not meant to live out our remaining years passively. Everything we know about older adults suggests that the more active they are, the happier and healthier they are.

In this chapter, we present self-help books, autobiographies, online self-help, films, Internet resources, and national support groups for people who are in their older years and, in some cases, for their children and caregivers (Box 5.1).

## ■ SELF-HELP BOOKS

**Strongly Recommended**

★★★★★ *Healthy Aging: A Lifelong Guide to Your Well-Being* (2005) by Andrew Weil. New York: Anchor

The concept of aging is viewed comprehensively in this book by integrative medicine pioneer Andrew Weil. There is no promotion of fighting age or submitting to age, but a fact-based description of what we truly know about what is good for us and what is not. Subjects include the standard topics such as physical activity, nutritional choices, sleep, and stress; however, these are discussed in the context of factors that apply in different age categories and how to maximize one's health at a given age. Not-so-conventional topics include attention to anti-inflammatory foods and supplements, memory, and an extensive appendix on dietary supplements, the model nutritional plan, and other reference material. The most highly rated book on aging in all of our national studies.

## BOX 5.1
## RECOMMENDATION HIGHLIGHTS

**SELF-HELP BOOKS**
- On aging from multiple and comprehensive perspectives:
  - ★★★★★ *Healthy Aging* by Andrew Weil
  - ★★★★ *You, Staying Young* by Michael F. Roizen and Mehmet C. Oz
- On aging successfully:
  - ★★★ *Aging Well* by George Vaillant
  - ★★★ *It's Better to Be over the Hill Than under It* by Eda LeShan
- On becoming an adult caregiver of aging parents:
  - ★★★ *The Emotional Survival Guide for Caregivers* by Barry J. Jacobs

**AUTOBIOGRAPHIES**
- On conversations about life and death:
  - ★★★★★ *Tuesdays with Morrie* by Mitch Albom
- On remaining active and contributing to society:
  - ★★★★ *The Virtues of Aging* by Jimmy Carter
  - ★★★ *The Last Gift of Life* by Carolyn G. Heilbrun
- On turning 50 and passing through menopause:
  - ♦ *Getting Over Getting Older* by Letty Cottin Pogrebin
- On taking care of aging parents:
  - ★★★ *Changing Places* by Judy Kramer
  - ♦ *A Bittersweet Season* by Jane Gross

**FILMS**
- On accepting aging, repairing relationships, and finding meaning:
  - ★★★★★ *On Golden Pond*
  - ★★★★ *About Schmidt*
  - ★★★ *Wrestling Ernest Hemingway*

**ONLINE SELF-HELP**
- For research-validated tests to determine risk for cognitive decline:
  - ★★★ *Positive Aging* www.positiveager.com

**INTERNET RESOURCES**
- On resources for those 55 and older:
  - ★★★★★ *NIH Senior Health* nihseniorhealth.gov
  - ★★★★★ *USA.gov Senior Citizens' Resources* www.usa.gov/Topics/Seniors.shtml
  - ★★★★ *American Association of Retired Persons (AARP)* www.aarp.org

**** *You, Staying Young: The Owner's Manual for Extending Your Warranty* (2007) by Michael F. Roizen and Mehmet C. Oz. New York: Free Press

"Aging and disease are not the same" is the theme of this pragmatic book on health and aging by two prominent physicians. The chapters are organized into two categories: the Major Aging Factors such as genetics, energy, viruses, toxins, and sun radiation, and what one can do to counteract the aging factors. The entire narrative is placed in the clever and interesting metaphor of our bodies as a city. The geography, which essentially cannot be changed, represents our bodies. The immune system is our police force, our arteries are highways, our brain is an electric grid, our skin is like the city parks contributing to our vibrancy, and yes, our fat is the landfill. Even though the metaphors are cute and clever, they are also functional in describing our systems and what we can do to keep them healthy. Highly valued and hugely popular.

**Recommended**

*** *Another Country: Navigating the Emotional Terrain of Our Elders* (2000) by Mary Pipher. New York: Riverhead.

Psychologist Pipher describes the transition into old age, which is what she means by "another country." She believes that the greatest shame of older adults is not being self-suf-ficient and keeping their feelings to themselves. The old must be valued, must be involved, must give back, and must be engaged in life. The book includes excerpts from sessions with Pipher's clients, interspersed with advice for sensitively communicating with the elderly. Pipher says that there is a huge cultural gap between Baby Boomers, who express their emo-tions openly, and their emotionally restrictive aging parents. Psychologists in our studies rated the book quite favorably but infrequently.

*** *Aging Well* (2002) by George Vaillant. Boston: Little Brown.

This book describes the most recent results from longitudinal studies of aging con-ducted by psychiatrist George Vaillant. Inspirational messages reveal how men and women can lead happier, more fulfilling, healthier lives as they grow older. Vaillant does a wonder-ful job of interspersing case studies and research results to provide an in-depth look at the mechanisms of aging well. Vaillant concludes that individual lifestyles play a greater role than genetics, wealth, or ethnicity in determining how happy people are as older adults. He describes in step-by-step fashion how people can change their lifestyle to lead a more fulfill-ing life as they age. This is an outstanding book and one that undoubtedly would have been given 5 stars if it had been rated by enough psychologists in our national studies.

*** *It's Better to Be over the Hill Than under It: Thoughts on Life over Sixty* (1990) by Eda LeShan. New York: Newmarket.

This book consists of what LeShan believes are her best columns from *Newsday* on a wide range of aging topics, related mainly to the social, psychological, and lifestyle aspects of aging. The articles are presented in three sections: Loving and Living, Memories, and Growing and Changing. The 75 essays range from "An Open Letter to the Tooth Fairy" to "Nothing Is Simple Anymore" and "Divorce after Sixty." Many life issues that have to be dealt with in old age are covered: money, love, sex, anger, facing mortality, work, marriage, friendship, retirement, holidays, grandparenting, and children. Woven through the essays is hope for older adults, hope that will allow them to love and grow and to keep their minds active and bodies alive. The real test for older adults, LeShan says, is not looking back but rather dealing with the present, no matter what the inevitable aspects of aging are, and anticipating each coming day. This 3-star book was favorably reviewed, deserving of 4 stars were it not for the small number of experts evaluating it. LeShan is a masterful writer who mixes wit with sage advice. The book proves especially good for older adults who feel caught in a rut and need their spirits lifted.

★★★ *Emotional Survival Guide for Caregivers: Looking After Yourself and Your Family While Helping an Aging Parent* (2006) by Barry J. Jacobs. New York: Guilford.

The story of two sisters caring for their mother during her cancer portrays the experience of millions of families undergoing recalibration. The book candidly discusses sadness, guilt, resentment, anger, and other feelings that no one wants to admit but that are normal in this circumstance. Two themes guide the narrative: (1) the relationships among the well and ill family members and the health professionals and (2) the individuals coping with defining commitment, accepting support, handling sacrifice, weighing hope and acceptance, fostering flexibility, protecting intimacy, and sustaining spirit. Each topic is discussed in one chapter; lots of questions and answers serve as tips for navigating each area.

★★★ *Enjoy Old Age: A Program of Self-Management* (1983) by B. F. Skinner and M. E. Vaughan. New York: Norton.

Vaughan, a former Harvard research associate and well-known expert on aging, and Skinner, a pioneer in behaviorism, combine their talents to assist older adults in making environmental changes to improve the quality of their lives. Specific areas covered include forgetfulness, thinking clearly and creatively, doing something about old age, getting along better with people, and dealing with the new emotions of aging. Advance planning and a positive approach can provide solutions to the problems of aging. Skinner describes his own solutions, and Vaughan contributes selections from the literature on aging. The book is written in a nonscientific way using everyday English. It is useful for people approaching or already in their 60s or 70s, or for those living or working with older people.

★★★ *Complete Guide to Health and Well-Being after 50* (1988) by Robert Weiss and Genell Subak-Sharpe. New York: Times Books.

The full title of this book is actually *The Columbia University School of Public Health Complete Guide to Health and Well-Being after 50.* The word *Complete* in the title is appropriate: the book provides information about an encyclopedic number of physical and mental health matters that older adults face. The topics range from medical and physical concerns such as heart disease, arthritis, and cosmetic surgery to psychological and lifestyle concerns such as coping with stress and retirement. This excellent guide provides solid descriptions of the health problems of the elderly and the best ways to deal with them. As would be expected in a book written by public health experts, it is strongly tilted toward a presentation and exploration of physical health; coverage of the psychological and social dimensions of aging is not as thorough and not as insightful.

★★★  *Aging Well* (1989) by James Fries. Reading, MA: Addison-Wesley.

Fries believes that we have the capability to age well, with grace, wisdom, energy, and vitality. Aging well is not an easy task, he says. It requires a basic understanding of the aging process, a good plan, work, and persistence. Part I, Vitality and Aging, communicates the value of pride and enthusiasm in preventing disease and provides a wealth of understanding about specific diseases such as arthritis and osteoporosis. Part II, General Concerns, describes five keys to a healthy senior lifestyle: selecting and dealing with doctors, sexual issues, retirement, chronic illness, and completing a plan that will ensure that your wishes are carried out after you die. Part III, Solutions, is a step-by-step guide to managing a full range of medical problems, including pain, urinary tract problems, and heart ailments. The book is optimistic, well written, and thorough. Fries's expertise on aging clearly comes through.

★★★  *Gift of Years: Growing Older Gracefully* (2010) by Joan Chittister. New York: BlueBridge.

"Death can come at any time: age comes as a true blessing," writes the author. This book concerns not the physical dimension of living but the mental and spiritual ones. Forty aspects of living through stages are presented by a 70-year-old who says she may have written the book too soon and reserves the right for a revision in 20 years. The topics of resentment, joy, regret, fulfillment, freedom, limitations, and productivity reframe the meaning of being versus doing. Life after organized work is not "non-life" but "new life." The message is a rich and meaningful perspective on charting new territory for healthy and valuable years that earlier generations did not have.

★★★  *Ageless Body, Timeless Mind: The Quantum Alternative to Growing Old* (1993) by Deepak Chopra. New York: Harmony.

Chopra, a bestselling author, offers an Eastern philosophical approach to the problems of aging. He combines mind–body medicine with current antiaging research. He states that a prolonged, fruitful life is not a question of mind over matter, but rather of mind and matter, mind and body, together as one with the universe. By intervening at the level where belief becomes biology, we can achieve our potential. Chopra offers step-by-step exercises to help create a healthy life. A separate chapter examines India's traditional medical system of Ayurveda. The book reveals how we can learn to direct the way our bodies metabolize time and reverse the aging process. A book for the layperson and professional interested in a blend of Eastern philosophy and Western scientific research.

★★★  *The Fountain of Age* (1993) by Betty Friedan. New York: Simon & Schuster.

The book looks at new possibilities and new directions for aging of both men and women. Some topics covered are women's living longer than men; physical, emotional, and environmental changes; and age as adventure. The author encourages older people not to buy into the myth that aging is a problem, a plight, a time of rapidly declining faculties. Friedan provides research and anecdotal evidence that the older adult years may be a period of true creativity. She discusses the tragic practice of early retirement, myths about menopause, early preparation for death, and overprotectiveness of family, friends, professionals, and the government. Creative ideas about health care, housing, work, and relationships are discussed. A book for all adults, but a critique of our society and aging that will definitely move the over-60 crowd.

★★★  *How to Live Longer and Feel Better* (1986) by Linus Pauling. New York: Freeman.

This book provides a regimen that the author believes will add years to your life and make you feel better. Linus Pauling, a two-time Nobel Prize winner, shows how vitamins work and how to make them work for you. Pauling especially believes that vitamin C is responsible for producing and maintaining the body's supply of collagen, which he calls the glue that holds the body together. He argues that megadoses of vitamin C and other critical vitamins can slow the aging process, make us look younger, and help us feel better. This book received 3 stars in the national studies, barely making it into the Recommended category. In the past, Pauling's ideas clashed with those of the medical establishment, but recently researchers are finding that the antioxidant vitamins may help slow the aging process and improve the health of older adults. Pauling portrays himself as a misunderstood, maligned maverick whose ideas will eventually be accepted by the medical community.

★★★  *What's Age Got to Do with It?* (2008) by Robin McGraw. Nashville, TN: Thomas Nelson.

Robin McGraw's mother died of a heart attack at age 58 while on the phone with her. This event set the context for the author's evaluation of self-care, doing all that is possible physically, spiritually, and emotionally to care for herself, not just those around her. Her mother was a kind and caring person who had devoted and ultimately sacrificed her well-being for her family, friends, and others. This experience changed McGraw, and her transformation is reflected in the subjects of fitness, nutrition, physical maintenance of self, spirituality, and other aspects of self-care. The author's discussion of balancing care for others with self-care lends a personal perspective that invites readers to apply these topics to their own lives.

### Diamond in the Rough

♦  *Your Renaissance Years* (1991) by Robert Veninga. Boston: Little, Brown.

This volume, subtitled *Making Retirement the Best Years of Your Life,* begins by describing the secrets of successful retirement and urging the reader to consider early retirement. Subsequent parts of the book focus on the retirement concerns of money, housing, health, leisure, relationships, and spirituality. Case histories of 135 retirees are interspersed throughout. *Your Renaissance Years* was positively rated in our national studies, but by only five psychologists; few of the mental health professionals were familiar with it. Nonetheless, it is a valuable, well-written, in-depth resource for coping effectively with retirement. (Also reviewed in Chapter 4 on Adult Development.)

### Not Recommended

★★  *20 Years Younger: Look Younger, Feel Younger, Be Younger!* (2011) by Bob Greene, Harold A. Lancer, Ronald L. Kotler, and Diane L. McKay. New York: Little, Brown.

## ■ AUTOBIOGRAPHIES

### Strongly Recommended

★★★★★ *Tuesdays with Morrie: An Old Man, a Young Man, and Life's Greatest Secrets* (1997) by Mitch Albom. New York: Doubleday.

Sportswriter Albom had been a student of sociology professor Morrie Schwartz 20 years earlier. Reunited after he saw Schwartz on *Nightline*, Albom finds that his former professor is dying from Lou Gehrig's disease. The book describes 14 Tuesday visits Albom made to his dying mentor and the content of their conversations. This moving bestseller deepens our understanding of life and death, is both funny and sad, and is as much about Albom's life as about his subject, who speaks for himself in *Morrie: In His Own Words*. (Also reviewed in Chapter 4 on Adult Development.)

★★★★ *The Virtues of Aging* (1998) by Jimmy Carter. New York: Ballantine.

The former president discusses aging in America, with special attention to the state of the Social Security system, health, exercise, and financial planning. Carter discusses the importance of family ties and describes ways in which older people can remain active and contribute to social betterment. Down to earth and easy to read, this book focuses on the wisdom that people accumulate over a lifetime and how it can be applied. President Carter personifies those whose reputation and good works increased following a formal retirement.

### Recommended

★★★ *Changing Places: A Journey with my Parents into their Old Age* (2001) by Judy Kramer. New York: Berkley.

Originally written as a series of newspaper columns, the book describes the aging of journalist Cramer's parents, their move into a nursing home, and their deaths. While holding a full-time job and caring for her own family, Kramer becomes her parents' caregiver, grappling on a daily basis with their medical appointments, Medicare paperwork, and bills. The book portrays with realism and tenderness the transition from being one's parents' child to becoming their caregiver, and the sandwich feeling of meeting demands from two families.

★★★ *The Last Gift of Life: Life Beyond Sixty* (1998) by Carolyn G. Heilbrun. New York: Ballantine.

The author had it all—a fine education, career, family, and great recognition. She was an English professor at Columbia, a noted feminist critic, and author of a well-known mystery series under the pseudonym Amanda Cross. However, when she was young, Heilbrun had vowed to take her life at age 70, in the belief that life after that was not worth living. The realization of how enjoyable and productive life had been in her 50s and 60s changed her mind. Now safely past 70, she had not lost her spirit, describing herself as "still dancing for joy" and free from earlier constraints and the pushes and pulls of family and career. Now she could fully be herself in a family context, as wife, mother, and grandmother. She is a great fan of e-mail and the Internet, describing how they expanded her universe. Heilbrun is a role model for younger women and an inspiration for older women.

★★★   *The Fountain of Age* (1993) by Betty Friedan. New York: Simon & schuster.

One of the major figures in the modern feminist movement and author of *The Feminine Mystique,* Friedan deconstructs current beliefs about aging, maintaining that it can be a time of adventure, exploration, fulfillment, and creativity. Combining the personal and the political with research findings, this book is a trenchant critique of the decline model of aging. A good book for a socially conscious reader. (Also rated earlier in this chapter as a self-help book.)

★★★   *I'm Not as Old as I Used to Be* (1998) by Frances Weaver. New York: Hyperion.

A sprightly account of life after 70 in which NPR commentator and senior editor of the *Today Show* Frances Weaver describes her battle with alcoholism after her husband's death. She went to a detox center and eventually achieved sobriety. Weaver returned to school, traveled, and began writing. She employs her keen wit to demonstrate how to be active and productive during life's later years. A good account of developing new interests after the age of 70.

★★★   *Getting Over Getting Older* (1997) by Letty Cottin Pogrebin. New York: Little, Brown.

In this book written when she was 55, Pogrebin, a founding editor of *Ms.* magazine and author of *Deborah, Golda and Me,* describes midlife as a time when time speeds up and the body slows down, when you are not old but no longer young. Her upbeat, sensitive, and funny book portrays the small highs and lows of midlife: losing a youthful appearance, discovering solitude, tiring more easily, needing reading glasses, bulging waistline, and running for more frequent bathroom visits. Throughout it all is a sense of sisterhood and feminist community. Aging brings medical emergencies, such as a breast biopsy. Because life no longer seems infinite, there is a heightened sense of living in the present.

### Diamond in the Rough

◆   *A Bittersweet Season: Caring for our Aging Parents—And Ourselves* (2011) by Jane Gross. New York: Knopf Doubleday.

Health journalist Jane Gross, author of the *New York Times* New Old Age blog, sensitively documents her struggle to care for her dying mother in a maze of frustrating federal and state programs and regulations plus problems in coordinating care with her brother. She cites relevant research on the biology and psychology of aging and gives advice to those seeking long-term care for a declining family member. Viewed in a broader context, this personal narrative is an indictment of our failing eldercare nonsystem and the toll it takes on caregivers. Although the role reversal between parent and child is a topic that most younger people are unwilling to discuss, the book leaves the reader informed and prepared rather than overwhelmed and defensive. The book ends with a 9-page list of resources. Published a few months before our latest survey, this book was not yet widely known and was therefore accorded a Diamond in the Rough.

# FILMS

### Strongly Recommended

★★★★★   *On Golden Pond* (1981) directed by Mark Rydell. PG rating. 109 minutes.

An 80-year-old retired teacher (Henry Fonda) becomes preoccupied with death and losing his faculties as his birthday is celebrated. He becomes anxious, irritable, and difficult to live with, but his wife (Katharine Hepburn) knows how to handle him and helps his alienated daughter (Jane Fonda) make the connections needed by both for resolution before his death. All three actors received Oscars. This film might prove most useful to those alienated from their parents and trying to communicate and to those parents. It might reinforce that there may not be time for healing unless one acts now. Deserving of the 5 stars it received in our national studies and deserving of another viewing by even the most cynical among us.

★★★★   *About Schmidt* (2002) directed by Alexander Payne. R rating. 125 minutes.

Jack Nicholson plays Warren Schmidt, who retires as an insurance executive at age 66. He sees an ad for connecting to an orphaned child in Africa and calls the number and signs up for the correspondence and support. As weeks go by, Schmidt comes home and finds his wife dead. His daughter is still planning to hold her wedding, however, and to a person Schmidt doesn't like. He attends the wedding and manages to get through the event only to be cornered by an attempted seduction by Kathy Bates, the mother of the son-in-law. Schmidt drives his RV back to his home in Omaha with a sense of emptiness. He finds in his mail a letter from the African boy, who drew stick figures of himself and Schmidt. The gesture touches Schmidt, and he begins to feel connected with humanity once again. This film is a poignant portrayal of meaning, relationships, and purpose among the aging.

### Recommended

★★★   *Wrestling Ernest Hemingway* (1993) directed by Randa Haines. PG-13 rating. 122 minutes.

A character study of two lonely old men trapped in the emptiness of their own lives. Frank and Walter meet in a park and gradually become friends but eventually separate after quarrels and misbehavior. In words and deeds, the two men discuss and accept the imminence of death. A sensitive film on a sensitive topic: aging and death.

★★★   *Cocoon* (1986) directed by Ron Howard. PG-13 rating. 117 minutes.

Disregard the subplot of visiting intergalactic aliens and focus on how the senior citizens of a Florida retirement community find an actual fountain of youth. They experience new vigor and possibilities. The movie is, of course, a fantasy and a denial of the negatives and losses of aging; nonetheless, it is an inspiring and perhaps helpful film about what may still be felt and lived.

★★★   *The Curious Case of Benjamin Button* (2008) directed by David Fincher. PG-13 rating. 166 minutes.

Unique aspects of aging are portrayed in the story of Benjamin Button, who mysteriously began life with several aging diseases that resulted in his being elderly at birth and growing younger. His mother died at childbirth, and his father gave him up to a childless couple. As he grew younger, he met the love of his life, Daisy, who was 12 at the time he was in his 50s. They developed a bond, and as the years went by, they met again and fell in love when they were both in their 40s. They lived together as partners for some years and then had a child together. As they aged apart, Benjamin left Daisy because he did not want his child to see him grow younger than she. They encountered each other at moments in time, the last being when Ben was a small child. The movie portrays the timelessness of love, commitment, and devotion. The storyline is certainly a unique one, but because of the juxtaposition of aging, it presents the meaning of life and loved ones in a chronologically backwards but poignant manner.

### Not Recommended

★★ *Space Cowboys* (2000) directed by Clint Eastwood. PG-13 rating. 130 minutes.

★★ *Grumpy Old Men* (1993) directed by Donald Petrie. PG-13 rating. 103 minutes.

## ■ ONLINE SELF-HELP

★★★ *Positive Aging* www.positiveager.com

This website contains several aging- and memory-related tests that can help adults decide whether they are at risk for age-related cognitive decline. The information can then be used by mental health professionals to develop treatments. The website presents information about healthy aging and also a blog where the principal author shares his expertise and advice. The tests and information are available free of charge.

## ■ INTERNET RESOURCES

While there are vast numbers of sites on aging, medical problems, and geriatric information, there is much less self-help on the Internet. These are the most clinically useful sites.

### General Websites

★★★★★ *National Institute on Aging* www.nia.nih.gov

From one of the U.S. National Institutes of Health comes this helpful and comprehensive government resource that offers hundreds of resources and articles related to aging and seniors. Includes dozens of booklets that can be downloaded or ordered on topics ranging from exercise, driving, and falls, to Alzheimer's, prostate problems, and the safe use of medicines (under "Health & Aging > Publications").

★★★★★ *USA.gov Senior Citizens' Resources* www.usa.gov/Topics/Seniors.shtml

This comprehensive U.S. government website provides links to hundreds of helpful senior resources and is a great place to start when searching for senior resources online.

★★★★ *New York Online Access to Health* noah-health.org

The New York Online Access to Health (NOAH) website offers a large directory of Internet resources on hundreds of health and related topics, including aging and general living. Type in "aging" or "Alzheimer's" (or any other topic that comes to mind) for dozens and sometimes hundreds of useful, relevant results. Results are not New York-specific.

★★★   *ElderWeb* www.elderweb.com

This research site for professionals and family members contains more than 4,500 links to eldercare and long-term care information, including legal, financial, medical, and housing issues and policy, research, and statistics.

★★★★   *Administration on Aging* www.aoa.gov

A website from the U.S. Department of Health & Human Services, this government resource provides information about government-funded programs focused on older Americans. It also runs the Eldercare Locator (eldercare.gov), designed to help a person easily find both local community resources as well as topical information resources.

★★★★   *American Association of Retired Persons* www.aarp.org

AARP is a nonprofit organization dedicated to addressing the needs and interests of persons 50 and older. Their website offers articles about aging as well as advocacy to help enhance the quality of life for all by promoting independence, dignity, and purpose.

★★★★★   *NIH Senior Health* www.nihseniorhealth.gov

Everything seniors need to know about their health from the U.S. National Institutes of Health, including topics such as diseases and conditions, healthy aging, memory, mental health concerns, vision and hearing, and much more. The website has been designed for ease of use with older adults in mind.

★★★★   *Healthy Aging* www.healthyaging.net

A website focused on providing positive information about healthy aging, with a focus on helping 50+-year-olds improve all aspects of their fitness—mental, physical, social, and financial.

★★★   *Senior Living* seniorliving.about.com

Senior Living from About.com is no longer updated with new content but is still a great resource for older adults who are looking for information about their health, relationships as we age, and jobs and financial advice.

## Psychoeducational Materials

★★★★★   *Social Gerontology* www.trinity.edu/_mkearl/geron.html

Written for the college educated, this page offers an introductory context and connections for understanding aging from a social psychology perspective. The website helps the reader understand aging in a helpful lifespan context.

★★★ *Alcohol and the Elderly* alcoholism.about.com/library/weekly/aa981118.htm?pid=2750&cob=home

This page has links to many others about alcohol and drug overuse in the elderly. They may help overcome denial in clients or families. Similarly, the upstream site, alcoholism.about.com/od/elder/Elderly_and_Alcohol.htm, offers over two dozen articles on this issue.

★★★★ *Attitudes: Key to Health, Happiness and Longevity* www.attitudefactor.com

The 20-item, 5-minute questionnaire asks about feelings of well-being, happiness, and hopefulness and then provides information on the longevity consequences of your answers. This could be useful feedback for unhappy persons who cannot commit to change. The site offers empirical support citations for this relationship and many readings.

★★★★ *Positively Aging blog* www.jannfreed.com/category/positively-aging

Understanding that learning is a life-long process that has the potential to result in wisdom, this blog by Jann Freed offers weekly tips and case stories.

★★★★ *Boomers on the Rise: Aging Well* blogs.psychcentral.com/aging

This blog, by Tamara McClintock Greenberg, PsyD, focuses on the complicated landscape of modern-day aging.

★★★★ *Healthy Aging Tips* www.helpguide.org/life/healthy_aging_seniors_aging_well.htm

A one-page article from the nonprofit HelpGuide about how to cope with change, finding meaning and joy as we age, staying connected with others, boosting vitality, and keeping our minds sharp.

★★★ *Senior Site* www.afb.org/seniorsitehome.asp

This site from the American Foundation for the Blind is a good resource for older adults concerned about their eyesight and eye health. Very detailed and easy to navigate and read.

## ■ SUPPORT GROUPS

**AARP (American Association of Retired Persons)**

Phone: 877-434-7598
www.aarp.org

**Alliance for Aging Research**

Phone: 202-293-2856
www.agingresearch.org

**American Parkinson's Disease Association**

Phone: 800-223-APDA or 718-981-8001
apdaparkinson.com

**American Society on Aging**

Phone: 415-974-9600
www.asaging.org

**Arthritis Foundation**

Phone: 800-283-7800
www.arthritis.org

**Department of Veterans Affairs**

www.va.gov
Publishes a resource guide for working with older adults.

**Gray Panthers**

Phone: 202-737-6637
www.graypanthers.org
For young and old adults working together.

**National Council on Aging**

Phone: 202-479-1200 or 800-424-9046
www.ncoa.org

**National Family Caregivers Association**

Phone: 800-896-3650
www.nfcacares.org

**National Hispanic Council on Aging**

Phone: 202-347-9733
www.nhcoa.org

**National Institute on Aging**

Phone: 800-222-4225
www.nih.gov/nia

**National Parkinson Foundation**

Phone: 1-800-327-4545
www.parkinson.org

**National Stroke Association**

Phone: 303-771-1700 or 800-STROKES
www.stroke.org

**Older Women's League**

Phone: 877-653-7966
www.owl-national.org
Membership organization that advocates on behalf of various economic and social issues
for midlife and older women.

**See also** Adult Development (Chapter 4), Death and Grieving (Chapter 18), and
Dementia/Alzheimer's (Chapter 19).

# CHAPTER 6

# ANGER

A nger is a powerful emotion. Everybody gets angry sometimes, but for most of us, it's mild anger a couple of times a week. Mild anger or annoyance often emerges if a loved one or a friend performs what we perceive to be a misdeed, whether it is being late, promising one thing and doing another, or neglecting a duty, for example. It's a part of life.

Anger disorders, on the other hand, are characterized as enraged, uncontrollable, and frequent. In the past, we have described such folks as possessing "fiery tempers"—becoming furious when they are criticized, when they are slowed down, when they are frustrated. In the present, we view chronic anger as a disorder that hurts others as well as themselves. Whether anger is an isolated problem or a symptom of another disorder, mental health professionals are increasingly treating it. Popular anger management techniques include relaxation, meditation, cognitive restructuring, empathy, problem solving, mindfulness, and communication skills.

In this chapter, we present the ratings and descriptions of anger self-help books and Internet resources, respectively (Box 6.1).

## ■ SELF-HELP BOOKS

### Strongly Recommended

★★★★★  *The Anger Control Workbook* (2000) by Matthew McKay and Peter Rogers. Oakland, CA: New Harbinger.

Psychologists McKay and Rogers provide a step-by-step, cognitive-behavioral approach for individuals seeking to control their anger. In 19 chapters, they describe how to identify, understand, respond to, and cope with hostile feelings. Especially recommended is learning how to relax in the face of physical tension in provocative situations; the authors state that it is almost impossible to get angry when you are able to relax your body. Numerous helpful exercises and worksheets are provided. This book is an excellent choice for those seeking to control their anger. Along with *The Dance of Anger* (reviewed below), *The Anger Control Workbook* was judged to be one of the best self-help books for anger.

★★★★★  *The Dance of Anger: A Woman's Guide to Changing the Patterns of Intimate Relationships* (reissue ed., 1997) by Harriet Lerner. New York: Harper Perennial.

This popular and prized book was written mainly for women about the anger in their lives, both their anger and that of the people they live with, especially men. It has sold more

**BOX 6.1**
**RECOMMENDATION HIGHLIGHTS**

**SELF-HELP BOOKS**

■ For advice and methods on reducing anger:

***** *The Anger Control Workbook* by Matthew McKay and Peter Rogers

**** *The Anger Workbook* by Lorrainne Bilodeau

**** *How to Control Your Anger before It Controls You* by Albert Ellis and Raymond Chip Tafrate

**** *Letting Go of Anger* by Ron Potter-Efron and Pat Potter-Efron

**** *Act on Life Not on Anger* (2006) by Georg H. Eifert et al.

■ For women who want to understand and moderate their anger:

***** *The Dance of Anger* by Harriet Lerner

■ For learning to control anger through cognitive therapy:

*** *Prisoners of Hate* by Aaron Beck

■ For coping with anger in different facets of life:

**** *Anger: The Misunderstood Emotion* by Carol Tavris

■ For helping children control their anger:

♦ *A Volcano in My Tummy* by Eliane Whitehouse and Warwick Pudney

**INTERNET RESOURCES**

■ For valuable information on anger management:

***** *How Can I Deal With My Anger?*
kidshealth.org/teen/your_mind/emotions/deal_with_anger.html

**** *Get Your Angries Out* www.angriesout.com

**** *How to Deal with Anger* www.mind.org.uk/help/diagnoses_and_conditions/dealing_with_anger

than a million copies and deservedly has been on the *New York Times* bestseller list. Lerner maintains that expressions of anger are not only encouraged more in boys and men than in girls and women but may be glorified to maladaptive extremes. By contrast, girls and women have been denied even a healthy and realistic expression of anger. Lerner argues that to express anger—especially openly, directly, or loudly—traditionally is considered to make a woman appear unladylike, unfeminine, and sexually unattractive. Lerner explains the difficulties women have in showing anger and describes how they can use their anger to gain a stronger, more independent sense of self. Rooted in both family systems and psychoanalytic theory, *The Dance of Anger* has nine chapters and an epilogue. Lerner describes the circular dances of couples, such as the all-too-familiar situation of the nagging wife and the withdrawing husband. The more she nags, the more he withdraws, and the more he withdraws, the more she nags. Lerner goes on to provide valuable advice about how to deal with anger when interacting with "impossible" mothers, with children, and in family triangles. This excellent guide is a compassionate exploration of women's anger and an insightful guide for turning anger into a constructive force that can reshape women's lives.

**** *Letting Go of Anger: The Ten Most Common Anger Styles and What to Do about Them* (1995) by Ron Potter-Efron and Pat Potter-Efron. Oakland, CA: New Harbinger.

The authors take a systematic approach to identifying and treating types of anger, often using cognitive-behavioral strategies. A questionnaire allows readers to categorize themselves into anger styles: masked anger, explosive anger, or chronic anger. Each chapter further describes several ways of manifesting anger within each of the three primary styles. Clarity and conciseness are strengths of this self-help resource. Each chapter outlines the characteristics of the anger style, typical examples of how the anger plays out, and remedies for counteracting anger. The suggested treatments are understandable and easily conducted by nonprofessionals.

**** *Anger: The Misunderstood Emotion* (revised and updated, 1989) by Carol Tavris. New York: Touchstone.

This excellent self-help book covers the wider terrain of anger and its manifestations. Indeed, it is hard to come up with any facet of anger—from wrecked friendships to wars— that Tavris does not address. The revised and updated edition includes new coverage of highway anger, violence in sports, young women's anger, and family anger, and it suggests strategies for getting through specific anger problems. The book consists of 10 entertaining chapters. In the first several chapters, Tavris debunks a number of myths about anger and highlights anger's cultural rules. She persuasively argues that "letting it all out" is not the best solution for defusing anger and effectively coping with stress. She dislikes pop-psychology approaches that tell people that anger is buried within them, and she argues that such notions are dangerous to the mental health of participants and to the social health of the community. She also sharply criticizes psychotherapy approaches that are based on the belief that inside every tranquil soul is a furious person screaming to get out. Later chapters present helpful ideas about anger in marital relationships and situations involving justice. In the final two chapters, Tavris tells readers how to rethink anger and make more adaptive choices. The book is well researched, and Tavris's delivery is witty and eloquent. People wanting to cope more effectively with the anger in their lives will find this book a welcome tonic.

**** *How to Control Your Anger before It Controls You* (1997) by Albert Ellis and Raymond Chip Tafrate. Secaucus, NJ: Birch Lane.

The treatment model of rational-emotive behavior therapy (REBT) developed by Albert Ellis has evolved over the years into many applications, all with the same underlying goal of controlling thoughts in order to control feelings. Ellis and his coauthor have adapted the REBT model to reducing or eliminating anger. They consider myths about dealing with anger, rational and irrational aspects of anger, and identifying self-angering beliefs. Multiple techniques are taught for thinking ways out of anger, as are well-described relaxation exercises and self-help forms that allow the reader to record experiences and self-guide through the cognitive-behavioral treatment of anger reduction. This practical volume is easy to read, understand, and apply. The REBT principles are presented with clarity in an inviting manner.

★★★★ *The Anger Workbook* (1992) by Lorrainne Bilodeau. Minneapolis: CompCare.

This information manual and workbook explains how to understand anger, see its usefulness, and have healthier anger. A cognitive-behavioral approach to anger is taken. The book presents a self-assessment questionnaire, followed by recommended changes in thought patterns and behaviors. The chapters are structured effectively for instruction; the several questionnaires are followed by chapters that address the potential clusters of answers the reader could have given and responds to them in a decision-making format. Concepts include taking a new perspective on anger, acknowledging the complexities of anger, understanding how anger goes awry, changing the experience of anger, and responding to another person's anger. This valuable and practical book clearly explains how to understand anger problems and how to move toward their resolution.

★★★★ *Act on Life, Not on Anger* (2006) by Georg H. Eifert, Matthew McKay, and John P. Forsyth. Oakland, CA: New Harbinger.

Acceptance and Commitment Therapy (ACT) is applied specifically to dealing with anger in this book. ACT principles teach the importance of accepting anger feelings and thoughts, but not acting on them. Failed techniques include keeping anger down and calming or distracting oneself—that is, trying to rid oneself of the anger. The three-part approach includes accepting the anger; choosing the values, outcome, and goals that one wants for life and for immediate direction; and then taking committed action toward the goals identified in step two. Each chapter offers a next step in the process and is accompanied by exercises that are practiced during the week. An instructional and systematic means of applying these principles is helpful.

**Recommended**

★★★ *Prisoners of Hate: The Cognitive Basis of Anger, Hostility, and Violence* (1999) by Aaron Beck. New York: Harper Perennial.

Psychiatrist Beck applies his cognitive therapy to helping individuals learn how to control their anger. Beck describes recognizable examples from everyday life of how people turn anger into hatred. He also tackles the history of hostility and violence on the part of societies and governments. His historical analysis of anger is somewhat tedious, though, especially for a self-help book. Beck argues that cognitive distortions involving hostile framing can lock the mind in a "prison of hate." He believes that hostility, anger, and violence can be greatly reduced when rational thinking overrides cognitive distortions. This valuable book was very highly rated by psychologists in our national studies and likely would have been given 5 stars if it had been rated more frequently.

★★★ *Angry All the Time: An Emergency Guide to Anger Control* (1994) by Ron Potter-Efron. Oakland, CA: New Harbinger.

This book was written for and about people who regularly function at a high level of anger. The author provides candid descriptions of the angry lifestyle, myths, and excuses for anger, along with a road map for breaking the cycle. Validating checklists enable the reader to clearly understand how to change. These include The Six Main Reasons People Stay Angry, The Violence Ladder, and a chapter for Partners of Angry People. This book hits anger behavior head on with a no-nonsense but understanding approach. The mental health experts in our study preferred Potter-Efron's later work, *Letting Go of Anger*, slightly more than this book. Refer to its review above in the "Strongly Recommended" listing.

★★★ *Anger Management for Everyone* (2009) by Raymond Chip Tafrate and Howard Kassinove. Atascadero, CA: Impact.

This self-help program on anger management is written for those who have difficulty managing their anger and those in work or personal relationships with them. The authors are psychologists who drew upon their many years of experience to develop this comprehensive model of changing anger responses through seven steps. The first section offers the basics on understanding anger, while the second section presents the seven steps. The third section discusses resources, relapse, and nine steps to a happier life. This book has humorous aspects, but is also a serious book about changing one's life with anger.

★★★ *When Anger Hurts* (1997) by Matthew McKay, Peter Rogers, and Judith McKay. Oakland, CA: Fine Communications.

This book presents a cognitive-behavioral approach to coping with anger. Subtitled *Quieting the Storm Within*, it is divided into three main sections that focus on understanding anger, building skills to cope with anger, and dealing with anger at home. The section on building skills to cope with anger contains a number of helpful strategies, including how to control stress step by step, how to keep anger from escalating, how to use healthy self-talk to deal with angry feelings, and how to engage in problem-solving communication when anger is harming relationships. The authors instruct readers in the specifics of keeping an anger journal.

★★★ *Rage: A Step-by-Step Guide to Overcoming Explosive Anger* (2007) by Ronald Potter-Efron. Oakland, CA: New Harbinger.

Written for individuals who experience uncontrollable or near-uncontrollable rage, this book fully explores the nature and causes of rage and tools to manage it. The approach teaches individuals how to control their rage now without prolonged experience. The author promotes the understanding of rage by explaining what he thinks are four types: survival rage, impotence rage, abandonment rage, and shame-based rage. The author leads the readers through the types of rage, the likely development, and the most relevant treatment for each person's actual needs. The book is well written and addresses a problem that most self-help books do not.

★★★ *The Anger Workbook for Teens* (2009) by Raychelle Cassada Lohmann. Oakland, CA: New Harbinger.

Thirty-seven exercises target the many facets of anger: understanding anger and what triggers it, observing the way one reacts to anger, and learning skills to overcome anger. Ten-minute daily worksheets offer personal anger profiles, how to notice physical symptoms, and other self-reflective activities. The exercises include such topics as coping with conflict, taking a mental vacation, releasing anger symbolically, and understanding family patterns. This book is written expressly for teens and projects an understanding of the life circumstances of being a teen and not knowing how to cope with anger.

★★★  *The Gift of Anger* (2011) by Marcia Cannon. Oakland, CA: New Harbinger.

The author takes a different perspective on anger: this book is not about resolving anger with others through communication or interpersonal connection, but rather about communicating with the self in a way that makes use of positive potential while reducing negative impulses. Anger is described in two phases, the first as a protective reaction offering a power boost for facing the challenge. The power boost removes inhibitions and provides a protective armor. The second phase outlines the seven-step method, with examples and exercises provided; topics include acknowledging anger, regaining emotional balance, giving oneself validation, identifying unmet needs, and understanding the other person's frame of reference. In closing, Cannon discusses being angry with oneself and offers a process to move through the feelings to gain resolution and forgiveness for oneself and for others.

★★★  *The Angry Book* (1969, reissued 1998) by Theodore Rubin. New York: Macmillan.

This early, psychoanalytically oriented book advocates the "let it all out" catharsis approach to anger. Rubin warns readers about the dangers that await them if they bottle up their anger and "twist" or "pervert" it. He says that a "slush fund" of accumulated, unexpressed anger builds up in the body, waiting for the opportunity to produce high blood pressure, depression, alcoholism, sexual problems, and other diseases. At the end of *The Angry Book*, Rubin asks readers 103 questions that are intended to give them therapeutic guidance. One of these questions is whether readers have ever experienced the good, clean feeling that comes after expressing anger, as well as the increased self-esteem and feeling of peace that such expression brings. The "let it all out" approach was widely accepted by many clinicians in the past, but it is less accepted today. Rubin's recommendations directly contradict the approaches advocated by cognitive-behaviorists in multiple books reviewed above. This book barely makes it into the 3-star category, and many experts see it as seriously dated.

### Diamonds in the Rough

♦ *A Volcano in My Tummy—Helping Children to Handle Anger* (1996) by Eliane Whitehouse and Warwick Pudney. Gabriola Island, BC: New Society.

This valuable workbook is written in a lesson-plan format that structures key anger concepts into activities for children age 6 through teens. The book is written for parents and teachers, with emphasis on use by teachers. The activities are well designed for the targeted age groups and demonstrate creativity and variety that could hold the attention of children, whether in school or at home. The purpose of the book is to help children become aware of their anger and learn safe, alternate responses to anger. Listed as a "Diamond in the Rough" because the few ratings it received in two of our studies were consistently high.

♦ *The Angry Self: A Comprehensive Approach to Anger Management* (1999) by M. M. Gottlieb. Phoenix: Zeig, Tucker, & Theisen.

Practical, step-by-step cognitive-behavioral, Ericksonian, and relaxation strategies are outlined to help control anger. This workbook includes extensive exercises and assignments that can be used effectively in anger control. It is placed in the "Diamond in the Rough" category for positive evaluations but low numbers of raters.

◆ *Anger Kills: Seventeen Strategies for Controlling the Hostility That Can Harm Your Health* (1994) by Redford Williams and Virginia Williams. New York: Harper Perennial.

The health costs to a person who experiences ongoing anger is the focus of *Anger Kills*, cited as a "Diamond in the Rough" for its modest number of raters but very high ratings. Hostility and its effect on individuals and those around them are outlined in factual terms and through scientific study. This area of study was pioneered by coauthor Redford Williams. A self-administered hostility questionnaire is followed by a roadmap of strategies to overcome hostility. Chapters are grouped by recommendations to alter thinking patterns, cope with volatile situations, react to others' hostility, improve relationships, and adopt positive attitudes. Cognitive-behavioral strategies are suggested and demonstrated through decision-making diagrams, making this book a good companion to cognitive-behavioral therapy on anger.

### Not Recommended

★★ *Anger: Deal with It, Heal with It, Stop It from Killing You* (1991) by Bill Defoore. Deerfield Beach, FL: Health Communications.
★★ *The Anger Workbook for Women* (2004) by Laura J. Petracek. Oakland, CA: New Harbinger.
★★ *What to Do When Your Temper Flares: A Kid's Guide to Overcoming Problems with Anger* (2007) by Dawn Huebner.

## ■ INTERNET RESOURCES

★★★★ *Anger* www.apa.org/topics/anger/index.aspx

This psychology topic from the American Psychological Association (APA) offers several articles about anger, as well as related resources on violence and bullying.

★★★★★ *How Can I Deal With My Anger?* kidshealth.org/teen/your_mind/emotions/deal_with_anger.html

This well-designed site from the Nemours Foundation is targeted to teenagers and kids, to help them better understand and recognize their anger. It also provides tips and advice on how to express and cope with angry feelings more effectively.

★★★★ *How to Deal with Anger* www.mind.org.uk/help/diagnoses_and_conditions/dealing_with_anger

A helpful single page from the U.K. charity Mind that helps people understand their anger, how to express it in a more healthy manner, and what to do with angry feelings.

★★★★ *Using Anger Management for Stress Relief* stress.about.com/od/relationships/a/anger_manage.htm

The About.com Stress Management site offers some good, accessible articles about anger management.

★★★★ *Get Your Angries Out* www.angriesout.com

Hundreds of articles by Lynne Namka offer anger management articles and helpful tips for adults, kids, parents, and teachers. Articles are well written and housed in a creative and accessible website.

★★★★ *Dealing with Anger* extension.unh.edu/family/documents/hcdvs103.pdf

This helpful four-page PDF from the University of New Hampshire Cooperative Extension is meant to help parents understand and cope with both their own and their children's anger.

★★ *Leonard Ingram's AngerMgmt.com* www.angermgmt.com

Although apparently not updated in years, this website from Leonard Ingram offers an interesting set of articles on anger and anger management, as well as an Anger Toolkit, and links to purchase his anger management DVDs, CDs and self-published books.

★★★ *Anger Management*

www.bbc.co.uk/health/emotional_health/mental_health/coping_angermanagement.shtml

This single page from the U.K.'s BBC provides a general, well-written overview of anger management, along with some simplistic advice.

★★★ *When Anger Hurts* by Mathew McKay, Peter D. Rogers, and Judith McKay psychcentral.com/lib/2011/anger-trigger-behaviors

This list of the verbal, gestural, facial, and other behaviors that trigger anger may be useful for people who do not recognize their anger triggers.

★★★ *Anger and Aggression* psychologicalselfhelp.org/Chapter7

This chapter of an online book offers a wide-ranging presentation (for example, marriage, prejudice, distrust, and gender) and cites a dozen therapeutic approaches and techniques.

★★★ *Why Am I So Angry?* arthritis.about.com/cs/emotion/a/anger.htm

Anger is a major component in flare-ups of rheumatoid arthritis. These four pages are a good introduction to the topic of anger for patients.

★★ *Plain Talk About…Dealing with the Angry Child*    www.kidsource.com/kidsource/content2/angry.children.html

An older fact sheet from the National Institute of Mental Health.

**See also** Stress Management and Relaxation (Chapter 37) and Violent Youth (Chapter 41).

# CHAPTER 7

# ANXIETY DISORDERS

A nxiety is a highly unpleasant feeling that comes in different forms. Sometimes it is a diffuse, vague feeling; at other times, it is a fear of something specific. People who have an anxiety disorder often feel motor tension (jumpy, trembling, or can't relax), are hyperactive (dizzy, their heart races, or they perspire), and are apprehensive.

All these anxiety symptoms exist, to a lesser or greater degree, in the spectrum of anxiety disorders: generalized anxiety disorder, phobias, panic disorders, hypochondriasis, obsessive–compulsive disorder, and posttraumatic stress disorder. The latter two disorders are covered in separate chapters: Posttraumatic Stress Disorder in Chapter 31, and Obsessive–Compulsive Disorder in Chapter 30. Also falling into the anxiety category is the controversial and rare diagnosis of dissociative identity disorder, previously known as multiple personality.

Controversy swirls around the causes of anxiety disorders. Some mental health experts, especially in the medical field, believe that anxiety is biologically determined and should be treated with medications. Other mental health experts, including many psychologists, argue that anxiety is primarily caused by what we experience and how we think. They maintain that anxiety reduction involves rearranging our environment and cognitively reinterpreting our world. The following self-help resources include both schools of thought.

As with the other chapters, we begin with a synopsis of our primary recommendations (Box 7.1) and proceed through the ratings and descriptions of self-help books, autobiographies, films, online self-help, Internet resources, and national support groups.

## ■ SELF-HELP BOOKS

### Strongly Recommended

★★★★★ *The Anxiety and Phobia Workbook* (2001, 3rd ed.) by Edmund J. Bourne. Oakland, CA: New Harbinger.

In the third edition of his workbook, psychologist Bourne describes specific skills needed to overcome problems with panic, anxiety, and phobias and provides step-by-step procedures for mastering these skills. The book contains a fair amount of descriptive material but emphasizes cognitive-behavioral skills, strategies, and exercises to foster recovery. Its approach is strongly holistic, focusing on multiple dimensions (e.g., body, behavior, feelings, mind, interpersonal relations, self-esteem, and spirituality). The latest edition offers additional information on medications, herbal supplements, and the patient's support

# BOX 7.1
## RECOMMENDATION HIGHLIGHTS

**SELF-HELP BOOKS**

■ For cognitive, behavioral, and social tools to reduce anxiety:

★★★★★ *The Anxiety and Phobia Workbook* by Edmund J. Bourne

★★★★★ *Mastery of Your Anxiety and Panic III* by Michelle G. Craske and David H. Barlow

★★★★★ *Mastering Your Fears and Phobias Workbook* by Antony, Craske, and Barlow

■ For helping the shy and socially anxious:

★★★★ *The Shyness and Social Anxiety Workbook* by Martin Anthony and Richard Swinson

■ For holistic and integrative approaches to anxiety:

★★★★★ *The Dance of Fear* by Harriet Lerner

★★★★ *Beyond Anxiety and Phobia* by Edmund J. Bourne

★★★★ *Feel the Fear and Do It Anyway* by Susan Jeffers

■ For reducing or eliminating panic attacks:

★★★★ *Don't Panic* by Reid Wilson

**AUTOBIOGRAPHIES**

■ For recovering from dissociative identity disorder:

★★★★ *A Mind of My Own* by Chris Costner Sizemore

■ For a treatment program for panic attacks:

★★★ *The Panic Attack Recovery Book* by Shirley Swede and Seymour S. Jaffe

♦ *The Anxiety Expert* by Marjorie Raskin

■ For recovering from hypochondria:

★★★ *Phantom Illness* by Carla Cantor

**FILMS**

■ For a riveting portrait of panic, obsession, and their toll:

★★★ *Black Swan*

■ For the (controversial) treatment of dissociative identity disorder:

★★★ *Sybil*

**ONLINE SELF-HELP**

■ For research-supported psychoeducation and treatment for anxiety conditions:

★★★★★ *FearFighter: Panic and Phobia Treatment* www.fearfighter.com

★★★★ *AnxietyOnline* www.anxietyonline.org.au

**INTERNET RESOURCES**

■ For valuable information on anxiety and panic disorders:

★★★★★ *Anxiety Disorders Association of America* www.adaa.org

★★★★★ *The Anxiety Panic Internet Resource* www.algy.com/anxiety/anxiety.php

★★★★★ *Anxiety, Panic and Phobias* psychcentral.com/disorders/anxiety

persons. For the layperson, this is a concise, practical, and comprehensive directory on how to reduce anxiety. This book is highly regarded and a widely known resource.

★★★★★ *Mastery of Your Anxiety and Panic III* (2000) by Michelle G. Craske and David H. Barlow. New York: Oxford University Press.

Barlow and Craske, nationally known researchers in the treatment of anxiety disorders, have updated their original self-help offering. The book is based on empirically supported and clinically proven treatments that cover the cognitive, behavioral, physical, and social aspects of anxiety. This third edition is easier to read, includes new methods for providing exposure to feared sensations, and offers a series of separate manuals (Therapist Guide, Client Workbook, Client Monitoring Forms, and Client Workbook for Agoraphobia). Record forms, case vignettes, and self-assessments are both numerous and useful. Questions and answers about medications are reviewed. This is an excellent and scientifically based self-help approach for anxiety-ridden patients, either as an independent self-help book or as an adjunct to psychotherapy.

★★★★★ *Mastering Your Fears and Phobias Workbook* (2006) by Martin A. Antony, Michelle G. Craske, and David H. Barlow. New York: Oxford University Press.

A workbook format is well suited for the topic of anxiety and phobias. This workbook, predicated on the book by Craske and Barlow reviewed above, first introduces the reader to the nature and development of phobias and then has the reader apply the knowledge to his or her own phobias. The treatment is explained and the process of changing thoughts and preparation for exposure to the phobia elements are introduced. Types of phobias are very interestingly described and compartmentalized as animals, situations (e.g., elevators, bridges), nature (e.g., storms), blood, needles, injury, and others (e.g., clowns, balloons). Readers are encouraged to use this material in conjunction with a psychotherapist and to work with only one phobia or psychological concern at a time. The approaches described in this book have been researched and determined to be effective. This book was rated not only rated highly but also by a high number of psychologists.

★★★★★ *The Dance of Fear* (2005) by Harriet Lerner. New York: William Morrow.

First published in 2004 under the name of *Fear and Other Uninvited Guests*, the author takes a measured and attentive look at the effects of fear, anxiety, and shame. There are no exercises or self-reflection as a primary theme; rather, the focus is on interactions with individuals who deal with these challenging feelings that disempower and often immobilize them. The poignant stories of different circumstances and contexts of fear resonate with the reader and even without a deliberate instructive approach become instructive. Lerner argues that each person must find the way to accept that fear and anxiety are part of living but should not be allowed to overshadow one's life. A high number of psychologists read and highly rated this book.

★★★★ *Beyond Anxiety and Phobia* (2001) by Edmund J. Bourne. Oakland, CA: New Harbinger.

Another excellent self-help resource by Edmund Bourne, who wrote *The Anxiety and Phobia Workbook* (reviewed above). This book covers the spectrum of mainstream and complementary approaches to self-enhancement, including using cognitive-behavioral methods, rearranging the environment, helping to define life purposes, embracing spirituality, using herbs, modifying diet, and incorporating yoga, massage, acupuncture, and meditation. This is a down-to-earth, easy-to-read workbook that includes appendices listing a variety of organizational and treatment resources. A useful self-help book for those interested in a mixture of traditional and alternative methods.

**** *The Shyness and Social Anxiety Workbook* (2002) by Martin Anthony and Richard Swinson. Oakland, CA: New Harbinger.

This highly rated resource was written to help people be more comfortable around others. The book provides worksheets and exercises that can be easily incorporated into daily life. Cognitive-behavioral, empirically supported techniques to combat social anxiety are presented in a step-by-step manner for the lay public. An excellent book: well organized, easy to read, and useful for those in or out of psychotherapy.

**** *Anxiety Disorders and Phobias: A Cognitive Perspective* (1985) by Aaron Beck and Gary Emery. New York: Basic.

This sophisticated book provides information about different types of anxiety and how sufferers can rearrange their thoughts to overcome crippling anxiety. Beck is an international expert on anxiety disorders and depression and one of the founders of cognitive therapy. Beck and Emery describe the nature of anxiety and how it is distinguished from fear, phobia, and panic. They believe that the core problem for anxiety sufferers is their sense of vulnerability and their ineffective cognitive strategies. The latter portion of the book contains a treatment program based on cognitive therapy that can help individuals cope with anxiety and phobias. Separate chapters tell readers how to change the way they develop images of themselves and their world, how to change feelings, and how to modify behavior. This highly rated volume received rave reviews in the academic community, but it is not primarily a self-help book. It is written at a high level of information that is appropriate for psychotherapists or graduate students. Only lay readers who are already fairly sophisticated about psychological problems or who seek an intellectual challenge will want to tackle this volume.

**** *When Perfect Isn't Good Enough* (2009) by Martin M. Antony and Richard P. Swinson. Oakland, CA: New Harbinger.

This subject of perfectionism is included in this chapter on anxiety because research has found ongoing similarities between perfectionism and the presence of anxiety, depression, and specifically social anxiety. Anxiety is often the driving factor in perfectionism. Treatments using the approach adopted in this book have been shown to significantly reduce social anxiety as well as perfectionism. This book develops for the reader an understanding of the types of perfectionism: unrealistically high expectations of oneself, unrealistically high expectation of others, and belief that others have unrealistically high expectations of oneself. Strategies for changing thoughts and behaviors and recalibrating one's perception of high standards are an important part of treating perfectionism and preventing its return. An emphasis is placed on the fact that this book is not intended to replace psychotherapy but is likely to be a companion.

★★★★　*When Panic Attacks: The New Drug-Free Therapy That Can Change Your Life*
(2007) by David D. Burns. New York: Morgan Road.

A clear and detailed explanation of cognitive therapy is presented with effective case examples. The primary causes of anxiety are described, including thoughts, avoidance, and passivity. Although such a multifaceted or integrative approach is typically adopted in formal treatment, this book attempts to do so in such a way that individuals may try the treatment plan on their own. Several techniques are presented, including the "What if," logic, humor, role play, and motivational techniques. Impressively, many "anxiety tools" are presented in the appendix, such as "the secrets of effective communication" form, an anxiety log, a cognitive distortion log, and a means of selecting techniques based on one's specific anxiety—be it shyness, OCD, panic attacks, or worry.

★★★★　*Feel the Fear and Do It Anyway* (reissue ed., 1992) by Susan Jeffers. New York: Fawcett.

This book offers positive and concrete techniques for turning fear, indecision, and anger into power, action, and love. The author helps people reach, understand, and convert negative paths of thinking that feed fear and inactivity. Jeffers uses a 10-step program to help convert negative thinking. Visualization techniques are one of the cognitive exercises that help people rid themselves of destructive fear. Other methods entail power vocabulary, turning decisions into no-lose situations, and adopting an optimistic perspective about life. The author's belief is that fear can be dealt with through reeducation. For those who struggle with their feelings of fear and indecision, this is a useful book.

★★★★　*Don't Panic: Taking Control of Anxiety Attacks* (revised ed., 1996) by Reid Wilson. New York: Harper & Row.

This book covers the diagnosis and treatment of panic, an anxiety disorder in which the main feature is recurrent panic attacks marked by the sudden onset of intense apprehension or terror. People who suffer from panic disorder may have feelings of impending doom but aren't necessarily anxious all the time. Wilson describes a self-help program for coping with panic attacks. In Part I, readers learn what panic attacks are like, how it feels to undergo one, and what type of people are prone to panic attacks. Advice is given on how to sort through the physical and psychological aspects of panic attacks. In Part II, readers learn how to conquer panic attacks, especially by using self-monitoring, breathing exercises, focused thinking, mental imagery, and deep muscle relaxation.

**Recommended**

★★★　*Overcoming Shyness and Social Phobia: A Step-by-Step Guide* (1998) by Ronald M. Rapee. Northvale, NJ: Jason Aronson.

Rapee educates, coaches, and guides those who struggle with social anxiety toward a more comfortable lifestyle. The nine thoughtful lessons are grounded in a systems perspective. The reader will be offered ways to learn, think, and act differently and to challenge and defeat the negative assumptions that limit personal growth. The author emphasizes learning and practice, and the case studies illuminate the path to change. A valuable self-help book for the general public and psychotherapy clients. In fact, had the book been more widely known by the mental health experts in our studies, it would have probably received a 4- or 5-star rating.

★★★  *An End to Panic* (1995, reissued 2000) by Elke Zuercher-White. Oakland, CA: New Harbinger.

The author's goal is to teach the cognitive-behavioral methods that have proven effective for panic disorders. In other words, changing one's style of thinking, believing, and behavior can help reduce anxiety. Medication is also discussed, as is a combination of medication and cognitive-behavioral therapy. Part I explains panic disorder and agoraphobia and sets the stage for the work ahead. Parts II and III review theory and practical methods to overcome panic, and Part IV works on mastering the techniques taught. This book is for people with panic disorders with or without agoraphobia and for people who want to prevent further panic attacks. Highly regarded by the psychologists in our national studies but not well known, which led to the 3-star rating.

★★★  *Worry: Controlling It and Using It Wisely* (1997) by Edward Hallowell. New York: Pantheon.

Worry is uniquely human. The author focuses on the many forms of worry (both destructive and productive), their underlying causes, and how these patterns can be changed. Illustrating his theories with case histories and therapy dialogues, Hallowell emphasizes the physical, not the psychological, aspect of worrying, which helps reduce the self-blame to which many worriers are prone. The treatment and preventive steps are holistic, eclectic, and straightforward. First comes awareness, which, over time, sets the stage for new pattern-making in the brain. Then, treatment consists of medication and psychotherapy as well as exercise, diet, and sufficient sleep. Another key to not excessively fretting is "connectedness"—to other people, to ideas, and to spirituality. The experts in our national studies were very positively disposed toward this integrated self-help resource; indeed, if more had rated it, it would have been a 4- or 5-star self-help book. A valuable aid to understanding and modifying one of the most common maladies.

★★★  *Stopping Anxiety Medication* (2009) by Michael H. Otto and Mark H. Pollack. New York: Oxford University Press.

Many people have dealt with anxiety and panic disorder through benzodiazepines such as Xanax, Librium, Klonopin, and Valium. The authors explain that these medications are difficult to discontinue and need to be tapered in a systematic way. It is strongly recommended that individuals wanting to discontinue these medications work with a psychologist or physician familiar with a tapering program. Although designed to taper benzodiazepines, this program is also effective with reduction of antidepressant medication. When tapering is too quick or not synchronized properly, the side effects can be strong enough that the individual relapses into medication use again. The workbook offers many opportunities to engage in exercises alone but also to collaborate with a mental health professional on the recovery.

★★★  *How to Control Your Anxiety before It Controls You* (1998) by Albert Ellis. Secaucus, NJ: Carol.

Ellis, one of the world's most influential psychologists, bases this book on his particular brand of cognitive-behavioral therapy known as rational-emotive behavior therapy. Ellis talks about how anxious feelings and behaviors go with specific kinds of anxiety-provoking thinking. You think, act, and feel together. That's the way, as a human, you behave. In the final three chapters, he emphasizes rational maxims and beliefs that can help change anxiety-provoking thinking, emotions, and actions. This book can be valuable for the average reader or can be used as a self-help resource during psychotherapy.

★★★  *Panic Disorder: The Facts* (1996) by Stanley Rachman and Padmal de Silva. New York: Oxford University.

This self-help resource book explains the experience, assessment, and treatment of panic attacks. The authors provide sound, practical advice to family members about choosing a therapist and self-help. Some of the common questions asked by people with panic disorder are reviewed. This book is a valuable and scientific resource for sufferers as well as their families. It can be integrated into a patient's treatment and is easy to read.

★★★  *Peace from Nervous Suffering* (1972, reissued 1990) by Claire Weekes. New York: Hawthorn.

This book concerns itself with one type of phobia—agoraphobia, the fear of entering unfamiliar situations, especially open or public spaces. It is the most common type of phobic disorder. Weekes maintains that the cure for agoraphobia involves four simple rules: face the phobia, don't run away from it; accept it, don't fight it; float past it, don't stop and listen in; and let time pass, don't be impatient. Weekes includes extensive case studies from around the world in which agoraphobics have overcome their fear of leaving the safety of their homes. Weekes's book was one of the first to deal with agoraphobia, and it helped many people recognize their problem; however, it is dated and misses many of the advances in psychological and medical treatments.

★★★  *Life without Fear: Anxiety and Its Cure* (1988) by Joseph Wolpe with David Wolpe. Oakland, CA: New Harbinger.

Joseph Wolpe, an international expert in the field of behavior therapy, provides a clear and authoritative account of the essential features of behavior therapy and its application to anxiety. With the help of his son David, a playwright, the two translate into nontechnical language information about behavior therapy and anxiety. Topics include useful and useless fears, how useless fears are developed, how thoughts and feelings are controlled by habit, how habits are formed and extinguished, coping in real-life situations, special behavior techniques for anxiety, getting help for behavior analysis, and the advantages and limits of behavior therapy. This book can be a useful self-help manual for adults engaged in behavior therapy for anxiety.

★★★  *Anxiety and Panic Attacks: Their Cause and Cure* (1985) by Robert Handly. New York: Fawcett Crest.

This text, about both panic attacks and agoraphobia, begins with the author's describing his own struggle with agoraphobia and the strategies he used to overcome it. Handly believes that five basic methods are involved in coping with anxiety and panic attacks: (1) using the creative powers of your unconscious mind to help yourself; (2) employing visualizations and affirmations to improve your self-image; (3) engaging in rational and positive thinking; (4) acting as if you are already who you want to be; and (5) setting goals to be the person you want to be. Handly also stresses the importance of physical health, fitness, and good nutrition in overcoming anxiety. This book has an easy-to-read writing style and provides in-depth analysis of one person's experience. However, it suffers from inattention to current developments in treating panic disorder and agoraphobia and from the rather loose inclusion of many different ideas that have not been well tested.

★★★ *Overcoming Social Anxiety and Shyness* (2008) by Gillian Butler. New York: Basic Books.

Social phobia or social anxiety is presented in the context of cognitive-behavioral therapy but in a self-help format. Shy individuals don't have ongoing social anxiety but rather specific or intermittent anxiety, whereas those with social anxiety are not necessarily shy. A clear and effective picture is painted of socially anxious people who fear at every turn that they will be embarrassed, humiliated, or devalued in a social setting. How and why does social anxiety develop? How does it apply to you, the reader, and what can be done to reverse it? This is the focus of the first part of the book, with the second being the treatment plan of learning to think differently, reducing self-consciousness, building self-confidence, and learning assertiveness.

★★★ *Overcoming Anxiety for Dummies* (2010) by Charles Elliott and Laura Smith. Hoboken, NJ: Wiley.

"For Dummies" doesn't treat the readers as dummies but is written in a conversational style that makes even the few techniques parts understandable and sensible. The material is extremely thorough and informative in explaining anxiety, its types and treatments, the role of stress, anxious thoughts, physical reactions, and how to detect anxiety. The latter content introduces the readers to self-assessments and comparison with common fears, reactions, and reasons for being stuck experienced by others. Unique aspects of this book are interesting icons that signal action statements, points to remember, and warning signals.

★★★ *The Anxiety Workbook for Teens* (2008) by Lisa M. Schab. Oakland, CA: Instant Help.

This workbook for teens takes a pragmatic and straightforward approach to combating anxiety. The 42 activities or chapters are presented in a clear and understandable way. Four origins of anxiety are explored: genetic, chemical, life events, and personality. The activities lead the reader in exploring these areas and then move into solutions, such as positive affirmations, seeing the big picture, the role of eating, talking or writing it out, and problem solving. Perfectionism, all-or-nothing thinking, and "should" statements are tip-offs that one is being influenced by stress, social pressures, or other events that enable anxiety.

★★★ *I Don't Want to Go to School: Helping Children Cope with Separation Anxiety* (2005) by Nancy Pando and Kathy Voerg. Far Hills, NJ: New Horizon.

This is a book for the child and the parent to read together. Stories about children who do not want to leave their mothers are effective ways to convey to children that their feelings are understood and are experienced by others. The stories are written for young children through elementary school. For parents, there are ideas and suggestions about handling their children's separation anxiety, such as (1) giving a concrete reminder of when the parent will be back, such as a sticker on a watch, (2) using transitional objects such as a scarf, stuffed animal, or picture of the mother and child together, (3) telling the child when the mother will be back in terms of time of day, and (4) not prolonging goodbyes.

★★★    *The Anxiety Disease* (1983) by David Sheehan. New York: Scribner.

This book astutely reviews the biological factors involved in anxiety and the effective treatment of anxiety disorders by appropriate drugs and behavior therapy. Sheehan describes a number of case studies from his psychiatric practice to illustrate how to recognize anxiety problems and successfully treat them. He believes that anxiety disorders progress through seven stages—spells, panic, hypochondriacal symptoms, limited phobias, social phobias, agoraphobia/extensive public avoidance, and finally depression—and that recovery from an anxiety disorder occurs in four phases—doubt, mastery, independence, and readjustment. Individuals go through the phases as their medications eliminate chemically induced panic attacks and therapy overcomes their avoidance tendencies. An interesting but dated book.

★★★    *The Good News about Panic, Anxiety, and Phobias* (1990) by Mark Gold. New York: Bantam.

This text, like that above, stresses the biological basis of anxiety disorders and their treatment with medications. Gold asserts that anxiety disorders are not the person's fault but rather the product of inherited dysfunctions in the biochemistry of the person's body. Gold recommends variations in drug therapy for different types of anxiety disorders. At the end of the book, he provides a state-by-state listing of resources and medical experts on anxiety disorders.

★★★    *Women Who Worry Too Much* (2005) by Holly Haxlett-Stevens. Oakland, CA: New Harbinger.

We don't know if women worry too much, but we know they worry about twice as much as men. This book considers worry and anxiety strictly from the female point of view and effectively covers important aspects of this phenomenon. For example, the book contrasts the male tendency to fight or flee, whereas women stand the ground and endure the threat, likely based on protection of home and children. Women are more aware of external cues while men are more aware of their internal sense. Thus, men rely more on themselves and women on others' cues. There are just a few examples of tailoring the treatment of worry to women.

### Diamonds in the Rough

♦   *The Sky Is Falling* (1996) by Raeann Dumont. New York: Norton.

This author provides information that will help the reader understand and cope with phobias, panic, and obsessive–compulsive behavior. Using case vignettes, Dumont alerts the reader to the danger of forming conclusions that increase anxiety without the benefit of rational thought. She explains how magical thinking evolves out of faulty cause-and-effect understanding. The book provides directions on planning and treatment programs. Clients, family members, and professionals will find this book to be informative and practical. It is a Diamond in the Rough because it was highly but infrequently rated in our national studies.

- ♦ *Overcoming Generalized Anxiety Disorder* (1999) by John White. Oakland, CA: New Harbinger.

Psychologist White has written separate client and therapist manuals on overcoming generalized anxiety disorders by means of relaxation, cognitive restructuring, and exposure. The client manual is a user-friendly workbook divided into 10 sessions/chapters, each addressed to a particular treatment method. Self-assessments, skill building, homework assignments, and cute illustrations fill each session/chapter. A valuable and evidence-based self-help resource that is not yet widely known among mental health professionals.

## Not Recommended

- ★ *Managing Social Anxiety Workbook* (2010) by Debra A. Hope, Richard G. Heimberg, and Cynthia L. Turk. New York: Oxford University Press.
- ★ *The Worry Cure* (2005) by Robert L. Leahy. New York: Three River Press.

## ■ AUTOBIOGRAPHIES

### Strongly Recommended

- ★★★★ *A Mind of My Own* (1989) by Chris Costner Sizemore. New York: William Morrow.

The protagonist of *Three Faces of Eve* describes her successful battle with multiple personality disorder. Now married with two children, the author has become a lecturer on mental health topics. A tale of hope and the success of psychotherapy, it has become a perennial favorite of those fascinated by—or suffering from—dissociative identity disorder. The book helps explain some of the puzzling aspects of the film and takes the reader further along in the author's life.

### Recommended

- ★★★ *The Panic Attack Recovery Book* (revised ed., 2000) by Shirley Swede and Seymour S. Jaffe. New York: New American Library/Dutton.

Jointly written by a former agoraphobic (Swede) and her psychiatrist (Jaffe), this updated edition outlines a treatment program that does not depend on medication. The PASS program is based on seven steps to recovery from panic attacks: a healthy balanced diet; relaxation; exercise; a positive attitude; imagination (pretending to feel confident); social support; and spiritual values (faith, hope, and forgiveness). The book is clearly written and an easy read and includes many helpful recommendations based on the personal experiences of Swede and the medical knowledge of Jaffe.

★★★  *Memoirs of an Amnesiac* (1990) by Oscar Levant. Hollywood, CA: Samuel French.

A famed pianist recounts a life with many mental and physical disorders. In a humorous and acerbic style, Levant describes his obsessive–compulsive disorder, phobias, and addiction to barbiturates. Chapter titles include "Total Recoil," "My Bed of Nails," and "Stand Up and Faint." Levant was treated with an enormous number of different drugs and had psychotherapy, several hospitalizations, and electroconvulsive therapy. Through it all, he appeared to lack the motivation to get well. The book would be most appropriate for someone with a multiplicity of disorders. (Also reviewed in Chapter 30 on Obsessive–Compulsive Disorder.)

★★★  *Phantom Illness: Recognizing, Understanding, and Overcoming Hypochondria* (1997) by Carla Cantor with Brian Fallon. New York: Houghton Mifflin.

Cantor's serious problems began when she crashed her car, killing a passenger. She became depressed and was briefly hospitalized. While in the hospital, her diagnosis was changed to hypochondria. The book describes her intense struggle with bodily preoccupations and the lessons she learned on the road to recovery. The author has collected a tremendous amount of material, which she shares with the readers. There are not many autobiographies on this disorder which often goes undiagnosed and untreated.

★★★  *Afraid of Everything: A Personal History of Agoraphobia* (1984) by Daryl M. Woods. Saratoga, CA: R & E.

A first-person account by a young woman with agoraphobia, the book includes information on what is known about the causes and treatment of the disorder. A helpful memoir in the self-help tradition, although dated with respect to treatments. Out of print and not easy to obtain.

### Diamonds in the Rough

♦ *The Anxiety Expert: A Psychiatrist's Story of Panic* (2004) by Marjorie Raskin. Bloomington, IN: Authorhouse.

In high school, after a beloved aunt contracts polio, the author decided to become a physician. She studied hard, earned high grades, completed medical school and a residency in psychiatry, and worked at leading hospitals. Yet despite all her achievements and mental health training, Raskin could not escape frequent anxiety and panic attacks. This book is her attempt, as an expert by both training and experience, to understand the reasons for her inner turmoil and to surmount them through years of successful therapy. In this warm and moving account, she describes her life as patient, physician, married woman, and single mother who combines parenting with a career in psychiatry.

♦ *The Earl Campbell Story: A Football Great's Battle with Panic Disorder* by Earl Campbell and John Ruane (1999). Toronto: ECW Press.

The author won the Heisman Trophy as the best college football player in the United States before going into professional football, where he received the NFL's most valuable player award for his first three seasons. He experienced his first panic attack 3 years after retiring from professional football. In spite of it, he became a successful executive in a meat-processing company and an inspiring speaker about panic and anxiety disorders. By showing that a strong-willed, award-winning athlete can achieve success after being diagnosed with a panic disorder, the book provides hope and helps to destigmatize the condition.

**Not Recommended**

   ★★   *Sybil* (1995) by Flora Rheta Schreiber. New York: Warner.

A reissue of a book that has become a classic in the multiple personality literature, now more accurately known as dissociative identity disorder. Sybil Dorsett purportedly had 16 separate personalities before her recovery. The dissociation is attributed to childhood abuse by her schizophrenic mother, which also produced unusual blackouts. With intensive psychotherapy, Sybil's personalities merged in 1965 when she was 42. It is difficult to sort out fact from fiction in the actions of Sybil's various personalities; indeed, some professionals believe that several of the personalities were created by hypnosis and pentothal. Recent research indicates that several of the book's claims are patently false (Nathan, 2011). Our mental health experts give the television movie higher marks than the book.

   ★★   *When Rabbit Howls: The Troops for Truddi Chase* (1987) by Truddi Chase. New York: Dutton.

The "troops" are the numerous personalities of the author. She did not know they existed until adulthood. Troop members speak of their empathy for Chase, who was abused from age 2 until age 16 by her stepfather. The troops, all 92 of them, speak in disjointed voices, and it is often difficult to keep them straight, leading many readers to find the book confusing. Not to mention that many professionals question the legitimacy of 92 distinct personalities.

## ▩ FILMS

**Recommended**

   ★★★   *Sybil* (1976) directed by Daniel Petrie. Not rated. 198 minutes.

The horrific physical and psychological abuse Sybil experienced as a child led to multiple personalities that served as protection, comfort, and survival through her tormented years. She commits herself to the journey of therapy with a caring and courageous psychotherapist who essentially reparents Sybil and gives her the healthier relationship that Sybil never had. This 1970s made-for-television movie features Sally Field as Sybil and Joanne Woodward as Dr. Wilbur. The book on which it is based remains contentious, but this moving film displays the extraordinary ways in which people survive and the miraculous healing power of human connection.

   ★★★   *Black Swan* (2010) directed by Darren Aronofsky. R rating. 108 minutes.

Nina (Natalie Portman), a prospective lead for the *Swan Lake* production of the New York City ballet, is blessed and cursed by a frustrated stage mother. Nina is an excellent dancer who performs the White Swan perfectly but does not possess the innate traits to dance the Black Swan role as convincingly. The director, Thomas, treats the dancers in ways that he thinks will bring out the persona he needs for the role. Thomas tantalizes and seduces Nina, ostensibly for the purpose of stretching her ability in the role. Nina becomes more and more frantic about winning the role because her competitor can dance both roles. Nina's actions to win reveal her panic and unrelenting anxiety, intensifying to the point where reality and delusion blur and Nina sees individuals morph into each other. Through a series of distorted perceptions and anxiety beyond her control, she imagines that she stabs her competitor while actually stabbing herself. She goes on with the dance and performs both roles perfectly. After the acclamation and standing ovations, she realizes she is bleeding and dying. Nina's story captures the desperation, the obsession with attaining perfection, and the terror of failing that characterize many individuals living with anxiety and panic disorder. The backdrop of the ballet offers a dramatic context for the silent pain and fear of many anxiety-ridden individuals who are living less dramatic lives but with the same intense obsessions and anxiety.

### Not Recommended

* ★ *Panic Room* (2002) directed by David Fincher. R rating. 112 minutes.
* ★ *Adaptation* (2002) directed by Spike Jonze. R rating. 114 minutes.
* ★ *What About Bob?* (1992) directed by Frank Oz. PG rating. 99 minutes.

### Strongly Not Recommended

† *High Anxiety* (1977) directed by Mel Brooks. PG rating. 94 minutes.

## ONLINE SELF-HELP

★★★★★ *FearFighter: Panic and Phobia Treatment* www.fearfighter.com

This resource was designed to provide online psychotherapy for a number of conditions, including panic disorder and generalized anxiety. A mental health professional selects the appropriate module and provides individuals with access to the system, where they complete online sessions. The treatment programs are designed as nine weekly cognitive-behavioral therapy sessions of 30 minutes per session. Support from professionals is necessary but minimal (1 to 2 hours).

★★★★ *AnxietyOnline* www.anxietyonline.org.au

This website is dedicated to the treatment of several anxiety conditions, including generalized anxiety disorder, social anxiety disorder, and panic disorder with and without agoraphobia. After free registration users are directed to take an extensive online assessment to determine the type and intensity of their anxiety. Based on these results, users are offered online either a free self-directed program or, in more severe cases, a therapist-assisted online program at a cost of $120. Those who use the therapist-assisted program maintain weekly e-mail contact with a therapist in addition to the online program. Based on the principles of cognitive-behavioral therapy, all programs provide users with education about their condition, exercises to build skills to manage their condition, and worksheets to track progress.

The program comprises 12 modules, with one to be completed per week for 12 weeks, but users are free to work at their own pace.

★★★  *eCouch* ecouch.anu.edu.au

This free online self-help resource was developed for users of all ages but has an aesthetic and language that is most appealing to youths. The programs are educational and helpful but are not to be used as a substitute for psychotherapy. The website contains a program for social anxiety as well as one for general anxiety. Users must complete the interactive educational phase before accessing the next set of modules. Users then move on to the second phase, where they learn to identify and correct their faulty thinking, develop problem-solving strategies, learn relaxation methods, and build social skills. The modules are based on the principles of interpersonal psychotherapy, behavior therapy, cognitive therapy, and meditation. The program also contains a workbook where users can practice their skills and track their progress.

★★★  *Fear Drop* www.feardrop.com

This free site is designed for people who suffer from specific phobias. It is currently available only for users with fears of spiders but will probably be updated to include other fears. Users are first required to register and complete an anxiety questionnaire. The program is designed as a 10-stage series of exercises based on the principles of graded exposure. In each exercise, users must follow a moving circle with their mouse and then rate their levels of anxiety and disgust at the beginning of the exercise and after 60, 120, and 180 seconds. Progressive stages present images of spiders in increasingly more anxiety-provoking situations. Users can monitor their progress on graphs that track their reported level of anxiety.

★★★  *Overcoming Anxiety, Panic, Fear, and Worry* www.anxietyhelp.com.au

This self-help DVD-based program is designed for the treatment of multiple anxiety disorders in 24 sessions. The package consists of DVD instruction and workbook exercises to be completed with each session. The sessions integrate elements of education, cognitive therapy, relaxation, behavior therapy, and nutrition. Users learn about their condition, learn to identify and change their thoughts, emotions, and behaviors, and learn assertiveness. Users can purchase the program as a full package with all 24 sessions and the hard-copy workbook for $570 and $460 for the workbook on CD. Users can also purchase 12 sessions for $260 or 6 sessions for $130. Additional packages are available to clinicians and organizations. With the purchase of a package, users have access to the online support group.

★★★  *The Panic Center* www.paniccenter.net

The Panic Center is a free online anxiety self-help program that contains many features available in other fee-based programs. After registration, users complete an anxiety test and are then given access to the program and the website's other features. The program is divided into two main sections. The first nine modules are called "The Panic Program" and modules 10 to 16 are called "The Auxiliary Sessions." The initial modules are based on cognitive-behavioral therapy and teach users about their condition, help them challenge their thinking, address their current avoidance behaviors, and begin graded exposure to anxiety-causing situations. Users are strongly encouraged to complete their homework as an integral part of their program. Program users can check their progress on a symptom tracker and also have access to the moderated message boards.

## ■ INTERNET RESOURCES

### General Websites

★★★★★ *The Anxiety Panic Internet Resource* www.algy.com/anxiety/anxiety.php

A dry sense of humor underlies a rich site with chat, forums, and loads of good-quality links to other Internet anxiety resources. Each of the anxiety disorders has a section with a brief but meaningful description and authoritative materials and handouts.

★★★★★ *Anxiety, Panic and Phobias* psychcentral.com/disorders/anxiety

Psych Central's comprehensive anxiety section includes symptom and treatment information on every anxiety disorder and phobia, as well as news and research updates, medication reviews, and online support groups.

### Psychoeducational Materials

★★★★ *The Causes of Anxiety and Panic Attacks* by Ron Rapee, Michelle J. Craske, and David H. Barlow www.algy.com/anxiety/files/barlow.html

This is a good overview article written by noted anxiety experts for their clients. The aim is to teach about the physical and mental components of anxiety so that "(1) you realize that many of the feelings which you now experience are the result of anxiety and (2) you learn that these feelings are not harmful or dangerous."

★★★★ *National Institute of Mental Health's (NIMH) Anxiety Disorders Library*   www.nimh.nih.gov/health/topics/anxiety-disorders

The National Institute of Mental Health offers a wealth of authoritative articles about anxiety disorders, written in neutral language and emphasizing the importance of government-funded research and breakthroughs (for instance, the "Science News" section mentions only research funded by the NIMH). Many of the articles are also available in Spanish.

★★★★★ *Anxiety Disorders Association of America* www.adaa.org

This national nonprofit organization offers a wealth of information and resources about anxiety disorders, with articles written in plain English. The site covers generalized anxiety disorder, obsessive–compulsive disorder, panic disorder and agoraphobia, social anxiety disorder, and specific phobias, as well as some related concerns. The organization also helps guide people to help through treatment and support groups and provides self-help psychoeducational articles on living with anxiety.

★★★★ *Madison Institute of Medicine* socialanxiety.factsforhealth.org

Their "Facts for Health" is a perfect introductory brochure on social anxiety with links, readings, and referrals. Emphasizes both medications and behavior therapy.

**** *Anxiety Attacks and Anxiety Disorders* helpguide.org/mental/anxiety_types_
symptoms_treatment.htm

This single page from the nonprofit HelpGuide provides a broad overview and understanding of anxiety disorders and panic attacks and provides some simple (and simplistic)
advice and tips on how you may be able to help reduce them.

*** *Social Phobia/Social Anxiety Association* www.socialphobia.org

Several informational brochures, fact sheets, a well-described audiotape series (20
hours, $360) on cognitive-behavioral therapy for sale, links, etc.

** *Panic Disorder, Separation, Anxiety Disorder, and Agoraphobia in Children and
Adolescents* by Jim Chandler, MD jamesdauntchandler.tripod.com/anxiety/pan-
icpamphlet.htm

This article offers information about panic and anxiety from a medical perspective, filled
with vignettes. Related articles at: jamesdauntchandler.tripod.com/table_of_contents

*** *Anxiety, Panic and Phobias—Royal College of Psychiatrists* www.rcpsych.ac.uk/
expertadvice/problems/anxietyphobias.aspx

A dozen articles about anxiety, panic, and phobias, including their treatments (which
cover cognitive-behavioral therapy, complementary and alternative medicines, and
antidepressants).

*** *Coping With Performance Anxiety* eeshop.unl.edu/anxiety.html

Focusing on musicians, this article is both interesting and thorough.

*** *Anxiety—American Psychological Association* www.apa.org/topics/anxiety/
index.aspx

A resource from the American Psychological Association that surprisingly covers only a
small number of anxiety topics and offers updated news in anxiety research.

*** *Social Anxiety Test* www.queendom.com/tests/access_page/index.
htm?idRegTest=3050

A 36-item online test for social anxiety. Probably most useful for organizing and understanding symptoms.

*** *Panic Disorder & Agoraphobia—About.com* panicdisorder.about.com

About.com offers a personal guide to panic disorder and agoraphobia with Katharina
Star, including a blog on the topic.

** *Anxiety Disorders* www.psychiatry.org/anxiety-disorders

A very brief section from the American Psychiatric Association about anxiety and anxiety disorders.

### Treatment

★★★★ *Panic Attack Treatment* www.psycheducation.org/anxiety/panic/introduction. htm

A brief guide to weighing medications and/or therapy, and siding with therapy; would make a fine handout for ambivalent clients.

★★★ *The Systematic Desensitization Procedure* www.guidetopsychology.com/sysden. htm

A very good presentation of the rationale and methods behind systematic desensitization by R. Richmond, PhD.

★★★ *Diaphragmatic Breathing* cmhc.utexas.edu/stressrecess/Level_Two/breathing. html

A helpful video that demonstrates this relaxation technique, which is often helpful with anxiety and panic attacks. It is contained within a larger stress-reduction self-help free online course.

★★★ *Shyness.com* www.shyness.com

This website from the Shyness Institute offers links to all aspects of shyness (and social anxiety) overseen by Lynne Henderson, PhD. The site offers brochures, questionnaires, program descriptions, book recommendations, and links to local programs.

★★ *Duke University's Program in Child and Adolescent Anxiety Disorder* www2. mc.duke.edu/pcaad

A Duke University Medical Center-affiliated site with information about their research and treatment programs that address anxiety disorders in children.

### Other Resources

★★★★ *Anxiety Self-Help Brochures* www.counselingcenter.illinois.edu/?page_id=7

These brochures from the University of Illinois may be helpful to people with an anxiety disorder: *Dissertation Success Strategies, Overcoming Procrastination, Perfectionism, Stress Management, Test Anxiety,* and *Time Management.*

## ■ SUPPORT GROUPS

### Agoraphobics in Motion (AIM)

Phone: 248-547-0400
www.aimforrecovery.com

### Anxiety Disorders Association of America (ADAA)

Phone: 240-485-1001
www.adaa.org

A nonprofit organization "whose mission is to promote the prevention and cure of anxiety disorders." The bookstore is excellent for its prices and the wide range of books.

### Emotions Anonymous

Phone: 651-647-9712
www.EmotionsAnonymous.org
Twelve-step program of recovery from emotional difficulties.

### Freedom from Fear

Phone: 718-351-1717
www.freedomfromfear.org

### National Anxiety Foundation

www.lexington-on-line.com/naf.html

### tAPir Registry

www.algy.com/anxiety
    This is a search engine for support groups. Although new, it is a wonderful idea and helps locate many people and organizations.

### Tourette Syndrome Association Inc. (TSA)

Phone: 718-224-2999
www.tsa-usa.org

**See also** Obsessive–Compulsive Disorder (Chapter 30), Posttraumatic Stress Disorder (Chapter 31), and Stress Management and Relaxation (Chapter 37).

# CHAPTER 8

# ASSERTIVENESS

The famous behavior therapist Joseph Wolpe said that there are essentially three ways to relate to others. The first is to be aggressive, considering only ourselves and riding roughshod over others. You count, but others don't. The second is to be nonassertive, always putting others before ourselves and letting others run roughshod over us. Others count, but you don't. The third approach is the golden mean—to be assertive, placing ourselves first, but taking others into account. That is, you count *and* other people count.

In most cultures, women have traditionally been socialized to be passive and men to be aggressive. In today's world, an increasing number of women have stepped up their efforts to reduce their passivity and be more assertive, and more men are choosing to be less aggressive. Most mental health professionals believe that our society would benefit from increased assertiveness by women and decreased aggression by men. Breaking out of traditional patterns, though, can be difficult and stressful. In the case of working hard to become more assertive, it's clearly worth the effort.

In this chapter, we present evaluative ratings and brief descriptions of self-help books and Internet resources on assertiveness (Box 8.1).

## ■ SELF-HELP BOOKS

### Strongly Recommended

★★★★★ *Your Perfect Right: A Guide to Assertive Living* (7th ed., 1995) by Robert Alberti and Michael Emmons. San Luis Obispo, CA: Impact.

This national bestseller, periodically updated, emphasizes the importance of developing better communication skills in becoming more assertive. Initially published in 1970, *Your Perfect Right* is presented in two main parts: Part I speaks to the self-help reader who wants to learn how to become more assertive; Part II is a guide for assertiveness training leaders that teaches techniques to help others become more assertive. In Part I, the reader learns how to distinguish assertive, nonassertive, and aggressive behavior and why assertive behavior is the best choice. Among the key components of assertive behavior are self-expression, honesty, directness, self-enhancement, not harming others, being socially responsible, and learned skills. Readers complete a questionnaire to evaluate their own level of assertiveness, and they learn about the obstacles they will face in trying to be more assertive. Step-by-step procedures are presented for getting started and for gaining the confidence to stand up for

**BOX 8.1**
**RECOMMENDATION HIGHLIGHTS**

**SELF-HELP BOOKS**

■ For practical and comprehensive training in assertion skills:

★★★★★ *Your Perfect Right* by Robert Alberti and Michael Emmons

★★★★ *Asserting Yourself* by Sharon Anthony Bower and Gordon H. Bower

★★★★ *Stand Up, Speak Out, Talk Back* by Robert Alberti and Michael Emmons

★★★★ *When I Say No, I Feel Guilty* by Manuel Smith

■ For women who want to become more assertive:

★★★★★ *The Assertive Woman* by Stanlee Phelps and Nancy Austin

■ For assertion and communication skills for children:

★★★ *Cool, Calm, and Confident* by Lisa M. Schab

♦ *Stick Up for Yourself* by Gershen Kaufman and Lev Raphael

**INTERNET RESOURCES**

■ For valuable information on assertiveness:

★★★ *Being Assertive in a Diverse World* www.counselingcenter.illinoisedu/?page_id=187

★★★ *Learn to Be Assertive* cmhc.utexas.edu/booklets/assert/assertive

★★★ *Assertiveness Skills Training Tips* www.assertiveness.org.uk

their own rights. An excellent chapter on soft assertions gives information about how to be more assertive with friends and family members. Interactions in school, work, and community are also covered, with tips on how to be assertive in those contexts. Readers learn how anger needs to be expressed in assertive, nonaggressive ways. An extensive annotated list of readings about assertiveness is provided toward the end of the book. *Your Perfect Right* is widely respected; almost 300 psychologists rated it. Indeed, some mental health professionals call it the assertiveness bible, they think so highly of it.

★★★★★ *The Assertive Woman* (3rd ed., 1997) by Stanlee Phelps and Nancy Austin. San Luis Obispo, CA: Impact.

This book is about how women can become more assertive. The third edition addresses the challenge for women to be assertive in the workplace, socially, at home, and with various sets of people with whom they come into contact. The topics of body image, attitude, power, compliments, saying no, and anger, among others, are approached with illustrative scenarios, checklists, and exercises that readers may use to learn the concepts presented. A strength of the book is that the authors adapt assertion principles to relevant contemporary contexts rather than to conventional scenarios. An effective question-and-answer section at the end of the book presents the questions that the authors have found women most frequently ask. This book is a 5-star resource specifically for women.

★★★★   *Stand Up, Speak Out, Talk Back* (1975, reissued 1982) by Robert Alberti and
Michael Emmons. New York: Pocket.

This book tackles the same problem as its sister publication, *Your Perfect Right*: how
to become more assertive by improving communication skills. The authors discuss
developing self-confidence and specific strategies that will help you become more assertive. Alberti and Emmons give artful advice on how to become assertive without stepping on others. Their 13-step assertiveness training program is based on the premise
that it is easier to change people's behavior than to change their attitudes. The steps
are clearly described and easy to understand. Readers learn some fascinating strategies
for using nonverbal behavior—eye contact, body posture, gestures, facial expressions,
voice, and timing—to present themselves more assertively. Readers are also taught how
to handle potential adverse reactions to their assertiveness, and situations are presented
in which they might not want to assert themselves, such as when interacting with overly
sensitive people. Not as well known or as highly regarded by our mental health experts
as the authors' *Your Perfect Right*, this book nonetheless is a solid, practical text on assertiveness training.

★★★★   *Asserting Yourself: A Practical Guide for Positive Change* (1991) by Sharon
Anthony Bower and Gordon H. Bower. Reading, MA: Addison-Wesley.

The authors maintain that some individuals lack communication and coping strategies
for everyday living and that these deficits are often the root of interpersonal conflict and
general unhappiness. The purpose of their program is to help individuals learn to change
their behavior in positive ways and to relate to others more effectively. Several self-tests
help the reader identify desired areas of change and goals. Then, the text focuses on success
exercises that the reader can do initially, followed by sample scripts for common situations
that can be practiced and, finally, ways to handle situations when people react negatively to
new assertive behaviors. In addition to the major focus of assertiveness training, the authors
address the often-accompanying problem of low self-esteem and conclude with a chapter
on how to develop friendships.

★★★★   *When I Say No, I Feel Guilty* (1975) by Manuel Smith. New York: Bantam.

This volume was written for people who feel that they are frequently being talked into
doing something they don't want to do. It falls into the category of assertiveness books
that emphasize the importance of learning better communication skills to become more
assertive. Its 11 chapters cover such important topics as how other people violate our
rights, an assertiveness bill of rights, the importance of persistence in becoming assertive, how to assertively cope with supervisors and experts, how to work out compromises and say "no," and how to be assertive in sexual encounters. Interspersed through
the book are 34 annotated dialogues that illustrate key skills, such as using calm persistence to get what we want, disclosing our worries to others, agreeing with critical truths
and still doing what we want, asserting our negative points, prompting criticism, and
keeping our self-respect. Many mental health professionals praise the book, comment-
ing about the down-to-earth advice and the many examples of timid people who gained
assertiveness skills.

**Recommended**

★★★  *The Assertiveness Workbook* (2000) by Randy Peterson. Oakland, CA: New Harbinger.

This book seeks to help people build their confidence, express their ideas, and say "no" without feeling guilty. Step-by-step methods assist individuals in standing up for their rights in work, love, and many other aspects of their lives. Cognitive-behavioral techniques help individuals to set and maintain personal boundaries, to be more open in relationships without getting hurt, and to defend themselves when they are criticized or asked to submit to unreasonable requests. This fine self-help book likely would have received a higher rating if it had been better known by more psychologists in our national studies.

★★★  *Don't Say Yes When You Want to Say No* (1975) by Herbert Fensterheim and Jean Baer. New York: Dell.

This behaviorally oriented book contains 13 chapters, 7 of which are devoted to the behavioral approach to assertiveness training. In the early chapters, the reader learns how to target assertiveness difficulties, use behavioral rehearsal and other strategies to learn to say "no," call on assertiveness training techniques to develop a social network of friends and acquaintances, and learn assertiveness skills that help at work. Other chapters explore a wide range of topics, some of which are not found in other assertiveness self-help books, including using assertiveness to combat depression, reduce eating disorders, and improve sexual relationships. The book was published some 35 years ago and has become dated in many ways; for example, in discussing mental disorders, the outmoded category of neurosis is used.

★★★  *Good-Bye to Guilt* (1985) by Gerald Jampolsky. New York: Bantam.

This self-help book presents an emotionally and spiritually based approach to becoming more assertive. Jampolsky uses the term *good-bye* for the process of letting go of guilt, fear, and condemning judgments. In Part I, the reader learns about the spiritual transformations involved in moving from fearfulness to forgiveness to unconditional love. In Part II, the majority of the book, 14 lessons apply the knowledge of Part I to real-life situations. Among the chapters are "Only My Condemnation Injures Me" and "In My Defenselessness My Safety Lies." Exercises such as becoming one with a flower introduce vivid images of the spiritual healing process.

★★★  *The Gentle Art of Verbal Self-Defense* (1980) by Suzette Elgin. Englewood Cliffs, NJ: Prentice-Hall.

This self-help book presents a communication skills approach to becoming more assertive. The 18 chapters train readers in verbal judo, which involves using an opponent's strength and momentum as tools for self-defense. Elgin describes four basic principles of verbal self-defense: (1) know that you are under attack; (2) know what kind of attack you are facing; (3) know how to make your defense fit the attack; and (4) know how to follow through. A number of examples and exercises help readers learn to use these principles. The book includes effective verbal strategies for seizing control of a situation, and the extensive exercises are good learning devices. However, the consensus of the mental health experts in the national studies was that the 4-star and 5-star books listed earlier do a better job of teaching assertiveness skills.

★★★ *Cool, Calm, and Confident: A Workbook to Help Kids Learn Assertiveness Skills* (2009) by Lisa M. Schab. Oakland, CA: Instant Help Books.

This book, written for children, takes a refreshing approach to developing a healthy way to interact with peers. Assertion, aggression, and passivity are described as the three primary ways to approach others for favors, inclusion, corrections, and other forms of engagement. Forty activities are offered. For example, three hypothetical children are described, each with one of these sets of characteristics. The reader is presented with a playground picture of the three and is asked to use a yellow crayon to circle the one he or she would most like to invite to a party or to be a friend. Other questions are asked about who will get to swing first and last. Another example is one of triples who are alike except that each is aggressive, passive, or assertive. The scenarios play out with what happens to each. These activities will be fun and interesting to children and will act as learning tools.

### Diamond in the Rough

♦ *Stick Up for Yourself: Every Kid's Guide to Personal Power and Positive Self-Esteem* (1990) by Gershen Kaufman and Lev Raphael. Minneapolis: Free Spirit.

Written for children ages 8 to 12, this book begins with the elusive concept of sticking up for yourself. The authors effectively use cognitive techniques in walking the child through definitions, explanations, and numerous scenarios with which the child can identify. Getting to know yourself is a central idea of the book, and the breadth and intensity of human feelings are discussed using short narratives, illustrations, short writing exercises, and questions to generate thinking (e.g., write about a time when you felt angry; tell what happened and what you did). A strength of the book is the section on learning to like yourself, which includes a self-esteem self-quiz, do's and don'ts, and good things to do for yourself. This book is cited as a Diamond in the Rough because few of our mental health experts were familiar with it, but it is particularly well presented and appropriate for the young.

### Not Recommended

★★ *Creative Aggression: The Art of Assertive Living* (1974) by George Bach and Herb Goldberg. Garden City, NY: Doubleday.
★ *Pulling Your Own Strings* (1977) by Wayne Dyer. New York: Crowell.
★ *Control Freaks: Who Are They and How to Stop Them from Running Your Life* (1991) by Gerald Piaget. New York: Doubleday.

### Strongly Not Recommended

† *Looking Out for Number One* (1977) by Robert Ringer. Beverly Hills, CA: Los Angeles Book Company.
† *Winning Through Intimidation* (1973) by Robert Ringer. Beverly Hills, CA: Los Angeles Book Company.

# ■ INTERNET RESOURCES

★★★ *Being Assertive in a Diverse World* www.counselingcenter.illinois. edu/?page_id=187

This article from the Counseling Center at the University of Illinois at Urbana-Champaign discusses the components of assertive behavior and how to improve one's assertiveness.

★★★ *Being Assertive: Reduce Stress, Communicate Better—Mayo Clinic* www.mayoclinic.com/health/assertive/SR00042

A two-page article that helps readers understand the differences between assertiveness and other kinds of behavior, like aggressive and passive behaviors.

★★★ *Being Assertive* www.moodjuice.scot.nhs.uk/assertiveness.asp

This website from the U.K.'s National Health Service is a single page that offers techniques to help improve one's assertiveness skills.

★★★ *Learn to Be Assertive* cmhc.utexas.edu/booklets/assert/assertive.html

This article from the University of Texas's counseling center includes topics on assertiveness, including "The 4 Types of Assertion" and "What Is Being Assertive?"

★★★ *Assertiveness Training* www.psychologicalselfhelp.org/Chapter13/chap13_18. html

This section of the book *Psychological Self-Help* deals with assertiveness and understanding its purpose in our relationships with others, as well as offering steps on how to achieve greater assertiveness in our lives.

★★★ *Assertiveness Skills Training Tips* www.assertiveness.org.uk

This set of articles from the Impact Factory covers the "art of saying no," understanding the differences between assertiveness and other things, and managing feelings. The articles offer sensible tips on becoming more assertive.

★★ *Become More Assertive* idiotsguides.com/static/quickguides/selfhelp/become_ more_assertive.html

This excerpt from *The Complete Idiot's Guide to Enhancing Your Social IQ* by Gregory Korgeski, PhD, offers down-to-earth (but perhaps overly simplistic) advice about improving your assertiveness.

**See also** Communication and People Skills (Chapter 17).

# CHAPTER 9

# ATTENTION-DEFICIT/ HYPERACTIVITY DISORDER

The diagnosis of attention-deficit/hyperactivity disorder (ADHD) has proliferated over the past two decades, with some experts asserting that this neurobehavioral disorder is finally being effectively diagnosed and others claiming that we are unduly labeling fidgety or misbehaving children. The attention-deficit part of the disorder is characterized by an inability to pay attention to details, a failure to sustain attention, easy distractibility, and forgetfulness in daily activities. Hyperactivity is characterized by fidgeting, squirming, talking excessively, moving around during sedentary activity, and impulsiveness, such as interrupting and displaying excessive impatience. ADHD is estimated to affect 3% to 5% of school-age children and occurs several times more frequently in males than in females.

ADHD can dramatically affect children's lives and, correspondingly, parents find their lives and families in turmoil. The symptoms become evident during early school years, when adjustment to group activities and norms becomes important. Academic achievement often declines, and behavioral problems in school develop. The child's inability to apply himself or herself to concentrated work often has the appearance of disinterest, lack of discipline, and contrary behavior. The symptoms of ADHD can shift in intensity and frequency, resulting in the parents' and teachers' perception of willfulness and deliberateness in oppositional behavior. The understandable fallout from ADHD includes family discord, discipline problems, and educational frustrations, while the child feels isolated, misunderstood, and sometimes rejected.

Originally seen as a childhood disorder, ADHD is now increasingly viewed as continuing, at least for many, into adulthood. In the past decade, increased attention has been brought to adults with ADHD. They suffer, as do their spouses, friends, and coworkers.

The self-help books, autobiographies, online self-help, websites, and support groups described in this chapter target children, adolescents, and adults suffering from ADHD as well as their families (Box 9.1).

## ■ SELF-HELP BOOKS

### Strongly Recommended

★★★★★  *Taking Charge of Adult ADHD* (2010) by Russell A. Barkley. New York: Guilford.

ADHD and attention-deficit disorder (ADD) are so overwhelmingly associated with childhood that little attention until recent years has been paid to adults who were not

**BOX 9.1**
**RECOMMENDATION HIGHLIGHTS**

**SELF-HELP BOOKS**

■ For parents of ADHD children:

***** *Taking Charge of ADHD* by Russell Barkley

■ For adults with ADHD:

***** *Taking Charge of Adult ADHD* by Russell Barkley

***** *Driven to Distraction* by Edward M. Hallowell and John J. Ratey

♦ *Adventures in Fast Forward* by Kathleen G. Nadeau

■ For teens with ADHD:

*** *ADHD and Teens* by Colleen Alexander-Roberts

■ For children with ADHD:

**** *Putting on the Brakes* by Patricia O. Quinn and Judith M. Stern

*** *Learning to Slow Down and Pay Attention* by Kathleen G. Nadeau and Ellen B. Dixon

**AUTOBIOGRAPHIES**

■ For coping strategies from parents of ADHD children:

**** *Parenting a Child with Attention Deficit/Hyperactivity Disorder* by Nancy S. Boyles and Darlene Contadino

*** *The Little Monster* by Robert Jergen

■ For advice from a psychotherapist who has ADHD:

*** *ADHD Handbook for Families* by Paul L. Weingartner

■ For insider descriptions of child and adolescent ADHD:

♦ *ADHD and Me* by Blake E. S. Taylor

**ONLINE SELF-HELP**

■ For computer-based programs to increase attention and listening:

**** *The Captain's Log Cognitive System* www.braintrain.com

**INTERNET RESOURCES**

■ For excellent general information about ADHD:

***** *Attention Deficit Disorder (ADD and ADHD)—Psych Central* psychcentral.com/disorders/adhd

***** *National Resource Center on ADHD* www.help4adhd.org

**** *Attention Deficit Disorder Association* www.add.org

diagnosed as children. This book targets those adult common characteristics (e.g., starting without waiting for directions, impulsive decision making, forgetting a task for something more appealing) that are not exactly the same as for children and offers typical scenarios in which ADD or ADHD is manifest in adults. Psychologist Barkley thoroughly explains the importance of an evaluation, how to approach an evaluation, where to go, what information needs to be provided, and what an evaluation will tell individuals. How ADD/ADHD affects one's work, relationships, education, and everyday life is described and a step-by-step way of managing the condition is presented. The book is well organized and encompasses what an adult needs to know about the condition. This book is enthusiastically recommended by our mental health experts, as is Barkley's self-help book for children with ADHD (reviewed next).

★★★★★  *Taking Charge of ADHD* (2000, revised ed.) by Russell A. Barkley. New York: Guilford.

Psychologist Barkley adopts an empathic stance toward parents of ADHD children, offering illustrations of how parents and children are misunderstood and misinformed. The purpose of this popular self-help resource is to describe how ADHD impairs the lives of parents and children and to empower parents to proactively take an executive role in decisions about their children. The theme of the book is upbeat: the author offers parents many practical and effective methods for managing their children, taking care of themselves as parents, becoming effective advocates for their children, and implementing techniques to help ADHD children succeed at school and feel better about themselves. This stellar book, which received a ringing endorsement from our mental health experts, is written for beleaguered parents who have not given up hope.

★★★★★  *Driven to Distraction: Recognizing and Coping with Attention Deficit Disorder from Childhood through Adulthood* (1994) by Edward M. Hallowell and John J. Ratey. New York: Simon & Schuster.

This superb book is written for people with ADHD, their family members, and others in their lives, with special focus on adults with ADHD. The experience of ADHD is realistically portrayed through case studies that illustrate specific problems, such as secondary symptoms of depression, low self-esteem, fear of learning new things, and the fear of diagnosis as an educational "death sentence." The reader is taught how to further a diagnosis, what one can do when the diagnosis is suspected, how to explain the diagnosis to children, and how to structure the child's daily life. There is a thorough description of treatment possibilities. The experience of ADHD and its effects on the relationships of adults, couples, the family, and schoolchildren is addressed. *Driven to Distraction* also presents an informative description of ADHD effects when coupled with anxiety, depression, learning disabilities, substance abuse, conduct disorders, and other conditions. An early and influential self-help book on ADHD throughout the lifespan.

★★★★  *Putting On The Brakes: Young People's Guide to Understanding Attention Deficit Hyperactivity Disorder* (2001) by Patricia O. Quinn and Judith M. Stern. New York: Magination.

This book speaks directly to children between the ages of 8 and 13 from a pediatric and educational perspective about their ADHD. The purpose is to give children a sense of control and encouragement that they can, in fact, achieve. Chapters on understanding ADHD ask a question such as What is ADHD?, How Do You Know If You Have ADHD?, and Are You The Only One? Then the chapter explains, using bullet formats, graphics, and symptom listings, what the child is likely experiencing and what it means. The second half of the book addresses ways children can gain a sense of control of their lives, including getting support, making friends, understanding medications, and becoming more organized. A letter of encouragement written to children concludes the book. An excellent activity book, *The Best of Brakes: An Activity Book for Kids with ADD* (2000), accompanies this book. This book speaks directly to children about their ADHD in an effective and positive way.

## Recommended

★★★   *Answers to Distraction* (1994) by Edward M. Hallowell and John J. Ratey. New York: Pantheon.

*Answers to Distraction* was written by Hallowell and Ratey shortly after they wrote *Driven to Distraction* and is a compilation of the questions they have been asked about ADHD since the publication of the first book (which is reviewed above). This highly readable text systematically focuses on ADD's impact on children, teachers, women, work, couples, and families. The chapter on ADD and Children clusters questions from parents, young children (ages 4–10), and adolescents (11–18) and answers them in an age-appropriate manner. Questions are effectively organized into topics of medication, creativity, diagnosis, addiction, and anger. The questions are clear and crisp, and the answers are informative. The authors take on the myths and stereotypes of ADD and offer, in the last section of the book, 100 tips on managing adult ADD, ADD in families, and ADD in couples. The recommendations are do-able and practical. This book was rated quite highly by those who had read it.

★★★   *ADHD and Teens* (1995, reissued 2002) by Colleen Alexander-Roberts. Dallas, TX: Taylor.

This volume is written for parents and, secondarily, for those working with ADHD teens. The roller-coaster ride of adolescence with ADHD is described by identifying problem areas, offering warning signs, suggesting coping techniques, and explaining improved parenting skills. The approach assumes a partnering of behavioral and educational models with medication for moderate to severe cases. The author also addresses the larger context of ADHD effects on family dynamics, school and peer interactions, and stages of development. Helpful chapters are included on coexisting special problems, such as substance abuse, sexuality, suicide risk, and oppositional defiant/conduct disorder. This book had not been read by many of our experts at the time of publication but was rated very highly by those who had read it.

★★★   *Learning to Slow Down and Pay Attention: A Book for Kids about ADD* (2nd ed., 1997) by Kathleen G. Nadeau and Ellen B. Dixon. Washington, DC: Magination.

This second edition of *Learning to Slow Down and Pay Attention*, written for children, retains the fundamental elements of the first but adds several strong areas, including many more "things I can do to help myself," increased focus on attentional problems without hyperactivity, and a greater emphasis on problems experienced by girls. The writing style, page layout, and funny cartoons lend themselves effectively to the interests of children. A checklist about the child at home, at school, and with friends and about the child himself or herself allows children to identify specific concerns and frustrations on which they can work with parents and teachers. "Things I can do for myself" is an excellent activity list that includes getting ready for school, paying attention, completing homework, controlling anger, solving problems, and making friends. A section on special projects that children can do with parents adds positive experiences.

★★★ *Mastering Your Adult ADHD* (2005) by Steven A. Safren, Carol A. Perlman, Susan Sprich, & Michael Otto. New York: Oxford University Press.

This approach to adult ADHD focuses directly on developing a self-help and treatment plan around cognitive-behavioral methods. The three major areas of symptoms are poor attention, high impulse, and high activity level. The treatment is well explained, and the authors offer techniques such as problem solving for managing tasks, gauging attention distractibility, and modifying the environment. The book is written in an academic style but is clear and explicit.

★★★ *Living with ADHD Children: A Handbook for Parents* (1998) by Peter H. Buntman. Los Alamitos, CA: Center for Family Life.

This handbook is written in a workbook format that presents the major topics concisely but thoroughly. The focus areas start with how it feels to be a parent and how the child feels to be coping with ADHD, moves into symptoms and other causes of hyperactivity that need to be ruled out, and then targets behavioral change. The instructional chapters teach the parent how to change the child's behavior, how to get the child to listen, how to work with self-esteem and school problems, and about medication. The last chapter is a compendium of questions from parents that is quite comprehensive.

★★★ *The ADHD Workbook for Kids* (2010) by Lawrence E. Shapiro. Oakland, CA: Instant Help Books.

The author directs introductory statements to the child readers, asking, "Do people tell you that you can do better when you've tried your best; do you have trouble keeping friends; do children tease you?" These questions will resonate with children and interest them in reading more. Activities for children and preteens are focused on four areas: learning self-control and how to stay out of trouble, overcoming school problems, making and keeping friends, and feeling good about oneself. Activities are interactive and allow the readers to insert their circumstances and characteristics into the questions and scenarios. Many decision and problem-solving situations and individual choices are presented in various scenarios and illustrate for readers how making the suggested improvement affects their relationships with individuals and with the environment.

★★★ *Overcoming ADHD* (2009) by Stanley I. Greenspan. Cambridge, MA: Da Capo Press.

A different approach is taken here: not on treatment but on understanding what drives ADHD and how parents can understand how their child is specifically affected by the sensory and motor aspects of ADHD. The audience is parents, who are asked in the book several sets of questions about their child (e.g., does the child over- or under-react to light, sound, touch, pitch of tone, sensations of any particular kind). In addition to sensory and motor characteristics, the role of emotions and other factors in regard to attention is explored;

self-esteem and family patterns are described; and the roles of the environment and medications are reviewed. Also distinct to this book is the view that attention is a learned characteristic, not an innate one. This perspective introduces a way of thinking about ADHD that differs from conventional models.

★★★ *The Gift of Adult ADD* (2008) by Lara Honos-Webb. Oakland, CA: New Harbinger.

A unique perspective is taken here: adult ADD is portrayed as encompassing a variety of gifts and strengths. Ways of thinking and acting that are often labeled as ADD deficits may actually be assets. Individuals are encouraged not to be defined by their ADD but to find the right environment in which their behaviors can be channeled into strengths. Several successful people are portrayed in interviews that highlight how, for example, daydreaming can be converted into creativity and dreams, which then materialize in success. Strengths of individuals with ADD are often humor, spontaneity, or cleverness, which also can be channeled into successful work, relationships, and life endeavors. Often those with ADD feel as though they are in "never-ending reform school" when they could be altering their environments to play on their strengths.

**Diamonds in the Rough**

♦ *Adventures in Fast Forward* (1996) by Kathleen G. Nadeau. New York: Brunner/ Mazel.

Adults with ADD symptoms are often anxious and confused about ADD. This highly readable and informative book is written for them. The early chapters are devoted to defining ADD and to explaining the scope of diagnosis and assessment; the latter chapters enumerate the treatment choices, including medication and psychotherapy. Two chapters on life management skills and social skills are very instructive in teaching individuals how to counteract ADD-related difficulties. Time-management techniques, stress management, money management, coping with hyperactivity and impulsivity, and memory techniques are among the life management skills recommended. Interpersonal behaviors including interrupting, distractibility, bluntness, hypersensitivity, poor listening skills, and missed social cues are among the problems described. Coping techniques for each problem behavior are suggested. Examples of ADD difficulties in the workplace are described, and modifications of behavioral patterns are recommended. This book was highly but infrequently rated in our studies, thus receiving the Diamond in the Rough designation.

♦ *Teenagers with ADD: A Parents' Guide* (1995) by Chris A. Zeigler Dendy. Bethesda, MD: Woodbine House.

The agony of being a parent of a child with undiagnosed ADD motivated the author to write this book for parents of adolescents who may not have been diagnosed as children. The distinctive contribution of this self-help resource, unlike many others, is the specific focus on the teen years (13–20) and the real-life vignettes of teenagers and parents who have experienced success as well as challenges. Neglected topics are discussed, including sports participation, driving privileges, speeding tickets, sleep disturbances, drug and alcohol use, and college attendance. Chapters include excellent "easy reference guides" that summarize the full content of the chapter and provide categorized listings of recommendations. These include a list of common learning problems and adaptations for home and school, guiding principles for parent–teen interpersonal interaction, and a warning list of problem behaviors that have potential for greater concerns. This text is an effective compendium for parents who want tools to help teens.

## ■ AUTOBIOGRAPHIES

### Strongly Recommended

**★★★★** *Parenting a Child with Attention Deficit/Hyperactivity Disorder* (1999) by Nancy S. Boyles and Darlene Contadino. Los Angeles: Lowell House.

The two authors, both parents of children with ADHD working as professionals in the field, have also collaborated on *The Learning Differences Sourcebook*. Here they present management, coping, and advocacy strategies for parents based on their own experiences and those of other parents. A self-help book as well as personal account, the book discusses test interpretation, diagnosis, and intervention strategies. A highly valued and practical volume with a strong insider's voice.

### Recommended

**★★★** *ADHD Handbook for Families: A Guide to Communicating with Professionals* (1999) by Paul L. Weingartner. Washington, DC: Child Welfare League of America.

An experienced therapist who works with ADHD children, Weingartner brings a personal perspective in that he has ADHD himself. He describes his coping mechanisms and the methods he uses to work with children and to educate parents about the disorder. A central theme of the book, encapsulated in its subtitle, is enhancing the family's ability to communicate and lobby effectively with health-care professionals. The thrust of the book is family empowerment through behavior management strategies, realistic goals, and effective reinforcement. Sample behavior contracts are presented. A very good and scientifically based approach that can benefit many parents of ADHD children.

**★★★** *The Little Monster: Growing Up With ADHD* (2004) by Robert Jergen. Lanham, MD: R&L Education.

Unlike many of the other authors with ADHD, Robert Jergen was not diagnosed until after he entered college and is able to describe undiagnosed ADHD from the child's perspective. He convincingly portrays how the constant rejection and criticism of his behavior undermined his feelings of self-worth. He did not see any point in living and twice tried to commit suicide. After he was properly diagnosed in college, Jergen decided to turn his ADHD into an asset and subsequently excelled in school and in his professional work. For him the question was not how to cure his ADHD but how to make the most of it. He offers practical suggestions for readers to accomplish a similar transformation of

ADHD into an asset. His book has received rave reviews from ADHD parents, teachers, and people with ADHD.

### Diamonds in the Rough

★★★ *Maybe You Know My Kid: A Parents' Guide to Helping Your Child with Attention Deficit Hyperactivity Disorder* (3rd ed., 1999) by Mary Fowler. Secaucus, NJ: Birch Lane.

Faced with the challenge of raising a son with ADHD, Mary Fowler researched the topic. The book describes theories in the field, available treatments, educational programs, and advocacy techniques related to the Americans with Disabilities Act. The new edition features recent material on treatments and on sources of assistance for families. Named a Diamond in the Rough because of its high rating but low number of ratings; our experts may have not been familiar with the revised edition.

★★★ *ADHD and Me: What I Learned from Lighting Fires at the Dinner Table* (2008) by Blake E. S. Taylor and Lara Honos-Webb. Oakland, CA: New Harbinger.

Blake was diagnosed with ADHD when he was 5 years old. The book, with an introduction by psychologist Lara Honos-Webb, was written during his last two years of high school. After graduation, he attended Berkeley. The book describes, often with a humorous touch, the world of teens with ADHD and how things look to them, which can explain why they act as they do. He puts into words the distractions and focus points that make their behavior seem odd and irrational. Blake has many useful tips for teens with ADHD and their parents. He was helped greatly by medication. Chapters have three sections: a noteworthy or funny incident in the author's childhood or adolescence (yes, he *did* light a fire at the dinner table) illustrating some manifestation of ADHD, the author's explanation of what was happening and why, followed by suggestions for family coping and remediation measures.

## ▓ ONLINE SELF-HELP

★★★★ *The Captain's Log Cognitive System* www.braintrain.com

This is a computer-based program designed to help users exercise areas of mental functions usually affected by ADHD. Interactive games and mental puzzles help users refine mental skills, including memory, attention, listening skills, processing speed, and others. Program cost begins at $495 and increases with the number of program users.

## ▓ INTERNET RESOURCES

### General Websites

★★★★★ *National Resource Center on ADHD* www.help4adhd.org

The National Resource Center on ADHD is a project of Children and Adults with Attention-Deficit/Hyperactivity Disorder (CHADD) and provides a wealth of information for all audiences—both children and adults—about ADHD. Well written and well researched, the articles are up to date and detailed.

★★★★★ *Attention Deficit Disorder (ADD and ADHD)* psychcentral.com/disorders/adhd

A comprehensive information center from Psych Central that offers dozens of articles about the diagnosis, causes, and treatments of ADHD in both adults and children. The site also offers two interactive quizzes on ADHD, a couple of blogs on ADHD, a support group, and updated news and research articles.

★★★ *The National Attention Deficit Disorder Association* www.add.org

This site offers dozens of articles under "Resources & Support," which vary in quality. There is much material for support and guidance of parents and children dealing with school, family, career, coaching, and treatment.

### Psychoeducational Materials

★★★ *Attention Deficit Hyperactivity Disorder*    www.nimh.nih.gov/health/topics/attention-deficit-hyperactivity-disorder-adhd

A basic information center from the National Institute of Mental Health, focused heavily on the government's role in funding new research and treatment advances (e.g., the Science News section mentions only NIMH-funded research). Articles tend to lack basic information about authors and about when they were written or last reviewed.

★★★★ *ADDvance* www.addvance.com

Because considerably fewer females have ADHD, this site may be of special value. Some of the articles and resources are specific to females—girls, students, and mothers—and the site also has a wealth of more generalized articles and links to additional online resources.

★★★ *Special Education Rights and Responsibilities* adhdnews.com/sped.htm

An article for child advocates and therapists looking for all the federal rules and policies and advice for writing IEPs and TIEPs for pursuing special educational services.

★★ *Born to Explore! The Other Side of ADD* borntoexplore.org

"ADD is a difference not a defect" is the theme here, for people who want to reframe their disorder as something more positive.

★★★ *ADHD: From A to Zoë* blogs.psychcentral.com/adhd-zoe

This blog by Zoë Kessler offers updated insights multiple times a week from someone who grapples with ADD. Often engaging and at times poignant, it's a helpful perspective for people who need the support of someone who's "been there."

★★★ *Social Security* adhdnews.com/ssi.htm

Offers advice on applying for Social Security disability benefits for a child with ADHD.

## Other Resources

★★★ *ADD Checklists and Forms* www.add-plus.com/forms.htm

Devised by John F. Taylor, PhD, these data collection forms can enhance communication with teachers and physicians. Checklists include Academic Problem Identification Checklist; Classroom Daily Report Form; Hyperactivity Screening Checklist; Medication Effectiveness Report Form; and Social/Emotional/Academic Adjustment Checklist.

★★★ *Job Information for People with ADD* add.about.com/msubjobs.htm?pid=2791&cob=home

Nine articles to assist in managing work issues, and a list of careers and information about each.

★★★ *ADDitude: Living Well with Attention Deficit* www.additudemag.com

A wealth of articles, information, and encouragement from the magazine of the same name. It's a big site with a lot of resources, including support groups, a directory of treatment professionals, and much more. Sadly, because it is so large, it suffers from confusing and overwhelming page layouts, and complicated navigation. Articles often lack attributions such as date of publication or authorship.

## ▪ SUPPORT GROUPS

### Attention Deficit Disorder Association (ADDA)

Phone: 847-432-ADDA
www.add.org

### Attention Deficit Information Network (AD-IN)

Phone: 781-455-9895
www.addinfonetwork.com

### CHADD: Children and Adults with Attention Deficit/Hyperactivity Disorder

Phone: 800-233-4050
www.chadd.org

### Council for Exceptional Children

Phone: 888-CEC-SPED
www.cec.sped.org

**Federation of Families for Children's Mental Health**

Phone: 703-684-7710
www.ffcmh.org

**HEATH Resource Center**

Phone: 800-544-3284
www.heath.gwu.edu

**Learning Disabilities Association of America**

Phone: 412-341-1515 and 412-341-8077
www.ldanatl.org
For people with learning disabilities and their families.

**National Association of Private Schools for Exceptional Children**

Phone: 202-408-3338
www.napsec.org
Provides referrals to private special education programs.

**National Information Center for Children and Youth with Disabilities**

Phone: 800-695-0285
www.nichcy.org

**See also** Child Development and Parenting (Chapter 15) and Violent Youth (Chapter 41).

# CHAPTER 10

# AUTISM AND ASPERGER'S

Autism spectrum disorders (ASD) are pervasive developmental syndromes affecting the acquisition of social and communication skills, before the age of 3. The disorders present in various forms and severities, ranging from a milder syndrome, Asperger's, to a more severe type, autism. The common threads along the autism spectrum involve problems in communication, social interaction, and rigid patterns of behavior.

Once viewed as rare, autism and its cousins afflict approximately 1 in every 100 children. But the prevalence rates are the result of improved diagnosis and are the subject of intense controversy and political lobbying, leading to wildly variable numbers. Nonetheless, everyone concurs on the need for accurate diagnosis and early intervention.

A rare but media-sensationalized version of ASD occurs with autistic savants who manifest extraordinary abilities. Dustin Hoffman's character in *Rain Man* typifies this fascinating disorder but leaves the public confused about the far more prevalent dysfunctions confronting those with autism.

This chapter gives the evaluative ratings and reviews of self-help books, autobiographies, films, online self-help, and Internet sites devoted to ASD, including a few on autistic savants (Box 10.1). The chapter concludes with a listing of national support groups.

## ■ SELF-HELP BOOKS

### Strongly Recommended

★★★★★ *The Complete Guide to Asperger's Syndrome* (2008) by Tony Attwood. Philadelphia, PA: Jessica Kingsley Publishers.

In this 5-star resource, Asperger's syndrome is thoroughly explained: how we came to understand the disorder, what the defining characteristics are, and in what way treatment can be effective. Complex aspects of the syndrome are impressively developed through understandable narrative and case examples on (1) understanding the expression of emotion, (2) the uniqueness of rare special interests, (3) language challenges, (4) motor coordination, (5) sensory sensitivity, (6) life after school, (7) long-term relationships, and (8) psychotherapy. In each chapter, Attwood presents moving depictions of differentiating characteristics of a person with Asperger's. Each area is addressed in detail with remedial and strategic plans. This book was familiar to many mental health experts in our national surveys and was deservedly rated highly.

## BOX 10.1
## RECOMMENDATION HIGHLIGHTS

**SELF-HELP BOOKS**

■ For a comprehensive overview for parents and professionals:

★★★★★ *The Complete Guide to Asperger's Syndrome* by Tony Attwood

■ For parents seeking treatment and resources:

★★★ *A Parent's Guide to Asperger Syndrome and High Functioning Autism*

♦ *The Autism Sourcebook* by Karen Siff Exkorn

**AUTOBIOGRAPHIES**

■ On autistic savants:

★★★★ *Born on a Blue Day* by Daniel Tammet

■ On Asperger's and autism:

★★★ *Atypical* by Jesse A. Saperstein

★★★ *Emergence* by Temple Grandin and Margaret M. Scariano

★★★ *Look Me in the Eye* by John Elder Robison

**FILMS**

■ On an autistic adult overcoming and thriving:

★★★★★ *Temple Grandin*

■ On young adults caring for those with spectrum disorders:

★★★★★ *Rain Man*

★★★★ *Mozart & the Whale*

★★★★ *What's Eating Gilbert Grape?*

**ONLINE SELF-HELP**

■ For building skills recognizing the emotions of other people:

★★★★ *Emotion Trainer* www.emotiontrainer.co.uk

■ For colorful animated games to teach social skills and other life lessons:

★★★★ *Whizkidgames.com* www.whizkidgames.com

**INTERNET RESOURCES**

■ For valuable information on autism:

★★★★★ *Autism Speaks* www.autismspeaks.org

★★★★★ *Left Brain/Right Brain—Autism News, Science, and Opinion*
leftbrainrightbrain.co.uk

**Recommended**

★★★ *A Parent's Guide to Asperger Syndrome and High Functioning Autism* (2002) by Sally Ozonoff, Geraldine Dawson, and James McPartland. New York: Guilford.

Parents of children with this syndrome will be given a solid framework through which to begin understanding and living with autism. The three authors provide clear, valuable descriptions of the diagnostic process, known causation, and treatment planning. Further, the authors lend support and direction to parents by discussing how a family continues to live their lives and to raise their child on a day-by-day basis. The authors strike a perfect balance between acknowledging the child's limitations while identifying and capitalizing on his or her strengths. Life at home, at work, and at school and social relationships are so important and are discussed thoroughly, including the adolescent and adult years. One of the better self-help books on higher-functioning kids on the autistic spectrum.

★★★ *The Social Skills Picture Book Teaching Play, Emotion, and Communication with Autism* (2003) by Jed Baker. Arlington, TX: Future Horizons.

Many autistic children have difficulty with language and attention; as a result, learning through verbal communication is not particularly effective for them. In this book, picture stories convert verbal and abstract information into concrete and visual material, which remains stable over time (auditory information is frequently lost through distraction). Visual pictures are most helpful to children who have problems with language processing, abstraction, and attention. The picture stories teach important social and communications skills, such as how to listen, maintain conversations, end conversations, introduce oneself, share in play, take turns, show interest in others' feelings, accept "no," try something new, and deal with teasing. A solid and unique self-help resource for families.

### Diamond in the Rough

◆ *The Autism Sourcebook: Everything You Need to Know About Diagnosis, Treatment, Coping, and Healing* (2005) by Karen Siff Exkorn. New York: Regan.

This book was just short of the number of professionals needed to rate it; however, those who did gave it a strong endorsement. *The Autism Sourcebook* is written for parents of children with autism who are under the age of 12. The author is the mother of an autistic boy and writes comprehensively about her experience: everything from getting the news, not knowing what to do, not getting definitive answers, finding the answers herself, making choices, dealing with the frustrations of the "runaround," and learning to become an advocate in education, medical, and legal venues. The focal areas are diagnosis, treatment, coping, and healing. Many frequently asked questions that don't have answers are addressed through the author's experience. A vast reference section ends the book. This book was clearly written from the heart of a mother who became a fierce advocate for her son, who today functions like most 8-year-olds.

### Not Recommended

★★ *1001 Great Ideas for Teaching and Raising Children with Autism or Asperger's* by Ellen Notbohm and Veronica Zysik

★★ *Engaging Autism* by Stanley I. Greenspan and Serena Wieder

## ■ AUTOBIOGRAPHIES

### Strongly Recommended

★★★★ *Born on a Blue Day: Inside the Extraordinary Mind of an Autistic Savant* (2007) by Daniel Tammet. New York: Free Press.

The author, a British writer, has a multiplicity of abilities and behaviors associated with Asperger's syndrome, including amazing calculating and linguistic abilities (he speaks

10 languages) and synesthesia, in which associations cross sensory boundaries. He describes some of the negative effects of his conditions as well: his obsessions, stereotyped movements, rocking, literalness, and endless distracting fascinations. He provides no explanations of his conditions other than a seizure at age 4 possibly creating unusual brain connections, and no program for behavior change, only descriptions of his unusual life, his alienation and marginality, and the celebrity his extraordinary calculating and linguistic feats have brought him.

### Recommended

★★★ *Emergence: Labeled Autistic* (1996) by Temple Grandin and Margaret M. Scariano. New York: Warner Books.

Temple Grandin has written several books on the role of autism in her life and her very successful career as an animal behaviorist designing livestock facilities. Some reviewers credit her with writing the first "insider account" of autism. She has written more recent books, such as *Thinking in Pictures* and *The Way I See It*, but this book captures the loneliness and separation of a child desperate for human contact while unable to relate to others. Her temper tantrums and difficulty communicating led to her placement in a special school for autistic children. Fortunately, Grandin had tremendous support from her mother and from outstanding teachers, a critical lesson of this book. Her mother and her teachers are as much the heroes of this tale as is the senior author. If not for the comparatively low number of raters, this autobiography would have earned a deserved 5-star, strongly recommended designation.

★★★ *Look Me in the Eye: My Life with Asperger's* (2008) by John Elder Robison. New York: Three Rivers Press.

The author grew up with an abusive alcoholic father and a schizophrenic mother. His younger brother, Augusten Burroughs, described the dysfunctional household in a bestselling book, *Running with Scissors*. Robison describes a lonely, isolated childhood in which he could not understand or relate to other people, who sometimes told him to "Look me in the eye," which became the book's title. He was the class clown and flunked out of high school. Although social inept, he discovered and honed his abilities to use logic and work with machines, leading to successful careers in developing sound systems, electronic games, and currently restoring classic cars. He did not identify himself as an "Aspergian" (his term) until he was in his 40s, by which time he had taught himself to compensate for his interpersonal difficulties and his lack of empathy. At book's end, he returns to his hometown and makes peace with his parents and his former schoolmates. This is an entertaining book about an unusual and talented person who views himself as having turned his liabilities to good use, but at considerable cost to himself and to others.

★★★ *Atypical: Life with Asperger's in 20 1/3 Chapters* (2010) by Jesse A. Saperstein. New York: Penguin.

Diagnosed at age 14 and self-identified as an "Aspie," the highest functioning of the autism spectrum, Jesse Saperstein writes with understanding and humor about his social awkwardness, especially when faced with the mysteries of interacting with the opposite sex, his responses to bullying and rejection, his self-doubts and compulsions to perform ritualistic behaviors, and the surprise engendered when he speaks his mind directly. Jesse learns that directness of speech may not be valued by others. He challenges and tests himself by hiking the Appalachian Trail, working as a substitute teacher and in a funeral home, being a successful fundraiser for teenagers with HIV/AIDS, and doing public speaking on behalf of people with autism spectrum disorders. Reflecting on these experiences (and also in his popular blog), Jesse has turned aspects of his condition into assets.

### Strongly Not Recommended

† *All I Can Handle: I'm No Mother Teresa: A Life Raising Three Daughters with Autism* (2010) by Kim Stagliano. New York: Skyhorse.

## ■ FILMS

### Strongly Recommended

★★★★★ *Temple Grandin* (2010) directed by Mick Jackson. PG rating. 103 minutes.

This is one of those truly uplifting films in which the lead character wins out against all odds. As reviewed above in her multiple books, Temple was a young girl diagnosed with autism, unable to speak until age 4, and with terrible problems in school, particularly with interpersonal interaction. She began visiting her aunt and uncle's farm for the summer and developed an affinity for the animals, particularly cattle. She was intrigued by the cattle press, which was used to settle the cattle. She put herself in it one day only to find that it calmed her and diminished her panic attacks. Some years later, Temple went to college and majored in animal husbandry. She made a cattle crush, which she called a "hug machine," and it became known for cradling autistic children and calming them. She had one in her dorm room. Temple went on to achieve a doctoral degree and is now on the faculty at Colorado State University and known for her development of methods to more humanely treat cattle that are being slaughtered. This is a wonderful story for those with autism, and particularly their parents. Temple began with the difficulties of most autistic children but between her resolve and her mother's dedication, she has achieved remarkable feats. This is a must-see movie for all parents of students with special conditions. One of the highest-rated films in all of our national studies.

★★★★★ *Rain Man* (1988) directed by Barry Levinson. R rating. 133 minutes.

This movie, which won multiple Academy Awards, is a moving portrayal of an autistic adult with savant mathematical abilities. Charlie (Tom Cruise) is told that his father died and that he inherited his prize rose bushes and his beloved 1949 Buick; an unknown beneficiary inherited the remaining $3 million. Charlie is furious but learns that the estate recipient is an autistic brother, Raymond (Dustin Hoffman), whom the father had never mentioned. Charlie kidnaps Raymond to make money, and they drive across the country because Raymond will fly only Qantas due to its excellent accident rating. Raymond demonstrates several characteristics of autism in a most believable and accurate way. He eats certain foods on certain days; all of his baseball cards and books must be in order; he must have certain types of snacks at a certain time of day and is afraid of smoke detector sounds. The longer Charlie is with Raymond, the less he cares about the money and the more he cares about Raymond. In the end, Charlie returns Raymond to the institute where Raymond wants to be and Charlie departs. For those who have connections to autism, this is a heartwarming and accurate movie that delivers the message that love and caring know no bounds. The two cautions here are that few people with autism possess savant abilities and that the ending implies most such people would prefer to live in a group home. These generalizations are not the case among many people with autism, who would be excellent employees, neighbors, and friends that others would be privileged to have.

★★★★    *Mozart & the Whale* (2005) directed by Petter Næss. PG-13 rating. 92 minutes.

This touching story goes to the heart of anyone with knowledge of Asperger's syndrome. Written by two people who have Asperger's, the screenplay presents the true story of Jerry and Mary. Jerry is a cab driver with special abilities in calculations and dates but has enormous difficulty in making decisions. Jerry wants so badly to be what he thinks of as normal and says he didn't know he had Asperger's until he saw *Rain Man*. Mary is a flamboyant artist with a knack for saying the wrong thing, and loudly. Jerry and Mary fall in love, and many hilarious as well as touching moments depict their difficulties. The focus of the movie is whether or not they can maintain their relationship while living with the many intense demands their challenges present. This film is excellent for family members and friends of people "on the spectrum." It gives possibly the most accurate and "insider" portrayal of living with Asperger's that is depicted in film or television today.

★★★★    *What's Eating Gilbert Grape?* (1993) directed by Lasse Hallström. PG-13 rating. 118 minutes.

The intensity of mixed feelings overwhelms Gilbert (Johnny Depp), a young man taking care of his autistic brother Arnie (Leonard DiCaprio), his morbidly obese mother, and two sisters who do work in their home, but leave him in charge of his brother. Gilbert loves Arnie and wants to protect him, but his own life is close to being out of control. Gilbert falls in love with Becky, who connects with Arnie and can calm him. Gilbert's frustration with his life and his responsibility and yet his love and protective nature toward Arnie are making his life impossible. The night of Arnie's 18th birthday, his mother goes to bed, dies, and is declared dead by her physician. The family doesn't want her to be ridiculed when people see her morbidly obese body, so the family removes the furnishings from the house and burns the house with the mother in it. The story ends with the sisters getting jobs elsewhere and Gilbert and Arnie driving away with Becky. The moving story demonstrates a caretaker's complicated set of feelings about his responsibilities in stark contrast to his dreams. Those with a person with autism in their lives will identify with the emotions and will likely feel affirmed and better informed.

### Recommended

★★★    *The Boy Who Could Fly* (1986) directed by Nick Castle. PG-13 rating. 114 minutes.

Millie, her mother, and her younger brother move to a small town after Millie's father dies. Next door lives Eric, an autistic boy, and his alcoholic uncle. Eric is at constant risk of being taken away to an institution because the alcoholic uncle does not take sufficient care of him. Eric has never spoken and doesn't communicate with anyone. Nevertheless, he is in Millie's class at school and the teacher asks Millie to keep an eye on him. Eric imitates Millie's expressions and shows fondness for her but doesn't engage. Eric often climbs on rooftops and imitates the action of jumping off and flying. One day Eric is taken from his uncle and placed in an institution. Millie and her family try to visit him but as the staff turn her away, she looks back and sees Eric trying to escape through the window, but he is restrained. Later Millie rescues him. Millie asks Eric if he can really fly, and he says yes. They jump together off the school roof and both fly around with all the community looking up at them. Eric returns Millie to her own window and tells her he must leave. Even though the flying gives the film a surreal feel, the story is filled with hope, belief in others and self, and caring that is a profound message for those connected to a person with autism.

## ■ ONLINE SELF-HELP

**** *Emotion Trainer* www.emotiontrainer.co.uk

Emotion Trainer is intended to help users better recognize and identify the emotions of other people based on facial expressions and descriptions of events. It is intended for use with individuals diagnosed with autism spectrum disorders, such as Asperger's syndrome. Once purchased, users are able to repeat unlimited trials during the one-year license period. Cost is $40 for a year's license and $8 for a renewal (after conversion from British pounds).

**** *Whizkidgames.com* www.whizkidgames.com

Researchers created this colorful animated site to teach social skills and lessons to children with moderate to severe autism. The site is associated with www.autismgames.com, a companion site where parents and teachers can provide the developers with feedback as they improve current games and develop new ones. Nine games are currently available that teach children principles such as dealing with change, taking turns, making decisions, grouping items, making eye contact, identifying emotions, and making a schedule. This site and games are available free of charge.

## ■ INTERNET RESOURCES

Since Asperger's is considered an ASD, most autism resources listed below also cover Asperger's (even if not specifically mentioned).

### General Websites

***** *Autism Speaks* www.autismspeaks.org

This nonprofit advocacy organization offers a wide range of both basic and more advanced information about ASD, including an entire section devoted to research and the science into understanding them. Especially helpful are the Family Services resources, which includes a "100 Day Kit" for those who have newly diagnosed family members.

**** *Autism Research Institute* www.autism.com

The Autism Research Institute is focused on conducting and fostering research into autism and publishes a scientific journal to help. The section entitled "Families" is full of dozens of articles and interviews to help people keep up to date and better understand autism. Its active discussion group, with over 1,300 members, is open to all.

**** *Autism Society* www.autism-society.org

The Autism Society, much like Autism Speaks, is devoted to helping people understand autism and improve their lives through advocacy and education.

*** *Autism Spectrum Disorders* www.nimh.nih.gov/health/publications/autism

The National Institute of Mental Health hosts a helpful section on autism, including delving into the science and current research, as well as discussing the myriad of treatment options available.

**** *Autism* health.nytimes.com/health/guides/disease/autism/overview.html

This resource from the *New York Times* is a surprisingly well-rounded page. Ignore the licensed content about autism from ADAM and instead check out the unique resources, which include multiple slide shows, an interactive feature, and Q&As with doctors.

** *National Autism Association* www.nationalautismassociation.org

You can't go wrong with the resources provided by the nonprofit National Autism Association, which includes the basics about ASD and also help for families through a multitude of programs and initiatives, as well as products that are sold to help support the organization. However, the emphasis on ads and products makes the site feel more like a storefront than a nonprofit.

**** *Asperger's Association of New England* www.aane.org

This nonprofit regional association for Asperger's syndrome is a reliable and helpful resource to learn more about Asperger's, including how the diagnosis is made, finding treatment, and understanding the types of treatments available. The "Articles and Resources" section offers a rich and diverse library of articles with targeted topic areas, including adults, teens, education, college, poetry, children & parenting, friends & family, and more.

**** *Asperger Syndrome* kidshealth.org/parent/medical/brain/asperger.html

This article, meant for parents, is from the Nemours Foundation (and a part of the larger, excellent KidsHealth resource) and offers a good overview of Asperger's and how it's treated.

*** *Autism and Asperger's Syndrome* www.aspergerssyndrome.org

This website from Dr. Lars Perner offers a wealth of knowledge and resources about both disorders, especially when it comes to the science and theory behind what causes autism and Asperger's. The articles may be a bit technical, but if you want to understand some of the theories of what causes autism, this is a great website to explore.

★★★★ *Asperger Syndrome Education Network (ASPEN)* www.aspennj.org

A regularly updated site, ASPEN is a great resource for information about Asperger's, including regularly updated news links and a library full of articles of general concern, for parents, and by people who have an ASD (under "Information About ASDs").

★★★ *WrongPlanet.net* www.wrongplanet.net

This website is a support community for people with autism and Asperger's but also offers a host of blogs with interesting commentary and insights from people with one of these concerns. The site can be a little confusing to navigate.

★★★★★ *Left Brain/Right Brain—Autism News, Science, and Opinion* leftbrainrightbrain.co.uk

This active and engaging blog from the U.K. offers commentary, politics, news, and dissection of ASD from multiple intelligent and thought-provoking perspectives. It features multiple contributors, making it a delight to read.

★★★ *Life with Asperger's* life-with-aspergers.blogspot.com

This eclectic blog from a father who, after his son's diagnosis with Asperger's, found out that he too had it, is interesting and insightful. It offers a personal perspective from someone who writes well and reviews news, movies, books, and more related to Asperger's, as well as sharing tidbits from his daily life living with this concern.

## ■ SUPPORT GROUPS

### Autism Genetic Resource Exchange

Phone: 866-612-2473
www.agre.org

### Autism Society of America

Phone: 301-657-0881 or 800-3AUTISM
www.autism-society.org

### Cure Autism Now Foundation

Phone: 888-282-4762
www.cureautismnow.org

### National Center on Birth Defects and Developmental Disabilities

Phone: 770-488-7150
www.cdc.gov/ncbddd/dd/ddaustism.htm

# CHAPTER 11

# BIPOLAR DISORDER

We all experience the routine ups and downs of life, but some people suffer from extreme and pathological mood swings. Bipolar disorder (BD), previously called manic-depression, is characterized by extreme mood swings between depression and mania. In the manic phase, people are exuberant, have tireless stamina, and tend toward excess. The manic symptoms—decreased sleep, racing thoughts, intense distractibility—may be so severe that people appear to be temporarily psychotic. In the depressed phase, people are fatigued, sad, indecisive, and hopeless. (Chapter 20 is devoted entirely to depression.)

As with most clinical conditions, there are multiple forms of BD. Bipolar I disorder is diagnosed when the person has experienced one or more manic episodes along with depression. Bipolar II disorder, by contrast, is diagnosed when the depression has been accompanied by at least one hypomanic episode but not a full-blown manic episode. Thus, rather confusingly, a person may receive a diagnosis of bipolar II disorder without having suffered through full-blown mania.

BD is increasingly seen as a brain or biological disease, but all experts acknowledge the reciprocal interaction of psychology and biology. Clinicians also increasingly see this volatile disorder showing up in older children and adolescents. And virtually all experts recommend a combination of medication, psychotherapy, family support, and self-help.

In this chapter we critically review the self-help books, autobiographies, films, and Internet resources dedicated to BD (Box 11.1).

## ■ SELF-HELP BOOKS

### Strongly Recommended

★★★★ *The Dialectical Behavior Therapy Skills Workbook for Bipolar Disorder* (2009) by Sheri Van Dijk. Oakland, CA: New Harbinger.

Individuals who either have been diagnosed with BD or think they may have characteristics of BD are the audience for this book. Even if one does not have the diagnosis, the skills taught here will probably prove helpful. Dialectical Behavior Therapy was developed for those with borderline personality disorder, but the life skills are useful to those with BP as well: (1) mindfulness or living in the moment rather than the past, (2) distress tolerance so that instant reaction is not the automatic response, (3) emotional regulation, and (4) interpersonal effectiveness. Individuals are strongly encouraged not to just read the book but also to engage in the written exercises, implement the suggestions, and apply the

## BOX 11.1
## RECOMMENDATION HIGHLIGHTS

**SELF-HELP BOOKS**
- For individual, families, and partners coping with bipolar disorder:
  - ★★★★ *The Dialectical Behavior Therapy Skills Workbook for Bipolar Disorder* by Sheri Van Dijk
  - ★★★ *The Bipolar Disorder Survival Guide* by David J. Miklowitz
  - ★★★ *Loving Someone with Bipolar Disorder* by Julie A. Fast and John D. Preston
- For parents and children:
  - ★★★ *The Bipolar Child* by Demitri F. Papolos and Janice Papolos
  - ★★★ *The Bipolar Teen* by David Miklowitz and Elizabeth L. George

**AUTOBIOGRAPHIES**
- For moving accounts of bipolar disorder:
  - ★★★★★ *An Unquiet Mind* by Kay R. Jamison
  - ★★★★ *A Brilliant Madness* by Patty Duke and Gloria Hochman
  - ★★★ *His Bright Light* by Danielle Steel
- For understanding the treatment of bipolar disorder:
  - ★★★ *Breakdown* by Stuart Sutherland
- For appreciating life with a bipolar parent:
  - ★★★ *Daughter of the Queen of Sheba* by Jacki Lyden

**FILMS**
- For witnessing and understanding bipolar disorder:
  - ★★★ *Blue Sky*
  - ★★★ *Michael Clayton*

**INTERNET RESOURCES**
- For excellent information on bipolar disorder:
  - ★★★★★ *Bipolar Disorder—Psych Central* psychcentral.com/disorders/bipolar
  - ★★★★ *Expert Consensus Guidelines: Treatment of Bipolar Disorder* www.psychguides.com/content/treatment-bipolar-disorder-2004
  - ★★★★★ *Bipolar Disorder* helpguide.org/mental/bipolar_disorder_symptoms_treatment.htm
  - ★★★★ *McMan's Depression and Bipolar Web* www.mcmanweb.com
  - ★★★ *Bipolar Burble* natashatracy.com

principles being taught. Chapters address important challenges for those with BD, such as acting versus reacting, surviving a crisis, soothing anxiety, and developing family skills. A top-rated self-help resource for BD, but the less-frequently-rated Miklowitz book reviewed next actually received the strongest endorsement in our national studies.

**Recommended**

★★★ *The Bipolar Disorder Survival Guide: What You and Your Family Need to Know* (2010, 2nd ed.) by David J. Miklowitz. New York: Guilford.

This self-help book was designed to help readers recognize the early warning signs of mania or depression and to secure the right medication and treatment. The author's research shows that education about BD and its treatment can actually alter the course of the illness, even though it stems from biological causes. Miklowitz offers much wise advice on preventing mood swings from dominating life and on remaining on track at home and at work. The most highly rated book on bipolar disorder in our national studies; it offers the right tools for both patients and families.

★★★ *Loving Someone with Bipolar Disorder* (2004) by Julie A. Fast and John D. Preston. Oakland, CA: New Harbinger.

This book is written for partners of those with bipolar disorder. The partner is encouraged to read and use the suggestions in the book before sharing with the patient, but at a time when the patient is healthy enough to participate. Partners frequently play multiple roles, such as caretaker and crisis manager. This book is not about what is wrong with the relationship but what BD has done to the relationship and how to shift the partner's role and find a balance. The treatment recommendations are holistic and include medication but also emphasize diet, exercise, sleep, lifestyle changes, and thought/behavior modification. Although this book was read by fewer mental health experts than some, the ratings were quite high.

★★★ *The Depression Workbook: A Guide for Living with Depression and Manic Depression* (1996) by Mary Ellen Copeland. Oakland, CA: New Harbinger.

A useful and comprehensive self-help book for unipolar and bipolar depression. Part I provides symptom outlines of depression and mania along with understanding the emotional context of these mood disorders. Part II offers information on how to secure family, professional, and social support systems. In Part III, Copeland reviews lifestyle and counseling techniques to build one's self-esteem. Part IV addresses suicide and prevention strategies. Part V provides a resource list on career planning, psychotherapy, diet, health, medications, sleep, substance abuse, self-esteem, and the like. This book represents a balanced and practical workbook for living with mood disorders.

★★★ *The Bipolar Workbook* (2006) by Monica Ramirez Basco. New York: Guilford.

Adults with BD will benefit from this book, whose purpose is to prevent recurrences of mood swings by learning the early warnings and acting quickly. Many of the recent writings on BD are meant for others than the adult with the condition; by contrast, the information and strategies offered here can be used by patients. The focus of *The Bipolar Workbook* is on charting a personal history of what makes the symptoms worse and what triggers them, identifying early warning cues, reducing symptoms by controlling thoughts and feelings, and reversing the meltdowns. Several false stereotypes of living with BD—such as giving up joy in life or the impossibility of having a desired career—are countered. The material is presented in a pragmatic but interesting and substantive style.

    ★★★   *The Bipolar Child: The Definitive and Reassuring Guide to Childhood's Most Misunderstood Disorder* (1999) by Demitri F. Papolos and Janice Papolos. New York: Broadway.

This book provides a balance of scientific knowledge, clinical experience, and family tales on children with BD. The authors walk the reader through the diagnostic dilemma, helping him or her to select treatments and to monitor the course of the disorder. Also helpfully discussed are the multiple causes of the disorder, the impact on the family, school concerns, dealing with adolescence, the timing of hospitalizations, and the insurance maze. The authors include clearly written and sensitive accounts of families who have lived with a bipolar child. There are few books dedicated to this child/adolescent problem, and *The Bipolar Child* is quite useful for those living with and caring for such children.

    ★★★   *The Bipolar Teen* (2007) by David Miklowitz and Elizabeth L. George. New York: Guilford.

Teens and moods seem to go together, but to extremes when those teens suffer from bipolar disorder. This valuable self-help resource offers management tools developed over years of research by the authors. The tools begin with understanding BD, getting an accurate diagnosis, and learning what the family can expect. Treatment, which includes medications, psychotherapy, and acceptance, is discussed in a clear and understandable way. The importance of keeping teachers, therapists, and professionals involved is discussed. The authors realized when researching adult BD that much less was understood about teens and what families can do; their work turned to developing assistance for the families of teens.

    ★★★   *When Someone You Love is Bipolar* (2009) by Cynthia G. Last. New York: Guilford.

An uncommon perspective is taken here on partnering with the person experiencing bipolar disorder: the author herself has BD and is a clinical psychologist. Last writes from her own experiences and those of her relationship with her husband, and from his perspective as well. As one might expect, this narrative is presented in personal format with case scenarios of other people and actual experiences between the author and her husband. What to expect, the course of the illness, when the partner is in denial, sticking with medications, preventing mood swings, and dealing with ups and downs make up a good part of the book. Specific suggestions provide valuable self-management and treatment recommendations, such as valuing the schedule of sleep enough that the person leaves parties early to stick to the sleep regimen.

**Not Recommended**

    ★★  *Bipolar Disorder: A Guide for Patients and Families* (1999) by Francis M. Mondimore. Baltimore: John Hopkins.
    ★★  *Bipolar Disorder for Dummies* (2005) by Candida Fink and Joe Kraynak. Hoboken, NJ: Wiley.

## ■ AUTOBIOGRAPHIES

**Strongly Recommended**

★★★★★  *An Unquiet Mind* (1997) by Kay R. Jamison. New York: Random House.

A psychologist known for her research on the relationship between bipolar disorder and creativity, Jamison discusses in this frank autobiography her own history of BD. It started in adolescence and is now controlled by lithium. Although the author had studied psychopathology, she did not connect what she learned in the lectures with her own life. Jamison acknowledges the risks of going public with her disorder while still working professionally in a medical school. She presents BD as a mixed blessing—it complicated her life but also contributed to her creativity, productivity, and empathy. A sensitive and compelling autobiography and deservedly rated with 5 stars.

★★★★  *A Brilliant Madness* (1993) by Patty Duke and Gloria Hochman. New York: Bantam.

Co-written by actress Duke and medical writer Hochman, the book details the disastrous effects of untreated BD on the young actress' life and career. Duke suffered through periods of wild euphoria and crippling depression for almost 20 years before being properly diagnosed and treated with lithium, to which she attributes her recovery. Duke's work in the mental health field and collaboration with a respected medical writer increase the book's credibility beyond the usual celebrity story. Hochman describes the different forms of affective disorders, treatments, and support groups available.

**Recommended**

★★★  *Skywriting: A Life Out of the Blue* (2005) by Jane Pauley.

There is far more information in this book about women in TV broadcasting and Jane Pauley's life and career (although not much about her marriage to Gary Trudeau) than about her bipolar episode in 2001, a side effect of steroid treatment for hives. She goes to a private hospital where she receives star treatment, and her bipolar condition is stabilized by lithium and other medications. The celebrity author's willingness to admit to a bipolar episode has helped to destigmatize the condition. Her conversational style makes the book a quick read.

★★★  *Call Me Anna: The Autobiography of Patty Duke* (1988) by Patty Duke with Kenneth Turan. New York: Bantam.

Patty Duke was a successful child actress but at the cost of normal contact with her family and with other children. She became a show-business legend but was an unfulfilled disturbed individual still searching for her lost childhood. She won three Emmy Awards and divorced three husbands and became notorious for tantrums, spending sprees, and promiscuous behavior. When her BD was diagnosed, she began receiving treatment with lithium, and it enabled her to become a successful wife, mother, and political activist. This book serves as a sequel to her *A Brilliant Madness*, reviewed earlier in this chapter, and contains more information on BD and her work in the mental health movement. An inspiring and brutally honest story.

★★★   *Daughter of the Queen of Sheba* (1998) by Jacki Lyden. New York: Viking Penguin.

Foreign correspondent Jacki Lyden describes her childhood in a dysfunctional family with a manic–depressive mother and a controlling stepfather who committed her mother and beat his stepdaughter. As a child, Lyden would find her mother wrapped in bed sheets with hieroglyphics drawn on her arms, convinced that she was the Queen of Sheba. Lyden and her sisters attempted to find treatment for their mother, who now functions on lithium.

★★★   *Breakdown: A Personal Crisis and a Medical Dilemma* (revised ed., 1987) by Stuart Sutherland. New York: Oxford University Press.

In this update of a 1976 account, psychology professor Sutherland describes his bipolar episodes (including a description of hypomania), experiences with psychodynamic and behavioral therapy, drug treatments, yoga, and two hospitalizations. This edition also presents the author's views on the way society treats the mentally ill, including ethical aspects of treatment. Simon Gray's book and play were based on *Breakdown*. A good description of the full range of available treatments. Drawing upon his background as a psychologist, the author discusses the history and rationale of the various treatments.

★★★   *His Bright Light: The Story of Nick Traina* (2000) by Danielle Steel. New York: Dell.

Novelist Steel sensitively depicts her son's brief life, his struggle with BD, and his tragic suicide at age 19. A brilliant and talented child, Nick was a good-looking, charming teenager who played in a rock band and experimented with drugs. His mother made repeated but unsuccessful attempts to find professional help for him. This was a time when it was unusual to diagnose a child with BD, and Steel could not persuade mental health professionals that her son had a serious disorder with a high risk of suicide. Nick's mental anguish is seen in his poems, songs, and diary notes included in the book. While this is a sad account of parental grief at the death of a child, it is also compassionate and respectful of Nick and his roller-coaster ride of a life. (Also cited in Chapter 39 on Suicide.)

★★★   *Pain: The Essence of Mental Illness* (1980) by Anna Eisenhart Anderson. Hicksville, NY: Exposition.

This repetitive, rambling book describes the author's life in and out of mental hospitals with a diagnosis of BD. Anderson describes herself as "a highly cultivated intellectual somewhat frail of body and very frail of mind." A recurring theme is that she viewed the hospital as her refuge and was happiest when she was there; as such, this book might be most useful for people apprehensive about hospitalization. The book is now dated and difficult to locate.

## Not Recommended

★   *The Loony-Bin Trip* (1990) by Kate Millett. New York: Simon & Schuster.

## ■ FILMS

### Recommended

★★★    *Blue Sky* (1994) directed by Tony Richardson. PG-13 rating. 101 minutes.

Hank (Tommy Lee Jones), Carly (Jessica Lange), and their teen children move from Hawaii to a military base in Alabama in the 1950s. Hank is at odds with his superior officers regarding atmospheric testing of nuclear explosives versus underground testing. Carly is volatile and flirtatious and has BD. The children are sad about moving to Alabama. Carly behaves erratically, acts seductively, and begins an affair with the base commander. The film is a superb portrayal of the effect of BD on their lives and on the small military community. Carly's illness was evident to all and, even though her unpredictable and sensational behavior brought him pain, Hank felt only love, compassion, and sadness for his wife and uncertainty about what he could do. Jessica Lange's role as Carly was intense and convincing, so much so that she won the Academy Award for Best Actress. This film offers those who either don't understand BD or perhaps have not known anyone with the disorder a close-up look at the toll taken by the disease and its impact on family members.

★★★    *Michael Clayton* (2001) directed by Tony Gilroy. R rating. 119 minutes.

Michael Clayton (George Clooney) is the closer for his high-powered law firm. He hates his work but is inextricably tied to the firm because he is a compulsive gambler, an alcoholic, and up to his ears in debt. Further, his addicted brother owes money to a dangerous loan shark and Michael is trying to pay that money back. His niche in the company is compromised when his law partner (Eden) leading a billion-dollar lawsuit has a meltdown, strips his clothes off, and says he can't be deceitful anymore by representing clients whose products kill people. Michael is asked to go in and clean up the situation. Michael is the lead figure in the film, but the secondary character Eden portrays a person with BD who has decided to stop taking his medication. Eden's medication had kept him in control of himself yet also numbed him to the complicity of defending the wrong side. His decision not to take his medications results in several scenes in which the viewers see a full manic attack and several phases of the condition across time. The central theme of the movie is the intrigue surrounding George Clooney's character and learning the outcome of the unseemly lawsuit. The side events of the Eden character, however, provide a window into the experience of the manic phase of BD.

★★★    *Garden State* (2004) directed by Zach Braff. R rating. 102 minutes.

Andrew is a TV actor taking lithium and other heavy medications since his mother's accident in which she became paraplegic. There was some question as to whether Andrew accidently pushed her or was in some way partially responsible. His psychiatrist father prescribed his medications and he did not question it. When his father calls to say that Andrew's mother had died, Andrew finds himself on a plane returning to New Jersey (the Garden State) after many years of absence. When he arrives he runs into many high school friends, but also Sam, a woman to whom he is immediately attracted. After the funeral, Andrew seeks out Sam and wants to spend the rest of his time with her. She is nonjudgmental, thoughtful, and interesting. He confides his medication use to her, and she suggests he take a holiday from his meds. For the first time in years, he feels alive and aware of feelings, other people, and experiences. The film's meaning regarding BD is mixed: it seems implied that Andrew was overmedicated for fear that his acting out and behavioral impulsivity were problems. As a result, Andrew was living in a medication stupor. On the other hand, the idea that a person with BD may be advised to shed any medication is misrepresentative and potentially harmful.

★★★   *Limitless* (2011) directed by Neil Burger. PG-13 rating. 105 minutes.

This film contains only a loose association with bipolar disorder in that the lead character, Eddie, comes across an old friend who offers him a drug called NZT, a designer pharmaceutical that enables persons to use 100% of their capacity to think and understand everything around them. Eddie becomes involved in multiple intrigues with other individuals taking the drug and with people pursuing him who want the drug. The effects are immediate but also are immediately gone after 24 hours or so. Eddie is a writer and finds that he can produce prolifically in short periods of time, so his publisher now has high interest in him. His other activities of doing day trading result in huge profits and he becomes known in the financial world and develops financial advising roles with companies. Suddenly the circumstances take a turn for the worse, and the individuals with whom Eddie has dealt regarding the drug are dead. He begins to worry about the long-term effects and what it means to his life. He decides to stop taking the drug altogether and to rely on his own innate abilities.

### Not Recommended

★   *Mr. Jones* (1993) directed by Mike Figgis. R rating. 114 minutes.

## ▓ INTERNET RESOURCES

### General Websites

★★★★★   *Bipolar Disorder* psychcentral.com/disorders/bipolar

A comprehensive condition center from Psych Central, this website offers hundreds of articles dealing with bipolar disorder, blogs, book reviews, bipolar and mood quizzes, daily-updated news and research articles, a peer-reviewed directory to other online bipolar resources, and a thriving set of support groups, along with much more.

★★★   *Internet Mental Health* www.mentalhealth.com/dis/p20-md02.html

Hosted by a Canadian psychiatrist, this site offers a varied but quality collection of linked articles. They are organized under many headings but include medical, legal, children, violence, deinstitutionalization, personal stories, patient education booklets, and so forth. Sadly, it doesn't appear this section has been updated in years.

★★   *BPSO-Bipolar Significant Others* www.bpso.org

The focus of this site is on supporting the "significant others" of those with BD. It offers dozens of reviewed links to other resources online. Sadly, it doesn't appear the site has been updated in years.

**Psychoeducational Materials**

★★★★★ *Bipolar Disorder* helpguide.org/mental/bipolar_disorder_symptoms_treatment. htm

This set of a half-dozen articles from the nonprofit HelpGuide about bipolar disorder covers topics including understanding the disorder, its treatment, helping a loved one with BD, finding support and self-help resources for BD, and a medication guide. Articles often end with a list of links to other resources online, but their lists are often very limited and not very useful.

★★★★ *Expert Consensus Guidelines: Treatment of Bipolar Disorder* www.psychguides. com/content/treatment-bipolar-disorder-2004

Treatment consensus guidelines for professionals from a group of bipolar researchers and experts; also offers a helpful patient and family guide. Although dated, the guidelines are generally still applicable and valid.

★★★★ *McMan's Depression and Bipolar Web* www.mcmanweb.com

John McManamy is a long-time advocate and sufferer of BD. For many years he has been providing a reliable resource about the disorder and to a lesser extent depression. The site features self-written articles, videos, and more. He also hosts a regularly updated blog and is an expert for another health website.

★★★★ *Depression and Bipolar Support Alliance* www.dbsalliance.org

This nonprofit advocacy and support organization offers dozens of articles on depression and BD, as well as information about their extensive community-based support groups and other online resources for emotional support and self-help.

★★★★ *The Balanced Mind Foundation* www.thebalancedmind.org

The nonprofit Child and Adolescent Bipolar Foundation renamed itself to focus on providing family resources for children and teens with all mood disorders. It does this through a library of articles on the topic, a set of forums, and an organization that works to promote education and awareness about childhood BD and depression.

★★★★ *About.com Bipolar Disorder* bipolar.about.com

This About.com website offers a wealth of resources and articles about BD, including a well-written "Get Help to Cope with Bipolar Disorder" guide for newcomers to the disorder. The site also offers resources for friends and family members of those with the disorder. The current editor of the site is a person who has suffered from BD, which makes the content more engaging in most cases.

★★★ *Bipolar World* bipolarworld.net

An older website that hasn't been as well updated as others, especially in recent years, it nonetheless provides some interesting resources, including an advice column and support groups for BD.

★★★   *Bipolar Burble* natashatracy.com

This blog from Natasha Tracy explores her experiences in dealing with her own BD. A nice look into the daily ups and downs of this concern from an excellent writer.

★★★   *Alternative Approaches to the Treatment of Manic-Depression* www.pendulum.org/articles/articles_misc_lisaalt.html

An overview suitable as an introduction to the use of nutrients, vitamins, and minerals in the treatment of BD.

### Other Resources

★★★   *Bipolar Health Information* www.cmellc.com/topics/bipolar.html

A list of articles on BD relevant to both professionals and laypeople published by *Psychiatric Times*.

★★★★   *Mood Charting* www.manicdepressive.org/tools_all.html

Gary Sachs, MD, offers three charting forms on his website: information on progress, symptom data, and mood charting. These could be very useful for assessment and treatment purposes.

★★★★   *The Secret Life of the Manic Depressive* topdocumentaryfilms.com/stephen-fry-the-secret-life-of-the-manic-depressive

This documentary film by comedian and actor Stephen Fry details his journey in documenting his own battle with BD while meeting many others who share their stories as well.

★★★   *Bipolar Beat* blogs.psychcentral.com/bipolar

One of the older and most regularly updated bipolar blogs, *Bipolar Beat* from Dr. Candida Fink and Joe Kraynak offers articles, Q&As, research updates, and more on all things bipolar from both a psychiatrist and a bipolar sufferer.

## ▓ SUPPORT GROUPS

### Child and Adolescent Bipolar Foundation (CABF)

Phone: 847-256-8525
www.bpkids.org

### Depression and Bipolar Support Alliance (DBSA)

Phone: 800-826-3632
www.DBSAlliance.org

### Depression and Related Affective Disorders Association

Phone: 410-955-4647
www.drada.org

### Manic Depressives Anonymous

Phone: 856-869-5508
www.manicdepressivesanon.org

### National Alliance for the Mentally Ill

Phone: 703-524-7600 or 800-950-NAMI (Hotline)
www.nami.org

**See also** Depression (Chapter 20) and Suicide (Chapter 39).

# CHAPTER 12

# BORDERLINE AND NARCISSISTIC PERSONALITY DISORDERS

Personality disorders are recurrent interpersonal patterns that exasperate other people and ultimately harm the afflicted person. It is frequently said that neurotics make themselves miserable, but those with personality disorders make everyone else miserable. Many types of personality disorders are recognized by mental health professionals, but we cover only two in this chapter—borderline personality disorder (BPD) and narcissistic personality disorder (NPD).

Individuals with borderline personality disorder typically exhibit mood swings, inappropriate anger, impulsivity, chronic feelings of emptiness, unstable relationships, identity disturbances, frenzied attempts to avoid abandonment, and risky behaviors (such as promiscuous sex, substance abuse, shoplifting). People with BPD also frequently engage in self-destructive acts, such as suicide attempts and cutting themselves. Borderlines are described as impulsive, unpredictable, and angry; their only stable feature seems to be instability. Approximately 2% of the general population suffers from this disorder. Of those diagnosed with BPD, nearly 75% are women.

The term *narcissistic* is derived from Narcissus, a handsome character in Greek mythology who could love only himself. One day Narcissus bent down to drink from a stream and saw his reflection in the water. He became so captivated with his own beauty that he stared at his reflection until he grew weak and died.

Individuals with narcissistic personality disorder suffer from a grandiose sense of self-importance, an unlimited need for admiration, and a lack of empathy for others. Their entitlement, arrogance, and interpersonal exploitation result in disrupted relationships with friends and family. However, most clinicians believe that narcissists are actually plagued by low and fragile self-esteem; they feel so bad about themselves that they behave in an opposite manner by acting so important. Up to 1% of the population displays NPD; approximately 75% of these individuals are men.

In this chapter, we review self-help books, autobiographies, films, and Internet sites addressing BPD and NPD (Box 12.1). Some of the self-help resources are written for patients and some are written for their families and loved ones.

## BOX 12.1
## RECOMMENDATION HIGHLIGHTS

### SELF-HELP BOOKS

■ For cognitive-behavioral skills training for BPD:

★★★★★ *Skills Training Manual for Treating Borderline Personality Disorder* by Marsha Linehan

■ For adult children of narcissistic or borderline parents:

★★★★★ *The Drama of the Gifted Child* by Alice Miller

★★★ *Surviving a Borderline Parent* by Kimberlee Roth and Freda B. Friedman

♦ *Trapped in the Mirror* by Elan Golomb

■ For understanding and managing relationships with people with BPD or NPD:

★★★ *I Hate You—Don't Leave Me* by Jerold Kreisman

★★★ *Disarming the Narcissist* by Wendy T. Behary

### AUTOBIOGRAPHIES

■ For insider accounts of the experience and treatment of BPD:

★★★★ *Girl, Interrupted* by Susanna Kaysen

★★★ *Welcome to My Country* by Lauren Slater

★★★ *Get Me Out of Here* by Rachel Reiland

★★★ *The Buddha and the Borderline* by Kiera Van Gelder

### FILMS

■ For NPD:

★★★★ *The Great Santini*

★★★★ *Sunset Boulevard*

★★★★ *Like Water for Chocolate*

■ For BPD:

★★★★ *Girl, Interrupted*

★★★ *Fatal Attraction*

★★★ *Margot at the Wedding*

### INTERNET RESOURCES

■ For valuable information on BPD and NPD:

★★★★ *BPD Central* www.BPDCentral.com

★★★★ *Facing the Facts* bpdfamily.com

★★★★ *Narcissistic Personality Disorder* www.narcissistic-abuse.com

★★★★ *Personality Disorders* psychcentral.com/personality

## ▓ SELF-HELP BOOKS

**Strongly Recommended**

★★★★★ *Skills Training Manual for Treating Borderline Personality Disorder* (1993) by Marsha M. Linehan. New York: Guilford.

This skills manual accompanies Linehan's professional text on Dialectical Behavior Therapy (DBT) for BPD. The manual presents lecture notes, discussion questions, exercises, and practical advice. Especially helpful are the reproducible client handouts and homework sheets on many of the skills borderline patients are learning. The manual is a step-by-step guide to teaching clients four broad sets of skills: interpersonal effectiveness, emotion regulation, distress tolerance, and mindfulness. An extremely practical and research-based guide for clinicians implementing skills training and for clients hoping to master these skills. Indeed, this self-help resource was one of the highest rated books in all of our national studies.

★★★★★ *Drama of the Gifted Child: The Search for the True Self* (1994) by Alice Miller. New York: Basic.

Originally published in German as *Prisoners of Childhood,* this book demonstrates how disturbed parent–child relationships negatively affect children's development. Miller tries to get parents to recognize the dangers of misusing their power. The title of the book is somewhat misleading in that *gifted* does not mean talented in ability or intellect; rather, it means sensitive and alert to the needs of others, especially to the feelings and needs of parents. As a result of parents' unintentional or unconscious manipulation of them, gifted children's feelings are stifled. While gifted children become reliable, empathic, and understanding in order to keep their parents happy, they end up never having experienced childhood at all. Miller believes that gifted children's sensitivity, empathy, and unusually powerful emotional antennae predispose them to be used by people with intense narcissistic needs. Miller argues that narcissistic individuals do not experience genuine feelings, and ultimately they destroy the authentic experiencing of genuine feelings in their children. *Drama of the Gifted Child* is beautifully written and can help gifted readers gain insight into their own feelings.

**Recommended**

★★★ *Surviving a Borderline Parent* (2004) by Kimberlee Roth and Freda B. Friedman. Oakland, CA: New Harbinger.

The experiences of adult children of a borderline parent are unique and singular in ways that lead them to feel disconnected, different, and alone. In fact, many can't explain why they feel uncomfortable when treated well. This self-help book is oriented specifically to those raised by a parent with BPD. Readers are offered a view of the present often riddled with guilt, anger, and resentment and then a promising look ahead to trusting oneself, setting boundaries, and breaking old habits. The borderline parent's chronic invalidations are recalled: looking to the child for unconditional love but loving the child only for achievements; abandoning or smothering the child; discounting the feelings of the child; not allowing emotion. The authors helpfully demonstrate how these parental conditions are still hurting the adult children in their contemporary relationships and in their self-view.

The authors take the adult children through steps of applying Dialectical Behavior Therapy principles to their own experiences.

★★★ *Disarming the Narcissist* (2008) by Wendy T. Behary. Oakland, CA: New Harbinger.

This self-help book poignantly describes the psychological damage of being in a relationship with a narcissist. Behary draws on the many narcissistic patients she has seen to explain their core characteristics and how they see the world: devoid of genuine interest in others, demeaning, entitled, self-absorbed, and unempathic. Cognitive therapy and specifically the maladaptive schema are well described as the means by which narcissistic individuals can be treated and healed. The latter part of the book focuses on those in relationships with narcissists and advances methods that have been shown to be effective in such relationships—showing compassion, communicating empathy, and validating the person (but not necessarily their behavior). A useful book for those living with narcissists.

★★★ *The Culture of Narcissism: American Life in an Age of Diminishing Expectations* (1974) by Christopher Lasch. New York: Norton.

Lasch provides a cultural assessment on how the concept of self has invaded contemporary society. A study of narcissism that takes a developmental look from birth to college, mixing sociology and individuality. Now somewhat dated, *The Culture of Narcissism* was a best-seller in the mid-1970s. The book is far more of a cultural critique than a self-help book, but its general point is well taken.

★★★ *I Hate You—Don't Leave Me* (1991) by Jerold Kreisman and Hal Straus. New York: Avon.

Psychiatrist Kreisman and writer Straus offer a diagnostic picture and treatment plan for the patient with BPD. The book title aptly captures the highly charged, hate–love relationship experienced by many of those living with people suffering from BPD. The authors describe how the person with a borderline personality creates chaos or adds to existing chaos within a family unit. The authors address comorbid disorders, seeking psychotherapy, communicating with the patient, and coping with BPD. A helpful resource for families and individuals wishing to better understand and live with BPD.

★★★ *The Borderline Personality Disorder Survival Guide* (2007) by Alexander L. Chapman and Kim L. Gratz. Oakland, CA: New Harbinger.

Those who have BPD or those caring about someone who does will learn what we know about and how to treat BPD by reading this book. The confusion, stigma, and mischaracterizations about BPD are explained in a clear fashion in the first part. Treatment methods are reviewed, with Dialectical Behavioral Therapy and Mentalization Therapy emerging as the primary recommendations. Even while seeking treatment, it is important to begin learning how to apply effective coping strategies. Exercises, techniques, and strategies are identified with which individuals can begin working on their own.

★★★   *Sometimes I Act Crazy: Living with a Borderline Personality Disorder* (2006) by
Jerold J. Kreisman and Hal Straus. Hoboken, NJ: Wiley.

The authors of *I Hate You—Don't Leave Me* (reviewed above) team up years later for
another self-help book on BPD. Anecdotes and narratives lead the reader through the
"symptom" chapters of this book, written for those with BPD and those close to them.
These "symptom" chapters also provide strategies for dealing with the common relationship challenges, such as coping with intense relationships, improving sense of self, managing impulsivity, containing negative thoughts, and coping with rage. Each chapter offers a
glimpse into what if feels like living with BPD. The authors also give guidance on how to
find the right professional help and how to select among the treatment options.

★★★   *Stop Walking on Eggshells: Taking Your Life Back When Someone You Care About
Has Borderline Personality Disorder* (1998) by Paul T. Mason and Randi Kreger.
Oakland, CA: New Harbinger.

This self-help book was explicitly written for family members and individuals in a relationship with someone diagnosed with BPD. *Stop Walking on Eggshells* begins by helping
people understand the character of a person with this diagnosis; feeling out of control is
one of the most common emotions in such a relationship. The book offers advice on how to
make the necessary changes within yourself and within your relationship. Establishing clear
boundaries, developing coping skills, and instituting a safety plan are among the strategies
discussed. The appendices contain reading lists and additional resources. This is a useful,
easy-to-read book on a neglected topic.

### Diamond in the Rough

◆   *Trapped In the Mirror* (1992) by Elan Golomb. New York: William Morrow.

This book is intended to help adult children of narcissists in the struggle for self. As the
author writes in the epilogue, "Because children of narcissists are raised to follow parental
dictates, to believe that what the parent thinks is right and to defer to authority, it is important for these individuals to break the habit of allowing other people to set their path." This
book presents various examples and offers methods to discover and maintain true identity. The author, a clinical psychologist, shares her own childhood development influenced
by narcissism. She knowingly demonstrates how narcissistic parents project onto their
child negative emotions and self-images. A good book for laypersons and therapists alike.
Highly but infrequently rated in one of our studies, meriting the Diamond in the Rough
designation.

## ■ AUTOBIOGRAPHIES

### Strongly Recommended

★★★★   *Girl, Interrupted* (1993) by Susanna Kaysen. New York: Random House.

Written 25 years after her hospitalization with probable diagnoses of BPD and depression, the author describes her self-mutilation and suicide attempts, problems with school

and work, where she was chronically afflicted with boredom and ennui, and her 18-month hospital stay. A perennial favorite of our college students, this popular book became a film showing how a rebellious and self-destructive teenager can end up in a psychiatric hospital. Trenchant observations of ward life. A great read but probably less valuable as a self-help resource.

## Recommended

★★★  *Get Me Out of Here: My Recovery from Borderline Personality Disorder* (2004) by Rachel Reiland. Center City, MN: Hazelden Publishing.

An inside view of what BPD is like, the chaos, seething anger, impulsiveness, outbursts, and continuing resentment, and the author's difficult struggle to overcome their negative effects. At one time suicidal, and later admitted to a psychiatric hospital for hitting her son, Reiland credits years of psychotherapy for getting her past traumatic childhood experiences and the effects of BPD on her life. Her psychotherapist is not spared her anger or abuse, yet persists in maintaining a caring and professional relationship. When she lashed out at the people around her, she found that, like her therapist, they did not reject her or confirm her intense feelings of abandonment. This hopeful book presents clinical information regarding symptoms and treatments for a condition once considered largely untreatable.

★★★  *The Buddha and the Borderline: My Recovery from Borderline Personality Disorder through Dialectical Behavior Therapy, Buddhism, and Online Dating* (2010) by Kiera Van Gelder. Oakland, CA: New Harbinger.

Clearly acknowledging how BPD negatively affects her life, Van Gelder describes her persistent search for a helpful form of psychotherapy. In understandable, honest, and sometimes humorous terms, she outlines the chaotic world of the borderline personality, the mercurial emotional shifts without reason, the negativity and anger, risky behaviors, and difficulty in maintaining relationships. She mentions the likelihood that the condition will be misdiagnosed and treatments misdirected. After much trial and error, she settles upon and is helped by Dialectical Behavioral Therapy, which uses the Buddhist principle of mindfulness. She joins a meditation group, which had a calming influence on her life. The book gives a hopeful outlook for BPD with this type of treatment. Van Gelder currently lectures about the utility of meditation and mindfulness in anger management and stress reduction.

★★★  *Welcome to My Country* (1997) by Lauren Slater. New York: Anchor Books/ Doubleday.

An unusual book: a combination of case studies, memoir, and literature bordering on poetry. Psychotherapist and former client Lauren Slater has experienced life on both sides of the desk. Now a psychologist, she spent much of her adolescence and young adulthood in a psychiatric hospital diagnosed with BPD. Sessions with her clients awaken memories of her own time in treatment. Like the work of Oliver Sacks, the book can be read as literature and will be most useful to individuals already in a helping profession or clients who want to understand the complexity, subjectivity, and uncertainties of treatment for serious mental disorder.

## ■ FILMS

### Strongly Recommended

★★★★ *The Great Santini* (1979) directed by Lewis Carlino. PG rating. 115 minutes.

A Marine pilot, the self-described "great Santini," is devoted to his family and troops but is an unpredictable and alcoholic narcissist. He must be in charge and victorious at home as well as at work. He subjects his codependent wife and resentful kids to white-glove inspections, verbal rants, and violent retributions in order to bolster his own self-esteem. He will not tolerate soft feelings or failures. One of his sons eventually takes a courageous stand and assertively defies his father's direct orders. *The Great Santini* is, at once, a harrowing film and an inspiring film. It is harrowing in its realistically dark portrayal of abuse and narcissism. Viewers will learn how families survive a domineering narcissist, perennially walking on eggshells and maneuvering around his abuse. However, the film is also inspiring in demonstrating the resilience of children and the possibility of escape. In both cases, it is a deeply emotional experience.

★★★★ *Sunset Boulevard* (1950) directed by Billy Wilder. Not rated. 110 minutes.

An aging star of silent movies, Norma Desmond (Gloria Swanson) harbors the narcissistic delusion that millions of fans still adore her and plans a comeback playing the lead in her own screenplay. William Holden plays a young screenwriter who exchanges admiration and sexual favors for the security she affords. In the end, though, the silent screen star's pathological possessiveness, jealousy, and entitlement get the best of both of them. A sad but accurate film about elderly narcissists, left only with their grandiosity.

★★★★ *Girl, Interrupted* (1999) directed by James Mangold. R rating. 127 minutes.

Based on Susanna Kaysen's memoir of the same title (reviewed above), the film traces her 18-month stay at a mental hospital in the 1960s. Susanna (Winona Ryder) is admitted following a probable suicide attempt, feeling depressed, directionless, and interpersonally alienated. She befriends the band of troubled women in her ward, addresses her borderline personality features in psychotherapy and in her relationships, and gradually pulls herself together. The ensemble cast is marvelous, especially Angelina Jolie as the resident antisocial. As a self-help resource, the film explores the hazy line between Susanna as a confused adolescent and as suffering from BPD. It is a film (and autobiography) especially popular among young women.

★★★★ *Like Water for Chocolate* (1993) directed by Alfonso Arau. R rating.
123 minutes. In Spanish with English subtitles

Family tradition dictates that Tita, the youngest daughter, remain unmarried and take care of her aging, self-absorbed Mama. But Tita falls in love with Pedro, who, bowing to the Mexican culture and Mama's wishes, marries Tita's older sister. Living in the same house, their love changes everything. Tita ultimately confronts the spirit of her narcissistic Mama and gains her autonomy despite the oppressive tradition. *Like Water for Chocolate* is a love story overflowing with romantic grandeur, but for self-help purposes it also realistically portrays the suffering of children of narcissist or tyrannical parents. The film vividly, if symbolically, displays Tita's liberation in wrenching free from her mother's oppression.

**Recommended**

★★★  *Notes on a Scandal* (2006) directed by Richard Eyre. R rating. 92 minutes.

A veteran teacher (played by Judi Dench) discovers that a younger teacher (Cate Blanchett) is carrying on an affair with a 15-year-old student. The veteran teacher manifests all of the cardinal features of BPD: seeking an intense friendship and nurturance with the younger teacher but also manipulating and betraying her. Dench's journaling and the narration brilliantly portray the internal experience of BPD, such as distorting the reality of relationships, obsessing about friendships, and fearing abandonment (even by her cat). At the conclusion of the film, we witness the repetitive interpersonal drama of the disorder as the veteran teacher grooms her next victim.

★★★  *Margot at the Wedding* (2007) directed by Noah Baumbach. R rating. 93 minutes.

Nicole Kidman plays the title character, who has separated from her husband and is spending time at her sister's home for a wedding. A cruel slice of family life ensues, with Margot demonstrating many features of BPD: labile mood, impulsive behavior, loose boundaries, chronic anger, and abandonment fears. Viewers are likely to be shocked when Margot laughs hilariously when describing a rape and chats nonchalantly about her history of abuse in front of children. Not much redeeming here, but an accurate portrayal of BPD and invalidating families of origin.

★★★  *Misery* (1990) directed by Rob Reiner. R rating. 107 minutes.

A horror and thriller flick based on a Stephen King novel. Kathy Bates stars as an obsessed and delusional fan who imprisons her favorite novelist and forces him to rewrite his latest novel to suit her tastes. He is bound, crippled, and drugged at her mercy. Bates displays classic borderline behaviors and deservedly won an Oscar for her role alternating between the extremes of a sweet nurse and a wicked torturer.

★★★  *Fatal Attraction* (1987) directed by Adrian Lyne. R rating. 119 minutes.

In probably the most eerily accurate portrayal of BPD in cinematic history, Glenn Close plays Alex, who has an affair with her married colleague and who will not let go of him. She engages in impulsive sex, intense anger, suicidal gestures, and disturbed interpersonal relationships alternating between idealization and devaluation. Her classic examples of borderline rage include throwing acid on her ex-lover's car, stalking his family, and cutting herself, all of it ending with violence. If you can ignore the contrived ending, the film brilliantly captures the psychological manifestations of borderline pathology (even though it never explains or treats it).

★★★  *Prozac Nation* (2001) directed by Erik Skjoldbj ærg. R rating. 95 minutes.

Lizzie (Christina Ricci) is a gifted Harvard student slowly descending into depression, abetted by drug abuse and a tumultuous sexual relationship. The latter behaviors suggest a concurrent borderline disorder, and the back story confirms the suspicion: emotional lability, attention seeking, abandonment fears, interpersonal manipulation, self-injurious behavior, and underlying self-loathing. A convincing depiction of comorbid depression and BPD and a positive message of recovery with extensive psychotherapy and medication. (Also reviewed in Chapter 20 on Depression.)

★★★ *White Oleander* (2002) directed by Peter Kosminsky. PG-13 rating. 109 minutes.

A narcissistic mother in a narcissistic rage kills her boyfriend with the deadly poison of her favorite flower (the white oleander) and winds up in prison for life. She systematically ignores her daughter's emotional needs and in fact sabotages the daughter's relationship with foster parents. Only in the end is the mother able to let her daughter move toward freedom and independence. Beautifully demonstrates a child's enduring love for a narcissistic parent even when the child realizes the parent is tragically flawed. A film likely to prove useful for children of aging narcissists.

★★★ *Vicky Cristina Barcelona* (2008) directed by Woody Allen. PG-13 rating. 96 minutes.

Penelope Cruz took home the Oscar for her performance as Maria Elena, a borderline personality in a story of two wealthy American women summering in Barcelona. Cruz's Spanish character is initially portrayed as a free-spirited, fun-loving, and adventure-seeking artist, but gradually the full symptom profile emerges: she is impulsive, labile, depressed, intermittently suicidal, and briefly dissociative. Although not central to the storyline of the two Americans and their love triangles, Cruz demonstrates the danger of crossing the line between passion and violence, between healthy spontaneity and unhealthy volatility. A disturbing portrait of a talented woman afflicted with BPD and the man who loves her.

★★★ *Roger Dodger* (2002) directed by Dylan Kidd. R rating. 106 minutes.

Living in Manhattan and working as an advertising writer, Roger Swanson is the archetype of a womanizer and a narcissistic personality. He lacks empathy, manipulates women, lies to clients, and lives only to satisfy his selfish whims. When his 16-year-old nephew visits from Ohio, Roger teaches him how to hunt and seduce women. Eventually, Roger learns from his nephew what relationships should entail. Despite the unrealistic ending, the film does convey the grandiosity, entitlement, and exploitation characteristic of those with NPD and the underlying narcissistic wound of Roger being rejected.

**Diamond in the Rough**

◆ *Unraveled* (2012) directed by Marc H. Simon. Not rated. 85 minutes

A powerful documentary that traces the house arrest and legal sentencing of Marc Dreier, the Manhattan lawyer who serially embezzled $450 million from hedge funds and clients. The film does not lecture or scold, but Dreier's own words satisfy virtually every diagnostic criteria of NPD. He admits to a "compulsion" to be recognized for his extraordinary accomplishments, to receive admiration, to feel special. His actions manifest his interpersonal exploitation and obvious paucity of empathy. The *New York Times* (April 12, 2012) enthused that *Unraveled* "is a mesmerizing one-man dive into narcissism, entitlement, and greed." Like all those suffering from personality disorders, Dreier is unable to concretely articulate the reasons for his self-destructive behavior or to recognize that he (not the system) is to blame. Designated as a Diamond in the Rough because it was released just as this book was going to press.

### Not Recommended

★★ *Black Snake Moan* (2006) directed by Craig Brewer. R rating. 116 minutes.
★★ *In the Company of Men* (1997) directed by Neil Labute. R rating. 97 minutes.
★ *Groundhog Day* (1993) directed by Harold Ramis. PG rating. 101 minutes.
★ *Phone Booth* (2003) directed by Joel Schumacher. R rating. 81 minutes.
★ *After Hours* (1985) directed by Martin Scorsese. R rating. 96 minutes.

### Strongly Not Recommended

† *Murder by Numbers* (2002) directed by Barbet Schroeder. R rating. 120 minutes.

## ■ INTERNET RESOURCES

### General Websites

★★★★ *BPD Central* www.BPDCentral.com

Lots of information, support, and stories for those who care about someone with BPD. The Basics of BPD (on the left) is about 10 pages of well-balanced information—an excellent starting place. Additional articles of helpful information are listed under topics in "Resources." However, often the site appears to be geared toward promoting its owner's books.

★★★★ *Facing the Facts* bpdfamily.com

This site is run by people who live with people who have BPD and offers not only helpful articles on the topic but also a select list of book reviews, links to additional online resources, and an active, thriving message board for support.

★★★★ *National Education Alliance Borderline Personality Disorder* www.borderlinepersonalitydisorder.com

This national advocacy group offers good information on its well-designed website for both sufferers and family members alike. In addition to a family-specific section, the organization has lists of books they recommend, as well as links to articles from around the web on BPD.

★★★★ *Narcissistic Personality Disorder* www.halcyon.com/jmashmun/npd/index.html

Joanna M. Ashmun's dozen or so essays here can extend readers' understanding enormously. In the first, she translates the DSM-IV into the familiar language of living with a narcissist. The second and third essays discuss how to recognize a narcissist by the traits displayed and excellent discussions of the traits. All presentations are well written, thoughtful, and sensitive.

**★★★★** *How to Spot a Narcissist* psychcentral.com/blog/archives/2008/08/04/how-to-spot-a-narcissist

An insightful article from Samuel Lopez deVictoria, PhD, filled with over 500 comments from readers who relate their own experiences with narcissism in their lives. Includes links to the symptoms of narcissism as well as a narcissistic personality quiz.

**★★★★** *Narcissistic Personality Disorder* www.narcissistic-abuse.com

Sam Vaknin is a narcissist who has written dozens of short essays that could be useful for getting a person with NPD to recognize and better understand his or her narcissism. Vaknin explores multiple aspects of society, history, and psychology through the lens of narcissism.

**★★★★** *Personality Disorders* psychcentral.com/personality

This section of Psych Central offers a rich library of informational articles on all personality disorders—including BPD and NPD—and provides an overview of normal and disordered personality. The site also features interactive quizzes on personality to help readers better understand their own personality traits.

**Psychoeducational Materials**

**★★★★** *Self-injury: You Are Not the Only One* users.palace.net/~llama/selfinjury

By the author of a book with the same name, the site offers support and links and much practical and helpful information on dozens of pages. Excellent for self-harmers who need to know they are not alone as well as those who need guidance and help more immediately. Sadly, the site hasn't been updated in many years.

**★★★★** *Borderline Personality Disorder* www.nimh.nih.gov/health/topics/borderline-personality-disorder/index.shtml

This resource from the National Institute of Mental Health provides a good overview from the government about the symptoms, causes, treatments, statistics, and research on BPD. The "science news" section links only to government-funded research in the news.

**★★★★** *Borderline Personality Disorder Demystified* www.bpddemystified.com

Offering a nice set of in-depth articles and information, this website from Robert O. Friedel, MD, covers topics including the history of the disorder, symptoms, and other disorders that may be co-occurring. The site's treatment section is a solid review of what to expect in treatment and is a must-read for the newly diagnosed.

**★★★★** *An Overview of Dialectical Behavior Therapy* psychcentral.com/lib/2007/an-overview-of-dialectical-behavior-therapy/all/1

Dialectical Behavior Therapy (DBT) is explained in a series of educational articles on this website. It also offers two blogs on the topic, "DBT Understood" and "The Emotionally Sensitive Person."

★★★★ *Kathi's Mental Health: Toddler Time* www.toddlertime.com/dx/borderline

There are dozens of articles (about half by Ms. Stringer) for clients, relatives, and professionals on this page. Every client will find much hope on this site.

★★★ *A Primer on Narcissism* www.mentalhelp.net/poc/view_doc.php/type/doc/id/419

A nice article covering definitions, dynamics, the major theorists' views, history of the disorder, family dysfunction, and traumas.

★★★★ *Voicelessness: Narcissism* voicelessness.com/narcissism.html

"Many people spend a lifetime aggressively trying to protect an injured or vulnerable self. Traditionally, psychologists have termed such people 'narcissists,' but this is a misnomer. To the outside world it appears that these people love themselves. Yet, at their core they don't love themselves—in fact, their self barely exists, and what part does exist is deemed worthless." So begins the webpage of Richard Grossman, PhD, who explores NPD and who offers several essays, moderated forums, and a reading list on NPD.

★★★ *You Owe Me! Children of Entitlement* by Lynne Namka, EdD www.angriesout.com/teach9.htm

About 10 pages on understanding children's selfish (narcissistic) behavior—its causes, dynamics, and management. It may be helpful to parents in understanding normal and abnormal behaviors or to adults in recalling their pasts.

★★★ *Self-confident Personality Type* ptypes.com/self-confident.html

After giving a list of nine characteristics of this type, there is much material on noteworthy people who had this type of personality. Useful to help distinguish high self-confidence from narcissism for family and friends.

★★★ *So, You're in Love With a Narcissist* by Alexandra Nouri alexandranouri.wordpress.com/2011/01/30/so-youre-in-love-with-a-narcissist-part-1

In 11 short essays, the author presents the pleasures, benefits, and the problems of living with a person with NPD in clear and ordinary terms. Rather bitter, but probably useful for partners who do not understand what is wrong with their relationship.

## ■ SUPPORT GROUPS

### BPD Central

Phone: 888-357-4355 or 800-431-1579
www.bpdcentral.com
Provides links to online groups for persons dealing with a loved one with BPD.

## BPDWORLD (Borderline Personality Disorder)

www.bpdworld.org
Mutual support for individuals with BPD provided through message boards.

## National Association for Personality Disorders

Phone: 888-482-7227 or 212-966-6514
www.tara4bpd.org

■ CHAPTER 13

# BULLYING

Bullying is a pattern of aggressive behavior encompassing verbal harassment, physical assault, social exclusion, and related threats. Unlike playground bullying, cyber bullying can occur 24/7, reaching from schools into homes. About one-third of all children bully and one in three children are bullied (CDC, 2011; DeVoe & Kaffenberger, 2005). As a result of bullying, many childhood victims suffer from psychological effects, such as anxiety, avoidance, helplessness, depression, poor self-esteem, and lower grades. As the headlines frequently report, bullying can even lead to tragic violence and suicide.

Far from an expected rite of passage, bullying is now properly recognized as a growing and prevalent problem. According to the World Health Organization, bullying is a public health crisis that requires the concerted efforts of families, educators, mental health professionals, and policymakers. In fact, bullying probably constitutes the number-one daily mental health concern of children and adolescents.

In this chapter, we critically review self-help books, autobiographies, films, online self-help, and Internet resources on bullying (Box 13.1). Our focus is primarily on bullying of children and adolescents, not on work or relational aggression among adults. We present self-help resources for all three roles related to bullying—bully, victim, and passive bystander—as well as their families.

## ■ SELF-HELP BOOKS

**Recommended**

★★★  *Bullies to Buddies* (2005) by Izzy Kalman. Staten Island, NY: Wisdom Pages.

Teachers, counselors, and parents as well as middle school children can all glean a different perspective on countering bullying through the approach recommended in this self-help book. In essence, the "victim" of bullying is armed with tools to empower himself or herself and to convert a bully into a buddy. Quizzes, drawings, multiple-choice tests, and activities reinforce the important principles. Kalman's view is that "When victims stop being victims, bullies stop being bullies." He advocates living by the Golden Rule and teaches students to turn anger into humor, fear into courage, and enemies into friends through verbal exchanges and body language. Internet bullying, sibling, and out-of-school bullying are all covered. The author suggests that defending against bullies rarely succeeds; instead, his proactive and strength-based methods reframe the bullying situations and enable the victim to end bullying. The best of the bullying self-help books according to our national studies,

## BOX 13.1
## RECOMMENDATION HIGHLIGHTS

### SELF-HELP BOOKS

▓ For bullied children and their parents:

    ★★★ *Bullies to Buddies* by Izzy Kalman

      ◆ *Bullies and Victims* by Suellen Fried and Paula Fried

▓ For children who are bullied:

      ◆ *Don't Pick on Me* by Susan Eikov Green

### AUTOBIOGRAPHIES

▓ On the pain of, and eventual triumph over, bullying:

      ◆ *Please Stop Laughing at Me* by Jodee Blanco

### FILMS

▓ On overcoming bullying through assertion and relationships:

    ★★★★ *My Bodyguard*

    ★★★★ *Karate Kid*

▓ On the brutal reality of bullying:

      ◆ *Bully* (2012)

### ONLINE SELF-HELP

▓ On helping bullied children respond by following the Golden Rule:

    ★★★ *Bullying: The Golden Rule Solution* protectingallgodschildren.com

### INTERNET RESOURCES

▓ For valuable information on bullying:

    ★★★★★ *Stop Bullying* www.stopbullying.gov

    ★★★★ *Dealing with Bullying—KidsHealth*

        kidshealth.org/teen/your_mind/problems/bullies.html#cat20128

but an approach that will surely not fit extreme and violent circumstances, as the author acknowledges.

### Diamonds in the Rough

    ◆ *Bullies and Victims: Helping Your Child Survive the Schoolyard Battlefield* (1998) by Suellen Fried and Paula Fried. New York: M. Evans.

    The authors survived peer abuse themselves and provide suggestions for parental intervention and constructive reactions. This book defines different forms of bullying and different levels of response to the bullying. Punctuated by short case studies, *Bullies and Victims* presents individual, family, school, and societal methods to reduce bullying. The book is characterized as a Diamond in the Rough because it was positively but infrequently evaluated in our national studies.

♦  *Don't Pick on Me: Help for Kids to Stand Up and to Deal with Bullies* (2010) by
Susan Eikov Green. Oakland, CA: Instant Help Books.

This child's book is chockfull of activities, games, and puzzles that promote learning
how to escape bullying. An early exercise, for example, explores what a bully is. Several
exercises provide the child with questions regarding how to recognize bullying (e.g.,
teasing, embarrassing, playing tricks, taking property, ganging up). The scenarios for
likely bullying are identified so that the child can walk through the possible bullying
experience, but this time with tools to combat it. Additional chapter themes include
don't put up with putdowns, being left out, don't bully back, cyber bullying, name calling, the silent treatment, and gossip. The author suggests practicing positive, 10-min-
ute exercises and role plays between parent and child. This self-help book receives a
Diamond in the Rough designation because it was well regarded but not well known
among psychologists.

♦  *Bullyproof Your Child for Life* (2007) by Joel Haber and Jenna Glatzer. New York:
Perigee.

One of this book's authors was bullied as a child and describes how conflicted he was
because his father insisted that fighting the bully was the sole solution. He recounts that
the tension, between the bullying and between himself and his father, was a most significant experience in his life. The co-author went on to specialize in bullying. Unlike homespun remedies of fighting back or coping in silence, the model advocated and taught
here involves parents and the child working together. Building resilience and confidence
through healthy interactions with parents is emphasized. The topics are quite varied
and include the bullyproofing prescription; how parents can break the cycle; school,
sport, camp, cyber, and special needs bullying. Bullying is often a family and systemic
problem; thus parents, children, and school personnel can work together to solve the
problem.

## ■ AUTOBIOGRAPHIES

### Diamond in the Rough

♦  *Please Stop Laughing at Me* (2010) by Jodee Blanco. Avon, MA: Adams
Media.

Heart-wrenching story of a young girl with strong needs for attention and belonging
who was constantly rejected by her school classmates. Transferring to a different school
did not help her, as her problems with peers followed her. Today, Blanco is an author
and an inspirational speaker who tours high schools speaking about bullying and runs
a successful PR firm with celebrity clients. She believes she would not be so successful
today if she had not been bullied in high school. While some readers were put off by the
author's self-righteousness and seeming narcissism, the book can show teachers what
students go through when they are taunted and rejected by peers, and victims of high
school bullying can learn that they are not alone and that success in life is possible after
graduation.

## ■ FILMS

### Strongly Recommended

★★★★  *My Bodyguard* (1980) directed by Tony Bill. PG rating. 96 minutes.

This inventive and believable film follows Clifford, a young teenage boy who has just moved to Chicago with his family. Everything with his family is smooth and comical, but it is a second storyline to the troubles Cliff faces at school. There he is extorted by a bully demanding protection money in order to keep the infamous and deadly Linderman away. Instead, Clifford cleverly pays Linderman to be his bodyguard. Soon the two become friends and Clifford learns about the horrors in Linderman's past that motivated him to become a bully. The film reveals the pain that often drives someone to act out as a bully and explores the possibility of friendship between bully and bullied.

★★★★  *Karate Kid* (1984) directed by John G. Avildsen. PG rating. 136 minutes.

This classic film is an ode to the underdog. After moving to a new home and school, Daniel runs into conflict with the local bullies and members of a rival dojo. His neighbor, Mr. Miyagi, takes a personal interest in him and begins to teach him karate. His unorthodox methods prove to be effective when Daniel faces his bully in the championship karate tournament. Remade in 2010 starring Jackie Chan as Mr. Miyagi, but we prefer the original movie for its messages of inner strength and discipline.

### Recommended

★★★  *Odd Girl Out* (2005) directed by Tom McLoughlin. PG-13 rating. 120 minutes.

Vanessa is a popular girl turned outsider after she is tricked into pursuing her friend's boy crush. She then becomes the victim of relentless verbal bullying and cyber bullying. Vanessa is tormented by her former friends until she suffers from severe stress and skips school to avoid their bullying. Her mother finally gets involved and takes the matter to the principal, but nothing can be done for nonphysical bullying. Their bullying drives Vanessa to attempt suicide; she survives but the girls do not relent. The situation continues until graduation, where the girls have planned their final humiliation. However, Vanessa stands up for herself in front of the entire class and their parents. The film ends as the crowd applauds Vanessa and the girls are left powerless. An accurate depiction of cyber and verbal bullying as well as the difficulty in remedying the situation. In the end, a classic example of the intimidation of words and relationships in schools and an rousing call to stand up for oneself.

★★★  *Knockout* (2011) directed by Anne Wheeler. PG rating. 95 minutes.

Dan Barnes, a retired pro boxer, works as a school janitor trying to escape his violent past. It is there that Dan meets Matthew Miller, a new student and the target of the bullies. Dan tries to help Matthew by teaching him how to box and stand up for himself. And in the process of teaching Matthew, Dan finds solace from his past in his new role as a teacher. Barely makes our recommendation list.

**Not Recommended**

> ★ *Revenge of the Nerds* (1984) directed by Jeff Kanew. R rating. 90 minutes.

**Diamond in the Rough**

> ♦ *Bully* (2012) directed by Lee Hirsch. R rating. 94 minutes.

Director Hirsch breathes life into the statistics by following the true stories of five victims of bullying. The documentary shows the violence these children endured and the indifferent reactions of teachers and administrators to the extraordinary acts of violence, including cursing, threats, and physical attacks. Two of the children were driven to suicide by their tormentors, and the film follows the victims' families struggle to cope. A Diamond in the Rough solely due to the film's release a few months after our last national study was completed. However, the film has already generated a lot of interest and received positive reviews from the critics. Not for the faint-hearted, as the brutal reality of bullying is on full display.

## ■ ONLINE SELF-HELP

> ★★★ *Bullying: The Golden Rule Solution* protectingallgodschildren.com

This online program is designed to help children respond when confronted by a bully. It is presented from a spiritual perspective and based on the Golden Rule of doing to others what you would have done to you. Children are encouraged to befriend the bullying child. The cost of the program is $10 for 60 days.

## ■ INTERNET RESOURCES

**General Websites**

★★★★★ *Stop Bullying* www.stopbullying.gov

You can't go wrong by checking out the U.S. government website that was developed by the Department of Health and Human Services to help clamp down on the increasing bullying problem among children and teens. It offers sections devoted to kids, teens, young adults, parents, and educators.

> ★★★★ *Dealing with Bullying—KidsHealth* kidshealth.org/teen/your_mind/problems/ bullies.html#cat20128

KidsHealth, funded by the Nemours Foundation, offers a comprehensive section specifically targeted toward teenagers. Well written for a teen audience, it offers a wealth of information and advice, including the topic of cyber bullying.

> ★★★★ *Bullies—PBS Kids* pbskids.org/itsmylife/friends/bullies

This web resource from the Public Broadcasting System is directed toward younger children but is well written and covers all the topics that a child will want to know about, including identifying a bully, how to handle it, and online bullying.

**★★★★**    *Bullying Stories* bullyinglte.wordpress.com

*Bullying Stories* is a blog that is about, well, bullying stories. People write about their personal experiences with bullying in heart-wrenching detail, putting very real faces onto this epidemic. The stories will break your heart and in the process help you better understand that you are not alone.

**★★★★**    *Workplace Bullying Institute* www.workplacebullying.org

Bullying isn't just a problem for teens and kids—it happens to adults as well. This resource from the Workplace Bullying Institute focuses on the topic of workplace bullying. It offers a number of helpful articles on the topic, as well as a regularly updated blog.

**★★★★**    *Bullying: Information for Parents and Teachers* www.lfcc.on.ca/bully.htm

This single, lengthy article is a comprehensive and intelligent perspective on bullying.

**★★★**    *Dealing with Bullying & Cyber-bullying* helpguide.org/mental/bullying.htm

This single-page article from the nonprofit HelpGuide is a good introduction to the topic, discussing why kids are generally bullied in the first place, as well as some simple tips for dealing with bullying (both for kids and their parents).

**★★★**    *The Nine Most Common Myths about Bullying* www.thedailybeast.com/news-
week/2010/10/14/the-nine-most-common-myths-about-bullying.html

An article from *Newsweek* discussing a set of common myths about bullying, such as bullying is easy to spot and all bullies have low self-esteem.

**★★★**    *Teens Against Bullying* www.pacerteensagainstbullying.org

This well-intentioned resource is designed in a hip manner to appeal to teens, yet it suffers from significant usability flaws that make some of its information and resources difficult to access because they're obstructed on the screen by website features. Otherwise, a very creative effort to help educate teens about the effects of bullying and providing response strategies.

**★★★**    *Steps to Respect: A Bullying Prevention Program* www.cfchildren.org/programs/
str/overview

This program is designed to reduce bullying and improve school climate.

# CHAPTER 14

# CAREER DEVELOPMENT

Too often we perceive developing a career plan as a one-time event, in which one makes a single major commitment. But each of us probably experiences life changes that require modifications in employment, adjustments in career goals, and sometimes a change of careers. In fact, the average worker now makes five or six job transitions in a lifetime.

Careers occupy a crucial role in our life satisfaction and our family relationships. Cost reductions and downsizing by businesses have translated into displacement and job loss. The workforce is rapidly becoming diverse, international, and service-oriented. Many jobs are more complex and technically demanding. Dual-career couples predominate. And now, more than ever, people are concerned about the role of work in their lives, wanting to strike the best balance between work and other life tasks.

Self-help resources on career development cover a number of topics, including career choice, job hunting, interviewing, career changes, dual-career families, and effective communication in the workplace. A large number of self-help books on specific components of work have been written—how to become a better salesperson, how to be an effective manager, how to improve the corporate workplace—but such books are not included here.

What follows are national ratings and evaluative descriptions of self-help books and Internet resources devoted to career development (Box 14.1).

## SELF-HELP BOOKS

### Strongly Recommended

★★★★★ *What Color Is Your Parachute?* (2010 edition) by Richard Bolles. Berkeley, CA: Ten Speed.

This extremely popular book about job hunting was first published in 1970. Since 1975, an updated edition has appeared annually. This is an enormously successful self-help book that has become the career seeker's bible. Bolles tries to answer concerns about the job-hunting process and gives many sources that can provide further information. Unlike many books on job hunting, *What Color Is Your Parachute?* does not assume that readers are recent college graduates seeking their first jobs; he spends considerable time discussing job hunting for people seeking to change careers. Bolles describes a number of myths about job hunting and debunks them. He also provides invaluable advice about where jobs are, what to do to get hired, and how to cut through the red tape and confusing hierarchies of the business world to meet the key people who make hiring decisions. The book has

## BOX 14.1
## RECOMMENDATION HIGHLIGHTS

**SELF-HELP BOOKS**

■ On career choice, job hunting, and interviewing:

★★★★★ *What Color Is Your Parachute?* by Richard Bolles

★★★ *Knock `Em Dead* by Martin Yate

♦ *Go Put Your Strengths to Work* by Marcus Buckingham

■ On turning conflict into career and interpersonal advancement:

★★★★ *Win–Win Negotiating* by Fred Jandt

■ On the meaning of work:

★★★ *Let Your Life Speak* by Parker J. Palmer

♦ *Lives without Balance* by Steven Carter and Julia Sokol

**INTERNET RESOURCES**

■ On everything you want to know about college and graduate school:

★★★★★ *Peterson's* www.petersons.com

★★★★★ *The Princeton Review* www.princetonreview.com

■ On finding your next career or expanding your existing one:

★★★★★ *Monster.com* www.monster.com

remained appreciably the same over the years, with updates as appropriate. Recent editions have added material on job hunting for those with physical disabilities, on the effective use of career counselors, and on finding a mission in life. This 5-star book was one of the most frequently rated books in our national studies—more than 300 mental health professionals evaluated it. It is indeed an excellent self-help book about job hunting and career change. Bolles writes in a warm, engaging, personal tone. His chatty comments are often witty and entertaining, and the book is attractively packaged with cartoons, drawings, and many self-administered exercises.

★★★★ *Staying the Course: The Emotional and Social Lives of Men Who Do Well at Work* (1990) by Robert Weiss. New York: Free Press.

This book is based on Weiss's interviews with 80 men, aged 35 to 55, in upper-middle-class occupations. Weiss explores the nature of the men's work and nonwork lives—their activities, relationships, goals, and stresses. He also delves into their psychological lives to discover what has motivated them to meet their obligations year after year after year. Weiss found that men who stayed the course had established social status and self-worth at work, had experienced emotional and social support from their marriages and families, and had benefited from loyal friendships. Weiss says that all too often in our society, successful men are portrayed as exploiters. He found this not to be the case. Successful men had made compromises with their youthful dreams and had developed respectful and caring relationships both in and out of the workplace. Their lives revolved around steady career advancement instead of ruthless ambition, and they cared more about family stability than sexual conquest. *Staying the Course* contains high-quality research, careful interpretation, and useful insights. However, there is something of a 1950s cast to Weiss's men and his interpretation of their lives. Many contemporary women and men will not accept some of the conclusions that can be drawn from Weiss's work, such as: If wives work, their jobs are secondary in terms of economics and status.

★★★★ *Win–Win Negotiating: Turning Conflict into Agreement* (1987) by Fred Jandt. New York: Wiley.

The main themes of this book are that conflict is inevitable but is not always bad and that, if everyone involved makes an honest effort, the conflict can be resolved. In the first four chapters, Jandt describes the basic nature of conflict and includes a self-assessment so that readers can determine how they deal with conflict and identify sources of conflict. He shows readers how to keep minor disagreements from turning into major battles. Jandt makes the important point that when one party is the "winner" in a conflict, in the long run both parties often lose when the losing party avoids future contact or tries to get even. Ultimately, the relationship dies. Thus, the goal is to develop a solution that will satisfy both parties and let the relationship continue in much the same way as in the past. *Win–Win Negotiating* is a good introduction to learning how opponents or adversaries think and how they negotiate their positions. Anyone who wants to learn about negotiating techniques and resolving conflict in the workplace can benefit from reading it.

**Recommended**

★★★ *Let Your Life Speak: Listening for the Voice of Vocation* (1999) by Parker J. Palmer. San Francisco, CA: Jossey-Bass

This half self-help book and half memoir focuses on the author's journey into self-understanding and search for purpose that served as the foundation for his pursuit of vocation. Palmer's message is found in the book's title "let one's life speak," a time-honored Quaker admonition to let your highest needs and goals drive your vocational choice. His journey to find his meaning was entangled in depression for some time, and this experience is woven here into his view of life's meaning. This book is not a practical guide to a career—in fact, anything but. However, this highly rated resource offers an inspiring and spiritual way to think about how one moves through life and how career choices are made.

★★★ *Shifting Gears* (1990) by Carole Hyatt. New York: Simon & Schuster.

Hyatt calls attention to research that indicates that most people go through several career changes. She uses the results of interviews with 300 individuals who succeeded in career transitions to develop a framework for self-guidance in making career transitions. She advises how to (1) adapt to today's marketplace, (2) determine your work style, (3) identify trigger points that require change, (4) explore and overcome the psychological barriers to change, and (5) learn strategies to define a career path and repackage yourself. This addition to the self-help literature was not well known among the mental health professionals—only 20 rated it—but they accorded it moderately positive value.

★★★ *Knock 'Em Dead* (2012) by Martin Yate. Holbrook, MA: Bob Adams.

This regularly updated guide to career development is subtitled *The Ultimate Job Search Guide* and is a perennial bestseller, with over 5 million copies sold. Earlier editions concentrated on the employment interview, but more recent editions have blossomed into coverage of the entire job search. Yate gives the best answers to a number of key questions likely to be asked in a job interview, such as: Why do you want to work here? How much money do you want? What can you do that someone else can't? What decisions are the most difficult for you? What is your greatest weakness? Why were you fired (if you lost your last job)? According to Yate, the best jobs go to the best-prepared rather than to the best-qualified candidates. Yate prepares the potential interviewee with the inside scoop on stress interviews, salary negotiations, executive search firms, and drug testing. He also provides advice about how to respond to illegal questions and other hardball tactics. In the more recent editions, Yate has added sections on "killer" résumés, networking, interview attire, and body language. This 3-star book has become more widely known since it was rated in one of our early studies, and it provides expert advice for job interviewing, especially on handling tough interviews.

★★★ *Do What You Love, the Money Will Follow* (1987) by Marsha Sinetar. New York: Dell.

This book is subtitled *Discovering Your Right Livelihood*, and that is what Sinetar tries to encourage readers to do. Sinetar strongly believes that people should try to find jobs that fulfill their needs, talents, and passions. She provides a step-by-step guide to doing so and includes dozens of real-life examples of how people have overcome their fears and found work that allows them to grow. Readers learn how to get in touch with their inner selves and true talents, evaluate and build their self-esteem, get rid of their "shoulds," overcome resistance, and get out of unfulfilling jobs and into fulfilling ones. *Do What You Love, the Money Will Follow* barely received a 3-star rating; that is, it was given mixed reviews. Some of the mental health professionals felt that Sinetar does a good job of helping people stuck in jobs they don't like to break free and find jobs they truly enjoy doing. Others said that Sinetar's approach borders on naïveté and might encourage people to leave jobs they probably shouldn't in search of the ultimate, perfect job.

### Diamonds in the Rough

♦ *Go Put Your Strengths to Work: Six Powerful Steps to Achieve Outstanding Performance* (2010) by Marcus Buckingham. New York: Free Press.

A simple concept but not one often practiced: play to your strengths and spend time building them, not remediating weaknesses. The six-step program offered by Buckingham is easy to follow and is intended to redirect energies to maximize success. The author suggests how to discover your true strengths, apply those strengths, volunteer on projects that emphasize your strengths, and capitalize whenever possible. The author contends that trying to improve weakness redirects your energy and time, when excelling in a special interest constitutes the key to business success. Many interesting exercises and activities make the pathway through this book interesting and applicable.

♦ *Lives without Balance* (1992) by Steven Carter and Julia Sokol. New York: Villard.

The authors describe the problem of unbalanced living because of outdated values and false premises. Among the destructive myths highlighted are the limitless credit card; you are the master of your own fate; think and grow rich; you can have it all; and you can do it all. Using catchy phrases, the authors evaluate four types of unbalanced lives: the downward slide, the never-ending treadmill, the uncontrollable escalator, and the roller coaster. Carter and Sokol also analyze image fixes, power fixes, glamour fixes, buying and selling fixes, job perks fixes, and status fixes—along with the problems entangled in the fixes. *Lives without Balance* was published between our national studies and, unfortunately, we neglected to secure experts' ratings on it. However, the book raises important issues and stimulates thought about the dimensions of work, careers, and meaning in life.

♦ *Career Mastery* (1992) by Harry Levinson. San Francisco: Berrett-Koehler.

This introspective exploration of career choices is not a how-to book, nor does it give advice on a job search. Rather, it is a psychological self-assessment and a values clarification that enables readers to decide how to direct themselves through a lifetime of careers. Topics involve the larger context of decision making, not a specific job but the direction the individual wants to go in shaping a professional future. These topics include how to cope with change in an organization, how to avoid self-blame, how to make sense of a failure, how to cultivate good work relationships, and how to relate to a good and to a problem boss. This book falls into the Diamonds in the Rough category because it received positive but infrequent ratings and because it reflects on the psychological aspects of work.

### Not Recommended

★★ *The Portable MBA* (1990) by Eliza Collins and Mary Devanna. New York: Wiley.
★★ *The Best Advice I Ever Got* (2011) by Katie Couric. New York: Random House.
★★ *The 100 Best Companies to Work for in America* (1994 revised ed.) by Robert Levering and Milton Moskowitz. New York: Signet.

## ■ INTERNET RESOURCES

There are numerous sites to post résumés, search for openings, locate recruiters, and apply for specialized jobs. None of these have been included here because they are not direct self-help resources and because they do not assist in psychotherapy; however, many of them have career-development sections that you should check out.

### General Websites

★★★★ *Peterson's* www.petersons.com

Peterson's is a good resource if you are considering college or graduate school, as it offers a wealth of information, resources, and articles to help you select your new school, how to finance it and make it affordable, admission tests, adult education, and more.

★★★★ *Career Interests Game* career.missouri.edu/students/majors-careers/skills-interests/career-interest-game

Using Holland's six types of personality, this site will suggest careers.

★★★★★ *Monster.com* www.monster.com

If you're looking for a job on the Internet, the venerable Monster.com remains one of the largest and most popular job and career development sites online. The site contains an extensive library of career articles and career tools, including guides to getting started with your first job.

★★★★ *Mind Tools* www.mindtools.com

This website was designed to enhance your workplace skills and help you understand how to advance in your career. Topics include learning leadership skills, time management, project management, organizational skills, stress management, and career building, among many others.

★★★★★ *The Princeton Review* www.princetonreview.com

Their specialty is coaching for the standardized admission tests to college and graduate schools, and the site offers a great deal of support, direction, and information on these. They also offer lots of good introductory advice on choosing a college or graduate program., as well as law, medical, and business schools.

★★★★ *MSN Careers* msn.careerbuilder.com/msn

This website from MSN and CareerBuilder offers resources for résumé writing, salaries, and finding the right career for your skillset and education.

★★★★ *Job Searching* jobsearch.about.com

This website from About.com guide Alison Doyle talks about all the basics a person needs to know about finding a job, composing good résumés and cover letters, as well as interviews and landing employment. A rich guide full of practical advice.

★★★ *Career Hub Blog* www.careerhubblog.com

This blog from a number of career experts provides a source of constantly updated entries about a wide range of career topics, including résumé writing, career change, interviewing, searching for a job, and more.

★★★★ *Career Shifters* www.careershifters.org

Many useful articles on improving and changing jobs in the "Expert Advice" section.

★★★ *Jobs and Career Development* managementhelp.org/careers

Hundreds of articles here about career development, interviewing, and everything you need to know about getting a job.

★★★ *Career Development Center* www.wpi.edu/Admin/CDC

Although this career development center is focused on college students (since it's published by the Worcester Polytechnic Institute), it nonetheless offers some career tools, articles, and advice that can be helpful to anyone. Click on "Students" to get started. (Every college and university has such a career resource, so if you're in school or graduating soon, check out your own school's local center for more personalized information.)

★★★   *The Riley Guide: Research for Career and Work Options* www.rileyguide.com

This site is eight links to the very best sites for job and career research. If you need the facts, here is how to find them on employers, education, salary, the future of different careers, career counselors, and so on.

# CHAPTER 15

# CHILD DEVELOPMENT AND PARENTING

Playwright George Bernard Shaw once commented that although parenting is an indispensible and crucial occupation, no test of fitness for it is ever imposed. If a test were imposed, some parents would turn out to be more fit than others. Most parents hope that their children will grow into socially mature individuals, but they often are not sure how to help their children reach this goal.

Child development and parenting are probably the largest categories of self-help resources. If parents are not confused about what to do before they visit a bookstore or surf the Internet to obtain information on parenting, they may well become confused when they see the bewildering array of advice. The ratings of the mental health experts in our national studies provide valuable advice about how to navigate the maze of parenting self-help books (Box 15.1).

In this chapter we evaluate self-help resources focusing on parenting children. Other chapters consider closely related topics, notably infants (Chapter 26), pregnancy (Chapter 32), families and stepfamilies (Chapter 23), and teenagers (Chapter 40). Entire chapters are also devoted to attention-deficit/hyperactivity disorder (Chapter 9) and violent youth (Chapter 41).

Because there are so many self-help resources on this topic, we had to make some decisions about which to include and exclude. We primarily included resources that deal with parenting in general rather than parenting strategies for specific problems. For example, we evaluate parenting books on discipline, but for the most part we do not rate books that exclusively cover such topics as learning or developmental disabilities. Of course, some parenting books include the specific topics in their overview of parenting and child development. We also were determined to highlight popular child-rearing resources that address fathers, as relatively few of them have historically done so (Fleming & Tobin, 2005). Even with these exclusions, be forewarned: this is one of the lengthiest chapters in the book. It is also, rewardingly, the chapter with the largest number of strongly recommended self-help resources.

## ■ SELF-HELP BOOKS

### Strongly Recommended

★★★★★ *Your Defiant Child: Eight Steps to Better Behavior* (1998) by Russell Barkley and Christine Benton. New York: Guilford.

This excellent self-help book, one of the most highly rated in all of our studies, is written for parents who have a child who is unyielding or combative. The book examines what

## BOX 15.1
## RECOMMENDATION HIGHLIGHTS

**SELF-HELP BOOKS**
- On the normal course of child development and coping with problems:
  ***** *To Listen to a Child* by T. Berry Brazelton
  ***** *Your Baby and Child* by Penelope Leach
  **** *A Mind at a Time* by Mel Levine
  *** *The Blessing of a Skinned Knee* by Wendy Mogel
- On parenting toddlers:
  ***** *Toddlers and Parents* by T. Berry Brazelton
- On parenting 3 to 6-year-olds:
  *** *Touchpoints* by T. Berry Brazelton and Joshua Sparrow
- On general parenting and communication skills:
  ***** *Between Parent and Child* by Haim Ginott
  ***** *How to Talk So Kids Will Listen and How to Listen So Kids Will Talk* by Adele Faber and Elaine Mazlish
  **** *Parent Effectiveness Training* by Thomas Gordon
  *** *Raising Resilient Children* by Robert Brooks and Sam Goldstein
- On effective discipline for children:
  ***** *Children: The Challenge* by Rudolph Dreikurs
  ***** *1–2-3 Magic* by Thomas W. Phelan
  *** *Living with Children* by Gerald Patterson
- On parenting defiant and difficult children:
  ***** *Your Defiant Child* by Russell Barkley and Christine Benton
  **** *Parenting the Strong-Willed Child* by Rex Forehand and Nicholas Long
  **** *The Difficult Child* by Stanley Turecki
- On the problem of children growing up too soon:
  **** *The Hurried Child* by David Elkind
- On parenting African-American children:
  ♦ *Raising Black Children* by James P. Comer and Alvin E. Poussaint

**FILMS**
- On pushing children and on children pleasing their parents:
  **** *Searching for Bobby Fischer*
- On discovering what is in a child's best interest:
  **** *Little Man Tate*
  **** *I am Sam*

**ONLINE SELF-HELP**
- On research-supported training to treat childhood encopresis:

**** *UCANPOOPTOO* www.healthsystem.virginia.edu/bmc/ucp2/flash/login.
  html
■ On evaluating a child's emotional response to injury and responding accordingly:
  *** *After the Injury* aftertheinjury.org

**INTERNET RESOURCES**
  ■ On parenting information in general:
  ***** *KidsHealth* www.kidshealth.org
  ***** *Parenthood.com* www.parenthood.com
  ***** *Facts for Families* www.aacap.org/cs/root/facts_for_families/facts_for_
  families

causes children to become defiant, when the defiance reaches problem proportions, and how to deal with the defiance. The authors' eight-step program emphasizes consistency and cooperation, as well as instituting changes through a system of praise, reward, and mild punishment. Parents learn how to establish effective discipline, communicate with children at a level they can understand, and reduce family stress. An exceptional resource. (Also reviewed in Chapter 41 on violent youth.)

***** *To Listen to a Child* (1984) by T. Berry Brazelton. Reading, MA: Addison-Wesley.

Brazelton's focus here is primarily on problematic events that arise in the lives of children. Fears, feeding difficulties, sleep problems, stomachaches, and asthma are among the problems that Brazelton evaluates. He assures parents that it is only when they let their own anxieties interfere that problems such as bedwetting become chronic and guilt-laden. Each chapter closes with practical guidelines for parents. This 5-star book is easy to read, includes well-chosen and clearly explained examples, and is warm and entertaining. The book's descriptions are not as detailed as those in some other books that focus on specific periods of development—for example, Brazelton's own *Toddlers and Parents*—but it is a very good resource for parents to refer to throughout the childhood years when normal problems emerge.

***** *Toddlers and Parents* (2nd ed., 1989) by T. Berry Brazelton. New York: Delacorte.

This Brazelton contribution traces normal child development and advises parents on how to handle typical problems and issues that arise during the toddler years. Each of the 11 chapters interweaves the narrative of an individual child's experiences (e.g., the birth of a sibling or a typical day at a day-care center) with Brazelton's moment-by-moment descriptions of what the child may be feeling, explanations of the child's behavior, and supportive suggestions for parents that help them cope with their own feelings as well as their child's behavior. Among the topics addressed by Brazelton:

  ■ The toddler's declaration of independence at about 1 year of age, a time when the toddler becomes alternately demanding and dismissing

- ◼ The nature of working parents' family life and their toddler's development at 18 and 30 months
- ◼ Life with a toddler of different ages in nontraditional families (divorced, stepfamily)
- ◼ Special considerations for withdrawn, demanding, and unusually active toddlers
- ◼ Coping with the 18-month-old's frequent "no's"
- ◼ The 30-month-old's developing self-control and self-awareness

All told, this is an excellent self-help book for the parents of toddlers. The writing is clear, and his tone is warm and personal. Brazelton not only provides parents with a guide to survival but helps them develop a sense of delight in the struggles and triumphs of their toddlers.

★★★★★ *Between Parent and Child* (1965) by Haim Ginott. New York: Avon.

This aging classic provides parents with a guide to improving communication with their children and understanding their children's feelings. Ginott's aim is to help parents understand the importance of listening to the feelings behind their child's communication. Ginott says that children who feel understood by their parents do not feel lonely and develop a deep love for their parents. Toward this end, he describes a communication technique he calls "childrenese," which is based on parents' respect for the child and statements of understanding preceding statements of advice or instruction. Since its publication in 1965, millions of copies of the book have been sold. *Between Parent and Child* has been praised for being simple and clear. Although four decades old, it continues to be one of the books that many mental health professionals recommend for parents. The book was updated in 2003 by Alice Ginott (Haim's widow and a psychologist herself) and H. Wallace Goddard, but the revision has never taken off as did the original.

★★★★★ *Children: The Challenge* (1964, reissued 1991) by Rudolph Dreikurs. New York: Hawthorn.

This aging classic is centrally concerned with effective and loving discipline. Dreikurs believes that parents have to learn how to become a match for their children by becoming wise to their children's ways and capable of guiding them without letting them run wild or stifling them. Unfortunately, says Dreikurs, most parents don't know what to do with their children. Dreikurs teaches parents how to understand their children and meet their needs. He stresses that the main reason for children's misbehavior is discouragement. Discouraged children often demand undue attention. Parents usually respond to this negative attention-getting behavior by trying to impose their will on the children, who in turn keep misbehaving. Dreikurs says that parents who get caught up in this cycle are actually rewarding their children's misbehavior. He tells parents to instead remain calm and pleasant when disciplining the child. Each of the 39 brief chapters involves a different type of discipline problem in which children misbehave and parents respond inappropriately. Dreikurs clearly spells out effective ways to handle each of these situations. He also recommends a "family council" for solving family problems. This book remains an excellent guide for parents to use in learning how to discipline their children more effectively. It is easy to read; the examples are clear and plentiful; the strategies for discipline are good ones. Although written five decades ago, *Children: The Challenge* is a golden oldie and a widely recommended book on parental discipline.

★★★★★ *How to Talk So Kids Will Listen and Listen So Kids Will Talk* (20th ed., 1999) by Adele Faber and Elaine Mazlish. New York: Avon.

This is a frequently revised, how-to book written to teach methods that affirm the dignity and humanity of parents and children. After years of conducting workshops on communication skills for parents, the authors assembled the many ideas, activities, and lessons learned into this book. Each chapter presents ways to put the principles into action and addresses topics such as dealing with children's feelings, cooperation, alternatives to punishment, autonomy and praise, and putting it all together. In their regularly revised editions, Faber and Mazlish include open-ended answers for reader response, cartoons that teach key principles, feeling and context exercises, parent–child role plays, and questions and answers. This is a good book for parent–child interaction that is both understandable and practical.

★★★★★ *1-2-3 Magic: Effective Discipline for Children 2–12* (2010) by Thomas W. Phelan.

This humorous book takes the reader through the 1-2-3 disciplinary approach with colorful and applicable illustrations. How to successfully start behaviors (e.g., cleaning room) and stop them (e.g., tantrums) are clearly described. The false assumption that the child is a little adult and the big mistakes parents make of showing too much emotion and explaining too much are played out in lighthearted but all-too-familiar scenarios. Phelan demonstrates established behavioral and Adlerian principles in novel ways. Updated every few years, this book has obtained deserved commercial success and impressive sales of more than a million copies. The book is written to instruct parents in accomplishing the program, but also to demonstrate empathic support of the challenges confronted by contemporary families.

★★★★ *Parenting the Strong-Willed Child* (1996) by Rex Forehand and Nicholas Long. Chicago, IL: Contemporary.

Parents of strong-willed children will learn a system of techniques and interactive skills that have been shown by research to be effective in improving child behavior. Well-accepted behavioral techniques are taught in clear and understandable terms. A 5-week program is outlined with step-by-step instructions that teach attending to the child, rewards, when to ignore the behavior, how to give directions, and how to implement an effective time-out. The program is then integrated with a focus on improved relationship, communication, and dealing with specific problem behaviors (e.g., tantrums, aggression, lying). This book will capture the interest of frustrated parents and will effectively lead parents through steps to improve their children's behavior.

★★★★ *The Difficult Child* (2nd revised ed., 2000) by Stanley Turecki. New York: Bantam.

This book tells parents how to more effectively deal with a child who has a difficult temperament. Turecki's book is based on his experience with thousands of families in the Difficult Children Program he created at Beth Israel Medical Center in New York City. He guides parents in identifying whether they have a difficult child, managing conflicts with their child, disciplining more effectively, obtaining support from schools, doctors, professionals, and support groups, and ensuring that they acknowledge and reward the difficult child's strengths. The revised second edition also addresses ADHD.

★★★★  *The Hurried Child: Growing Up Too Fast Too Soon* (2001, 3rd ed.) by David
       Elkind. Reading, MA: Addison-Wesley.

This book describes a pervasive and harmful condition that many children experience—
growing up too fast and too soon. Psychologist Elkind believes that many parents place
excessive pressure on children to grow up quickly. He says that parents too often push children to be "superkids," competent to deal with all of life's ups and downs. He believes that
parents have invented the superkid to alleviate their own anxiety and guilt. But he doesn't
just blame parents; he also faults schools and the media. Elkind argues that many parents
expect their children to excel intellectually and demand achievement early in their lives.
Excessive expectations are both academic and athletic: parental pressures let children know
that to be fully loved they have to win. In response, Elkin recommends respecting children's
own developmental timetables, encouraging children to play and fantasize, making sure
that expectations and support are in reasonable balance, and being polite. This 4-star book
highlights an important theme and provides insightful analysis: parents want children to be
stars but don't give them the necessary time and support.

★★★★  *Parent Effectiveness Training: The Proven Program for Raising Responsible Children*
       (2000) by Thomas Gordon. New York: Three Rivers Press.

First published in 1970, this book has been revised on multiple occasions, most recently
in 2000 on the 30th anniversary of its initial appearance. It is designed to educate parents
about the nature of children's development and to help them communicate more effectively
with them. The book opens with a discussion of how parents are blamed but not trained
(which underscores the rationale for Gordon's Parent Effectiveness Training [PET]).
Gordon advocates an authoritative parenting strategy that involves being neither permissive nor punitive but rather being nurturing and setting clear limitations. Gordon provides
especially good advice about how to communicate more effectively with children. Included
in his recommendations are how to engage in active listening, how to make frank statements of feeling without placing blame, and how to deal with children's problems. Gordon's
approach enables parents to show children how to solve their own problems rather than
inappropriately accusing or blaming children. The widespread popularity of this 4-star book
was reflected in the large number of respondents who rated the book—more than 250. The
book and the PET course, taught through numerous parenting groups and classes across
the country, have helped millions of parents gain a better understanding of their children
and learn to communicate more effectively with them. Despite its age, it remains one of the
best books available for improving parent–child communication. The 4 million copies in
circulation attest to both its popularity and its effectiveness.

★★★★  *Dr. Spock on Parenting* (1988) by Benjamin Spock. New York: Simon &
       Schuster.

This book is primarily a collection of articles that Dr. Spock wrote for *Redbook* magazine
in the 1970s and 1980s. Topics include anxieties in our lives, being a father today, divorce
and its consequences, the new baby, sleep problems, discipline, stages of childhood, difficult relationships, behavior problems, influencing personality and attitudes, and health and
nutrition. In a chapter on discipline, Spock rebuts the criticism leveled at *Dr. Spock's Baby
and Child Care* that he encourages parents to be too permissive. Spock says that he never
promulgated such a philosophy and believes that parents should deal with their children in

firm, clear ways. This 4-star book is easy to read and generally dispenses sound parenting advice. The consensus of our experts in the national studies, however, was that several of the preceding books would be better choices on general approaches to parenting.

★★★★   *A Mind at a Time* (2003) by Mel Levine. New York: Simon & Schuster.

The subject of this self-help book, neurodevelopmental system, may not immediately elicit familiarity and interest from parents and teachers, but reading even one segment draws the reader into a caring, warmhearted, and positive way of thinking about children's learning and about problems with learning. For example, Levine comments that many educators and researchers declare that learning is practically over at the age of 6, or at least remediation of problems must occur early. Sound and convincing examples of adolescents and young adults triumphing over learning problems are cited from the author's clientele. Important aspects of learning such as memory, language, problem solving, critical thinking, social thinking, memory, and attention each are thoroughly discussed with case examples and practical tips for parents. This is a very "can do" presentation of learning and learning problems that will be a helpful guide to parents and middle-school age to older children.

**Recommended**

★★★   *Living with Children* (3rd ed., 1987) by Gerald Patterson. Champaign, IL: Research.

This behavior modification approach to disciplining children has an unusual style for a self-help book. It is written in a programmed instruction format that makes the material easy to learn, according to Patterson. Main ideas are broken down into small units or items. Parents are asked to respond to the items actively rather than just read them. Four sections tell parents how learning takes place, how to change undesirable behavior, how normal children have normal problems, and what the problems of more seriously disturbed children are like. Patterson explains how reinforcement works and the importance of rewarding children immediately. Parents learn to develop a plan for changing their child's undesirable behavior. They begin by observing and recording the child's behaviors; detecting what led up to the behaviors and what followed them; and noting how the parents responded when the child behaved in undesirable ways. Parents then learn to respond to the child's behaviors differently than they have in the past. Time-out from positive reinforcement figures prominently in replacing the child's negative behaviors with positive ones. This simple but powerful book helps parents replace a child's undesirable behaviors with desirable ones by rearranging the way they respond to the child. Its 3-star rating is somewhat misleading: the book secured very positive ratings but was not rated frequently enough to reach the 4-star or 5-star categories.

★★★   *The Blessing of a Skinned Knee* (2008) by Wendy Mogel. New York: Penguin Books.

This delightful and heartwarming story about child rearing, parenting, and priorities mixes stories from the author/psychologist's psychotherapy practice, her self-reflections as a mother, and the teachings of Judaism. It all converges into a humorous and moving self-help message about what the true blessings are. In her practice, Mogel began to notice over time that parents were more expectant, driven, and achievement-focused for their children than seemed healthy. Mothers were disappointed when their children did not have a diagnosable problem that could be fixed and instead just had a natural limitation that suggested the child was not perfect. The blessings, which are the focus of each chapter, represent the healthy growth of our children—for example, (1) the blessing of acceptance: getting to know your unique and ordinary child; (2) the blessing of a skinned knee: God doesn't want us to overprotect our children; and (3) the blessing of longing: teaching your child to have an attitude of gratitude. There are nine blessings, all of which are presented through wonderful stories and end in a valued moral.

★★★  *Touchpoints: Three to Six* (2001) by T. Berry Brazelton and Joshua Sparrow. Cambridge, MA: Perseus.

This book describes effective parenting techniques for children age 3 to 6 years. Teaming with child psychiatrist Joshua Sparrow, leading pediatrician T. Berry Brazelton addresses key issues in this developmental time frame, such as sibling rivalry, bedwetting, tantrums, and lying. Especially helpful are strategies for staying emotionally calm when children engage in these behaviors. The second half of the book provides approximately 200 pages of advice for parents on topics like ADHD, divorce, computers, bad habits, and sadness. Brazelton's other self-help books are rated as 4-star and 5-star books, and this recent book would have also reached 5-star status if it had been known by more psychologists.

★★★  *Raising Resilient Children* (2001) by Robert Brooks and Sam Goldstein. New York: Contemporary.

This book seeks to help parents focus on their children's strengths rather than ruminating about their children's weaknesses. The authors argue that children's resilience has its most important roots in the home, nurtured by parents who provide their children with healthy doses of empathy, optimism, respect, unconditional love, listening skills, and patience. Detailed steps are given for rewriting negative parenting scripts, teaching and modeling empathy, and creating opportunities for children to behave in responsible ways. This excellent self-help book likely would have been designated a 4-star or 5-star resource had been it more frequently rated in our national studies.

★★★  *The Mother Dance: How Your Children Change Your Life* (1999) by Harriet Lerner. New York: Harper Perennial.

Psychologist Lerner writes about the experience of being a mother and all of the changes that it entails, beginning with pregnancy and continuing through birth, power struggles, guilt, anxiety, relationship challenges, and other aspects of motherhood. The book is especially helpful for mothers-to-be as a guide for what they are likely to experience in the future. Also, women who already are mothers can gain a better understanding of their experiences as mothers by reflecting on the experiences that Lerner frames.

★★★  *Positive Discipline A–Z* (1993) by Jane Nelsen, Lynn Lott, and H. Stephen Glenn. Rocklin, CA: Prima.

This book addresses 1,001 solutions to everyday parenting problems. The text covers parenting children of any age but focuses on children younger than teenagers. Part I consists of helpful parenting tools that set the stage for use of the positive discipline solutions to daily concerns in Part II. The tools are well explained and include how to direct your child's behavior using natural consequences, honesty, saying no, and a sense of humor. The book also covers beliefs behind behavior. The text is guided by Adlerian principles and implements the approach successfully.

★★★ *Supernanny: How to Get the Best from Your Children* (2005) by Jo Frost. New York: Hyperion.

This humorous book turns out to be a no-nonsense, logical, and effective model for facing the common obstacles in child rearing. The author, Frost, also has a TV show and other books, and so many people are familiar with her style. Ten rules rule the roost in regard to boundaries, meals, toilet training, going to bed, and other daily activities that can do a parent in if not armed with tools on how not to let a 5-year-old "get the best of you." The take-home messages entail no heat-of-the-moment behaviors, use of positive encouragement, and one-on-one time every day with the child. Troubleshooting methods and how to apply them are offered.

★★★ *How to Discipline Your Six- to Twelve-Year-Old without Losing Your Mind* (1991) by Jerry Wyckoff and Barbara Unell. New York: Doubleday.

As its title suggests, this book falls into the category of parenting discipline. The authors define discipline as a teaching system that leads to orderliness and control. Chapters focus on such topics as social problems, school problems, noise, children wanting their own way, irresponsibility and disorganization, sleeping and eating, hygiene problems, self-image problems, and activities. Each chapter begins with the statement of a problem followed by a brief description of how the problem can be prevented. Then the authors tell parents how to solve the problem. A "what not to do" section is also included. Although the book's title indicates that it is about discipline, in reality the book is a general parenting guide that provides suggestions for preventing and solving typical childhood problems. The experts' 3-star ratings convey the impression that the book does a good job of providing parents with concrete advice in an easy-to-read format.

### Diamonds in the Rough

♦ *Common Sense Parenting* (1996) by Ray Burke and Ron Herron. Boys Town, NB: Boys Town.

Many parents doubt their effectiveness as parents. This book is written for those parents who desire to improve their parenting skills with what the authors call a blueprint for parenting: practical, down-to-earth teaching and unconditional love coupled with spending time together. The skills material is systematically presented in an understandable manner using the following format: presentation of skill, examples of how to use it, how not to, and a variety of typical situations. The book is applicable to children of any age and includes skill development topics such as positive and negative consequences, praise, clear expectations, making decisions, and teaching self-control. This book is included as a Diamond in the Rough because it received very high ratings albeit from a small number of psychologists.

♦ *Raising Black Children* (1992) by James P. Comer and Alvin E. Poussaint. New York: Plume.

Written by a pair of highly respected experts on Black children, this book argues that African-American parents face additional difficulties in raising emotionally healthy children because of problems related to minority status and income. Comer and Poussaint's guide contains almost 1,000 child-rearing questions they have repeatedly heard from Black parents across the income spectrum. Among the topics on which they offer advice are how to improve the child's self-esteem and identity; how to confront racism; how to teach children to handle anger, conflict, and frustration; and how to deal with the mainstream culture and still retain a Black identity. This is an excellent self-help book that presents pertinent suggestions not found in most child-rearing books. Virtually all other child-rearing books are written for White, middle-class parents and do not deal with many of the problems faced by Black parents, especially those from low-income backgrounds.

- ♦ *Parenting Young Children: Systematic Training for Effective Parenting (STEP) of Children under Six* (1997) by Don C. Dinkmeyer and Gary D. McKay. Circle Pines, MN: American Guidance Service.

This is the accompanying text for the STEP (Systematic Training for Effective Parenting) program that has trained tens of thousands of parents across the country to communicate more effectively with their children. Dinkmeyer and McKay believe that democratic child rearing is the best strategy for parents. In democratic child rearing, both parent and child are socially equal in the family and mutually respect each other. The authors explain why children misbehave (to get attention, achieve power, mete out revenge, or display inadequacy). They suggest family activities and encourage parents to develop parenting goals. Parents are told how to get in touch with their own emotions and understand their children better. Encouragement, communication skills, and discipline methods that develop responsibility are advocated. This book received a very high positive rating but was evaluated by only eight respondents. It is brief (less than 100 pages) and somewhat sketchy without the accompanying parenting course that it is designed to supplement. Several mental health professionals mentioned that its exercises and goal-setting strategies are especially effective, but that the depth of coverage and extensive examples in other books make them more attractive on their own. The best use of this book is in conjunction with the parent training workshops developed by the authors.

- ♦ *Perfect Madness: Motherhood in the Age of Anxiety* (2006) by Judith Warner. New York: Penguin Books.

Many mothers—full-time mothers, part-time working mothers, double-duty mothers and professionals—were interviewed by the author about being a mother today. Warner describes a feeling of almost all of the interviewees as a "choking cocktail of anxiety and guilt" zapping their energy and leaving them at the end of the day feeling wrong or substandard. "The feeling has many faces but no name; it's not depression or oppression, it's just a mess." This sentence expresses the message of this book, which is built around the interviews conducted by the author. Stay-at-home mothers felt as though they were not being successful moms; working mothers felt the same. The commonality across all was quite stark. This is not a book of tips on being a better parent or pulling double duty, but rather about the lives of mothers, expectations of themselves and by other, and existential angst.

### Not Recommended

- ★★ *Parent Power! A Common Sense Approach to Parenting in the 90's and Beyond* (1990) by John K. Rosemond. Kansas City, MO: Andrews and McMeel.

**Strongly Not Recommended**

† *Battle Hymn of the Tiger Mother* (2011) by Amy Chua. New York: Penguin Books.
† *In Praise of Stay at Home Moms* (2009) by Laura Schlessinger. New York: HarperCollins.

## ■ FILMS

**Strongly Recommended**

★★★★ *Searching for Bobby Fischer* (1994) directed by Steven Zaillian. PG rating. 110 minutes.

When a 7-year-old boy and his father discover that he has a gift for chess, the boy begins a conflicted journey to become the next Bobby Fischer. His father and coach relentlessly drive him to become ruthless, single-minded, and competitive beyond a level of decency that the boy and his mother value. The boy accommodates the wishes of his father and coach for a while, but when he and his mother realize that his very life is at stake, he returns to playing chess in the local park and makes difficult but confirming choices. This is a compelling morality tale about and for parents who drive their children, children who feel the pressure and desire to please their parents, and families learning to cherish the true value of nurturance.

★★★★ *Little Man Tate* (1991) directed by Jodie Foster. PG rating. 99 minutes.

Young Fred Tate and his single-parent mother are a working-class family. They love each other and find great enjoyment in their lives. Tension and uncertainty arise when the mother realizes that Fred is a genius and, though she can give him the safety and caring, she cannot provide the intellectual stimulation he requires. She sends him to a school for the gifted where his teacher focuses only on his intellectual abilities. Only when the two women work together for Fred's welfare will he truly grow and learn. The film is about the decision of what is best for one's child and how to balance the many dimensions of a child's growth.

★★★★ *I am Sam* (2001) directed by Jessie Nelson. PG-13 rating. 132 minutes.

The title character has the mental capacity of a 7-year-old and a daughter with a homeless woman, who abandons father and daughter. Sam raises his daughter, but as she reaches age 7 herself, Sam's intellectual limitations begin to impede his daughter's academic performance. The state authorities remove the daughter, and Sam sues for custody. In the process, we learn about genuine parental love and the priority of a child's needs. Despite the predictable plot, a tender parable about parenting.

**Recommended**

★★★ *Big* (1989) directed by Penny Marshall. PG rating. 104 minutes.

Twelve-year-old Josh yearns to be older so that he can be taken more seriously, especially by Cynthia, who has stolen his heart. After being rejected by Cynthia at the carnival, he wanders over to the wish machine, where his wish to grow up fast is granted. The next morning, he wakes up as an adult. He remains an imaginative, fun-loving, spontaneous youngster in an adult existence. We are reminded that adults could use a good dose of Josh's qualities in order to enjoy life more and to truly connect with others and with life. Josh's compelling honesty and virtuosity play out in a corporate advertising environment to remind us of the power of basic morality and good deeds.

★★★　*Parenthood* (1990) directed by Ron Howard. PG-13 rating. 124 minutes.

The common yet terribly difficult challenge of raising children is effectively illuminated through the eyes of the main character, Gil (played by Steve Martin). Gil is the son of Frank, whose other three adult children continue to bring their problems home to father, and Gil has three children of his own for whom he wants to be a better dad than his was. Frank discovers that not rescuing his adult children is in fact the only way to help save them. Gil learns that bringing home the bacon and being home for the family are in a continuing balance. This is a film that lets parents know they are not alone in their uncertainties, anxieties, and dreams.

**Not Recommended**

★★　*Baby Boom* (1987) directed by Charles Shyer. PG rating. 110 minutes.

## ■ ONLINE SELF-HELP

★★★★　*UCANPOOPTOO* www.healthsystem.virginia.edu/bmc/ucp2/flash/login.html

This site provides parents with a child-focused guided training program for encopresis. The colorful animated site is intended for parents together with their children. Following the initial three core modules (60–90 minutes), there are 27 additional 5- to 10-minute modules to be completed over the following two weeks. Interactive elements, educational tutorials, and quizzes teach topics related to normal bowel movements. A mental health professional can help parents select the modules to complete based on their child's needs.

★★★　*After the Injury* aftertheinjury.org

This free website can help adults who are caring for children after an injury. The site provides information about how children experience injury or trauma and a questionnaire to rate how their child is reacting to the injury. Resources on the site allow parents to develop a customized care plan for their child. The site includes useful links to additional resources and information on how to find outside help for the adult and child.

## ■ INTERNET RESOURCES

**General Websites**

★★★★★　*KidsHealth* www.kidshealth.org

KidsHealth is an outstanding website that has three distinct sections—one for parents, one for kids, and one for teens, with information tailored for each age group. Underwritten by the Nemours Foundation, the site offers resources that are interactive (for kids), engaging, well written, and regularly updated.

★★★★★ *Parenthood.com* www.parenthood.com

A comprehensive source for pregnancy, parenting, and child-care articles and websites. Features include hundreds of articles about parenting, pregnancy, your baby, your child, and dozens of videos.

★★★★★ *Tufts University Child and Family Webguide* www.cfw.tufts.edu

This directory from Tufts University indexes hundreds of websites with parenting, child, and family information. Includes topics such as having a baby, picking schools, understanding child development and behavior problems, and much more.

★★★★ *Parenting Today—Child Development Institute* www.childdevelopmentinfo.com

This site offers hundreds of articles on every aspect of development, school, parenting, and disorders. The child development and child psychology sections could easily substitute for a book on these subjects.

## Psychoeducational Materials

★★★ *Parent Information Sheets for School Success* www.sdpirc.org/content/parents/parentinformationsheets.htm

Dozens of well-written articles on everything from adolescence, behavior and discipline, early childhood, to homework help, math, reading, violence, school success, and more.

★★★★ *DrGreene.com* www.drgreene.com

This resource from the pediatrician Alan Greene, MD, offers a wealth of insight and wisdom from his many years as both a doctor and a parent. Includes categories of parenting, prenatal, newborn, infant, toddler, preschooler, school age, and teen, so goes beyond just an infant resource.

★★★★★ *Today's Parent* www.todaysparent.com

A large website with thousands of articles, organized according to pregnancy, baby, toddler, kid, and teen categories, along with health, activities, recipes, general parenting topics, and a dozen blogs to keep you current on the latest parenting trends.

★★★★★ *Facts for Families* www.aacap.org/cs/root/facts_for_families/facts_for_families

Almost a hundred fact sheets on almost any topic of relevance to adolescents and children from the American Academy of Child and Adolescent Psychiatry. While largely well written and accurate, some of the fact sheets were out of date and didn't always reflect the latest research trends.

★★★★　*Parents* www.parents.com

The website of the magazine of the same name hosts all sorts of parenting articles and resources, much of it taken from the print publication. Like most offerings, it divides up the parent's world according to the child's development level, but also includes general articles on parenting and offers a section on food and recipes.

★★★★　*Family Life Library* www.ksre.ksu.edu/p.aspx?tabid=22

The categories of children and parenting are suitable as handouts and brochures from a Kansas State University program.

★★★★　*Cambridge Center for Behavioral Studies* www.behavior.org

The Parenting section under the "Help Centers" offers several good essays as well as collections of articles.

★★★★　*Children* by Kalman Heller, PhD www.drheller.com/index.html

There are dozens of well-written essays under "Parenting and Marital Advice" by a now-retired psychologist.

★★★　*Family Keys: Self-Care Resources for Children and their Families* parenting.uwex.edu/family-keys

These 13 brochures cover such topics as family rules, phone skills, first aid, safe at home, nutritious snacks, and the like. Developed by the University of Wisconsin, they are at a simple reading level, making them easy to understand.

**Specific Aspects of Parenting**

★★★★★　*Project NoSpank* www.nospank.net

A superb site for those who wish to campaign against paddling in the schools (and spanking in general) and designed to educate both parents and education policymakers.

★★★★　*People, Places, and Things That Help You Feel Better*　www.kidshealth.org/kid/feel_better/index.html

If you need readings for children about going to the hospital, dentist, or other medical service, the 20 here are excellent.

★★★★　*Contact a Family* www.cafamily.org.uk

Information and support for people caring for children with rare disorders. If parents need this kind of material, this is the only place to get it.

**** *Dealing with Feelings* www.kidshealth.org/kid/feeling/index.html

There are 50 readings here of about four pages each. They really deal with contexts, not just labeled emotions. Examples are "A Kid's Guide to Divorce," "Am I Too Fat or Too Thin?", "Are You Shy?," and "Why Am I So Sad?"

**** *National Center for Fathering* www.fathers.com

Under "Fathering Tips" are about 30 practical tips, plus hundreds of brief and sometimes sappy essays on stages, responsibilities, and functions. It is best as a source of beginning ideas or expanding some men's ideas of what it could mean to be a father.

**** *Foster Care and Adoptive Community* www.fosterparents.com

While the site offers support through chat and boards, one of the highlights are the dozens of articles under "Articles." They are information-packed and relevant.

*** *So What Are Dads Good For?* www.prismnet.com/~duanev/family/dads.html

A fine essay with insight and guidance for the confused.

**See also** Infant Development and Parenting (Chapter 26) and Teenagers and Parenting (Chapter 40).

# CHAPTER 16

# CHRONIC PAIN

N early one in four Americans suffers from chronic pain, defined by distressing physical pain lasting more than six months (Pizzo & Clark, 2012). Chronic pain costs the United States about $500 billion each year, but more than the financial expense, pain wreaks havoc with the quality of life of its sufferers and their families.

The pain itself is only part of the corrosive chronic pain syndrome, which entails a host of ailments that viciously perpetuate the cycle of despair. Financial, legal, medical, and work problems attendant to chronic pain frequently give rise to anxiety and depression. The pain exacerbates sleep and exercise difficulties, which only intensify the pain experience. Without medications, many chronic pain patients cannot function, but with medications, they frequently complain of fatigue, concentration difficulties, and intense constipation.

Chronic neck and back pain, fibromyalgia, and complex regional pain syndrome (and its earlier label "reflex sympathetic dystrophy") establish the focus of this chapter. Self-help materials addressing the pervasive side effects of medication, physical therapy, and marital difficulties are also included, as well as self-help resources for families coping with a member's chronic pain. Unfortunately, complete coverage of every cause and consequence of chronic pain is beyond the scope of this chapter, so chronic headaches and arthritis pain are not directly addressed.

In this chapter, we critically review self-help books, online self-help, and Internet resources on chronic pain, concluding with a list of national support groups (Box 16.1).

## ■ SELF-HELP BOOKS

### Strongly Recommended

★★★★★ *Managing Pain Before It Manages You* (2008) by Margaret A. Caudill and Herbert Benson. New York: Guilford.

Chronic pain is comprehensively and effectively counterpunched in this self-help book. The writing style conveys a true respect for the experience with which chronic pain patients live. The overarching attitude is one of hope and seriousness about overcoming pain and a resolve that one doesn't just "have to put up with it." The mind–body–environment connection is presented as foundational and important in recovery. To understand chronic pain means to understand chronic stress. Health researchers Caudill and Benson advance a multipronged self-help program: cognitive therapy, attitude, nutrition, active listening, coping, helping relationships, and problem solving. Many supplemental materials and techniques

## BOX 16.1
## RECOMMENDATION HIGHLIGHTS

**SELF-HELP BOOKS**

▪ For managing chronic pain:

★★★★★ *Managing Pain Before It Manages You* by Margaret A. Caudill and Herbert Benson

★★★★ *The Pain Survival Guide* by Dennis W. Turk and Frits Winter

★★★ *Managing Chronic Pain* by John Otis

**ONLINE SELF-HELP**

▪ For learning research-supported skills crucial to pain management:

★★★★ *Goalistics* pain.goalistics.com

**INTERNET RESOURCES**

▪ For valuable information on chronic pain:

★★★★ *American Chronic Pain Association* www.theacpa.org

★★★★ *Power Over Your Pain* www.poweroveryourpain.com

are provided to assist readers and as a resource guide for loved ones (e.g., common types of chronic pain; work conditions such as chair, keyboard, monitor; and lighting). The highest-rated resource for self-management of pain in our studies.

★★★★ *The Pain Survival Guide* (2006) by Dennis W. Turk and Frits Winter. New York: Guilford.

A singular contribution of this book is the candid description of the ineffective and sometimes deprecating way medical professionals treat individuals with chronic pain. The hopeful message is that chronic pain sufferers, once armed with the tools and knowledge of this book, will become experts on their own pain management. With the skills presented here by internationally recognized pain expert Turk, the person can prevent pain from controlling his or her life. Some pain may be inevitable, but suffering is not. Key self-help methods include correcting problems with sleep, fatigue, negative thinking, and inadequate pacing. Tips, activities, behavioral logs, and other active components add to the interest and effectiveness of this splendid self-help book.

### Recommended

★★★ *The Mindfulness Solution to Pain* (2009) by Jackie Gardner-Nix and Lucie Costin-Hall. Oakland, CA: New Harbinger.

Mindfulness has become a popular method of psychotherapy in recent years, and this book applies the principles of mindfulness and meditation to diminishing the effects of chronic pain. We are reminded here of the difference between awareness and thinking. Thinking about the pain is hypothesized, within a mind–body connection context, to increase or irritate the pain. Many case examples are given of individuals who practiced mindfulness by focusing their awareness on their chronic pain. As negative memories and emotions come into the mind, individuals develop insight through the awareness of pain and can then work with a professional or, as this book encourages, can work independently on the experiences that caused the pain rather than trying to work on the pain itself. Paradoxically, many patients found that this process relieved or ended their chronic pain.

★★★ *Coping with Chronic Illness* (2010) by H. Norman Wright and Lynn Ellis. Eugene, OR: Harvest House.

Chronic pain of some type accompanies chronic illness; however, this book features first-person stories about the impact of a chronic illness. One of the cases cites a therapist telling the patient, "Chronic illness is like a career; you can do poorly or well." *Well* means learning to cope in a way that manages the illness. Many patients express the frustration of not being believed when others doubt or question the condition because they can't see "invisible symptoms" of pain. Interactions with the medical community are frequently chronicled as "pitiful" because the default response is "there is nothing we can do." What they can do is described in this book: explanations of differing treatments designed for specific medical conditions are given. No single treatment plan or technique is recommended—rather, an overview of the often lonely and frustrating experience of chronic pain and how to find help that can make a difference.

★★★ *Managing Chronic Pain* (2007) by John Otis. New York: Oxford University Press.

This book offers a particular treatment plan for controlling chronic pain. The treatment is cognitive-behavioral therapy that can also be applied to many other diagnoses. The application to chronic pain, however, involves a specific and tailored procedure for reduction of chronic pain. Important elements of the treatment include learning muscle relaxation and imagery, improving sleep, managing anger, reconstructing negative thoughts, pacing one's activities, and building in pleasant activities. The automatic negative thoughts typically entail feeling misunderstood by everyone, feeling frustrated that there is no help, and feeling isolated. This treatment would need to be conducted with a mental health professional, although many of the activities and preparatory activities in the book can be conducted on one's own.

**Not Recommended**

★★ *Sick and Tired of Feeling Sick and Tired* (2000) by Paul J. Donoghue and Mary Elizabeth Siegel. New York: Norton.

## ■ ONLINE SELF-HELP

★★★★ *Goalistics* pain.goalistics.com

Goalistics is an online pain management program designed for people with chronic pain. Based on individualized assessments, the program creates a customized learning plan that prioritizes the four learning centers at the heart of the program. The learning centers help users address their thinking, better manage their emotions, learn relaxation, and make behavioral changes in their daily lives. In each learning center users view a multimedia introduction, set goals, complete the interactive activities, utilize rewards, and learn pacing to maintain pain management and increased activity. Users track their progress with daily log-ins to rate their mood, pain level, and activity level. The cost of the program is $29.95 for a year-long membership. The site also contains an online support group that visitors can join free of charge without purchasing the program.

★★★   *Pain Action* www.painaction.com

This website is designed for people with chronic pain and is available free with registration. Based on an initial self-directed test, users are provided with a customized home page. From that page, users can access learning modules that teach them various aspects of pain management, including relaxation, physical exercises, and emotional coping strategies. A tracking function allows users to track their pain and completed lessons.

## ■ INTERNET RESOURCES

### General Websites

★★★★   *American Chronic Pain Association* www.theacpa.org

This nonprofit advocacy organization offers a wealth of resources for people with chronic pain or a loved one with chronic pain, including a set of pain management tools, a consumer's guide to pain medications and treatment, understanding the various medications prescribed for pain, and a brief encyclopedia of common conditions that may have chronic pain as a symptom. The site also offers an interactive pain log to help you track your pain day to day.

★★★★   *Power Over Your Pain* www.poweroveryourpain.com

This website, from St. Jude Medical, acts as a resource for people living with chronic pain, with dozens of articles and related resources.

★★★★   *Chronic Pain Health Center—Spine Health* www.spine-health.com/conditions/chronic-pain

This resource center from Spine Health offers a comprehensive set of articles for those dealing with chronic pain. Includes chronic pain videos, a provider directory, and an active online support group.

★★★★   *Pain Management Health Center* www.spine-health.com/treatment/pain-management

This pain management center offers dozens of useful articles about pain basics, causes, diagnosis, treatment, and common pain medications, as well as a section about living with pain.

★★★   *American Pain Foundation* www.painfoundation.org

The American Pain Foundation is a national nonprofit advocacy organization that helps people dealing with all types of physical pain, ranging from acute, back and cancer pain, to fibromyalgia, neuropathy, and Lyme disease. Their website offers information on all of these kinds of pain and more, as well as pain resources and more.

★★★    *The American Academy of Pain Medicine* www.painmed.org

This professional association has a nice set of consumer-oriented articles under the "Patient Center" section. While it deals with more than just chronic pain, it's a good resource to check out.

★★★    *Chronic Pain Australia* www.chronicpainaustralia.org.au

This resource from Down Under offers a good set of articles under "Fact Sheets," as well as personal stories under "Resources, Pain Stories."

★★    *Pain Connection* www.painconnection.org

This nonprofit organization is focused on helping people with chronic pain, as well as their families, by providing resources, information, and support. The most helpful component of their website, which is primarily focused on their organization, may be the "Newsletter" section.

## ▓ SUPPORT GROUPS

### American Chronic Pain Association

Phone: 800-533-3231
www.theacpa.org

### American Pain Foundation

Phone: 888-615-7246
www.painfoundation.org

### American Society for Action on Pain

www.actiononpain.org

### Men with Fibromyalgia

Menwithfibro.com

### National Chronic Pain Outreach Association

Phone: 540-862-9437
www.chronicpain.org

### National Fibromyalgia Association

www.FMaware.com

**National Pain Foundation**

www.nationalpainfoundation.org

**Pain Connection**

www.painconnection.org

**Reflex Sympathetic Dystrophy Syndrome Association**

www.rsds.org

# CHAPTER 17

# COMMUNICATION AND PEOPLE SKILLS

We get things done by talking with family, friends, colleagues, and neighbors. When someone doesn't quite grasp what we are saying, we often let it go, the talk continues, and nobody pays much attention. But some conversations have critical outcomes that hinge on the effectiveness of the conversation—a job interview, a business meeting, a marriage proposal, a family decision. In these circumstances, ineffective communication can have serious negative consequences: we don't get the job, don't convince our business colleagues, don't get engaged, and don't collaborate as a family.

Sometimes strained conversations reflect genuine differences between people. On many occasions, though, strained conversations develop when people simply are miscommunicating. Their conversations could readily be improved by understanding the nature of interpersonal communication and by acquiring people skills.

Communication and people skills are hot items on self-help lists. Whether it is general interpersonal abilities, or female–male communication, or negotiating agreements, humans seem to crave "knowing" one other. In this chapter, we review self-help books, films, and Internet sites devoted to these quintessentially human skills (Box 17.1).

## ■ SELF-HELP BOOKS

### Strongly Recommended

★★★★ *Boundaries: When to Say Yes, When to Say No to Take Control of Your Life* (1992) by Henry Cloud and John Townsend. Grand Rapids, MI: Zondervan.

A boundary is a personal line that defines identity and responsibility. In this fine book, Cloud and Townsend define several types of boundaries (e.g., physical, mental, emotional, and spiritual) and help people clarify their boundaries. This is accomplished in various ways, such as setting limits and changing how one feels about setting boundaries. The authors take a biblical and psychological approach to constructing healthy boundaries. Under the Law of Exposure, the authors remind us that the entire concept revolves around the fact that we exist in relationships. An excellent resource for individuals looking to clarify boundaries, especially for those interested in blending psychology and scripture.

## BOX 17.1
## RECOMMENDATION HIGHLIGHTS

**SELF-HELP BOOKS**

■ On learning communication and people skills:

**** *The Dance of Connection* by Harriet Lerner

**** *How to Communicate* by Matthew McKay et al.

**** *People Skills* by Robert Bolton

**** *The New Peoplemaking* by Virginia Satir

*** *The Messages Workbook* by Martha Davis et al.

■ On improving female–male communication:

**** *You Just Don't Understand* by Deborah Tannen

**** *Intimate Strangers* by Lillian Rubin

■ On defining boundaries and clarifying responsibilities:

**** *Boundaries* by Henry Cloud and John Townsend

■ On negotiating agreements:

**** *Getting to Yes* by Roger Fisher and William Ury

■ On the healing power of confiding in others:

*** *Opening Up* by James Pennebaker

■ On overcoming shyness and being less lonely:

**** *Shyness* by Philip Zimbardo

**** *Intimate Connections* by David Burns

■ On friendship and its important roles in our lives:

**** *Just Friends* by Lillian Rubin

**FILMS**

■ On demonstrating love and triumph over adversity:

***** *Children of a Lesser God*

■ On inspiring creativity and individuality at a cost:

**** *Dead Poets Society*

**INTERNET RESOURCES**

■ For information on improving communication skills:

***** *The New Conversations Initiative* www.newconversations.net

**** *Mind Tools* www.mindtools.com/page8.html

---

**** *You Just Don't Understand: Women and Men in Conversation* (1990) by Deborah Tannen. New York: Ballantine.

As its title implies, this book is about how women and men communicate—or all too often miscommunicate—with each other. *You Just Don't Understand* reached number one on several bestseller lists. Tannen shows that friction between women and men in conversation often develops because as girls and boys they were brought up in two virtually distinct cultures and continue to live in those two very different cultures. The two gender cultures are rapport talk (female culture) and report talk (male culture). Rapport talk is the language of conversation and a way of establishing connections and negotiating relationships, which women feel more comfortable doing. Report talk is public speaking, which men feel more comfortable doing. Tannen illustrates miscommunication in male–female relationships with several cartoons about a husband and wife at the breakfast table. Harmful and unjustified misinterpretations might be avoided by understanding the conversational styles of the other gender. The problem, then, may not be an individual man or even men's styles but the difference between women's and men's styles. This excellent 4-star self-help book has been especially taken up by women who, after reading the book, want their partner to read it too. Tannen's book is solidly written, well researched, and entertaining.

★★★★ *The Dance of Connection* by Harriet Lerner (2002). New York: Quill.

This book examines the verbal challenges of life's most painful conversations with a special emphasis on women's experiences. Lerner counsels women on how to speak out in such stressful circumstances as when their husband is having an affair or when friends jeopardize their relationship by becoming roommates. She provides advice on how to complain, how to request, how to apologize, and how to listen and set limits on the extent to which one is willing to listen to others' negativity. Another excellent resource from psychologist Lerner, who also wrote *The Dance of Anger.*

★★★★ *Intimate Strangers* (revised ed., 1990) by Lillian Rubin. New York: Harper & Row.

This book focuses on intimacy and communication difficulties between women and men. Rubin tackles a relationship problem that confronts many women and men—their inability to develop a satisfying intimate relationship with each other. Rubin says that male–female differences in intimacy are related to the fact that it is primarily mothers who raise children and are the emotional managers of the family. Because girls identify with mothers and boys with fathers, females develop a capacity for intimacy and an interest in managing emotional problems, and males do not. Rubin supports her ideas with a number of case studies derived from interviews with approximately 150 couples. Rubin provides detailed insights about the nature of intimacy and communication problems in sexual matters and in raising children. She concludes that the only solution to the intimacy gulf between females and males is for every child to be raised and nurtured by two loving parents, not just the mother, from birth on. That is, Rubin's culprit is the nonnurturant father, who, she says, has to change his ways and serve as a nurturing, intimate role model committed to managing emotional difficulties. While this 4-star resource is reviewed in this chapter, its contents also apply to several other categories, including marriage, love, and intimacy.

★★★★ *The New Peoplemaking* (1988) by Virginia Satir. Palo Alto, CA: Science and Behavior Books.

This book is aimed at improving communication with a select group of people in your life—family members. Virginia Satir, a pioneer in family therapy, originally published

*Peoplemaking* in 1972 and then revised it for 1988 publication. Based on her extensive observations as a leading family therapist, Satir describes four areas that can lead to troubles for families: self-worth, communication, family system, and link to society. In her observations, troubled families invariably have low levels of self-worth, communication patterns that are indirect or dishonest, rigid systems of rules, and relations with the rest of society in fearful and blaming ways. Satir encourages readers to explore their own family dynamics to see how they stack up in regard to the four areas. Although dated in some areas, *The New Peoplemaking* still contains some valuable advice, especially for couples who want to communicate effectively and for parents who want to communicate with their children.

★★★★  *How to Communicate: The Ultimate Guide to Improving Your Personal and Professional Relationships* (1997) by Matthew McKay, Martha Davis, and Patrick Fanning. New York: Fine.

The premise of this book is that communication makes life work. The book tells what to do about communicating rather than what to think about. The emphasis is on skills (e.g., basic skills, advanced skills, conflict skills, social skills, family skills, public skills). The authors recommend that you read the basic and advanced skills chapters first, then go on to the specific chapters appropriate to your relationships and position in life. Contained in the basic skills section are listening, self-disclosure, and expressing skills. In the advanced skills section is information on body language, paralanguage (vocal component), hidden agendas, and clarifying skills. For adults and older adolescents looking to improve their communication style, this 4-star book is worthwhile.

★★★★  *Shyness* (1987) by Philip Zimbardo. Reading, MA: Addison-Wesley.

This book is dedicated to overcoming social isolation and becoming more gregarious. What does psychologist Zimbardo say shy people can do about their situation? First, they have to analyze their shyness and figure out how they got this way. Possible reasons include negative evaluations, fear of being rejected, fear of intimacy, and lack of adequate social skills, among others. Second, they need to build up their self-esteem. To help with this, Zimbardo spells out 15 steps to becoming more confident. Third, shy people need to improve their social skills. To accomplish this, Zimbardo describes several behavior modification strategies, tells how to set realistic goals, and advocates working hard toward achieving these goals. *Shyness* received a robust 4-star rating as a well-known (164 respondents), excellent self-help book for shy people. It gives sound advice, is free of psychobabble, and is easy to read.

★★★★  *Intimate Connections: The New Clinically Tested Program for Overcoming Loneliness* (1985) by David Burns. New York: Morrow.

This book, a program for overcoming loneliness, is written by David Burns, famous for *Feeling Good*, on depression. Psychiatrist Burns believes that loneliness is essentially a state of mind that is primarily caused by the faulty assumption that a loving partner is needed before one can feel happy and secure. Burns says that the first step in breaking free from loneliness is learning to like and love oneself. He also distinguishes between two types of loneliness: situational loneliness, which lasts for only a brief time and can be healthy and motivating; and chronic loneliness, which persists and results from problems that have plagued people for most of their lives. Among the topics Bums touches on are how to make social connections, how to get close to others, and how to improve one's sexual life. Checklists, worksheets, daily mood logs, and a number of self-assessments are found throughout the book, which received a 4-star rating. This is a good self-help book—full of straightforward advice and helpful examples—for helping people overcome their loneliness.

★★★★ *Just Friends: The Role of Friendship in Our Lives* (1985) by Lillian Rubin. New York: Harper & Row.

Author Rubin, who penned *Intimate Strangers*, which was evaluated earlier in this chapter, examines the nature of intimacy and friendship in this book. Rubin analyzes the nature of the valued yet fragile bond of friendship between women, between men, between women and men, between best friends, and in couples. She says that unlike many other relationships, friendship is a private affair with no rituals, social contracts, shared tasks, role requirements, or institutional supports of any kind. Rubin believes friends are central players in our lives, not just in childhood but in adulthood as well. Friends give us a reference outside of our families against which we can judge and evaluate ourselves; they help us develop an independent sense of self and support our efforts to adapt to new circumstances and stressful situations. This is an insightful analysis of the important and often-overlooked role that friends play in our lives. However, some critics said that Rubin exaggerates sex differences in friendships and fails to provide sufficient practical tools for enhancing friendships.

★★★★ *People Skills* (reissue ed., 1986) by Robert Bolton. New York: Touchstone.

This book, dedicated to improving human communication, is presented in four main parts. Part I, the Introduction, describes a number of skills for bridging gaps in interpersonal communication and barriers to communicating effectively. Part II, Listening Skills, explains how listening is different from merely hearing, how to develop the important skill of reflective listening, and how to read body language. Part III, Assertion Skills, outlines a number of valuable techniques to help a person become more assertive in relationships. Part IV, Conflict Management Skills, discusses how to effectively manage conflict in many different circumstances. *People Skills* received a 4-star rating in our studies even though it was originally published in 1981. However, a number of the mental health professionals concluded that it remains one of the best general introductions to communication skills.

★★★★ *Getting to Yes: Negotiating Agreement without Giving In* (1991 revised ed.) by Roger Fisher and William Ury. New York: Penguin.

This concise book (only about 150 pages) offers a step-by-step method for arriving at mutually acceptable agreements, whether between parents and children, neighbors, bosses and employees, customers and business managers, or tenants and landlords. Fisher and Ury describe how to separate people from the problem; emphasize interests, not positions; develop precise goals at the outset of negotiations; work together to establish options that will satisfy both parties; and negotiate successfully with opponents who are more powerful, refuse to play by the rules, or resort to dirty tricks. The book is based on the method of principled negotiation developed as part of the Harvard Negotiation Project. This method helps people evaluate issues based on their merits instead of regressing to a haggling process in which each side says what it will and won't do. It teaches negotiators to look for mutual gains whenever possible. Although written more than two decades ago, this 4-star book remains one of the best easy-to-read resources for learning how to negotiate effectively in a wide range of situations.

### Recommended

★★★   *That's Not What I Meant! How Conversational Style Makes or Breaks Relationships* (1986, reprinted 1991) by Deborah Tannen. New York: Ballantine.

This book provides a broader understanding of the inner workings of conversation than Tannen's earlier-reviewed book, *You Just Don't Understand.* Tannen believes that different conversational styles are at the heart of miscommunication. But conversational confusion between the sexes is only part of the picture. Tannen shows that growing up in different parts of the country, having different ethnic and class backgrounds, being of different ages, and possessing different personality traits all contribute to different conversational styles that can cause disappointment, hurt, and misplaced blame. *That's Not What I Meant!* received a 3-star rating in one of our studies, just missing a 4-star rating. This is a good self-help book that provides a rich understanding of how conversational styles make or break relationships. Compared to *You Just Don't Understand,* this book includes more basic information about communication skills in general, which are covered in other books, although Tannen does a better job of describing these skills than most other authors.

★★★   *Opening Up: The Healing Power of Confiding in Others* (1997) by James Pennebaker. New York: Guilford.

As its subtitle indicates, this book concerns the healing power of confiding in other people. It deals with (a) why suppressing inner turmoil has a devastating effect on health, (b) how denial of mental pain can cause physical pain, and (c) why talking or writing about troubling thoughts protects us from the internal stresses that cause physical illness. Psychologist Pennebaker's advice is not based only on his own opinions: for several decades, he has studied thousands of people in many different contexts to learn how confessing troubling feelings and experiences benefited health. What is surprising about Pennebaker's findings is that the benefits of confession occur whether you tell your secrets to someone else or simply write about them privately. Pennebaker is especially adept at pinpointing how the hard work of inhibiting troublesome thoughts and feelings gradually undermines the body's defenses. *Opening Up* received a 3-star rating in our national study, probably because it was not well known at the time it was rated.

★★★   *Difficult People: How to Deal with Impossible Clients, Bosses and Employees* (1990) by Roberta Cava. Toronto: Key Porter.

This book addresses the stress of dealing with rude, impatient, emotional, persistent, and aggressive people. You learn to control your moods by not allowing other people to give you negative feelings, which you do by improving your people skills. The author first helps identify emotional behavior by having you answer specific questions, examine techniques for specific stressful situations, look at consequences of behavior, and examine approaches to conflict resolution. Reviewed are basic communication skills, communication skills for specific situations, gender influences, and ratings of your listening and speaking skills. Three chapters address difficult clients, supervisors, coworkers, and subordinates. For adults finding themselves faced with difficult people, this book could provide some informative advice and practical skills.

★★★ *Coping with Difficult People* (1981) by Robert Bramson. New York: Dell.

In this self-help resource, Bramson describes and presents strategies for coping with the following types of difficult people:

- The Hostile Aggressive, who bullies by bombarding, making cutting remarks, or throwing tantrums
- The Complainer, who gripes incessantly but never gets any closer to solving the problem
- The Silent Unresponsive, who is always reasonable, sincere, and supportive to your face but never comes through
- The Negativist, who responds to any proposal with statements like "It will never work"
- The Know-It-All, who is confident that he or she knows everything there is to know about anything worth knowing
- The Indecisive, who delays any important decision until the outcome is certain and refuses to let go of anything until it's perfect—which is never

Bramson outlines a six-step plan to cope with these people and make life less stressful. This recommended book is entertaining reading, and the author uses a lot of catchy labels to get his points across and grab the reader's attention, such as describing Know-It-Alls as bulldozers and balloons and Hostile Aggressives as Sherman tanks, snipers, and exploders. Written several decades ago, *Coping with Difficult People* has been successful, with sales of more than 500,000 copies. The mental health experts in our national studies recommended the book for improved understanding of people in work settings rather than family settings; since the author's background is in managerial consulting, many of the examples come from work settings.

★★★ *Games People Play* (1964) by Eric Berne. New York: Grove.

Psychiatrist Berne was the founder of Transactional Analysis, an approach to under-standing interpersonal relationships that emphasizes communication patterns. He main-tained that people live their lives by playing out games in their interpersonal relationships. People play games to manipulate others, avoid reality, and conceal ulterior motives. Berne analyzes 36 different games, which he divides into seven main categories: life games, mari-tal games, sexual games, party games, consulting room games, underworld games, and good games, which involve social contributions that outweigh the complexity of underlying moti-vation and manipulation. *Games People Play* received a 3-star rating in one of our national studies. On the positive side, many characterize the book as a self-help classic that has been a huge bestseller. It was one of the most frequently rated books in our studies. People who read it will find numerous examples that apply to their own lives. Berne connects with read-ers through catchy, witty writing. You can read about the sweetheart, the threadbare, the schlemiel, the stocking game, the wooden leg, and the swymd (see what you made me do). Although the book is now more than four decades old, some psychotherapists continue to strongly recommend it to clients who are having communication problems and use Berne's Transactional Analysis in their practice. On the other side, this book has steadily faded in professional popularity, and many will find it dated in content and tone. Some critics opine that Berne overdramatizes the role of game playing in intimate relationships, that the parent–adult–child aspect of Berne's approach is overly simplistic, and that the games reiterate traditional male and female orientations.

★★★ *Messages Workbook: Powerful Strategies for Effective Communication at Work and Home* (2004) by Martha Davis, Kim Paleg, and Patrick Fanning. Oakland, CA: New Harbinger.

This workbook targets a broad spectrum of situations, relationships, and environments in which we spend most of our time. Common problematic communication deficits are identified and then necessary skills are taught to rectify them. Exercises and other activities are included in the book, and the authors provide ample opportunity to practice the requisite skills. The book focuses primarily on three areas: (1) laying the foundation (e.g., hearing what others are saying, regulating emotions, learning to disclose), (2) conflict (e.g., fighting fair, asserting one's self, negotiating conflict, and coping with differential power), and (3) social (e.g., meeting new people, communicating in small groups, overcoming state fright). The book's strengths are found in the thoroughness in which the authors explain and implement these essential communication skills.

★★★ *Stop! You're Driving Me Crazy* (1979) by George Bach and Ronald Deutsch. New York: Berkley.

This self-help resource covers a broad array of communication strategies to help, in the authors' words, "keep the people in your life from driving you up the wall." It spells out Bach's catchy concept of "crazymaking." Crazymaking describes a variety of harmful communication patterns that are passive–aggressive in nature. Passive–aggressive individuals consciously like, love, or at least respect each other but unconsciously undermine rather than build up the morale and mental well-being of friends, lovers, or spouses. Some examples of passive–aggressive crazymaking: A husband stirs up a screaming fight and then wants to make passionate love; a boss gives an employee a promotion and then says, "You're worthless;" and a young woman tells her mother that she is on a crash diet and the mother then offers her a piece of chocolate cake. The authors help readers cope with and eliminate such crazymaking techniques. On the borderline between 2 and 3 stars, this book just managed the 3-star rating. An early success that achieved bestseller status in the early 1980s, its popularity has waned. Several of our experts criticized the book for being too sensational, gender-biased, and difficult to read in places.

**Diamond in the Rough**

♦ *The Talk Book: The Intimate Science of Communicating in Close Relationships* (1988) by Gerald Goodman and Glenn Esterly. New York: Ballantine.

Talk is an essential tool for ensuring the success of all close relationships, and *The Talk Book* is about ways to improve face-to-face communication. The authors describe six communication tools that contribute to using talk more effectively: disclosures, reflections, interpretations, advisements, questions, and silences. These talk tools fashion most of the meaning in everyday conversation. Understood well, they can help improve close relationships. Each chapter ends with a section that includes several tested methods for improving mastery of talk and making sense of another person's talk. This resource made the Diamonds in the Rough category: it was rated positively but by too few experts. This is a solid book on conversation skills written by a leading expert. Its main drawbacks are its length (almost 400 pages of small type) and encyclopedic tendencies.

**Not Recommended**

- ★★ *How to Start a Conversation and Make Friends* (2001 revised ed.) by Don Gabor. New York: Simon & Schuster.
- ★★ *Men Are from Mars, Women Are from Venus* (1992) by John Gray. New York: HarperCollins.
- ★★ *How to Argue and Win Every Time* (1995) by Gerry Spence. New York: St. Martin's.
- ★ *Body Language* (1970) by Julius Fast. New York: Pocket Books.
- ★ *How to Win Friends and Influence People* (rev. ed., 1981) by Dale Carnegie. New York: Simon & Schuster.
- ★ *Are You the One for Me?* (1998) by Barbara DeAngelis. London: Thorsons.

**Strongly Not Recommended**

† *Mars & Venus on a Date* (1997) by John Gray. New York: HarperCollins.

## ■ FILMS

**Strongly Recommended**

★★★★★ *Children of a Lesser God* (1987) directed by Randa Haines. R rating. 119 minutes.

Marlee Matlin, who is hearing impaired, won an Academy Award for her performance as a young hearing-impaired woman who refuses to read lips or try to learn to speak. She encountered a teacher of the deaf who is both attracted to her and single-minded in implementing his ideas that the deaf should read lips and speak. The film is a love story, but more a story of triumph over adversity and the struggle for control between two people. Those who live with physical or emotional obstacles will find spirit and love winning out in this excellent 5-star film.

★★★★ *Dead Poets Society* (1990) directed by Peter Weir. PG rating. 129 minutes.

John Keating (Robin Williams) is a brilliant and inspiring English teacher who returns to the New England private school that he attended as a youth. He brings poetry, literature, and pursuit of life to his students and in so doing brings to life their spirit, self-confidence, and independence. The school doesn't approve of his teaching style. When a student is encouraged to confront his parents about his career direction and the parents remove him from the school, the boy commits suicide. The death is subsequently blamed on Keating. The film reminds us that the exhilaration of learning through spontaneity, nurtured curiosity, and creativity is to be cherished; the rebelliousness and individuality that often result from unbridled growth must be handled conscientiously. Also reviewed under Teenagers and Parenting (Chapter 40).

**Not Recommended**

★★ *He Said, She Said* (1990) directed by Ken Kwapis and Marisa Silver. PG-13 rating. 115 minutes.

## ■ INTERNET RESOURCES

**Psychoeducational Materials**

★★★★★ *The New Conversations Initiative* www.newconversations.net

Here you will find a seven-chapter workbook and reader in communication skills by Dennis Rivers, MA, entitled "The Seven Challenges Workbook." Each topic takes only a few pages and is stated as a challenge: listening more attentively and responsively; explaining your conversational intent and inviting consent; expressing yourself more clearly and completely; translating complaints and criticisms into requests; asking more open-ended and more creative questions; expressing more appreciation; and making better communication an important part of everyday living. This might be used as self-help exercises or assigned as homework in treatment.

★★★★ *Mind Tools* www.mindtools.com/page8.html

A career website that offers dozens of articles about how to improve one's communication skills. The skills you can learn through this website are applicable not only within the workplace, but also in your relationships with others more generally.

★★★★ *Effective Communication* helpguide.org/mental/effective_communication_skills.htm

A helpful one-page guide from the nonprofit HelpGuide that may be useful in improving communication skills in both business and relationships.

★★★ *Online Training Program on Intractable Conflict* www.colorado.edu/conflict/peace/index.html

This free online course, which is no longer updated, nonetheless provides dozens of helpful articles about conflict resolution and improving communication skills more generally.

★★★★ *Arguing and Relationships: Introduction* www.queendom.com/articles/articles.htm?a=8

This two-page article presents a set of guidelines for constructive arguing.

★★★ *Interpersonal Communication Skills* www.queendom.com/tests/access_page/index.htm?idRegTest=2288

This is a self-help interactive quiz that consists of 25 questions to help a person assess his or her communication skills. The quiz provides instant feedback and is free.

★★★★   *9 Steps to Better Communication Today* psychcentral.com/blog/ archives/2009/04/14/9-steps-to-better-communication-today

A single article offering nine helpful tips to improve your communication skills with your partner or significant other.

### Other Resources

★★   *Toastmasters International* www.toastmasters.org

This international voluntary group offers free or low-cost training, feedback, and practice making speeches to business, civic, and other groups. There are chapters everywhere. Click on "Speaking Tips" for 10 tips for successful public speaking.

**See also** Love and Intimacy (Chapter 27) and Marriage (Chapter 28).

# CHAPTER 18

# DEATH AND GRIEVING

The famous psychotherapist Erich Fromm once commented that "Man is the only animal that finds his own existence a problem he has to solve and from which he cannot
escape." He went on to say that "in the same sense man is the only animal who knows he must
die." Our life does ultimately end, reaching the point when, as Italian playwright Salvatore
Quasimodo says, "Each of us stands alone at the heart of the earth pierced through by a ray
of sunlight, and suddenly it is evening!" In the end, the years do steal us from ourselves and
from our loved ones.

Compared to people in many other cultures around the world, Americans are death
avoiders and death deniers. We are rarely prepared to cope with the overwhelming emotions and upheavals that fear, despair, and grief bring into our lives. Because we are such
a death-avoiding and death-denying culture, many people might expect this chapter to be
depressing. We think you will not find that to be the case. Self-help writers who dispense
advice on coping with the sadness of death balance the sadness with love, support, and
spiritual healing.

In this chapter, we review self-help books, autobiographies, films, online self-help, and
Internet sites on the topics of death, loss, and grief (Box 18.1). These resources address coping with loss of any kind, including death, impending death (one's own or someone else's),
and grieving in general. A listing of pertinent support and self-help groups concludes the
chapter.

## ■ SELF-HELP BOOKS

### Strongly Recommended

★★★★★ *How to Survive the Loss of a Love* (2nd ed., 1991) by Melba Colgrove, Harold
     Bloomfield, and Peter McWilliams. Los Angeles: Prelude.

This book provides suggestions for coping with the loss of a loved one, through death
or otherwise. Since the first edition appeared in 1976, the authors have experienced, among
them, the death of a parent, a major stroke, serious car accidents, a bankruptcy, a lawsuit,
and an impending divorce. Consequently, the authors view loss broadly. They subdivide
loss into four categories: (1) obvious losses, such as death of a loved one, divorce, robbery,
and rape; (2) not-so obvious losses, such as moving, loss of a long-term goal, and success
(loss of striving); (3) loss related to age, such as leaving home, loss of youth, loss of hair, and

## BOX 18.1
## RECOMMENDATION HIGHLIGHTS

**SELF-HELP BOOKS**

- On coping with loss of any kind, including death:
  - ***** *How to Survive the Loss of a Love* by Melba Colgrove et al.
  - ***** *How to Go on Living When Someone You Love Dies* by Therese Rando
  - **** *The Grief Recovery Handbook* by John W. James and Frank Cherry
  - **** *Recovering from the Loss of a Child* by Katherine Donnelly
  - **** *Staring at the Sun* by Irvin D. Yalom
- On a spiritual approach to death and grief:
  - ***** *When Bad Things Happen to Good People* by Harold Kushner
- On coping with death (your own or someone else's):
  - **** *Working It Through* by Elisabeth Kübler-Ross
  - *** *On Death and Dying* by Elisabeth Kübler-Ross
- On helping children cope with grief:
  - ***** *On Children and Death* by Elisabeth Kübler-Ross
  - **** *Learning to Say Good-By* by Eda LeShan
  - **** *Talking about Death* by Earl Grollman
  - **** *Helping Children Grieve* by Theresa Huntley
- On sudden infant death syndrome:
  - *** *Sudden Infant Death* by John DeFrain et al.
- On life (and death) lessons:
  - **** *Life Lessons* by Elizabeth Kübler-Ross and David Kessler
- On grieving the loss of a pet:
  - *** *Saying Goodbye to the Pet You Love* by Lorrie A. Greene and Jacquelyn Landis

**AUTOBIOGRAPHIES**

- On grieving a spouse's death:
  - ***** *A Grief Observed* by C. S. Lewis
  - ***** *The Year of Magical Thinking* by Joan Didion
- On grieving a mother's death:
  - **** *Motherless Daughter* by Hope Edelman
- On grieving a child's death:
  - ***** *Death Be Not Proud* by John Gunther
  - *** *After the Death of a Child* by Ann Finkbeiner
  - *** *Lament for a Son* by Nicholas Wolterstorff
- On living while dying:
  - ***** *Letting Go* by Morrie Schwartz
  - **** *The Wheel of Life* by Elisabeth Kübler-Ross & Todd Gold

## FILMS

- On denial of grief and eventual recovery:
  - ★★★★★ *Ordinary People*
  - ★★★ *The Accidental Tourist*
- On grieving a loss and choosing life:
  - ★★★★★ *Corrina, Corrina*
  - ★★★★ *Truly, Madly, Deeply*
  - ★★★★ *Steel Magnolias*
- On the death of a child and the desire for revenge:
  - ★★★★ *In the Bedroom*
- On choosing how to live one's life:
  - ★★★★ *The Bucket List*
  - ★★★★ *A River Runs through It*

## ONLINE SELF-HELP

- On learning about bereavement and correcting faulty thinking:
  - ★★★ *eCouch* ecouch.anu.edu.au

## INTERNET RESOURCES

- On advice on grief and loss:
  - ★★★★ *Grief & Loss* www.aarp.org/relationships/grief-loss
- On information and links on end-of-life care:
  - ★★★★★ *Growth House* www.growthhouse.org
  - ★★★★ *Hospice Net* www.hospicenet.org

menopause; and (4) limbo losses, such as awaiting medical tests, going through a lawsuit, and having a loved one missing in action. The presentation is unusual for a self-help book. Poetry, common sense, and psychological advice are interwoven throughout more than a hundred very brief topics that are organized according to the categories of understanding loss, surviving, healing, and growing. Topics include it's OK to feel, tomorrow will come, seek the comfort of others, touching and hugging, do the mourning now, when counseling or therapy might be helpful, nutrition, remaining distraught is no proof of love, pray, meditate, contemplate, keep a journal, take stock of the good, and your happiness is up to you. This has been a highly successful book, selling more than 2 million copies. The content is clear, succinct, and helpful, and it covers a vast range of situations involving loss. It has helped people cope with many types of loss.

★★★★★ *When Bad Things Happen to Good People* (1981, reissued 1997) by Harold Kushner. New York: Schocken.

Rabbi Kushner provides a spiritual perspective on death, dying, and grief. He addresses the historic question: If God is just and all-powerful, why do good people suffer? Some conventional explanations of why bad things happen are that it's God's punishment for our sins,

God is teaching us a lesson, or it's all part of a divine plan that is beyond our comprehension. Kushner writes that God provides us with the strength to endure. Although theologically guided, this is not a book about God and theology but rather about one man's personal tragedy and his view of God, humans, and life, written in an informal and easy style. The mystery of tragedy is not answered, but readers are brought a little closer to accepting the mystery and, in turn, feel a little more comforted. A book for any adult, but especially for those experiencing the emotional and spiritual conflicts that accompany life's many tragedies. A highly regarded, bestselling source of solace.

★★★★★ *On Children and Death* (reprint ed., 1997) by Elisabeth Kübler-Ross. New York: Collier.

This internationally known thanatologist writes about how children and their parents can cope with death. Death is the culmination of life, the graduation, the goodbye before another hello, the great transition. The material in this book represents a decade of working with dying children of all ages, their families, and friends. Kübler-Ross advises not to shield surviving children from the pains of death, but to let them share to the extent that they can. Among the topics addressed are death's influence on having other children, the spiritual aspects of working with dying children, and attending funerals. A valuable 4-star book for the general public, particularly for people caring for a dying child.

★★★★★ *How to Go on Living When Someone You Love Dies* (1991) by Therese Rando. New York: Bantam.

Originally published as *Grieving* in 1988, this book advises people about ways to grieve effectively when someone they love dies. Rando believes that there is no wrong or right way to grieve because people are so different. She describes a variety of ways to grieve and encourages readers to select the coping strategy best for them. Part I, Learning about Grief, identifies what grief is, how it affects people, what factors influence grief, and how women and men experience grief differently. Part II, Grieving Different Forms of Death, explains how grief often varies depending on what caused the death. Part III, Grieving and Your Family, addresses the inevitable family reorganization following a family member's death and how to cope with the death of specific family members: spouse, adult loss of a parent, adult loss of a sibling, and loss of a child. Part IV, Resolving Your Grief, offers specific recommendations for getting through bereavement rituals and funerals, including information about funeral arrangements and talking about loss to others. Part V, Getting Additional Help, explains how to find effective professional and self-help groups. This 5-star resource is an excellent self-help book for learning how to cope with the death of a loved one. There are no pat, overgeneralized suggestions on how to grieve. Rando covers a variety of grief circumstances and dispenses easy-to-understand, practical advice for each.

★★★★ *The Grief Recovery Handbook: A Step-by-Step Program for Moving beyond Loss* (1988) by John W. James and Frank Cherry. New York: Harper & Row.

The coauthors stress that grief is a growth process. In this book, acceptance of grief is presented as a positive reaction to loss that helps prepare the griever for recovery. The five stages of grief are gaining awareness, accepting responsibility, identifying recovery communications, taking action, and moving beyond loss. This book is for adults who are dealing with the approaching reality of death or in the process of dealing with loss. Although it received a 4-star rating in the national studies, its rating was high enough for 5 stars, but insufficient numbers of experts were familiar with it. A fine, practical resource.

★★★★ *Life Lessons* (2000) by Elisabeth Kübler-Ross and David Kessler. New York: Simon & Schuster.

The two authors write poignantly and passionately about life lessons, the ultimate truths that are the secrets to life itself. Kübler-Ross wanted this, her declared last book, to be about life and living, not death and dying. Each chapter includes richly described stories of people who experienced one of these life lessons. The perspective of the book might best be conveyed by citing some of the messages of life stories. On love: If you are loved by many, surely you would love yourself—but alas this is often not true. On relationships: We think we have relationships with relatively few people, but we have relationships with everybody we meet. On power: Power is not derived from position in life or money, but from authenticity, strength, integrity, and grace externalized. On the final lesson: Michelangelo said that beautiful sculptures were already there inside the stones. He simply removed the excess.

★★★★ *Talking about Death: A Dialogue between Parent and Child* (3rd ed., 1991) by Earl Grollman. Boston: Beacon.

This brief book (about 100 pages) is appropriate for children of all faiths. It consists of dialogues between parents and children and is divided into two main parts: The Children's Read-Along, which uses simple language so that even 5- to 9-year-olds can understand its messages about death and dying; and The Parent's Guide to Talking about Death, which provides answers for children's anticipated questions about death. Parents are urged to be straightforward with their children and are also helped to come to terms with their own feelings of loss. Highly regarded by our mental health experts, it received a 4-star rating and is a solid self-help resource.

★★★★ *Learning to Say Good-By* (1976) by Eda LeShan. New York: Macmillan.

This book was written to help children cope with the death of a parent. LeShan believes that children are resilient and can live through anything as long as they are told the truth and are allowed to share their suffering with loved ones. The book is a letter to children from LeShan, and it helps children understand what they are probably feeling, what their surviving parent is probably feeling, and why family members are behaving so strangely. Topics addressed include what happens immediately following a parent's death, feelings of grief, recovering, and how death teaches us about life. Although written for children, *Learning to Say Good-By* can help a surviving parent better understand children's feelings during this time of emotional upheaval. In our death-avoiding culture, LeShan's message is an important one: Children should be allowed to see our grief and should have the privilege of expressing their own grief in their own time. LeShan is an excellent writer, and she sensitively communicates with children.

★★★★ *Working It Through* (1982) by Elisabeth Kübler-Ross. New York: Macmillan.

An earlier Kübler-Ross book on death and grieving, *Working It Through* is based on workshops for people dealing with death, people who are terminally ill, people who have lost a loved one, and people who are involved with the dying. Sensitive photographs by Mal Warshaw complement the personal and emotional stories. The narratives cover a wide range of grieving experiences, such as emotions as our friends, the significance of music, the loss of a child, suicide, and spiritual awareness. A book especially for those touched by death or wishing to understand the dying process more fully.

★★★★　*Recovering from the Loss of a Child* (1982) by Katherine Donnelly. New York: Macmillan.

This book tells parents and other family members how to cope with the death of a child. It features excerpts from interviews with parents and siblings of children who died from illness, accident, and suicide. Part I describes family members' and friends' experiences with grief. Part II is devoted to organizations that help bereaved families. A basic theme of the book is that the loss of a child of any age is tragic and a terrible loss for all members of the family. This 4-star book presents a sensitive portrayal of a family's struggle to cope with the loss of a child; there is also an extensive list of support organizations.

★★★★　*Helping Children Grieve* (1991) by Theresa Huntley. Minneapolis: Augsburg Fortress.

As the title suggests, this book is about helping children cope with death—their own and the death of a loved one. Huntley presents a developmental approach: she begins by discussing how children under 3 years of age understand death, and then describes how death is perceived by children aged 3 to 6 years, 6 to 10 years, 10 to 12 years, and in adolescence. Huntley says that children of different ages have different thoughts about the nature of death. For example, toddlers come to understand death as an extension of "all gone," while 10-year-olds often view a loved one's death as a punishment for some misdeed. Advice is given on how to talk about death with children, and common behaviors and feelings children show when faced with death are discussed. Adults are advised to encourage children to ask them questions about death and to answer these questions as honestly as possible. This 4-star resource gives adults sound, clear advice about helping children cope with their own death or the death of a loved one.

★★★★　*Staring at the Sun* (2009) by Irvin D. Yalom. San Francisco, CA: Jossey-Bass.

Psychiatrist Irving Yalom is no stranger to ideas that throw us into self-reflective and introspective states only to emerge with greater awareness of the human experience. Drawing upon his profound understanding of his patients and himself, he offers us the insight that terror of death (or death anxiety) is an element of our being much more so than we think. The purpose of his book is to help the reader overcome death anxiety and, in the process, discover the importance of awakening to each moment of life and of developing compassion for self and for others. Yalom discusses his own process of dealing with death anxiety and offers advice to psychotherapists working with patients in this realm.

**Recommended**

★★★　*A Time to Say Good-Bye: Moving Beyond Loss* (1996) by Mary McClure Goulding. Watsonville, CA: Papier-Mache.

In this book, a psychotherapist recounts her own journey of mourning the death of her husband. Goulding shares what she has learned in her years of experience, covering such topics as grief, loneliness, and retirement unshared with the mate whom she worked beside for so long. The book is her narrative of her 3½ years of mourning at her own speed. She speaks about the love of family, friends, and community and the love of self that nurtured her and still supports her today. She no longer defines herself solely by whom she lost. For widows and widowers working out feelings of mourning and at the same time going on with living, this book can be encouraging and a reminder to be patient and loving to themselves. Highly rated but not well known by mental health professionals.

★★★   *Living through Personal Crisis* (1984) by Ann Stearns. Chicago: Thomas More.

This self-help resource provides advice about coping with many different kinds of loss, especially the death of a loved one. Using case studies to document her ideas, Stearns stresses that it is common for the bereaved to blame themselves and that the grieving person will undoubtedly experience such physical symptoms as aches and pains or eating and sleeping problems. Stearns advises readers not to hide their feelings but to get them out in the open, to be good to themselves, and to surround themselves with caring people. Stearns suggests when to seek professional help, how to find it, and how to evaluate progress. She closes the book with the image of a bird rising from the ashes as a metaphor for overcoming the sense of loss, but she reminds readers that their scars will never completely disappear. An appendix answers commonly asked questions about grieving. This book provides a good overview of how grief works in variety of loss circumstances (loss of limb, rape, loss of personal possessions in a fire, as well as the death of a loved one).

★★★   *Sudden Infant Death: Enduring the Loss* (1991) by John DeFrain, Linda Ernst, Deanne Jakub, and Jacque Taylor. Lexington, MA: Heath.

Sudden infant death (SIDS) occurs when an infant stops breathing, usually during the night, and dies suddenly without apparent cause. SIDS is the major cause of infant death from birth to 1 year of age. The tragic loss of a baby to SIDS affects families in many ways, and it is the authors' intention to help these families recapture the meaning and direction of their lives. The book's contents are based on interviews with 392 mothers, fathers, and siblings who have directly experienced the devastation of SIDS. The book recounts stories of the day the baby died and how parents mistakenly feel an overwhelming sense of guilt that their baby died of neglect. Grief symptoms, the effects of SIDS on marital relationships, and the suffering of grandparents are also covered. Suggestions are given for how friends and family members can be supportive. The fear of having another child and having it die is dealt with at length. This 3-star book provides extensive knowledge and personal stories about SIDS. The book also will prove helpful to friends of a family who experience SIDS, providing them with knowledge and support strategies.

★★★   *On Death and Dying* (1969) by Elisabeth Kübler-Ross. New York: Macmillan.

This bestseller is about facing one's own death and about negotiating the stages of dying. In the 1960s, Kübler-Ross and her students studied terminally ill patients to learn how they faced and coped with the crisis of their own impending death. Kübler-Ross and her staff interviewed 200 patients, focusing on them as human beings rather than bodies to be treated. Kübler-Ross concluded that people go through five stages as they face death:

1. Denial and isolation: The person denies that death is really going to take place.
2. Anger: The dying person's denial can no longer be maintained and gives way to anger, resentment, rage, and envy.
3. Bargaining: The person develops the hope that somehow death can be postponed or delayed.
4. Depression: The person accepts the certainty of death but is unhappy about it.
5. Acceptance: The person develops a sense of peace about accepting the inevitable and often wants to be left alone.

Kübler-Ross presents the five stages in considerable detail and discusses the effects of impending death on the dying person's family. Suggestions for therapy with the terminally ill are included. *On Death and Dying* received a 3-star rating in our studies, just missing the 4-star category. The book was one of the most frequently rated in our first study: 355 mental health professionals evaluated it. It is a classic in the field of death and dying, and Kübler-Ross's approach has helped millions of people cope effectively with impending death. Critics of the book say that no one has been able to confirm that people go through the stages of dying in the order Kübler-Ross proposes, but Kübler-Ross feels that she has been misinterpreted, saying that she never intended the stages to be taken as an invariant sequence toward death. Her other two books reviewed in this chapter fared better in our national studies.

★★★ *Gentle Willow: A Story for Children about Dying* (2004) by Joyce C. Mills. Washington, DC: Magination Press.

This story is written for children who may lose a special person but also for children who may not survive their own illness. A willow tree is ill and its friends, Amanda and the squirrel, search for a way to make the tree better. This metaphor for loss displays feelings of anger and sadness but introduces compassion and love for the willow and the value of caring when an impending loss occurs. The illustrations are an essential part of the story in the portrayal of the changing emotions of Amanda and the love her friends have for each other.

★★★ *Saying Goodbye to the Pet You Love* (2002) by Lorrie A. Greene and Jacquelyn Landis. Oakland, CA: New Harbinger.

Written by a psychologist who specializes in bereavement, this self-help book is both touching and informative. It is written for adults, children, elderly, and those who have working dogs. The author recognizes that the love, attachment, and myriad of feelings we have for our pets are not inferior to those feelings we have for fellow humans. She notes that when people are insensitive to the loss of a pet, the diminishment of the pet is not what is seen but the "socially sanctioned insensitivity to human suffering." Some of the topics discussed include feeling guilty, the questions of quality of life, making a final decision, the special role in human lives of working dogs, coping for children, and resources for the elderly. The author has anticipated or rather experienced all of the emotions we have at these stages of relationship with our pets and shares them with us in a sensitive and caring way.

★★★   *How We Die* (1994) by Sherwin B. Nuland. New York: Knopf.

The author attempts to show that death with dignity is a myth and talks about the painful realities of death. His intention is to depict death in its biological and emotional reality, as seen by those who are witness to it and felt by those who experience it. His hope is that frank discussion will help us deal with the aspects of death that frighten us the most. Nuland also talks about responsibility and choices that we have as we exit our own lives. Ultimately, the dignity that we see in dying must grow out of the dignity with which we have lived our lives. For those interested in the physiological process of death, and the accompanying emotions, this is an informative and insightful book.

★★★   *The Widow's Handbook* (1988) by Charlotte Foehner and Carol Cozart. Golden, CO: Fulcrum.

Following the deaths of their husbands, Foehner began studying financial investment and tax preparation, and Cozart started her first full-time job. The book provides emotional support for widows, offers suggestions for rearing children, tells widows how to care for themselves, and discusses changes in relationships, but its main emphasis is on the financial and procedural issues widows are likely to encounter. Making funeral arrangements, selecting an attorney and a financial advisory team, performing an executor's duties, filing claims for life insurance and survivor benefits, getting credit and checking accounts in order, and maintaining a house and auto are some of the practical topics covered. The authors include sample letters widows need to write and examine questions that crop up. This 3-star book is very good at what it attempts—providing widows with sound advice about financial and procedural matters—but it includes only minimal advice about the psychological and emotional dimensions of coping with the loss of a husband.

### Diamonds in the Rough

♦   *Ambiguous Loss: Learning to Live with Unresolved Grief* (1999) by Pauline Boss. Cambridge, MA: Harvard University Press.

Ambiguous loss is defined as one of two conditions: (1) individuals are physically absent but psychologically present, as in the case of MIAs, kidnapping victims, and immigrants who leave their families for better lives or (2) individuals who are physically present but psychologically absent, as in the case of those with Alzheimer's, addictions, chronic mental illness, and traumatic brain injury. The grief of loved ones is frozen and cannot be resolved. Family therapy is described as a means of working with the family in making decisions in the face of uncertain and incomplete information, of understanding that ups and downs become more accentuated and frequent, and of the value of family members hearing each other out. Boss discusses resolving loss and the difficulty in making sense of it. The hopeful message conveyed is that ambiguity can make people less dependent on stability and more tolerant of spontaneity and uncertainty. The author calls this concept the "benefits of doubt." This book accurately identifies and sensitively portrays the struggles of those living with ambiguous loss. As with the following three books in this chapter, *Ambiguous Loss* was very favorably rated but infrequently rated in our studies, thus achieving a Diamond in the Rough designation.

- *When Children Grieve* (2001) by John W. James and Russell Friedman with Leslie Landon Matthews. New York: HarperCollins.

How adults can help children deal with loss is the purpose of this book. Losses include death of grandparents, death of a pet, a major move, divorce of parents, injury to the child, or death of a friend or relative. Six myths keep adults and children stuck in grief: don't feel bad, replace the loss, grieve alone, be strong, keep busy, and time heals all wounds. These concepts form the foundation for a stepwise instruction through grieving and recovery. The authors define completion of a grieving experience as communicating the undelivered emotions that attach to any relationship that changes or ends. Adults are urged to help children identify those relationships that are incomplete, and an emotional energy checklist is provided for guidance in talking through the energy-laden experiences. A 74-item questionnaire is offered to help adults understand how they are communicating with children about loss.

- *The Needs of the Dying* (2007) by David Kessler. New York: HarperCollins.

Accompanying a loved one to the point of death is described in caring and sensitive concepts through the work the author has done with the bereaved and with patients facing death. The movement of death from the home to the hospital and increasingly to hospice give us a background on how we treat the dying process. Kessler describes how we treat the dying by keeping information from them, whispering to others, and even stepping out of the room every time a decision has to be made, which in one case resulted in the loved one calling out, "I'm not dead yet. Don't treat me as though I were." The author reminds us that every person is still living until he or she dies and should be treated as such, with his or her needs being a priority.

- *Grieving As Well As Possible* (2010) by Mardi Horowitz. Sausalito, CA: GreyHawk.

Psychiatrist Horowitz sensitively discusses the death of a loved one, awareness of the many ways one will be affected by that loss, and the multitude of ways one can cope with it. The process from sudden bad news to rebuilding self-coherence is presented in personalized stories. Interestingly, the author says that there are "official" stages of grief but people should think in terms of their own stages and that they will skip around and may need to go back to an earlier stage. Attending to oneself first and finding an authentic listener are emphasized here. Helping children and teens deal with the loss when they can't really tell you what they need, dealing with others, and feeling guilty for surviving are important topics addressed thoroughly in the book. Most importantly, being responsive to oneself and children, expecting the unpredictable, and going easy on oneself and loved ones are the valuable take-home messages.

### Strongly Not Recommended

† *Widowed* (1990) by Joyce Brothers. New York: Simon & Schuster.
† *Final Exit: The Practicalities of Self-Deliverance and Assisted Suicide for the Dying* (1991) by Derek Humphrey. Eugene, OR: Hemlock Society.

## ■ AUTOBIOGRAPHIES

### Strongly Recommended

★★★★★ *A Grief Observed* (1961) by C. S. Lewis. New York: Seabury.

This is a poignant tale of loss and spiritual search following the death of a spouse. The movie *Shadowlands* is based on it. Both the book and the movie describe the humanizing of Oxford don and famed writer C. S. Lewis following the death of his wife, Joy Gresham, from cancer. Originally published under the pseudonym of N. W. Clerk just before Lewis's own death, *A Grief Observed* reveals the inner turmoil of his grief. The author says that he wrote these memoirs as a "defense against total collapse, a safety valve." This 5-star autobiography presents profound human experience from the spiritual perspective of a gifted writer. It offers no advice for recovery but presents a moving description of human vulnerability. Lewis's personal loss will benefit many readers, especially those who feel themselves distant from ordinary human affairs.

★★★★★ *Letting Go: Morrie's Reflections on Living While Dying* (1997) by Morrie Schwartz. New York: Dell.

Also published under the title *Morrie: In His Own Words*, this book describes the last years of sociologist Morrie Schwartz after he learned at age 75 that he had Lou Gehrig's disease, which is progressive and incurable. Schwartz became a participant-observer as his physical abilities declined, tape-recording his observations, impressions, and memories. He became known to a wider public after appearing three times on Ted Koppel's TV show *Nightline* to discuss his life, dying, and Lou Gehrig's disease. The book is a wise, compassionate account of living as a dying person.

★★★★★ *The Year of Magical Thinking* (2007) by Joan Didion. New York: Knox Doubleday.

"Life changes fast. Life changes in an instant. You sit down for dinner and life as you know it ends." Those lines begin this well-known author's account of the unexpected death of her husband and collaborator of 40 years, the noted writer John Gregory Dunne, at the dinner table while their child lay gravely ill in hospital. "Magical thinking" is her name for the temporary craziness that overcame her, in which Didion imagines her husband isn't dead, still talks to her, will be coming home. She knows that this isn't true but the craziness is part of her coming to terms with what happened. She is realistic about her own failure to accept reality. She recounts all the tricks and circumlocutions she used to resist acceptance of her husband's death. She wrote the book with brutal honesty while she was still in the experience rather than waiting for recovery. Writing the book within the first year of her husband's death was part of the recovery process. The agony continued as Didion immersed herself in her daughter's deteriorating condition. There is probably more detail than most readers will need about medical procedures, but this is a book of loss, vulnerability, and grief for the ages.

★★★★★ *Death Be Not Proud: A Memoir* (1998) by John Gunther. New York: HarperCollins.

Classic, moving story of Johnny Gunther, a promising 16-year-old diagnosed with a serious brain tumor. Written by his father, it is a chronicle of hope as the tumor shrinks, pain as it resumes growing, the nobility of the struggle, Johnny's optimism and patience during a succession of invasive treatments, and courage as he says his final good-byes. An inspiring and affirming account, especially good for parents and for teens. The key message is to live life to the fullest as Johnny had done.

★★★★ *The Wheel of Life: A Memoir of Living and Dying* (1998) by Elisabeth Kübler-Ross & Todd Gold. New York: Touchstone.

Elisabeth Kübler-Ross, the noted authority on dying and promoter of the hospice movement, recounts her life growing up in Switzerland, becoming a physician and psychiatrist, moving to the United States, and conducting her pioneering studies of death and dying. Her research initially encountered considerable opposition because, she maintains, people refuse to accept their own mortality. Having had several strokes, she is prepared to face her end and considers this to be her final book. There are also sections more controversial than the description of her career and strokes, and these deal with near-death and out-of-the-body experiences, communicating and channeling spirits, and other aspects of the paranormal.

★★★★ *Motherless Daughter* (1995) by Hope Edelman. New York: Delta.

The author was 17 when she lost her mother. After finishing college and working as a journalist, Edelman realized that she was still grieving. She turned this experience first into a magazine article and then into this book, which attracted a large amount of media attention. Often described as the first book specifically on loss of a mother, *Motherless Daughter* discusses the experience of women who lost their mothers either as children or as adults.

**Recommended**

★★★ *After the Death of a Child: Living with Loss through the Years* (1998) by Ann Finkbeiner. Baltimore: Johns Hopkins University Press.

The author's only child died in 1987. She describes her grief and the methods she used to cope with the loss. She interviewed other parents who had lost children to collect additional material for this book. Highly rated, but infrequently so, in our national studies. Had it been better known, *After the Death of a Child* would have probably emerged as a 5-star selection.

★★★ *Lament for a Son* (1987) by Nicholas Wolterstorff. Grand Rapids, MI: Eerdmans Publishing.

With brutal honesty, Yale philosopher Nicholas Wolterstorff puts his grief in all its confusing detail on paper in this small and moving book. He lost his 25-year-old son to a tragic mountain-climbing accident and wrote this heartfelt book to give voice to his grief. The autobiography makes readers feel part of a community of mourners, particularly for those who have lost a loved one and don't have the right words to speak. Wolterstorff has the words: "And now he's gone. That future which I embraced to myself has been destroyed. He slipped out of my arms. For twenty-five years I guarded and sustained and encouraged him with these hands of mine, helping him to grow and become a man of his own. Then he slipped out and was smashed." "Instead of rowing, I float. The joy that comes my way I savor. But the seeking, the clutching, the aiming, is gone.....What the world gives, I still accept. But what it promises, I no longer reach for. I've become an alien in the world, shyly touching it as if it's not mine. I don't belong anymore." Wolterstorff does not hide his memories or try to "get over" them; they are witness to his love for his son.

★★★   *A Widow's Story: A Memoir* (2011) by Joyce Carol Oates. New York: HarperCollins.

For most readers, this will not be a comforting self-help book. True, one would not expect this from this famous author of 50 dark novels. In elegant but not elegiac prose, Oates tries to make sense of the sudden loss of her husband of 48 years, writer and editor Raymond Smith, who was admitted to a noted hospital for what seemed like a routine case of pneumonia and acquired an infection that killed him. There is wisdom, insight, and good writing but not relief to be found in these pages. The book shifts back and forth in time as she faces old memories and finds new routines. Oates describes the shock, anguish, rage, and disorientation of widowhood; she became preoccupied with suicide and started using antidepressant medication. At one point, she considered having a T-shirt imprinted with:

YES MY HUSBAND DIED, YES I AM VERY SAD, YES YOU ARE KIND TO OFFER CONDOLENCES, NOW CAN WE CHANGE THE SUBJECT?

She found relief in continuing to teach her classes and taking over the garden and other communal household tasks that had been done by her husband.

### Diamonds in the Rough

◆   *Eric* (2000) by Doris Lund. New York: HarperCollins Perennial.

The death of a child isn't easy to understand or write about. *Eric* is the reissue of a classic book made into a movie in the 1970s about a vibrant and athletic 17-year-old diagnosed with leukemia. Written by his mother, it chronicles Eric's struggle to avoid despair and make the most of the remaining time, to live his dying, and sensitively portrays the pain of the family as they pass through stages of shock, disbelief, rage, grief, and acceptance. A moving and cathartic book for anyone who has a family member with leukemia or is faced with a child's death.

◆   *Hannah's Gift: Lessons from a Life Fully Lived* (2002) by Maria Housden. New York: Doubleday Dell.

Beautifully written story of a 3-year-old girl diagnosed with terminal cancer, the succession of unsuccessful treatments, her death, and the family's coming to terms. Hannah was an outgoing, excited child whose infectious curiosity and joy changed the lives of those who met her. Hannah demanded to be treated in the hospital as an individual, to wear her Mary Janes in the operating room, and to know the names of her physicians. The book is about child as teacher and about a parent's pain, joy, and dignity when faced with the incomprehensible. A touching, uplifting book.

## ■ FILMS

### Strongly Recommended

★★★★★ *Ordinary People* (1980) directed by Robert Redford. R rating. 124 minutes.

This is a movie about grieving and the denial of grief. A privileged family loses its prize son, and the parents' withdrawal becomes too extreme for their other son. In his isolation, he cuts his wrists and is hospitalized for months. When he returns, nothing has changed. His father's cheerfulness is all pretense; his mother's self-preoccupation is a stone wall. This stirring but ultimately hopeful film, winner of a bushel of Academy Awards, tragically illustrates how some families respond psychologically and interpersonally to loss and how the stress of loss makes them more of what they were before.

★★★★★ *Corrina, Corrina* (1994) directed by Jesse Nelson. PG rating. 115 minutes.

A light-hearted and warm-hearted film focusing on a withdrawn 8-year-old child whose mother has died. Her father hires Corrina, a sassy housekeeper played by Whoopi Goldberg, who coaxes the daughter back to life and shows the survivors a whole new way of living. A valuable resource for demonstrating children's reactions toward death and for reminding us all that life can again blossom following the death of a family member.

★★★★ *The Bucket List* (2008) directed by Rob Reiner. PG-13 rating. 97 minutes.

This film follows two men, Edward Cole (Jack Nicholson) and Carter Chambers (Morgan Freeman), who hold nothing in common but their terminal lung cancer. However, the unlikely match decides to leave the hospital to complete their life dreams, the eponymous "bucket list." Carter's cancer progresses to his brain, and he dies on the operating table. At Carter's funeral, Edward, whose cancer is now in remission, delivers a eulogy stating that the little time they spent together was the best of his life. Soon after, Edward decides to complete the rest of Carter's bucket list, including reunification with his own long-estranged daughter. Warm and wise, if a bit formulaic, in which the prospect of death forces us to rediscover ourselves and what truly matters.

★★★★ *Steel Magnolias* (1990) directed by Herbert Ross. PG rating. 118 minutes.

This is both a woman's picture and a picture of women. Six friends joke, gossip, and support each other for several years in a small Louisiana town in the early 1980s. They cry and fight and make up and get their hair done at the beauty parlor that is the center of their lives. When a tragic death strikes, their grieving is wonderful to watch: character tells, and strength is required. This may be an excellent movie to show survival in the face of tragedy, although the comedy is the main focus of the movie.

★★★★ *In the Bedroom* (2001) directed by Todd Field. R rating. 130 minutes.

The Fowlers (Sissy Spacek, Tom Wilkinson) are a respectable, upper-middle-class Maine couple whose 21-year-old-son falls in love with a young woman separated but not yet divorced from her husband. The separated husband is pathologically jealous and violent, resulting in the murder of the Fowlers' son. The unthinkable tragedy tears the Fowlers apart, and the film traces their loss, rage, and quest for revenge. The grief is palpable; Wilkinson's character expresses more loss and helplessness than any words could ever convey. *In the Bedroom* is wrenching emotional drama, as sensitive and accurate a portrayal of grief for a child as ever filmed. The movie was nominated for an Oscar for best picture, and its two main characters were also nominated for best actress and best actor.

★★★★   *A River Runs through It* (1988) directed by Robert Redford. PG rating. 123 minutes.

This movie is about how one can chose to live one's life. In the words of movie critic Roger Ebert, "Fly-fishing stands for life in this movie. If you can learn to do it correctly, to read the river and the fish and yourself, and to do what needs to be done without one wasted motion, you will have attained some of the grace and economy needed to live a good life. If you can do it and understand that the river, the fish and the whole world are God's gifts to use wisely, you will have gone the rest of the way."

★★★★   *Truly, Madly, Deeply* (1991) directed by Anthony Minghella. PG rating. 105 minutes.

A London couple is truly, madly, and deeply in love, but then one of them dies. The spouse is heartbroken, left alone in a house filled with rats and repairmen, until her love reappears as a ghost. This romantic comedy centers on the memory of a loved one and ignoring life for the dead. An intelligent and realistic film for people who have suffered the loss of a true love and those who need to let the past go in order to move forward.

**Recommended**

★★★   *Unstrung Heroes* (1995) directed by Diane Keaton. PG rating. 93 minutes.

A dramatic comedy in which a boy coming of age grapples with a dying mother and rebels against his father. He goes to live with his two pleasantly crazy uncles, who support him through his ordeal and help him thrive. The mother is very loving, but sadly abandons him by dying. A quirky yet moving film, probably best as a self-help resource for those who have relocated following a parent's death.

★★★   *My Life* (1993) directed by Bruce Joel Rubin. PG-13 rating. 112 minutes.

A successful advertising executive whose wife is pregnant learns that he is dying and doesn't know how to deal with the unfinished business in his life (particularly his feelings of anger toward his family) or the fact that he may never see his child. He is able to reach out to his unborn child by making videotapes. His wife is shown as a pillar of strength, his doctors as automatons. There are many truthful and poignant moments in this unabashed tearjerker, but contrivances ultimately take over, especially toward the end. The film could be used to illustrate loss, grief, and unfinished business if the responses to them are not taken too realistically.

★★★   *Rabbit Hole* (2010) directed by John Cameron Mitchell. PG-13 rating. 91 minutes.

A married couple mourns the death of their 4-year-old son, and the mother, Becca, decides to rid her life of anything related to her son. Husband Howie, on the other hand, becomes angry with Becca's behavior and desires to have another child. The two attend a self-help group and choose different paths in their lives. Becca becomes fixated on the comic book artist who drove the car that killed her son, while Howie finds a sympathetic ear in a fellow support group member. They reunite in new undertakings and begin to accept the death of their son. The film demonstrates that grief takes many paths and that spending time apart may lead to a thriving relationship.

★★★    *The Accidental Tourist* (1989) directed by Lawrence Kasdan. PG rating. 121 minutes.

On the surface, this acclaimed film is about a man who is shattered by the death of his son and withdraws from any emotional contact. His wife leaves him, and he lives a safe but routine life until he meets a kooky, assertive woman who draws him out of his shell. Sounds like a typical Hollywood romance. This film could illustrate a style of coping with death and its negative consequences. It also shows how the man brings himself finally to choose between isolation and routine in his shell or love and risk in a new relationship. The film can be used with couples because it illustrates how the nature of the man's marriage, calm but distant, is too weak to support the couple's needs after their tragedy. The wife needs to talk, but the husband needs to be alone and deny his feelings.

★★★    *The Summer of '42* (1971) directed by Robert Mulligan. PG rating. 103 minutes.

A nostalgic look back at an adolescent boy's infatuation with an older woman who shares a sexual experience with him after her husband is killed in World War II and then disappears. The film illustrates how she, desperate for companionship in her despair over her husband's absence and then his sudden and tragic death, reaches out to the boy.

★★★    *The Lion King* (1995) directed by Roger Allers and Robert Minkoff. G rating. 87 minutes.

Sure, it is a cartoon, and one without people in it, too. But the story is a wonderful one of how courage, assumption of adult responsibilities, and friends can triumph over loss, evil, and treachery. The evil Scar has the king killed and drives the young prince out so that he can become king. The prince lives a carefree life until his father's ghost commands him to return and seek revenge. The film can illustrate how an individual need not be defeated by deaths and losses and can prevail by "growing up" and taking on social responsibilities.

★★★    *My Girl* (1992) directed by Howard Zieff. PG rating. 102 minutes.

An 11-year-old girl has become hypochondriacal and as eccentric as her father. He copes with her mother's death in childbirth by isolation and contact only with the dead; she copes by a preoccupation with death, the meaning of life, and her imaginary diseases. She becomes close to a boy and shares puppy love, philosophical questions, and much of her time. When he dies, she is submerged in guilt—she feels like she killed him and her mother—and she is alone. Through her grieving and sharing with others, she develops new friends and accepts her father's new girlfriend. She struggles and achieves a normal (early) adolescent's life. While imperfect, this film can be valuable in suggesting the complexities of grief in families.

**Diamond in the Rough**

♦ *Moonlight Mile* (2002) directed by Brad Silberling. PG-13 rating. 146 minutes.

A couple loses their only daughter and embrace her fiancé as if he were their own child. He, in turn, begins a relationship with a woman mourning her boyfriend's three years as an MIA in the Vietnam conflict. Four people grieving death in their respective ways and learning about the bittersweet nature of human relationships. Mother Susan Sarandon's initial responses to the death of her daughter—burning self-help books on grief and complaining that she is angry at friends who offer sympathy and also angry at those who say nothing—will resonate with many viewers. Oscar-caliber acting by a fine cast in a telling tale of mourning and recovery.

**Not Recommended**

★★ *Message in a Bottle* (1999) directed by Luis Mandoki. PG-13 rating. 126 minutes.
★★ *Ghost* (1991) directed by Jerry Zucker. PG-13 rating. 122 minutes.

## ONLINE SELF-HELP

★★★ *eCouch* ecouch.anu.edu.au

This free bereavement and loss program provides youths with information and support during a loss. Through an interactive presentation, users initially learn about the bereavement process and then move on to learning to identify and correct their faulty thinking. The program also contains a workbook where users can practice skills and track their progress. The sequential modules integrate principles from cognitive therapy and meditation. The website is designed with a look and in a language comfortable for young users, but the programs will prove useful for users of all ages.

## INTERNET RESOURCES

**General Websites**

★★★★★ *Growth House* www.growthhouse.org

This rich site has thousands of articles covering end-of-life care, palliative medicine, and hospice care.

★★★★ *End of Life & Palliative Care* www.rwjf.org/en/topics/rwjf-topic-areas/end-of-life.html

A helpful website from the Robert Wood Johnson Foundation that is ideal for those who are searching for information about better care at the end of life.

★★★ *GriefNet* www.griefnet.org

This website offers a large resource directory, a few articles, and dozens of support groups.

★★★★ *The Compassionate Friends* www.compassionatefriends.org

This large nonprofit is for those who have lost a child. They publish many books and booklets (see "Resources") for the bereaved.

## Psychoeducational Materials

### Grieving

★★★★ *Life after Loss: Dealing with Grief* cmhc.utexas.edu/griefloss.html

An overview about grief and loss written for college students published by the University of Texas at Austin.

★★★ *Grief and Loss* www.counselingcenter.illinois.edu/?page_id=175

A set of guidelines suitable as a handout for explaining the nature and process of grief and loss.

★★★★ *Safe Crossings Foundation* www.safecrossingsfoundation.org

This site is for children who are facing the loss of a loved one. The website interactively explores many feelings and offers activities and ways to memorialize the loss.

★★★★ *Grief & Loss* www.aarp.org/relationships/grief-loss

A rather comprehensive site from the American Association of Retired Persons, there are many articles and resources found on this site.

★★★★ *End of Life* www.mayoclinic.com/health/end-of-life/MY00365

This in-depth resource from the Mayo Clinic offers a wealth of resources about end-of-life issues, including grief and coping with the loss of a loved one's life.

★★★★ *Coping with the Loss of a Pet* www.avma.org/public/PetCare/Pages/pet-loss.aspx

The pain associated with the death of a beloved pet is often underappreciated and under-responded to. The brochure "Making the Decision" is complete. Also useful is the brochure "Grief and Pet Loss" by Margaret Muns, DVM, at www.petloss.com/muns.htm

★★★ *Bereavement* www.rcpsych.ac.uk/expertadvice/problems/bereavement.aspx

A good overview leaflet about bereavement aimed at general readers.

★★★ *Mothers in Sympathy and Support* www.misschildren.org

The MISS Foundation is a nonprofit focused on providing support to grieving families, along with advocacy and education to help reduce infant and toddler deaths.

★★★    *WidowNet* www.widownet.org

The first three articles are helpful: "Dumb Remarks and Stupid Questions," "Getting through the Holidays," and "You Know You're Getting Better When…" You can also find a support group near you here.

### Dying
★★★★    *Caring Connections* www.caringinfo.org

The site offers articles about end-of-life issues, legal aspects, and state-specific advance directives.

★★★★    *End of Life Issues* www.acponline.org/patients_families/end_of_life_issues

This resource provided by the American College of Physicians offers a wealth of resources for consumers about end-of-life issues, including living with a life-threatening issue, dealing with pain, and making medical decisions for a loved one.

★★★★    *Funeral Consumers Alliance* www.funerals.org

A consumer-oriented site with lots of information to help make responsible and efficient choices about funerals, cemeteries, and caskets.

### Other Resources
★★★★    *Hospice Net* www.hospicenet.org

This site provides dozens of articles on end-of-life issues.

★★★    *A Heartbreaking Choice* www.aheartbreakingchoice.com

A website that offers resources, information, and support for women who have terminated a pregnancy due to the mother's health or a poor prenatal diagnosis, or for the health of another fetus.

## ▩ SUPPORT GROUPS

### Compassionate Friends

Phone: 877-969-0010
www.compassionatefriends.org
This is the major organization for parents who have lost a child.

### Concerns of Police Survivors (COPS)

Phone: 573-346-4911
www.nationalcops.org
This group was created to reach out to surviving families of America's law enforcement officers killed in the line of duty.

### Mothers Against Drunk Driving (MADD)

Phone: 800-ASK-MADD
madd.org/home
For victims of drunk drivers.

### Parents of Murdered Children

Phone: 513-721-5683
www.pomc.org

### Partnership for Caring: America's Voices for the Dying

Phone: 800-989-9455
www.partnershipforcaring.org
"The inventor of living wills in 1967, it is dedicated to fostering communication about complex end-of-life decisions. The nonprofit organization provides advance directives, counsels patients and families, trains professionals, advocates for improved laws, and offers a range of publications and services."

### Pet Loss Hotline

Phone: 877-394-CARE
www.vetmed.illinois.edu/CARE
"It's okay to love and miss your pet." Provides a support mechanism for grieving people who have experienced pet loss.

### SHARE Office (Pregnancy and Infant Loss Support)

Phone: 800-821-6819
www.nationalshareoffice.com

### Society of Military Widows

Phone: 800-842-3451
www.militarywidows.org

### TAPS (Tragedy Assistance Program for Survivors)

Phone: 800-959-TAPS
taps.org
"TAPS serves all those affected by a death in the line of military duty and works with parents, children, spouses, and friends."

# CHAPTER 19

# DEMENTIA/ALZHEIMER'S

The majority of older adults in the United States are living longer, more active lives, but some older adults are declining mentally and physically to the point of needing continuous help. Many of these older adults are suffering from dementia, which commonly refers to impairment in more than one aspect of cognitive functioning, always including memory dysfunction and personality alterations (Lezak, 1995).

By far the most prevalent and best known of the dementias is Alzheimer's disease, a progressive and irreversible brain disorder. It is characterized by a gradual deterioration in memory, reasoning, language, and physical functioning. About 19% of people 75 to 84 suffer from Alzheimer's. Rates of dementia increase exponentially with age; the consensus among scholars is that 30% of North Americans aged 85 and older are living with dementia (Gatz, 2007).

A family caring for a dementia patient assumes a great deal of responsibility. The condition typically begins so gradually that often the family is unaware that anything is wrong until work problems pile up or a sudden disruption in routine leaves the person disoriented, confused, and unable to deal with the unfamiliar situation. The first sign is usually a decline in recent memory. Families caring for loved ones diagnosed with dementia need to be educated and prepared to cope with a number of predictable and unpredictable behaviors. Family distress tends to be chronic and high. There will come a time when the family has to decide what level of care their family member needs and the most appropriate setting in which to provide that care.

In this chapter, we present the experts' consensual ratings and our brief descriptions of self-help books, autobiographies, and films on this crippling disease (Box 19.1). Listings of Internet resources and national support groups round out the resources.

## ■ SELF-HELP BOOKS

### Strongly Recommended

***** *The 36-Hour Day: A Family Guide to Caring for Persons with Alzheimer's Disease, Related Dementing Illness and Memory Loss in Later Life* (3rd ed., 1999) by Nancy Mace and Peter Rabins. Baltimore: Johns Hopkins University.

This book, now in its third edition, is a family guide to caring for persons with Alzheimer's and related diseases. The authors say that for those who care for a person with Alzheimer's

## BOX 19.1
## RECOMMENDATION HIGHLIGHTS

**SELF-HELP BOOKS**

■ For families caring for a person with Alzheimer's:

★★★★★ *The 36-Hour Day* by Nancy Mace and Peter Rabins

★★★ *The Hidden Victims of Alzheimer's Disease* by Steven Zarit et al.

♦ *When Your Loved One Has Alzheimer's* by David L. Carroll

♦ *A Caregiver's Guide to Alzheimer's Disease* by Patricia Callone et al.

**AUTOBIOGRAPHIES**

■ For moving accounts of caring for a spouse with Alzheimer's:

★★★★ *Elegy for Iris* by John Bayley

★★★ *The Diminished Mind* by Jean Tyler and Harry Anifantakis

■ Ongoing diary record of the early stages:

♦ *Alzheimer's from the Inside Out* by Richard Taylor

♦ *Losing my Mind* by Thomas DeBaggio

**FILMS**

■ For superb portrayals of Alzheimer's and its impact on the spouse:

★★★★★ *Iris*

★★★★★ *Away from Her*

★★★ *Do You Remember Love?*

■ For repairing relationships while a parent descends into dementia:

★★★ *Memories of Me*

**INTERNET RESOURCES**

■ For valuable information on Alzheimer's:

★★★★★ *The Alzheimer's Association* www.alz.org

★★★★ *Alzheimer's Disease* psychcentral.com/disorders/alzheimers

or related diseases, every day seems as if it is 36 hours long. This is a guide for the home care of older adults in the early and middle stages of these diseases. The family is assisted in recognizing the point beyond which home care is no longer enough and is guided in choosing a nursing home or other care facility. Various support groups that have been formed to help families with an Alzheimer's member are also described. This 5-star book is an excellent guide for families who have a relative suffering from Alzheimer's. It provides practical advice with specific examples that help readers learn how to care for an impaired relative on a day-to-day basis. *The 36-Hour Day* is one of the highest-rated self-help books in all of our national studies.

## Recommended

★★★   *The Hidden Victims of Alzheimer's Disease: Families under Stress* (1985) by Steven Zarit, Nancy K. Orr, and Judy M. Zarit. New York: New York University.

The authors offer families support and advice in caring for a person with Alzheimer's disease. Specific situations and interventions are addressed, including stealing, incontinence, asking repetitive questions, lowered sexual inhibitions, and inappropriate public behavior. Also covered are positive psychosocial approaches to dementia, causes of memory loss, and how to assess for dementia. The section on caring for the caregivers is especially good. This book has been written primarily for practitioners working with patients and their families in community settings. It may also serve the needs of family members working with organizations devoted to Alzheimer's disease. Besides recognizing and dealing with Alzheimer's disease, the book addresses individual counseling, family meetings, support groups, and special treatment concerns (e.g., drugs, placement, and patients without families). A valuable 3-star resource that would have received 4 stars had it been more frequently rated.

★★★   *The Alzheimer's Caregiver: Dealing with the Realities of Dementia* (1998) by Harriet Hodgson. Minneapolis: Chronimed.

The chronic and debilitating nature of Alzheimer's is sensitively captured in Hodgson's book. As an Alzheimer's patient's mental abilities deteriorate, the caregiver's responsibilities and emotional challenges escalate. The caregiver needs to learn how to cope with this consuming process and to care for himself or herself without guilt. Various problems covered in the book are home care, assisted living, anticipatory grief, legal complications, personal struggles, Alzheimer's depression, health-care costs, and the family system. Appendices provide self-assessment. This 3-star book is clearly and effectively aimed at caregivers.

## Diamonds in the Rough

♦   *When Your Loved One Has Alzheimer's: A Caregiver's Guide* (1989) by David L. Carroll. New York: Harper & Row.

The author covers a variety of Alzheimer's topics, notably understanding the disease, reviewing medical care and coverage, preparing the family home, maintaining the caregiver's emotional health, and getting help. The information and techniques in these pages are designed to be used on several levels—practical, psychological, and spiritual. Some of the day-to-day problems discussed in the book are the person's temper tantrums, incontinence pads, embarrassing scenes in public settings, motor difficulties, and impaired memory. This book is written expressly for caregivers as a how-to manual. Favorably rated but not widely known by the mental health experts in our studies, thus meriting the Diamond in the Rough designation.

♦   *A Caregiver's Guide to Alzheimer's Disease* (2005) by Patricia Callone, Barbara Vasiloff, Roger Brumback, Janaan Manternach, and Connie Kudlacek. New York: Demos.

The development of dementia/Alzheimer's, a broad range of information, and a complete resource guide are the primary components of this comprehensive book on dementia/

Alzheimer's. The explanation of dementia/Alzheimer's is not technically written but is able to convey just what happens within the brain during the disease development. Particularly valuable is the segmenting of stages of the disease so that typical symptoms are explained with examples of how these deficits play out, for example between an adult daughter and her father, at each of the stages. The areas affected by the disease—memory, language, social skills, judgment/reasoning, ambulation—are followed throughout each stage. The book format is very clear and useful. The information section discusses frequently asked questions, when to tell others, legal concerns, living environments, changing roles, and the topics that any caretaker involved with this disease will need to know. The book gives the reader valued information and a true sense of what needs to be known and understood.

♦ *Learning to Speak Alzheimer's: A Groundbreaking Approach for Everyone Dealing with the Disease* (2004) by Joanne Koenig Coste. New York: First Mariner.

Positive and "can do" are not words that are typically associated with taking care of a person with Alzheimer's, but this self-help book does. The author's husband, at an early age, developed Alzheimer's, and this book traces her path from frustration and despair to comfort and a respectful environment. The foundation of her success may reside in her five tenets of care for Alzheimer's: make the physical environment work for the person; realize that communication, although altered, is still possible; capitalize on the remaining skills; make the behavior changes that allow living in the person's world; and enrich the person's life. An extensive list of foods that are more accommodating for those with Alzheimer's is given in the back of the book. This approach does give the reader some sense of regained control in a world where nothing has been under control.

## ■ AUTOBIOGRAPHIES

### Highly Recommended

★★★★ *Elegy for Iris* (1999) by John Bayley. New York: St. Martin's.

A moving account of the literary courtship and unconventional union between Oxford don and literary critic John Bayley and renowned philosopher and novelist Dame Iris Murdoch. Using his talents for elegant prose, Bayley recounts his wife's descent into unknowing darkness and the caretaking role he was forced to take, in which he performed nobly. An impressive book not only for the perceptive account of Alzheimer's, but also because the author and the subject are important literary figures. This beautiful book shows how Bayley played the hand he was dealt with grace and dignity, never losing respect or love for his partner.

### Recommended

★★★ *The Diminished Mind: One Family's Extraordinary Battle with Alzheimer's* (1991) by Jean Tyler and Harry Anifantakis. Blue Ridge Summit, PA: Tab Books.

Jean Tyler recounts her husband Manley's devastating battle with Alzheimer's disease. Manley Tyler was a loving husband and a respected elementary school principal before the onset of Alzheimer's. Jean Tyler sensitively describes the pain and grief of her husband's slow 15-year decline and his eventual death. Alzheimer's hits most older adults much later than it did Manley Tyler: he was only 42 years old when he first showed symptoms. Jean Tyler relates the progressive deterioration of memory and judgment that made it impossible for him to complete even the simplest of tasks and made him increasingly prone to hostile behavior and paranoia. This 3-star autobiography not only speaks volumes about the emotionally draining losses involved in Alzheimer's, but it also carries some important messages for the survivors of an Alzheimer's victim, who can emerge from the experience with fond memories of their loved one and a stronger understanding of what it means to be human.

### Diamonds in the Rough

♦ *Alzheimer's, A Love Story: One Year in My Husband's Journey* (1997) by Ann Davidson. Secaucus, NJ: Birch Lane.

At the age of 50, Julian Davidson, a Stanford professor of physiology and medical researcher, was diagnosed with Alzheimer's. This book is his wife's account of the year in which she and her husband came to terms with his increasing deficits. Together, sharing where possible what was happening, they went through stages of confusion, anger, grief, mourning for what was lost, to acceptance. Told in 56 vignettes, some bittersweet, even humorous, and rich with honest dialogue, this splendid book captures the progressively debilitating effects of this disorder on the daily lives of clients and their families. Very favorably rated by mental health professionals, but unfortunately not well known by them.

♦ *Losing my Mind: An Intimate Look at Life with Alzheimer's* (2002) by Thomas DeBaggio. New York: Free Press.

Most books on progressive memory loss have been written by family members, but this is written by the patient himself. DeBaggio had several things going for him in this remarkable autobiography. He had been a journalist and freelance writer and author of several garden books, was diagnosed with Alzheimer's at a relatively early age (57), and started writing the book on the day he received the diagnosis. He describes the cognitive deficits as they appear on a daily basis, especially the losses in communication skills, and how they affected his life and his family. Long-term memories of his childhood seem more vivid than what is happening around him. He tells of the hopelessness he feels, knowing that things will only get worse. Keeping a journal helped DeBaggio cope. Sometimes he writes out of desperation to try to record even if he cannot comprehend what is occurring. This is a wonderful book for caregivers and those fearful of developing Alzheimer's. It does not sugarcoat the condition but shows that sentience (reflection) and family life can continue. One of the few books that fell through the cracks and was not represented in our national surveys, but we include and recommend it here.

♦ *Alzheimer's from the Inside Out* (2006) by Richard Taylor. Baltimore, MD: Health Professions Press.

At age 61, clinical psychologist Richard Taylor was diagnosed with Alzheimer's and decided to chronicle the progression of his condition from its early stages for as long as he could. This collection of essays describes life after diagnosis with insight and occasional flashes of sardonic wit, including his difficulties in communication, loss of independence, inability to perform familiar tasks, and changed relations with other people. He describes what it feels like to be talked about but ignored personally by others in the room. There are lists of recommended readings, Web addresses, and relevant social services agencies. This is a fine book for people given this diagnosis and their caregivers.

## ■ FILMS

### Strongly Recommended

★★★★★  *Iris* (2001) directed by Richard Eyre. R rating. 97 minutes.

A tender depiction of novelist's Iris Murdoch's descent into Alzheimer's. The film is a series of flashbacks from the perspective of Iris's husband, John Bayley, and is based on his acclaimed book *Elegy for Iris* (reviewed above). The earlier scenes depict Iris as a vibrant young woman, a revered British writer and philosopher; the later scenes, in stark and sad contrast, show here as a helpless and confused victim of Alzheimer's ravages. Sensitively rendered, it is simultaneously a love story and a dementia tale. *Iris* was deservedly one of highest-rated movies in our national studies.

★★★★★  *Away from Her* (2006) directed by Sarah Polley. PG-13 rating. 110 minutes.

A bittersweet film about a married man and his struggles with his wife's Alzheimer's. Grant's wife, Fiona, checks into a nursing home after deciding she has become too much of a risk to herself. Fiona soon forgets her husband and grows fond of another nursing home patient. That patient is forced to leave due to financial difficulties, and Fiona becomes depressed. Touched by the relationship between his wife and the patient, Grant decides to reunite them. This film will probably prove valuable for those married to someone with Alzheimer's.

★★★★★  *The Notebook* (2004) directed by Nick Cassavetes. PG-13 rating. 123 minutes.

The movie unfolds in a nursing home, where an elderly man reads a story to an old woman. The story depicts the romance of a youthful Noah Calhoun and Allie Hamilton. An indigent Noah and wealthy Allie spend a pastoral summer together until Allie moves away to college. Since she never receives any letters from Noah, Allie assumes it's the conclusion to their relationship. Years later, Allie becomes engaged to another man and decides to visit Noah's home. Allie stays with Noah for a few days and resists returning to her fiancé. The film shifts back to the nursing home, where the man and woman are an aged Noah and Allie, with Allie suffering from dementia. Allie remembers that she left her fiancé and is now married to Noah. The film reveals that Allie had herself written the story with instructions for Noah to read it to her. Unfortunately, Allie shortly loses these memories and forgets Noah once again.

### Recommended

★★★  *Do You Remember Love?* (1985, made for TV) directed by Jeff Bleckner. Not rated.

Joanne Woodward won an Emmy for her portrayal of a middle-aged college professor who begins to suffer from Alzheimer's disease. The effects on her husband and family are superbly shown in an Emmy-winning script. Realistic and touching at the same time.

★★★  *Memories of Me* (1989) directed by Henry Winkler. PG-13 rating. 105 minutes.

After his own heart attack, a heart surgeon seeks to reconcile with his father in order to put his own life back in order. That fathers and sons have superficial and (especially in this movie) joking relationships is not news, but the way they struggle and partly succeed in deepening their relationship is funny and memorable. The son's response to his father's early Alzheimer's is also illuminating at times.

## ■ INTERNET RESOURCES

### General Websites

★★★★★  *The Alzheimer's Association* www.alz.org

The Alzheimer's Association offers an extensive resource for people, caregivers, and families who are dealing with Alzheimer's. This is the best place to start learning about the disease.

★★★★  *Alzheimer's Outreach* www.zarcrom.com/users/alzheimers

The best resources on this website are the four Alzheimer's directories—Caregiving, Alzheimer's, Nursing/Nursing Home Information, and Health Care Issues. They offer a great deal of detailed practical information. Unfortunately, the articles on the website rarely carry author attribution or dates.

★★★★★  *Alzheimer's Association of New South Wales (Australia)* www.fightdementia. org.au

The articles found under "Understanding Dementia" are well written and cover most topics for people interested in learning more about dementia and Alzheimer's.

★★★★  *The Alzheimer's Disease Education and Referral Center* www.nia.nih.gov/ alzheimers

This is the Alzheimer's section of the National Institute on Aging of the National Institutes of Health. The Fact Sheets (under "Publications") offer reliable government information and are a good starting place.

### Psychoeducational Materials

★★★★  *Alzheimer's Center* www.mayoclinic.com/health/alzheimers-disease/ DS00161

From the Mayo Clinic, this site offers about a dozen short articles about different aspects of the disease from a health perspective. You can find a wealth of articles under the "In-Depth" tab on risk assessment, genetics, caregiving, and more.

★★★ *Memory and Dementia* www.rcpsych.ac.uk/mentalhealthinfo/alzheimersandde-mentia.aspx

Fact sheets and brochures discussing appropriate memory expectations, the role of anxiety and depression in lessening recall, aspects of dementia, self-help tips, and readings.

★★★★ *AARP Foundation* www.aarp.org/aarp-foundation

This site features articles focusing on living well and independently despite the burdens of age, loss, and disease, with a focus on those age 50+ who are especially vulnerable.

★★★★ *ALZwell Caregiver Support* www.alzwell.com

One of the older Alzheimer's disease resources online, this comprehensive site is still regularly updated and offers many resources designed for supporting caregivers.

★★★★ *Ageless Design* www.agelessdesign.com

The site helps you to Alzheimer's-proof your house and offers special products, a newsletter, and related products and resources.

★★★★ *The Caregiver's Handbook* by Robert S. Stall, MD www.acsu.buffalo.edu/~drstall/hndbk0.html

Although not updated in some time, this online book offers dozens of pages of detailed and practical ideas for caregivers about nutrition, emotions, personal care, and legal and financial issues.

★★★★ *Alzheimer's Disease* psychcentral.com/disorders/alzheimers

A helpful introduction to Alzheimer's disease, this condition center from Psych Central includes a Caregiver's Guide to Alzheimer's as well as dozens of other articles. The recent news and research briefs section is a good way to stay up on the latest developments in Alzheimer's research.

★★★ *Dementia and Alzheimer's Care* helpguide.org/elder/alzheimers_disease_dementias_caring_caregivers.htm

A single page from the nonprofit HelpGuide that provides a wealth of information about preparing and planning for Alzheimer's and related diseases of aging.

★★ *Alzheimer's Foundation of America* www.alzfdn.org

Although a noble nonprofit organization, the website offers few unique resources to those with Alzheimer's or their family members. However, there is a great deal of information about the organization itself here, which may be useful for those looking to get more involved in the advocacy, research, and policy issues of this disease.

## ▨ SUPPORT GROUPS

### Alzheimer's Disease Education and Referral Center (ADEAR)

Hotline: 800-438-4380
www.nia.nih.gov/alzheimers
Information, referrals, publications, and information about clinical trials.

### Alzheimer's Research Forum

www.alzforum.org

### National Family Caregivers Association

Phone: 800-896-3650
www.nfcacares.org

### National Niemann–Pick Disease Foundation

Phone: 877-287-3672
www.nnpdf.org

**See also** Aging (Chapter 5) and Death and Grieving (Chapter 18).

# CHAPTER 20

# DEPRESSION

D epression is a frequently used and abused term. When someone looks at your gloomy face and asks you what is wrong, you might respond, "I feel depressed about myself, about my life." Everyone is down in the dumps some of the time, but most people, after a few hours, days, or weeks, snap out of a despondent mood.

However, some people are not as fortunate. They suffer from major depression, a mood disorder that involves feeling deeply unhappy, demoralized, self-derogatory, and unenergetic. A person suffering from major depression often does not feel physically well, loses stamina, has a poor appetite, is listless, and experiences a sleep disorder. (The extreme mood swings of bipolar disorder or manic-depression are covered in Chapter 11.) Experts acknowledge the reciprocal interaction of both psychology and physiology in causing depression, and most believe in the superiority of a combination of medication and psychotherapy.

In this chapter, we critically review the voluminous body of self-help books, autobiographies, films, online self-help, and Internet resources related to depression (Box 20.1). Our primary concern is with major depression, but we also cover seasonal affective disorder (SAD), dysthymia, and postpartum depression.

## ■ SELF-HELP BOOKS

### Strongly Recommended

★★★★★  *The Mindful Way through Depression* (2007) by Mark Williams, John Teasdale, Zindel Segal, and Jon Kabat-Zinn. New York: Guilford.

Mindfulness-based cognitive therapy is applied to depression in this superb self-help resource. The importance of the mind–body connection, particularly in emotion, is elaborated and the effectiveness of this approach with chronic depression (actually, any mood condition) is described. The psychologist-authors thoroughly explain mindfulness and awareness with clear and understandable case applications to depression. Buttressed by several research studies, the authors encourage readers not to dispel depression by thinking it away or pushing it out of the mind but by paying attention and focusing on the sensation itself. That makes the experience a different one and begins the end of depression. An attractive and evidence-based alternative to the cognitive therapy self-help books that dominate the depression category.

## BOX 20.1
## RECOMMENDATION HIGHLIGHTS

**SELF-HELP BOOKS**

- For alleviating depression through cognitive-behavioral methods:

    ★★★★★ *Feeling Good* by David Burns

    ★★★★★ *The Feeling Good Handbook* by David Burns

    ★★★★★ *Mind Over Mood* by Dennis Greenberger and Christine A. Padesky

    ★★★★★ *Control Your Depression* by Peter Lewinsohn et al.

    ★★★★ *The Cognitive-Behavioral Workbook for Depression* by William J. Knaus

- For reducing depression by mindfulness and practical directives:

    ★★★★★ *The Mindful Way Through Depression* by Mark Williams et al.

    ★★★★ *When Living Hurts* by Michael D. Yapko

- For converting depression into new sources of growth:

    ★★★★ *When Feeling Bad Is Good* by Ellen McGrath

- For treating seasonal affective disorder:

    ★★★ *Winter Blues: Seasonal Affective Disorder* by Norman E. Rosenthal

- For identifying and remediating men's depression:

    ★★★ *I Don't Want to Talk About It* by Terrence Real

- For helping parents cope with a teenager's depression:

    ♦ *Overcoming Teen Depression* by Miriam Kaufman

**AUTOBIOGRAPHIES**

- For sensitive descriptions of severe depression and near suicide:

    ★★★★★ *Darkness Visible* by William Styron

    ★★★★ *Undercurrents* by Martha Manning

    ★★★ *The Beast* by Tracy Thompson

    ★★★ *My Depression: A Picture Book* by Elizabeth Swados

- For a personal yet comprehensive look at depression:

    ★★★ *The Noonday Demon* by Andrew Solomon

- For accounts of postpartum depression:

    ★★★ *Down Came the Rain* by Brooke Shields

    ★★★ *Behind the Smile* by Marie Osmond and others

**FILMS**

- For harrowing, systemic portraits of depression among women:

    ★★★★ *A Woman Under the Influence*

    ★★★★ *The Hours*

- For a moving portrait of a dysthymic everyman:

    ★★★ *American Splendor*

(Continued)

**ONLINE SELF-HELP**

■ For research-supported online self-assessment and self-treatment:

★★★★★ *Beating the Blues* www.beatingtheblues.co.uk

★★★★★ *COPE Depression and Stress Treatment* www.ccbt.co.uk

★★★★ *MoodGYM* www.moodgym.anu.edu.au

★★★★ *Living Life to the Full* www.llttfi.com

**INTERNET RESOURCES**

■ For excellent general information on depression:

★★★★★ *Expert Consensus Guidelines: Pharmacotherapy of Depressive Disorders in Older Patients* www.psychguides.com/depression

★★★★★ *Depression* psychcentral.com/disorders/depression

■ For valuable information on postpartum depression:

★★★★★ *Postpartum Progress* postpartumprogress.com

★★★★★ *Feeling Good: The New Mood Therapy* (revised ed., 1999) by David Burns. New York: Avon.

The cognitive therapy that psychiatrist Burns describes in this updated self-help classic is the most popular form of psychological treatment for depression. Cognitive therapists believe that people become depressed because of faulty thinking, which triggers self-destructive moods. Examples of faulty thinking are all-or-nothing thinking (if a situation is anything less than perfect, it is a total failure), discounting the positive (positive experiences don't count), magnification (exaggerating the importance of problems and shortcomings), and personalization (taking personal responsibility for events that aren't entirely under one's control). In *Feeling Good*, Burns outlines techniques people can use to identify and combat their faulty thinking. These techniques have been extensively tested in published research studies; indeed, this is one of the few books in the entire self-help literature that can boast about its demonstrated effectiveness (Ackerson et al., 1998; Cuijpers, 1997). It is peppered with self-assessment tests, self-help forms, and charts. The self-assessment techniques include the widely used Beck Depression Inventory, an anger scale, and a dysfunctional attitude scale. The self-help forms and charts include a daily record of dysfunctional thoughts, an antiprocrastination sheet, a pleasure-predicting sheet, an anger cost/benefit analysis, and an antiperfection sheet. It is an outstanding self-help book that has sold more than 2 million copies since its original publication in 1980. Burns's easy-to-read writing style, extensive use of examples, and enthusiasm give readers a clear understanding of cognitive therapy and the confidence to try its methods.

★★★★★ *Mind Over Mood: Change How You Feel by Changing the Way You Think* (1995) by Dennis Greenberger and Christine A. Padesky. New York: Guilford.

The authors have taken the nuts and bolts of cognitive therapy and spelled out in a step-by-step fashion how a layperson can utilize these methods in dealing with depression, anxiety, anger, panic, guilt, and shame. Strategies described in this book can also help solve relationship problems, handle stress better, improve self-esteem, and become less fearful and more confident. The book helps the reader identify and make necessary changes in the relationship among thoughts, emotions, behavior, body changes, and events in one's life. Each chapter contains practice exercises. This 5-star cognitive therapy manual can be truly helpful for adults suffering from depressive complaints—truly a matter of "mind over mood."

★★★★★ *The Feeling Good Handbook* (revised ed., 1999) by David Burns. New York: Plume.

In this sequel to *Feeling Good*, Burns says that one of the most exciting recent developments is the discovery that cognitive therapy, which he calls the new mood therapy, can help people with the entire range of mood problems they encounter in their everyday lives. These include feelings of inferiority, procrastination, guilt, stress, frustration, and irritability. In this handbook, Burns explains why we are plagued by irrational worries and how to conquer our worst fears without having to rely on addictive tranquilizers or alcohol. Burns also describes the important application of cognitive therapy in recent years to problems in personal relationships, especially marital and couple relationships. *The Feeling Good Handbook* asks readers to complete a number of self-assessments once a week, just as patients do, to monitor progress. The assessments ask about thoughts, feelings, and actions in a variety of circumstances that typically make people feel angry, sad, frustrated, or anxious. There are two main differences in *The Feeling Good Handbook* compared to the original book: it covers a wider array of problems (anxiety and relationships as well as depression), and it includes daily logs to fill out. This 5-star resource can be used as an adjunct to *Feeling Good* or independent of it. In either case, it is a valuable and prized self-help book.

★★★★★ *Control Your Depression* (1996) by Peter Lewinsohn, Ricardo Munoz, Mary Ann Youngren, and Antonette Zeiss. Englewood Cliffs, NJ: Prentice-Hall.

This self-help resource, also in the cognitive-behavioral tradition, is intended to teach a way of thinking about depression as well as controlling it. The book is presented in three parts: Part I explains how depressed people think; Part II provides step-by-step procedures to control depression; and Part III is about ensuring success. Techniques include self-control, relaxation, pleasant activities planning, and modifying self-defeating thinking patterns. There are illustrations of how to gauge progress, maintain gains, and determine the need for further help. *Control Your Depression* has been shown in controlled research to work effectively in many cases (Cuijpers, 1998). This 5-star resource is a solid, research-based self-help book for treating depression.

★★★★★ *Cognitive Therapy and the Emotional Disorders* (1976) by Aaron Beck. New York: International Universities Press.

This text, as the title implies, presents a cognitive therapy approach to depression and other emotional disorders. Aaron Beck pioneered the cognitive therapy approach to depression. He describes the cognitive triad that consists of negative thoughts about the self, ongoing experience, and the future. Beck believes that systematic errors in thinking, each of which darkens the person's experiences, produce depression. These errors include drawing a conclusion when there is little or no evidence to support it; focusing on an insignificant detail while ignoring the more important features of a situation; drawing global conclusions about worth or performance on the basis of a single fact; magnifying small bad events and minimizing large good events; and incorrectly engaging in self-blame for bad events. Cognitive therapy attempts to counter these distorted thoughts. People are taught to identify and correct the flawed thinking and are trained to conquer problems and master situations they previously thought were insurmountable. This valuable 5-star book was written primarily for professionals rather than a self-help audience. Many of the ideas in Beck's book are presented in a much easier-to-read fashion in Burns's *Feeling Good* and Greenberger and Padesky's *Mind Over Mood*. Beck's book will thus appeal primarily to the clinical community and to the knowledgeable layperson.

★★★★   *When Living Hurts: Directives for Treating Depression* (1994) by Michael
        D. Yapko. New York: Brunner/Mazel.

This book presents brief and practical methods for treating depression. Yapko believes that depression can be managed, and when it is well managed, it doesn't hurt as much or for as long. Given are directives and strategies intended to help the clinician intervene actively and provide catalysts for learning to interrupt the cycle of depression. The first part of the book provides a theoretical overview; the second part describes 91 directives; and the third part presents case narratives that illustrate applications of the directives. This excellent 4-star book is largely a reference book for clinicians; if a client were to use it as a self-help resource, it should probably be used in conjunction with a professional. Yapko's *Breaking the Patterns of Depression* (reviewed below) is a more conventional self-help book.

★★★★   *When Feeling Bad Is Good* (1994) by Ellen McGrath. New York: Bantam.

This book provides a program for women to convert "healthy depression" into new sources of growth. McGrath challenges the cultural myth that feeling bad must necessarily be negative and introduces a new perspective on women's depression. A woman's healthy depression may be a realistic and appropriate emotional response to the unhealthy culture in which she lives. McGrath identifies six types of healthy depression: victimization depression, relationship depression, age-range depression, depletion depression, body image depression, and mind–body depression. This valuable 4-star book is appropriate for women of all ages, ethnicities, and socioeconomic strata.

★★★★   *The Cognitive Behavioral Workbook for Depression* (2006) by William J. Knaus.
        Oakland, CA: New Harbinger.

The workbook utilizes a combination of three popular and effective treatments for depression: cognitive therapy, cognitive-behavioral therapy, and rational-emotive therapy. The reader is introduced to the definition, criteria, and characteristics of depression and participates in a self-assessment. How to recognize depressive thinking, use reasoning, understand cognitive distortions, and then learn the depressive thinking themes such as hopelessness and helplessness prepares the groundwork for the treatment. Common problems, such as perfectionism, emotional stress, and low frustration tolerance, are explored and the cognitive-behavioral model is applied to these conditions. The workbook includes interesting and reflective exercises that promote the understanding of depression. This book would probably be best utilized in conjunction with psychotherapy because of the complexity of the applications.

**Recommended**

★★★ *You Can Beat Depression: A Guide to Prevention and Recovery* (2001, 3rd ed.) by John Preston. San Luis Obispo, CA: Impact.

In the third edition of this valuable book, the author helps readers appreciate that all depression is not alike (for example, chronic versus acute depression). After providing a clearer understanding of depression, Preston guides readers through various treatment choices, such as brief therapy, self-help approaches, family therapy, medication, and cognitive changes. Relapse-prevention programs are also addressed for the person who is working to maintain or improve gains. This 3-star book would actually be a 4-star selection if not for the fact that relatively few mental health professionals rated it. A useful resource for people trying to understand and make choices about treating their depression.

★★★ *Winter Blues—Seasonal Affective Disorder: What It Is and How To Overcome It* (1998) by Norman E. Rosenthal. New York: Guilford.

A book for patients, spouses, and family members who wish to better understand and cope with seasonal affective disorder. Psychiatrist Rosenthal begins with a self-test to evaluate the level of seasonal affective disorder and then reviews the effectiveness of antidepressant medication, light therapy, St. John's wort, and a nutritional regimen. Light therapy, the author's research area, is particularly favored. There is also a step-by-step guide on coping with the disorder all year around.

★★★ *Getting Un-Depressed: How a Woman Can Change Her Life through Cognitive Therapy* (revised ed., 1988) by Gary Emery. New York: Touchstone.

Cognitive therapy presented in this book is designed to help women cope effectively with depression. The risk for women of developing depression is about double that of men. Emery explains what depression is and how cognitive therapy can help. He describes how women can get immediate relief from their symptoms and improve their state of mind. Next, the author focuses on ways to overcome common complications of depression (weight gain, alcohol and drug dependency, and relationship problems). After this, women learn that they can avoid future depression by working on the psychological causes of depression, which according to Emery are underlying negative beliefs and ineffective ways of handling stress. Finally, Emery outlines how women can lead more self-reliant and self-directed lives. This 3-star book, just missing the 4-star rating, is a popular and practical application of cognitive therapy to depression for women.

★★★ *I Don't Want to Talk About It: Overcoming the Secret Legacy of Male Depression* (1997) by Terrence Real. New York: Scribner.

Feeling the stigma of depression's "unmanliness," many men hide their condition not only from family and friends but also from themselves. Real believes that by directing their pain outward, depressed men hurt the people they love and frequently pass their condition on to their children. Real mixes in his own experiences with depression, as a son of a depressed, violent father and the father of two young sons. By integrating personal and professional experiences, Real teaches men how they can unearth their pain, heal themselves, restore relationships, and break the legacy of abuse. A useful self-help book specifically for men.

★★★   *How to Stubbornly Refuse to Make Yourself Miserable about Anything, Yes Anything!* (1988) by Albert Ellis. New York: Lyle Stuart.

This internationally respected psychologist, originator of rational-emotive behavioral therapy (REBT), contends that we create our own feelings and choose to think and feel in self-harming ways. Ellis's goals here are to show people how to express and control their emotional destinies, how to stubbornly refuse to make themselves miserable, how to use scientific reasoning, and how to effectively change their emotional and behavioral problems. The book certainly covers depression and misery, but it is broader in its coverage. This 3-star book can be helpful for laypersons who are self-motivated or who are already involved in cognitive-behavior therapy.

★★★   *Hand-Me-Down Blues: How to Stop Depression from Spreading in Families* (1999) by Michael D. Yapko. New York: Golden.

The family is a powerful system, both for unwittingly teaching depression and for helping to overcome it. Psychologist Yapko advocates a shift away from medications as the sole solution for depression toward the curative role of family therapy. He emphasizes that "depression can be relived with a family approach as family members are brought together to relieve their distress by learning to help each other and to avoid blame as the whole family reacts to depression." This book presents a realistic and family approach to the management of depression.

★★★   *Overcoming Depression: A Cognitive Therapy Approach for Taming the Depression BEAST* (1999) by Mark Gilson and Arthur Freeman. Albany, NY: Graywind.

The depression BEAST is a treatment acronym: "B" for body and biology; "E" for emotions; "A" for action; "S" for situations and vulnerability; and "T" for thoughts. A final chapter focuses on the role of hope. The book adopts an integrative but largely cognitive perspective to the treatment of depression. It is educational, easy to read, and practical. In all, a useful self-help resource for depressed individuals and their families.

★★★   *How to Cope with Depression* (1989, reprinted 1996) by Raymond DePaulo and Keith Ablow. New York: Ballantine.

Subtitled *A Complete Guide for You and Your Family*, this book is primarily about the biological causes of depression and the treatment of depression through drug therapy. Part I, Depression: What We Know, defines depression and bipolar disorder (the authors call it manic–depressive illness) and describes the causes of depression as biological. Part II, The Experience of Depression, portrays the nature of depression from the perspective of the patient, the family, and the physician. Part III, The Four Perspectives of Depression, evaluates the disease perspective, the personality perspective, the behavior perspective, and the life-story perspective, and Part IV, Current Treatments, presents the authors' view of how depression should be treated. This 3-star book was not widely known in our studies, and its title notwithstanding, it is less a guide to coping with depression than a primer on possible causes, treatments, and professional perspectives. The authors make clear their own view: Depression is a physical disease with genetic and biological causes that can be successfully treated only through drug therapy. Other therapies are given token discussion.

★★★   *Breaking the Patterns of Depression* (1997) by Michael D. Yapko. New York. Doubleday.

The author's dual foci are on the initial treatment and the prevention of depressive disorders. Yapko provides over 100 activities to help learn the skills necessary for becoming and remaining depression-free. Readers are asked to participate in the activities listed in each chapter. Action steps are emphasized throughout.

★★★   *When the Blues Won't Go Away* (1991) by Robert Hirschfeld. New York: Macmillan.

This book concerns one form of depression—dysthymic disorder (DD)—that is long-lasting and relatively mild. In the early chapters, Hirschfeld describes the rut that people with DD get themselves into and what they do to stay in that rut. Many characteristics of DD resemble those of major depression, but DD's symptoms are less severe and usually last longer. People with DD continue to function at home and work, but not at the level they once did. Most of the book is devoted to getting rid of DD, and Hirschfeld does an excellent job of presenting a variety of treatment strategies. The author outlines self-help strategies and therapies that are tailor-made for such problems. He also discusses antidepressant medications, and he shows how a combination of drug therapy and psychotherapy can be effective. This 3-star resource came out just before one of our studies was conducted, so only a few mental health professionals rated it. We believe that *When the Blues Won't Go Away* provides a well-balanced analysis of a specific type of depression—long-lasting, relatively mild depression.

★★★   *Understanding and Overcoming Depression: A Common Sense Approach* (1999) by Tony Bates. Freedom, CA: Crossing.

The author offers a heartwarming message that builds self-esteem and gives us a trust in ourselves. In 128 pages, Bates overviews the signs and causes of depression and argues that hopelessness is the major obstacle to overcoming depression. The recovery plan includes cognitive work on self-image and a relapse-prevention/maintenance plan. Pharmacological therapy and psychotherapy are briefly addressed. This book is a useful and—as the title declares—common sense self-help book.

★★★   *Listening to Prozac* (1997) by Peter D. Kramer. New York: Penguin.

This best-selling author guides us into the scientific study of biology and personality. Kramer explains the historical debate over what drives us as human beings—nature versus nurture. He then shares his psychiatric and philosophical observations about the influence of a medication like Prozac on a patient's outlook and self-image. His focus is limited mainly to explaining the impact of mood-altering drugs on the modern sense of self: What is Prozac's influence on personality, work performance, memory, dexterity? Does it affect character rather than illness? For the professional and layperson interested in the ongoing debates about mind versus body and nature versus nurture, this is a stimulating read. However, it is not intended as a self-help guide.

**Diamonds in the Rough**

♦ *Overcoming Teen Depression: A Guide for Parents* (2001) by Miriam Kaufman. Buffalo, NY: Firefly.

This self-help book was explicitly written for the parents of depressed teenagers. The author reviews the signs of teen depression, its various types, comorbid conditions, and suicide risks. She usefully discusses indications for psychotherapy, selection of a therapist, the purposes of psychopharmacology, and the possibilities of alternative treatments, such as herbal medicines. A practical and reassuring book for parents and family members. If *Overcoming Teen Depression* had been read by more experts in our national studies, it would have certainly received a rating of 3 or more stars.

♦ *Overcoming Depression One Step at a Time* (2004) by Michael E. Addis and Christopher R. Martell. Oakland, CA: New Harbinger.

This workbook leads the reader through a self-guided approach to reducing depression employing Behavioral Activation Therapy. Its primary thrust is that once depression is identified and understood, the reader conducts self-evaluations with the help of exercises and other tools. A clear and helpful system of TRAP entails identification of the trigger, the response to the trigger, the avoidance of how the individual escapes the trigger but doesn't escape the depression, followed by the consequence. A key element is the importance of positive and rewarding responses when the individual makes a positive change. Behavioral activation has been shown repeatedly to work for depression in the clinic with minimal psychotherapist contact, and we have every reason to think that many laypersons can do likewise with this book.

**Not Recommended**

★★ *You Mean I Don't Have to Feel This Way?* (1991) by Colette Dowling. New York: Scribner.
★ *The Good News about Depression: Cures and Treatments in the New Age of Psychiatry* (1995 revised ed.) by Mark S. Gold. New York: Villard.

## ■ AUTOBIOGRAPHIES

**Strongly Recommended**

★★★★★ *Darkness Visible: A Memoir of Madness* (1992) by William Styron. New York: Vintage.

In beautifully written prose, novelist William Styron describes his gradual recognition of debilitating depression, his descent into despair, his suicidal impulses, hospitalization, and recovery. One of the best portrayals of the loneliness and despair of major depression ever written. The book illustrates the benefits of brief hospitalization: "For me," he writes, "the real helpers were seclusion and time" afforded by brief hospital stays. This book is widely known and very positively evaluated in our national studies—and short enough to be read by someone suffering from depression.

**★★★★** *Undercurrents: A Therapist's Reckoning with Her Own Depression* (1994) by Martha Manning. San Francisco, CA: HarperSanFrancisco.

In her late 30s, psychotherapist Manning experienced a severe unipolar depression. Symptoms included sleep disturbance, lack of energy, and suicidal impulses. Neither psychotherapy nor drugs seemed to help. Reluctantly, she underwent electroconvulsive therapy (ECT; previously known as "shock therapy"), which lifted the depression. Afterwards, she learns that it is difficult to convince her colleagues and her friends that ECT was a beneficial treatment. The book takes some of the fear out of ECT and demonstrates how the experience of depression can deepen understanding of the human condition. Manning writes, "In these flashes of insight, I understand for a moment that one of the great dividends of darkness is an increased sensitivity to light." A very sensitive account by a therapist who was compelled to switch roles and become a patient.

## Recommended

**★★★** *The Beast: A Journey through Depression* (1996) by Tracy Thompson. New York: Plume.

Drawing on notes in a journal she kept from adolescence onward and her considerable research skills as a reporter for the *Washington Post,* Thompson writes of her struggles with the depression, suicidal thoughts, and inner demons that have been with her since adolescence. She was treated with psychotherapy and various drugs, including Prozac and imipramine. A compassionate and well-written account told with openness and candor that captures the emotional depths of depression. The book is particularly useful in showing that one can have a serious, chronic depression and still maintain a successful career. Very highly but infrequently rated by the mental health experts in our studies, resulting in the 3-star summary.

**★★★** *The Noonday Demon: An Atlas of Depression* (2002) by Andrew Solomon. New York: Simon & Schuster.

Superbly written and well researched, this combined memoir and compendium by National Book Award winner Andrew Solomon has become an instant classic on depression. His own serious bouts of depression, his desire to end his life, and the many treatments he had undergone led him to explore the condition in medical, historical, and cross-cultural contexts. He interviewed psychotherapists and researchers, other people with depression, drug makers, and philosophers and read accounts of famous literary figures who had serious depression. To understand the many expressions of depression, he visited mental hospitals and traveled to Senegal, Cambodia, and Greenland. The book covers both unipolar and bipolar disorders and describes treatment modalities across the spectrum, including drugs, talk therapies, alternative herbal and homeopathic remedies, diet and exercise, and electroconvulsive therapy. Concluding with a chapter titled "Hope," this moving, empathic, and comprehensive work is a milestone among books on depression. Although its average rating would have merited 5 stars, this autobiography is not widely known and did not collect sufficient ratings for a 5-star designation.

**★★★** *On the Edge of Darkness* (1995) by Kathy Cronkite. New York: Dell.

Following her own bout with depression, Kathy Cronkite undertook research into the disorder and produced this combination autobiography and self-help book. Most of the book involves interviews with celebrities who suffered from depression, including Mike Wallace, Kitty Dukakis, Rod Steiger, and William Styron. Cronkite also talked to researchers and describes therapeutic options for adults and children with depression. The interviewees recommend seeking treatment sooner rather than later, as untreated depression is likely to worsen, bringing with it risks of suicide. Learning that successful people have suffered from the disorder and come through the experience will benefit many readers, especially in overcoming the "No one has ever felt like this before" feelings so typical of serious depression.

★★★ *Down Came the Rain: My Journey through Postpartum Depression* (2006) by Brooke Shields. New York: Hyperion.

Actress Brooke Shields had difficulty becoming pregnant and tried in vitro fertilization. After a miscarriage, she and her husband tried again and had a baby girl. Depression and anxiety began immediately after the C-section delivery and continued unabated. She felt unable to connect with her baby, resented the baby, became angry at family and friends for not understanding what was in her head, felt alone and hopeless with unwanted images of harming Rowan, and was scared of being along with her baby for fear of what she might do. Shields began thinking of suicide as preferable to harming her baby. Antidepressant drugs, a trained nurse, and caring friends helped lift the crushing depression. The takeaway is that postpartum depression is a serious and potentially fatal disorder that is treatable, better sooner than later.

★★★ *The Bell Jar* (1995) by Sylvia Plath. Cutchogue, NY: Buccaneer.

Plath was a prize-winning poet who received much acclaim during her lifetime and afterward. This autobiographical novel, published only a month before her suicide in 1963, recounts the young woman's hospitalization for severe depression while she was a summer intern at a New York City magazine. She is given shock treatments and spends time in private psychiatric hospitals. Her multiple hospitalizations left her fearful of treatment, especially shock treatment. The book is regarded as a literary classic in its sensitive description of inner pain so great it leads to suicide. This is not a hopeful book as Plath's tragic end is already known, but it can awaken readers to danger signs in themselves and others.

★★★ *Behind the Smile: My Journey out of Postpartum Depression* (2007) by Marie Osmond, Marcia Wilkie, and Judith Moore. New York: Grand Central Publishing.

Writing this candid and revealing autobiography was cathartic for entertainer Marie Osmond. She wrote the book to inform other women going through the devastating personal effects of postpartum depression without knowing what it is and where to get help. For too long this condition, popularly called "the baby blues," has been a taboo subject. Osmond hopes to bring it out of the closet. Co-author Judith Moore is also Osmond's physician. Several readers remarked that Dr. Moore's section alone is worth the price of the book. Her chapter contains information not only on appropriate antidepressant medication but also on alternative homeopathic remedies such as vitamins and herbal supplements, along with addresses where these can be obtained. Dr. Moore includes a section on the father's experience in living with postpartum depression.

★★★ *My Depression: A Picture Book* (2005) by Elizabeth Swados. New York: Hyperion.

Mood disorders are especially common among highly creative people. Writer, composer, theater director, and artist Elizabeth Swados experienced multiple episodes of severe depression. In this short book, she illustrates these experiences using hand-drawn line drawings with brief captions that convey, better than words alone, an inside view of depression. Unlike word books, which a depressed person is not likely to read, these drawings depicting the interior landscape of depression can reach a person in the midst of a depressive episode. They would also prove useful in acquainting teenagers with the disorder.

## Not Recommended

★★ *Prozac Nation: Young and Depressed in America* (1997) by Elizabeth Wurtzel. New York: Riverhead.

## ■ FILMS

### Strongly Recommended

★★★★ *A Woman Under the Influence* (1974) directed by John Cassavetes. R rating. 155 minutes.

A harrowing film that charts the emotional breakdown of a housewife and the effects of her depression on her blue-collar family. Peter Falk plays a distant, inexpressive construction worker flummoxed by his wife's (Gena Rowland's) fragile mental condition. When her condition threatens the well-being of their children, he has her committed to a psychiatric hospital for several months. The film poignantly demonstrates one person's sense of depressive desperation, a partner's inability to provide emotional support, and the devastating consequences. The heart-wrenching performances leave a lasting impression.

★★★★ *The Hours* (2002) directed by Stephen Daldry. PG-13 rating. 114 minutes.

A beautiful and haunting film that depicts three women suffering from depression: Virginia Woolf (Nicole Kidman) writing her book *Mrs. Dalloway* in the 1920s in England; Laura Brown (Julianne Moore) reading that book in the 1950s in Los Angeles; and Clarissa Vaughan (Meryl Streep) throwing a party in the 2000s in New York City for a dying friend, who has nicknamed her Mrs. Dalloway. The various plots come together in the end and address the universal question of whether it is better to live for your own happiness or for others. The film ends where it began: Virginia Woolf committing suicide by putting stones in her pockets and walking into the river. Why must so many characters die in novels? "So that we all appreciate life." A beautifully acted and achingly accurate portrayal of women and depression, *The Hours* shows the tragic pain and gender-linked causes of depression across the decades. (Also reviewed in Chapter 39 on Suicide.)

**Recommended**

★★★  *American Splendor* (2003) directed by Shari Springer Berman & Robert Pulcini. R rating. 101 minutes.

A tragic-comedy inspired by the life of the late Harvey Pekar, who wrote a series of dark autobiographical comic books titled *American Splendor*. A file clerk becomes a wildly successful comic-strip writer but continues to suffer from chronic depression, characterized by pessimism, negativity, cynicism, loneliness, and hoarding. A moving portrait of an everyman (played by Paul Giamatti), it uncannily portrays the sad, monotonous life of dysthymia (chronic but mild depression) and the value of coping through creative work and soul mates.

★★★  *Prozac Nation* (2001) directed by Erik Skjoldbjærg. R rating. 95 minutes.

This film fares better than the book on which it was based (listed above) in our national studies. Lizzie (Christina Ricci) is a gifted Harvard student slowly descending into depression, abetted by drug abuse and a tumultuous sexual relationship. Paraphrasing a character in one of Hemingway's stories, Lizzie describes depression as coming on "gradually, then suddenly. That's how depression hits. You wake up one morning afraid that you're going to live." Her reliance on medication leads her to observe, "Sometimes it feels like we're all living in a Prozac nation." After a lengthy period of medication, psychotherapy, and a suicide attempt, Lizzie improves and returns to the world. A fine example of the devastation of depression in young adults and of the effectiveness of combined treatment (psychotherapy plus medication).

## ■ ONLINE SELF-HELP

★★★★★  *Beating the Blues* www.beatingtheblues.co.uk

Based on the principles of cognitive-behavior therapy, users of this interactive self-help program complete eight sessions at a rate of one per week. Between sessions, users complete homework and skill-building activities. The program contains multimedia presentation of case studies to illustrate the principles presented in each week's module. The interactive modules will teach users about depression and anxiety, help them identify and modify automatic thoughts, challenge their thinking, develop and practice behavior changes, and monitor their progress. Weekly progress is available for users to keep track of their progress or share with a mental health professional. It is currently available in the United Kingdom and also has limited availability in the United States to people insured with the University of Pittsburgh Medical Center Health Plan. Individual users are provided an activation code to access the program.

★★★★★  *COPE Depression and Stress Treatment* www.ccbt.co.uk

COPE is created by the same company that developed the FearFighter and OCFighter online self-help programs. This program follows a similar format. Following a brief screening by a mental health professional, users are directed to the nine-step online program. It is intended as an early form of intervention and not for users who are already in face-to-face psychotherapy for depression. This program is currently available only in the United Kingdom.

★★★★ *Living Life to the Full* www.llttf.com

This interactive online program is the newest version of a program previously called Overcoming Depression. In addition to the change in name, the program has undergone additional revisions. The program developers intend to make LLTTF available to mental health professionals for use with their clients. This will allow practitioners to walk through elements of the program with clients, provide feedback, and receive electronic updates about patient progress. Based on the principles of CBT, the program consists of 6 interactive modules that allow clients to input data creating a personalized experience. Modules include education about depression, creating an action plan, challenging thoughts, learning new skills, and planning for the future. Pricing for the program is not yet finalized for the United States version. For the purpose of comparison, the British version cost $100 per user when purchased alone and $880 for a package of 10 users. Increasingly larger packages result in progressively lower per user costs.

★★★★ *MoodGYM* www.moodgym.anu.edu.au

This free program is intended for users with mild to moderate depression. Users with elevated scores are referred to live professionals. This program provides demonstrations, information, and mood exercises. Users then complete exercises that are stored in an electronic workbook.

★★★ *The Depression Center* www.depressioncenter.net

The Depression Center program is available free of charge to registered users. After completing the initial depression and anxiety test, users can access the program from their start page called My Program. The program consists of modules 1 through 9 (called The Depression Program) and 10 through 18 (called The Auxiliary Sessions). The initial modules are based on cognitive-behavioral therapy and teach users about their condition, help them challenge their thinking, address their current behaviors, and examine their core beliefs. Users are strongly encouraged to complete their homework as an integral part of their program. The Auxiliary Sessions address specific issues related to depression (such as grief) or teach skills such as relaxation, resolving disputes, and addressing worry. Users can check their progress on the mood tracker and they also have access to the moderated message boards. Many users completed the program in 16 weeks.

★★★ *Good Days Ahead* www.mindstreet.com

This interactive DVD-ROM provides users with practical tools for building self-esteem, controlling moods, and coping with stress. The program provides video clips of actors portraying interpersonal interactions as well as professional commentary. The program also includes assignments to be completed by the user based on cognitive-behavioral therapy. Cost is $99 for individual self-help use. Packages are also available to professionals for use in their practice.

★★★ *Little Prince Is Depressed* www.depression.edu.hk

This free depression program is primarily designed for adolescents and is available in several languages, including English. It unfolds as an animated story with multiple stops at which the main character learns about depression, treatment options, and strategies to address depression. The program includes a depression self-test and a "post office" stop where a user can send someone an e-card. It is not stated but implied that a user might send a card to someone in order to reach out for help due to depression.

★★★    *The Low Down* www.thelowdown.co.nz

This free program designed for adolescents is based in New Zealand. The website provides a self-test where users can assess their level of depression. This site contains a lot of multimedia and video elements. It also contains information about depression, the personal stories of famous people and the general public alike. Users can communicate with the "Lowdown Team" via text or email or by posting on the website's message board. The site includes music by Kiwi artists who are also website contributors.

★★★    *MyRay* www.myray.com

MyRay is a free online cognitive-behavioral therapy-based self-help program for depression. Users are invited to take a self-test and, based on those results, are offered recommendations for healthy eating, exercise, and time management. Users are provided with instructions on exercises for breathing and muscle relaxation. Users are instructed to return to the site weekly and complete the exercises. Progress is charted on graphs and records are kept of scores on tests. E-group is available for users to post new questions or to review/ respond to other users' posts.

★★★    *My Mood Monitor* mymoodmonitor.com

This free website is a self-directed screening test for depression, anxiety, and bipolar disorder. Based on a person's answers, this site offers a simple test to indicate a person's risk for having one of the four conditions. Visitors to the site have the option to print out their results and take them to their health-care professional to determine if a diagnosis is appropriate and to develop a treatment plan.

★★★    *The Reawakening Center* www.reawake.com

This free interactive website is an online self-help resource for depression. No registration is required. Site visitors can take a test to measure their level of depression. The site contains a series of animated interactive presentations to address the barriers that prevent people from seeking treatment for depression. The presentations integrate principles of cognitive therapy with motivation. The site also contains educational material about depression and useful links to related topics.

## ■ INTERNET RESOURCES

### General Websites

★★★★★    *Depression* psychcentral.com/disorders/depression

A comprehensive condition center from Psych Central, this website offers hundreds of articles dealing with depression, blogs, book reviews, depression quizzes, daily updated news and research articles, a peer-reviewed directory to other online depression resources, and a thriving set of support groups, along with much more.

**** *Wing of Madness: A Depression Guide* www.wingofmadness.com

An enormous collection of sensible and accurate information, started in 1995. However, since moving to a blog format, it's a little more difficult to navigate and find information related to a specific topic.

*** *Psychology Information Online: Depression* www.psychologyinfo.com/depression

This site from Donald J. Franklin, PhD, offers about two dozen articles on depression. Although regularly updated, the articles are short and offer little else.

*** *Internet Mental Health: Major Depressive Disorder* www.mentalhealth.com/dis/p20-md01.html

This website links to dozens of resources that are weighted toward an academic, clinical, or research audience, including consensus treatment guidelines and recent research reviews. The page carries no update date and appears to be only occasionally updated (last update was over 2 years ago).

## Psychoeducational Materials

### General Sites on Depression
***** *Depression* nimh.nih.gov/health/topics/depression

From the National Institute of Mental Health, this page offers a dozen brochures organized by audience (adolescents, employers, senior citizens, and women) and by topic (bipolar, suicide, comorbidity, etc.).

***** *Expert Consensus Guidelines: Pharmacotherapy of Depressive Disorders in Older Patients* www.psychguides.com/depression

This set of pharmacotherapy treatment guidelines from experts in geriatric depression are tailored to older adults. The accompanying 12-page guide for patients and families is, although a bit dated, still a valuable resource.

**** *Depression in Children and Adolescents: What It Is and What to Do about It* by Jim Chandler, MD www.jameschandlermd.com

Click on "Pediatric Psychiatry Pamphlets" to get to the section on depression information and vignettes written for the public and teens. The section "What Can be Done?" is about behavioral interventions.

**** *Depression and Bipolar Support Alliance* www.dbsalliance.org

This nonprofit advocacy and support organization offers dozens of articles on depression and bipolar disorder, as well as information about their extensive community-based support groups, and other online resources for emotional support and self-help.

**** *Dr. Deb* drdeborahserani.blogspot.com

While Dr. Deborah Serani, a psychologist and psychoanalyst, blogs about many topics, her book is entitled *Living with Depression,* so most of her blogging is on depression and topics of interest to people with depression. Always interesting, the blog provides helpful, real-life tips in living with depression.

**** *Fighting the Darkness* fightingthedarkness.blogspot.com

This blog from Jamie, mother of two, is about her battle with depression for over two decades. Interesting and constantly updated, its one of the best depression blogs online.

*** *Depression Articles* www.selfhelpmagazine.com/article/depression

A set of depression articles from *Selfhelp Magazine* that unfortunately have little organization or dates.

**** *Understanding and Treating Depression* www.counselingcenter.illinois. edu/?page_id=146

A brief, balanced, and complete overview from the University of Illinois at Urbana-Champaign.

### Medication Treatment
**** *Antidepressants* helpguide.org/mental/medications_depression.htm

A single article from the nonprofit HelpGuide that provides a helpful overview about everything you need to know about taking medications for depression.

**** *Are You Considering Medication for Depression?* www.cmhc.utexas.edu/depressionmedications.html

An article offering relevant questions and their answers about antidepressants that is well written. It might make a useful handout to read before a medication evaluation.

### Psychotherapy
There are a wealth of general psychotherapy resources available online that describe the process and types of psychotherapy. They are not covered here but instead appear in Chapter 34, Self-Management and Self-Enhancement.

**** *Depression Treatment: Psychotherapy* psychcentral.com/lib/2006/depression-treatment

This article covers all aspects of the treatment of depression, including psychotherapy. Also check out this editorial about why psychotherapy is often the best treatment choice for depression: psychcentral.com/depress3.htm

### Postpartum Depression
★★★★★   *Postpartum Progress* postpartumprogress.com

This amazing blog from parenting writer and advocate Katherine Stone offers not only daily entries and insights, but also a frequently asked questions section, survival tools, and a set of reference articles about postpartum disorders, such as postpartum depression, anxiety, psychosis, and more. A rich, detailed and constantly updated resource.

★★★★   *Postpartum Support International* www.postpartum.net

This website is designed to help women with perinatal mood and anxiety disorders, most commonly postpartum depression. Lots of good articles and links to support resources on the site.

★★★   *This Isn't What I Expected* www.psychologytoday.com/blog/isnt-what-i-expected

This blog from Karen Kleiman, LCSW, offers an eclectic, irregularly updated view of postpartum depression issues and opinion.

### Seasonal Affective Disorder (SAD)
★★★★   *Seasonal Affective Disorder* www.mayoclinic.com/health/seasonal-affective-disorder/DS00195

This resource from the Mayo Clinic offers brief but informative articles about symptoms, risk factors, and treatments for SAD, as well more articles under the "In-Depth" tab.

## ■ SUPPORT GROUPS

### Depression and Bipolar Support Alliance

Phone: 800-826-3632 or 312-642-0049
www.dbsalliance.org

### Depression and Related Affective Disorders Association

www.drada.org

### Emotional Health Anonymous

Phone: 626-287-6260
Fellowship of people who meet to share experiences, strengths, and hopes with each other so they may solve common mental health problems.

### Emotions Anonymous

Phone: 651-647-9712
www.emotionsanonymous.org
Fellowship for people experiencing emotional difficulties.

**National Alliance for the Mentally Ill**

Phone: 703-524-7600 or 800-950-NAMI (Hotline)
www.nami.org

**National Foundation for Depressive Illness**

Phone: 800-239-1264
www.depression.org

**National Organization for Seasonal Affective Disorder**

Phone: 800-826-3632
www.nosad.org

**Postpartum Support International**

Phone: 503-894-9453
www.postpartum.net
To increase the awareness of the emotional changes women often experience during pregnancy and after the birth of a baby.

**Recovery International**

Phone: 866-221-0302
www.recovery-inc.com
A community mental health organization that offers a self-help method of will training.

**See also** Bipolar Disorder (Chapter 11) and Suicide (Chapter 39).

# CHAPTER 21

# DIVORCE

D ivorce has become epidemic in our society: almost half of new marriages end up in divorce. For those involved, separation and divorce are complex and emotionally charged, and its stresses place men, women, and children at risk for psychological and physical difficulties. Separated and divorced adults have higher rates of behavioral disorders, admission to psychiatric hospitals, substance abuse, suicide, and depression than their married counterparts. Many separations and divorces immerse children in conflict, and as a consequence, the children are more likely to have school-related problems, especially at the beginning of the separation and divorce.

Self-help resources on divorce fall into four main categories: for divorced or divorcing parents; for the children of divorced or divorcing parents; for divorced or divorcing adults in general; and child custody. This chapter presents self-help books, films, online self-help, Internet resources, and support groups directed to all those involved in divorce.

## ■ SELF-HELP BOOKS

**Strongly Recommended**

★★★★★   *The Boys and Girls Book about Divorce* (1985) by Richard Gardner. New York: Bantam.

This treasured book is written for children to help them cope with their parents' separation and divorce. It is appropriate for children age 10 years and older. Most of what psychiatrist Gardner tells children in the book comes from his therapy experiences with children of divorced parents. Gardner talks directly to children about their feelings after the divorce, who is and is not to blame for the divorce, parents' love for their children, and how to handle angry feelings and the fear of being left alone. Then he tells children about how to get along better with their divorced mother and their divorced father. Gardner also covers the important topic of getting along with parents who live apart, sensitively handling such difficult issues as playing one parent against the other and what to do when parents try to use the child as a weapon. The final chapter explains to children what to expect if they see a psychotherapist. Written at an appropriate reading level for its intended audience, the book also features a number of cartoon-like drawings, which adds to its appeal for children. It has survived the test of time and remains a superb resource for divorced or divorcing parents to give to their 10-year-old and older children.

## BOX 21.1
## RECOMMENDATION HIGHLIGHTS

### SELF-HELP BOOKS

- For young children in divorced families:
  - ***** *Dinosaurs Divorce* by Laurene Brown and Marc Brown
- For older children and adolescents in divorced families:
  - ***** *The Boys and Girls Book about Divorce* by Richard Gardner
  - **** *How It Feels When Parents Divorce* by Jill Krementz
- For divorced parents to help children:
  - **** *Growing Up with Divorce* by Neil Kalter
  - *** *Helping Children Cope with Divorce* by Edward Teyber
  - *** *Helping Your Kids Cope with Divorce* by M. Gary Neuman
  - *** *The Truth About Children and Divorce* by Robert E. Emery
- For those undergoing divorce:
  - *** *Crazy Time* by Abigail Trafford
- For those wanting to examine the research controversy on the effects of divorce:
  - **** *The Unexpected Legacy of Divorce* by Judith Wallerstein et al.
  - **** *Coping with Divorce, Single Parenting, and Remarriage* by E. Mavis Hetherington

### FILMS

- On the pain of divorce and the need to attend to children:
  - ***** *The Squid and the Whale*
  - **** *Kramer vs. Kramer*
- On women making the postdivorce transition and redefining themselves:
  - **** *An Unmarried Woman*
- On inevitable changes in marriages and friendships:
  - *** *The Four Seasons*

### ONLINE SELF-HELP

- For free information and self-help for youth dealing with divorce:
  - *** *eCouch* ecouch.anu.edu.au

### INTERNET RESOURCES

- For complete and supportive sites for people going through or considering divorce:
  - **** *Divorce—Psychology Today* www.psychologytoday.com/basics/divorce
  - **** *Divorce Support* www.divorcesupport.com
  - **** *Smart Marriages* www.smartmarriages.com

★★★★★ *Dinosaurs Divorce: A Guide for Changing Families* (1986) by Laurene Brown and Marc Brown. Boston: Little, Brown.

This book, designed for children living in divorced families, grew out of the Browns' experiences with divorce as parent and stepparent, and for Laurene, as a child herself. *Dinosaurs Divorce* is a 30-page, full-color picture book that takes children through the experience of divorce in a dinosaur family. The topics include why parents divorce, how children feel when their parents divorce, what happens after the divorce, what it's like to live with one parent, what it's like to visit the other parent, having two homes, celebrating holidays and special occasions, telling friends, meeting parents' new friends, and having stepsisters and stepbrothers. The book is simple and easy for children to understand. Much of it can be read and understood by children who are in elementary school. Parents can read and discuss the pictures and words with younger children.

★★★★ *How It Feels When Parents Divorce* (1984) by Jill Krementz. New York: Knopf.

Jill Krementz, a writer and photographer, presents 19 children's experiences with the divorces of their parents. Krementz interviewed and photographed 19 children aged 7 to 16. The title of each of the chapters is a child's name. Each chapter opens with a full-page photograph of the child, followed by the child's experience in a divorced family. The children talk about the changes in their lives, their hurt, their confusion, and the knowledge they gained. The book is mainly geared toward children and adolescents—it is at about the same reading level as Gardner's *The Boys and Girls Book about Divorce*—although divorced parents can also benefit from the children's descriptions of their experiences. The children's stories reflect their vulnerability and resilience. Eight-year-old Lulu reflects, "I suppose they needed the divorce to be happy, but there were times when I thought it was stupid and unfair and mean to me." Many mental health professionals find it an excellent self-help book for older children and adolescents.

★★★★ *The Unexpected Legacy of Divorce* (2001) by Judith Wallerstein, Sandra Blakeslee, and Julia Lewis. New York: Hyperion.

This book provides a variety of descriptions of people's experiences with divorce at different points in their lives. The authors describe how people still define themselves as children of divorce up to 30 years after their parents' divorce. The unexpectedly negative results of divorce reported here made this book a controversial and certainly sobering reevaluation of the decision to divorce. The authors assert that many children of divorce make bad choices in relationships or avoid relationships altogether. The book is based on tracking approximately 100 children of divorced parents into their adult lives.

★★★★ *Coping with Divorce, Single Parenting, and Remarriage* (1999) edited by E. Mavis Hetherington. Mahwah, NJ: Erlbaum.

A leading divorce researcher edited this book and a number of leading researchers contributed chapters. The book is a research book far more than a self-help book. However, if you want to read more about what leading researchers in this area are studying, the book is a good choice.

**★★★★**  *Surviving the Breakup* (1996) by Judith Wallerstein and Joan Kelly. New York: Basic Books.

Based on their Children of Divorce Project, Wallerstein and Kelly describe how children, adolescents, and their parents cope with divorce. Especially helpful are the authors' portrayals of how children of different ages cope with divorce and the ways that parents can help them. A fine, 4-star self-help guide by the lead author of *The Unexpected Legacy of Divorce* (reviewed above).

**★★★★**  *Growing Up with Divorce* (1990) by Neil Kalter. New York: Free.

This book is written for divorced parents and provides information to help their children avoid emotional problems. It is especially designed to counteract the long-term effects of divorce on children, many of whom struggle with emotional difficulties for years after the actual divorce itself. Kalter's book offers parents practical strategies for helping children cope with the anxiety, anger, and confusion that can occur immediately or can develop over a number of years. Kalter nicely shows how a child's level of psychological development influences the specific ways that he or she experiences, understands, and reacts to the stress of divorce. The book includes in-depth accounts of the experiences of children from infancy through adolescence. Kalter gives step-by-step instructions to parents about how to speak to their children in indirect and nonthreatening ways and tells them what to say in specific situations. A splendid self-help book for divorced parents.

**Recommended**

**★★★**  *Crazy Time: Surviving Divorce* (1982) by Abigail Trafford. New York: Harper & Row.

As a result of her own painful experience with divorce, journalist Trafford began recording the many stories she heard from others who were going through divorce. Each story was different, yet each fit a pattern. Trafford identifies and describes the developmental stages of divorce, crazy time, and the recovery. *Crazy Time* is the author's term for the two years immediately following a divorce, in which unpredictable and inexplicable emotions take over and the roller-coaster ride begins. Each topic is approached through the true-life experiences of many interviewees. The personalized style of the book gives an intimate feeling to the stories and the people who lived them. *Crazy Time* received a sterling evaluation from those experts familiar with it, but the low number of ratings reduced its overall rating.

**★★★**  *Helping Children Cope with Divorce* (revised ed., 2001) by Edward Teyber. New York: Wiley.

Teyber provides good strategies for parents to help their children through a divorce as unscathed and emotionally strong as possible in the face of stressful circumstances. Parents learn about ways to minimize stress, explain the divorce, establish custody and visitation plans, and shield the children from parental conflicts. A wise and sensible book in the divorce field characterized by ideology and polarization. If this self-help book had been more widely known among mental health professionals, it may have reached 5-star status.

★★★   *The Good Divorce* (1995) by Constance Ahrons. New York: Harper Collins.

Based on her longitudinal study of postdivorce families, Ahrons provides hope that divorced spouses can handle their breakup in a way that will help both the adults and children involved to be as emotionally healthy as they were before the divorce. The book especially provides helpful information for couples in which "staying together for the sake of the children" is not a viable option.

★★★   *Helping Your Kids Cope with Divorce* (1998) by M. Gary Neuman with Patricia
       Romanowski. New York: Times.

This parents' book on divorce through a child's eyes explains how children think and feel about divorce and, more importantly, how they interpret what has happened. The central concept is that more often than not the child is thinking differently than the parent thinks. The result is that children blame themselves and make distorted attributions about why it happened, what their role was, and what will happen to them now. Activities teach parents how to stop reasoning and to start communicating by knowing how to find out what the child thinks and feels through art, play, activities, and simply asking different questions. A chapter each is devoted to age-specific information on the infant and toddler to the 17-year-old. Other topics include fighting, the first day of the divorce, moving, custody and visitation, and divorce-related changes (e.g., finances, home, changing schools, child care).

★★★   *For Better or For Worse: Divorce Reconsidered* (2002) by E. Mavis Hetherington
       and John Kelly. New York: Norton.

Hetherington and Kelly paint a very different picture of divorce than Judith Wallerstein in her *The Unexpected Legacy of Divorce* (reviewed above) and *Second Chances* (reviewed below). Based on Hetherington's extensive research on more than 1,400 families over three decades, the authors argue that while divorce can be destructive in the short term, it can also be positive, creating new opportunities for long-term growth. Readers are taken through the stages of divorce, single parenthood, remarriage, and stepfamily life and are given many recommendations for how to cope with the stress involved. Excellent strategies are provided for both adults and children. Many excerpts from cases in Hetherington's study are provided to illustrate various aspects of divorce.

★★★   *The Truth about Children and Divorce* (2006) by Robert E. Emery. London:
       Penguin.

Putting children first is a concept on which all would agree, but doing so is more difficult for parents who are engaged in intense emotional decisions. This book is written for the divorcing parents and offers commonsense suggestions that are rarely at the forefront of thinking when a divorce is under way. Some of the themes are: (1) keep the children out of the middle, especially emotionally; (2) a divorce begins a grieving process for both parents and the child, but other emotions often crowd out this important aspect; (3) an unsuccessful marriage doesn't have to lead to an unsuccessful divorce; and (4) instead of dwelling on the failed marriage, begin thinking about the new relationship as parents sharing children and needing a new beginning. These and other positive perspectives are presented by the author, who has worked with divorcing parents for years and presents his accumulated experience here.

★★★   *Second Chances: Men, Women, and Children a Decade after Divorce* (revised ed., 1996) by Judith S. Wallerstein and Sandra Blakeslee. Boston: Houghton Mifflin.

This book is based on a long-term study of divorced couples and their children. Wallerstein and associates examined how 60 families fared five years after divorce. In *Second Chances*, Wallerstein and Blakeslee describe the reevaluation of 90% of the original 60 families 10 years after divorce, with some analysis of their lives at the 15-year mark. Additional commentary is included about divorced families who are seen at the California clinic Wallerstein directs. The authors argue that divorce is emotionally painful and psychologically devastating for a large proportion of children. In their view, divorced parents who are struggling to meet their own needs often fail to meet their children's needs; through their own instability and continuing conflict with each other, divorced parents add to the psychological burdens of their children. Interview excerpts are interwoven with clinical interpretations and research findings to tell the emotionally difficult story of the long-term negative effects of divorce on children. The book, although recommended, is sober reading for many divorcing parents.

★★★   *The Divorce Book* (2001) by Matthew McKay, Joan Blades, Richard Gosse, and Peter Rogers. Oakland, CA: New Harbinger.

The authors—psychologists and lawyers—combined their expertise to help adults negotiate the painful legal and emotional hurdles of divorce. Their book distinctively provides information about the legal aspects of ending a marriage, including conflict resolution, divorce mediation, and custody arrangements.

★★★   *The Parents' Book about Divorce* (revised ed., 1991) by Richard Gardner. New York: Bantam.

Gardner, a leading expert on divorce, provides helpful information about the psychological and emotional aspects of divorce. He takes parents through a chronological timetable of the circumstances involving divorce, telling parents how and when to tell children about an impending separation, strategies for informing friends and teachers, and guidelines for adapting to new homes and stepfamilies. Although rated favorably in our national studies, this book pales in comparison to the exceptional ratings accorded to Gardner's *The Boys and Girls Book about Divorce* (reviewed above).

★★★   *Two Homes* (2003) by Claire Masurel and Katy McDonald Denton. Cambridge, MA: Candlewick Press.

This children's book is meant to help children navigate their parents' divorce in a warm and positive way. The illustrations are effectively matched to the narrative, which is focused not on what is missing but on what children do have in their new "two homes." The comfort items, such as having one's toothbrush in both places, emphasize the love, caring, and belonging that children have in their two homes. The story is presented through Alex, the young boy telling the story. The concept does not try to diminish the difficult part of divorce for children but gives comfort about his new life with his parents.

★★★   *Creative Divorce* (1973) by Mel Krantzler. New York: Signet.

This book, anchored in the 1970s, is about divorced individuals' opportunities for personal growth. When he was 50 years of age, Krantzler and his wife separated after 24 years of marriage. He describes his ordeal—self-pity, guilt, loneliness, and helplessness—and how it helped him grow as a person. The author also draws on the experiences of his male and female clients. Krantzler considers divorce the death of a relationship, requiring a mourning period followed by reflective self-evaluation and planning. The self-destructive patterns that many divorced adults engage in are portrayed, as when men say they want companionship but pursue women as sexual objects. The book was a bestseller in the 1970s, but its popularity has declined since then, and many readers may regard it as both dated and too optimistic.

★★★ *Chicken Soup for the Soul: Divorce and Recovery* (2008) by Jack Canfield, Mark Victor Hansen, and Patty Hansen. Cos Cob, CT: Chicken Soup for the Soul.

The *Chicken Soup* series is well known for taking a topic and stirring in the ingredients of humor, sadness, relief, anxiety, and optimism. These emotions and insights are shared by many of the contributors, each of whom tell their divorce story in homespun and personal ways. The stories range from humorous to despairing, and most have mixed elements. The format of a personal story to convey a principle, a moral, or other guiding benchmark is almost always a successful choice because we like to hear about others' trials and triumphs.

### Not Recommended

★ *Mars and Venus Starting Over* (1998) by John Gray. New York: HarperCollins.

## ■ FILMS

### Strongly Recommended

★★★★★ *The Squid and the Whale* (2005) directed by Noah Baumbach. R rating. 81 minutes.

Walt and Frank, two bright boys attempting to navigate adolescence, are caught in the middle of their parents' messy divorce. Walt decides to live with his father, and Frank remains with his mother in the family home. The boys take sides and develop stress symptoms as this bohemian family dissolves. Walt plagiarizes songs and breaks ties with his girlfriend after his father urges him to play the field. Frank begins drinking and masturbating in school. In the midst of dealing with their own problems, the boys must also maintain a connection with their parents, who have both entered into new relationships. The boys' turmoil demonstrates the toll that divorce can take on children and serves as a call for parents to pay particular attention to how their children are coping. A useful film for any family undergoing the stress of separation or divorce.

★★★★ *Kramer vs. Kramer* (1979) directed by Robert Benton. PG rating. 105 minutes.

Wife leaves marriage; husband assumes care of their 5-year-old son; father discovers the responsibilities and joys of parenting; wife returns and fights for custody of son. The ensuing legal proceedings are bitter and cruel, resulting in a decision favoring the mother and ordering the father to relinquish custody. But then the Kramers negotiate a mature arrangement on their own that attends to the needs of the child and themselves. A powerful film, recipient of five Academy Awards, that vividly demonstrates multiple realities of marriage, divorce, and custody: adult self-involvement with work (the father), search for identity (the mother), avoiding heartrending custody battles, attending to the child's needs during custody, the pain of nasty legal battles, and ultimately the superiority of working cooperatively.

★★★★  *An Unmarried Woman* (1978) directed by Paul Mazursky. R rating. 124 minutes.

An affluent Manhattan lawyer suddenly informs his steadfast wife that he doesn't love her and is leaving their 20-year marriage. The wife, accustomed to defining herself in terms of her husband, makes the difficult transition to being an unmarried woman, developing a mature identity, and learning to love without losing herself. One of the earliest and still best films that realistically depict women redefining their postdivorce identities. Also beautifully explores the loving relationship between a mother and her teenage daughter.

**Recommended**

★★★  *The Four Seasons* (1981) directed by Alan Alda. PG rating. 107 minutes.

Three middle-aged couples are lifelong friends and vacation together until one of the men decides to divorce his wife. He brings his young girlfriend on their next vacation, a cruise around the Virgin Islands, and the other two couples are both disturbed and envious of the couple's romantic relationship. The divorced wife subsequently accuses her lifelong friends of deserting her, and the three couples continue to support one another, adapt, and struggle through the travails of life and marriage. The film uses Vivaldi's *Four Seasons* as a metaphor for the development and inevitable changes in their lives and marriages. Useful for illustrating the interpersonal ramifications of divorce and accepting changes in friends.

★★★  *The Good Mother* (1989) directed by Leonard Nimoy. R rating. 104 minutes.

A divorced mother falls in love with a man who naively allows the woman's young daughter to touch his penis, resulting in the divorced father's filing a suit for custody. Although the psychologists conclude that the child has suffered no harm and that she is securely attached to the mother, the lawyer convinces the mother to make her boyfriend the scapegoat in order to maintain the relationship with her daughter. A provocative and sad film showing the challenges of intimacy for single parents and the charge of sexual molestation being used as a weapon by a former spouse.

★★★  *Husbands & Wives* (1992) directed by Woody Allen. R rating. 107 minutes.

A film in which art imitated life. Woody Allen and Mia Farrow endured a public battle over Allen's affair with Farrow's adopted daughter. A few months later, Allen released this film, starring himself and Farrow acting out a virtually identical plot: an unhappy marriage crumbles when the husband strays with a much younger woman (in this case, a student). In the film, a friend of Allen's character discards his longtime wife for an aerobics instructor, shocking their friends and planting seeds of marital dissolution all around. *Husbands & Wives* is a lacerating comedy, an honest look at conflicts that beset many marriages. It is a story about the fragility of relationships and the foolishness of older men seeking to recapture their youth with younger women.

★★★    *Starting Over* (1979) directed by Alan J. Pakula. R rating. 105 minutes.

This honest film casts Burt Reynolds as a newly divorced man struggling to adjust to single life in the late 1970s. Reynolds plays an unsuccessful writer torn between his neurotic girlfriend (Jill Clayburgh) and his flighty, sexy ex-wife (Candice Bergen). The man is vulnerable, indecisive, and confused—at one point suffering a hilarious anxiety attack in public. Wonderfully acted (the female leads were nominated for Oscars) and quirkily entertaining, *Starting Over* only disappoints with an abrupt ending. A valuable self-help resource for sharing ambivalent feelings about an ex-spouse and about the indecision of reconciliation. Also useful for discussing coping with single life and dating again.

★★★    *Mrs. Doubtfire* (1994) directed by Chris Columbus. PG-13 rating.
119 minutes.

An idealistic and fun-loving father clashes with a sensible and sedate mother in marriage and then in divorce when the mother is awarded custody of their three children. The father transforms himself into an elderly English nanny, Mrs. Doubtfire, and is hired to care for the children. That's when the hijinks begin. Nicely demonstrates the genuine pain and loss of divorce, parental devotion to children despite the end of a marriage, and the realistic struggles to accommodate everyone's needs in postdivorce families.

★★★    *Bye Bye Love* (1995) directed by Sam Weisman. PG-13 rating. 106 minutes.

Three divorced California fathers attempt to juggle their children's and their own needs over a weekend. No enviable role models here, but the film will trigger discussion of the difficult postdivorce adjustment and balancing multiple needs in limited time.

**Not Recommended**

★    *First Wives' Club* (1996) directed by Hugh Wilson. PG rating. 102 minutes.

**Strongly Not Recommended**

†    *The War of the Roses* (1990) directed by Danny DeVito. R rating. 116 minutes.

## ■ ONLINE SELF-HELP

★★★    *eCouch* ecouch.anu.edu.au

This free online self-help resource offers a divorce and separation program for youth. It provides information about divorce as well as self-help modules on problem solving, cognitive retraining, dealing with anger, and physical activity. Youths complete interactive modules where they identify their own thinking. The program also contains a workbook where users can practice skills and track their progress. The website is designed with a look and in a language comfortable for young users but the programs are probably useful for all ages.

## ■ INTERNET RESOURCES

### General Websites

★★★★ *Divorce* www.psychologytoday.com/basics/divorce

This resource from the commercial *Psychology Today* offers helpful resources and articles about all areas of divorce, from the initial breakup of the marriage to the aftermath. It also covers special topics, such as divorce and children, as well as remarriage. The articles come from the print edition of the magazine (so some are dated) but are usually well grounded, with practical advice.

★★ *Divorce Magazine* www.divorcemag.com

This is a large resource but a very confusing website to navigate, with lots of links seemingly listed just to increase search engine traffic. Easier-to-navigate websites are available that offer far more information.

★★★ *Divorceinfo.com* www.divorceinfo.com

Although a simple site created by an individual, it addresses all the issues with good, if short, articles on a wide variety of divorce-related topics. Hundreds of articles to explore that are easy to digest.

★★★★ *Divorce Support* www.divorcesupport.com

This site offers lots of articles, chats, information links, and other resources. Organized by state so it is easy to find information specific to you, but click on "Articles" to get to the general library of divorce information.

★★★ *Divorce Online* www.divorceonline.com

A great many articles not only on the legal and financial aspects of divorce, but also about the psychological and emotional aspects of divorce.

★★★ *Frequently Asked Questions about Divorce* www.divorcecentral.com/resource/faq. html

Frequently asked questions and their answers about the emotional, legal, parenting, and financial aspects of divorce. Although these FAQs haven't been updated in many years, it remains a good starting place for understanding the different aspects and consequences of getting a divorce.

★★★★ *Smart Marriages* www.smartmarriages.com

Click on "Articles, Reports, Research item" to find dozens of helpful articles that provide eye-opening information about marriage, divorce, and remarrying. This is an especially useful resource for those on the fence about divorce.

★★★    *The Relationship and Personal Development Center* www.relationshipjourney.com

Dawn Lipthrott, LCSW, offers readers dozens of helpful articles about divorce and relationships.

★★★    *Bill Ferguson's How to Divorce as Friends* www.divorceasfriends.com

Ferguson combines legal and relationship advice in brief selections from his book. Includes an occasional blog and an online course.

### Legal Aspects
★★★★★  *Divorce Helpline* www.divorcehelp.com

Although this is a commercial site designed to sell books and make referrals, the brief articles in the Reading Room are educational about both legal matters and emotions. The Short Divorce Course is an alternative to the courts and should certainly be considered.

★★★★    *Nolo* www.nolo.com/legal-encyclopedia/family-law-divorce

Nolo sells high-quality do-it-yourself legal guides. Their Legal Encyclopedia offers numerous complete and well-written readings on various legal aspects of divorce.

★★★★    *Flying Solo* www.lifemanagement/flyingsolo

Click on "Divorce Separation" in the text or the left column. Over 100 articles dealing primarily with the legal and financial side of divorce, taxes, some tips, FAQs, and so on. Some are difficult to read, but most are to the point and some are unique.

### Kids and Custody
★★★    *Helping Children Understand Divorce* by Sara Gable and Kelly Cole    muextension.missouri.edu/xplor/hesguide/humanrel/gh6600.htm

This article discusses the stresses on kids and their likely reactions to divorce.

★★★★    *Coping with Separation and Divorce: A Parenting Seminar* by Judy Branch, MS, and Lawrence G. Shelton, PhD www.dartmouth.edu/~eap/library/COPEhandbook22oct09.pdf

A PDF that covers all the issues of divorce in a downloadable and easy-to-read handbook and curriculum guide.

★★★    *Your Parents' Divorce* www.counselingcenter.illinois.edu/?page_id=173

A brief but good pamphlet from a university counseling service.

★★★    *Learning to "Get Along" for the Best Interest of the Child* by Hedy Schleifer, MA www.hedyyumi.com/2010/07/learning-to-get-along-for-the-best-interest-of-the-child

An essay suitable as a handout to explain the value of counseling for kids after a divorce. Parts of the article emphasize Imago Relationship therapy.

## ■ SUPPORT GROUPS

### ACES (Association for Children for Enforcement of Support)

Phone: 800-739-2237
www.childsupport-aces.com

### Children's Rights Council

Phone: 301-459-1220
www.crckids.org
Concerned parents provide education and advocacy for reform of the legal system regarding child custody.

### North American Conference of Separated and Divorced Catholics

Phone: 906-482-0494
www.nacsdc.org

**See also** Child Development and Parenting (Chapter 15), Families and Stepfamilies (Chapter 23), and Marriage (Chapter 28).

# CHAPTER 22

# EATING DISORDERS

We are a nation obsessed with food, spending an extraordinary amount of time think-ing about it, gobbling it, controlling it, avoiding it. Taken to extreme, our food issues turn into pathological behaviors. Eating disorders include binge eating (consuming huge quantities at one time), anorexia nervosa (the relentless pursuit of thinness through starva-tion), and bulimia (a binge-and-purge eating pattern). In fact, about 3% of U.S. teens have suffered from one of these disorders (Swanson et al., 2011).

Eating disorders are far more common in women than in men. The most extreme case is anorexia nervosa, in which about 90% of cases are female. If one adds in general preoccupa-tion with weight and body image, then practically all women socialized in the United States harbor deep concerns about their eating.

In this chapter, we critically review self-help books, autobiographies, films, online self-help, Internet resources, and support groups on eating disorders (Box 22.1). We assiduously avoid the Pro-Ana (pro-anorexia) websites and online groups that extol eating disorders; these encourage deception and perhaps exacerbate symptoms.

## ■ SELF-HELP BOOKS

### Strongly Recommended

★★★★ *Dying to Be Thin: Understanding and Defeating Anorexia Nervosa and Bulimia* (2001 updated ed.) by Ira M. Sacker and Marc A. Zimmer. New York: Warner.

This book is about the secrets and private worlds of anorexics and bulimics. The authors have included sections on personal histories information for the person with an eating dis-order and his or her families, friends, and teachers, as well as resources. By reading this book, you will see how people can carry dangerous secrets for a long time before they admit that the secret has taken control of their lives. For people who may think or know they suf-fer from an eating disorder, or those connected with someone with an eating disorder, this book provides insight, motivation, and knowledge about the complexity of eating disor-ders. One of the highest-rated books on eating disorders in our national studies.

### Recommended

★★★ *The Hunger Within: A Twelve-Week Guided Journey from Compulsive Eating to Recovery* (1998) by Marilyn Ann Migliore with Philip Ross. New York: Main Street.

## BOX 22.1
## RECOMMENDATION HIGHLIGHTS

**SELF-HELP BOOKS**

■ For a research-supported treatment of binge eating:

★★★ *Overcoming Binge Eating* by Christopher G. Fairburn

■ For the practical treatment of eating disorders:

★★★★ *Dying to Be Thin* by Ira M. Sacker and Marc A. Zimmer

★★★ *The Anorexia Workbook* by Michelle Hefner and Georgia I. Eifert

★★★ *Eat, Drink, and be Mindful* by Susan Albers

■ For transitioning from compulsive eating to a healthy lifestyle:

★★★ *The Hunger Within* by Marilyn Ann Migliore with Philip Ross

★★★ *Healing the Hungry Self* by Deirdre Price

■ For sociocultural and familial roots of eating disorders:

★★★ *Bulimia/Anorexia* by Marlene Boskind-White and William White, Jr.

★★★ *The Golden Cage* by Hilde Bruch

**AUTOBIOGRAPHIES**

■ On the development of eating disorders:

★★★★★ *Feeding the Hungry Heart* by Geneen Roth

★★★★ *Breaking Free from Compulsive Eating* by Geneen Roth

■ On the realities of anorexia and bulimia:

★★★ *Starving for Attention* by Cherry B. O'Neill

★★★ *My Life So Far* by Jane Fonda

■ On life as a recovering anorexic:

◆ *Gaining* by Aimee E. Liu

**FILMS**

■ On the familial origins and drastic consequences of anorexia:

★★★★★ *The Karen Carpenter Story*

★★★★ *Best Little Girl in the World*

■ On the intersections of women, food, and identity:

★★★★ *Eating*

**ONLINE SELF-HELP**

■ For a research-supported, 8-week program for bulimia:

★★★★ *Overcoming Bulimia Online* www.overcomingbulimiaonline.com

■ For family members and friends of those struggling with anorexia:

★★★ *Overcoming Anorexia: Effective Caring* www.overcominganorexiaonline.com

**INTERNET RESOURCES**

■ For valuable information on eating disorders:

★★★★★ *National Eating Disorders Association* www.nationaleatingdisorders.org

★★★★★ *Bulimia Nervosa Resource Guide* www.bulimiaguide.org

★★★★ *Eating Disorders—Psych Central* psychcentral.com/disorders/eating_disorders

This book shows the on-and-off dieter how his or her individual struggle with eating is a response to feelings of emotional deprivation established in childhood. It provides a step-by-step program that explores the core reasons for overeating, identifies triggers that precipitate bingeing, and shows how to break the cycle of yo-yo dieting. The book includes motivational sayings, guided weekly sessions, exercises to stay on track, a hunger awareness diary, a vicious cycle worksheet, and weekly food-for-thought programs. A person who eats compulsively is enacting an emotional script, and the script is what has to be changed. This is a 12-week program with three stages. For people who have ridden the roller coaster of compulsive eating, this book may prove to be helpful.

★★★ *Healing the Hungry Self: The Diet-Free Solution to Lifelong Weight Management* (1998) by Deirdre Price. New York: Plume.

This book provides a comprehensive program for healthy eating using a variety of physical, mental, emotional, and spiritual concepts. The author addresses the difference between physical and emotional hunger, the importance of three (or more) meals a day, recognizing danger zones, alternatives to food in coping with emotions, and sensible exercise programs. There are case studies, self-help tests, charts to monitor progress, checklists, and a 6-week plan. Adults or adolescents wishing to modify their dietary lifestyles will find practical and useful advice in this 3-star resource.

★★★ *Overcoming Binge Eating* (1995) by Christopher G. Fairburn. New York: Guilford Press.

Fairburn is a well-known authority on eating disorders. His book has two main parts. The first part reviews the current scientific literature about binge eating, and the second part offers a structured cognitive-behavior self-help manual to treat binge eating problems. Given the reluctance of people with eating disorders to reveal their problem to anyone, the book could be a safe and helpful first step in accepting help and beginning treatment. The author advises friends and therapists on how they can use this book most effectively. Had this book been more frequently rated in our studies it would have probably reached a 4-star status. In any case, *Overcoming Binge Eating* is an exceptional resource with research-supported treatment strategies.

★★★ *The Twelve Steps and Twelve Traditions of Overeaters Anonymous.* (1995). Rio Rancho, NM: Overeaters Anonymous.

This book is devoted to detailed discussions of the Twelve Steps and Twelve Traditions used in Overeaters Anonymous (OA). This is a program of physical, emotional, and spiritual recovery based on the original Alcoholics Anonymous principles. The often-moving writing explains how OA's principles help members recover and how the fellowship functions. The common bonds shared by OA members are the disease of compulsive eating from which all have suffered, and the solutions found are in the principles embodied in the 12 steps. This book, in concert with an OA group and psychotherapy, will prove helpful to people who find the spiritual emphasis of 12-step programs congenial.

★★★  *The Golden Cage* (reprinted ed., 2001) by Hilde Bruch and Catherine
      Steiner-Adair. Cambridge, MA: Harvard University Press.

*The Golden Cage* symbolizes the high expectations many anorexic women feel. They feel like a sparrow, a very ordinary bird, which is meant to fly free, not to be viewed as an exotic, beautiful bird in a cage. Psychiatrist Bruch originally wrote the book 30 years ago; it has been periodically reprinted. She describes the profile of many of the youngsters with whom she worked who grew up in high-socioeconomic-status families and for whom there were high expectations and rigid parental control. The core characteristics of anorexia are viewed as fear of failure to live up to expectations, not being good enough, and being disappointing. The resulting self-concept is not being deserving of what they have been given materially and at the sacrifice of the family. The youngsters start to take pride in self-deprivation and self-discipline; in fact, they come to view the hunger state as rewarding. Bruch believes that most medication, behavioral modification, and psychoanalytic therapies miss the mark. The effective treatment plan is one in which self-concept and self-valuing are primary treatment goals. Although many mental health experts agree with Bruch's major points, they also believe that the book is dated and neglects the research-supported effectiveness of cognitive-behavioral therapy and select medications.

★★★  *Bulimia/Anorexia* (3rd ed., 2000) by Marlene Boskind-White and William C.
      White, Jr. New York: Norton.

This third edition of this book, first published in 1993, reflects the continuing phenomenon of girls and women in body image crisis and self-concept despair. The evolving process of an eating disorder is traced from childhood to teen years, in which self-concept is determined largely by social interaction skills and acceptance begins to suffer with pressure to conform. The college years for this population also reflect pressure to conform, use of food as a coping mechanism, and a struggle between total control and no control. Treatment myths about bulimia are described. Psychotherapy for bulimia focuses on decision making, conformity, and movement away from self-sabotage. Psychotherapy for anorexia addresses relationship with therapist, consciousness raising, changing the ways one thinks, and anger control. The negative sociocultural roots of anorexia and the treatment of eating disorders within managed care are significant additions to the new edition.

★★★  *The Anorexia Workshop* (2007) by Michelle Hefner and Georgia I. Eifert.
      Oakland, CA: New Harbinger.

This book is written primarily for those who suffer from anorexia and secondarily for family/friends and for psychotherapists. The workshop is a "how to" book on the application of ACT (Acceptance and Commitment Therapy) to anorexia. ACT has been an increasingly popular treatment with several difficult problems, such as substance abuse. In this case, the treatment is clearly and methodically explained such that the average reader can understand and apply it. The overarching message is that most therapies try to make individuals change their thoughts and feelings as part of the treatment plan; by contrast, ACT emphasizes acceptance and observation of thoughts and feelings and commitment to identifying what one values in life and working toward that goal. The exercises and worksheets are critical for the usefulness of the book. Consideration of professional assistance is encouraged, but the book is written so that it can be a stand-alone guide for self-help in dealing with anorexia.

★★★   *Fat Is a Family Affair* (1996) by Judi Hollis. Cedar City, MN: Hazelden.

This book covers a number of eating disorders, including the bingeing and vomiting of bulimia, the starvation of anorexia nervosa, and compulsive overeating. Hollis recommends a 12-step program as the best treatment for eating disorders. The book is presented in two main parts: Part I, The Weigh In, and Part II, The Weigh Out. The Weigh In discusses how eating disorders evolve and provides a self-test to determine if you have an eating disorder. Hollis believes that most people with eating disorders are surrounded by 10 or 12 codependent people who, for reasons of their own, are enmeshed in trying to help or change the eating disorder but instead only perpetuate it. Hollis includes many success stories of people who have followed her advice. Special attention is given to the family's role in eating disorders. This 3-star book promotes Overeaters Anonymous, which has helped many individuals learn to change their eating habits. But critics didn't like the preachy tone of the book and the codependency explanations.

★★★   *Eat, Drink, and be Mindful* (2009) by Susan Albers. Oakland, CA:
          New Harbinger.

A mindful approach to eating is the theme and purpose of this book. Rather than focusing on an eating disorder *per se*, Albers integrates Acceptance and Commitment Therapy (ACT) with cognitive-behavioral therapy, the latter when individuals want to begin changing their behavior. Acceptance and being mindful of what one eats, not having a judgment about eating, is the goal. Rather than eating what is on the plate, one would focus on each bite and think about the eating process. As a result, one may decide that eating all that is on the plate is not necessary. This is a different and interesting perspective on mindful attention.

★★★   *Helping Your Teenager Beat an Eating Disorder* (2004) by James Lock and Daniel
          LeGrange. New York: Guilford Press.

Written for parents, this self-help book advocates that parents should be involved in the care of their children's possible eating disorder. Many sources have discouraged parental involvement; on the contrary, this approach points out that the problem is much greater than we should expect a teenager to deal with even with a professional involvement. How to be involved effectively without seeming to hover or control the teenager is discussed thoroughly here. The key elements for parents are understanding eating disorders and that teenage thinking on such a subject could be distorted or only partially accurate. How to engage in a treatment plan with one's teenager and how to stay on the same page as a family are masterfully discussed.

★★★   *Why Weight? A Guide to Ending Compulsive Eating* (1989, reissued 1993) by Geneen Roth. New York: Plume.

Geneen Roth founded the Breaking Free workshops that help people cope with eating disorders. She overcame her own compulsive overeating several years ago. First, she put an end to constant dieting that inevitably led to weight gain. She eliminated her compulsive overeating by developing seven eating guidelines that form the core of her Breaking Free program: eat only when hungry, sitting down, without distractions; eat only what you want, until you are satisfied, in full view of others and with enjoyment. The 16 chapters include written exercises that help compulsive overeaters become aware of what they are doing and that provide information on the emotional basis of overeating. Questions are asked about how it would feel to be thin, how it really felt to diet and binge all those years, and how the overeater can learn to eat only when physically hungry. Each chapter also contains charts and lists that focus on what is eaten, why, and when, and feelings associated with food. The 3-star book is full of helpful exercises for overeaters, is free of psychobabble, and provides insights about the nature of eating problems.

★★★   *When Food Is Love* (1991) by Geneen Roth. New York: Dutton.

This book explores the relation between eating disorders and close relationships. It was written by Geneen Roth, the author of *Why Weight?* (reviewed above) and several autobiographies (reviewed in the next section). The book focuses on how family-of-origin experiences contribute to the development of eating disorders. Roth reveals her own childhood abuse, which led to compulsive overeating in adulthood and prevented her from having a successful intimate relationship with a man. According to Roth, similar patterns are found in people who are compulsive overeaters and lack intimacy in their life: excessive fantasizing, wanting what is forbidden, creating drama, needing to be in control, and the "one wrong move syndrome" (placing too much importance on doing the absolutely correct thing at this moment). This 3-star book does a good job of explaining how inadequate close relationships and eating disorders are linked. Critics say that Roth does not adequately consider biological and sociocultural factors that determine eating disorders.

★★★   *Food for Thought* (1980) by the Hazelden Foundation. New York: Harper & Row.

Subtitled *Daily Meditations for Dieters*, this book presents a spiritual approach to eating disorders. The Hazelden Foundation is based near Minneapolis and is known primarily for its alcohol treatment program. Through short daily meditations, *Food for Thought* offers encouragement to anyone who has ever tried to diet, people who overeat or have an eating disorder, and members of Overeaters Anonymous. Each day's brief reading addresses the concerns of people with eating disorders. The book is especially designed for use by individuals who go to Overeaters Anonymous meetings, and it will have special appeal to individuals who want a spiritual approach to eating problems.

★★★   *Feeling Good about the Way You Look* (2006) by Sabine Wilhelm. New York: Guilford.

Body image and physical appearance are often unrelated perceptions: body image reflects how one internally evaluates looks, whereas appearance is perceived by others more objectively. This theme underlies psychologist Wilhelm's purpose of helping those whose body image is distorted, thus resulting in personal, occupational, and interpersonal limitations. Other health problems that often accompany body image concerns are social phobias, obsessive-compulsive disorder, and eating disorders. Individuals are encouraged to think about change and what they want to change, to name thoughts, to reflect on core beliefs, and to be self-reflective on how to move ahead.

### Diamond in the Rough

 ♦  *Anatomy of Anorexia* (2000) by Steven Levenkron. New York: Norton.

The intrusive dominance of anorexia in the lives of girls and their families is the thrust of this sensitive book. Levenkron discusses milestones in the development of the disease, including the effects on the family system, evaluating readiness for college, treatment formats, transferential dynamics, an authoritative/nurturing therapeutic alliance, and the effects of incest on anorexia development. The etiology of anorexia is explained as a failure by the family system to engender trust, healthy dependency, and a positive attachment to the parent figure. The subsequent development of perfectionism, mistrust, and emotional insecurity as preludes to anorexia is poignantly described. Each chapter features case vignettes that demonstrate the powerful effect of anorexia. Written in the psychodynamic and family systems traditions, this book is intended for mental health professionals to help them identify anorexia before it is too late. The author's earlier book, *The Best Little Girl in the World* (1978), was made into a movie by the same name and is reviewed later in this chapter.

### Not Recommended

★★ *You Can't Quit Eating until You Know What's Eating You* (1990) by Donna LeBlanc. Deerfield Beach, FL: Health Communications.

★★ *Weight Watchers Stop Stuffing Yourself* (1999) by Weight Watchers. New York: Weight Watchers.

 ★ *Brave Girl Eating* (2010) by Harriett Brown

 ★ *Love Hunger: Recovery from Food Addiction* (1990) by Frank Minirth, Paul Meier, Robert Helmfelt, Sharon Sneed, and Don Hawkins. Nashville, TN: Thomas Nelson.

 ★ *Just a Little Too Thin* (2006) by Michael A. Strober and Meg Schneider. Cambridge, MA: Da Capo Press.

### Strongly Not Recommended

 † *The Love-Powered Diet* (1992) by Victoria Moran. San Rafael, CA: New World Library.

## ■ AUTOBIOGRAPHIES

### Strongly Recommended

★★★★★ *Feeding the Hungry Heart: The Experience of Compulsive Eating* (1993) by Geneen Roth. New York: NAL/Dutton

This classic book precedes the author's subsequent writing and audios on compulsive eating, including *Why Weight?* and *Breaking Free from Emotional Eating* (see below). It is not a diet book; Roth declines to offer quick fixes. Progress is seen as gradual and setbacks are to be expected and should not be sources of shame and guilt. This is an inspiring, personal book in which Roth shares her own eating and weight struggles; many readers say that it changed their lives. Roth is nonjudgmental; she doesn't blame compulsive eaters and makes them feel they are not alone in this struggle. There are many others who share a food obsession. Thinness is not seen an absolute value; readers should be satisfied with who they are.

★★★★ *Breaking Free from Compulsive Eating* (1993) by Geneen Roth. New York: NAL/ Dutton.

Speaking from personal experience, the author of numerous books about eating and dieting advises readers about how they can free themselves from compulsive eating. She outlines the techniques developed in her weight loss workshops. Roth shows women struggling with weight management that they are not alone and maintains that self-understanding can bring self-acceptance.

**Recommended**

★★★ *My Life So Far* (2005) by Jane Fonda. New York: Random House.

Jane Fonda has played so many roles on stage and in life that it seems disingenuous to fit her into a single topical chapter. She is the daughter of a famous couple, the wife of three gifted and powerful men, a talented actress, a fitness guru, a political radical, and much more. She was one of the first celebrities to openly admit her eating disorder. In the 1970s she went public with what she termed her "bulimarexia," a binge-and-purge cycle that lasted several decades. She sometimes engaged in self-induced vomiting 10 or more times per day. At other times she fasted, comprising the "arexia" part of her neologism. She attributes her eating disorder to, among other reasons, the way that Hollywood equates thinness with beauty: "For 25 years, I could never put a forkful in my mouth without feeling fear, without feeling scared." It took decades for her to get over this fear and her search for a perfect appearance and to accept that good is good enough. Unfortunately, there is not major coverage of her eating disorder in this autobiography; now that she is in recovery, it didn't seem so important. Nonetheless, the discussion of her life trajectory shows how her appearance interacted with her career and was critical in laying the groundwork of her eating disorder.

★★★ *Starving for Attention* (1995) by Cherry Boone O'Neill. Center City, MN: Hazelden Foundation.

The daughter of singer and TV personality Pat Boone gives a frank first-person account of her eating disorders, including the lies and deceptions that accompanied them. She suffered from both anorexia and bulimia and confronts the reader with the harsh realities and twisted perceptions of body image in both conditions as well as the health problems due to being underweight in anorexia and the binge–purge cycle of bulimia. There is also a detailed discussion of her personal life, career, and religious faith, which she believes helped her to overcome both eating disorders.

★★★   *Wasted: A Memoir of Anorexia and Bulimia* (2006) by Marya Hornbacher.
New York: HarperCollins.

This is a frank look inside the world of an eating disorder—a scary story of body image distortion, compulsive dieting, and self-induced vomiting, repeated daily with no seeming end other than starvation and death. Hornbacher suffered from a combined anorexia and bulimia, in which the perfectionism and mental purity of the anorexic lived together with the self-disgusting ritual binges and vomiting of the bulimic. At one point, the amount of vomit she spewed out plugged the family sewer system. At another point, she claims to have reduced her weight to 52 pounds and describes the many ways she hid her eating disorders from others. Hornbacher was hospitalized and treated but not cured. The book ends with her still emaciated and resigned to a continuing struggle with her demons. This is not an optimistic book but instead a graphic description of the downside of eating disorders.

★★★   *Am I Still Visible? A Woman's Triumph over Anorexia Nervosa* (1983) by Sandra
Harvey Heater. White Hall, VT: Betterway.

The author, who teaches preschool reading, describes the development and treatment of her anorexia. She also provides a history of the disorder and theories and describes treatment options. Mental health professionals applauded this autobiography; however, the book is out of print and not easy to obtain.

### Diamonds in the Rough

♦   *Good Enough: When Losing Is Winning, Perfection Becomes Obsession, and Thin
Enough Can Never Be Achieved* (1998) by Cynthia N. Bitter. Penfield, NY:
HopeLines.

The author grew up in a difficult family situation. Her father had a bipolar disorder, and her mother was in denial about it. At age 14, she developed anorexia, binge–purge type, which almost resulted in her death, and this condition did not end until she was 39. The book describes the numerous medical complications of the disorder, the self-destructive behaviors, the food obsessions, and the benefits of therapy, both inpatient and outpatient, that helped her finally overcome her disorder. Positively rated in our national surveys but not well known.

♦   *Gaining: The Truth about Life after Eating Disorders* (2008) by Aimee E. Liu.
New York: Grand Central.

Her earlier memoir *Solitaire* describes the anorexia that plagued Aimee Liu during her high school and college years. This is the coverage of most first-person narratives describing an eating disorder. This sequel, written almost 30 years later, describes her life as a recovered anorexic (her term), although in Alcoholics Anonymous one would say "recovering" anorexic. Liu acknowledges that symptoms of the disorder remain but are currently under control. The book is a mix of memoir, interviews with present and former anorexics, and a distillation of current research, with sections on the role of genetics and environmental factors in eating disorders, a chapter on media images that equate thinness with beauty, and the role of personality dispositions. The interviews revealed the daily struggle of people still in the throes of the disorder and were helpful to Liu in "connecting the dots," identifying factors leading to her anorexia and how she was able to overcome it. She shows how people can use the control and perfectionism associated with an anorexic lifestyle to gain career and personal success. Liu is nonjudgmental without being patronizing or overly clinical.

## ■ FILMS

**Strongly Recommended**

★★★★★ *The Karen Carpenter Story* (1989, made for TV) directed by Richard Carpenter III and Joseph Sargent. Not rated. 100 minutes.

Anorexia is portrayed as a family-based disorder that led singer Karen Carpenter to feel little control over her life, except over the food she ate. Her brother Richard was designated the talented one of the family, and when Karen's voice overshadowed Richard's, she felt she had betrayed her parents' dream. The complexity and power of eating disorders come through effectively and accurately. This 5-star film biography of a pop star may serve as a warning sign and a valuable model for adolescent girls.

★★★★ *Best Little Girl in the World* (1981, made for TV) directed by Sam O'Steen. Not rated.

Being the second daughter and following a troublesome older sister set Casey up for unrealistically high expectations of herself that place her on a trajectory toward self-starvation. When hospitalized, Casey meets two people, a fellow patient and a psychotherapist, who give her hope, support, and motivation. This story portrays the road to recovery and the need to confront longstanding familial conflicts.

★★★★ *Eating* (1990) directed by Henry Jaglom. R rating. 110 minutes.

A birthday party attended by women friends sets the stage for candid self-disclosures about relationships, food, money, food, loneliness, food, men, and food. In other words, many aspects of women's lives are revealed and shared, particularly women's love–hate relationship with eating. The characters are familiar and real people—people who make the subject seem ordinary, natural, and at times very funny. Subtitled *A Very Serious Comedy about Women and Food,* this movie is also rated under Women's Issues (Chapter 42).

**Recommended**

★★★ *For the Love of Nancy* (1994, made for TV) directed by Paul Scheider.

Nancy is an anxious high-school graduate whose social isolation, constant exercising, and sudden temper tantrums were clear signs of an addictive behavioral cycle, but no one heard. The familiar pattern of family attempts to force eating, resulting in further restraint from food, is well illuminated. The story poignantly reveals that the family must experience healing and positive change before anorexia can be treated. This is a touching story with an overarching message that, in many cases, the family is the patient.

★★★  *Center Stage* (2000) directed by Nicholas Hytner. PG-13 rating. 115 minutes.

An intimate look at three young women studying at the American Ballet Academy. All three face problems along their paths involving relationships, sex, identity, competition, and the constant pressure to perform and remain thin. One of the three women develops bulimia, and she denies that she is hurting her body. More about the quest for autonomy than eating disorders, this film illustrates important themes for young women about living life on one's own terms instead of adhering to parental controls or pleasing boyfriends.

### Not Recommended

★★  *Thin* (2006) directed by Lauren Greenfield. Not rated. 102 minutes.

## ONLINE SELF-HELP

★★★★  *Overcoming Bulimia Online* www.overcomingbulimiaonline.com

This online self-help program is designed to help people struggling with bulimia. Designed as an 8-week program, it contains multimedia elements and interactive elements that help users identify their own behavior patterns and thoughts about eating. The program helps users develop a healthy eating plan, develop problem-solving skills, and learn assertiveness. Price is $99.

★★★  *Overcoming Anorexia: Effective Caring* www.overcominganorexiaonline.com

This online program is designed to be used by family members and loved ones of people diagnosed with anorexia nervosa. It provides users with information about the condition, treatment options, and strategies for intervening with a family member. Based on the principles of cognitive-behavioral therapy, the program presents video clips of family members interacting with someone who has anorexia. Cost of the program is $100.

## INTERNET RESOURCES

The Internet is full of eating disorders websites, but so many of them lead to treatment centers simply interested in trying to get your business. We've filtered through them to bring you some of the surprisingly few useful online resources below.

### General Websites

★★★★★  *National Eating Disorders Association* www.nationaleatingdisorders.org

This national nonprofit advocacy and education organization offers a wealth of educational materials with clear explanations and well-written articles. Topics are in-depth and wide-ranging and are often categorized based upon age and gender groups, making them age- and gender-appropriate. The usual organization-specific information is here too, such as NEDA events and programs. The site is well designed and easy to navigate as well.

**★★★★** *Eating Disorders—Psych Central* psychcentral.com/disorders/eating_disorders

An in-depth educational center about all kinds of eating disorders—anorexia, bulimia, binge eating, etc.—offering a wide array of mental health-oriented topics, such as symptoms, causes, and treatments. Q&As, an active online support group, and a blog on body image round out the site's offerings.

**★★** *Something Fishy* www.something-fishy.org

Although at one time one of the premier independent, consumer-run eating disorder sites online, since being acquired by a company that runs eating disorder treatment centers, it's gone downhill. Features a still-active support group community as well.

## Psychoeducational Materials

**★★★★** *Eating Disorders—KidsHealth* kidshealth.org/parent/emotions/feelings/eating_disorders.html

This resource from the nonprofit Nemours Foundation not only provides an age-appropriate introduction to the topic of eating disorders for children and teenagers, it also offers more age-specific topics for parents and teens. Well designed and easy to read, the articles are informative and up to date.

**★★★★★** *Bulimia Nervosa Resource Guide* www.bulimiaguide.org

This website from the nonprofit ECRI Institute is a comprehensive resource for patients and their families to better understand bulimia, risk factors, prevention, causes, symptoms, treatments, and much more. Dozens of articles can be found here, including checklists and understanding how to maximize health insurance benefits to pay for bulimia treatment (which is often an inpatient experience).

**★★★★** *Eating Disorders—Mayo Clinic* www.mayoclinic.com/health/eating-disorders/DS00294

Like all Mayo Clinic informational resources online, their section on eating disorders is well written in short articles that provide not only the usual basics (symptoms, causes, treatments) but also some in-depth materials as well.

**★★★** *Anorexia Nervosa and Related Eating Disorders* www.anred.com

The factual materials here are numerous, detailed, and fairly well organized. However, the site is frustrating in its lack of authorship and dates on articles, and its layout is reminiscent of websites from the 1990s.

**★★★** *Mirror, Mirror* www.mirror-mirror.org/eatdis.htm

Offers some interesting articles and resources on eating disorders, including myths and realities about them and a "survivors wall" (that sadly hasn't been updated in years).

★★★   *Anorexia Nervosa* www.helpguide.org/mental/anorexia_signs_symptoms_
causes_treatment.htm

This single page from the nonprofit HelpGuide is a good overview of the disorder, its signs and symptoms, risk factors, and finding treatment. It also offers links to a few additional Internet resources about anorexia.

★★★★   *Eating Disorders* www.nimh.nih.gov/health/publications/eating-disorders

An up-to-date guide to eating disorders from the National Institute of Mental Health.

★★★   *The Mindful Eating Program* www.cmhc.utexas.edu/mindfuleating.html

This page not only describes mindful eating but also offers information on intuitive eating, emotional eating, body image, and many related topics.

## ■ SUPPORT GROUPS

### Compulsive Eaters Anonymous

Phone: 562-342-9344
www.ceahow.org
A 12-step recovery program.

### Food Addicts Anonymous

Phone: 561-967-3871
www.foodaddictsanonymous.org
To find a local group, visit the website or call the World Service Office.

### Food Addicts in Recovery Anonymous

Phone: 781-321-9118
www.foodaddicts.org

### National Association of Anorexia Nervosa and Associated Disorders

Phone: 847-433-4632
www.anad.org
For persons with eating disorders.

### National Eating Disorders Association

Phone: 206-382-3587
nationaleatingdisorders.org
For persons with eating disorders, their families, and friends.

### Overeaters Anonymous (OA)

Phone: 505-891-2664
www.oa.org
A 12-step self-help fellowship. Free local and online meetings are listed on the website.

### We Insist on Natural Shapes (WINS)

Phone: 800-600-WINS
www.winsnews.org
A nonprofit organization dedicated to educating adults and children about what normal, healthy shapes are.

**See also** Women's Issues (Chapter 42).

# CHAPTER 23

# FAMILIES AND STEPFAMILIES

"A friend loves you for your intelligence, a mistress for your charm, but your family's love is unreasoning; you were born into it and are of its flesh and blood. Nevertheless, it can irritate you more than any group in the world," observed French philosopher André Maurois. Families who do not function well together often foster maladjusted behavior on the part of one or more members.

In this chapter we limit our evaluation to general books on families and stepfamilies, especially those that examine how families or blending families can be a source of distress. Other chapters cover the family's role in a number of specific areas, such as abuse (Chapter 2), addictions (Chapter 3), child development and parenting (Chapter 15), divorce (Chapter 21), love and intimacy (Chapter 27), marriage (Chapter 28), and teenagers (Chapter 40).

Children born in the United States today have a 40% chance of living at least part of their lives in a stepfamily before they are 18 years of age. Stepfamilies are a heterogeneous group—about 65% are stepfather families, about 20% are stepmother families, and about 15% are so-called blended families to which both partners bring children from previous marriages. And many stepfamilies produce children of their own. We review a number of self-help resources directed specifically at stepfamilies and blended families.

Following our summary of recommended self-help resources (Box 23.1), we consider in detail books, films, and Internet resources related to families and stepfamilies. We emphasize several positive cinematic portrayals of stepfamilies, as they are typically depicted in a negative or mixed way in popular films (Leon & Angst, 2005). A list of national support groups rounds out the chapter.

## ■ SELF-HELP BOOKS

### Strongly Recommended

★★★★★ *Old Loyalties, New Ties: Therapeutic Strategies with Step-Families* (1988) by Emily Visher and John Visher. New York: Brunner/Mazel.

This book is designed to help families and stepfamilies cope more effectively. Visher and Visher argue that remarried families are not imperfect copies of nuclear families but are rather family systems created from the integration of old loyalties and new ties. They outline special therapeutic strategies they believe are most effective with stepfamilies, such as helping stepfamily members enhance their self-esteem, reducing a sense of helplessness, teaching negotiation, and encouraging mutually rewarding dyadic relationships, all designed to

## BOX 23.1
## RECOMMENDATION HIGHLIGHTS

### SELF-HELP BOOKS

- For a wide variety of family and stepfamily circumstances:
  - **** *Old Loyalties, New Ties* by Emily Visher and John Visher
  - *** *The Shelter of Each Other* by Mary Pipher
- For a family systems approach to solving family problems:
  - **** *The Family Crucible* by Augustus Napier and Carl Whitaker
- For stepfathers:
  - **** *Step-Fathering* by Mark Rosin
- For blended families:
  - **** *Step by Step-Parenting* by James D. Eckler
  - *** *Stepfamilies* by James H. Bray and John Kelly
- For creating two stable and happy homes for children of divorce:
  - *** *Mom's House, Dad's House* by Isolina Ricci

### FILMS

- On surviving victimization and wanting more for our children:
  - ***** *The Joy Luck Club*
- On familial bonding and moral growth in caring for family members:
  - **** *Rain Man*
  - **** *What's Eating Gilbert Grape?*
- On the enduring value of flawed family relationships:
  - ***** *Life as a House*
  - **** *Terms of Endearment*
  - **** *Pieces of April*
- On the costs, struggles, and possibilities of remarriage:
  - **** *Stepmom*
- On healing a strained parental relationship by helping others:
  - **** *Fly Away Home*
- On second chances and choosing a family:
  - **** *The Family Man*

### INTERNET RESOURCES

- For excellent general information for families:
  - **** *Families.com* www.families.com
  - **** *Working Mother* www.workingmother.com
- On blended families/stepfamilies
  - **** *National Stepfamily Resource Center* www.stepfamilies.info

achieve greater integration and stability in the stepfamily. Concrete ways in which thera-pists can help stepfamilies with specific types of problems are also described. Among them are how to deal with the many changes and losses in their lives, identify realistic beliefs so that expectations are manageable, resolve loyalty conflicts, develop adequate boundaries, cope with life-cycle discrepancies and complexities, and create a more equal distribution of power. Many case studies illustrate the authors' therapy strategies. This is a very good book about remarried families, but it was written primarily for a professional audience rather than a self-help audience. Nonetheless, it is well written, and the self-help reader can gain considerable insight into the dynamics of remarried families and therapy strategies.

**★★★★** *Step by Step-Parenting: A Guide to Successful Living with a Blended Family* (2nd ed., 1993) by James D. Eckler. White Hall, VA: Betterway.

This book, as is evident from its title, concerns blended families, families to which each adult has brought children from a previous marriage. The book reflects both the adjustments that made author James Eckler's blended family a successful one and his years of experience as a minister and pastoral counselor. A wide array of issues are covered, including the games stepchildren play, the rights of the stepparent, name changes, the pros and cons of adoption, discipline, stepsibling rivalries, marital communication, grandparents, and dealing with chil-dren at different developmental levels (preschool, elementary school, and adolescence). Our mental health experts said that this is a good self-help book for blended families—it presents a balanced approach and includes detailed discussions of blended families' stressful experi-ences and wise strategies for successful living in a blended family.

**★★★★** *Step-Fathering* (1987) by Mark Rosin. New York: Simon & Schuster.

This was among the first self-help books to describe the stepfather family from the stepfather's perspective. Rosin draws on his own experiences as a stepfather and in-depth interviews with more than 50 stepfathers to help men cope effectively in a stepfather fam-ily. Chapters take stepfathers through such topics as the adjustment involved in becoming a stepfather, the problems of combining families, how to handle discipline and authority, communication with the wife/mother, dealing with the other father, money matters, ado-lescent stepchildren, and the rewards of stepfathering. The expert consensus is that this is a fine self-help book for stepfathers. It is well written and includes insightful examples that most stepfathers will be able to relate to.

**★★★★** *The Family Crucible* (1978) by Augustus Napier and Carl Whitaker. New York: Harper & Row.

This book presents a family systems approach to solving family problems. In family sys-tems therapy, the family unit is viewed as a system of interacting individuals with different subsystems (husband–wife, sibling–sibling, mother–daughter, father–sibling–sibling, and so on). A basic theme is that most problems that seem to be the property of a single individ-ual evolved from relationships within the family. Therefore, the best way to solve problems is to work with the family rather than the individual. Napier and Whitaker say that prob-lem families have in common certain general patterns: acute interpersonal or intrapersonal stress, polarization (family members at odds with each other) and escalation (the conflict intensifies), triangulation (one member is the scapegoat for other members who are in con-flict but pretend not to be), diffusion of identity (no one is free to be autonomous), and fear of immobility, which Napier and Whitaker equate with fear of death (of the family). The authors describe in considerable detail how they used family systems therapy with a particular family—an angry adolescent and other equally distressed family members. This book is widely considered to be one of the classics in family systems therapy. However, it is written mainly for a professional audience and is somewhat dated.

**Recommended**

    ★★★  *Families: Applications of Social Learning to Family Life* (revised ed., 1975) by Gerald Patterson. Champaign, IL: Research.

This volume presents a behavioral approach to improving children's behavior and family functioning. To begin, Patterson explains some important behavioral concepts like social reinforcers, aversive stimuli, and accidental training. Time-out procedures and behavioral contracts are integrated into a step-by-step reinforcement management program for parents to implement with their children. Behavioral management strategies are also tailored to children with specific problems. This book was very favorably evaluated by our mental health experts, but by only 12 of them, thus leading to a lower rating. Mental health professionals of a behavioral persuasion described this book as exceptionally good for parents who want to improve a child's behavior, especially the behavior of a child who is aggressive and out of control.

    ★★★  *The Shelter of Each Other: Rebuilding Our Families* (1996) by Mary Pipher. New York: Grosset/Putnam.

This is not a how-to book but a how-to-think book that sensitively exposes the breadth of family struggles. Psychologist Pipher brings us face to face with a culture in which parents sell Girl Scout cookies to colleagues because Girl Scouts can't go door to door anymore and with an electronic revolution that has resulted in making media personalities more recognizable than neighbors. Pipher organizes the stories of families around the three central themes of character, will, and commitment. Through these themes, she brings hope that we as families and as community can shelter each other and decide the future and the culture we want, now that we see what we have become. This book was highly rated in our national study but was evaluated by only 14 experts, thus receiving a modest 3-star designation.

    ★★★  *Mom's House, Dad's House* (1997) by Isolina Ricci. New York: Fireside.

Written by a family therapist who directs the Family Court services for the California judicial branch, this fine book provides guidance for creating two happy, stable homes for children of divorce. Legal, emotional, and practical aspects are examined. Advice includes how to talk to a former mate, steps to building a positive co-parenting relationship, and when to use mediation. Self-tests, checklists, strategies, and extensive examples are included. Had this book been more frequently rated in our studies, it would have been a 4- or 5-star resource.

    ★★★  *Love in the Blended Family: Stepfamilies* (1991) by Angela Clubb. Deerfield Beach, FL: Health Communications.

This self-help resource concerns stepmother families, not blended families in the accepted sense of the term. At the beginning of the book, Clubb tells readers that what they are reading is biased because it is written by a stepmother and second wife. Her husband brought two children to the newly formed stepmother family, and the Clubbs subsequently had two children of their own. Thus, the book is primarily about relationships and experiences in one stepmother family, although Clubb does occasionally bring in mental health experts' views on stepfamily issues. This 3-star effort clearly shows Clubb's professional background as a writer; the book reads in places like a finely tuned novel. Many of the problems and issues Clubb has experienced in her stepmother family are those that any stepmother has to face.

★★★  *The Second Time Around: Why Some Second Marriages Fail* (1991) by Louis Janda and Ellen MacCormack. New York: Carol.

Janda and MacCormack conducted a study of more than a hundred people who were in second marriages, which furnished much of the material in this book. Readers learn that a majority of individuals in stepfamilies find the adjustment to be more difficult than they anticipated. Janda and MacCormack believe that many people expect too much when they enter a stepfamily, and they say that stepchildren make any second marriage a challenge. The book received a 3-star rating because it was positively reviewed, but by only 10 respondents. The few mental health professionals who knew about it opined that it included a number of good examples of stepfamily problems and how to solve them effectively.

★★★  *Strengthening Your Stepfamily* (1986) by Elizabeth Einstein and Linda Albert. Circle Pines, MN: American Guidance.

This 133-page book contains five comprehensive chapters. Chapter 1 describes stepfamily structure and how it is different from previous family structure. The authors discuss common stepfamily myths and unrealistic expectations. Chapter 2 focuses on the couple relationship and how to communicate more effectively and share feelings. Chapter 3 examines strategies for creating positive relationships between stepparents and stepchildren. Chapter 4 explores children's feelings and behaviors in stepfamilies and offers guidelines for helping children cope more effectively. Chapter 5 discusses making a stepfamily function well and gives hints for dealing with issues that range from daily routines to holiday celebrations. The book was positively but infrequently rated in our national studies. This is an easy-to-read overview of stepfamily problems and ways to solve them.

★★★  *Blending Families: A Guide for Parents, Stepparents, Grandparents, and Everyone Building a Successful New Family* (1999) by Elaine F. Shimberg. New York: Berkley.

This self-help resource takes a unique approach in viewing stepfamily dynamics. Interviews, surveys, and discussion groups were conducted, and the resulting information is distilled in this book. The information is presented in a practical fashion, with ideas and perspectives offered directly by stepfamily members about what worked for them and what strengthened their families. The book contains reflective quotes from adult children of stepfamilies looking back on their experiences as well as contemporary quotes by stepfamily members. The author intended the book to be a practical guide based on actual successes and shortcomings of people who have lived in a stepfamily system. The content of the book is not directed only at stepparents, but also at stepchildren and extended family members.

★★★ *Stepfamilies* (1999) by James Bray and John Kelly. New York: Broadway.

The results of a 9-year project on the development of stepfamilies are presented clearly through the three types of stepfamilies and the identification of cycles through which they move. This book provides good advice for easing the conflicts of stepfamily life and coping with the stress of divorce. Bray includes many emotionally laden stories of stepfamilies to illustrate both how to cope and how not to cope with life in a stepfamily. The ups and downs of different types of stepfamilies are described. Special focus is given to important aspects of the stepfamily structure, such as bridging the insider–outsider gap, the stepmother, the nonresidential parent, and adolescence. This is a splendid book for stepfamilies.

★★★ *Back to the Family* (1990) by Ray Guarendi. New York: Basic.

Subtitled *How to Encourage Traditional Values in Complicated Times,* this book is the result of a study sponsored by the Children's Hospital in Akron, Ohio, to identify the characteristics of healthy, adaptive families. One hundred happy families were nominated by award-winning educators in the National/State Teachers of the Year organization. Guarendi distilled information from interviews with the families and developed a how-to manual for parents who want to build a happy home. The interviews reveal how families can mature through good and bad times and how parents in happy, competent families sifted through various types of child-rearing advice to arrive at the way they reared their own children. At times the book is inspirational, but families frequently need more than a pep talk to solve their problems.

★★★ *Adult Children: The Secrets of Dysfunctional Families* (1988) by John Friel and Linda Friel. Deerfield Beach, FL: Health Communications.

This book is primarily intended for adults who grew up in dysfunctional families and suggests what they can do to improve their lives. Modeled after the 12-step program of Alcoholics Anonymous, it tries to shed light on why adults who grew up in dysfunctional families developed problems as adults—problems such as addiction, depression, compulsion, unhealthy dependency, stress disorders, and unsatisfying relationships. Five sections discuss (1) who adult children are and what their symptoms are, (2) family systems and how dysfunctional families get off track, (3) how the dysfunctional family affects the child, (4) a model of codependency, and (5) recovery. *Adult Children* barely received a 3-star rating; many mental health experts frown on the codependency approach of the authors.

**Not Recommended**

★★ *Smart Stepfamily: Seven Steps to a Healthy Family* (2006) by Ron L. Deal. Bethany House.

★★ *Bradshaw on the Family* (1988) by John Bradshaw. Deerfield Beach, FL: Health Communications.

## ■ FILMS

**Strongly Recommended**

★★★★★ *The Joy Luck Club* (1994) directed by Wayne Wang. R rating. 138 minutes.

This is a film about neither joy nor luck, but about hope and triumph of the will. When one of a group of four Chinese immigrant women dies, the event prompts the recollections of great hardships, despair, and loss and, most importantly, the effect these experiences had on their relationships with their own daughters. Two of the dominant themes are the effects of feelings of self-worthlessness on women's lives and mothers' desire for a better life for their children. This heartwarming 5-star film transcends culture, race, and generations.

★★★★★ *Life As a House* (2001) directed by Irwin Winkler. R rating. 125 minutes

Kevin Kline is an architect who learns he will soon die and tries to finish his life's tasks: reconnecting with his 16-year-old, drug-using, and suicide-chasing son; making amends with his ex-wife who has her own marital troubles; and turning the shack he inherited from his father into a house. While veering into maudlin, the movie reminds us that we cannot erase our pasts nor ignore how we repeat our family dynamics. This superbly acted film underscores the centrality and urgency of attending to family relationships while we can.

★★★★ *The Family Man* (2000) directed by Brett Ratner. PG-13 rating. 125 minutes.

In a milder remake of *It's a Wonderful Life*, Nicholas Cage plays a successful and talented businessman. He is happily living his single life until he magically awakens on Christmas morning married to the girlfriend (Téa Leoni) he abandoned 13 years before. He now has a house in New Jersey, two adorable kids, a minivan (instead of his Ferrari), and a job selling tires for his father-in-law. He struggles with wanting his old life back but slowly recognizes the pleasures of domestic bliss. The film's strongest points are that it is a *marital* love story and that any life is a mixture of pleasure and pain. It may be superficial at times, but it contains a core of genuine warmth and could help with marital reconciliation.

★★★★ *Terms of Endearment* (1983) directed by James L. Brooks. PG rating. 130 minutes.

This film dominated the Academy Awards in 1983, but its popular acclaim should not overshadow its therapeutic value and portrayal of characters who struggle with enmeshment, marital infidelity, and loss in a poignant and heart-wrenching way. The mother, Aurora, is overprotective, dominant, and consumed by running her daughter's life, while the daughter is overattached and dependent. A midlife relationship changes Aurora, while infidelity and sickness change her daughter. The film's enduring messages are the value of (flawed) love, strength in (flawed) relationships, and familial survival through pain.

★★★★ *Rain Man* (1988) directed by Barry Levinson. R rating. 130 minutes.

Twenty-something self-centered Charlie, disinherited by his deceased father, discovers that he has an autistic older brother, Raymond, who has inherited the father's $3 million. The real story, however, is about Charlie's learned selflessness, the brothers' fraternal bonding, and Charlie's moral growth as he learns to care for Raymond. Raymond is tragic and funny, a survivor and yet fragile; he has built a life of required predictability that Charlie can penetrate only momentarily. This film realistically portrays mental illness and what it means to the life of a family. *Rain Man* deservedly garnered four Academy Awards in 1988, including Best Picture.

★★★★   *Fly Away Home* (1996) directed by Carroll Ballard. PG rating. 107 minutes.

Adolescent Amy loses her mother in an auto accident and must move from her home in New Zealand to Canada to live with her father, with whom she has a strained relationship. When Amy finds a gaggle of geese that follow her around and will not fly on their own, she and her father join forces to nurture the geese and teach them how to fly. This is a classic story of the healer who is healed through caring for others. Amy and her father find common ground and common values in assisting others and in identifying with the desire to fly free.

★★★★   *What's Eating Gilbert Grape?* (1994) directed by Lasse Hallstrom. PG-13 rating. 118 minutes.

The energy, the relationships, and the purpose of life for the members of the Grape family are driven by disabilities. The father committed suicide; the mother subsequently ballooned to 500 pounds and developed agoraphobia; and one son suffers from autism. The mother places herself squarely in the lives of the family, while the breadwinning son becomes responsible for all family members. This story is about family loyalty, community caring, fraternal caretaking, a mother's letting go, and most of all, the power of internal strength. (Also reviewed in Chapter 10 on Autism.)

★★★★   *Pieces of April* (2003) directed by Peter Hedges. PG-13 rating. 80 minutes.

April (Katie Holmes), a raffish young woman and the black sheep of her family, lives in a dingy tenement with her boyfriend in the lower east side of Manhattan. She plans to reconnect with her mother, who suffers from breast cancer, and the rest of her dysfunctional family by inviting them for Thanksgiving dinner. April encounters a series of inconveniences that interfere with the success of the holiday dinner. This sentimental film focuses on reunion and terminal illness and was nominated for both Academy and Golden Globe awards. Poignant and funny flick about family dysfunction that will resonate with most viewers.

★★★★   *Stepmom* (1998) directed by Chris Columbus. PG-13 rating. 123 minutes.

This film has much to offer about the costs, struggles, and possibilities of remarriage—if you can ignore the unrealistic aspects of finances, relatives, and the mother's (Susan Sarandon) terminal illness. *Stepmom* realistically shows how the kids may suffer. Twelve-year-old Anna's brattiness is so annoying and yet so clearly an expression of the conflicts of a child who loves both her divorced parents. The film shows how a successful professional woman, the stepmom (Julia Roberts), feels limited by the new responsibilities of children not her own. She does all that might be expected of a stepmom but loves her work and won't give it up. The birth mother is a paragon who places her children's needs above her own and cannot understand the stepmom's "neglect." In the end, the birth mother's impending death resolves the kids' divided loyalties and the conflicts between herself and the stepmom. The struggles of all are realistically portrayed, but viewers should be cautioned that the Hollywood solution of killing off the birth mother is an unrealistic copout to complicated relationships.

★★★★   *Radio Flyer* (1992) directed by Richard Donner. PG-13 rating. 120 minutes.

Life becomes horrific for Mike and Bobby when their mother marries an alcoholic man who physically and verbally abuses them. They escape into their own world as they dream of turning their Radio Flyer wagon into an airplane in order to fly away. The film reveals the pain of physical abuse, living with substance abuse, the denial of the mother about what is happening, and the valiant attempts of young children to insulate their mother from pain. This is a story for everyone who has walked this path and for people who have experienced the resilience of children in an abusive home. (Also reviewed in Chapter 2 on abuse.)

**Recommended**

★★★ *The Father of the Bride* (1991) directed by Charles Shyer. PG rating. 114 minutes.

George and Nina are the parents of a daughter who has grown up when they weren't looking. The daughter has distressed her father by announcing her engagement. The film continues with the antics of wedding plans, costs, and invitations, but underneath is the story of a father who sees himself losing his little girl and fighting it by complaining about expense, potential flaws in the fiancé, and the bossiness of the wedding coordinator. The film is touching and funny and speaks to all families moving through adult–child transitions.

## ■ INTERNET RESOURCES

### *Families (General)*
★★★★ *Families.com* www.families.com

A general commercial site covering all things family-related, with resources, articles and blogs on parenting, pregnancy, family, entertainment, and health.

★★★★ *FamilyLife.com* www.familylife.com

A Christian-based website, it offers many helpful articles and resources about marriage, parenting, faith, occasions and family. Some may find the website's tone a bit off-putting, such as a recent article's title, "How Can You Honor Parents When You Feel They Don't Deserve It?"

★★★★ *Working Mother* www.workingmother.com

*Working Mother* magazine's website is a solid resource for family information too. While slick and glossy like its magazine counterpart, the site is constantly updated and focuses on moms who want to have it all—a career and family. The blogs help bring a personal perspective to achieving this balance, while article topics range from family time and family travel to financial planning and health concerns.

★★★ *Fathering Magazine* www.fathermag.com

This site offers hundreds of articles on topics ranging from new fathers, to the joy of fathers, the importance of fathers, single fathers, and more. The site might be ideal for expanding and validating a father's view of his role, but sadly it apparently hasn't been updated recently.

### Blended Families/Stepfamilies

**★★★★** *National Stepfamily Resource Center* www.stepfamilies.info

Although apparently not regularly updated, this center from Auburn University still offers a great set of resources and educational articles for stepfamilies, including fact sheets and a directory of state-based support groups for people needing more information and assistance.

**★★★** *Guide to Step-parenting and Blended Families* www.helpguide.org/mental/ blended_families_stepfamilies.htm

This single page from the nonprofit HelpGuide offers a good overview of the topic. The resource tends to simplify complex issues, however, such as how to bond with a new blended family, and dealing with differences in blended families.

**★★** *Stepfamily in Formation* www.stepfamilyinfo.org

There are hundreds of pages of information and ideas here, covering almost every family topic. There is a lot to read, but it is generally well-written material from Peter Gerlach, MSW. The site is difficult to navigate, however, and will take you back to the era of 1990s Web design.

**★★★★** *Supporting Stepfamilies* www.ianrpubs.unl.edu/sendIt/ec476.pdf

This 61-page downloadable PDF workbook from the University of Nebraska has 20 activities and lessons for parents and children in a blended family. An excellent resource.

**★★★★** *Divorce and the Family in America* by Christopher Lasch www.theatlantic.com/ magazine/archive/1966/11/divorce-and-the-family-in-america/5942

For those needing a historical perspective on family and divorce, this is an interesting and lengthy historical perspective from 1966.

**★★★** *Parenting Apart: Patterns of Childrearing after Marital Disruption* by Frank Furstenberg, Jr., and Christine Winquist Nord users.tpg.com.au/users/resolve/ ncpreport/furstenberg%281985%29.html

A good national survey of the qualities of family relations. It clearly shows that a former spouse's remaining active with the kids is a very positive influence. Could be motivational for some clients.

**★★★** *Wicked Stepmothers, Fact or Fiction?* www.siskiyous.edu/class/engl12/stepmom.htm

A paper that details the pervasiveness and harm done by culturally transmitted stereotypes of stepmothers. It may be thought-provoking for some. See also *The Evil Stepmother* by Maureen F. McHugh at my.en.com/~mcq/stepmother.html

**★★★** *Blended Families* by Willard F. Harley, Jr., PhD priscillasfriends.org/studies/ blended.html

An essay on resolving conflicts in blended families.

★★★   *Stepfamily Information* www.positive-way.com/step.htm

This site has four helpful resources: an introduction with a number of good suggestions, Tips for Stepfathers, Tips for Stepmothers, and Tips for Remarried Parents.

★★★   *Stepfamilies on TV: Step by Step* psychcentral.com/lib/2012/stepfamilies-on-tv-step-by-step

An article by Marie Van Dam about the 1990s television sitcom *Step by Step* that may help differentiate media portrayals from reality.

### Single-Parent Families
★★★   *Single Rose: Article Database* www.singlerose.com/articles

Hundreds of articles are available on this website covering many aspects of being a single mom. Topics include child development, parenting, self-improvement, dating, cooking, health and fitness, and much more.

★★   *Parents Without Partners: Visiting Authors* www.parentswithoutpartners.org/resources-authors.html

A list of dozens of topical articles that are unfortunately organized by author, not topic, so it makes finding articles relevant to your needs challenging.

### Adoption
★★★   *Shared Journey* www.sharedjourney.com

This website offer materials on infertility and adoption, including a mini-textbook on infertility's medical aspects.

★★★★   *Adoption Library* library.adoption.com

There are hundreds of articles on the topic of adoption here, in a well-organized list and an attractive website.

★★★   *The Adopted Child* aacap.org/page.ww?name=The+Adopted+Child&section=Facts+for+Families

A brief article from the American Academy of Child & Adolescent Psychiatry on telling a child about his or her adoption.

## ■ SUPPORT GROUPS

### Concerned United Birthparents (CUB)

Phone: 800-822-2777
www.cubirthparents.org
For adoption-affected people.

## Families Anonymous

Phone: 800-736-9805
www.FamiliesAnonymous.org
12-step fellowship for relatives and friends concerned about substance abuse and behavioral problems.

## National Foster Parent Association

Phone: 253-853-4000 or 800-557-5238
www.nfpainc.org
Support, education, and advocacy for foster parents and their children. Advocates for child support enforcement and collection.

## Parents without Partners

Phone: 561-391-8833
www.parentswithoutpartners.org

## Stepfamily Association of America

Phone: 800-735-0329
www.stepfamilies.info
Information and advocacy for stepfamilies.

**See also** Child Development and Parenting (Chapter 15), Divorce (Chapter 21), and Teenagers (Chapter 40).

# CHAPTER 24

# GAY, LESBIAN, AND BISEXUAL ISSUES

Closets are for clothes, and as this realization spreads so does the number of people acknowledging their homosexual orientation. The acronym GLBT (gay, lesbian, bisexual, transgender) denotes a variety of sexual orientations beyond heterosexuality. However, you will not find information for transgender individuals in this chapter due to space restrictions.

The burgeoning acceptance of GLB individuals in our society today heralds a movement, albeit a slow one, that awareness, sensitivity, and respect for others are gaining a toehold on the way we engage with the world. This increased attention and growing acceptance have led to a profusion of self-help resources for GLB individuals, their families, and their allies. But GLB individuals still face a difficult journey, and most of the self-help resources we review here offer guidance in doing so.

Research does not offer any conclusive statistics on the prevalence of homosexuality in the population. Still, the classic Kinsey studies of the 1950s found that, based on lifetime sexual experiences, 10% of men could be considered gay and 2% to 6% of women as lesbian. About 11% of the population would be characterized as bisexual in behavioral terms. Let's not become consumed with statistics but acknowledge that sexual orientation cannot be strictly bifurcated as it exists along a continuum. As Dr. Kinsey said, "The world is not to be divided into sheep and goats."

In this chapter, we present self-help books, autobiographies, films, Internet resources, and support groups for GLB individuals, their families, and their allies (Box 24.1). The majority of the resources offer guidance in coming out, but there are also materials on how to deal with the aftereffects for individuals and their families.

## ■ SELF-HELP BOOKS

### Recommended

★★★ *Coming Out, Coming Home* (2010) by Michael C. Lasala. New York: Columbia University Press.

The full range of family dynamics involved before, during, and after coming out are explored through interviews that the author, a gay man and a psychotherapist, conducted with 65 families of young adults and their parents. The format of questioning and interactive responding brings the reader into personal and revealing accounts of earlier stages

## BOX 24.1
## RECOMMENDATION HIGHLIGHTS

**SELF-HELP BOOKS**

■ For parents of GLB children:

★★★ *Coming Out, Coming Home* by Michael C. Lasala

★★★ *Always My Child* by Kevin Jennings and Pat Shapiro

■ For GLB partners:

♦ *Permanent Partners* by Betty Berzon

**AUTOBIOGRAPHIES**

■ For family responses to a son coming out:

★★★ *The Family Heart* by Robb Forman Dew

**FILMS**

■ For powerful stories on accepting homosexuality and then loss:

★★★★★ *Milk*

★★★★★ *Angels in America*

★★★★ *Brokeback Mountain*

★★★★ *Torch Song Trilogy*

■ For a popular film on bisexual experimentation:

★★★★ *Kissing Jessica Stein*

■ For an intriguing look at underground lifestyle of gay men:

★★★ *Paris Is Burning*

**INTERNET RESOURCES**

■ For valuable information on LGBT health and wellness:

★★★★ *Gay Health—NHS Choices*

www.nhs.uk/Livewell/LGBhealth/Pages/Gayandlesbianhealth.aspx

■ For support to LGBT individuals, families, and friends:

★★★★ *GLBT National Help Center* www.glnh.org

★★★★ *Parents, Families and Friends of Lesbians and Gays* www.pflag.org

of the family discovery and also to conversations between the parents and youth today. The young adults retell the story of when they realized they were gay or lesbian and what that means, now and then. The subjects' relationships with their parents when they were younger and now is poignantly presented. These are useful stories of resiliency, intimacy, and family dynamics across the spectrum.

★★★ *Always My Child* (2002) by Kevin Jennings and Pat Shapiro. New York: Fireside.

Parents of LGBT children are guided through the world their children inhabit in this self-help book. The tone expresses unconditional love, as reflected in the title. Jennings and Shapiro help parents make the home a safe harbor and then describe parents' role in supporting the child: sexuality, society, friends, children of color, and recognizing signs of depression, suicide, and drug abuse are discussed. Beneficially, the authors explain that sexual orientation is the only minority status that the parents don't share with the child. As a result, most parents don't automatically identify with the discrimination and abusive treatment the child may have experienced. Sample dialogues are offered that give parents some direction in conversations regarding parental acceptance, telling the grandparents, and advocating for their beloved child.

### Diamond in the Rough

♦ *Permanent Partners: Building Gay and Lesbian Relationships* (1988) by Betty Berzon. New York: Dutton.

This book was written from the personal and professional experiences of the author, a psychotherapist. Written for gay and lesbian couples, her purposes are to assist them in seeing the relationship stressors that may inhibit growth and to develop new options for dealing with those stressors. The wide-ranging topics include establishing compatibility, identifying the effects of internalized homophobia, improving communication with partners, negotiating out of power struggles, fighting constructively, dealing with sexual conflicts and financial arrangements, having children, and accommodating changes in the partnership. Among the obstacles explored are the lack of visible long-term same-sex couples as role models, the paucity of support from society, and the guidance gap that has not provided adequate advice on building a life with another man or another woman. This book was highly but infrequently rated in two of our national studies, thus meriting a Diamond in the Rough designation.

### Not Recommended

★★ *GLBTQ* (2011) by Kelly Huegel. Minneapolis, MN: Free Spirit.

## ■ AUTOBIOGRAPHIES

### Diamond in the Rough

♦ *The Family Heart: A Memoir of When Our Son Came Out* (1995) by Robb Forman Dew. New York: Random House.

Novelist Dew writes frankly and sensitively about the effects on her life and that of her family when her son, home from college, announced that he was gay. She acknowledges a fear that her son will be assaulted or develop AIDS, her own and others' ignorance and homophobia, and the end of dreams about her son's conventional marriage complete with grandchildren. In the larger society, things have improved since the book was written in all these areas, but the underlying issues remain contentious and potentially disruptive to family cohesion. Dew and her husband come out themselves as parents of a gay son and are active in PFLAG, a support organization. This book offers insight into parental expectations and adjustments to the new reality.

## ■ FILMS

### Strongly Recommended

★★★★★ *Milk* (2008) directed by Gus Van Sant. R rating. 128 minutes.

This biographical film follows Harvey Milk (Sean Penn), the first openly gay politician to be elected to office. Driven to politics after viewing the persecution of homosexuals in San Francisco and a desire to effect change, Milk preached a message of acceptance and urged LGB people to come out of the closet. The film documents the opposition that Milk faced from the conservative front as well as the many relationships he forms along the way, especially with Michael White. White and Milk form a complex working relationship in which they provide each other political and personal support. However, as White spirals down after losing his political position, he takes his rage out on Milk. Just as Milk is celebrating a political victory, White enters City Hall with a concealed weapon and assassinates Milk and another victim. The film artfully depicts the rise and determination of this iconic figure, the emergence of the gay movement, and the stubborn resistance to gay rights. Deserving of the numerous accolades and the extravagant ratings it received in our national studies.

★★★★★ *Angels in America* (2003) directed by Mike Nichols. MA rating. 352 minutes.

This epic television miniseries takes place during the Reagan era as the AIDS epidemic was in its full and deadly swing. The six-part drama was adapted from two award-winning plays written by Tony Kushner that were originally performed on Broadway. Set in Manhattan during the 1980s, the film follows the interconnected lives of a band of male gay characters, several open, others closeted, and two suffering from AIDS. A young man dying of AIDS is visited on several occasions by an Angel (played by Emma Thompson), while an older hospitalized man (played by Al Pacino), in strong denial about his AIDS, is repeatedly visited by a Ghost (played by Meryl Streep) of a woman he sent to the electric chair. A stellar cast, a searching story, and an alternately touching and saddening masterpiece on being gay in America.

★★★★ *Brokeback Mountain* (2005) directed by Ang Lee. R rating. 134 minutes.

Ennis and Jack, two Wyoming men, fall in love and endanger their lives because of it. After meeting during a summer job when they were both 19, the two quickly develop feelings for one another but must part ways as the summer ends. Because of the strongly anti-homosexual world in which they live, their lives would be threatened if they were open about their relationship. Instead, the men both attempt to live a "straight" life and settle down with women, but their strong attraction persists. The two men regularly meet to be together under the guise of fishing trips. Times passes and Ennis's marriage fails, but the fear remains. The two men are never able to be honest with themselves or one another and thus remain apart. This popular film aptly portrays the devastating effects that homophobia and its associated violence can exert on closeted individuals. A melancholy ache pervades this powerful award-winning drama.

★★★★ *Torch Song Trilogy* (1989) directed by Paul Bogart. R rating. 117 minutes.

A story of gay men struggling to tell their families and friends about their mutual love. Tragedy strikes when one is murdered in a senseless killing. The theme is more about love and relationship struggles than about homosexuality. The movie shows the importance of being loved for who we are versus being loved conditionally. A highly regarded film, it is a celebration of the tenacity of the human spirit with its often-thwarted search for love and acceptance.

**Recommended**

★★★  *Beautiful Thing* (1996) directed by Hettie Macdonald. R rating. 90 minutes.

Two London teenagers in a housing project realize they are gay. Jamie, a quiet intro-
vert, is drawn to the athlete Ste but does not act on his feelings. However, the plot begins
to move after Jamie's mother takes pity on Ste and lets him sleep in their home after he
was beaten by his alcoholic father. While living under the same roof, the teenagers quickly
develop feelings for one another. Though both struggling to accept their orientation, they
help each other navigate the new worlds of dating and homosexuality. Their sweet romance
highlights the similarities among all teen romances but the additional danger in many gay
relationships.

★★★  *Kissing Jessica Stein* (2002) directed by Charles Herman-Wurmfeld. R rating.
       94 minutes.

Jessica Stein is a fastidious perfectionist who, after a series of hapless dates with hopeless
men, "chooses" to be lesbian. She dates a bisexual, Heather Juergensen, whose personality
is the opposite, experienced and cool. Jessica works enthusiastically with the novelty of lesbian sexuality, but her anxiety never enables her to commit and her ambivalence toward her
ex-boyfriend never leaves her. Full of sophisticated wit and graceful humor, the film does
feature a few serious issues about coming out to family members. This film could serve as a
light introduction to bisexual experimentation, the matrix of relational and sexual choices,
and the discovery that one is not as straight as she (or he) thought.

★★★  *Big Eden* (2002) directed by Thomas Bezucha. PG-13 rating. 118 minutes.

Big Eden is a small and gay-friendly town in northwestern Montana where a successful New York artist, Henry, has returned to care for his grandfather, who has just suffered a
stroke. While in Big Eden, Henry runs into his best friend and the former stud of his high
school, Dean. Henry is forced to confront his unrequited loving feelings for Dean. A love
triangle soon forms as Pike, the painfully shy owner of the local general store, develops feelings for Henry. The people of Big Eden then conspire to bring Henry and Pike together. Its
sweet warmth in an implausibly tolerant Western town has made this film a favorite of gay
and lesbian film festivals.

★★★  *Paris Is Burning* (1992) directed by Jennie Livingston. No rating. 78 minutes.

This film depicts an underground lifestyle in Manhattan where gay men work in fashion
and dance shows to earn money. During the day they prepare for the shows, and in the
evening they perform. There are multiple story lines with different endings. More of a documentary than a commercial film, but it is effective in reminding viewers of the centrality of
accepting people for who they are.

★★★  *In & Out* (1997) directed by Frank Oz. PG-13 rating. 90 minutes.

Howard, a small-town English teacher and football coach, is outed as gay when a former
student thanks him in his speech at the Oscars. His fiancée, Emily, is crushed as the entire
town begins to gossip. The situation escalates when reporters invade the town looking for

Howard and searching for the "real story." Despite Howard's assurances of his heterosexuality, everyone assumes Howard is gay. In one last attempt to restore his heterosexuality, Howard proceeds with the wedding. Emily flawlessly recites her vows but when Howard is prompted to do so, he simply says, "I'm gay." The wedding is immediately called off and Howard is later fired from his teaching job, but still attends the graduation ceremony to support his students. After learning that Howard was dismissed for being gay, all of his students proclaim that they are gay and Howard's family and friends follow suit and show support for the teacher. This movie provides an uplifting and comedic spin to the difficult process of coming out.

★★★  *The Boys in the Band* (1970) directed by William Friedkin. R rating. 120 minutes.

A gathering of gay men at a birthday party turns into a sharing of intimate feelings and needs. At the end of the party, two of the men struggle with their personal relationships. A movie that can be comforting for those who struggle with their sexual identity. An early and influential movie on gay relationships.

★★★  *Prayers for Bobby* (2009) directed by Russell Mulcahy. Unrated. 91 minutes.

The film follows a mother and son as they both come to grips with his homosexuality. Mary Griffith is a devout Christian woman and raises her children by the teachings of the Presbyterian Church. However, life for the family changes when her son Bobby comes out. Bobby's brothers and father slowly come to terms with his orientation, but his mother remains adamant that there is a cure. She takes Bobby to a psychiatrist and urges him to seek solace in church activities. Bobby continues to suppress his behaviors and becomes depressed and withdrawn. Filled with guilt, Bobby moves away with his cousin and finds a boyfriend, David. The weight of his mother's disapproval and seeing David with another man finally becomes too much for David to bear. He falls off a freeway bridge and is killed instantly. The family is devastated, and Mary begins to question herself and her Church's stance on homosexuality. She slowly reaches out to the gay community, comes to terms with her son's homosexuality, and becomes an advocate for gay rights. Based on a book of the same name, this movie raises profound questions about religious intolerance.

**Strongly Not Recommended**

†  *I Now Pronounce You Chuck & Larry* (2007) directed by Dennis Dugan. PG-13 rating. 115 minutes.

## ■ INTERNET RESOURCES

**General Websites**

★★★★  *Gay Health—NHS Choices* www.nhs.uk/Livewell/LGBhealth/Pages/Gayandlesbianhealth.aspx

This website from the U.K.'s National Health Service focuses mostly on LGBT general health and wellness issues but also has resources about mental health and bullying.

**** *Sexual Orientation* www.pamf.org/teen/sex/orientation

This resource from the Palo Alto Medical Foundation offers a few pages of helpful materials directed toward young adults and teens about sexual orientation, gender identity, and LGBT topics such as coming out, relationships, and family acceptance, among others.

**** *It Gets Better Project* www.itgetsbetter.org

The "It Gets Better Project" is a resource funded by the nonprofit Iola Foundation designed to help LGBT youth understand that often their teenage and young adult years are emotionally the hardest years of their life. The site focuses on videos of people who share their own inspirational messages and personal stories about making it through this time in their lives.

*** *Issue: Coming Out* www.hrc.org/issues/coming-out

The Human Rights Campaign is a nonprofit advocacy organization working for LGBT equal rights around the world. It has a set of helpful informational articles and sections on the site, such as this one about coming out.

**** *Gay Life* gaylife.about.com

Gay Life, from About.com Ramon Johnson, is a particularly good resource for gay men but also offers information and resources about gay marriage and coming out. In the coming out section, the site offers tips for doing so, coming out stories, what to expect from family and friends, and how to deal with school and work issues.

*** *COLAGE* www.colage.org

This website is for people with a LGBT parent and hosts resources such as private mailing list discussion groups, local chapters, and guides to various topics. The "Media & Fun" section hosts some personal story videos and short films.

**** *GLBT National Help Center* www.glnh.org

The GLBT National Help Center offers free and confidential telephone and online counseling and access to local resources. Their resource directory contains over 15,000 local community resources. Everything is free.

**** *Parents, Families and Friends of Lesbians and Gays* www.pflag.org

This national nonprofit organization has over 350 local affiliates in the United States and helps to promote the health and well-being of LGBT persons through support, advocacy, and education. The website offers a great deal of information about the services the organization offers, how to find local support, and articles about major LGBT issues, such as family acceptance, marriage, the workplace, and more.

## ■ SUPPORT GROUPS

### ACT UP (AIDS Coalition to Unleash Power)

Phone: 212-966-4873
www.actupny.org

### COLAGE (Children of Lesbian and Gays Everywhere)

Colage.org

### Dignity/USA

Phone: 800-877-8797 or 202-861-0017
www.dignityusa.org
Organization of lesbian, bisexual, and gay Catholics and their families and friends.

### Family Equality Council

Phone: 617-502-8700
www.familyequality.org

### Gay Men's Health Crisis

Phone: 212-807-6655
www.gmhc.org
Information is available in Spanish and Creole.

### LLEGO (National Latino/a Lesbian and Gay Organization)

Phone: 202-408-5380
www.llego.org

### National Gay and Lesbian Task Force

Phone: 202-393-5177
www.thetaskforce.org

### !OUTPROUD! (The National Coalition for Gay, Lesbian and Bisexual Youth)

Phone: 415-460-5452
www.outproud.org

### PFLAG (Parents, Families, and Friends of Lesbians and Gays)

Phone: 202-467-8180 or 216-691-4357
Pflag.org

**Rainbow Room**

Phone: 860-278-4163
A 24-hour, **national** help line for **gay** and questioning teens.

**The Trevor Project**

Phone: 866-488-7386
www.thetrevorproject.org
Committed to end suicide among LGBTQ youth by providing resources such as 24/7 crisis intervention lifeline, digital community, and advocacy/educational programs.

# CHAPTER 25

# HAPPINESS

"Don't worry, be happy!" go the words of the popular tune by Bobby McFerrin, "'Cause when you worry, your face will frown, and that will bring everybody down." Is McFerrin's cheerful optimism an effective strategy?

In the 1990s, a number of psychologists began recommending *positive illusions*—that is, happy people often entertain high opinions of themselves, give self-serving explanations for events, and hold exaggerated beliefs about their ability to control the world around them. In the 2000s, a number of other psychologists began touting *positive psychology*—a movement that builds on the strengths and virtues that enable individuals to thrive. The practice of psychology had become quite focused on pathology and disease. Coupled with continued evidence for mind–body connections, positive psychology took flight in both the professional literature and in the self-help section.

Martin Seligman, one of the parents of the movement and author of a number of self-help resources on happiness, believes that psychology over the past 100 years has subscribed to a "rotten to the core" notion of human nature. Humans are neurotic, if not evil, deep down. This belief system has lead to a half-baked psychology that solely focuses on the alleviation of suffering. By helping people discover their significant strengths, positive psychology promises a more comprehensive approach that promotes growth and happiness. Humans can do more than survive; we can thrive and flourish.

The line of demarcation between teaching happiness, on one side, and achieving life goals, on the other, proves a murky gray. Self-help materials that explicitly invoke *happiness, optimism,* or *subjective well-being* (the research jargon) in their title, subtitle, or stated aim are featured in this chapter, while materials focused more generally on improving one's life are reviewed in Chapter 34, Self-Management and Self-Enhancement. This chapter reviews books, autobiographies, online self-help, and Internet resources dedicated to promoting happiness (Box 25.1).

## ■ SELF-HELP BOOKS

### Strongly Recommended

★★★★★ *Learned Optimism: How to Change your Mind and Your Life* (1992, reissued 1998) by Martin Seligman. New York: Pocket.

This approach to positive thinking is based on psychological research rather than spiritual belief. Seligman argues that optimism and pessimism are not fixed, inborn

## BOX 25.1
## RECOMMENDATION HIGHLIGHTS

**SELF-HELP BOOKS**

■ On promoting happiness with optimistic thinking:

★★★★★ *Learned Optimism* by Martin Seligman

★★★ *Positive Illusions* by Shelley Taylor

■ On understanding the human condition and happiness:

★★★★ *Stumbling on Happiness* by Daniel Gilbert

★★★ *The Art of Happiness* by the Dalai Lama and Howard C. Cutler

★★★ *The Power of Now* by Eckhart Toll

**AUTOBIOGRAPHIES**

■ For personal explorations and models of happiness despite travails:

★★★ *The Happiness Project* by Gretchen Rubin

◆ *The Tao of Willie* by Willie Nelson and Turk Pipkin

**INTERNET RESOURCES**

■ For excellent research, talks, and tips on happiness:

★★★★★ *The Happiness Project* www.happiness-project.com

★★★★★ *Authentic Happiness* www.authentichappiness.sas.upenn.edu

psychological traits but rather are learned explanatory styles—habitual ways we explain things that happen to us. Pessimists, says Seligman, perceive a defeat as permanent, catastrophic, and evidence of personal inadequacy; optimists, by contrast, perceive the same mishap as a temporary setback, something that can be controlled, and rooted in circumstances or luck. Seligman's positive message is that since pessimism is learned, it can be unlearned. Included are self-tests to determine the reader's levels of optimism, pessimism, and depression. Seligman reviews a great deal of research on explanatory styles, concluding that optimists do better in school, in athletics, and at work because they persist even in the face of setbacks, while equally talented pessimists are less likely to stay the course. Seligman also reviews research to demonstrate that pessimists have weaker immune systems, have more health problems, and are more likely to be depressed. This 5-star resource is an excellent self-help book on positive thinking. It is well documented but not overly academic.

★★★★ *Stumbling on Happiness* (2007) by Daniel Todd Gilbert. New York: First Vintage Books.

This is not a book about achieving happiness but rather a fascinating journey into the human psyche. It explains in interesting detail our penchant for living, at least part of the time, in the future, our presumption to prepare for our future selves even though experience tells us our future selves usually don't like the decisions our present selves make, and that we enjoy the illusion of controlling the future by planning. Harvard psychologist Gilbert notes that a common question of what can humans can do that other animals can't do is often answered with "use tools" or "develop language." The definitive answer is "think about the future." We stand alone in that capacity. The author also speculates about a permanent presence and the experience that might be. This stellar book is not a recipe for happiness, but it gives the reader much to think about regarding our brain's capacity and how we use it.

### Recommended

★★★ *Positive Illusions: Creative Self-Discipline and the Healthy Mind* (1989) by Shelley Taylor. New York: Basic.

Taylor's main themes are similar to Seligman's (reviewed above): Facing the complete truth about ourselves is often not the best mental strategy. The healthy human mind has a tendency to block out negative information; positive illusions help us cope. Taylor believes that creative deceptions are especially beneficial when we are threatened by adversity. Taylor describes research on cancer patients, disaster victims, and other people facing crises to portray how mental and physical well-being can be improved by having an unrealistically positive view of one's self and abilities. This book was positively rated but by too few respondents to make the 4-star or 5-star categories. It is a good book on positive thinking, but one that becomes too formal and academic in places. However, the quality of Taylor's documentation is outstanding, and intellectual readers will enjoy the book.

★★★ *The Art of Happiness: A Handbook for Living* (1998) by the Dalai Lama and Howard C. Cutler. New York: Riverside.

The authors avow that "The very purpose of our life is to seek happiness...I think that the very motion of our life is toward happiness." This book of deep reflection and Buddhist insight was written for those seeking more happiness. Although the narrative is more philosophy than self-help, the Dalai Lama assists in finding sources of internal peace, training the mind, and reclaiming one's inner state of happiness. The book closes with reflections on living a spiritual life.

★★★ *The Power of Now: A Guide to Spiritual Enlightenment* (2004) by Eckhart Toll. Novato, CA: New World Library.

The central theme of this book is that in today's complex world, most of us allow our minds to be consumed with thinking; our minds are so geared to thinking that it seems impossible that we could ever suspend thinking and just "be." Toll explains that thinking and consciousness are not synonymous and that we have given our consciousness over to thinking rather than experiencing. He notes that some say they are more influenced by emotions than thinking. His approach makes the case that emotions are keyed to thoughts and are the physical manifestation of thoughts. What we feel reflects how we are thinking at the moment. The exercises and worksheets as well as the outline throughout the book aid the reader in moving toward this view of our world and our lives. Many psychologists viewed the book favorably, but many also complained that Toll writes in an obscure, arcane style with practically no research evidence for his spiritual claims.

★★★ *A Short Guide to a Happy Life* (2000) by Anna Quindlen. New York: Random House.

The title fits the size of this self-help book; its 50 pages are composed of pictures and brief reflections. Anna Quindlen, author of best-selling novels and winner of a 1992 Pulitzer Prize, humbly offers her insights on what helps constitute a "happy life." She reveals her beliefs on what makes her life happy, emphasizing the twin imperatives of simplicity and clarity. Position and perspective are two other themes in her book. A brief book for anyone interested in working toward happiness in his or her life.

★★★ *What's Right with You* (2005) by Barry L. Duncan. Deerfield Beach, FL: Health Communications.

The process of change tends to gravitate to the question of what is wrong with us. Seeking change in our lives inevitably draws us into diagnostic classification of some sort. This author proclaims that what is right with us is our strength, resiliency, and power to move forward. Psychologist Duncan recounts case scenarios of patients, with the underlying theme that people can draw from resources that already exist to successfully pursue their goals. The treatment approach presents six steps: challenging the idea of dysfunction, validating our own struggles and strength, finding a change partner or someone who will support our goals, not underestimating our own ideas, giving ourselves a chance, and empowering ourselves. The appendix is composed of many activities and exercises the author has amassed over the years.

★★★ *How to Live 365 Days a Year* (1975, reissued 2002) by John Schindler. Englewood Cliffs, NJ: Prentice-Hall.

This book takes the stance that illnesses and problems in life arise out of emotions. The book is divided into two main parts. In Part I, How Your Emotions Make You Ill, readers learn that emotions produce most physical diseases and also about the "good" emotions and the "bad" emotions. Part II, How to Cure Your Emotionally Induced Illness, describes how to attain emotional maturity in many different areas of life—family, sexuality, and work, for example. *How to Live 365 Days a Year* received a 3-star rating. On the positive side, it presents some important ideas about how emotional difficulties cause illness and how to take control of emotional life, but on the negative side, it is dated and inferior to more modern books.

★★★ *The Present* (2003) by Spencer Johnson. New York: Doubleday.

This self-help resource is based on the story of an old man who lived across the street from a youngster and engaged in a conversation about "The Present." The boy was most curious but then went on his way and, as he grew up, he came back to the old man to learn more about how to acquire the present. The book then discusses the importance of "The Present" in the gifts of the present—peace of mind, feeling more alive, being more productive or prosperous or whatever else is most valued by any given person. The story invites self-reflection, value assessment, and prioritizing.

**Not Recommended**

★★ *The Power of Optimism* (1990) by Alan McGinnis. San Francisco: Harper & Row.

★ *The Power of Positive Thinking* (1952) by Norman Vincent Peale. New York: Ballantine.

## ■ AUTOBIOGRAPHIES

### Recommended

★★★ *The Happiness Project: Or, Why I Spent a Year Trying to Sing in the Morning, Clean my Closets, Fight Right, Read Aristotle, and Generally Have More Fun* by Gretchen Rubin (2011). New York: HarperCollins.

Rubin had a stellar education and privileged background before becoming a writer. She was editor-in-chief of the *Yale Law Journal*, served as a law clerk for Supreme Court Justice Sandra Day O'Connor, and wrote bestselling biographies of Winston Churchill and John F. Kennedy; her husband was a successful hedge fund manager. This book describes her yearlong exploration of happiness, with clearly specified goals of improving her marriage and parenting, plus advancement in other areas. She distills what she learned from reading works in philosophy and positive psychology and trying out various techniques she came across in her reading, such as being nice to her husband for a week. Well regarded by most mental health professionals but probably not the best self-help autobiography for people in less privileged circumstances.

### Diamond in the Rough

♦ *The Tao of Willie: A Guide to Happiness in Your Heart* (2007) by Willie Nelson and Turk Pipkin. New York: Penguin Grove.

Willie Nelson is an acclaimed country-western singer who has sold over 100 million records; his friend and golfing buddy Turk Pipkin is the author of 10 books. Together they fashion down-to-earth homilies from the ups and downs in Willie's life and what he learned from them. He wants readers to live happier lives, but he is realistic about the prospects that anyone will take his advice: "Because something works for me doesn't mean it will for you, especially in large doses." Nelson describes the wisdom he found in Eastern religions, particularly the *Tao Te Ching* by Lao Tzu. This is a happy book, with jokes and song lyrics scattered through the easy-to-read chapters, making a satisfying blend of wit and folk wisdom.

### Not Recommended

★★ *Eat, Pray, Love: One Woman's Search for Everything Across Italy, India, and Indonesia* (2007) by Elizabeth Gilbert. New York: Penguin.

## ■ ONLINE SELF-HELP

★★★ *Live Life to the Full* www.llttf.com

This free site is designed not to help users with any specific problems but rather to make changes and be happier. The site provides users with life skills, including understanding emotions, practical problem solving, and identifying helpful and unhelpful behaviors. Users are also provided with help in making healthy changes in their sleep, diet, and exercise patterns. A tracking program allows users to track their mood using three mood-assessment tools. Books are available by the author to supplement the program, but not required.

## ■ INTERNET RESOURCES

★★★★★ *The Happiness Project* www.happiness-project.com

*The Happiness Project* by Gretchen Rubin is a companion to her book of the same name (reviewed above). In an active blog, the author posts tips she has learned from consulting with experts, researchers, and others to find ways to help increase happiness in our own lives. A creative work full of videos and more, the author also encourages us to join in with our own Happiness Challenge.

★★★★★ *Authentic Happiness* www.authentichappiness.sas.upenn.edu

*Authentic Happiness* is the website of Dr. Martin Seligman, one of the fathers of modern happiness psychology research. Here you'll find a wealth of resources, upcoming talks, questionnaires, and theories about well-being (the psychological term for happiness), as well as the opportunity to participate in happiness research.

★★★★ *Dr. Ellen Kenner* www.drkenner.com

While most professionals' websites are little more than digital brochures for their practice, author and clinical psychologist Dr. Kenner takes a different route. She offers free weekly podcasts answering people's advice questions and is the host of *The Rational Basis of Happiness*, a radio show available in many areas as well as through the website.

★★★★ *TED: Talks on Happiness* www.ted.com/talks/tags/happiness

TED (Technology, Entertainment and Design), a project of the nonprofit Sapling Foundation, hosts annual conferences featuring engaging and entertaining speakers to an audience that pays out big bucks to attend. This section of their website features dozens of videos of TED speakers on the topic of happiness. TED videos are usually fun to watch because the talks are always under 20 minutes in length, and the organization preps speakers to ensure their talks don't bore.

★★★★ *This Emotional Life: Happiness* www.pbs.org/thisemotionallife/topic/happiness

This engaging PBS series looked at a series of topics related to our emotional lives in depth, including happiness. The website features video from the series, interviews, blog posts, and more and is a great way to get a solid introduction to the topic.

★★★★★ *Daily Challenge* challenge.meyouhealth.com

The *Daily Challenge*, from a company called MeYou Health, focuses on helping people make small, incremental, daily changes in their life in order to take on the bigger changes in life. The philosophy is that tackling a big life change—such as "increasing happiness"—all at once is nearly impossible. The website sends a "daily challenge" to individuals who sign up (it is generally something they can do with little effort) and then asks them to rate their success and comment on the challenge. Different tracks allow people to focus on different life aspects, such as emotional health, they'd like to tackle. It's a great idea that is well implemented.

★★★★   *The Positivity Blog* www.positivityblog.com

This blog from layperson Henrik Edberg focuses on the positive, with entries that target becoming happier, simplifying one's life, getting in shape, and living more consciously. Regularly updated with usually interesting content, Edberg also sells his own self-esteem and productivity courses on the site.

**See also** Self-Management and Self-Enhancement (Chapter 34).

# CHAPTER 26

# INFANT DEVELOPMENT AND PARENTING

I n this chapter we evaluate self-help resources that focus on parenting infants. In other chapters we examine parenting and other periods of development: pregnancy in Chapter 32, childhood in Chapter 15, and adolescence in Chapter 40.

Infancy is a special period of growth and development, requiring extensive time and support by caregivers. Unlike the newborn of some species (the newborn wildebeest runs with the herd moments after birth!), the human newborn requires considerable care. Good parenting requires long hours, interpersonal skills, and emotional commitment. Many parents learn parenting practices and baby care from their parents—some of which they accept, some of which they discard. Unfortunately, when parenting practices and baby care are passed on from one generation to the next, both desirable and undesirable practices are perpetuated.

Many parents eagerly, perhaps anxiously, want to know the answers to such questions as: How should I respond to the baby's crying? Is there a point at which I can spoil the baby? What are normal developmental milestones for my child? How should I stimulate my young child intellectually? What discipline methods are most effective and yet most humane? Many parents turn to self-help resources on parenting for answers and advice on the best way to handle their children—and those who do find no shortage of written and Internet resources.

Here are the clinician-recommended self-help books and Internet resources on infant development and parenting (Box 26.1).

## ■ SELF-HELP BOOKS

### Strongly Recommended

★★★★★ *What To Expect: The Toddler Years* (1996) by Arlene Eisenberg, Heidi E. Murkoff, and Sandee E. Hathaway. New York: Workman.

It is unimaginable that there is a question that could be asked that is not answered in this book. As is the case for its predecessor, *What To Expect The First Year*, by the same authors and reviewed in this chapter, this book has an encyclopedic level of information that is well organized and understandable. Each chapter is subheaded "What your toddler may be doing now," "What you may be concerned about," "What it's important to know,"

---

**BOX 26.1**
**RECOMMENDATION HIGHLIGHTS**

---

**SELF-HELP BOOKS**

■ For sound general advice on parenting infants:

★★★★★ *Infants and Mothers* by T. Berry Brazelton

★★★★★ *What Every Baby Knows* by T. Berry Brazelton

★★★★★ *Dr. Spock's Baby and Child Care* by Benjamin Spock and Michael Rothenberg

★★★★ *The Happiest Baby on the Block* by Harvey Karp

■ For month-to-month descriptions of infant development and care:

★★★★★ *What to Expect the First Year* by Arlene Eisenberg et al.

★★★★★ *What to Expect: The Toddler Years* by Arlene Eisenberg et al.

★★★★★ *Your Baby and Child* by Penelope Leach

■ For a broad-based nonmedical approach to parenting infants and children:

★★★★★ *The First Three Years of Life* by Burton White

★★★★★ *The First Twelve Months of Life* by Frank Caplan

★★★ *Baby 411* by Denise Fields and Ari Brown

**INTERNET RESOURCES**

■ For comprehensive sources of parenting information:

★★★★★ *Zero to Three* www.zerotothree.org

■ For excellent sites on bonding, brain development, and no spanking:

★★★★★ *The Natural Child Project* www.naturalchild.org

★★★★★ *Project NoSpank* www.nospank.net

■ For valuable information on infants:

★★★★★ *BabyZone* babyzone.com

---

and "What it's important for your toddler to know." Each chapter highlights a particular month in the 2-year span, and final chapters address safety, feeding, toilet learning, injuries, special needs, toddlers with siblings, and child care. Descriptions are conversational and inviting, as though one were sitting down with the authors over a cup of coffee. The authoritative, practical, and engaging presentation ensures continued high appeal for this series of books.

★★★★★ *Infants and Mothers* (revised ed., 1983) by T. Berry Brazelton. New York: Delta.

This book concerns the infant's temperament, developmental milestones in the first year of life, and the parents' (especially the mother's) role in the infant's development. Pediatrician Berry Brazelton describes three different temperamental or behavioral styles: active baby, average baby, and quiet baby. He takes readers through the developmental milestones of these three different types of babies from birth to 12 months. Most of the chapters are titled with the babies' ages: The Second Month, The Third Month, and so on. In every chapter, Brazelton tells mothers the best way to parent the different types of babies. He advises the mother to be a sensitive observer of her baby's temperament and behavior, believing that this strategy will help the mother chart the best course for meeting the infant's needs. This 5-star book is now considered a classic. Brazelton's approach is well-informed, warm, and personal.

★★★★★ *What Every Baby Knows* (1987) by T. Berry Brazelton. Reading, MA: Addison-Wesley.

This self-help book is based on the Lifetime cable television series that Brazelton hosts, and like the series, it is a broad approach to parenting infants that is organized according to the experiences of five different families. Brazelton presents in-depth analyses of the families and their child-rearing concerns, such as how to handle crying, how to discipline, how to deal with the infant's fears, sibling rivalry, separation and divorce, hyperactivity, birth order, and the child's developing sense of self. The descriptions of each family include the circumstances of the family's visits to Dr. Brazelton and lengthy excerpts of pediatrician–parent dialogues, interspersed with brief explanatory notes. Each family also is shown two years later so we can see how they resolved their child-rearing difficulties and where they are at that point. In this 5-star book, Brazelton dispenses wise advice to parents. He does an excellent job of helping parents become more sensitive to their infants' needs and of providing parents with sage recommendations on how to handle a host of problems that may arise.

★★★★★ *Dr. Spock's Baby and Child Care* (1998, 7th ed.) by Benjamin Spock and Steven J. Parker. New York: Pocket.

Initially published in 1945, this is one of the classics of self-help literature. Spock was considered America's baby doctor for decades, and this book was perceived by many to be the bible of self-help books for parents of infants and young children. It offers a broad approach to infant and child development. It has more medical advice than most of the other books in the infant and parenting category, but it also includes a number of chapters of child-rearing advice. The material includes advice on feeding, daily care, illnesses, first aid, nutrition, single-parent families, breastfeeding, the role of fathers in the child's development, and a myriad of other topics. The book has retained its political flavor: the authors fervently state that children should not play with toy guns or watch cowboy movies, they advocate a nuclear freeze, and they argue for abolishing competitiveness in our society. Across almost six decades, more than 30 million copies of this book have been sold, placing it second on the nation's overall bestseller list (after the Bible). The book's enthusiasts say that it is extremely well organized and serves as a handy guide for parents to consult when they run into problems with their infant or child. The medical advice is outstanding. However, some critics maintain that Spock's approach to discipline is still too permissive.

★★★★★ *The First Three Years of Life* (20th ed., 1995) by Burton White. New York: Fireside.

This book presents a broad-based, age-related approach to parenting infants and young children. White strongly believes that most parents in the United States fail to provide an adequate intellectual and social foundation for their children's development, especially between the ages of 8 months and 3 years. White provides in-depth discussion of motor, sensory, emotional, sociability, and language milestones. He divides the first 3 years into stages. For each of the stages, White describes the general behavior and educational development of the young child and parental practices that he does and does not recommended. His goal is to provide parents with the tools to help every child reach his or her maximum level of competence by structuring early experiences. White presents advice about such child-rearing topics as sibling rivalry, spacing children, types of discipline, and detection of disabilities. Appropriate toys and materials are listed, and how to obtain professional testing of a child is outlined. His recommendations about which toys parents should and should not buy, how to handle sibling rivalry, and how to discipline children are also excellent. This 5-star book has been a very popular self-help book; however, White has been criticized in the past because he essentially does not think mothers should work outside the home during the child's early years. Critics say White's view places an unnecessary burden of guilt on the high percentage of working mothers with infants.

★★★★★ *What to Expect the First Year* (1996) by Arlene Eisenberg, Heidi Murkoff, and Sandee Hathaway. New York: Workman.

This is an encyclopedic (almost 700 pages) volume of facts and practical tips on how babies develop, how to become a better parent, and how to deal with problems as they arise. The authors give chatty answers to hypothetical questions arranged in a month-by-month format. The book is full of questions commonly asked by parents. What to buy for a newborn, first aid, recipes, adoption, low-birthweight babies, and the father's role also are discussed. Some of the book's enthusiasts called it the best one on the market for parents of infants in their first year of life. The book covers an enormous array of topics that concern parents and generally provides sound advice.

★★★★★ *Your Baby and Child: From Birth to Age Five* (revised ed., 1997) by Penelope Leach. New York: Knopf.

This book describes normal child development from birth to 5 years of age and provides suggestions for parents about how to cope with typical problems at different ages in infancy and the early childhood years. Leach describes the basics of what parents need to know about feeding, sleeping, eliminating, teething, bathing, and dressing at each period of early development—during the first 6 months, 6 to 12 months, 1 to 2½ years, and 2½ to 5 years. Nontechnical graphs of growth rates are easy to interpret. Leach also explores the young child's emotional world, telling parents what children are feeling and experiencing in different periods of development. Despite describing normal development in different periods, Leach carefully points out individual variations in growth and development. She concludes that when parents have a decision to make about their child, their best choice is usually to go "by the baby"—their sensitive reading of what the child's needs are—rather than "by the book" or what is generally prescribed for the average child. The final pages of the book are a handy illustrated guide to first aid, accidents, safety, infectious diseases, and nursing. Leach's extensive experience with children comes through in her sensitive, 5-star suggestions for how to handle children in the early years of life. The material is extensive, well organized, and packed with more than 650 well-executed charts, drawings, and photographs.

★★★★★   *The First Twelve Months of Life* (revised ed., 1995) by Frank Caplan. New York: Bantam.

This is a broad-based, developmental milestone approach to infant development in the first year of life. A month-by-month assessment of normal infant development is provided. The timetables in the book are presented in a rather rigid way—the author does warn the reader to use them not in that way but rather as indicators of appropriate sequences of growth. Feeding, sleeping, language, physical skills, guidance, parental emotions, and learning stimulation are among the topics covered in depth. Each chapter contains a detailed developmental chart outlining the appropriate sensory, motor, language, mental, and social developmental milestones for that month. The book also includes 150 photographs. This 5-star book is well organized, well written, and easy to follow. Although Caplan warns readers not to take the timetables for developmental milestones as gospel, it's almost impossible not to do so because that is the way the book is organized.

★★★★   *The Happiest Baby on the Block* (2003) by Harvey Karp. New York: Bantam.

This practical, humorous, yet very serious recipe for calming babies seems to be a magic answer, as proclaimed by many parents. The pediatrician/author recounts his experience in training and in subsequent practice in which there was no treatment for "fussy or colicky" babies. The author was drawn to research existing solutions and to venture into other cultures and ancient child-rearing practices He came upon several answers, which he has formulated into the calming effect and five steps. The steps are accompanied by stories of parents whose lives, they say, were changed by this and other advice given to them by the author. There is a helpful addendum on general baby-raising tips and other resources.

**Recommended**

★★★   *Baby 411* (2011) by Denise Fields and Ari Brown. Boulder, CO: Windsor Peak.

Possibly every conceivable question is answered by this book. It is written for first-time parents or even second-time ones, given all the information and the differences among children. The authors present the material in an interpersonal and informal way, yet it is clear, well described, and categorized in a way that makes the information readily accessible. The 16 chapters include nutrition, liquids, solids, "the other end," sleep, vaccines, infections, common diseases, and first aid—and then under, for example, first aid, possibly 20 circumstances that can occur. This compendium is quite comprehensive and easily interpretable; in fact, it would have received 4 or 5 stars had more professionals rated it.

★★★   *The Baby Book* (2003) by William Sears and Martha Sears. Boston: Little, Brown.

A unique theme of this book is attachment parenting. Five attachment tools are introduced: connecting with your baby early, reading and responding to your baby's cues, breastfeeding your baby, carrying your baby, and sharing sleep with your baby. Frequently asked questions about this approach are discussed. The 28 chapters thoroughly discuss stages of the first two years of life. Specific features of child care are presented, including parenting a colicky baby, postpartum adjustments, baby's sleep difficulties, twins, the adopted baby, toilet training, mild medical emergency needs, and day care. This book thoroughly addresses the key components of child rearing in early years; *The Baby Book* is written for parents and those working in collaboration with parents.

★★★ *The Father's Almanac* (2nd ed., 1992) by S. Adams Sullivan. Garden City, NY: Doubleday.

*The Father's Almanac* is a guide for the day-to-day care of children written primarily for fathers. It begins before the child is born and includes a discussion of childbirth classes. The father's role at birth and during infancy is chronicled, as is his relationship with the child during the preschool years. The traditional role of the father is emphasized by Sullivan. For example, one chapter devoted to "Daddy's Work" describes how business travel or commuting cuts into the time the father has to spend with his children. Another chapter stresses the importance of the father's being supportive of the mother. Other chapters focus on the father's play with children, building things with them, learning with them, and hints about photographing the family. This 3-star resource includes a great deal of practical advice for helping fathers interact with their young children effectively.

★★★ *Becoming a Calm Mom* (2009) by Deborah Roth Ledley. Washington, DC: American Psychological Association.

Being a calm new mother is certainly not a naturally occurring event: the author learned after talks with her friends and other new moms that they all were anything but calm. Nonetheless, she and many new mothers thought they were expected to put on a smile and say all is terrific. The author discloses her experience—and that of many women with whom she has worked in psychotherapy and in her support groups—that the change from being a career woman to a full-time mother is a significant transition. Difficulties with breastfeeding, crying, and other challenges are common but not spoken about for fear of being seen as a "bad mother." This book walks the reader through several key areas of first-year child rearing. After sharing the six calm mom strategies, she turns to questions of experiencing surprising emotions, loss of identity, loss of time, and self-care topics.

## ■ INTERNET RESOURCES

### General Websites

★★★★★ *Zero to Three* www.zerotothree.org

The National Center for Infants, Toddlers and Families is a national nonprofit organization designed to help professionals and parents improve the lives of infants and toddlers. The website offers a wealth of helpful information on childhood development basics, toddler mental health, language and literacy, nutrition, brain development, sleep, play, and many more topics. It also covers issues of maltreatment (such as child abuse and neglect), public policy, and choosing quality child care.

★★★★★ *BabyCenter* www.babycenter.com

This offering from Johnson & Johnson is a large commercial site that has everything related to early childhood a parent would need. Information is divided into helpful categories: getting pregnant, pregnancy, baby, toddler, preschooler, big kid, and for you (the parent). Some of the innovative content, such as a week-by-week description and helpful guide to a baby's development, is engaging and interesting. The site also offers smartphone apps, as well as a thriving community and blogs.

★★★★★ *BabyZone* babyzone.com

An enormous commercial website from Disney for any kind of question related to babies from preconception and pregnancy to infancy and toddlerhood. The baby and pregnancy sections include not only the usual array of articles but also slideshows, expert Q&As, quizzes, and a mom-to-mom community.

★★★★ *National Network for Child Care* www.nncc.org

A service of Iowa State University, this website offers hundreds of articles, under "Learn about early childhood," on topics such as nutrition and diet, activities and learning, child care, school, public policy, and more. Sadly, it appears the website hasn't been updated in years, but it remains a helpful and valuable resource.

★★★★ *DrGreene.com* www.drgreene.com

This resource from the pediatrician Alan Greene, MD, offers a wealth of insight and wisdom from his many years as both a doctor and a parent. Includes categories of parenting, prenatal, newborn, infant, toddler, preschooler, school age, and teen, so goes beyond just an infant resource.

**Psychoeducational Materials**

★★★★★ *Today's Parent* www.todaysparent.com

A large website with thousands of articles, organized according to pregnancy, baby, toddler, kid, and teen categories, along with health, activities, recipes, general parenting topics, and a dozen blogs to keep you current on the latest parenting trends. The baby and toddler sections cover all the usual topics any new parent will be thankful to read up on.

★★★★★ *Project NoSpank* www.nospank.net

A superb site for those who wish to campaign against paddling in the schools (and spanking in general) and designed to educate both parents and education policymakers.

★★★★★ *Parenthood.com* www.parenthood.com

A comprehensive source of pregnancy, parenting, and child-care articles and websites. Features include hundreds of articles about parenting, pregnancy, your baby, your child, baby names, and dozens of videos.

★★★★ *The Natural Child Project* www.naturalchild.org

This website seeks to help parents raise children with dignity, respect, understanding, and compassion. Article topics include Attachment Parenting, Babies, Breastfeeding, Child Advocacy, Learning, Living with Children, and Sleeping. Unfortunately, articles often don't have dates, so it's unclear how often the website is updated.

★★★★  *Parenting* parenting.uwex.edu

This extensive parenting resource from the University of Wisconsin-Extension is organized in a helpful manner: Parenting the First Year, Parenting the Second and Third Years, Parenting the Preschooler, Parenting your Unique Child, and so on. The articles are in the form of downloadable PDF newsletters.

★★★★  *Brain Wonders* main.zerotothree.org/site/PageServer?pagename=key_brain

This interesting section in the *Zero to Three* website from a nonprofit organization explains brain development from 0 to 3 years.

**See also** Pregnancy (Chapter 32) and Child Development and Parenting (Chapter 15).

# CHAPTER 27

# LOVE AND INTIMACY

For centuries, philosophers, songwriters, and poets have been intrigued by love. Only recently, though, have psychologists turned their attention to love and offered recommendations on how to improve your love life and your intimacy.

Love is a vast and complex territory of human behavior. Much of romantic love and physical intimacy has traditionally occurred in the context of marriage, a topic to which we devote the next chapter (Chapter 28). In this chapter, we cover self-help books, films, and Internet resources devoted to love and intimacy (Box 27.1), which admittedly overlaps with the following chapter. Indeed, simply because of the immense pool of resources, we chose not to review the thousands of autobiographies touching on the subject.

## ■ SELF-HELP BOOKS

### Strongly Recommended

★★★★★ *Love Is Never Enough* (1988) by Aaron Beck. New York: Harper & Row.

This volume presents a cognitive therapy approach to love from one of the founders of cognitive therapy. Beck tells couples how to overcome misunderstandings, resolve conflicts, and improve their relationship by following cognitive therapy strategies. Beck first helps partners understand the specific self-defeating attitudes that plague their troubled relationships. Then he applies his cognitive therapy to what he labels the most common marital problems:

- How negative perceptions can overwhelm the positive aspects of marriage
- The swing from idealization to disillusionment
- The clash of differing perspectives
- The imposition of rigid expectations and rules
- How partners fail to hear what is said and often hear things that are not said
- How automatic negative thinking leads to conflict
- How partners cognitively distort a relationship that drives couples apart

In the second half of the book, Beck presents a number of different cognitive methods to fit the specific needs of couples. The book was written primarily as a self-help guide to improve love relationships, and it remains the highest-rated book in its category. Practical, inspiring, and clear.

---

**BOX 27.1**
**RECOMMENDATION HIGHLIGHTS**

---

**SELF-HELP BOOKS**

- On improving relationships with communication and cognitive therapy:
  - ★★★★★ *Love Is Never Enough* by Aaron Beck
  - ★★★★ *The Relationship Cure* by John Gottman and Joan DeClaire
- On the nature of love and the forms of love:
  - ★★★★ *The Art of Loving* by Erich Fromm
  - ★★★★ *The Triangle of Love* by Robert Sternberg
- On improving relationships by understanding yourself and previous relationships:
  - ★★★★ *The Dance of Intimacy* by Harriet Lerner
  - ★★★★ *The Dance of Connection* by Harriet Lerner
  - ♦ *In the Meantime* by Iyanla Vanzant
- On improving relationships by learning effective communication:
  - ★★★★★ *The 5 Love Languages* by Gary Chapman
  - ★★★★ *I Only Say This Because I Love You* by Deborah Tannen
- On seeking partners and maintaining a loving relationship:
  - ★★★★ *Keeping the Love You Find* by Harville Hendrix

**FILMS**

- On changing romantic partners as couples grow old together:
  - ★★★ *The Four Seasons*
- On the complexity and challenge of heterosexual relationships:
  - ★★★ *When Harry Met Sally*

**INTERNET RESOURCES**

- On understanding love:
  - ★★★★ *The Nature of Attraction and Love*
    www.psychologicalselfhelp.org/Chapter10/chap10_10.html
- On dating, relationship, and love advice:
  - ★★★★ *Relationships* www.psychologytoday.com/topics/relationships
  - ★★★★ *YourTango* www.yourtango.com

---

★★★★  *5 Love Languages* (2010) by Gary Chapman. Chicago, IL: Northfield.

After learning that the author is a marriage therapist, the passenger beside him on the plane asked, "What happens to love after the wedding?" The author's reply to this fundamental problem is that different people express love and caring in different languages. Just as children learn a primary language and then others, people have a particular language through which they receive love and caring. The five love languages are affirmation, quality time, receiving gifts, acts of service, and physical touch. Many case scenarios exemplify the principles and describe how this understanding can make significant differences in the lives of couples who are not speaking the same language. A bestseller, and deservedly so.

★★★★    *The Relationship Cure* (2002) by John Gottman and Joan DeClaire. New York: Crown.

Leading researcher John Gottman describes how happiness is based on everyday communication that involves emotion. Gottman says that this happiness depends on what he calls "bids" and how other people respond, or fail to respond, to such approaches. Gottman puts forth a five-step program to show readers how to become a master "bidder" in emotional communication. Numerous case studies, sample dialogues, and self-assessments are included. A superb, research-supported book that would have probably reached 5-star status had more psychologists in our studies rated it.

★★★★    *The Dance of Intimacy: A Woman's Guide to Courageous Acts of Change in Key Relationships* (1989) by Harriet Lerner. New York: Harper Perennial.

Written for women and about women's intimate relationships, *The Dance of Intimacy* weaves a portrait of our current self and relationships that Lerner believes is derived from longstanding relationships with mothers, fathers, and siblings. Drawing on a combination of psychoanalytic and family systems theories, Lerner tells women that if they are having problems in intimate relationships, they need to explore their upbringing to find clues to the current difficulties. Women learn how to avoid distancing themselves from their families of origin and overreacting to problems. Lerner intelligently tells women that they should balance the *I* and the *we* in their lives and be neither too self-absorbed nor too other-oriented. To explore unhealthy patterns that have been passed down from one generation to the next, Lerner helps women create a "genogram," a family diagram that goes back to the grandparents or earlier. This is an outstanding self-help book on understanding why close relationships are problematic and how to change them in positive ways. It does not give simple, quick-fix strategies. Lerner accurately avows that change is difficult, but she shows that it is possible.

★★★★    *The Dance of Connection* (2002) by Harriet Lerner. New York: HarperCollins.

Continuing the themes of *The Dance of Intimacy* (reviewed above), psychologist Lerner describes the importance of positively connecting with the people who matter most to us in life. She analyzes the most stressful problems people face when others hurt them and tells readers how to take a conversation to a more positive level when we feel desperate. Individuals learn when to let things go as well as the steps to take when they face betrayals and inequities in relationships.

★★★★    *Keeping the Love You Find* (1993) by Harville Hendrix. New York: Pocket.

Hendrix describes a self-help program for singles who seek a loving, rewarding romantic relationship. He especially focuses on how to maintain a positive relationship with someone you love over the long term. Although the book's title and the writing may appear a little slick, the mental health professionals in our studies consistently rated this book positively.

★★★★  *The Art of Loving* (1956, reissued 2002) by Erich Fromm. New York: Harper & Row.

This philosophical and psychological treatise on the nature of love was penned by Erich Fromm, a well-known psychoanalyst and social philosopher. He describes love in general, as well as different forms of love. In Fromm's view, love is an attitude that determines the relatedness of the person to the whole world, not just toward one love object. Love is an act of faith, a commitment, a complete giving of oneself. There are no quick fixes for developing love; rather, Fromm argues that learning to love is a long and difficult process, requiring discipline, patience, sensitivity to self, and the productive use of skills. Fromm stresses that although the principle underlying capitalistic society and the principle of love are incompatible, love is the only sane and satisfactory solution to the human condition. As such, this book is very different from most of the books evaluated in our national studies; it doesn't include the usual exercises, case histories, and clinical examples. Rather, it tackles the complex question of what love is and how society can benefit if people learn how to love more effectively. Widely regarded as a classic, this is an intellectually challenging piece that is not written in the style of many other self-help and resource books.

★★★★  *I Only Say This Because I Love You* (2001) by Deborah Tannen. New York: Random House.

Tannen explains how individuals can avoid or redirect conversations and circumstances with their loved ones that rapidly become destructive. She provides many examples of conversations that have gone sour and discusses numerous strategies for communicating more effectively with people you love. A fine self-help book with interesting examples.

★★★★  *The Triangle of Love* (1987) by Robert Sternberg. New York: Basic Books.

The three sides of love's triangle are the fire of sexual and romantic passion, the close emotional sharing of intimacy, and the enduring bond of commitment. The type and quality of a relationship depend on the strength of each side of the triangle in each partner and how closely the partners' triangles match. Sternberg argues that each side has its own timetable. For example, passion dominates the early part of a love relationship, while intimacy and commitment play more important roles as relationships progress. In the author's view, the ultimate form of love combines the passion, intimacy, and commitment. Sternberg gives specific guidelines for improving love relationships and includes a "love scale" for measuring one's own love. An insightful perspective on the nature of love, this book gives good advice about how to achieve perfect love, but it includes more academic discussion than is typical of self-help books. Nonetheless, Sternberg's analysis of love's nature is much easier reading than Fromm's *The Art of Loving*.

### Recommended

★★★  *Fear of Intimacy* (2001) by Robert Firestone and Joyce Catlett. Washington, DC: American Psychological Association.

Based on their extensive clinical experience, the authors argue that relationships fail not for commonly given reasons but rather because psychological defenses formed in childhood act as barriers to closeness in adulthood. Numerous case studies are used to illustrate the childhood precursors of adult relationship problems. A bit academic for a self-help book, but favorably rated by mental health experts who were familiar with it; in fact, had it been more widely known, it would have probably obtained a 4-star designation.

★★★ *Obsessive Love: When It Hurts Too Much to Let Go* (2002) by Susan Forward and Craig Buck. New York: Bantam.

This book is for people who are obsessive lovers and their "other." Obsessive love is not really love at all, according to Forward and Buck, but rather a pathological compulsion. They believe that obsessive love is caused by rejecting parents or separation problems in childhood. According to the authors, obsessive love occurs about equally in women and men and takes different forms: worshiping someone from afar, fantasizing about saving a troubled partner, or refusing to let go of a lover who has broken off a relationship. The authors intelligently tell obsessive lovers who are violence-prone to see a psychotherapist immediately rather than simply relying on a self-help book. For obsessive lovers who are not violence-prone, they recommend detailed logging of emotions, a 2-week vacation from contact with the other, and a probing self-evaluation in which the obsessive person asks himself or herself tough questions about whether anything in the relationship can be salvaged.

★★★ *Do I Have to Give Up Me to Be Loved by You?* (1983) by Jordan Paul and Margaret Paul. Minneapolis: CompCare.

This best-selling self-help book advocates probing and understanding the unspoken motivations behind what we do to solve our relationship problems. Using their intention therapy as a base, the authors tell readers how to become aware of self-created obstacles and develop more intimate relationships. A number of exercises help couples work on their power struggles, sexual expectations, and many other marital problems.

★★★ *Creating Love: The Next Great Stage of Growth* (1992) by John Bradshaw. New York: Bantam.

This bestselling author writes on the many dimensions of love and demystifies the belief that love is easy and a given among blood relatives. To paraphrase Bradshaw, love is difficult and requires hard work and honesty. The reader is forced to evaluate and perhaps surrender counterfeit love in exchange for the soul-building work of real love. Bradshaw addresses how to create love in various relationships (e.g., with God, parents, children, friends, spouses, work, and self). This 3-star book brings to the surface the mystical, spiritual, and soulful characteristics of love and will probably be useful to people who have struggled with uncertainty about love.

★★★ *Soul Mates: Honoring the Mysteries of Love and Relationship* (1994) by Thomas Moore. New York: HarperCollins.

Moore, a former Catholic monk turned bestselling author, reawakens the reader to discernment and nurturance of the soul in an effort to cultivate loving relationships. He looks at relationships from a position of mystery, religion, and theology, believing it is a mistake to talk authoritatively about mysteries. Moore's objective is to help individuals change well-entrenched ideas of what it means to love and be one with others in friendship, marriage, and community. This book would probably be best received by religiously and spiritually oriented readers.

    ★★★   *The Love Dare* (2008) by Stephen Kendrix and Alex Kendrix. Nashville, TN: B&H.

Another book written from a Christian frame of reference, it is grounded in Scripture that speaks to love and other virtues that are important in relationships. The "dare" is the challenge of meeting a different dare each day for 40 days. The first day's dare, for example, is to refrain from saying anything negative or critical for 24 hours. Each day carries a dare that is meant to both reveal the effect of withholding criticism, in this example, but also to begin building positive patterns in the relationship. The book includes sections on thoughts and behaviors that block prayer and questions that partners can ask each other in the service of being positive and caring. Both patience and kindness are presented as fundamental qualities of any healthy relationship, and these are exemplified in scenarios throughout the book.

    ★★★   *Going the Distance: Secrets of Lifelong Love* (1991) by Lonnie Barbach and David Geisinger. New York: Plume.

The advice rendered here is appropriate for a wide range of couples, from people just embarking on a close intimate relationship to people who want to renew their commitment to marital partners. According to Barbach and Geisinger, we bring the scars of old psychic wounds to any new relationship; a good close relationship is a healing one; and even individuals with a long history of troubled relationships can learn the skills needed to make a marriage work. The authors stress the importance of chemistry, courtship, trust, respect, acceptance, and shared values. They also suggest methods for overcoming commitment phobias, strategies to resolve power conflicts for control, and ways to improve a couple's sex life. A 50-item compatibility questionnaire helps couples evaluate how well suited they are. Solid advice and well written, even if standard fare for relationship books.

    ★★★   *Women Who Love Too Much* (1985) by Robin Norwood. New York: Pocket.

This volume was one of many bestselling self-help books in the 1980s that blame many of women's problems on a male-dominated society. Among the characteristics of a woman who loves too much are a childhood in which her emotional needs were not met, willingness to assume the majority of blame for a relationship's problems, low self-esteem, and a belief that she has no right to be happy. Such women choose men who need help, inevitably causing their marriage to become troubled. These women are addicted to pain, says Norwood, just as an alcoholic is addicted to liquor. The first step to recovering from a relationship addiction is to back off from the partner—quit nagging and stop making demands—and start focusing on her own problems. Norwood advocates finding a support group and leaving the relationship if necessary. *Women Who Love Too Much* headed the *New York Times* bestseller list for 37 weeks. It can inspire women who are trapped in bad relationships to evaluate their situations and chart better courses for their lives. On the other hand, critics say that it attributes women's problems disproportionately to men and doesn't adequately deal with what happens to a woman once she "recovers."

★★★ *A Return to Love* (1992) by Marianne Williamson. New York: HarperCollins.

This book is a spiritual journey back to our natural tendency to love. Bestselling author Williamson argues that we have frequently been taught to detach, to compete, and to dislike ourselves. Through her psychological, emotional, and spiritual approach, she encourages us to relinquish our social fears and accept back into our hearts the love we have been denying. This is a book about the practical application of love and its daily practice. An inspiring book for the spiritually minded and for those seeking a life based on the practice of love.

**Diamond in the Rough**

♦ *In the Meantime: Finding Yourself and the Love That You Want* (1998) by Iyanla Vanzant. New York: Simon & Schuster.

The author focuses on the vision and purpose humans need to find their way through life. Vanzant asks: As you are working to achieve a state of love, what do you do in the meantime? Mental housekeeping is the answer—for example, repairing past hurts, addressing fears, and correcting inaccurate information that stand in the way of finding true love. Vanzant states that love will come to us, but most of us won't recognize it since love rarely shows up in the place we expect it or looks the way we expect it to look. She reinforces the point that true self-love needs to be in place in order to find the love that you want. Taking each experience and learning more about yourself is part of what to do in the meantime. But it's not easy: reflection, evaluation, and unlearning require a willingness to do the grunge work. A highly but infrequently rated book for adults trying to understand themselves and willing to learn in the meantime.

**Not Recommended**

★★ *Relationship Rescue: A Seven-Step Strategy for Reconnecting With Your Partner* (2000) by Philip McGraw. New York: Hyperion.

★★ *Loving Each Other* (1984) by Leo Buscaglia. Thorofare, NJ: Slack.

★★ *Men Who Hate Women and the Women Who Love Them* (1986) by Susan Forward. New York: Bantam.

★★ *Men Who Can't Love: When a Man's Fear Makes Him Run from Commitment* (1987) by Steven Carter. New York: Evans.

★ *When Someone You Love Is Someone You Hate* (1988, reprinted 1996) by Stephen Arterburn and David Stoop. Dallas: Word.

★ *What Smart Women Know* (1990) by Steven Carter and Julia Sokol. New York: Evans.

**Strongly Not Recommended**

† *Mars and Venus in the Bedroom: A Guide to Lasting Romance and Passion* (1995) by John Gray. New York: HarperCollins.

† *Women Men Love, Women Men Leave* (1987) by Connell Cowan and Melvyn Kinder. New York: Clarkson N. Potter.

† *What Every Woman Should Know about Men* (1981) by Joyce Brothers. New York: Simon & Schuster.

† *Straight Talk, No Chaser* (2010) by Steve Harvey. New York: HarperCollins.

## ■ FILMS

**Recommended**

★★★  *The Four Seasons* (1982) directed by Alan Alda. PG rating. 107 minutes.

This film provides a realistic view of small-group dynamics—that is, the group members' relationship to each other and also the subset relationships of each person to his or her partner. Three couples have taken their vacations together for many years when one couple suddenly divorces. The man brings his new wife to the group's holiday, thereby challenging the nature of their relationships and the meaning of love. The film highlights the foibles of growing up and older together in very funny scenarios while also capturing the spirit of lifetime romantic changes. Also reviewed in the Divorce chapter (Chapter 21).

★★★  *When Harry Met Sally* (1989) directed by Rob Reiner. R rating. 95 minutes.

Harry and Sally run into each other every five years or so and find themselves at differing points in their romantic relationships. They repeatedly discuss the possibility of being friends, but Harry proclaims that men and women can't be friends because of the inevitability of sex. The uncertainty of their relationship and their commitment and caring for each other are the themes of this story. The complexity and challenge of contemporary relationships between men and women is revealed in funny yet poignant ways.

★★★  *The Way We Were* (1973) directed by Sydney Pollack. PG rating. 118 minutes.

Tearjerker in which a man and woman meet and fall in love years after their friendship in college. They find themselves with conflicting political and ideological perspectives that eventually drive them apart. The movie demonstrates the challenges of love and the difficulties of holding on to one's beliefs while accepting differences in a partner. The story is energetic, sad, and hopeful; in the end, it chronicles coping with interpersonal loss based on principles.

★★★  *The Story of Us* (1999) directed by Rob Reiner. R rating. 96 minutes.

Bruce Willis and Michelle Pfeiffer have been married 15 years and seem to get along for the sake of their wonderful children. After the kids leave for summer camp, they start a trial separation. The movie focuses on how they cope with the separation and understand their marriage. He is a disorganized and laidback comedy writer who finds her too rigid; she is a crossword puzzle writer who finds him irresponsible. The marriage is told in a series of flashbacks, including some high points, endless screaming fights, and times of bland distance. While any married person will find several things to relate to and will appreciate the marital therapy sessions, the couple shows little growth and little insight. In the end, the couple decides to remain married, but it is a sobering, nonromantic picture of a struggling marriage.

★★★  *Sleepless in Seattle* (1994) directed by Nora Ephron. PG rating. 100 minutes.

The despair over a spouse's death and the search for a soulmate drive this heartwarming and funny story. Sam's wife died, leaving Sam and son Jonah adrift. Sam's initial abdication of a love life and his awkward attempts to console his son are realistic portrayals of families in turmoil. Holding out for the real thing so that love conquers all and the irrepressibility of a child's mission to make his family complete are the dual lessons of this story.

**Not Recommended**

★★ *Pretty in Pink* (1986) directed by Howard Deutch. PG-13 rating. 96 minutes.

★ *Serendipity* (2001) directed by Peter Chelsom. PG-13 rating. 90 minutes.

**Strongly Not Recommended**

† *9½ Weeks* (1987) directed by Adrian Lyne. R rating. 113 minutes.

## ■ INTERNET RESOURCES

**Love and Romance**

★★★★ *The Nature of Attraction and Love* www.psychologicalselfhelp.org/Chapter10/chap10_10.html

This article from the late psychologist Clay Tucker-Ladd, PhD, discusses how romantic and companionate love are different and therefore each must be understood uniquely.

★★★★ *Relationships* www.psychologytoday.com/topics/relationships

With the support of dozens of blogs related to this topic, *Psychology Today*'s website (a companion to the company's print magazine) offers hundreds of articles on relationships, love, and intimacy. With so many writers, however, sometimes the writing can be of variable quality, and the topics will be of varying interest to consumers.

★★★★ *YourTango* www.yourtango.com

YourTango is a one-stop commercial website that offers a very glossy, mainstream offering for relationships, dating, and love advice. Well designed and easy to navigate, the site's articles range from engaging and entertaining, to informative and advice-oriented. May not appeal to all, but worth checking out nonetheless for a lighter take on love.

★★★★ *Relationships & Sexuality* psychcentral.com/relationships

This center from Psych Central offers a wealth of relationship articles on love, couplehood, communication, sexuality, and much more from a variety of diverse mental health professionals. It's all wrapped in an attractive website with quizzes, blogs, and an active support community.

★★★★ *SIRC Guide to Flirting* www.sirc.org/publik/flirt.html

This lengthy article from the Social Issues Research Centre reviews what behavioral science tells us about flirting and how to do it. The article covers everything about flirting and beginning relationships and may be helpful for the overly ideational but socially inexperienced college-educated reader or others with social anxiety.

★★★★  *Erotic Talk* www.sexuality.org/talk.html

Wondering how to engage in erotic talk with your partner? This website provides an article that summarizes advice from multiple books on this topic. It is sex-positive, and, toward the end, gets into perhaps too much detail about phone sex operations.

★★★  *Love Bytes* www.psychologytoday.com/blog/love-bytes

This blog from John Buri, PhD, on *Psychology Today* talks about love from many different, and often engaging, perspectives.

★★★  *Love and Relationships* dataguru.org/love

The term "love" is packed with multiple meanings and yet we cling to it and use it frequently. This site features numerous articles about love, communication, and relationships, including articles about different types of love, nonverbal signals, and more. Unfortunately the site has no dates on it, so it's unclear how updated the information is.

★★★  *Shelia's Kissing Booth* www.kissingbooth.com

This is an eclectic personal site that focuses on articles related to kissing (no surprise), romance, love, and dating. Shelia Lee, the site's creator, is a married romantic and enjoys writing about these topics on her regularly updated blog on the site as well.

★★★  *LovingYou.com* archive.lovingyou.com

This large commercial website features thousands of articles about love, romance, passion, inspiration, as well as sections on beauty, recipes, travel, and more.

★★★  *Rekindle Romance* www.positive-way.com

The website offers a wealth of relationship resources for couples, including a section entitled "Romance and Passion." Article topics cover rekindling romance, finding intimacy, and expressing love.

★★★  *Advice on Flirting* www.sexuality.org/flirtadv.html

A collection of tips from a discussion group and a book on flirting.

### Dating: In Person and Online

★★★★  *Ask HeartBeat.com* www.askheartbeat.com

This website is devoted to "black male/female and interracial romantic relationships" and is tailored toward anyone looking for such relationship and dating advice.

★★★★   *The Rebuttal from Uranus* susanhamson.wordpress.com

John Gray's *Men Are from Mars, Women Are from Venus* and subsequent books have been on the bestseller lists for many years. This site offers intelligent and devastating critiques (unfortunately not well organized or easy to navigate) from archivist and mom Susan Hamson.

★★★★   *Singles Coach* www.singlescoach.com/blog

Readers will find many well-written advice columns and articles here, written by psychotherapist Nina Atwood, which contain many down-to-Earth suggestions.

★★★   *Guys Guide to Girls* by Philip Ovalsen www.philipov.com/guys1.htm

This online book, although not updated, is full of musings on love, shyness, writing letters, and other social skills. The first four essays are gently written and supportive; the last two give good advice on using the Internet to find romance.

★★★   *Out of the Cave: Exploring Gray's Anatomy* by Kathleen Trigiani web2.airmail. net/ktrig246/out_of_cave

"This series of five essays takes a macroscopic look at the Mars and Venus phenomenon and concludes that we don't have to settle for Dr. John Gray's worldview. This site is ideal for people who are interested in gender issues but don't have time to read the major literature."

★★   *The Straight FAQ: One Straight Male's Thoughts and Advice on Successful Use of Internet Personals* by Dean Esmay www.faqs.org/faqs/personals/straightfaq/ part1

This dated FAQ article includes general helpful advice about online dating but is focused on online classified ads, which are rarely used any more. For gay men, a companion FAQ is at www.faqs.org/faqs/personals/gayfaq/part1

**See also** Marriage (Chapter 28) and Sexuality (Chapter 35).

# MARRIAGE

The changes in American marital patterns have been revolutionary, not evolutionary. Just 50 years ago, people married in their teens and early twenties, had children, and stayed together for the rest of their lives. Men worked outside the home and were the breadwinners; women worked inside the home and cared for the children.

In today's world, many people marry later or not at all. When they do get married, many couples postpone children until both partners have developed their careers. Or they choose to remain childless. Divorce captures 40% of all first marriages and 50% of subsequent marriages. Couples want their relationship to be deep and loving, and if it isn't, they increasingly see a psychologist or marriage counselor or consult a self-help resource to improve their marital relationship.

In this chapter we present the evaluative ratings and narrative descriptions of self-help resources on marriage. The content of this chapter obviously overlaps with the preceding chapter on love and intimacy, but if the focus of the resource is marriage or couplehood, we placed it here (Box 28.1).

## ■ SELF-HELP BOOKS

### Strongly Recommended

★★★★★ *Why Marriages Succeed or Fail* (1994) by John Gottman. New York: Simon & Schuster.

Based on research conducted over a number of years with hundreds of couples, the principles presented in this book diagnose, interpret, and predict the success or failure of a marriage with a high degree of accuracy. Psychologist Gottman, an internationally known researcher, effectively and systematically describes the three types of marriage styles and how healthy or unhealthy each may be depending on the interaction. The four warning signs that a marriage is spiraling downward are described (criticism, contempt, defensiveness, and stonewalling) and in concluding chapters, four keys to improving a marriage and reversing the spiral are discussed. Gottman's advice is logical, clear, and research-based. Quizzes allow couples to self-identify the status of their marriages. According to our mental health experts, a very valuable and research-based self-help book.

---

**BOX 28.1**
**RECOMMENDATION HIGHLIGHTS**

---

**SELF-HELP BOOKS**

■ On the origins of healthy and unhealthy marriage styles:

★★★★★ *Why Marriages Succeed or Fail* by John Gottman

★★★★ *Intimate Partners* by Maggie Scarf

■ On solving marital problems and improving the relationship:

★★★★★ *Seven Principles for Making Marriages Work* by John Gottman and Nan Silver

★★★★ *Divorce Bustin g* by Michele Weiner-Davis

★★★★ *Getting the Love You Want* by Harville Hendrix

★★★ *Fighting for Your Marriage* by Howard Markman and associates

★★★ *The Hard Questions* by Susan Piver

★★★ *Reconcilable Differences* by Andrew Christensen and Neil Jacobson

■ On pastoral marital counseling:

◆ *Love for a Lifetime* by James Dobson

**FILMS**

■ On the challenges and complexities of a loving (lesbian) marriage:

★★★★ *The Kids are All Right*

■ On the depressing brutality of a deteriorating marriage:

★★★★ *Revolutionary Road*

**INTERNET RESOURCES**

■ For valuable information and advice about marriage:

★★★★ *Parenting and Marriage Articles* www.drheller.com

★★★★★ *About.com Marriage* marriage.about.com

★★★★ *The Relationship Learning Center* www.relationshipjourney.com

---

★★★★★ *The Seven Principles for Making Marriages Work* (2000) by John Gottman and Nan Silver. New York: Crown.

This outstanding self-help book received very high ratings. Written by leading marriage researcher John Gottman (who also wrote *Why Marriages Succeed or Fail,* reviewed above) and based on his extensive research, this book provides a number of positive strategies for helping couples to understand their problems and make their relationship work. Gottman's principles for making a marriage work include establishing love maps, turning toward each other instead of away, letting your partner influence you, solving solvable conflicts, overcoming gridlock, and creating shared meaning. Extensive examples and self-assessments are included. His two books received among the highest ratings for this category in our national studies.

**★★★★**  *Intimate Partners: Patterns in Love and Marriage* (1986, reprinted 1996) by Maggie Scarf. New York: Ballantine.

This book tells readers how to solve their marital problems, especially by understanding the stages of development and the family of origin. Scarf charts the lives of five married couples in depth, categorizing them according to their life stage: idealization, disenchantment, child-rearing and career-building, child-launching, and the retirement years. She starts with relative newlyweds and ends with a couple who have finished rearing their children and are free to focus on each other once again. Interviews with 32 couples are woven through the book. Scarf emphasizes the importance of a couple's birth families, configurations, and genograms (diagrams of lines of attachment between marital partners and their parents, grandparents, and siblings) to illuminate how people often repeat the past. Unfulfilled needs are powerful, unconscious forces that shape a marriage from the beginning and continue to dominate it throughout the marriage stages. Scarf does an excellent job of encouraging partners to examine their stages of marriage and their families of origin.

**★★★★**  *Getting the Love You Want* (1988) by Harville Hendrix. New York: Henry Holt.

This book is based on workshop techniques that Hendrix has developed to help couples construct a conscious marriage—a relationship based on awareness of the unresolved childhood conflicts that cause individuals to select particular spouses. The author tells readers how to conduct a 10-week course in couples therapy in the privacy of their homes. In a stepwise fashion, he teaches readers how to communicate more clearly and sensitively, to eliminate self-defeating behaviors, and to focus attention on meeting their partners' needs. Hendrix's goal is to transform the downward spiral of the power struggle into a mutually beneficial relationship of emotional growth. This 4-star book is superb for marital partners engulfed in conflict. Hendrix does an excellent job of helping the reader become aware of longstanding family influences on current close relationships.

**★★★★**  *Divorce Busting* (1992) by Michele Weiner-Davis. New York: Summit.

This book advocates a brief, solution-oriented approach to keeping a marriage together. Author Weiner-Davis says that divorce is not the answer to an unhappy marriage. She says she came to this conclusion after observing that former spouses often continue to be unhappy after the divorce. Weiner-Davis's approach focuses on the present and the future and on actions rather than feelings. It is accomplished in brief rather than lengthy therapy or problem-solving sessions. (In her practice, she sees most couples for only four or five sessions.) *Divorce Busting* offers step-by-step strategies that couples can follow to make their marriage loving again. Brief case histories show how couples have used Weiner-Davis's approach to solve their marital difficulties. The steps can be followed alone or with a spouse. The therapeutic techniques are well translated into everyday language that the reader will easily comprehend.

**Recommended**

**★★★**  *The Hard Questions* (2007) by Susan Piver. New York: Tarcher/Putman.

The questions are those asked by couples thinking about a committed relationship and also those who already have done so. Piver stresses the importance of honesty and kindness in addressing these questions. The 100 questions focus on home, money, work, sex, heath, family, children, friends, and spirituality. At a pace that is suitable for a few questions at a time, the couple shares their answers to each question. The process of answering these questions takes the couple through a learning, growth, and intimacy experience in itself.

★★★   *Fighting for Your Marriage* (revised ed., 2001) by Howard Markman, Scott Stanley, and Susan Blumberg. New York: Wiley.

Based on the Prevention and Relationship Enhancement Program (PREP), this book provides couples with strategies for handling conflict more constructively, protecting happiness, and reducing the chances of breaking up. Markman is a leading figure in the study of marital relationships. This one is a research-based and practical self-help book.

★★★   *Reconcilable Differences* (2000) by Andrew Christensen and Neil Jacobson. New York: Guilford.

Two leading researchers in couple therapy describe why couples have the same fights over and over again and how to reconcile their differences. Couples learn how to defuse arguments, accept differences, and change for the better. The authors describe concrete steps for developing compassionate acceptance of some of their partner's behaviors. Numerous case studies provide insights about differences and how to deal with them. Each chapter concludes with relevant couple exercises. As is the case for *Fighting for Your Marriage* (above), this is a research-based and practical self-help book.

★★★   *The Power of Two Workbook* (2003) by Susan Heitler and Abigail Hirsch. Oakland, CA: New Harbinger.

Couples and partners interested in improving communication skills and conflict resolution skills will find these exercises, questions, and techniques helpful. The authors recommend writing out and completing the exercises, not just reading them. The communication factors include talking directly, respecting boundaries, listening effectively, understanding and receiving anger, avoiding traps, handling upsets, and providing mutual support. The pragmatic approach is easy to follow and to understand.

★★★   *I Love You, Let's Work It Out* (1987) by David Viscott. New York: Simon & Schuster.

The cycle of working it out in Viscott's book begins with commitment and communication. The central focus is diagnosing and interpreting what couples argue about, how they argue, and what their individual and joint styles of interacting reveal about how to work out problems. Protective styles (dependent, controlling, and competitive) are analyzed in relationship to couples' styles, and an interaction is predicted and described for each. Working it out means that once the dynamics and interactions that maintain conflict are understood, couples can break the cycle and make different choices. This text presents an interactive, organized system for understanding conflict patterns and lends itself to cognitive approaches toward solutions.

★★★   *Getting It Right the First Time* (2004) by Barry McCarthy and Emily J. McCarthy. New York: Brunner-Routledge.

These recommendations come for those in a first marriage or committed relationship and preferably in the first two years. The topics discussed are important for the health, respect, and continued shared commitment within the relationship. Resolution of conflict, sexual problems, parenting, career conflicts, in-laws, and divorce prevention are addressed through exercises that couples can do together. The topics share a theme of trouble-shooting and tackling problems early on.

★★★ *Husbands and Wives: Exploring Marital Myths* (1989) by Melvyn Kinder and Connell Cowan. New York: Clarkson N. Potter.

The major problem in most marriages, the authors maintain, is that each partner tries to change the other instead of focusing on improving his or her own behavior. Kinder and Cowan call their approach "self-directed marriage"; it emphasizes the importance of each partner's taking responsibility for his or her own happiness and replacing other-directed blame with acceptance. The authors tell marital partners to accept their differences, become friends, and rediscover the enjoyment of marital life.

★★★ *All You Need Is Love and Other Lies about Marriage* (2005) by John W. Jacobs. New York: HarperCollins.

Jacobs reviews several explanations for the challenges of marriage through both an historical and societal lens. Marriage was easier 100 years ago because of a life expectancy of 47 in 1900, briefer marriages, and fewer empty nesters. Further, personal and emotional satisfaction was not an expectation of marriage until recent years. The seven lies about marriage are presented together in a chapter; for example, when you marry, you create your own family. This book intends to demystify and debunk unrealistic expectations about marriage.

★★★ *Getting Together and Staying Together* (2000) by William Glasser and Carleen Glasser. New York: Harper Collins.

Why some marriages make it and others fail is examined here. Based on William Glasser's choice theory, partners learn how to create loving, long-lasting relationships. This book was not a strong entry in the Recommended category.

**Diamonds in the Rough**

♦ *We Love Each Other but…* (1999) by Ellen Wachtel. New York: Golden.

Intimate relationships are most often lost because of failure in basic, daily interactions, not because of major events. This self-help resource directs the reader to just those basics and tells how to regain the fundamental elements of the relationship that brought the two people together in the first place. There are no exercises, activities, or artificial interventions. Instead, Wachtel suggests how to think and act differently toward problems so that both partners will be heard and understood. She offers four basic truths about being in relationships and identifies seven areas of conflict that have emerged as most common in her work with couples. Very do-able solutions are offered for each problem, accompanied by numerous examples from the author's experience with couples who enhanced their relationships. This book was highly rated in two of our studies but not yet well known. It is a wise and comforting book.

♦ *Love for a Lifetime* (1998) by James Dobson. Sisters, OR: Multnomah.

James Dobson, a psychologist widely known for his many books on marriage and parenting, has written this book for adult singles, engaged couples, and those married less than 10 years. The author's objectives are to identify the major pitfalls that undermine a relationship and to make suggestions on how to avoid them. Christian principles frame the narrative, and his perspectives on relationships, money, sex, and family are consistent with Christian teachings. Topics addressed are controversial either in Christian teaching or in general society, such as premarital sex, divorce, homosexuality, and gender differences. The teachings of this book will be helpful to people looking for guidance in relationship building within conventional Christian beliefs. Diamond in the Rough status is given to this book because of its moderately high but infrequent ratings in two of our studies.

### Strongly Not Recommended

† *The Proper Care and Feeding of Husbands* (2006) by Laura Schlessinger. New York: Harper.

† *10 Stupid Things Couples Do to Mess Up Their Relationships* (2002) by Laura Schlessinger. New York: Harper.

## ■ FILMS

### Strongly Recommended

★★★★ *The Kids Are All Right* (2010) directed by Lisa Cholodenko. R rating. 106 minutes.

This complex film follows a married lesbian couple and their two adolescent children. Conflict arises when the children of this upper-middle-class couple seek out their biological father, Paul. The introduction of Paul threatens the foundation of the family. The struggle of the family demonstrates the universal difficulties all married couples face but also highlights the love that binds them and the complexities of lesbian relationships. This realistic depiction of marriage and family makes for an honest and thought-provoking film.

★★★★ *Revolutionary Road* (2008) directed by Sam Mendes. R rating. 119 minutes.

Desperation grows between this young couple after they marry and move to the suburbs in Connecticut. Frank and April Wheeler believed marriage would allow them to fulfill all their fantasies, but instead they have fallen into a boring routine. They both want something more and plan to move to Paris but cannot make the move. Just as this is happening their neighbor Helen asks if her son, John, can come to their home for dinner. John has been away at a psychiatric hospital, but as the couple soon finds out, his only disorder is being brutally honest. Over the course of the meal he shows the Wheelers their true reality and mocks the delusions they have been living under. John's introduction into the film/story helps to dispel the marriage of fairy tales and fantasies attached to it and reveal the true nature of the troubled marriage. Not as brutal as *Who's Afraid of Virginia Woolf?* but nearly as powerful and depressing.

## ■ INTERNET RESOURCES

### Psychoeducational Materials

**★★★★** *Relationship Information for Couples* www.positive-way.com/relation.htm

This site has a number of short, practical sections on improving a relationship, with good ideas about issues like Warning Signs, Hidden Issues and Expectations, Expressing Your Feelings, Who's the Boss, How to Love Your Mate, Rekindle Romance, Relate to Create Happiness, Men, Housework, Better Sex, and Problem Solving. Each section has guidelines and suggestions, and often questionnaires, all of which appear useful.

**★★★★** *Parenting and Marriage Articles* www.drheller.com

Over 100 well-written articles on various aspects of married life, like conflict, gender, marital therapy, fair fighting, etc., from retired psychologist Kalman Heller, PhD.

**★★★★** *Marriage—A Many-Splendored, Sometimes Splintered, Thing* by Daniel Wayne Matthews, PhD ncsu.edu/ffci/publications/1996/v1-n4–1996-fall/marriage. php

A helpful article in which Matthews presents the challenges couples face when they marry, myths, financial and in-law issues, and more. It makes for a helpful premarital review.

**★★★★★** *About.com Marriage* marriage.about.com

This site from About.com guides Sheri and Bob Striof is regularly updated and full of useful marriage information for both newly married couples and those celebrating 10 or 20 years of marriage. Tabs organize information according to Getting Married, Staying Married, and Love & Sex, with dozens of insight and engaging articles in each. It's a well-developed, rich resource full of advice and information for even the best of marriages.

**★★★★** *YourTango* www.yourtango.com

YourTango is a one-stop commercial website that offers a very glossy, mainstream offering for relationships, marriage, and love advice. Well designed and easy to navigate, the site's articles range from engaging and entertaining, to informative and advice-oriented. May not appeal to all, but worth checking out nonetheless for a lighter take on love and marriage.

**★★★★** *The Relationship Learning Center* www.relationshipjourney.com

Dawn Lipthrott, LCSW, offers readers dozens of helpful articles about divorce and relationships under "Resources & Links."

**★★★** *Love Doc* www.psychologytoday.com/blog/love-doc

This blog from Frances Cohen Praver, PhD, a clinical psychologist and relational psychoanalyst, on *Psychology Today* offers weekly insights into sex, love, relationships, and marriage.

★★★  *Traditional Family Values* by Peter McWilliams www.james-l-drush.com/jd/tra-ditionalfamilyvalues.htm

This article debunks the myths of perfect families of the 1950s, which may be useful to clear out assumptions of what marriage was and should be.

### Affairs/Infidelity
★★★  *The Other Woman* www.gloryb.com

This is a support and informational site for the partner of the married person having an affair. It presents all sides and offers personal stories, endings, and a large FAQ. The "MM to English Dictionary" is an interesting read. The site, however, suffers from numerous pop-up ads that gets in the way of the content.

★★★★  *How to Survive Infidelity* www.marriagebuilders.com/graphic/mbi5525_qa.html

While Willard F. Harley, Jr., PhD, on the Marriage Builders website appears to be against affairs, he writes well about the emotional issues. Here are about a dozen articles he wrote in response to letters and FAQs about affairs. All of these may be useful to people who need to see all sides of an affair.

★★★★  *Articles about Affairs* www.vaughan-vaughan.com/affairsmenu.html

Peggy Vaughn, author of a book on affairs, offers a wealth of good but brief essays on many different aspects of affairs.

### Alternatives to Marriage
★★★★  *Alternatives to Marriage Project* www.unmarried.org

This is a nonprofit organization advocating for quality and fairness for people who are single, who choose not to marry, who cannot marry, or who live together. It offers a number of different articles about alternatives to marriage and still experience loving, rewarding relationships, as well as offering information about the organization itself.

### Other Resources

★★★★  *Marriage Encounter* marriage-encounter.org

Marriage Encounter is a weekend marriage-improvement workshop for married couples that is based on Judeo-Christian concepts. It has programs all over the country and in every kind of church.

★★★  *PAIRS* www.pairs.com

The PAIRS (Practical Application of Intimate Relationship Skills) Foundation offers educational workshops to help couples improve their marriage. The workshops vary from 1 day to 1 week in length. They have a companion project website called the Fatherhood Channel at fatherhoodchannel.com

## ■ SUPPORT GROUPS

### Association for Couples in Marriage Enrichment

Phone: 800-634-8325
www.bettermarriages.org

### No Kidding!

Phone: 604-538-7736
www.nokidding.net
Mutual support and social activities for married and single people who either have decided not to have children, are postponing parenthood, or are unable to have children.

### Smart Marriages' Directory of Marriage Education Programs

www.smartmarriages.com
This is a searchable listing of about 150 local and national programs with annotations and complete addresses.

**See also** Families and Stepfamilies (Chapter 23), Love and Intimacy (Chapter 27), and Sexuality (Chapter 35).

# CHAPTER 29

# MEN'S ISSUES

The male of the human species—what is he really like? What does he want and need? At no other point in human history have males and females been placed under a psychological microscope the way they have been in the past 40 years. It began with the emergence of the women's movement and its confrontation with male bias and discrimination against women. As a result, women were encouraged to develop their own identity, establish their own independence, and break away from patriarchal conventions.

In response to women's efforts to change themselves and to change men, men developed their own movement. The men's movement has not been as political or as activist as the women's movement. Rather, it has been more of an informal emotional, spiritual movement that reasserts the importance of masculinity and urges men to explore their own identities, free themselves from stereotypical expectations, and foster healthier relationships. The men's movement has also been a psychological movement that recognizes that men need to be less violent and more nurturing but still retain their masculine identity.

Self-help resources on men's issues traverse a large and heterogeneous group of materials. The early men's movement books focused on coping with fluctuating gender roles, while men's books in the 1990s relied on mythological and spiritual accounts of man's recapturing his true identity. The self-help resources in the 2000s emphasized liberation from societal myths and reconstructing the definition of masculinity. The most recent resources increasingly address why men die younger than women and how a "macho" worldview of taking risks and ignoring health symptoms lead men to outrank women in all 15 leading causes of death (except Alzheimer's; Williams, 2003). In what follows, we critically review self-help books, films, and Internet resources on the expansive topic of men' issues (Box 29.1).

## ■ SELF-HELP BOOKS

### Strongly Recommended

★★★★  *Real Boys: Rescuing Our Sons from the Myths of Boyhood* (1998) by William
       Pollack. New York: Henry Holt.

The author explores this generation of boys' feelings of sadness, loneliness, and confusion while they try to appear tough, cheerful, and confident. Pollack takes the reader through the stages of childhood and adolescent development, ferreting out truth from

---

## BOX 29.1
## RECOMMENDATION HIGHLIGHTS

### SELF-HELP BOOKS

- On rescuing sons from the destructive myths of boyhood:
  - ★★★★ *Real Boys* by William Pollack
- On understanding men's life cycles:
  - ★★★★ *Seasons of a Man's Life* by Daniel J. Levinson
- On improving the quality of men's identity and life:
  - ★★★ *Being a Man* by Patrick Fanning and Matthew McKay
  - ★★★ *Masculinity Reconsidered* by Ronald Levant and Gini Kopecky
- On healing male victims of childhood abuse:
  - ★★★★ *Victims No Longer* by Mike Lew

### FILMS

- On identity development and father–son rapprochement:
  - ★★★★★ *Billy Elliot*
  - ★★★★★ *October Sky*
- On caring for an aging father and dissolving their lifelong distance:
  - ★★★★★ *I Never Sang for My Father*
  - ★★★ *Nothing in Common*
- On the magic of baseball for men and recapturing youth:
  - ★★★★ *Field of Dreams*
- On men's competitiveness and life decisions in the business world:
  - ★★★★ *Up in the Air*
  - ★★★ *Glengarry Glen Ross*

### INTERNET RESOURCES

- For valuable information on men's health issues:
  - ★★★★★ *The Good Men Project* goodmenproject.com
  - ★★★★ *Men at Midlife* www.midlife-men.com
  - ★★★★ *Men's Health Magazine* www.menshealth.com
  - ★★★★ *National Coalition for Men* www.ncfm.org

---

myth, and recognizing the cultural and relational influences on male sexuality and behavior. Discussed is how to let real boys be real men by revising the "Boys' Code" and still feeling connected. Pollack writes about what boys are like, how to help them, and what happens if they aren't helped. Negative influences include early and harsh disconnection from family, mixed messages, and outdated models, rules, and assumptions that are making boys sick. Parents, teachers, and professionals actively connected with boys will find this book valuable and revealing. *Real Boys* was very favorably evaluated by our mental health experts and was among the highest rated of the books in this category. (Also reviewed in Chapter 41, Violent Youth.)

★★★★   *Victims No Longer* (2004) by Michael Lew. New York: HarperCollins

This book is intended for male victims of childhood sexual, emotional, or physical abuse or rape and also their partners. The author is a psychotherapist who works particularly with men who are living with and working through these traumas. Male abuse has only in recent years been recognized as a problem so that men even as adults are conflicted about acknowledging their experiences and the shame and guilt that often accompany the disclosure. All topics are discussed with respect and affirmation of men whose stories are told throughout the book. The chapters address child sexual abuse, stereotyping of masculinity, aftereffects of survival, and strategies to promote recovery. A fine self-help resource on a neglected and sensitive topic.

★★★★   *Seasons of a Man's Life* (1978) by Daniel J. Levinson. New York: Ballantine.

This national bestseller is reviewed in Chapter 4 (Adult Development) but merits a brief mention here. It outlines a number of stages men pass through, including the midlife crisis. Levinson describes the stages and transitions in the male life cycle from 17 to 65 years of age.

**Recommended**

★★★   *Being a Man: A Guide to the New Masculinity* (1993) by Patrick Fanning and Matthew McKay. Oakland, CA: New Harbinger.

This is a practical book about what men can do to improve the quality and length of their lives. Filled with assurance and assistance, the book addresses multiple topics, such as appreciating gender differences, relating to one's father, clarifying and acting on values, finding meaningful work, making male friends, and raising children. The authors convincingly argue that identity is strongly determined by whether an individual was born a boy or girl and by who the person's parents were. A person can't change these circumstances but can understand them better. For any man who wishes to evaluate the quality and context of his life, and for the woman wishing to understand a man in context, this is an interesting and practical book. Indeed, its 3-star rating underestimates its value according to the psychologists who evaluated it highly; had more known of it, this would surely be a 4-star or perhaps a 5-star resource.

★★★   *Man Enough: Fathers, Sons and the Search for Masculinity* (1993) by Frank S. Pittman. New York: Putnam.

In this book, masculinity is conceptualized as a group activity, as a cultural concept. Masculinity is different for each generation. It is supposed to be passed on from father to son. If a boy does not have men in his family, his need for mentors begins early. When children try to get close to their fathers, the practice of masculinity frequently gets in the way. Psychiatrist Pittman writes tellingly of the plight of men who didn't get the fathering they needed to make them comfortable with their masculinity and of the healing of men who have rediscovered the forgotten profession of fatherhood. This book was rated favorably but relatively infrequently, resulting in its relegation to the 3-star category. It is an enlightening and helpful resource for men at any stage of their development.

★★★  *The Hazards of Being Male* (1976) by Herb Goldberg. New York: Signet.

Published in 1976, this was the first self-help book for men to come out after the woman's movement began to take hold. Goldberg became a central figure in the early development of the men's movement in the 1970s and early 1980s, mainly as a result of his writing about men's rights in this book and *The New Male*. Psychologist Goldberg argues that a critical difference between men and women creates a precipitous gulf between them: women can sense and articulate their feelings and problems, but men—because of their masculine conditioning—can't. The result in men is an armor of masculinity that is defensive and powerfully maintains self-destructive patterns. Goldberg says that most men have been effective work machines and performers, but about everything else in their lives suffers. Goldberg believes that millions of men are killing themselves by striving to be "true men," a heavy price to pay for masculine privilege and power. Goldberg encourages men to: (1) Recognize the suicidal success syndrome and avoid it; (2) Understand that occasional impotence is nothing serious; (3) Become aware of their real desires and get in touch with their own bodies; (4) Elude the bonds of masculine role-playing; (5) Relate to women as equals rather than serving as women's guilty servant or hostile enemy; and (6) Develop male friendships. This 3-star book is definitely dated, but it still delivers important messages to men.

★★★  *Masculinity Reconstructed* (1995) by Ronald Levant and Gini Kopecky. New York: Dutton/Plume.

One of psychology's leading experts on masculinity and men's relationships, Ronald Levant considers American men to be in a crisis because of their inability to establish positive relationships, especially with women. He believes this crisis has developed because men lack adequate emotional empathy and tend to act rather than feel. Levant provides a number of strategies to help men develop insights into the emotional aspects of their lives and establish more positive relationships with women.

★★★  *Act Like a Lady, Think Like a Man* (2009) by Steve Harvey. New York: HarperCollins.

These observations about men came out of a radio talk show hosted by the author. The call-in questions from women about understanding men were handled with humor for some time, but then Harvey realized the pattern of questions and the true importance to these women of asking for help with relationships. He began to treat their questions with respect and seriousness, which resulted in the writing of this book. Men's relationships, motivations, needs, and priorities are discussed as though all men are alike, and the author says this is true to an extent. The writing style is kind and the advice reaches out in a supportive way to the reader.

★★★  *The New Male: From Self-Destruction to Self-Care* (1980) by Herb Goldberg. New York: Signet.

The themes of Goldberg's second book on men's issues are similar to the first (reviewed above). In Part I, "He," Goldberg evaluates the traditional male role and its entrapments. In Part II, "He and She," he explores the traditional relationship between men and women. Part III, "He and Her Changes," analyzes how changes in women's roles brought about by the women's movement have affected men. Part IV, "He and His Changes," provides hope for men by elaborating on how men can combine some of the strengths of traditional masculinity—such as assertiveness and independence—with increased exploration of the inner self, greater awareness of emotions, and more healthy close relationships with others to become more complete men. Dated in content and examples, this 3-star book expresses the timeless message of challenging men to explore their inner selves, get in touch with their feelings, and pay more attention to developing meaningful relationships.

★★★   *Chicken Soup for the Father's Soul* (2001) by Jack Canfield, Mark Donnelly, Jeff Aubery, and Mark Hansen. Deerfield Beach, FL: Health Communications.

Contributions about the nature of fatherhood are provided by famous fathers, including Bill Cosby. Moments of pride and fulfillment are described in a series of stories about fathers. There is little direct advice or assistance, but much inspiration.

★★★   *Fire in the Belly* (1991) by Sam Keen. New York: Bantam.

While Goldberg's books were the men's movement bibles in the 1970s and 1980s, two authors ushered in a renewed interest in the men's movement in the 1990s—Sam Keen and Robert Bly. (Bly's book *Iron John* is listed in the Not Recommended category.) Keen's theme is that every man is on a spiritual journey to attain the grail of manhood. He provides a road map for the journey, advising men on ways to avoid the dead ends of combative machismo and the blind alleys of romantic obsession. Keen says that he wrote *Fire in the Belly* because men have lost their vision of what masculinity is. Keen's answer is that men's true identity is fire in the belly and passion in the heart. Although this book was a *New York Times* bestseller, it received only a 3-star rating in our national studies. Virtually all books on men's issues—and women's issues—are controversial and inflame feelings in the opposite sex. On the positive side, our experts applauded Keen's efforts to get men to reexamine their male identity, to incorporate more empathy into their relationships, and to reduce their hostility. On the other side, Keen's critics, especially female critics, didn't like his trashing of androgyny, his exaggeration of gender differences, and the mysticism that permeates the book. Keen adopts a Jungian perspective on man's inner journey to find himself, a perspective that is filled with symbols and metaphors that are not always clearly presented.

### Diamond in the Rough

♦   *Fatherloss: How Our Sons of All Ages Come to Terms with the Death of Their Dads* (2001) by Neil Chethik. New York: Hyperion.

This book analyzes men's anxieties about the deaths of their fathers. It especially tackles the cultural expectation that men are supposed to respond to loss with emotional strength and not grieve openly, which places them at risk for not adequately coping with death. Chethik describes how John F. Kennedy, Jr., Ernest Hemingway, and other well-known men coped with the death of their fathers. The author also gives strategies for preparing for the loss of a father, coping immediately after his death, grieving, and preparing a son for a father's own death. Favorably but infrequently rated in our latest national study, leading to the Diamond in the Rough designation.

**Not Recommended**

  ★★ *Straight Talk to Men* (2000) by James Dobson. New York: W Publishing.
  ★★ *Iron John: Straight Talk About Men* (1990) by Robert Bly. New York: Vintage.
   ★ *Why Men Don't Get Enough Sex and Women Don't Get Enough Love* (1990) by Jonathan Kramer and Diane Dunaway. New York: Pocket.

**Strongly Not Recommended**

  † *What Men Really Want: Straight Talk from Men About Sex* (1990) by Susan Bakos. New York: St. Martin's.
  † *Ten Stupid Things Men Do to Mess Up Their Lives* (1997) by Laura Schlessinger. New York: Cliff Street.

## ■ FILMS

**Strongly Recommended**

  ★★★★★ *I Never Sang for My Father* (1969) directed by Gilbert Cates. PG rating. 92 minutes.

A son tries to care for an aging father, accepting his father's eccentricities and changing the quality of their relationship before it's too late. The difficulties of disclosure, of admitting lifelong hurt, and of finding a way to dissolve the distance between them are the universal tasks undertaken by the father and son. The moving story is a realistic glimpse into the complexity and the fundamental challenges of father–son relationships. This 5-star resource is one of the most favorably rated of all films in our national studies.

  ★★★★★ *Billy Elliot* (2000) directed by Stephen Daldry. PG-13 rating. 110 minutes.

Set in a harsh northern England mining town, this is the uplifting story of 11-year-old Billy's (Jamie Bell) struggle to find his way and be true to himself against his family's and his community's homophobia and anticultural attitudes. Billy is forced to take boxing lessons at great cost to his poor family to toughen him but accidentally discovers that his real talent lies in ballet dancing. Although encouraged by the dance teacher, he and she know that the others will see this as unmanly if not homosexual in their unremittingly macho world. Billy tries to keep his secret but reveals himself and copes with his father, whose love eventually overpowers his archaic beliefs. The dancing is absolutely wonderful, as is the music and the happy ending earned by the father's and son's courage. Deservedly rated a 5-star movie.

  ★★★★★ *October Sky* (1999) directed by Joe Johnston. PG rating. 108 minutes.

An exhilarating story of the power of the human spirit conveyed through a young West Virginia boy whose life in the coal fields stands in stark contrast to his goal of launching a rocket. The boy's dream represents escape and triumph for the coal miners whose lives are painfully and realistically portrayed. They rally around the boy and support his science achievements and his attempt to go to the national science fair, but the father, who loves his son, does not believe science is a realistic "out." The eventual success of the boy and his father's change of heart are characterized in this true story. The boy grew up to become a NASA scientist, as portrayed in his book *Rocket Boys*. This is a wonderful film for adolescents struggling with identity and for the approval of their fathers.

**** *Field of Dreams* (1989) directed by Phil Alden Robinson. PG rating. 106 minutes.

Reminiscence about the glory days of baseball is its secondary theme, but the real story is the magic of baseball for boys and men. For them, baseball was another world, a cherished world. An Iowa farmer, Ray, builds a magical field in his cornfield, and the ghosts of professional ballplayers show up and compete in games. This is a warm and poignant film about men who connect to other men (and Ray to his father) through the special love of baseball.

**** *Up in the Air* (2009) directed by Jason Reitman. R rating. 109 minutes.

George Clooney flies around the country firing people, dreaming of reaching 10 million frequent flier miles, and loving every minute of it. Meanwhile, he is emotionally removed from his family of origin and emotionally unavailable to others, going so far as to deliver motivational speeches on relieving oneself of emotional baggage and entanglements. When an ambitious new colleague implements a cost-cutting program to conduct the layoffs via videoconferencing, Clooney begins to question his life decisions. This film is an excellent portrayal of how a self-absorbed, alexithymic man begins to regret his tragic criteria of "success."

**Recommended**

*** *Antwone Fisher* (2002) directed by Denzel Washington. PG-13 rating. 120 minutes.

A fatherless sailor prone to outbursts is sent to a childless psychiatrist for treatment. Although closed to his feelings at first, the young man opens up to reveal a trauma-filled childhood. The psychiatrist father-figure (Denzel Washington) helps him confront his horrific past and emotionally adopts the young man, taking him home for Thanksgiving. Characterized as a "male weepie" (like *Field of Dreams*), this true story leads many men to cry for their own loss and the deep father–son bond. (Also reviewed in Chapter 2 on Abuse.)

*** *Glengarry Glen Ross* (1992) directed by James Foley. R rating. 100 minutes.

The four salesmen in a real estate office (Jack Lemmon, Alan Arkin, Ed Harris, and Al Pacino) are forced into a sales contest by their big bosses downtown. The pressure is immense, the sales leads are worthless, and in desperation they commit a stupid robbery that makes things even worse. Their desperation is palpable and pitiful. The film keenly displays the pressure and competitiveness experienced by many men in the business world. If someone does not understand what male workers feel, this film will explain it.

★★★ *Nothing in Common* (1986) directed by Garry Marshall. PG rating. 118 minutes.

David is in his mid-30s and has been estranged from his critical, cynical father for many years. Suddenly, he learns that his mother is leaving his father. His father is scared but belligerent, lonely but angry, and his father needs him. Resentment, reconciliation, acceptance, and dealing with old pain are all part of the dynamics between David and his father. David learns that his unresolved problems with his father have to be faced in order to begin healing.

★★★ *Disney's The Kid* (2000) directed by Jon Turtletaub. PG rating. 101 minutes.

An angry, alone, and empty "image consultant" is revisited by his 8-year-old self and together they revisit their pasts, especially a playground defeat. They revise the past by having the man teach the boy fighting skills and standing up for his rights. Unfortunately, the movie suggests that the solution for interpersonal conflict is fighting skills rather than cooperation and compromise. Nonetheless, the movie does show with some humor and tenderness a man and a boy trying to help each other improve themselves. A sweet "inner child" story.

★★★ *American Beauty* (1999) directed by Sam Mendes. R rating. 122 minutes.

Kevin Spacey has lived a life lost. He loses his pointless job, his wife is chronically irritable and having an affair, his daughter is disaffected and distant, and then he falls in lust with his daughter's girlfriend. These events lead him to radically alter his life, running wild in sheer freedom. This Academy Award-winning film is, at once, a compelling satire of suburban life and a hopeful tale of how a man might recapture his life, gain the confidence to rebel, and reestablish dignity.

★★★ *City Slickers* (1992) directed by Ron Underwood. PG-13 rating. 110 minutes.

Three urban men, friends since adolescence, take a cattle-drive vacation in the midst of their various midlife crises. Billy Crystal is approaching his 40th birthday and reevaluating his life and masculinity. This funny film is best at demonstrating the bonds among male friends, revealing their middle-age complaints and choices, and acknowledging male perseverance when "the chips are down."

★★★ *Tootsie* (1983) directed by Sydney Pollack. PG rating. 116 minutes.

Michael (Dustin Hoffman), an out-of-work actor, takes on the identity of a female character, Dorothy, and wins a part in a daytime soap opera. He meets Julie (Jessica Lange) on the set, and they become women friends, although Michael has strong romantic feelings for her. Living the life of Dorothy and having relationships as a female dramatically transforms Michael's perspective about women, men, and himself. This is a touching and funny story of gender roles and subsequent insights into the subtle but significant differences in how we relate as men and women.

★★★ *The Rape of Richard Beck* (1985, made for TV) directed by Karen Arthur. Not rated.

Richard Beck (Richard Crenna) is a big-city cop who is insensitive and uncaring, particularly to women. He rejects the trauma and violation of rape until he himself is raped.

He is thrown into the same experience of humiliation and rage as the women he has known who have been victims of sexual assault. Although flawed, this film is one of the few that depicts the rape of a man; the reversal of a familiar story is eye-opening. The film conveys compassion and caring for all victims of sexual assault.

## ■ INTERNET RESOURCES

### General Websites

★★★★★ *The Good Men Project* goodmenproject.com

An alternative to the dumbed-down men's magazines, the Good Men Project grew out of a documentary film in 2009 and is now an engaging male-oriented website that offers thought-provoking and interesting articles, updated regularly. Yes, it covers sports, sex, and relationships, but it also has topics on ethics, education, families, conflict, and even fiction. A fascinating website that should be on any man's regular reading list.

★★★★ *Men at Midlife* www.midlife-men.com

This website from Noel McNaughton offers not only his experience with making it through a midlife crisis but also a wealth of articles on spirituality, depression, stages of life, your life's mission, health, personal stories, and more. Although primarily aimed at a male audience, some of the articles and topics are relevant and valuable for women too.

★★★ *Men's Stuff: The National Men's Resource* www.menstuff.org

"A free international resource covering all six major segments of the men's movement (men's rights, mythopoetic, pro-feminist, recovery, re-evaluation counseling, and religious)," the website offers hundreds of articles dealing with men's issues. Unfortunately, the site doesn't appear to be updated very often any longer, and the confusing layout is from the 1990s.

★★★ *AskMen* www.askmen.com

A slick, commercial online magazine designed for men that covers a wealth of (mostly) shallow topics but throws in occasional helpful tips and articles about recent research findings. There is probably something on the website that will entertain any man, at least for a little while.

★★★ *Dumb Little Man* www.dumblittleman.com

An interesting and at times engaging magazine-like blog that provide tips about how to live, increase one's productivity, or be amused. Click on "Categories" to find specific topics of interest.

★★ *MenWeb: Men's Voices Magazine* www.menweb.org

*MenWeb*, an online magazine, offers lots of articles and interesting interviews but hasn't been updated in some time. Its design leaves much to be desired as well.

## Psychoeducational Materials

### Health and Sexuality

**★★★★** *Men's Health Magazine* www.menshealth.com

The website of the print magazine of the same name features articles from the magazine as well as online-only features such as daily news, blogs, and top 10 lists. Resources are divided into Fitness, Sex & Women, Health, Nutrition, Weight Loss, and Grooming. A rich, always-updated resource, but it tends toward the shallow end of reading.

**★★★** *Online Sexual Disorders Screening for Men* psych.med.nyu.edu/patient-care/ sexual-disorders-screening-test-men

A 10-item interactive test on male sexual disorders.

**★★★★** *Men's Health—WebMD* men.webmd.com

A comprehensive and constantly changing resource from the folks at WebMD, it offers news, discussions, and blogs of relevance to men, along with a Men's Health Guide and additional health and sexuality topics.

**★★★** *Men's Health—Mayo Clinic* www.mayoclinic.com/health/mens-health/ MY00394

This health resource from the venerable Mayo Clinic won't steer you wrong when it comes to basic health information tailored to men. This is basically a compilation of resources available on the Mayo Clinic website.

### Fathers and Child Support

These sites were created mainly to assert fathers' rights against the perceived overemphasis on mothers' rights and their political and legal manifestations. The sites tend to be hostile toward mainstream legal proceedings and mental health practices.

**★★★★** *Fathers Rights to Custody: Information to Assist Fathers in Gaining Custody* www.deltabravo.net/custody/guide.php

Here you can read a complete *Guide to the Parenting Evaluation Process* and dozens of articles on coping with the divorce and custody processes, as well as download many materials to help you make a case for father custody.

**★★★★** *Separated Parenting Access & Resource Center* www.deltabravo.net

Hundreds of articles may be found on this site about parenting while separated, including information about custody evaluations and divorce.

**★★★** *American Coalition for Fathers and Children* www.acfc.org

This is a small website for political action and education advocating for equal rights in the family law system because "children need both parents."

*Men's Rights/Backlash*
    ★★★★    *National Coalition for Men* www.ncfm.org

The National Coalition for Men is the oldest men's rights organization in the world. Its large website acts as an information resource for men's issues, ranging from media bias and fathering to false accusations and domestic violence.

    ★★    *The Men's Defense Association* www.mensdefense.org

A handful of articles covering the Men's Manifesto, father custody, and fact sheets.

## ■ SUPPORT GROUPS

Several of these entries are based on a list by David R. Throop (throop@vix.com) and posted to *The World Wide Web Virtual Library* as Men's Organizations.

### Coalition for the Preservation of Fatherhood

Phone: 617-723-3237
www.fatherhoodcoalition.org

### Men's Defense Association

Phone: 651-464-7887
www.mensdefense.org
Book distributors, nationwide attorney referral, and newsletter publishing.

### National Center for Men

Phone: 516-942-2020; activism/message line: 503-727-3686
www.nationalcenterformen.org
Men's rights, male choice, fathers' rights.

### National Fathers' Resource Center

Phone: 214-953-2233
www.fathers4kids.org
They publish *Father Times.*

### National Men's Resource Center

www.menstuff.org

### National Organization for Men

Phone: 415-259-6343 or 510-655-2777
www.orgformen.org
For men seeking equal rights in divorce, custody, property, and visitation laws.

## Promise Keepers

Phone: 1-866-766-6473
www.promisekeepers.org
Born-again Christian men's movement.

## MaleSurvivor

Phone: 800-738-4181
www.malesurvivor.org
They publish a newsletter for male sexual abuse survivors.

**See also** Child Development and Parenting (Chapter 15), Divorce (Chapter 21), and Sexuality (Chapter 35).

# CHAPTER 30

# OBSESSIVE-COMPULSIVE DISORDER

An obsession is a persistent and intrusive thought or image. A compulsion is a repetitive or ritualistic behavior. When frequent and severe, they form obsessive-compulsive disorder (OCD), an anxiety disorder that afflicts about 2% of the population.

In severe form, OCD presents in mainly two groups of ritualistic behavior. Washers, the largest group, are people who feel contaminated when exposed to certain stimuli, such as dirt, sex, and bodily secretions. In turn, they avoid the contaminants at all costs or engage in the compulsive behavior of excessive cleaning. Checkers are people who repetitively check, count, or perform stereotyped actions to avoid a future "disaster."

About 10% to 15% of the population suffers from some OCD features. Some of these people suffer from obsessive-compulsive personality, in which they are preoccupied with orderliness, perfectionism, and control. Some are consumed with ruminations, a word whose first meaning is "chewing the cud." Ruminant animals, such as cattle and goats, chew a cud composed of regurgitated, partially digested food—not a very appealing image of what people who ruminate do with their thoughts, but an exceedingly apt one. Recent years have brought many advances in our understanding of OCD and the development of effective treatments for it. The most popular treatments are exposure therapies, cognitive-behavioral therapy (CBT), and medications, typically the antidepressant and antianxiety medications.

In this chapter, we review expert opinions on the dozens of self-help books, autobiographies, films, online self-help, and Internet sites on OCD. But first, our Recommendation Highlights (Box 30.1).

## ■ SELF-HELP BOOKS

### Strongly Recommended

★★★★★ *S.T.O.P. Obsessing: How to Overcome Your Obsessions and Compulsions* (1991) by Edna B. Foa and Reid Wilson. New York: Bantam.

Two authorities on the treatment of anxiety disorders present a cognitive-behavioral approach. The book begins with a questionnaire to understand and analyze the severity of obsessions and compulsions. Included is a self-help program to overcome the milder symptoms and a more intensive 3-week program for severe symptoms. Guidelines to help

## BOX 30.1
## RECOMMENDATION HIGHLIGHTS

**SELF-HELP BOOKS**

■ For top-notch, cognitive-behavioral programs for treating OCD:

★★★★★ *S.T.O.P. Obsessing* by Edna B. Foa and Reid Wilson

★★★★ *Mastery of Obsessive-Compulsive Disorder* by Michael J. Kozak and Edna B. Foa

★★★★ *Overcoming Obsessive-Compulsive Disorder* by Gail Steketee

■ For children and their parents battling OCD:

★★★★ *What to Do When Your Brain Gets Stuck* by Dawn Huebner

■ For balanced and comprehensive approaches to OCD:

★★★★★ *The OCD Workbook* by Bruce M. Hyman and Cherry Pedrick

★★★★ *Obsessive–Compulsive Disorders* by Steven Levenkron

■ For self-help guidance on trichotillomania:

★★★ *The Hair-Pulling Problem* by Fred Penzel

**AUTOBIOGRAPHIES**

■ For a funny and acerbic recounting of OCD and phobias:

★★★ *Memoirs of an Amnesiac* by Oscar Levant

■ For a fine memoir of OCD:

♦ *Rewind, Replay, Repeat* by Jeff Bell

■ For an interesting take by an OCD therapist who treats OCD patients:

♦ *The Boy Who Finally Stopped Washing* by John B.

**FILMS**

■ For a humorous film on OCD and its interpersonal impact:

★★★★ *As Good as It Gets*

■ For a tragic film on OCD and its persistence:

★★★ *The Aviator*

**ONLINE SELF-HELP**

■ For self-assessment and professional-guided online treatment:

★★★★★ *OCFighter: Online Treatment for OCD* www.ocfighter.com

★★★★ *OCD STOP!* www.anxietyonline.org.au

**INTERNET RESOURCES**

■ For comprehensive information on OCD:

★★★★★ *Obsessive-Compulsive Disorder—Psych Central* psychcentral.com/disorders/ocd

★★★★ *Obsessive-Compulsive Disorder—About.com* ocd.about.com

★★★★ *Obsessive-Compulsive Disorder—Anxieties.com* anxieties.com/ocd.php

determine whether a person needs professional help are presented with clarity and practicability. Our mental health experts consistently agreed that this book is very useful for people with obsessions and compulsions.

★★★★★ *The OCD Workbook* (2010) by Bruce M. Hyman and Cherry Pedrick. Oakland, CA: New Harbinger.

This workbook is one of the very few that actually deserves its title: it presents a self-directed program. Even though advice on finding professional help is provided, the program is built for individuals to implement themselves. The contents are clearly organized into sections: what is OCD; what are the symptoms and causes; what are the treatment options; how does one use cognitive-behavioral methods for treatment; self-assessment; and challenging beliefs. Additionally, the authors present conditions that often occur simultaneously with OCD and describe the centrality of family involvement. This workbook does prescribe a treatment of choice (CBT) and offers coping strategies and ways to prevent relapse. A practical, 5-star self-help workbook.

★★★★ *Mastery of Obsessive-Compulsive Disorder* (2004) by Michael J. Kozak and Edna B. Foa. New York: Oxford University Press.

The treatment plan presented here is meant to be employed by professional therapists, not through individual application. Theories of OCD, the administration of CBT, and the role of medication are directed to psychotherapists who have some familiarity with the material. The program is quite complete and includes assessment of OCD and related conditions. The program guides the professional to discuss the treatment with clients (e.g., exposure and ritual prevention), conduct in vivo treatment, include social support, prevent relapse, and address resistance. An important part of exposure therapy, and this book is the treatment contract.

★★★★ *Overcoming Obsessive-Compulsive Disorder: A Behavioral and Cognitive Protocol for the Treatment of OCD* (1999) by Gail Steketee. Oakland, CA: New Harbinger.

Prolific researcher Steketee offers a step-by-step, session-by-session treatment plan for OCD. The book includes worksheets, homework assignments, in-session exercises, and didactic materials. As the subtitle states, it is research-based CBT that relies heavily on exposure and cognitive therapy. Steketee also provides a relapse-prevention program to maintain treatment gains. An appendix features a number of individual and family symptom inventories.

★★★★ *What to Do When Your Brain Gets Stuck: A Kid's Guide to Overcoming OCD* (2007) by Dawn Huebner. Washington, DC: Magination.

This delightfully illustrated story of a boy who has OCD is meant to be used by parents and child as well as therapist and child. The story is developmentally appropriate and has a reading level of 8 years. The cover draws the reader in by showing a boy and his friends at the fair, and he is throwing darts at balloons labeled, "repeat, wash, count." Obsessive thoughts are called "sticky thoughts," and children take the role of "super sleuth" in tracking down their OCD symptoms. Many interactive exercises and illustrations reinforce the fun and adventure of using the book in therapy and at home.

★★★★　*Getting Over OCD: A 10-Step Workbook for Taking Back Your Life* (2009) by Jonathan S. Abramowitz. New York: Guilford.

Although a self-help plan designed to be conducted by the individual, this book is advanced in presentation and would best be used by those with some rudimentary understanding of CBT and by those disciplined enough that adherence can be ensured during the exposure treatment. Developing one's own tailored plan, identifying thinking errors, and defeating avoidance behaviors are the primary aspects of the program. Well regarded by our national experts but requiring more knowledge and discipline than most self-help books.

★★★★　*Obsessive–Compulsive Disorders* (1992) by Steven Levenkron. New York: Warner.

Levenkron believes OCD is the personality's attempt to reduce anxiety, which may stem from a painful childhood or a genetic tendency toward anxiousness. He believes that people can reduce their obsessions and compulsions if they follow four basic steps: (1) Rely on a family member or a therapist for support and comfort, (2) Unmask their rituals, (3) Talk in depth to trusted family members or a therapist, and (4) Control their anxiety. This is a useful, balanced self-help book but is getting a tad dated.

**Recommended**

★★★　*Brain Lock* (1996) by Jeffrey M. Schwartz and Beverly Beyette. New York: Regan.

The author presents a four-step method to defeat irrational impulses by a process of relabeling, reattributing, refocusing, and reevaluating. The same treatment methods can be applied to substance abuse, pathological gambling, and compulsive sexual behavior. Each chapter features a nice summary of key points, and the book provides a useful OCD Patient Diary. Had the book been rated by more reviewers in our national study, it would probably have earned a 4-star evaluation.

★★★　*Freedom from Obsessive-Compulsive Disorder* (2004) by John Grayson. New York: Berkley Publishing.

This approach allows individuals to conduct the treatment themselves, although the best ways to identify a therapist are also noted. The program is interactive and is intended to demystify OCD through self-evaluations and self-directed methods. Some topics include what people fear and then what they do about it, medication, accepting the uncertainty of what will happen, how to control the internal OCD voice, and how to focus on specific symptoms such as checking and washing. An interesting and likely helpful component to the book is called "Therapy Scripts," a topic listing in the back of the book that refers individuals to a page and a significant passage on that page. For example, a notation under the topic of uncertainty is a reference to "The Fiddler on the Roof" and an analogy made to that story.

★★★ *Coping with OCD* (2008) by Bruce M. Hyman and Troy DuFrene. Oakland, CA: New Harbinger.

The expression "the mind is at war with itself" is the metaphor for this self-directed approach to mild to moderate OCD. The treatment includes a gradual exposure to distressing thoughts and techniques to restructure thinking. The authors term OCD "the doubting disease" and offer a clear explanation of the relationship between obsessive thoughts and compulsive behavior that is not always included in OCD definitions. The role of friends and family members in coping and in treatment is emphasized. Short tips and brief exercises are encouraged, one being "talking back to the obsessive voice."

★★★ *The Hair-Pulling Problem* (2003) by Fred Penzel. New York: Oxford University Press.

Trichotillomania is described as a mysterious, rarely understood disorder that is not easily treatable because few psychotherapists work with the condition. This self-help plan can be conducted independently but also as a companion to formal treatment. The content combines scientific data and the author's expertise in working with this condition, resulting in a balance that is clear and engaging. The chapters address what trichotillomania is and its cause, how to know when therapy is warranted, and what to do for your child with trichotillomania. Useful information is offered on hair itself and the factors that come into play regarding hair. Penzel outlines what therapies don't work, which ones might, and which do.

### Diamonds in the Rough

♦ *Obsessive-Compulsive Disorder for Dummies* (2008) by Charles Elliott and Laura Smith. Hoboken, NJ: Wiley.

This hands-on approach, the hallmark of the "Dummy" books, provides helpful guidance through this complicated subject. Tools that facilitate the message are case illustrations to make specific points, use of icons to signal a tip, and a polished writing style. Foundational chapters include "Ins and Outs" of understanding OCD, treatment options, targeting specific forms of OCD, and helping others. Exercises are made user-friendly by framing as self-handicapping monitoring, the exposure staircase, and others that reduce intimidation. The last section includes "10 Quick Tricks, 10 Steps after Getting Better, and 10 Secrets." These and other entries add to reader interest and curiosity.

♦ *Obsessive-Compulsive Disorder: The Facts* (1998) by Padmal de Silva and Stanley Rachman. New York: Oxford University Press.

A sensible and straightforward book both for individuals suffering from OCD and their family members. Written by two clinical psychologists known for their work in anxiety disorders, the book comprehensively covers the causes, symptoms, diagnosis, and treatment of OCD. In this second edition, the authors cover compulsive hoarding and obsessive-compulsive behavior in children. This valuable self-help resource is classified as a Diamond in the Rough because it was favorably but infrequently rated in our studies.

♦ *Obsessive-Compulsive Disorders: A Complete Guide to Getting Well and Staying Well* (2000) by Fred Penzel. New York: Oxford University Press.

This book has been described as "near-encyclopedic" for the sufferers of obsessive-compulsive spectrum disorders. Penzel addresses the broad spectrum of these disorders, from obsessive-compulsive to body dysmorphic disorder to trichotillomania (compulsive hair pulling). He details cognitive-behavioral treatments and leading medications and offers family advice. This book is an effective self-help resource for professionals and laypersons. It was highly rated but not frequently by our mental health experts, thus receiving the designation of Diamond in the Rough.

# ■ AUTOBIOGRAPHIES

### Recommended

★★★ *Memoirs of an Amnesiac* (1990) by Oscar Levant. Hollywood, CA: Samuel French Trade Books.

A famed pianist recounts a life with many mental and physical disorders. In a humorous and acerbic style, Levant describes his obsessive-compulsive disorder, phobias, and addiction to barbiturates. Chapter titles include "Total Recoil," "My Bed of Nails," and "Stand Up and Faint." Levant was treated with an enormous number of different drugs and underwent psychotherapy, several hospitalizations, and electroconvulsive therapy. He was a better pianist and writer than he was a client, since he lacked the motivation to get well. Perhaps writing the book had cathartic value. Also reviewed in Chapter 7, Anxiety Disorders.

### Diamonds in the Rough

♦ *Rewind, Replay, Repeat: A Memoir of Obsessive-Compulsive Disorder* (2007) by Jeff Bell. Center City, MN: Hazelden Publishing.

Jeff Bell had a successful career in commercial radio and for six years struggled with OCD, describing his life at the time as one of fear, torment, agony, and shame. His marriage, his career, and his sanity were all at risk. Bell uses the metaphor of a tape recorder playing and replaying in his brain. He classifies the different categories of OCD as hoarders, checkers, doubters, and hand washers. Bell was a combination doubter and checker; he didn't believe his senses, so he felt compelled to check repeatedly to see that nothing was amiss, and worried constantly about things that he might have done. Internal voices made him a hostage to these logically absurd repetitions. Eventually Bell found a cognitive-behavioral therapist skilled at working with OCD. The book is honest, heartfelt, humorous at times, and very readable. Praised by the mental health professionals familiar with it.

♦ *The Boy Who Finally Stopped Washing: OCD from Both Sides of the Couch* (2008) by John B. New York: Cooper Union Press.

Writing under the pseudonym John B., the author is both an OCD sufferer and a psychotherapist who has worked with hundreds of OCD cases. The book's title builds on the bestselling self-help book *The Boy Who Couldn't Stop Washing*, implying that with proper psychotherapy the boy can stop the repetitive ritualistic behaviors characteristic of OCD. The book outlines therapeutic techniques helpful in such cases, including Exposure and Response Prevention (E/RP), which the author uses in his practice. In this hopeful book, the author describes his patients' accounts of how OCD has affected their relations with other people and how they reacted when he revealed himself as a fellow OCD sufferer.

## ▓ FILMS

### Strongly Recommended

★★★★   *As Good as It Gets* (1997) directed by James L. Brooks. PG-13 rating. 138 minutes.

Jack Nicholson's portrayal of a nasty, selfish bigot with a mix of anxiety symptoms (compulsions and phobias) won him an Oscar because of the humanizing experiences with his neighbor and the only waitress he can trust. Nicholson performs many of the individual and social symptoms of OCD, including obsessive hand washing and avoiding imagined contamination. Probably useful to show that even a person crippled by symptoms can find the courage to reach out and improve (if not cure) his relationships, especially with the help of caring others (Helen Hunt, who won an Oscar as the waitress; an ugly dog; and Jack's long-suffering neighbor).

### Recommended

★★★   *The Aviator* (2004) directed by Martin Scorsese. PG-13 rating. 170 minutes.

An award-winning biopic of Howard Hughes (1905–1976), from his early years to his tragic descent into madness. Directed by Martin Scorsese and starring Leonardo DiCaprio, *The Aviator* traces the genesis of Hughes' genius and OCD. In fact, the film begins with a scene featuring the 9-year-old Hughes being bathed by his mother, who warns him of disease: "You are not safe." His compulsions and obsessions develop over the course of his life; in one exchange, Hughes orders, "I want 10 chocolate chip cookies. Medium chips. None too close to the outside." His contamination fears, obsessions with details, quest for perfection, and abuse of alcohol and opiates in a futile attempt to self-medicate leave him a mad hermit toward the end of his life. An effective film for showing the multiple factors that contribute to OCD (e.g., genetic loading, overprotective mother, reinforcement for cleanliness), the amazing productivity and perseverance of some OCD sufferers, the exacerbation of symptoms over time, and the torture of untreated OCD.

★★★   *Matchstick Men* (2003) directed by Ridley Scott. PG-13 rating. 116 minutes.

Roy Waller is a con artist (played by Nicholas Cage) who has netted over $1 million selling overpriced "water filtration systems" to unsuspecting people. But his personal life is not so profitable: Roy suffers from OCD, agoraphobia, tics, and panic attacks that lead him into psychotherapy. He is approached by his abandoned 14-year-old daughter, Angela, who rejuvenates him and inspires him to live an honest life. But then Roy learns that Angela is, in fact, part of an elaborate con played on him. No matter; a happier, honest, and married

Roy emerges from his debilitating anxiety. The film superbly illustrates the incapacitating symptoms of severe OCD as well as his therapy sessions that express the internal conflicts of anxiety-plagued patients.

## ■ ONLINE SELF-HELP

★★★★★ *OCFighter: Online Treatment for OCD* www.ocfighter.com

This resource was designed to provide online treatment for OCD. A mental health professional provides individuals with access to the system, where they complete online sessions. The treatment programs are designed as 10 weekly sessions of 30 to 40 minutes each and are based on the principles of CBT and exposure and response prevention. Support from professionals is minimal (1 hour per intervention). This program is currently available only in the United Kingdom but will probably be available soon in other countries.

★★★★ *OCD STOP!* www.anxietyonline.org.au

This website is dedicated to the treatment of several forms of anxiety, including OCD. After free registration, users are directed to take an extensive online assessment to determine the type and intensity of their anxiety. Users with mild anxiety are offered the choice of the free online program or the therapist-assisted program. Those with higher anxiety are offered the therapist-assisted program at a cost of $120. Users who use the therapist-assisted program maintain weekly email contact with a therapist in addition to the online program. Based on CBT principles, all programs provide users with education about their condition, interactive exercises to build skills to manage it, and worksheets to track progress. The program is designed with 12 modules to be completed at a rate of one module per week, but users can work at their own pace.

★★★ *H-C Compulsive Hoarding Community* health.groups.yahoo.com/group/H-C

This is an online support group for people interested in changing their compulsive hoarding behavior. This private unlisted group permits up to 115 members at a time. New applicants are waitlisted as room becomes available when previous members leave. Users are expected to be active members and post on the discussion boards at least once a month and actively make changes in their behavior within 60 days of joining the group. The discussion boards are reviewed and moderated by a psychologist. There is no fee to join.

★★★ *Live OCD Free* App available for Apple iPhone and iPad

This application is designed for people in treatment for OCD. With this program, users can customize and set up practice exercises based on the principles of exposure with response prevention (ERP). Users can set up timed reminders, track their levels of anxiety, and track various elements of progress all on their iPhone or iPad. The program also permits users to email their progress to a professional with whom they are working. Live OCD Free comes in two versions: adult and child. The child's version is presented in a children-friendly format. The program is available for $79.99 on iTunes.

★★★  *StopPicking* www.stoppicking.com

This Web-based self-help program is intended for people with body-focused repetitive behaviors such as skin picking, nail biting, cheek biting, and lip biting. Once registered, users will have a start page that will serve as a summary of their progress. The site allows users to update their behaviors daily and track their progress through the program and toward their goals. As users progress through the program, the questions become increasingly detailed. The program also provides tailored coping strategies to address urges based on the assessments. Users move from the intervention phase to the maintenance phase after consistently achieving their goals for 4 weeks. Authors of the site report that most users require 7 to 10 weeks to complete the first two modules. Subscription cost is $29.95 per month.

★★★  *StopPulling* www.stoppulling.com

This Web-based program is designed for individuals 12 years and older suffering from trichotillomania. Once registered, users will have a start page that will serve as a summary of their progress. The site allows users to update their behaviors daily and track their progress. As with StopPicking (described above), the program provides tailored coping strategies to address urges. Current subscription is approximately $25 per month.

## ▓ INTERNET RESOURCES

### General Websites

★★★★★  *Obsessive-Compulsive Disorder* psychcentral.com/disorders/ocd

This condition center from Psych Central offers a wide range of educational and reference information on OCD, including symptoms, differential diagnoses, treatments, medications, and more. The site also features updated news and research briefs on OCD, an interactive screening quiz, clinical trial opportunities, a blog, and an active support group for people with this disorder.

### Psychoeducational Materials

★★★★  *Obsessive-Compulsive Disorder—Anxieties.com* anxieties.com/ocd.php

This online self-help program is designed with the layperson in mind and provides a half-dozen pages of goal-directed information and exercises to help a person with obsessive-compulsive behavior. Part of a larger commercial site overseen by Reid Wilson, PhD.

★★★★  *Obsessive Compulsive Disorder* www.nursece.com/courses/35

This resource from the National Center of Continuing Education is an online course that is designed for nurses but is actually of benefit to anyone who wants to become familiar with OCD. Well written and appears to be updated regularly.

★★★★  *Obsessive-Compulsive Disorder (OCD)* www.nimh.nih.gov/health/topics/
obsessive-compulsive-disorder-ocd

The National Institute of Mental Health offers up its usual consumer-oriented website for OCD, with the basics of symptoms, treatments, and statistics well covered here. Less impressive is their science news feed, which lists only research updates from NIH-funded sources.

★★★★  *Obsessive-Compulsive Disorder (OCD)* helpguide.org/mental/obsessive_com-
pulsive_disorder_ocd.htm

This resource from the nonprofit HelpGuide is a single page of general information about OCD, including the symptoms, types of treatment, and some self-help strategies to try. As with most HelpGuide resources, it's a bit simplistic in its suggestions, and the resources listed at the end of the article leave out a lot.

★★★★  *Obsessive-Compulsive Disorder* ocd.about.com

This resource from About.com guide Owen Kelly, PhD, like most About.com sites, offers a good comprehensive overview of OCD, including risks and causes, treat-ment, and living with OCD. It also has articles on related concerns, like hoarding and trichotillomania.

★★★★  *International OCD Foundation* www.ocfoundation.org

This nonprofit advocacy, research, and patient education organization is focused on OCD. It hosts an annual conference, and its website is full of helpful information for the newly diagnosed patient. Lots of information can be found in the "About OCD" section, as well as in the "Resources" category.

★★★★  *Obsessive–Compulsive Disorder* www.mayoclinic.com/health/obsessive-
compulsive-disorder/DS00189

A condition center from the Mayo Clinic, the site provides a wealth of reliable, solid information about OCD, including more detailed articles and topics under the "In-Depth" tab.

★★★  *OCDTalk* ocdtalk.wordpress.com

This blog from mom Janet Singer (whose son had OCD) is reliably updated a few times a month with personal perspectives, commentary, and news on OCD.

★★★  *Obsessive Compulsive Disorder* www.ocdonline.com/articlesphillipson.php

These dozen articles by Steven Phillipson, PhD, provide some interesting topical per-spectives from a clinician who treats OCD, including an introduction to cognitive-behav-ioral therapy, hair pulling (trichotillomania), treatment strategies, and more.

## ■ SUPPORT GROUPS

### Anxiety Disorders Association of America (ADAA)

Phone: 240-485-10001
www.adaa.org

### International Obsessive–Compulsive Foundation

Phone: 617-973-5801
www.ocfoundation.org
Their Internet site is broad, with research, book reviews, chat, newsletters, and conferences.

### National Alliance for the Mentally Ill

Phone: 703-524-7600 or 800-950-NAMI (Hotline)
www.nami.org

### Obsessive–Compulsive Anonymous

Phone: 516-739-0662
Obsessivecompulsivesanonymous.org
Twelve-step self-help group for people with OCD.

**See also** Anxiety Disorders (Chapter 7) and Stress Management and Relaxation (Chapter 37).

# CHAPTER 31

# POSTTRAUMATIC STRESS DISORDER

Posttraumatic stress disorder (PTSD) is a complex and serious anxiety condition that affects approximately 2% to 5% of the American population. As the name suggests, PTSD follows exposure to a traumatic stressor involving actual or threatened death or serious injury, witnessing an event that involves death or injury, or learning about such a trauma experienced by a family member or friend. Typical traumatic stressors are military combat, sexual assault, abduction, terrorist attack, incarceration, natural disasters, and severe accidents.

PTSD symptoms include re-experiencing of the traumatic event, avoidance of situations associated with the trauma, and increased arousal. The traumatic event can be re-experienced in various ways, such as recurrent nightmares or flashbacks. Triggering events, such as anniversaries of the trauma, can lead to intense psychological distress or physical symptoms. The PTSD victim may make deliberate efforts to avoid thinking or talking about the event and will avoid activities, situations, or people who provoke recollections of it.

In this chapter, we feature professionals' ratings on self-help books, autobiographies, films, online self-help, and Internet resources regarding PTSD (Box 31.1). The self-help resources cover the assessment and treatment of PTSD, the core experiences of trauma survivors, survival guilt, and PTSD as a result of rape, childhood abuse, and physical attacks. We conclude the chapter with a listing of support groups.

## ■ SELF-HELP BOOKS

### Strongly Recommended

★★★★★ *Trauma and Recovery* (1997) by Judith Lewis Herman. New York: Basic.

Truth-telling and secrecy are the "twin imperatives" that define psychological trauma and that form the basis of the recovery model described in this book. Herman thoughtfully describes the dialectic of the comfort of denial and the indomitable need to speak. Fundamental commonalities are identified between those who survive domestic and sexual violence (the traditional sphere of trauma for women) and those who survive war and political imprisonment (the traditional sphere of trauma for men). The stages of recovery—establishing safety, reconstructing the trauma story, and reuniting survivors with their communities, significant others, and themselves—are described and set the stage for a conceptual framework for psychotherapy and more accurate diagnoses. The core experiences

## BOX 31.1
## RECOMMENDATION HIGHLIGHTS

**SELF-HELP BOOKS**

▪ For survivors of trauma:

 ★★★★★ *Trauma and Recovery* by Judith Lewis Herman

 ★★★★ *I Can't Get Over It* by Aphrodite Matsakis

 ★★★ *Life After Trauma* by Dena Rosenbloom and Mary Beth Williams

 ★★★ *The PTSD Workbook* by Mary Beth Williams and Soili Poijula

 ★★★ *Reclaiming Your Life from a Traumatic Experience* by Barbara Rothbaum et al.

 ★★★ *Writing to Heal* by James W. Pennebaker

▪ For victims of sexual abuse:

 ★★★ *Reclaiming Your Life After Rape* by Barbara Olasov Rothbaum and Edna B. Foa

▪ For couples experiencing trauma:

 ◆ *Healing Together* by Suzanne B. Phillips and Dianne Kane

**AUTOBIOGRAPHIES**

▪ For recovering from combat stress:

 ◆ *I Can Still Hear Their Cries, Even in My Sleep* by Everett McFall

▪ For recovering from rape:

 ◆ *Telling* by Patricia Weaver

 ◆ *I Am the Central Park Jogger* by Trishi Meili

**FILMS**

▪ On rape's torment and the judicial system's insensitivity:

 ★★★★ *The Accused*

▪ On war-related PTSD:

 ★★★★★ *In the Valley of Elah*

 ★★★ *The Messenger*

 ★★★ *Born on the Fourth of July*

 ★★★ *The Deer Hunter*

▪ On recovery from non-combat PTSD:

 ★★★ *Fearless*

 ★★★ *Reign Over Me*

**ONLINE SELF-HELP**

▪ For Web-based assessments and stepped care for PTSD:

 ★★★ *AnxietyOnline* www.anxietyonline.org.au

 ★★★ *PTSD Coach* App available for Apple and Android

▪ For kids coping with emotional consequences of an accident:

 ★★★ *So You've Been in an Accident* kidsaccident.psy.uq.edu.au

**INTERNET RESOURCES**

■ For comprehensive information on traumatic experiences:

★★★★★ *National Center for PTSD* www.ptsd.va.gov

■ For excellent information on traumatic stress:

★★★★ *Post Traumatic Stress (PTSD)* ptsd.about.com

★★★★ *The International Society for Traumatic Stress Studies* www.istss.org

of trauma, disempowerment, and disconnection are key therapeutic components of the recovery model and are treated as healing properties in each survivor's re-entry. This is an excellent resource, though quite academic as a self-help book.

★★★★　*I Can't Get Over It: A Handbook for Trauma Survivors* (1996) by Aphrodite Matsakis. Oakland, CA: New Harbinger.

The author presents a full range of assessment and treatment options for PTSD. Her initial focus is to explain the diagnostic criteria, biochemical variables, feelings and thoughts of the trauma, concepts of victimization, and types of triggers that evoke memory of the trauma. The healing process is framed as a growth rather than deficit model. Two special features of the book are customizing the growth model to specific types of trauma (e.g., crime, suicide, combat, domestic violence) and using the exercises and questionnaires sprinkled throughout. The author effectively explains the model through stages and processes and then offers practical and do-able suggestions. Even though *I Can't Get Over It* was not written as a workbook, the exercises and questionnaires give it an action-oriented, problem-solving perspective.

### Recommended

★★★　*Reclaiming Your Life After Rape* (1999) by Barbara Olasov Rothbaum and Edna B. Foa. Albany, NY: Graywind.

PTSD after rape is the focus of this cognitive-behavioral workbook that lends itself both to self-help and therapy use. The book begins with a diagnostic explanation of PTSD followed by an individualized assessment. Although the treatment options later in the workbook are solely cognitive-behavioral, a section is devoted to describing various therapeutic models. The second half of the workbook describes in understandable detail cognitive-behavioral treatments, including systematic desensitization, anxiety management, imaginal and in vivo exposure, and cognitive restructuring. A chapter on "other techniques" describes role playing, thought stopping, assertiveness, and self-talk. Complex principles of cognitive-behavioral treatment are effectively presented and are accompanied by worksheets, assessment forms, and other application tools. This book is based upon years of outcome research conducted by psychologist Foa and colleagues and was one of the highest-rated self-help resources in our national studies; only the comparatively low number of ratings kept it from achieving 5-star status. Rothbaum and Foa have also co-authored a book for practitioners treating PTSD entitled *Treating the Trauma of Rape: A Cognitive-Behavioral Therapy for PTSD*.

★★★ *The PTSD Workbook* (2002) by Mary Beth Williams and Soili Poijula. Oakland, CA: New Harbinger.

This is one of the few books written after September 11, 2001, and although it does not focus on that tragedy, the trauma and the aftermath are exemplified in the authors' approach to trauma. The book begins by helping readers understand the impact of PTSD on their lives, followed by descriptions of many creative exercises (e.g., drawing, journaling, identifying strengths), questions to be answered, and healing activities. Williams and Poijula explore re-experiencing trauma (e.g., dealing with flashbacks, nightmares, triggers of trauma), physical aspects, and associated symptoms (e.g., survivor guilt, shame, loss), with resulting recommendations for healing. A final section is devoted to complex PTSD and different means of coping with this chronic variation of trauma impact. The message of this book comes across powerfully in its workbook format and valuable content.

★★★ *Life After Trauma: A Workbook For Healing* (1999) by Dena Rosenbloom and Mary Beth Williams with Barbara E. Watkins. New York: Guilford.

Safety, trust, control, and connectedness are the basic human needs called into question as a result of a trauma. The book is designed to help individuals live their lives since the trauma (not relive the trauma) by assessing the status of each of their basic needs and working through ways to reevaluate and change those that have suffered as a result of the trauma. Each basic need is evaluated, and individualized means for change are designed. Specific attention is paid to the importance of self-care and coping with triggers of the past trauma. Strengths of the book are its workbook format and its flexibility as either a self-help guide or adjunct to therapy (with a letter to the therapist in an appendix).

★★★ *Reclaiming Your Life from a Traumatic Experience* (2007) by Barbara Rothbaum, Edna Foa, and Elizabeth Hembree. New York: Oxford University Press.

Treatment for trauma has evolved in recent years, with exposure being a core component of most treatments. The authors have written extensively about a particular type of exposure called "prolonged exposure and social processing." This book presents the reader with this approach to trauma treatment and offers a clear explanation of the model. The treatment is organized into a number of sessions that contain prescribed exercises and interactions. In vivo practice of those experiences that are reminiscent of the event is followed by imaginal experience of the trauma event. This treatment has gained widespread recognition for its effectiveness and is preferably conducted in conjunction with a psychotherapist.

★★★ *After the Storm* (2006) by Kendall Johnson. Alameda, CA: Hunter House.

The book reads as a preparedness guide for dealing with crises of all kinds. The backdrop takes us through the strife and many trials that we have endured societally, politically, and economically and brings the implications down to our own individual preparedness. The broad spectrum of emergency services is reviewed, as well as what to do during a crisis and the aftermath (e.g., self, child, elder care). Specific types of crisis care are discussed and procedures for involvement are identified. The author provides an impressive list of emergency resources.

★★★   *Writing to Heal* (2010) by James W. Pennebaker. Oakland, CA: New Harbinger.

This therapeutic method, offered by a research psychologist, is a refreshing departure from the usual therapies of choice. Expressive writing represents a healing art and activity largely supported by Pennebaker's years of research. A series of directed writings asks individuals to write about their traumas in the book. The exercises are not general statements but are targeted to the trauma content. The author prepares the reader with basic techniques of writing and how to look back on what has already been written. In the last phase, the stories take on a final editing, moving the individual in his or her perspective on the trauma. This is a treatment approach for all but is particularly suitable to those who enjoy writing and those who have difficulty with self-expression.

★★★   *Victims No Longer* (2004) by Michael Lew. New York: HarperCollins

This book is intended for male victims of childhood abuse and was reviewed in the Men's Issues chapter (Chapter 29) as well. Lew is a psychotherapist who works particularly with men living with and working through these traumas. Male abuse has only in recent years been recognized as a problem, so that men even as adults are conflicted about acknowledging their experiences and the shame and guilt that often accompany the disclosure. All topics are discussed with respect and affirmation of men whose stories are told throughout the book.

★★★   *Prolonged Exposure Therapy for PTSD Teen Workbook* (2008) by Kelly R. Chrestman, Eva Gilboa-Schechtman, and Edna B. Foa. New York: Oxford University Press.

These exercises are modified from adult prolonged exposure to suit the age range of 13 to 18 years. The treatment variation is based on two areas: real-life experiments and recounting memories. Teens identify areas of their lives that were interrupted in some way by the trauma: emotional, physical, leisure, friends, and school. The real-life experiments gradually ask the teens to put themselves in situations that remind them of the trauma but are not the trauma situations. The teens then rate the stress level before, during, and after the event while staying in the situation for, if possible, half an hour. Recounting the trauma involves going over the trauma in one's head and identifying the worst moment and staying in that thought for a period of time. These exercises are, according to the authors, best accomplished with the assistance of a mental health professional.

★★★   *Overcoming the Trauma of Your Motor Vehicle Accident* (2006) by Edward B. Blanchard and Edward J. Hickling. New York: Oxford University Press.

Exposure therapy is applied here specifically to those who survived or witnessed a motor vehicle accident. The authors have researched this area for many years and have included many case studies from their practices that illustrate the treatment. The purpose of the book is to reduce the emotional distress of the memory of the accident and the many ways those reactions are still affecting the individuals (e.g., startle response, hypervigilance). The authors recommend that the exposure be conducted with a professional who can help with the activities in this workbook.

**Diamonds in the Rough**

♦ *Roadmap to Resilience: A Guide for Military, Trauma Victims, and Their Families* (2012) by Donald Meichenbaum.

Noted psychologist Don Meichenbaum wrote and self-published this book to discuss the differences between the 70% of individuals, both military and civilian, who show resilience and the 30% who manifest persistent psychological problems. He provides evidence-based ways to bolster resilience in six domains: physical, interpersonal, emotional, cognitive, behavioral, and spiritual. Just released as this book goes to press, *Roadmap to Resilience* is based on the author's 40 years of experience working with trauma survivors and includes numerous action plans and a comprehensive resource guide.

♦ *Survivor Guilt: A Self-Help Guide* (1999) by Aphrodite Matsakis. Oakland, CA: New Harbinger.

Guilt in this book is defined as a negative feeling created by the belief that one should have thought, felt, or acted differently. Survivor guilt is explained in terms of common causes and its devastating effects. Existential survivor guilt (guilt from continuing to live) is differentiated from content survivor guilt (guilt for acts committed to stay alive). Matsakis reviews the psychological consequences for the survivor, including eating disorders, depression, anger, suicidal feelings, and substance abuse. Part Two of the book focuses on healing and the critical aspects of the process. Each chapter includes self-assessment guides that facilitate evaluation of the chapter topic. This book is intended for survivors and mental health professionals who work with them. Favorably but infrequently rated in our national studies, leading to the Diamond in the Rough status.

♦ *Healing Together: A Couple's Guide to Coping with Trauma and Posttraumatic Stress.* (2009) by Suzanne B. Phillips and Dianne Kane. Oakland, CA: New Harbinger.

The impact of trauma on couples and their relationship is poignantly expressed through cases of clients seen by the author, particularly firefighters at 9/11. The loss brought on by trauma is explained as a stress greater than an individual's coping skills. Trauma from natural disasters, war, accident, crime, violence, and the many other means of sudden stress are discussed in the context of the couple's relationship. Understanding the impact of the trauma, communicating needs, managing anger, recapturing lost intimacy, and other key elements of healthy relationships can be brought back into the lives of the couple. A well-regarded but infrequently rated resource on a topic seldom discussed in trauma self-help books.

**Not Recommended**

★★ *Energy Tapping for Trauma* (2007) by Fred P. Gallo. Oakland, CA: New Harbinger.

## ■ AUTOBIOGRAPHIES

### Diamonds in the Rough

♦ *I Am the Central Park Jogger: A Story of Hope and Possibility* (2004) by Trisha Melli. New York: Scribner.

In April 1989 five teenage boys were arrested and accused of raping and beating jogger Trisha Melli and leaving her for dead in New York's Central Park. When found, she was in a coma with serious brain injury. The book dwells less on the horrific attack (which she did not remember) and the perpetrators than on the slow healing process and her life after the assault. Melli maintains a positive attitude throughout, drawing strength from family and friends, not letting the assault drag her down. This inspiring book has the appropriate subtitle "A Story of Hope and Possibility."

♦ *I Can Still Hear Their Cries, Even in My Sleep: A Journey into PTSD* (2007) by E. Everett McFall. Parker, CO: Outskirts Press.

The author served as a medical corpsman in Vietnam during 1966-67. He cared for the wounded and collected body parts after explosions had scattered them around the countryside so that they could be properly matched and delivered to relatives back home. When he showed symptoms of PTSD and considered suicide, a psychotherapist advised him to keep a journal. This small book contains heart-wrenching field observations and his poems describing the debilitating and mind-numbing realities of combat, the sights, screams, and smells of the battlefield, and the corpsman's grisly job. McFall believes that his journey to recovery still is not finished. There are tips for veterans and their families for managing stress and a resource section that includes guidelines for filling out VA forms.

♦ *Telling: A Memoir of Rape and Recovery* (1999) by Patricia Weaver Francisco. New York: HarperCollins.

In 1981, while her husband was away, an intruder broke into Francisco's home and raped her. She went into counseling, but it was unable to relieve her pain. Eventually her marriage broke up, which she attributes to the rape. She carried the story inside her for more than 15 years before writing this frank memoir. She describes the horror of the assault as well as its aftermath. Francisco attended rape and domestic violence trials to collect additional material for the book. This well-researched and moving account was brand-new at the time of one of our studies and thus not yet widely known, leading to a rating of Diamond in the Rough

♦ *Miles to Go Before I Sleep: A Survivor's Story of a Terrorist Hijacking* (2001) by Jackie Nink Pflug. Center City, MN: Hazelden.

Accompanying her students to a basketball tournament, special education teacher Jackie Pflug's flight was hijacked. While negotiations proceeded on the ground, she was chosen for execution by the hijackers, shot in the head, and thrown out of the plane onto the tarmac. Fifty-eight passengers died as a result of the hijacking and the harrowing rescue attempt. Jackie Pflug survived but suffered substantial brain injury; she provides this inspiring account of her continuing struggle to retrieve the skills she lost. The book provides valuable insights about courage, PTSD, and the slow, painful process of recovering lost abilities.

The author became the special education client she was originally trained to teach. This autobiography was released the year before one of our studies and did not receive sufficient ratings to make it into the formal ratings (Appendix C), but we are pleased to recommend it nonetheless.

## ▓ FILMS

### Strongly Recommended

★★★★★ *In the Valley of Elah* (2007) directed by Paul Haggis. R rating. 121 minutes.

An award-wining, 5-star film based on the 2003 murder of Richard Davis, a young soldier who had just returned to America after deployment in Iraq. His father, Hank (Tommy Lee Jones), and a female detective piece together the evidence and events that led to Richard's disappearance. Together they discover the dirty secrets and dehumanization of war, both for the invaded country and for the soldiers serving there. Richard's murder and multiple side stories illustrate the ravages of combat PTSD on the home front. The horrors of war, the indifference of the military, and the tragic consequences of PTSD are on full display. By the end of the film, the patriotic father, himself a proud veteran, understands that the country is indeed in distress. Probably the best movie on war-related PTSD ever made.

★★★★ *The Accused* (1988) directed by Jonathan Kaplan. R rating. 110 minutes.

Rape victims are often seen as complicit in their rape, particularly by the traditional male-dominated judicial system, and especially when they act provocatively and are intoxicated. Jodie Foster is repeatedly raped in a bar in front of cheering men. She escapes and seeks legal help. Kelly McGillis, the public prosecutor, is unsympathetic to a woman so different from her and, at first, betrays Foster by accepting a reduced charge. Through their continuing relationship, the movie makes the point that no matter how a woman acts, she still has the right to say "no" and to be heard. The film also convincingly shows the torment of trauma and the potential retraumatization associated with an insensitive judicial system.

### Recommended

★★★ *The Messenger* (2009) directed by Oren Moverman. R rating. 113 minutes.

Sergeant Will Montgomery has been seriously injured in Iraq and has been returned to complete his tour of duty in the United States while recuperating. He is assigned to the Casualty Notification Team, despite his lack of training or experience. Will is tutored by a strict career soldier (Woody Harrelson) in the proper protocol for delivering the lethal news to loved ones and gradually learns to cope with the emotions of the next of kin. But he is unprepared for the reaction of a woman whose husband is killed in Iraq. Will then struggles with an ethical dilemma when he becomes romantically involved with a widow of a fallen officer. *The Messenger* received high ratings in our national studies, probably due to its superb acting and realistic story, but it is not particularly strong in showing PTSD per se.

★★★ *Fearless* (1993) directed by Peter Weir. R rating. 122 minutes.

An ordinary man (Jeff Bridges) survives a plane crash that kills many passengers. He realizes that his assumptions about how life works and should be lived can be questioned.

He comes to feel invulnerable but is laid low by a tiny accident. A psychologist cannot help much and his wife offers loving support for his withdrawal and confusions, but only a fellow survivor can offer understanding. Their relationship avoids the sexual, and the movie shows how each grows. His PTSD and anxiety symptoms are shown and treated in group therapy. The film richly illustrates the psychic consequences of trauma and the ways we can overcome it with the help of our friends when conventional psychotherapy fails.

★★★   *Born on the Fourth of July* (1990) directed by Oliver Stone. R rating. 145 minutes.

The true story of a patriotic and excitement-seeking small-town boy who volunteers to fight in Vietnam only to return wheelchair bound. Abandoned and condemned by his fellow citizens, he falls into drug use and PTSD but eventually finds himself by understanding the larger political picture and participating in antiwar activism. The movie might be used to show the possibility of redemption and making the best of a terrible situation by facing reality and seeing the truth beyond the culturally supported images.

★★★   *The Fisher King* (1991) directed by Terry Gilliam. R rating. 137 minutes.

Jeff Bridges is a radio talk-show host whose listener goes on a shooting spree. Jeff quits his job and descends into a drinking binge but is rescued by Robin Williams as a homeless man searching for the Holy Grail. Williams' character was traumatized by witnessing the death of his wife. Although an interesting and occasionally funny film, *The Fisher King* is not quite convincing or accurate about PTSD. (Also reviewed in the Schizophrenia chapter, Chapter 33.)

★★★   *Brothers* (2009) directed by Jim Sheridan. R rating. 105 minutes.

Captain Sam Cahill (Tobey Maguire) is shot down in a helicopter and presumed dead in Afghanistan. While imprisoned by the enemy, Sam endures unspeakable and unbearable horrors, returning home with severe PTSD. Demons possess him: detached, silent, suspicious, without enthusiasm or emotion. Back home, his ne'er-do-well brother has attempted to redeem himself by caring for Sam's wife and two young daughters. Sam's PTSD gets the best of him: he destroys a kitchen, pulls a gun on his brother, nearly commits suicide, and is admitted to a psychiatric hospital. Maguire's performance is right on, down to his emaciated body and mental hell. War is hell alright—right in the kitchen. *Brothers* reminds us that even when the troops return home their war is far from over, for them and their loved ones.

★★★   *Reign Over Me* (2007) directed by Mike Binder. R rating. 124 minutes.

Charlie Fineman (Adam Sandler) lost his entire family on 9/11 and in subsequent years lost most of himself, retreating into a childlike existence. Meanwhile, his college roommate has a great career, a loving wife, and delightful children but feels unfulfilled and isolated. They reunite and help each other rebuild their respective lives. The fabulous Liv Tyler plays a sensitive psychologist who helps Charlie acknowledge his profound loss and craft a new adult life. More about the curative power of friendship than PTSD itself, but the film does demonstrate the chronic regression that can accompany severe PTSD.

★★★ *The Client* (1994) directed by Joel Schumacher. PG-13 rating. 117 minutes.

Street-smart 11-year-old Brad Renfro watches a suicide and learns information that puts his life in danger from the gangsters and politicians of a Southern Gothic town. He seeks out a lawyer, Susan Sarandon, and they bond and grow with each other. The film presents the boy's traumatization as well as showing the healing power of relationships.

★★★ *The Deer Hunter* (1978) directed by Michael Cimino. R rating. 182 minutes.

Three working-class guys from a small town go to war and are greatly and differently affected by the experience. We witness the most graphic of atrocities as they change. One is scarred but matures and can no longer kill even the deer he used to hunt. The other two are damaged, one physically and the other mentally. The film illustrates the way a person can endure PTSD and develop, even in the most hostile of environments, into a better human being. Winner of five Academy Awards.

★★★ *Full Metal Jacket* (1988) directed by Stanley Kubrick. R rating. 118 minutes.

The film moves from the induction into the military of naive recruits, through hellish training to toughen them, and into the war in Vietnam—the battles, killing, prostitution, drugs, and alcohol. A haunting film that may demonstrate the genesis of PTSD, but not much else of clinical utility. Vivid scenes of the horrors of war and warriors mark a realistic, apolitical, and complex film.

**Not Recommended**

★★ *Beloved* (1998) directed by Jonathan Demme. R rating. 175 minutes.
★★ *The Legend of Bagger Vance* (2000) directed by Robert Redford. PG-13 rating. 127 minutes.
★★ *The Hurt Locker* (2008) directed by Kathryn Bigelow. R rating. 131 minutes.
★ *Angel Eyes* (2001) directed by Luis Mandoki. R rating. 104 minutes.

## ■ ONLINE SELF-HELP

★★★ *AnxietyOnline* www.anxietyonline.org.au

This website is dedicated to the treatment of several anxiety conditions, including PTSD. After free registration, users are directed to take an extensive online assessment to determine the type and intensity of their anxiety. Based on these results, users are offered online either a free self-directed program or, in more severe cases, a therapist-assisted online program at a cost of $120. Users who utilize the therapist-assisted program maintain weekly email contact with a therapist in addition to the online program. Based on the principles of cognitive-behavioral therapy, all the programs provide users with education about their condition, exercises to build skills to manage their condition, and worksheets to track progress. The program consists of 12 weekly modules.

★★★ *PTSD Coach* App available for Apple and Android

This program is intended as an additional support for people currently in treatment for symptoms of PTSD. It was developed by the Veterans Administration National

Center for PTSD and the Department of Defense's National Center for Telehealth and Technology. The program provides users with education about PTSD and tools to help manage their symptoms. Features include a screening instrument for self-assessment, relaxation exercises to address symptoms of anxiety or anger, and links for additional support. The program is available free of charge. Current reviews of the software indicated that users were generally pleased with the program, but there were some glitches with the smartphone apps.

★★★  *So You've Been in an Accident* kidsaccident.psy.uq.edu.au

This website is designed for children and adolescents who are recovering emotionally following an accident. Upon entering, users select either the Kids or Adolescents version of the program. The seven modules, based on cognitive-behavioral therapy, help users identify their feelings, note their personal strengths, develop problem-solving strategies, and develop positive self-talk. Youths are encouraged to reach out to others and seek help if they are feeling distress.

## ■ INTERNET RESOURCES

### General Websites

★★★★★  *National Center for PTSD* www.ptsd.va.gov

This resource from the U.S. Department of Veterans Affairs is a comprehensive website focused on PTSD in military veterans. Click on the "Public" section to find hundreds of consumer-oriented articles on PTSD, including assessment, treatment, coping, women-specific, and articles to help friends and family better understand what a veteran is going through. The constantly updated site also features research resources and videos.

★★★  *David Baldwin's Trauma Information Pages* www.trauma-pages.com

Although at one time one of the best trauma resources online, it apparently hasn't been updated in years. Still a useful resource, however, with lots of articles about PTSD, and trauma in general.

### Psychoeducational Materials

★★★★  *Sidran Institute* www.sidran.org

This site provides numerous online resources for survivors, families, and professionals. Check under the "Resources" section to get started.

★★★★  *Post Traumatic Stress (PTSD)* ptsd.about.com

This resource from About.com Matthew Tull, PhD, offers a rich and deep library on the symptoms and diagnosis of PTSD and its treatment, as well as learning to better cope with the disorder. Causes are also covered, and articles written for loved ones and family members are offered to help them better understand the PTSD sufferer's experiences.

**★★★★** *The International Society for Traumatic Stress Studies* www.istss.org

There are some helpful articles under the "For the Public" section about traumatic stress, including videos and fact sheets.

**★★★★** *PTSD Alliance* www.ptsdalliance.org

A collaboration of four organizations concerned with trauma's effects, this site offers dozens of short informative materials for family, therapists, and the media.

**★★★★** *Post-traumatic Stress Disorder (PTSD)* www.mayoclinic.com/health/post-traumatic-stress-disorder/DS00246

This section of the Mayo Clinic website offers a reliable set of articles about PTSD's symptoms, causes, risk factors, complications, treatments and drugs, alternative medicine, and coping with the disorder, among other topics.

**★★★★** *Posttraumatic Stress Disorder* psychcentral.com/disorders/ptsd

This condition center from Psych Central offers a wealth of information about PTSD, including symptoms, causes, differential diagnosis, treatment, myths and facts, and FAQs about PTSD. It also offers personal stories, daily updated news and research briefs, and two active self-help support groups.

**★★★** *ChildTrauma Academy* www.childtrauma.org

You can find dozens of sophisticated articles on traumatized children for parents and caregivers in the "Articles" section.

**★★★** *Post-traumatic Stress Disorder* helpguide.org/mental/post_traumatic_stress_disorder_symptoms_treatment.htm

This single article from the nonprofit HelpGuide offers a helpful overview about PTSD, such as the signs and symptoms, causes, and treatment. There are a bunch of simple self-help tips at the end of the article, as well as a handful of related resources.

## ■ SUPPORT GROUPS

We have been unable to identify any national support groups specifically for PTSD. Similarly, the authors of the impressive *Self-Help Sourcebook* (White & Madara, 1995, p. 167) write that, "Regrettably, we are unaware of any model or national self-help support groups that have yet been formed" for PTSD and accident victims. As a result, the following list is largely composed of educational and professional groups, as opposed to self-help groups per se.

### Anxiety Disorders Association of America (ADAA)

Phone: 240-485-10001

www.adaa.org
Dedicated to promoting the prevention and cure of anxiety disorders; their bookstore is excellent for its prices and the wide range of books.

## Emotions Anonymous

Phone: 651-647-9712
www.emotionsanonymous.org

## International Society for Traumatic Stress Studies (ISTSS)

Phone: 847-480-9028
www.istss.org
More of a professional organization than a self-help association, but a valuable source of reliable information.

## National Center for Post-Traumatic Stress Disorder

Phone: 802-296-6300
www.ptsd.va.gov

## National Organization for Victim Assistance

Phone: 202-232-6682
www.try-nova.org
Support for victims of violent crimes and disaster.

## PTSD Support Services

Phone: 719-687-4582
ptsdsupport.net

## Trauma Survivors Anonymous

Phone: 706-649-6500

**See also** Abuse (Chapter 2) and Anxiety Disorders (Chapter 7).

# CHAPTER 32

# PREGNANCY

Although Sara and Jim did not plan to have a baby right away, they did not take any precautions to prevent it, and it was not long before Sara was pregnant. They found a nurse–midwife they liked and invented a pet name—Bibinello—for the fetus. They signed up for birth preparation classes, and each Friday night for 8 weeks they faithfully practiced for contractions. They moved into a larger apartment so that the baby could have its own room and spent weekends browsing through garage sales and secondhand stores to find good prices on baby furniture—a crib, a high chair, a stroller, a changing table, a crib mobile, a swing, a car seat.

Jim and Sara also spent a lot of time talking about what kind of parents they wanted to be, what their child might be like, and what changes the baby would make in their lives. One of their concerns was that Sara's maternity leave would last only 6 weeks. If she wanted to stay home longer, she would have to quit her job, something she and Jim were not sure they could afford.

These are among the many scripts and questions expectant couples have about pregnancy, and there have been many resources created to help expectant parents like Sara and Jim better understand pregnancy and make more informed decisions about their offspring's health and well-being, as well as their own. We review, in this chapter, the most useful self-help books, films, Internet resources, and support groups for doing so (Box 32.1).

## ■ SELF-HELP BOOKS

### Strongly Recommended

★★★★★ *What to Expect When You're Expecting* (2002, 3rd ed.) by Arlene Eisenberg, Heidi Eisenberg Murkoff, and Sandee E. Hathaway. New York: Workman.

This third edition of the best-selling "pregnancy bible" reflects advances in obstetrical practice but just as importantly incorporates new or expanded areas suggested by the readers: alternative birthing, second pregnancies, postpartum depression, more on common pregnancy symptoms, and advice on traveling while pregnant. This is a month-by-month, step-by-step guide to pregnancy and childbirth. The authors are a mother–daughters team, and their book was the result of the unnecessarily worry-filled pregnancy of the second author (Heidi Murkoff). The book tries to put expectant parents' normal fears into perspective by giving them comprehensive information and helping them enjoy this transition in their lives. *What to Expect When You're Expecting* is an excellent self-help book for expectant

**BOX 32.1**
**RECOMMENDATION HIGHLIGHTS**

**SELF-HELP BOOKS**

■ On a month-by-month, step-by-step map of pregnancy:

★★★★★ *What to Expect When You're Expecting* by Arlene Eisenberg et al.

■ On pregnancy in general:

★★★★★ *The Complete Book of Pregnancy and Childbirth* by Sheila Kitzinger

♦ *The Girlfriends' Guide to Pregnancy* by Vicki Iovine

♦ *The Working Woman's Pregnancy Book* by Marjorie Greenfield

■ On becoming a father:

♦ *The Expectant Father* by Armin A. Brott and Jennifer Ash

**FILMS**

■ On handling teenage pregnancy and adoption:

★★★★ *Juno*

■ On enduring pregnancy with the support of friends:

★★★ *Where the Heart Is*

■ On making a life-threatening decision to maintain pregnancy:

★★★ *Steel Magnolias*

**INTERNET RESOURCES**

■ On pregnancy:

★★★★★ *New York Online Access to Health* www.noah-health.org/en/pregnancy

★★★★★ *Planned Parenthood* www.plannedparenthood.org

★★★★ *Pregnancy & Childbirth* pregnancy.about.com

■ On postpartum depression:

★★★★★ *Postpartum Progress* postpartumprogress.com

parents, walking them through the 9 months of pregnancy and childbirth. It is reassuring and thorough.

★★★★★ *The Complete Book of Pregnancy and Childbirth* (1996) by Sheila Kitzinger. New York: Knopf.

This comprehensive guide to pregnancy and childbirth emphasizes an active and informed stance to giving birth. The expectant mother prepares for an active role in childbirth by learning about the changes that are occurring in her body, childbirth options, and who does what to her and why. Expectant parents learn about the early weeks of pregnancy and the emotional and physical changes they are likely to experience at this time. Kitzinger educates expectant mothers about prenatal care and medical charts. She describes common worries of expectant mothers, lovemaking during pregnancy, and the father's role. The author recommends relaxation and breathing exercises and provides advice about medical checkups. She covers what happens during the stages of labor, support during labor, coping with pain, the option of gentle birth, and what to expect in the first few hours and days after birth. The book has numerous charts, drawings, and photographs. The book's enthusiasts especially liked Kitzinger's holistic approach to pregnancy and her emphasis on women's choices.

**Recommended**

★★★  *What to Eat When You're Expecting* (1986) by Arlene Eisenberg, Heidi Murkoff, and Sandee Hathaway. New York: Workman.

The book, written by the authors of *What to Expect When You're Expecting* (reviewed above), is based on 20 years of practical application in the Eisenberg family. They present the "best odds" diet, which they believe increases the probability of having a healthy baby. The book describes the mother's nutritional needs during pregnancy and how they affect the baby. Daily recommended portions are given. The expectant mother learns how to assess her eating habits and how to alter them if they are not good. Almost 100 pages of recipes and a lengthy appendix of nutritional charts are also included. The book is well written and easy to read, and the nutritional plan for expectant mothers is sound, albeit perhaps slightly dated.

★★★  *Pregnancy After 35* (1976, reissued 1984) by Carole McCauley. New York: Pocket.

The older mother faces unique medical and emotional problems during pregnancy. This book is based on medical journal articles and interviews with physicians, psychologists, midwives, and older couples to address the special concerns of pregnancy in older women. Women over 35 learn about genetic counseling, risk factors, and psychological issues that arise throughout pregnancy. The book was published in 1976 and is dated, especially in terms of nutritional advice. And, of course, it does not cover a number of tests that have been developed in recent years to assess the likelihood of having a healthy baby.

★★★  *The Well Pregnancy Book* (revised ed., 1996) by Mike Samuels and Nancy Samuels. New York: Summit.

This guide to pregnancy and childbirth emphasizes a holistic approach. It provides an overview of childbirth practices in different cultures and serves as an expectant parents' guide to pregnancy, childbirth, and the postpartum period. The authors cover nutrition and fitness, physical changes in the expectant mother and the offspring, and the medical aspects of hormonal and bodily changes in pregnant women. This book is better used in cases of uncomplicated pregnancies rather than high-risk ones. Critics also said that the book is too simplistic and is poorly organized.

★★★  *From Here to Maternity* (1986) by Connie Marshall. Citrus Heights, CA: Conmar.

This self-help book is a general guide to pregnancy that emphasizes childbirth preparation and selection of a health-care team. Its purpose is to improve the expectant couple's ability to communicate knowledgeably with their health-care team. The book's three parts deal with (1) emotions during pregnancy, the expectant mother's body and prenatal growth, drug use, and choosing breast or bottle feeding; (2) selecting a doctor; and (3) labor and delivery. *From Here to Maternity* received a 3-star rating, but some critics thought the book to be superficial and poorly illustrated.

## Diamonds in the Rough

- *The Girlfriends' Guide to Pregnancy* (1995) by Vicki Iovine. New York: Pocket Books.

Pregnancy books are so "detached, calm, neat, and moderate" that the author would never ask a physician about the indelicate matters that her girlfriends discuss freely. Ninety percent of the good information she received came from girlfriends, not the experts. This is the backdrop for the hilarious *Girlfriends' Guide* that does, in fact, discuss every phase of pregnancy. Some topics are circumspect responses to serious concerns, such as being scared, fearing miscarriage, or worrying that something might be wrong with the baby. Other topics are funny responses to light-hearted concerns, such as the likelihood of stretch marks, fear of turning into the husband's mother, and baby arrival anxiety (e.g., "What if the baby doesn't like me?"). The conversational style of the book is like lunch with a candid best friend. Much factual information is offered here; myths are dispelled; rumors are confirmed or denied; and lies about pregnancy are revealed. This book takes a funny, bold, but also knowledgeable view of pregnancy. In our earlier edition, this book was a Diamond in the Rough and for the same reasons it remains one: it was not rated frequently enough in our studies, but those who did know it rated it very highly.

- *1000 Questions About Your Pregnancy* (1997) by Jeffrey M. Thurston. Arlington, TX: Summit.

The author is an associate professor of OB/GYN at a major medical school. As a function of practice and teaching, he has developed answers to the 1,000 questions presented in this book. This easy-to-read reference gives the facts about pregnancy and childbirth and adds a little humor on the side. Questions are sequential by developmental stage of pregnancy, yet are subgrouped by subject areas (e.g., morning sickness, tests of fetal functioning, drugs, childbirth classes). Fact and opinion are carefully differentiated and the information given is consistent with the recommendations of the American College of Obstetricians and Gynecologists. This Q&A book is accurate and useful but was not well known among mental health professionals, thus qualifying for Diamond in the Rough status.

- *Mindful Motherhood: Practical Tools for Staying Sane During Pregnancy and Your Child's First Year* (2009) by Cassandra Vieten. Oakland, CA: New Harbinger.

The principles of mindfulness are applied to early motherhood in this relatively recent offering. The first section of the book offers the basics (e.g., enhancement of awareness) and activities of mindfulness (e.g., yoga, meditation), which facilitate a changing perception about what is important. The author reminds mothers that they already know how to mother their infants but have just not made the time and space to become aware of what they already know and who they already are. The author highlights nonstriving, curiosity, acceptance, and motherhood not as it should be but as it is. Not well known, but a fresh take on ancient challenges.

◆ *The Expectant Father: Facts, Tips, and Advice for Dads-to-Be* (2010) by Armin A. Brott and Jennifer Ash. Abbeville.

Another hidden gem, this time designed for the expectant father. The engaging prose informs, reassures, and identifies with the anxieties of fathers-to-be. The newest edition features sections on infertility treatments, artificial insemination, cesarean sections, epidurals during childbirth, and more. Co-authored by the host of the "Positive Parenting" talk show and numerous books on fatherhood, this volume is chock-full of practical advice and humorous cartoons. The best self-help guide for men according to our experts.

◆ *The Working Woman's Pregnancy Book* (2008) by Marjorie Greenfield. New Haven, CT: Yale University Press.

Pregnancy and work may not be a common topic but is one that greatly affects working women. As the author expresses, "crawling up the learning curve" involves many decisions. This book is a toolkit of information on almost all matters of import and decision making during that time: medical care, life on the job before the birth, maternity leave, returning to work, breast feeding, and others. The comprehensive appendices list medical, developmental, and physical information regarding conditions, medicines, symptoms, genetic factors, and all manner of information that will assist mothers in navigating the first year. Favorably evaluated in our latest national study but not widely known, thereby earning the status of a Diamond in the Rough.

## ▦ FILMS

**Recommended**

★★★★ *Juno* (2007) directed by Jason Reitman. PG-13 rating. 96 minutes.

This film follows the pregnancy of the young and quick-witted Juno. A determined 16-year-old, she decides it is time for her to experiment with sex and enlists the help of her best friend Paulie, who is not thrilled at the idea. Soon thereafter Juno discovers she is pregnant and is left to make a decision. After a trip to an abortion clinic, she decides to have the child but knows she cannot raise it. She looks to the ads for adoptive parents in the Penny Saver. She finds Vanessa and Mark, a broken couple composed of a woman consumed with the idea of a child and a husband who is still one himself. The film has an unorthodox ending but is nonetheless happy as Vanessa raises her new son as a single mother and Juno and Paulie can finally be two teens in love. A delightfully quirky sermon about pregnancy, motherhood, and love.

★★★ *Where the Heart Is* (2000) directed by Matt Williams. PG-13 rating. 120 minutes.

Natalie Portman portrays a very pregnant 17-year-old, escaping to California and hoping for a new life with her selfish and unreliable musician boyfriend. He dumps her in Oklahoma. With the assistance of an assortment of odd women, she lives in the Wal-Mart and delivers there, and eventually becomes part of a makeshift family of support. The plot is too busy and full of holes, but the characters shine through. The folksy warmth about pregnancy and the message of nonstandard family love are the lasting lessons.

★★★ *Steel Magnolias* (1990) directed by Herbert Ross. PG rating. 118 minutes.

This movie spans several years in the lives of a group of women whose central meeting place is a beauty salon. One of the central characters, a diabetic woman, gives birth to a child her physician warned her not to have and subsequently lapses into a terminal coma (which is why this film is also considered in the Death and Grieving chapter, Chapter 18). More generally, the film is about the support of good friends, accepting loss, and learning to grow beyond differences. Through troubling times, there is a rebirth of relationship and newfound support.

### Not Recommended

* ★ *Father of the Bride II* (1995) directed by Charles Shyer. PG rating. 106 minutes.
* ★ *Knocked Up* (2007) directed by Judd Apatow. R rating. 129 minutes.
* ★ *Nine Months* (1995) directed by Chris Columbus. PG-13 rating. 102 minutes.
* ★ *Baby M* (1988, made for TV) directed by James Stephen Sadwith. PG rating. 128 minutes.

## ■ INTERNET RESOURCES

Expecting mothers should be aware of the "mommy blogger" category. While we don't list any of these blogs below (because they come and go so quickly, it's unlikely any blog we list will still be around a few years after this book is published), you can find up-to-date mommy blogs by simply typing the term "mommy blogs" into Google or your favorite search engine.

### General Websites

★★★★★ *New York Online Access to Health* www.noah-health.org/en/pregnancy

The New York Online Access to Health (NOAH) website offers a large directory of Internet resources on hundreds of health and related topics, including pregnancy, labor, and delivery. Includes information about prepregnancy health care, medications during pregnancy, nutrition, medications, and many more subjects. Results are not New York-specific.

★★★★★ *BabyZone* babyzone.com

An enormous commercial website from Disney for any kind of question related to babies from preconception and pregnancy to infancy and toddlerhood. The pregnancy section includes not only the usual array of articles but also includes slideshows, expert Q&As, quizzes, and a mom-to-mom community.

★★★★ *Pregnancy & Childbirth* pregnancy.about.com

This site from About.com is led by Robin Elise Weiss, LCCE, and covers all the usual pregnancy topics in a straightforward and matter-of-fact manner. These topics include getting pregnant, pregnancy basics, labor, your pregnant body, prenatal care, twins and multiples, complications, postpartum, and pregnancy loss, among many others.

**** *Infertility* infertility.about.com

This commercial site from About.com is led by Rachel Gurevich and covers a wealth of infertility topics, including trying to conceive and all sorts of conception subjects, trouble with getting pregnant, and possible infertility treatments. A large and helpful site.

**** *Top 10 Free Pregnancy iPhone Apps* www.mypregnancybaby.com/top-10-free-pregnancy-iphone-apps

If you want an app for your iPhone to help you with your pregnancy, check out this helpful list. Using a search term like "pregnancy apps" or "Android pregnancy apps" in Google can help you find a more updated list in the future.

## Psychoeducational Materials

***** *Parenthood.com* www.parenthood.com

A comprehensive source of pregnancy, parenting, and child-care articles. Features include hundreds of articles about parenting, pregnancy, your baby, your child, baby names, and dozens of videos.

**** *OBGYN.net: The Universe of Women's Health* www.obgyn.net

OBGYN.net is a commercial website designed by obstetricians and gynecologists primarily for other medical professionals, but it offers a wealth of information that, although sometimes technical, is also helpful to laypeople. Some of the topics covered in the "Women and Patients" section include contraceptives, medications, infertility, grief, pregnancy and birth, raising children, sexuality and reproductive health, and fitness. Patients who still have medical questions after looking elsewhere can probably find the answer here.

*** *BabyCenter—Advice for New Dads* www.babycenter.com/advice-for-new-dads

This commercial site offers a few dozen fine articles from preconception to baby's first year tailored for new dads.

## *Medical Aspects*

**** *Pregnancy Calendar* www.justmommies.com/pregnancy_calendar.php

"Find out what is going on with your baby during your pregnancy and what changes to expect in mom during pregnancy. Our pregnancy calendar will give you details on your baby's development and what is happening to mom during her pregnancy." A great and engaging feature for expecting moms.

**** *StorkNet's Week-by-Week Guide to Your Pregnancy!* www.pregnancyguideonline.com

Similar to the *Pregnancy Calendar* (above) but also includes Fetal Development, Maternal Changes, Checkups, Readings, and Ideas for Dad. Instead of a day-by-day calendar, it's a week-by-week one.

### Getting Pregnant and Infertility
★★★★★  *Plus-Size Pregnancy Website* plus-size-pregnancy.org/firstindex.html

This website features many articles and links to resources on preparing for and being pregnant, complications, clothing, and breast feeding. Superb links and support for the large woman.

★★★★  *Infertility FAQ* www.fertilityplus.org/faq/infertility.html

This is a well-organized and superb overview of the medical aspects that should be understood before exploring the psychological ones. It also covers online news groups, books and readings, and how to join online groups.

★★★  *Infertility Resources* www.ihr.com/infertility

This website features hundreds of articles on infertility.

### Pregnancy Loss
★★★  *A Heartbreaking Choice* www.aheartbreakingchoice.com

A website that offers resources, information, and support for women who have terminated a pregnancy due to the mother's health, a poor prenatal diagnosis, or for the health of another fetus.

### Unwanted Pregnancies
★★★★★  *Planned Parenthood* www.plannedparenthood.org

This national nonprofit organization offers a great deal of resources about women's health and pregnancy under "Health Info & Services."

★★★★  *Adoption.com* www.adoption.com

This large commercial site offers a wealth of resources and thousands of articles related to adoption, adoptees, birth parents, parenting, and reunion.

★★★  *Option Line* optionline.org

This helpline is run by two faith-based organizations and provides information about pregnancy, emergency contraception, and, to a limited extent, abortion (but will not refer women for abortion services).

### Birth Defects
★★★★  *March of Dimes* www.marchofdimes.com

This well-known nonprofit organization offers many helpful resources on its website under the categories of "Pregnancy," "Baby," and "Research." It also offers information about its organization and advocacy efforts and volunteer opportunities.

### Childbirth Educators and Doulas
Doulas are trained to provide emotional, physical, and educational support to women and their families during and after childbirth.

★★★    *DONA International* www.dona.org

A good website to learn more about doulas.

★★★    *Association for Pre- & Perinatal Psychology and Health* www.birthpsychology.com

This professional association helps to advocate for the health and mental health of babies and offers some interesting articles under "Libraries."

### Postpartum Depression
★★★★★    *Postpartum Progress* postpartumprogress.com

This amazing blog from parenting writer and advocate Katherine Stone offers not only daily entries and insights but also a FAQ section, survival tools, and a set of reference articles about postpartum disorders, such as postpartum depression, anxiety, psychosis, and more. A rich, detailed, and constantly updated resource.

★★★★    *Postpartum Support International* www.postpartum.net

This website is designed to help women with perinatal mood and anxiety disorders, most commonly postpartum depression. Lots of good articles and links to support resources on the site.

★★★    *This Isn't What I Expected* www.psychologytoday.com/blog/isnt-what-i-expected

This blog from social worker Karen Kleiman offers an eclectic, irregularly updated view of postpartum depression issues.

## ▧ SUPPORT GROUPS

### Compassionate Friends

Phone: 877-969-0010
www.compassionatefriends.org
Their mission is to assist families in their grieving following the death of a child and to provide information to help others be supportive.

### National Organization on Fetal Alcohol Syndrome

Phone: 202-785-4585
www.nofas.org
Grassroots coalition of families and professionals concerned with fetal alcohol syndrome.

### Helping After Neonatal Death (HAND)

Phone: 888-908-HAND or 408-995-6102
www.handonline.org

"HAND ... is a non-profit, volunteer group founded in the early 1980's to provide support and information to bereaved parents, their families and friends following a miscarriage, stillbirth, or newborn death." They have many local chapters.

### National Abortion Federation

www.prochoice.org
Phone: 800-772-9100
Provides information and referrals regarding abortions; financial aid.

### National Adoption Center

Phone: 800-TO-ADOPT
www.adopt.org/adopt
Information on adoption agencies and support groups. Network for matching parents and children with special needs.

### Planned Parenthood

Phone: 800-230-7526 (referrals) or 800-829-7732 (administration)
www.plannedparenthood.org
Referrals to local Planned Parenthood clinics nationwide.

### Pregnancy Crisis Hotline

Phone: 800-238-4269
www.bethany.org
Information and counseling for pregnant women. Referrals to free pregnancy test facilities, foster care, and adoption centers. Sponsored by Bethany Christian Services.

### Pregnancy Hotline

Phone: 800-848-5683
Free, confidential information for pregnant women, shelters for women, baby clothes, adoption referrals.

### Resolve

Phone: 703-556-7172
www.resolve.org
For those coping with infertility, this is the oldest and largest organization.

**See also** Infant Development and Parenting (Chapter 26) and Sexuality (Chapter 35).

# CHAPTER 33

# SCHIZOPHRENIA

Schizophrenia, a serious mental disorder that afflicts about 1% of the population, is characterized by disorganized thinking, impairment in reality testing, hallucinations, and delusions. Many scientific and academic books are available describing this disorder; however, the resources reviewed in this chapter were explicitly chosen for their usefulness to individuals and families coping with schizophrenia in their daily lives.

In recent years, mental health professionals have come to realize what laypersons touched by schizophrenia have known all along: that schizophrenia can have as devastating an effect on family and friends as on the mentally ill individuals themselves. Because the onset is typically during the late teens and early 20s, family and friends experience a deterioration of a loved one for whom the early years were normal. The person they had come to know is experiencing a metamorphosis before their very eyes. Parents and caretakers of schizophrenic children suffer emotional upheaval while also being responsible for seeking medical and psychological assistance, dealing with trauma within the family, and attending to financial, social, educational, and employment changes. Siblings of the mentally ill find their worlds turned upside down because their needs have suddenly become low priority. Extended family and friends are at loss, confused about what to do or not to do.

The self-help resources reviewed here are primarily directed to patients, family, and friends who seek direction that is often not provided by systems or individuals with whom they consult. We consider the ratings and descriptions of, in turn, self-help books, autobiographies, films, online self-help, and Internet resources, followed by an alphabetical listing of national support organizations (Box 33.1).

## ■ SELF-HELP BOOKS

### Strongly Recommended

★★★★★ *Surviving Schizophrenia: A Manual for Families, Consumers, and Providers* (2001, 4th ed.) by E. Fuller Torrey. New York: HarperPerennial.

The author, a renowned expert on schizophrenia, is both a psychiatrist and the brother of a person diagnosed with schizophrenia. As a result, this book is written with a personal perspective and also with accurate medical information. The important aspects of this disease are addressed factually and with encouragement. The view from the inside, the view from the outside, what the disease is not, and FAQs are examples of topics discussed in an understandable and respectful way. The decline in outpatient services, rehabilitation,

## BOX 33.1
## RECOMMENDATION HIGHLIGHTS

**SELF-HELP BOOKS**

- For families:

    ★★★★★ *Surviving Schizophrenia* by E. Fuller Torrey

    ★★★ *The Complete Family Guide to Schizophrenia* by Kim Mueser and Susan Gingerich

    ★★★ *How to Cope with Mental Illness in Your Family* by Diane T. Marsh and Rex M. Dickens

- For understanding the disorder and patient advocacy:

    ★★★ *Helping Someone with Mental Illness* by Rosalynn Carter with Susan K. Golant

    ♦ *Understanding Schizophrenia* by Richard S. E. Keefe and Philip D. Harvey

**AUTOBIOGRAPHIES**

- For a classic story of a teen's fantasy world and psychotherapy:

    ★★★★★ *I Never Promised You a Rose Garden* by Joanne Greenberg

- For a successful career and life of a schizophrenic person:

    ★★★★ *The Center Cannot Hold: My Journey Through Madness* by Elyn R. Saks

- For friends and families trying to help the chronic mentally ill:

    ★★★ *The Soloist* by Steve Lopez

- For memoirs and diary notes of youngsters suffering from schizophrenia:

    ★★★ *When the Music's Over* edited by Richard Gates and Robin Hammond

    ★★★ *Autobiography of a Schizophrenic Girl* by Marguerite Sechehaye

**FILMS**

- For inspiring stories of brilliant schizophrenics:

    ★★★★★ *A Beautiful Mind*

    ★★★★ *Shine*

    ★★★★ *Proof*

- For examples of friendship despite schizophrenia:

    ★★★★★ *The Soloist*

    ★★★★ *Birdy*

- For a healing search despite mental disarray:

    ★★★★ *The Fisher King*

**ONLINE SELF-HELP**

- For free screening, self-help modules, and goal setting:

    ★★★ *Get Real* www.ontrack.org.au

**INTERNET RESOURCES**

- For just about anything you want to know:

    ★★★★★ *Schizophrenia.com* www.schizophrenia.com

    ★★★★ *Schizophrenia* psychcentral.com/disorders/schizophrenia

housing, and other needed assistance leads to a closing section on how to be an effective advocate. This 5-star book is widely regarded as a top self-help book on the subject.

### Recommended

★★★ *Coping with Schizophrenia* (1994) by Kim T. Mueser and Susan Gingerich. Oakland, CA: New Harbinger.

This book is a comprehensive guide for families and individuals living with chronic mental illness and for whom retaining some independence for the individual remains crucial. Until recent years, the families of the mentally ill have been denied explanations and have been shut out of treatment planning. A movement toward family education has begun, and this book is a significant contribution to helping family members improve their quality of life. The authors thoroughly present the disease and offer recommendations for coping and making decisions. The text provides an overview of diagnosis, symptoms, medication, side effects, and early warning signs of relapse. Other sections focus on solving problems, managing stress, establishing household rules, and dealing with depression, anxiety, and alcohol and drug use. The practical format, replete with numerous checklists and exercises, allows family members to gauge the progress of themselves and the mentally ill member. Final chapters focus on the family quality of life, the importance of siblings, and planning for the future. An excellent self-help resource that, had it been better known, would have obtained a 4- or a 5-star rating.

★★★ *The Complete Family Guide to Schizophrenia* (2006) by Kim Mueser and Susan Gingerich. New York: Guilford.

This guide, written by the psychologist and the social worker who authored the book just reviewed, brings recent research developments and treatments to the fore. Schizophrenia is often written about in complex and detailed terms because it is complex, and writers have a difficult time converting all the information to a conversational yet substantive text. This book is useful in terms of format and content for family members and those who care for someone with schizophrenia. More emphasis is placed on relapse prevention and the toll the disease takes on the family and what can be done to minimize those negative effects. Either this book or the authors' earlier effort (*Coping with Schizophrenia*) will prove valuable, but our nod goes to the more recent and updated one.

★★★ *How to Cope with Mental Illness in Your Family: A Self Care Guide for Siblings, Offspring, and Parents* (1998) by Diane T. Marsh and Rex M. Dickens. New York: Jeremy P. Tarcher/Putnam.

This book is written from the point of view of a family affected by mental disorder. One of the authors is a psychologist who works with families of the mentally ill, and the other author is an adult who grew up with a mentally ill sibling. The book is directed to family members, particularly the siblings and adult children of the mentally ill. It describes the effect of the illness on the childhood and adolescence of the siblings and the effect that living with this disease may have on a person's worldview. Experiences of siblings are cited as illustrative of how they learned to cope and how they managed losses. Chapters are devoted to such topics as how the illness disrupts the family, the emotional burden of daily problems, peer relationships, vulnerability, and adaptation across developmental stages. The concluding focus is on strengths, coping skills, and hope for family members developed through support groups and other resources.

★★★  *Helping Someone With Mental Illness* (1998) by Rosalynn Carter with Susan K. Golant. New York: Random House.

This refreshing first-person narrative gives a sense of storytelling between two people. Former First Lady Rosalynn Carter tells her story of initial involvement in mental health in 1970 and the motivating factors that continue to sustain her work. Chapters discuss the biological and psychological nature of mental illness, triggers, symptoms, and warning signs. The major mental illnesses of schizophrenia, bipolar disorder, obsessive-compulsive disorder, anxiety, and depression are addressed. The authors articulate the importance of understanding mental illness in the workplace, with insurance and managed care, and in advocacy through the media and the public. Important information is summarized about new medications and treatment potential, risk factors, and protective factors. This is a sensitive and personally written book on helping someone with mental illness.

### Diamond in the Rough

♦  *Understanding Schizophrenia: A Guide to the New Research on Causes and Treatment* (1994) by Richard S. E. Keefe and Philip D. Harvey. New York: Free.

In this self-help resource, schizophrenia is presented as research understood it in the mid-1990s. A valuable feature of the text is that it serves as a handbook for ongoing reference during the course of the illness and selection of treatments. It provides a description of the nature of schizophrenia, the impact on self and families, state-of-the-art treatments, and clinical advances. This book is a useful tool to help families gauge the knowledge and ability of the professionals with whom they are working. *Understanding Schizophrenia* remains a Diamond in the Rough, as it was in our earlier edition, because it continued to receive very high ratings from those who read it—but it is dated in many respects, including the sections on medications.

## ■ AUTOBIOGRAPHIES

### Strongly Recommended

★★★★★  *I Never Promised You a Rose Garden* (1976) by Joanne Greenberg. New York: New American Library.

Originally published under the pseudonym "Hannah Green," this slightly fictionalized version of the author's three years as an adolescent treated for schizophrenia is a classic in the mental health field. It is a sensitive portrayal of the relationship between a young girl in the throes of paranoid delusions, creating a fantasy world called the Kingdom of Yr, and her wise, comforting therapist. The treatment section is dated in not covering the use of the newer psychotropic drugs. Following the book's success, the author came out publicly, revealed her true name, and became active in the mental health movement. She acknowledges that the book was written deliberately to counteract attempts to romanticize mental illness. The book succeeds in that respect and does much more. There are not many schizophrenic clients who can find and afford a therapist as wise and patient as the one described in the book, but their relationship can serve as a useful model of what the relationship can be under the best conditions. An especially moving book for teens.

**** *The Center Cannot Hold: My Journey Through Madness* (2008) by Elyn R. Saks. New York: Hyperion.

This is a book about and by a person with schizophrenia who is managing a successful career and personal life, refusing to be defined by her thought disorder. Her symptoms began at age 8, when she started feeling that her perceptions, thoughts, and feelings were disconnected. In college she fought off bizarre thoughts and neglected her personal appearance but still graduated as class valedictorian. She sensitively describes the mental changes that she struggled against in which her consciousness gradually lost its coherence and her continuing struggle to hold at bay the voices and the delusions. At times she lost the battle and was hospitalized. This provided her with an inside look at the quixotic practices and policies of mental health systems in the United States and in England, where she did graduate work. She was occasionally put into restraints and forcibly given psychotropic drugs, which she resisted, but now accepts that she must take them to quiet the voices and clear up the inner confusion. She is also very positive about the role of psychoanalysis in maintaining her contact with reality: "While medication had kept me alive, it had been psychoanalysis that helped me find a life worth living." Saks holds an endowed professorship of law and psychiatry, has written several books, and has won prestigious awards for her work on mental health law. She is also happily married. The juxtaposition of her serious thought disorder with her many accomplishments is a beacon light to mental health clients, their families, and the mental health professions.

**** *Out of the Depths: An Autobiographical Study of Mental Disorder and Religious Experience* (1960) by Anton T. Boisen. New York: Harper.

This older book briefly describes the author's breakdown when he was a young theology student. He found a cause in his illness and dedicated himself to the mental health movement. An interesting account of the relationship between mental illness and religious experience. Boisen believed that many religious leaders, including George Fox, Swedenborg, and John Bunyan, went through a psychotic experience. In his research, he assessed religious factors in 173 schizophrenic patients at Worcester State Hospital. He published several books on religion and was active in the mental health movement. Most useful for those with low self-esteem who feel they cannot meet their own standards.

**** *Too Much Anger, Too Many Tears: A Personal Triumph Over Psychiatry* (1992) by Janet Gotkin and Paul Gotkin. New York: HarperPerennial.

Janet exhibits many symptoms of schizophrenia, tries suicide on several occasions, is hospitalized numerous times, and receives drug treatment, electroconvulsive therapy, and individual psychotherapy. Her recollections of her hospitalizations and treatment are interesting and often insightful. However, she rejects the diagnosis of schizophrenia and maintains that the treatments were not helpful. Both authors are active in the Mental Patients Liberation Movement. Critiques like these are more useful for social reform than for personal assistance. The book will confirm the negative stereotypes held by those disenchanted with the mental health system.

### Recommended

&#9733;&#9733;&#9733;  *The Soloist: A Lost Dream, an Unlikely Friendship, and the Redemptive Power of Music* (2008) by Steve Lopez. New York: Putnam.

Steve Lopez, a reporter for the *Los Angeles Times*, is looking for a story. When he hears Nathaniel Ayers, a homeless mentally ill African-American man in his fifties, playing classical music on a two-string violin on the street in front of a statue of Beethoven, he has his story and more. Lopez learns that Ayers had been a promising student at Julliard until he developed a disabling paranoid schizophrenia, refused medication and psychotherapy, and went to live on the streets. Lopez wants to help Ayers, thinking this would be a good story. The story turns out to be a roller-coaster ride of small successes and devastating setbacks. Lopez interviews Ayers' relatives and former music teachers at Julliard and learns the realities of life on the streets for the homeless mentally ill and how difficult it is to assist a person who doesn't seek or want help. He also realizes the healing powers of music, Ayers' tenuous connection to reality, and how much their friendship has given to both of them. This is a very good book for understanding how difficult, frustrating, and yet rewarding working with the long-term mentally ill can be.

&#9733;&#9733;&#9733;  *Nobody's Child* (1992) by Marie Balter and Richard Katz. New York: Perseus.

At age 17 Marie Balter was diagnosed with schizophrenia and spent the next 17 years of her life at Danvers State Hospital. With the help of friends, she was released. She subsequently found an apartment, got married, obtained a PhD from Harvard, and became a vocal advocate for mental health patients. Recently she returned to Danvers as an administrator. The book presents a very hopeful message in showing that there can be potential for achievement and career enhancement among long-term mental health clients.

&#9733;&#9733;&#9733;  *The Eden Express* (1988) by Mark Vonnegut. New York: Dell.

Now a pediatrician, Mark Vonnegut, a child of the 1960s and the son of a famous novelist, eloquently describes his hippie life on a British Columbia commune, his breakdown and diagnosis of schizophrenia, and the precarious road to recovery. In a note for this reprinting, Vonnegut believes that using today's definitions, he would probably be diagnosed as having a mood disorder. Whatever his diagnosis, the author suffered an acute episode that cleared and did not return. An engaging story of madness and eventual recovery. Vonnegut's optimism will have particular resonance to young people and will demonstrate that a crazy period in a young person's life will not necessarily result in lifelong disability.

&#9733;&#9733;&#9733;  *When the Music's Over: My Journey into Schizophrenia* (1996) edited by Richard Gates and Robin Hammond. New York: Plume.

This disorganized, semifictional account documents the brief life of David Burke, a young Australian who, before he committed suicide, asked his former psychology instructor, Richard Gates, to edit his notes for publication. Much of the manuscript was written while Burke was in a variety of jails, mental hospitals, and halfway houses. Both the disjointed format and the text illustrate the bizarre thinking characteristic of paranoid schizophrenia.

★★★  *Father, Have I Kept My Promise? Madness as Seen from Within* (1988) by Edith Weisskopf-Joelson. West Lafayette, IN: Purdue University.

A psychology professor describes in diary form her episode of paranoid schizophrenia, admission to a state hospital for a year, and life afterward as a teacher at Purdue University. The author is an inspiring person who positively views her breakdown as leading to constructive changes in her life. A hopeful book in describing how a person with problems starting in childhood can mature and go on to have a successful career in mental health.

★★★  *An Angel at My Table: An Autobiography, Volume Two* (1984) by Janet Frame. New York: George Braziller.

*An Angel at My Table* is a sequel to *Faces in the Water*, a fictional account of life in a mental hospital published almost 30 years after the author was discharged from the last of her five hospitalizations. Frame is an accomplished New Zealand writer with an international reputation for fiction. The first volume of her autobiography traces her difficult childhood; this second volume covers her life at college and her treatment for schizophrenia; and the third volume covers her subsequent literary career. Because the author and her present physician doubt the accuracy of the original diagnosis of schizophrenia, the book seems most suitable for those who experience loneliness and have difficulty fitting in.

★★★  *Autobiography of a Schizophrenic Girl: An Astonishing Memoir of Reality Lost and Regained* (1994) by Marguerite Sechehaye. New York: NAL/Dutton.

A reprint of a classic account of a young girl's schizophrenia compiled from case materials by her therapist Marguerite Sechehaye. The book has been republished several times under different titles and with different author names. Told in the young patient's own words, Renee describes bizarre perceptual experiences and feelings of unreality that started at age 5. Similar to the protagonist in *I Never Promised You a Rose Garden*, Renee is brought back to reality with the aid of a caring therapist, whom Renee called Mama. Not as tight a narrative as *Rose Garden*, but still a good description of the thought disorder characteristic of childhood schizophrenia and of a skilled therapist's treatment.

★★★  *The Quiet Room: A Journey out of the Torment of Madness* (1996) by Lori Schiller and Amanda Bennett. New York: Warner.

Expanded from an article in the *Wall Street Journal*, this gripping account of Schiller's descent into schizophrenia and recovery, based on diary notes, is accompanied by interviews with family members and mental health practitioners. The book is particularly strong in demonstrating the effects of Lori's disorder on her friends and family, whose views are presented in the book. A sensitive inside view of a young woman's struggle against hallucinations and delusions.

# ■ FILMS

### Strongly Recommended

★★★★★ *The Soloist* (2008) directed by Joe Wright. PG-13 rating. 117 minutes.

This popular film fared better in our national studies than the book on which it was based (reviewed above). A Los Angeles newspaper columnist discovers a homeless, mentally ill man (Nathaniel, played by Jamie Foxx) with extraordinary musical talent, but they run headlong into the cruel realities of public funding and treatment of chronic mental illness and homelessness. In the end, they overcome the system, create possibilities, and become better people for their friendship. In the end, too, as the film credits indicate, Nathaniel sleeps inside and the columnist continues to write, but 90,000 homeless people sleep on the streets of greater Los Angeles. A touching and realistic tale of paranoid schizophrenia, underfunded public services, and the redemptive power of friendship.

★★★★★ *A Beautiful Mind* (2001) directed by Ron Howard. PG-13 rating. 136 minutes.

Russell Crowe plays the mathematician John Nash, whose work eventually wins a Nobel Prize but whose life is savaged by schizophrenia. His hallucinations and paranoid delusions are remarkably well portrayed. The disorder never takes precedence over Nash as a lovable, albeit limited, human. Treatment is shown positively, although the methods were then primitive and only partly effective. This Academy Award-winning film is hopeful about recovery but does not shy away from showing the terrible pain of Nash and his loving wife. An honest and beautiful film based on the book of the same title.

★★★★ *Birdy* (1985) directed by Alan Parker. R rating. 120 minutes.

A powerful story about friendship and helping others survive the effects of the Vietnam War. One of the veterans suffers from catatonic schizophrenia, probably arising from both life and war experiences. These friends are fighting not only to overcome the ravages of war but also to rise above their lower socioeconomic existence in South Philadelphia. They refuse to abandon each other, and they celebrate their male bonding. This self-help resource was enthusiastically recommended by psychologists in our national studies as well as by movie critics.

★★★★ *Shine* (1996) directed by Scott Hicks. PG-13 rating. 105 minutes.

The true and inspiring story of David Helfgott, an Australian piano prodigy whose brilliant career is interrupted by an unspecified mental illness, probably schizophrenia or bipolar disorder. As a child and then as an adult, he struggles to separate and individuate from his domineering father. The movie is described as glorious, powerful, and extraordinary. It takes you from David's childhood to his adulthood and shows all the joys and sorrows of this brilliant man's complex disorder.

★★★★ *Proof* (2005) directed by John Madden. PG-13 rating. 100 minutes.

A brilliant but schizophrenic mathematician (played by Anthony Hopkins) at the University of Chicago and his adult daughter (Gwyneth Paltrow) grapple with his mental disorder and her fear that she may inherit it. Following her father's death, the daughter deals with a former student of her father who seeks an important mathematical proof among the deceased's papers. The film then concentrates on their relationship and its rupture and eventual resolution. An excellent film for capturing the fears and burdens of family members of those suffering from schizophrenia.

**** *The Fisher King* (1991) directed by Terry Gilliam. R rating. 137 minutes.

A substance-abusing talk-show host finds himself on the outs. His life is dramatically turned around when he meets a man who has been traumatized by witnessing the death of his wife. In what appears to be a psychotic state (or severe posttraumatic stress disorder), this man attempts to rediscover the meaning in life by searching for the Holy Grail. Both men struggle with their own demons, but together they secure the Grail and find healing. The movie is funny and inspiring but at times quite confusing. (Also reviewed in the Posttraumatic Stress Disorder chapter, Chapter 31.)

### Recommended

*** *Benny and Joon* (1994) directed by Jeremiah Chechik. PG rating. 100 minutes.

The predominant themes here are accepting people and their limitations, struggling with mental illness, and learning to let go in a relationship. Benny and Joon is a love story; it reminds us that there is someone in the world for everyone. It reinforces the myth that love will conquer all. The movie creators walk a thin line between comedy and tragedy in their efforts to demonstrate the plight of a woman with schizophrenia. Overall, it emerges as a likable and effective comedy/drama.

*** *Spider* (2002) directed by David Cronenberg. R rating. 98 minutes.

Ralph Fiennes' title character is a man suffering from the disorganized type of schizophrenia. Spider is disoriented, incoherent, and isolated; he rarely speaks, so we can only guess or project his internal experience, as the opening credits suggest with its images of Rorschach inkblots. This dark but psychological movie received a tepid rating from mental health professionals; other films probably offer more on the topic. But *Spider* offers a compelling portrait of the symptoms of disorganized schizophrenia and the inconclusive fates of many of those suffering from it.

### Not Recommended

* *Mad Love* (1995) directed by Antonia Bird. PG-13 rating.

## ■ ONLINE SELF-HELP

*** *Get Real* www.ontrack.org.au

This free online self-help program is designed for people who are concerned about the reality and clarity of their thinking. The program contains a quiz where users can compare their level of unusual thinking with that of others. The program consists of three modules presenting information about schizophrenia, addressing realistic possibilities to odd experiences, and deciding if professional help is recommended. The program contains video clips and interactive elements where users identify their own thoughts and experiences. In addition, users identify and create plans to increase their activity and positive life experiences.

## ■ INTERNET RESOURCES

### General Websites

★★★★★ *Schizophrenia.com* www.schizophrenia.com

This long-time website offers a wide range of in-depth information about schizophrenia, including personal stories, research, and discussion areas. Unfortunately, articles appear to lack author attribution, references, or even dates of publication, so it's difficult to tell how up to date or accurate the information is. The list of Early Schizophrenia Diagnosis and Treatment Centers is unique.

★★★★ *Schizophrenia* psychcentral.com/disorders/schizophrenia

This condition center from Psych Central offers a wide range of resources and information about schizophrenia, including its symptoms, causes, treatments, updated news and research, and an online support group.

### Psychoeducational Materials

★★★★ *Schizophrenia* www.nimh.nih.gov/health/topics/schizophrenia

The National Institute of Mental Health has a well-written government informational section on its website about schizophrenia, including information about the latest NIMH-backed discoveries in research.

★★★★ *The Experience of Schizophrenia* www.chovil.ca

Ian Chovil is a person with schizophrenia who has taken the time to gather an eclectic set of charts, graphs, and fact pages about many aspects of schizophrenia, including outcomes, prevalence, and medication compliance. It's a good-sized site with a lot of information on it, but sadly it hasn't been updated in many years.

★★★★ *Schizophrenia* www.mentalhealth.com/dis/p20-ps01.html

This condition center from Internet Mental Health covers a breadth of topics associated with schizophrenia, focusing a lot of attention on research findings and links to medication guidelines, consensus treatment guidelines, and the like. It may be a bit much for the ordinary layperson to digest, and it apparently hasn't been updated in years.

**★★★★**  *Schizophrenia: A Handbook for Families* www.athealth.com/Consumer/disorders/schizophreniahandbook.html

A simple but effective guide for families who are grappling with schizophrenia in their family for the first time. Answers questions most newly diagnosed people might have as well.

**★★★★**  *The Center of Reintegration* www.reintegration.com

A good resource from a social rehabilitation perspective with material on clubhouses, independent living, and family issues.

**★★★★**  *Understanding Schizophrenia* www.mind.org.uk/help/diagnoses_and_conditions/schizophrenia

The U.K. charity Mind has a wonderful website devoted to mental disorders, and their section on schizophrenia is a great overview to this disorder. Simple, straightforward, and relatively brief, this is a great start for friends or family members who have just learned of someone with a schizophrenia diagnosis.

**★★★**  *Center for Psychiatric Rehabilitation at Boston University* www.bu.edu/cpr

A useful website for people in recovery. Check out the section about workplace accommodations for psychiatric disabilities: www.bu.edu/cpr/reasaccom/index.html

**★★**  *Schizophrenia* www.cmellc.com/topics/schiz.html

A few articles about negative symptoms in schizophrenia, adolescent psychosis, and medications and quality of life with schizophrenia.

## ▮ SUPPORT GROUPS

**Brain and Behavioral Research Fund**

Phone: 516-829-0091
www.narsad.org

**National Alliance for the Mentally Ill (NAMI)**

Phone: 800-950-NAMI or 703-524-7600
www.nami.org
Support, information, conferences, and referrals; NAMI considers schizophrenia to be a brain disease.

**National Mental Health Association (NMHA)**

Phone: 1-800-273-TALK
www.nmha.org

**National Mental Health Consumers' Self-Help Clearinghouse**

Phone: 800-553-4539 or 215-751-1810
www.mhselfhelp.org

**National Schizophrenia Foundation**

Phone: 517-485-7168
www.NSFoundation.org

**Recovery Inc.**

Phone: 312-337-5661
www.recovery-inc.com

# CHAPTER 34

# SELF-MANAGEMENT AND SELF-ENHANCEMENT

Starting with the earliest human writings, self-help has advanced strategies to promote adaptation, to achieve life goals, and to manage undesirable behaviors. Some self-help writers suggest avoiding negative people; some preach trust in God; some teach positive thinking; and some advocate perceiving reality as accurately as possible.

In a way, all self-help resources are about self-improvement. But in this chapter, we critically consider a multitude of self-help books and Internet resources devoted to self-management and self-enhancement (Box 34.1). This is admittedly a broad topic—indeed, so broad and inclusive that we purposely excluded films and autobiographies because they number in the hundreds. In this edition, we have dedicated a new chapter just to the many self-help resources devoted to happiness (Chapter 25).

## ■ SELF-HELP BOOKS

### Strongly Recommended

★★★★★ *Get Out of Your Mind and Into Your Life* (2005) by Steven C. Hayes and Spencer Smith. Oakland, CA: New Harbinger.

The self-help book introduces and applies Acceptance and Commitment Therapy (ACT). Trying to change conditions that are not reasonably or predictably likely to change is defeating and sidetracks us from enjoying life. This principle takes the reader through the process of first defining and understanding the concepts involved in ACT and then focusing on several common problems, such as avoidance and thinking. Avoidance takes energy and doesn't change anything; thinking preoccupies the individual with trying to force a change within when acceptance would allow energy and focus for healthier values. The recommended exercises here are useful; the material is organized so that an individual can use it independently or in concert with formal treatment.

★★★★★ *The Last Lecture* (2008) by Randy Pausch and Jeffry Zaslow. New York: Hyperion.

This moving story is told by the first author, who at the time of writing had advanced pancreatic cancer and was living his remaining months with what was most important to

## BOX 34.1
## RECOMMENDATION HIGHLIGHTS

**SELF-HELP BOOKS**

■ On the success—and limitations—of changing behavior:

★★★★★ *What You Can Change and What You Can't* by Martin Seligman

■ On improving life functioning and self-esteem:

★★★★★ *Get Out of Your Mind and Into Your Life* (2005) by Steven C. Hayes and Spencer Smith

★★★★★ *The 7 Habits of Highly Effective People* by Steven Covey

★★★★ *Ten Days to Self-Esteem* by David Burns

■ On the stages of change and what to do when:

★★★★ *Changing for Good* by James Prochaska et al.

■ On a cognitive approach to self-management:

★★★★ *A New Guide to Rational Living* by Albert Ellis and Robert Harper

★★★★ *Feel the Fear and Do It Anyway* by Susan Jeffers

★★★★ *What to Say When You Talk to Yourself* by Shad Helmstetter

■ On optimizing natural healing and bodily functioning:

★★★★ *Spontaneous Healing* by Andrew Weil

■ On learning to respond to life with ease:

★★★★ *Don't Sweat the Small Stuff . . . and It's All Small Stuff* by Richard Carlson

■ On conquering procrastination:

★★★★ *Overcoming Procrastination* by Albert Ellis and William Knaus

■ On women's self-enhancement and not blaming mothers:

★★★★ *Don't Blame Mother* by Paula Caplan

**INTERNET RESOURCES**

■ On cultivating self-management:

★★★★★ *Psych Central* psychcentral.com

★★★★ *Selfhelp Magazine* www.selfhelpmagazine.com

★★★★ *Psychology Today* www.psychologytoday.com/basics/self-help

★★★★ *Pick the Brain* www.pickthebrain.com

him. An invitation to deliver a lecture at Carnegie Mellon was not how his wife wanted to spend their remaining time, but the author was drawn to telling his story and imparting his final words or "last lecture." His lecture was given from the context of fulfilling childhood dreams, but he realized the most important thing is how people live their lives today. More inspiration than practical self-help, but riveting.

★★★★★ *The 7 Habits of Highly Effective People* (1989) by Steven Covey. New York: Simon & Schuster.

Covey's bestselling and influential book provides an in-depth examination of how people's perspectives and values determine how competently they perform in their business and personal lives. Covey argues that to be quality leaders in an organization, people must first become quality-oriented, identifying the underlying principles that are important in their lives and evaluating whether they are living up to those standards. Covey lists seven basic habits that are fundamental to anyone's efforts to become quality-oriented: (1) Be proactive instead of reactive; (2) Begin with the end in mind; (3) Put first things first; (4) Think win/win; (5) Seek first to understand, then to be understood; (6) Synergize; and (7) Sharpen the saw (renewal). This 5-star resource is a breath of fresh air among the superficial quick-fix books that populate the checkout counters across the nation. Covey's choices of personal, family, educational, and professional examples to illustrate the habits of highly effective people are excellent. Critics, however, said that no research has been conducted to confirm that these actually are the seven core habits of competent individuals.

★★★★★ *What You Can Change and What You Can't* (1993) by Martin Seligman. Connecticut: Fawcett.

Seligman, a leading authority on depression and optimism, also wrote this 5-star self-help resource. This book provides a wealth of scientific thought and scholarly opinions about the effects of biology, genetics, heredity, environment, and self-motivation on how we think and change. There are certainly limits on what we can change, but Seligman repeatedly reminds us that there is much we can do within those boundaries to influence our quality of life. In several chapters, Seligman gives his own evaluation of treatments for various disorders (e.g., anxiety, anger, depression). This book is written at a higher level than most self-help manuals but will be very informative for the interested general public.

★★★★ *Feel the Fear and Do It Anyway* (1987, reprinted 1996) by Susan Jeffers. Connecticut: Fawcett.

This book applies a cognitive approach, much of it based on Ellis's rational-emotive therapy, to coping with fear. Jeffers believes that most inaction, whether it involves changing jobs, breaking off a relationship, or starting a relationship, stems from the fear of not being able to handle whatever comes along. She says that fear never completely goes away. Fear should be a sign to us that we are being challenged, and we should confront the fear by taking reasonable risks. Jeffers does a good job of showing how faulty thinking is the source of most people's unreasonable fears, and she gives valuable advice about how to modify such irrational thinking.

★★★★ *Changing for Good* (1995) by James O. Prochaska, John C. Norcross, and Carlo C. DiClemente. New York: Avon.

The authors bring their 20 years of federally funded research and 50 years of collective knowledge to bear on behavior change. The book is organized around the stages of change: precontemplation, contemplation, preparation, action, and maintenance. This scientific approach to self-change helps identify the stage of change for a particular problem and then reviews the common obstacles, best change methods, and interpersonal support for that particular stage. One of the few self-change books to be based on and backed by scientific research, this 4-star resource will be helpful to laypersons who wish to understand the stages of change and valuable to the professionals working with them. (In the interest of full disclosure, *Changing for Good* was co-written by one of the co-authors of *Self-Help That Works*.)

★★★★   *Ten Days to Self-Esteem* (1999) by David D. Burns. New York: Harper Collins.

Psychiatrist Burns is the author of the bestselling *Feeling Good: The New Mood Therapy.* This book is a valuable resource for developing self-esteem and discovering the secrets of joy in daily life. In a clear and practical fashion, Burns offers 10 steps to self-esteem: the pride of happiness; you feel the way you think and you can change the way you feel; how to break out of a bad mood; the acceptance paradox; getting down to the root causes; how to improve self-esteem; the perfectionist's script for self-defeat; a prescription for procrastination; and practice, practice, and practice. This self-help book is filled with logs, charts, and step-by-step guides to enhance self-esteem.

★★★★   *A New Guide to Rational Living* (1975) by Albert Ellis and Robert Harper. Englewood Cliffs, NJ: Prentice-Hall.

This cognitive approach to self-enhancement is co-written by Albert Ellis, a well-known psychologist and prolific author of self-help books. His rational-emotive therapy states that people develop psychological problems because they use irrational beliefs to interpret what happens to them and their world. In this view, people disturb themselves by thinking in self-defeating, illogical, and unrealistic ways. According to Ellis and Harper, years of lengthy psychotherapy are not needed to attack the root of emotional problems. They believe that rational-emotive therapy can quickly help people learn how to detect their irrational thinking, overcome the influence of the past, erase dire fears of failure, conquer anxiety, and acquire self-discipline. The book is filled with conversations between irrational thinkers and therapists and the subsequent interchanges that led to successful living. This valued 4-star book is widely known (evaluated by 238 psychologists) and came close to making a 5-star rating. The book's enthusiasts say that Ellis's approach is very effective in motivating people to restructure their thinking and rid themselves of irrational beliefs. The 1970s examples are now dated, but the content is classic.

★★★★   *Spontaneous Healing: How to Discover and Enhance Your Body's Natural Ability to Maintain and Heal Itself* (1995) by Andrew Weil. New York: Knopf.

This author and physician describes the mechanisms of the body's healing system; simply put, the body can heal itself because it has a healing system. Weil delineates the ways an individual can optimize the functioning of his or her own system and incorporate alternative medicines and treatments to enhance the healing system. Using clear and concise language, this bestseller explains how the healing system operates and provides information on how foods, environments, and lifestyles can maintain well-being. Included is an 8-week program that can help the body's natural healing powers. Weil cleverly combines current Western medical practice with alternative treatments (e.g., acupuncture, biofeedback, guided imagery, and herbal medicine). For the general public interested in the study of the internal healing system, this book provides a wealth of knowledge.

★★★★   *What to Say When You Talk to Yourself* (1986) by Shad Helmstetter. Scottsdale, AZ: Fine.

The author examines the literature on success and finds some missing ingredients: permanent solutions, knowledge of mind–brain functions, and word-for-word directions for programming the unconscious mind. Helmstetter concludes that the only solution that includes all three ingredients is self-talk and goes on to outline five levels of self-talk, the highest being the level of universal affirmation. The author spells out the self-talk strategies of silent self-talk, self-speak, self-conversation, self-write, tape-talk, and creating self-talk tapes. Favorably evaluated but not particularly well known, this book presents some helpful strategies for coping with stressful circumstances, especially for negative thinkers and people low in motivation. Helmstetter spells out what to say to yourself to improve your life instead of just being a cheerleader like so many motivational self-help authors. Critics contend that the material about the nonconscious mind is fuzzy.

**** *Don't Sweat the Small Stuff... and It's All Small Stuff* (1997) by Richard Carlson. New York: Hyperion.

A small bestselling book about simple ways to keep the little things from taking over your life. Carlson argues that when you learn the habit of responding to life with more ease, problems that seem insurmountable will begin to seem more manageable, and even the biggies won't throw you off track as much as they once did. The book consists of 100 strategies, covered in a single page each, to replace old habits of reaction with new habits of perspective. Many of the strategies apply not only to isolated events but also to many of life's most difficult challenges. For teens and adults who wish to live life more reflectively and fully.

**** *Overcoming Procrastination* (1977) by Albert Ellis and William Knaus. New York: Institute for Rational Living.

Subtitled *How to Think and Act Rationally in Spite of Life's Inevitable Hassles*, the book applies rational-emotive therapy to the task of combating procrastination. Ellis and Knaus begin by explaining what procrastination means and then turn to its main causes—self-downing, low frustration tolerance, and hostility. They recommend a cognitive approach to overcoming procrastination and outline the basic ideas of Ellis's rational-emotive therapy. The last chapter includes a psychotherapy transcript of a psychologist and procrastinator and shows how rational-emotive therapy helped the client. *Overcoming Procrastination* just barely received a 4-star rating, but it presents a creative, practical approach to solving procrastination.

**** *Don't Blame Mother: Mending the Mother–Daughter Relationship* (1989) by Paula Caplan. New York: Harper & Row.

The thesis here is that society and psychology have shortchanged mothers, blaming them far too often and too much for their children's problems. Caplan argues that daughters are taught to criticize the work of mothering and to make their mothers the scapegoats. Caplan believes that myths of idealization give rise to impossible expectations and set mothers up for failure. However, mothers and daughters can move beyond these troublesome stereotypes and negative perceptions and gain a new appreciation for each other and their relationship. She gives advice on identifying conflicting messages and myths that weaken the mother–daughter bond. Caplan also underscores the value of women sharing experiences with other women as a means of personal change and self-improvement. Just making the 4-star rating, this book rejects the notion especially popular among those with a codependency perspective that blaming one's mother is a means of psychological growth. *Don't Blame Mother* is a much-needed antidote. This is an excellent self-help book on mother–daughter relationships, especially how to improve them in the adult years.

**Recommended**

★★★ *Opening Up: The Healing Power of Expressing Emotions* (1997) by James W. Pennebaker. New York: Guilford.

Opening up one's emotions is not "just getting feelings off one's chest" but a research-based means of releasing pain and restoring health. Psychologist Pennebaker explains various strategies for opening up, including his own extensive research on expressive writing. Case studies demonstrate the hidden price of silence and the reciprocal interaction of mind and body. An excellent resource for professionals and a useful self-help book. *Opening Up* would have received a 4- or 5-star rating had it been read by more experts in our national studies.

★★★ *Self-Directed Behavior: Self-Modification for Personal Adjustment* (2002) by David L. Watson and Roland G. Tharp. Belmont, CA: Wadsworth.

This book is, at once, a popular textbook and a valuable self-help resource. The authors take the behavioral position that all behavior is learned, practiced, and rewarded. Many behaviors are learned without awareness in childhood, but as adults, we can still acquire the skills necessary to function positively. The book teaches new actions, coping methods, and problem-solving skills. The book can be used by the general public but is probably optimally used under the guidance of a mental health professional. *Self-Directed Behavior* was very favorably evaluated in our studies; in fact, it would have received a rating of 4 stars if it had been read by more professionals.

★★★ *Drive: The Surprising Truth About What Motivates Us* (2011) by Daniel H. Pink. New York: Riverhead.

This book on motivation is motivating largely because it recounts interesting experiments from early research and recent work on the topic. The author differentiates the various types of motivation and heralds intrinsic motivation as standing equally with biological and reward/punishment motivation. Autonomy, mastery, and purpose are explained as the three critical elements of success. Chapters are written with a twist of humor but with sound observations, such as "why the carrot and the stick don't work," seven business thinkers who get it, and 20 conversation starters that keep you thinking.

★★★ *Emotional Intelligence* (1994, reprinted 1997) by Daniel Goleman. New York: Bantam.

This bestselling book reviews the importance of social and emotional competencies (e.g., self-awareness, self-discipline, and empathy) that can determine the quality of life. A *New York Times* reporter and social psychologist, Goleman gives equal weight to one's emotional quotient (EQ) and intelligence quotient (IQ). Goleman discusses how to understand and bolster emotional intelligence, which can be nurtured throughout life. Heavy on science reporting at times, this book has a more scholarly flair than most but appeals widely to educated laypersons. The book is written about EQ and has little "how to." Frequently rated in our national studies, it almost made the 4-star listing.

★★★ *The 60-Second Shrink* (1997) by Arnold A. Lazarus and Clifford N. Lazarus. San Luis Obispo, CA: Impact.

The internationally known psychologist Arnold Lazarus and his son distill 100 complex mental health topics into a back-pocket reference book for those who desire to cope more effectively with life's stressors. Depending on need, this book lends itself to time-efficient selective reading. It is a technically eclectic, scientifically based, problem-solving self-help book, usable by professionals and laypersons alike. Topics traverse the mental health landscape: healthy thinking, action steps, relationship building, effective communication, handling emotions, stress reduction, weight management, and choosing various psychotherapies, for example. This valuable 3-star resource just missed making the 4-star category.

★★★ *Staying Rational in an Irrational World* (1991) by Michael Bernard. New York: Carol.

This book applies cognitive therapy to a number of different life domains—love, dating, sex, work, children, parents, women's issues, homosexuality, and death and dying. The basic theme of rational-emotive therapy is that to cope effectively, we need to replace irrational thinking with rational thinking. The book includes many examples in which individuals learn to talk to themselves more effectively and think in more rational ways. Two final chapters include an interview with Ellis about rational-emotive therapy and a long list of Ellis's books, tapes, and talks. The book is now, however, quite dated.

★★★ *Positive Addiction* (1985) by William Glasser. New York: HarperCollins.

William Glasser became famous in the 1960s and 1970s for founding a school of therapy known as reality therapy—a results-oriented treatment designed to help people cope with their immediate environment. In *Positive Addiction*, Glasser turns from psychotherapy to the problems virtually all of us have in developing our potential. Glasser argues that every person can overcome self-imposed weaknesses by engaging in positive addictions or activities, such as running and meditation, that help people to lose their consciousness. Glasser says that when people do this, they "spin free" and almost mystically arrive at new strategies for coping with life. By contrast, negative addictions are escapes from the pain of striving for things people want but doubt they can accomplish, such as career or athletic achievements. This 3-star resource contains ideas much more popular in the 1970s than today. *Positive Addiction* was written in 1976, and frequent references to well-known people of that time— Jimmy the Greek and Tim Galloway (*Inner Tennis*), for example—seriously date the book. Critics also say that in places the book regresses into mystical explanations.

★★★ *You Can Heal Your Life* (2009) by Louise Hay. Carlsbad, CA: Hay House.

This messages here are inspiration, energy, worth, and a can-do attitude. Even though the chapter titles are simple—What is the problem? Where did it come from? Is it true? What do we do now?—the answers are not. The author's answer to "Is the problem true" is "yes if you believe it and no if you don't." She, of course, is speaking about one's own value of self, thoughts and feelings about self, and early markers for those patterns. After a series of these self-reflective questions, the author tells her own story with an authentic message with which many will identify. Hay's critics complain that she relies excessively on autobiographical and quasi-mystical sources, largely ignoring the scientific evidence.

★★★   *Talking to Yourself: Learning the Language of Self-Affirmation* (revised ed., 1991)
by Pamela Butler. New York: Harper Collins.

Butler says that each of us experiences an inner self as a distinct person speaking to us. Each of us engages this inner person in a dialogue throughout our lives as we make decisions, set goals, and feel satisfied or dejected. Butler believes that our self-esteem is strongly influenced by such inner speech. In this book, Butler provides a number of specific strategies for changing our self-talk and making it work better. Topics include anger and self-talk, sex and self-talk, and gender and self-talk. A 3-star resource, this book provides good advice about how to improve the way we talk to ourselves.

★★★   *Life's Little Instruction Book* (1991) by H. Jackson Brown. Nashville, TN:
Rutledge Hill.

This book of instruction was inspired by a father's love for his son and his desire to guide his son along life's many paths. The instructions start with (1) compliment people every day and ends with (511) call your mother. A compact booklet filled with 511 one-liners that might prove helpful for an adolescent or adult looking for good advice or recalling consensual wisdom of the ages.

★★★   *Life Strategies: Doing What Works, Doing What Matters* (1999) by Phillip C.
McGraw. New York: Hyperion.

In this bestseller, Dr. Phil offers Ten Laws of Life: (1) You Either Get It or You Don't; (2) You Create Your Own Experience; (3) People Do What Works; (4) You Cannot Change What You Do Not Acknowledge; (5) Life Rewards Action; (6) There Is No Reality, Only Perception; (7) Life Is Managed, It Is Not Cured; (8) We Teach People How To Treat Us; (9) There Is Power In Forgiveness; and (10) You Have To Name It Before You Can Claim It. He also discusses A Guided Tour of Your Life, The Seven-Step Strategy, and Finding Your Formula. Experts in our national studies found it to be a valuable but oversimplified recipe for self-enhancement.

★★★   *All I Really Need to Know I Learned in Kindergarten: Uncommon Thought on
Common Things* (1998) by Robert Fulghum. New York: Ivy.

This bestselling author's approach is to find wonderment and meaning in the smallest of life's experiences. Presented with wit and humor, Fulghum's book is one that you can read a little, put down, pick up later, and put down again without worrying about the plot resolution or missing the overarching theme. His simple rules of life gleaned from early years in kindergarten—for example, share, play fair, clean up, say you're sorry, don't take things that aren't yours—are extrapolated into adult life. When you go out into the world, it is best to hold hands and stick together. The author concludes the book with, "Peace is not something you wish for; it's something you make, something you do, something you are, and something you give away." A valued, insightful, but perhaps overly simplistic book that received a 3-star evaluation in one of our national studies.

★★★   *Change Your Brain, Change Your Body* (2010) by Daniel G. Amen. New York:
Three Rivers.

Amen holds that careful and deliberate attention to the brain will solve many psychological and physical problems. The author offers ten principles to change your brain. This sounds ominous, but the explanation includes nutrition, exercise, willpower, hormones, and other components of healthy living. New thinking skills, making changes in interpretation, and other suggestions promote the notion that we can affect our psychological well-being through cognitive and biological means.

★★★  *Change Your Thoughts—Change Your Life* (2009) by Wayne W. Dyer. Carlsbad, CA: Hay House.

The ancient teachings of Tao are compiled in this self-help resource by bestselling author Wayne Dyer, who spent a year studying Tao. He states that his life and how he lives it were changed forever by these teaching of the importance of joy, love, nature, and peacefulness. Eighty-one Tao verses make up a single chapter. For example, the first teaching is "Living the mystery." The modern-day application would suggest enjoying and accepting the mystery of the Tao, not reacting with judgment or interpretation. It also would mean resisting the need to name and label all of our experiences. Each chapter takes the same format of application to contemporary events, such as our penchant for generating anxieties and judgments.

★★★  *Excuses Be Gone* (2011) by Wayne W. Dyer. Carlsbad, CA: Hay House.

The ingrained belief that one cannot change our thinking habits (because we are too old or because of heredity) is challenged with specific questions and principles. Seven steps lead individuals through the process for changing the most intractable patterns: Is the excuse true? Where did it come from? What is the payoff for the excuse? What would my life look like without the excuse? Can I access cooperation in shedding the habit? How do I reinforce the new way of being? Case examples help the reader walk through the excuse-rejecting paradigm.

★★★  *Chicken Soup for the Soul* (1991) by Jack Canfield and Mark Victor Hansen. Deerfield Beach, FL: Health Communications.

These bestselling authors have selected a number of stories to illuminate life paths and motivate us to pursue a fulfilling lifestyle. Each of the 101 stories is designed to open our minds and hearts to our potential. The stories are presented in seven sections: love, learning to love yourself, parenting, learning, living your dream, overcoming obstacles, and eclectic wisdom. This 3-star, entertaining book can be read at length or for 15 minutes and will leave one feeling inspired.

★★★  *Simple Abundance: A Day Book of Comfort and Job* (1995) by Sarah Ban Breathnach. New York: Warner.

*Simple Abundance* is a book of 366 evocative essays—one for every day of the year—written for women who wish to live by their own lights. The author describes the order of the essays as progressing from creating a manageable lifestyle to living in a state of grace. The essays are intended to help readers take stock in their life and find out what is working and what is not. This book is written mainly for women but is a treasure of wisdom for all.

★★★  *Who Moved My Cheese?* (1998) by Spencer Johnson. New York: Putnam.

This brief and bestselling book offers a metaphor on the difficulties of change, organizational and individual. Four characters (Sniff, Scurry, Hem, and Haw) live in a maze and look for cheese to nourish them. The four characters are intended to represent the simple and the complex parts of ourselves. Cheese is the metaphor for what you want in life (job, money, relationship, etc.). The maze is where you go to find what you want. The characters are faced with unexpected changes and challenges. This small but metaphoric book provides indirect advice on effectively moving through the maze of life.

★★★ *I'm OK, You're OK* (1967, reissued 1996) by Thomas Harris. New York: Avon.

This 1960s bestseller presents transactional analysis as a means to self-management. Transactional analysis maintains that people are responsible for their behavior in the present and future regardless of what has happened to them in the past. It distinguishes three main components in each person's makeup: the Parent, the Adult, and the Child. The Parent involves the many don'ts and a few do's of our early years. The Child represents spontaneous emotion. Both Parent and Child have to be kept in proper relation to the Adult, whose function is maintaining reality through decision making. The goal of transactional analysis is strengthening and emancipating the Adult from the Parent and the Child. Harris identifies four life positions that underlie people's behavior: (1) I'm not OK—You're OK, the anxious dependency of an insecure person; (2) I'm not OK—You're not OK, a position of despair or giving up; (3) I'm OK—You're not OK, the criminal position; and (4) I'm OK—You're OK, the response of mature adults who are at peace with themselves and others. Harris believes that most people unconsciously operate from the I'm not OK—You're OK position. The 3-star book is extremely well known and was immensely successful when it was published. Despite its popularity, it received a tepid evaluation from mental health professionals. Some experts still praise the book, but all agree that its popularity has waned dramatically.

★★★ *Unlimited Power* (1986) by Anthony Robbins. New York: Fawcett Columbine.

This book is based on the neurolinguistic programming claim that people can be programmed in ways that will make them highly successful. Robbins advocates a host of mental, emotional, and physiological programming strategies, especially developing confidence in the mind's power. To convince people of their mental powers, Robbins recommends firewalking, a barefoot jaunt over hot coals. A basic step in becoming successful, he says, is selecting a successful person as a model and learning about how the person became successful and how he or she conducts his or her life. Essential to Robbins's "ultimate success formula" are clarity of desired goals, energy, passion, persistence of action, effective communication skills, and altruistic motives. Mental health professionals said this book has some good points mixed with some bad points. A good point is that Robbins' enthusiastic approach can motivate people to develop their talents and to select a competent model to emulate. The bad points are that research has generally not supported the postulates of neurolinguistic programming, that the mind-over-matter firewalking demonstrations are misleading (scientists have demonstrated that people can walk across hot coals without getting burned if they move quickly enough), and that Robbins' claims that just about anyone can develop "unlimited power" are unsubstantiated and outlandish.

### Diamond in the Rough

♦ *Success Is a Choice: Ten Steps to Overachieving in Business and Life* (1997) by Rick Pitino with Bill Reynolds. New York: Broadway.

Pitino, a respected basketball coach, believes that success is not about shortcuts. He maintains the need to aim higher and work harder than ever before in order to succeed. His 10-step program teaches people to build self-esteem, identify goals, and use a positive attitude to accomplish what they want. Being better comes in many forms. Pitino speaks to the importance of communication, role models, and turning adversity into advantage. Before working on this 10-step program, a plan of attack needs to be formalized. Pitino ends his book: "Your real journey begins now." This book, a Diamond in the Rough because of its favorable but infrequent ratings, is for adolescents and adults who are willing to study and work hard to achieve their goals.

### Not Recommended

- ★★ *Your Maximum Mind* (1987) by Herbert Benson. New York: Random House.
- ★★ *Self-Matters: Creating Your Life From the Inside Out* (2001) by Phillip C. McGraw. New York: Simon and Schuster.
- ★★ *Tough Times Never Last, but Tough People Do!* (1983) by Robert Schuller. New York: Bantam.
- ★★ *Magnificent Mind at Any Age* (2009) by Daniel G. Amen. New York: Three Rivers Press.
- ★★ *Your Erroneous Zones* (1976) by Wayne Dyer. New York: Funk & Wagnalls.
- ★ *Be a Better You* (2007) by Joel Osteen. New York: Running Press Book Publishers.
- ★ *Just Who Will You Be?* (2008) by Maria Shriver. New York: Hyperion
- ★ *How to Stop Worrying and Start Living* (1944) by Dale Carnegie. New York: Simon & Schuster.
- ★ *One Month to Live* (2008) by Kerry Shook and Chris Shook. Colorado Springs, CO: WaterBrook Press.
- ★ *Steps to the Top* (1985) by Zig Ziglar. Gretna, LA: Pelican.
- ★ *Awaken the Giant Within* (1991) by Anthony Robbins. New York: Fireside.

### Strongly Not Recommended

- † *Stop Whining, Start Living* (2008) by Laura Schlessinger. New York: HarperCollins.
- † *The Secret* (2006) by Rhonda Byrne. Hillsboro, OR: Beyond Words.

## ■ INTERNET RESOURCES

When it comes to self-help resources online, there's a lot of self-promotional material from people looking to sell CDs, DVDs, e-books, and self-published books. It's more than a little challenging to separate the wheat from the chaff, especially if you're just searching Google. However, there are few self-help websites that are based in empirical evidence or emphasize psychological science. Therefore, we focus on self-help sites that are based more in science or at least acknowledge the importance of research evidence on their sites.

The general topic of psychotherapy is also covered in this section because although it isn't a self-help resource per se, general websites on psychotherapy offer a great deal of information that can also be useful in your own recovery, or to make the decision to seek professional help.

**General Websites**

★★★★★ *Psychological Self-Help* psychologicalselfhelp.org

This is an online book published by the late psychologist Clay Tucker-Ladd, PhD. While lengthy and at times wordy, it nonetheless offers a wealth of grounded self-help techniques that are well referenced in psychological research. The book encompasses 15 chapters and can be read online, searched, or downloaded chapter by chapter (so you can focus on one topic you're interested in), or the whole book can be downloaded. Topics cover the breadth of human experience, from stress, anxiety, depression, anger, and fears, to morality, values, dating, love and marriage, and everything in between. The entire resource is free, and although no longer updated, it remains a valuable and valid guide.

★★★★★ *Psych Central* psychcentral.com

This commercial website, online since 1995, offers mental health and psychology information, much of it in the form of self-help resources to empower patients and concerned family members or friends to find the help they need. The breadth of topics covered is extensive and includes not only mental health disorders but also more general psychological concerns dealing with relationships, parenting, childhood development, stress management, and more. Articles are usually written by professionals, and library, news, and reference articles carry citations or sources. Updated daily with research and news briefs, as well as dozens of blogs.

★★★★ *Selfhelp Magazine* www.selfhelpmagazine.com

This Internet resource offers thousands of articles, many written by professionals and referenced, on a wide variety of self-help topics ranging from aging, anxiety, depression, and dreams, to sex, stress, psychotherapy, and women, among many others.

★★★★ *Psychology Today* www.psychologytoday.com/basics/self-help

Although much of *Psychology Today*'s content could be helpful to an individual seeking out self-help resources, this section devoted to Self-Help is a nice collection of articles on self-reinvention, setting and achieving goals, becoming more mindful and happy, and improving your relationships, among other topics. It also features more than a half-dozen blogs on the same topic, although some appear to be rarely updated.

★★★ *LifeHacker* lifehacker.com

This popular mainstream blog features helpful tips on everything from improving your computer's performance to helping you get to sleep faster. Its lack of focus is reflected in an eclectic design that is apparently meant to ensure you don't find the information you're looking for (hint: scroll down to the bottom of the page to find the site's categories).

★★★ *Emotional Intelligence* eqi.org/eitoc.htm

This website from Steven Hein, PhD, offers a lot of information about this topic in dozens of articles.

★★★★    *Pick the Brain* www.pickthebrain.com

A handy self-improvement website that focuses on topics valuable to people in any stage of their life, from motivation and personal productivity, to psychology and self-education.

★★★★    *Mayo Clinic* www.mayoclinic.com/health/HealthyLivingIndex/ HealthyLivingIndex

Each of these Healthy Living centers has many articles suitable for education. You can select materials on sexually transmitted diseases (use the Diseases & Conditions A-Z list as well), sexual dysfunctions, infertility, or other topics. They are all well written and quite thorough.

★★★★    *Emotional Intelligence Test* www.queendom.com/tests/access_page/index. htm?idRegTest=3037

This lengthy but accurate, well-designed interactive test with multiple choices provides results that help a person better understand his or her level of emotional intelligence.

★★★    *Guide to Psychology* www.guidetopsychology.com

This guide to clinical psychology from Raymond L. Richmond, PhD, covers psychological practice, clinical issues, social issues, personality and identity, and stress management and offers specific self-help techniques and exercises. A large and interesting site, but articles lack dates.

### Psychotherapy

★★★★    *Psychotherapy* psychcentral.com/psychotherapy

This overview of psychotherapy from Psych Central offers both information about common psychological therapies and engaging blog entries about the psychotherapy process.

★★★    *Beck Institute* www.beckinstitute.org

The venerable Beck Institute offers an informative website that provides basic information about cognitive-behavioral therapy (CBT). It also offers information about CBT training and workshops it offers.

**See also** Happiness (Chapter 25).

■ CHAPTER 35

# SEXUALITY

Although we can talk about sex with each other, we often don't. Sex in America still comes cloaked in mystery, and as a nation we are neither knowledgeable about sex nor comfortable talking about it. While many people manage to develop a mature sexuality, even those who do handle sex maturely have periods of vulnerability and confusion. Many people wonder and worry about their sexual attractiveness, their ability to satisfy their sexual partner, and whether they will be able to experience their sexual fantasies. Our worries are fueled by media stereotypes of sexual potency and superhuman sexual exploits. Sexual concerns also prevail because of our inability to communicate about sex directly with one another.

In this chapter, we critically examine self-help books and websites devoted to sexuality in its many manifestations (Box 35.1). We omit films on sexuality since there would literally be thousands of possibilities.

## ■ SELF-HELP BOOKS

**Strongly Recommended**

★★★★★  *Becoming Orgasmic: A Sexual Growth Program for Women* (revised ed., 1988) by Julia Heiman and Joseph LoPiccolo. New York: Prentice-Hall.

This excellent resource offers women permission, encouragement, and behavioral exercises to become more sexually fulfilled. The book leads women through a personal sex history to understand their own sexual feelings and experiences, includes self-touch exercises for learning how to relax and gain sexual pleasure, and presents advice for sharing pleasures with a partner. The topics include looking at oneself, vaginal exercises, erotic literature, fantasizing, using a vibrator, and intercourse. Attention is also given to potentially related conditions such as menstrual cycling, pregnancy, and general gynecological health. *Becoming Orgasmic* is a popular and effective self-help resource for preorgasmic women.

★★★★  *For Each Other: Sharing Sexual Intimacy* (1982) by Lonnie Barbach. Garden City, NY: Anchor.

*For Each Other*, like its precursor, *For Yourself*, is written for and about women who wish to improve their sexual fulfillment. This book focuses on sexual concerns within the sexual

## BOX 35.1
## RECOMMENDATION HIGHLIGHTS

### SELF-HELP BOOKS

■ For improving sexual relationships and communication:

**** *For Each Other* by Lonnie Barbach

**** *Rekindling Desire* by Barry and Emily McCarthy

**** *Illustrated Manual of Sexual Therapy* by Helen Kaplan

*** *Sexual Awareness* by Barry McCarthy and Emily McCarthy

■ For men:

*** *The New Male Sexuality* by Bernie Zilbergeld

♦ *Male Sexual Awareness* by Barry McCarthy and Emily McCarthy

■ For women:

***** *Becoming Orgasmic* by Julia Heiman and Joseph LoPiccolo

*** *For Yourself* by Lonnie Barbach

*** *For Women Only* by Jennifer Berman and Laura Berman

### INTERNET RESOURCES

■ For excellent information on topics pertaining to sexuality:

***** *Kinsey Confidential* kinseyconfidential.org

***** *Sex, Etc.* www.sxetc.org

***** *Sexual Health* health.howstuffworks.com/sexual-health

relationship with a partner. Basic aspects of sexuality and the cultural context in which women learn about sexuality are reviewed; orgasmic problems and recommendations are described; and general level of sexual interest is discussed. Various exercises that the author has found effective in her practice are suggested for each problem area. The subject of female sexuality is approached candidly and in support of the women for whom this book is written.

**** *Illustrated Manual of Sexual Therapy* (1987) by Helen Kaplan. New York: Brunner/Mazel.

Kaplan espouses an integrated approach to improved sexual functioning through couples therapy and use of specific sexual exercises, which are outlined in this book. She does not incorporate psychotherapeutic strategies with the sexual exercises; however, an important context for the sexual aspects is an understanding of how the activities promote the relationship. Strategies are offered to counteract the difficulty some couples may have actually trying out these therapeutic exercises. Specific techniques are targeted for specific dysfunctions—for example, orgasmic problems and premature ejaculation. The narrative is accompanied by numerous drawings that show couples or therapists using this manual to carry out the exercises. A favorite of sex therapists for training, it is too academic and graphic for most couples.

**★★★★** *Rekindling Desire* (2003) by Barry and Emily McCarthy. New York: Brunner-Routledge.

Inhibited sexual desire afflicts 35% of couples together for more than two years. The cause of inhibited desire is often that couples were sexual at the beginning of the relationship but drifted into infrequent sexual experiences with each other. Once that pattern is set, it is difficult to break. The authors have developed a treatment plan that includes nurturing anticipation, enhancing intimacy, and offering nondemanding touch. The program is designed to be conducted with a psychotherapist. Suggestions are made for getting past the reticence of working with a couples or sex therapist. An excellent self-help resource about a challenge for many long-term couples.

### Recommended

**★★★** *The New Male Sexuality: A Guide to Sexual Fulfillment* (1999 revised ed.) by Bernie Zilbergeld. New York: Bantam.

*The New Male Sexuality* presents a number of methods to improve male sexuality and disposes of a number of myths that have victimized men. One common myth Zilbergeld attacks is that all that men really want is sexual intercourse. When men want something else, such as love and sensitivity, they are inhibited by the stereotype. Many men have gotten themselves into a losing situation by adopting superhuman standards for measuring their genitals, sexual performance, and satisfaction. Zilbergeld's book is not a sex guide full of gimmicks or gymnastics; it does not try to impose a lifestyle on anyone; and it does not accept the premise that all men are the same. Instead, Zilbergeld explains the most common sex problems, the importance of touching, how to relax in sexual situations, how to be sensitive to your sexual partner, and sex for older adults and disabled individuals. The newer edition also covers erectile dysfunction medications and recent medical discoveries. A series of exercises—verbal and physical—encourages men to understand their sexual feelings and preferences. Although rated by only 18 of our experts, its rating was one of the highest obtained in our national studies. Far above the crowd of how-to sex books, it is a literate, thoughtful analysis of male sexuality that can enhance the sexual lives of many men.

**★★★** *For Women Only* (2001) by Jennifer Berman and Laura Berman. New York: Henry Holt.

Two sisters, one a urologist and one a psychologist, joined forces to write this book and to forge a new direction in medical and psychological practice for women with sexual dysfunction. Their view is that women have been treated in masculine terms for sexual concerns that have been typically been labeled emotional, relational, or due to fatigue from child rearing. They consider women's sexual concerns to have both medical and emotional roots. The Bermans arm women with the information they need about their bodies to provide them with a full spectrum of treatment options. They demasculinize sexual concerns with different categorization: hypoactive sexual desire, sexual arousal disorder, orgasmic disorder, and sexual pain. They further suggest that many of the same health problems that apply to men's sexual concerns are applicable to women, including high blood pressure, diabetes, and high cholesterol. This book is comfortable to read; it offers a holistic and positive viewpoint on women's sexual concerns.

★★★　*The New Joy of Sex* (1991) by Alex Comfort. New York: Crown.

This book is the revision and expansion of *The Joy of Sex,* published in 1973, which sold more than 8 million copies. It was a manual of uninhibited sexual techniques with boldly explicit illustrations. *The New Joy of Sex* continues the uninhibited approach to sexual expression and explicit illustrations that characterized its predecessor, along with new material on AIDS and sexually transmitted diseases (including a stern lecture on the importance of using condoms). Topics such as sexual experimentation, fantasy activity, locations for sexual experiences, and serious topics such as AIDS, frigidity, erectile dysfunction, and others are discussed. This well-known book (rated by 173 psychologists) is educational and can help people rid themselves of sexual anxieties and achieve greater sexual satisfaction. However, it's definitely more for liberal thinkers than conservative ones.

★★★　*Making Love: A Man's Guide* (1984) by Barry White. New York: Signet.

As its title implies, this book is designed to help men improve their lovemaking and sexual skills. *Making Love* advises men about what they can give women, the role of appearance in sex, women's sexual hang-ups, how to make women feel like making love, foreplay, intercourse, women's sexual anatomy, what to do after having sex, how to keep sex exciting, and what to do about sexual problems. This is mainly a how-to book with specific recommendations to help men become better lovers. Although the book provides some good suggestions in places, too often it regresses to pop-psych descriptions of sexuality. The consensus of the mental health professionals is that Zilbergeld's *New Male Sexuality* is a much better choice.

★★★　*Making Love: A Woman's Guide* (1983) by Judith Davis. New York: Signet.

Davis points out that at one time the woman was supposed to be the passive partner in making love, always waiting for the man to make the move and following his lead after that. She says that the rules have changed in today's world—that women can now take a more active, assertive role and can enjoy sex. This sexual how-to guide for women provides explicit instructions on how to become better lovers and attract men sexually. Some mental health professionals consider this to be a helpful guide for women who are too inhibited sexually, but others complain that the book contains too many sensationalist comments. In either case, it has become quite dated.

★★★　*Sexual Awareness: Enhancing Sexual Pleasure* (1993, revised 2002) by Barry
　　　　McCarthy and Emily McCarthy. New York: Carroll & Graf.

This book is written for couples who want to improve their sexual communication and functioning. Basic skills are presented within major book sections about increasing comfort and pleasure, enhancing sexual satisfaction, and overcoming sexual problems. The authors integrate the research findings of Masters and Johnson with strategies consistent with social-learning theory. A variety of exercises are proposed for each presenting concern. The exercises are meant to provide choices and alternatives to couples as well as ways they can explore, learn, and improve their sexual relationships. *Sexual Awareness* received very favorable ratings but relatively few evaluations, thus resulting in a 3-star designation.

★★★    *The Soul of Sex* (1998) by Thomas Moore. New York: HarperCollins

The author describes *The Soul of Sex* as a book about sexuality that contains no information on biology, anatomy, or health and little about techniques and relationships. He says that the human soul is a composite of meanings: emotions, dreams, wishes, fears, a past, culture, thought, and fantasy. Therefore, he directs the reader to the soul of sex, meaning not the physical only, but a more spiritual and complex integration of all aspects of self. This book is written in a poetic, narrative form that draws on Greek mythology, English literature, and other sources that allow symbolic representation in expressing meaning and interpretation. The author is a psychotherapist who intends this book to be read by psychotherapists, clients, and others who are drawn to his broader perspective of sex.

★★★    *What Really Happens in Bed* (1989) by Steven Carter and Julia Sokol
        Coopersmith. New York: M. Evans.

This self-help book presents a broad-based approach to improving sexual competence and relationships for both women and men. It tries to cut through sexual expectations often based on myths and romantic fantasies. The authors interviewed several hundred women and men to provide a profile of what people are really doing and saying in their sexual lives. Section I, "Talking About Sex," explodes a number of sexual myths and unrealistic expectations and explores why people are reluctant to talk about what really happens in bed. Section II, "Sexual Life Patterns and Stages," examines the single life and temporary sexual solutions, sexual fantasies and experimentation, marriage and sex, extramarital affairs, and what people can learn to improve their sex lives. The book includes a number of excerpts from the interviews the authors conducted. On the positive side, it cuts through many sexual myths and includes extensive material about communication and relationships. On the negative side, critics faulted the authors for the unscientific nature of their interviews.

★★★    *For Yourself: The Fulfillment of Female Sexuality* (1975) by Lonnie Barbach. New
        York: Doubleday.

Barbach addresses the worries of nonorgasmic women and tells them how they can achieve orgasm. Barbach attacks the negative cultural belief that women should not enjoy sex. She presents a number of exercises that will enable women to achieve orgasm, and each exercise is accompanied by an explanation of why it can be effective as well as pitfalls to avoid. The book also includes many examples from the sexual lives of women the author has counseled in her sex therapy groups. This book was very positively rated, but by relatively few experts in our studies. The book's enthusiasts said that Barbach sensitively and clearly explains to women how they can achieve a more satisfactory sex life. The book is becoming dated, however.

★★★    *The New Love and Sex After 60* (2002) by Robert N. Butler and Myrna I. Lewis.
        New York: Ballantine.

In the 2020s, 20% of the population in the United States will be over the age of 65. This book is written for those who are now over 60 years, the early Baby Boomers. Increasingly people in this age category are seeking professional help in order to maintain a satisfying sexual component to their relationships. The content of the book does, in fact, discuss some of the factors that are of more concern for older individuals than for the general population. The narrative is respectful, sensitive, and yet candid and straightforward. Normal physical changes are discussed along with common medical problems and how they affect sexuality. Erectile dysfunction is readily treated today and suggestions are made for ongoing care. An interesting take on an increasing challenge.

### Diamonds in the Rough

♦ *The Family Book About Sexuality* (1989) by Mary S. Calderone and Eric W. Johnson. New York: Harper & Row.

The authors cite the proliferation of misinformation and myth about sexuality as an important reason to write this book. They want people to understand the sexual part of their lives, the role sex plays in all lives, and the new information learned from research about sexuality. The topic is comprehensively discussed—from the human sexual response, reproduction, and family planning, to the family and its role, people with special problems, and sexually transmitted diseases. The second half of the book is what the authors call the "Concise A–Z Encyclopedia," which defines and describes approximately 100 words related to sexuality. This combination of encyclopedia and information guide makes this book unique and useful for those who want to understand the subject more accurately. This book is included as a Diamond in the Rough because of its high rating, albeit by a small number of respondents.

♦ *Male Sexual Awareness* (1998) by Barry McCarthy and Emily McCarthy. New York: Carroll & Graf.

A comprehensive approach to male sexuality within the wider context of developmental, relational, and physical dimensions of men's lives. General sexual functioning is addressed in topics such as performance expectations, sexual capacity, loss of sexual desire, masturbation, sexual trauma, contraception, and sexual fantasies. Medical and health issues are described in the sections on vasectomy, ejaculatory problems, STDs, HIV, and other difficult subjects. Relational aspects of sexuality span divorce and widow status, marriage, extramarital experience, sexual orientation, and working through new roles in the "gender wars." *Male Sexual Awareness* was accorded a Diamond in the Rough classification because it was not read by the requisite number of mental health professionals but was rated highly by those who did read it.

### Strongly Not Recommended

† *Dr. Ruth's Guide to Good Sex* (1983, reissued 1994) by Ruth Westheimer. New York: Warner.
† *Dr. Ruth's Guide to Erotic and Sensuous Pleasures* (1991) by Ruth Westheimer and Louis Lieberman. New York: Warner.

## ■ INTERNET RESOURCES

### General Websites

★★★★★ *Sexual Health* health.howstuffworks.com/sexual-health

This resource from the folks at the Discovery Channel and How Stuff Works is a pretty interesting and comprehensive library of sexual health information, including large sections on the male and female reproductive systems, contraception, sexual dysfunction, and human sexuality. A nice, well-rounded resource with a balance of engaging and scientific articles.

***** *Kinsey Confidential* kinseyconfidential.org

You can't go wrong when the website about sexuality is from the renowned Kinsey Institute. Although a bit confusing to navigate, the website is still a valuable resource. Click on the "Resources" tab to explore their health library and find answers to your sex questions, or subscribe to their podcast.

**** *Society for Human Sexuality* www.sexuality.org

This is a helpful website that has frank talk about positive sexuality in categories such as "Learning More," including Erotic Massage, Erotic Talk, Sex Toys, and G-Spot Play. Other topics and areas may too intense for some, such as BDSM (Bondage, Discipline, Slave, Master), Hosting Erotic Events, and Polyamory. Although apparently regularly updated, pages don't reflect any current dates.

**** *Sexuality Information and Education Council of the United States* www.siecus.org

This nonprofit organization is dedicated to positive sexuality, and does so through education, advocacy, and other activities. Primarily meant for educators and policymakers, you can find information about abstinence-only programs, adolescent and teen sexuality and pregnancy, sexually transmitted diseases, sexual orientation, and reproductive health topics here.

*** *iVillage: Love & Sex* www.ivillage.com/love-sex

This section of the commercial site iVillage offers a wealth of consumer-oriented and magazine-friendly articles on sexuality. The articles are often pretty shallow and glossy and are in an annoying slideshow format, but the topics are diverse and may appeal to a wider audience.

*** *SexEd Library* www.sexedlibrary.org

The SexEd Library is a surprising resource offering hundreds of lesson plans (meant for educators, but helpful to anyone) culled from throughout the Internet on topics such as human development, relationships, personal skills, sexual behavior, sexual health, society and culture.

*** *Health & Sex Center* www.webmd.com/sex-relationships

This resource from WebMD covers all aspects of human sexuality and health, but also delves into topics of relationships. There's a lot of content here, but it's under a confusing index page that doesn't make it easy to navigate or find what you're looking for.

### Psychoeducational Materials

***** *Go Ask Alice! Sexuality* goaskalice.columbia.edu/sexual-and-reproductive-health

Go Ask Alice is a free service of the Health Services at Columbia University, and its section on sexuality is a great way to explore and learn about a wide range of sexuality topics, including kissing, masturbation, orgasms, sex toys, fetishes, erotica, and alternative sexuality. It's done in a straightforward advice-column manner, so the answers aren't always in depth, but they are right on target.

★★★★★ *Coalition for Positive Sexuality* www.positive.org

This positive sexuality website offers an online tour (called "Just Say Yes") with about 12 topics of special concern to sexually active teens (should I have sex?, safe sex, birth control, homosexuality, pregnancy, and STDs) presented without preaching or moralizing. The website, oriented toward teens and young adults, also discusses topics such as HIV, abortion, sin, and abstinence.

### Sexually Transmitted Diseases (STDs)
★★★★★ *American Social Health Association* www.ashastd.org

The nonprofit American Social Health Association for the past century has been one of the "go to" resources for information about sexually transmitted diseases and infections, so it's not surprising that their website offers a wealth of information on these topics. Everything you'd ever want to know about STDs and STIs can be found here, including myths about them. The organization also offers an extensive library of articles on sexual health.

★★★★ *AVERT: AIDS Education and Research Trust* www.avert.org/teens.htm

The "Teens' Pages" section from this U.K. charity organization is a set of linked pages with good-quality information for teenagers on puberty, AIDS, HIV, homosexuality, relationships, and so on.

### Birth Control
★★★★★ *Birth Control* www.plannedparenthood.org/health-topics/birth-control-4211.htm

A comprehensive review from the nonprofit Planned Parenthood organization of every birth control method, including the latest methods. Each article is detailed and descriptive, offering a photo and videos of the method under discussion.

★★★★★ *Emergency Contraception* ec.princeton.edu

For those who need to prevent pregnancy after unprotected sexual intercourse, all the emergency contraception methods are discussed here.

★★★★★ *New York Online Access to Health* www.noah-health.org/en/pregnancy/contraception

The New York Online Access to Health (NOAH) website offers a large directory of Internet resources on hundreds of health and related topics, including family planning and birth control. Includes information about what is family planning, contraceptive methods, barrier methods, hormonal methods, and natural methods of birth control. Results are not New York-specific.

★★★ *Ann Rose's Ultimate Birth Control Links* www.ultimatebirthcontrol.com

A good resource that covers many birth control methods. It hasn't been updated in years, however, and some links are broken, while some newer methods aren't discussed at all.

### Aging and Sexuality
★★★★  *Better Senior Sex* www.helpguide.org/elder/sexuality_aging.htm

This guide from the nonprofit HelpGuide offers a single article about tips for enjoying a healthy sex life as you age. The article offers its usual array of helpful if not always simple tips for seniors to improve their sex life.

### For Teens
★★★★★  *Info for Teens* www.plannedparenthood.org/info-for-teens

This site from the nonprofit Planned Parenthood can be a source of solid social and medical information for curious teens. Answers are also offered in video format, something that is often more appealing to younger people.

★★★★★  *Sex, Etc.* www.sxetc.org

This excellent website from Rutgers University is oriented to teens and offers a frank discussion of sexuality, relationship, birth control, love, and more. It is constantly updated and is designed for adolescents, presenting information in a way that isn't boring or staid.

★★★  *Puberty 101* www.puberty101.com

Using a Q&A format, this site from J. Geoff Malta, MA, offers clear and complete answers to difficult and important questions. Apparently the site is no longer updated, but it is still a helpful resource.

## ■ SUPPORT GROUPS

This is a heterogeneous listing of groups. Some are support groups, some are consciousness-raising groups, and some are political activism groups.

### Augustine Fellowship, Sex and Love Addicts Anonymous

Phone: 781-255-8825
www.slaafws.org
A 12-step fellowship based on AA for those who desire to stop living out a pattern of sex addiction, obsessive-compulsive sexual behavior, or emotional attachment.

### CDC Info

Phone: 1-800-232–4636
www.cdc.gov/cdc-info

### Codependents of Sex Addicts (COSA)

Phone: 866-899-COSA
www.cosa-recovery.org

A 12-step program for those in relationships with people who have compulsive sexual behavior.

## Family Pride Coalition

Phone: 617-502-8700
www.familyequality.org

## GLBT National Help Center

Phone: 888-843-4564
www.glbtnationalhelpcenter.org

## NARAL (National Abortion and Reproductive Rights Action League)

Phone: 202-973-3000
www.naral.org

## National Advocacy Coalition on Youth and Sexual Orientation

Phone: 202-319-7596
www.nyacyouth.org

## National Association of People with AIDS

Phone: 866-846-9366
www.napwa.org

## NOW (National Organization for Women)

Phone: 202-628-8669
www.now.org/index.html

## Planned Parenthood

Phone: 212-541-7800
www.plannedparenthood.org

## Society for the Scientific Study of Sexuality

Phone: 610-443-3100
www.sexscience.org

**See also** Love and Intimacy (Chapter 27), Marriage (Chapter 28), and Teenagers and Parenting (Chapter 40).

# CHAPTER 36

# SPIRITUAL AND EXISTENTIAL CONCERNS

M ental health professionals and self-help authors have recently rediscovered the centrality of spirituality, but understanding spirituality is not new. More than 400 years ago, St. Ignatius compiled his notes into the *Spiritual Exercises,* a practical guide on discernment and living a life of spirituality.

Spirituality is far more than formalized religion. It's not simply a prayer we say on the Sabbath, but a prayerful life we live with our family and neighbors. Spirituality is inevitably concerned with the elusive search for the purpose and meaning of life. These existential concerns focus on life's ultimate questions—freedom, existence, meaning, authenticity, and death. Life, existence itself, is in a constant state of becoming; to live in the moment is a dynamic process of person and environment experiencing life.

In this chapter, we critically consider self-help books and Internet resources devoted to an assortment of spiritual and existential concerns. But first our recommendation highlights (Box 36.1).

## ■ SELF-HELP BOOKS

### Strongly Recommended

★★★★★ *Man's Search for Meaning* (revised ed., 1998) by Viktor Frankl. New York: Pocket.

Viktor Frankl, a professor of psychiatry at the University of Vienna, pursues an existential approach to self-fulfillment. After Frankl survived the German concentration camp at Auschwitz, he founded a school of psychotherapy called *logotherapy*, which maintains that the desire to find a meaning in life is the primary human motive. Frankl's mother, father, brother, and wife died in the concentration camps. Frankl emphasizes each person's uniqueness and the finiteness of life. He thinks that examining the finiteness of existence and the certainty of death adds meaning to life. Frankl believes that the three most distinct human qualities are spirituality, freedom, and responsibility. Spirituality, in his system, does not have a religious underpinning; rather, it refers to a human being's uniqueness—to spirit, philosophy, and mind. Freedom is the freedom to make decisions, but with the freedom to make decisions comes responsibility for those decisions. Logotherapists often ask clients

## BOX 36.1
## RECOMMENDATION HIGHLIGHTS

### SELF-HELP BOOKS

■ For an existential approach to life and self-fulfillment:

★★★★★ *Man's Search for Meaning* by Viktor Frankl

■ For rediscovering the joy of everyday life:

★★★★ *Finding Flow* by Mihaly Csikszentmihalyi

■ For a spiritual approach to meaning and self-fulfillment:

★★★★ *The Road Less Traveled* by M. Scott Peck

★★★★ *When All You Ever Wanted Isn't Enough* by Harold Kushner

■ For an inner-healing mind–body approach to self-improvement:

★★★★ *Peace, Love, and Healing* by Bernie Siegel

■ For finding one's way out of psychological pain:

★★★ *The Power of Now* by Eckhart Tolle

■ For prayer and a religious approach to self-fulfillment:

♦ *Sacred Contracts* by Caroline Myss

### INTERNET RESOURCES

■ For information on spirituality:

★★★★★ *Beliefnet* www.beliefnet.com

★★★★ *Spirituality & Practice* www.spiritualityandpractice.com

such questions as why they exist, what they want from life, and what the meaning of their life is. Originally published in 1946, *Man's Search for Meaning* is a 5-star classic that still commands a great deal of respect among mental health professionals. This book challenges readers to think about the meaning of their lives. The reading is rough going at times, but for those who persist and probe Frankl's remarkable insights, the rewards are well worth the effort.

★★★★ *Finding Flow: The Psychology of Engagement with Everyday Life* (1997) by Mihaly Csikszentmihalyi. New York: Basic.

Csikszentmihalyi (pronounced "chik-sent-mee-high-yee") has been investigating "flow" for more than three decades. Flow is the state of deep enjoyment that people feel when they have a sense of mastering something. Supported by a number of research studies, this self-help resource addresses how people can better structure their everyday lives in joyful ways. What we do in our day can largely determine what kind of life we live, and how we emotionally experience what we do is even more important. When in flow, what we feel, what we wish, and what we think are in harmony. This excellent 4-star book offers engaging, research-supported information on creating and discovering flow in everyday life. The quality of life depends on what we do with what we have.

**★★★★** *When All You Ever Wanted Isn't Enough* (1986) by Harold Kushner. New York: Summit.

Harold Kushner, rabbi and author of *When Bad Things Happen to Good People* (evaluated in Chapter 18), here offers a spiritual message of self-fulfillment. Subtitled *The Search for a Life That Matters*, the book maintains that material rewards create almost as many problems as they solve. Kushner believes that sooner or later we come face to face with a big question: What am I supposed to do with my life? We want to be more than just brief biological flashes in the universe that disappear forever. Kushner argues that there is no one big answer to the meaning of life, but that there are answers. And the answers are found in filling our day-to-day existence with meaning, with the love of friends and family, and with striving for integrity, instead of just reaching for the pot of gold. Kushner spends considerable time analyzing the biblical book of Ecclesiastes because it asks us to think about life. Kushner believes, like Ecclesiastes, that life is its own reward.

**★★★★** *Peace, Love, and Healing* (1989) by Bernie Siegel. New York: Harper & Row.

Bernie Siegel, a surgeon and the bestselling author of *Love, Medicine and Miracles,* offers an inner resource for self-healing. Siegel believes that the medical field has ignored the power of self-healing for too long and argues that modern medicine and self-healing are not mutually exclusive. Among the self-healing techniques he recommends are meditation, visualization, relaxation, and developing peace of mind. Siegel describes a number of exceptional patients who used self-healing to improve their physical and mental well-being. Although *Peace, Love, and Healing* received a 4-star rating, it is controversial in the medical field. Some physicians feel that Siegel exaggerates the power of self-healing and that his ideas may keep some people from seeking medical treatment. Siegel's supporters among the mental health professionals said that he has inspired many patients, nurses, medical students, and even some physicians to look at healing in a larger context and to look at illnesses in new ways.

**★★★★** *The Road Less Traveled* (1978) by M. Scott Peck. New York: Simon & Schuster.

This spiritual and psychological book was on bestseller lists for more than 10 years. Psychiatrist Peck begins by stating that life is difficult and that we all suffer pain and disappointment. He counsels us to face up to life's difficulties and not be lazy. Indeed, Peck equates laziness with original sin, going on to say that people's tendency to avoid problems and emotional suffering is the root of many mental disorders. Peck also believes that people are thirsting for integrity in their lives. They are not happy with a country that has "In God We Trust" as a motto and at the same time leads the world in the arms race. To achieve integrity, says Peck, people need to move spirituality into all aspects of their daily lives. Peck speaks of four tools to use in life's journey: delayed gratification, acceptance of responsibility, dedication to the truth, and balance. After a thorough analysis of each, Peck explores the will to use them, which he calls love. Then he analyzes the relationship of growth and religion, which leads him to examine the final step of the road less traveled: grace. By grace, Peck means the whole range of human activities that support the human spirit. This immensely popular 4-star resource has developed a cultlike following, especially among young people. Peck has obviously recognized the need for an integrated, spiritually oriented existence. While many of Peck's ideas are not new, he has succeeded in packaging them in contemporary American language that has enormous appeal.

**Recommended**

★★★ *The Power of Now: A Guide to Spiritual Enlightenment* (1999) by Eckhart Tolle. Novata, CA: New World Library.

Although written in simple language and in a Q&A format, this book takes the reader on a spiritual and religious journey. We are not our mind; we can find our way out of psychological pain when we surrender to the now. Tolle helps us see that our relationships are yet another doorway into spiritual enlightenment if we use them wisely, if we use them to become more conscious and therefore more loving human beings. The result is real communication between self and others looking to be truly present. Drawing on the teachings of religious masters such as Jesus and Buddha, the book is designed to facilitate the spiritual journey through life.

★★★ *Further Along the Road Less Traveled* (2nd ed., 1998) by M. Scott Peck. New York: Touchstone.

Peck, the best-selling author of *The Road Less Traveled* (reviewed above), starts this book with the phrase "Life is complex." He describes the road each person has to travel as a rocky wilderness through which we must carve out our own individual paths. Searching for individual meaning and the center of spirituality is woven throughout this book. The author encourages us to glory in the mystery of life and not to be dismayed. Peck's book is interesting for the self-motivated layperson and the mental health professional. The author applauds the scientific advances of medicine but cautions about the danger of losing the centrality of psychological wisdom and of neglecting our spirituality.

★★★ *Care of the Soul* (1992) by Thomas Moore. New York: HarperCollins.

Moore, a former Catholic monk and now a psychotherapist, makes the case for the loss of the soul as the great malady of the 20th century. The soul is embodied in genuineness and depth and is revealed in attachment, love, and community. This bestselling book is about living a soulful life. Moore repeatedly distinguishes between "spirituality" and "soul." Those interested in the influence of philosophy and religion coupled with a modern view of spirituality and soulfulness will find this book both challenging and enlightening.

★★★ *The Third Jesus: The Christ We Cannot Ignore* (2009) by Deepak Chopra. New York: Three Rivers Press.

Jesus left an unsolved riddle for 2,000 years: Why are His teachings impossible to live by? We struggle with the Golden Rule of "do unto others as you would have others do unto you." Therein lies the conundrum: empathic and authentic caring for others is beyond the capability and perhaps motivation for most people. Chopra proposes that our striving for this state and then falling short of it prevents a higher level of functioning within ourselves and with others. The book is written not from a conventional religious perspective but one of self-awareness and purpose of life. As with all of Chopra's books (including the one reviewed below), it is filled with spiritual guidance on cultivating mind–body wellness.

\*\*\* *The Seven Spiritual Laws of Success: A Practical Guide to the Fulfillment of Your Dreams* (1994) by Deepak Chopra. San Rafael, CA: Amber-Allen.

This book shatters the myth that success is the result of hard work, planning, and driving ambition. Chopra distills the path to a successful and fulfilling life into seven spiritual principles. Essentially, personal understanding and harmony promote fulfilling relationships. The overriding message is that once we understand our true nature and live in harmony with natural law, a sense of well-being, health, enthusiasm, and satisfaction will flow effortlessly. It is for anyone looking for a spiritual and relational take on living a successful life.

\*\*\* *Your Sacred Self* (2001) by Wayne W. Dyer. New York: Quill.

Popular self-help author Dyer concerns himself here with the sacred self, in which the spirit triumphs over the ego. Dyer advances a three-step plan: preparing for the sacred journey; implementing the keys to higher awareness; and transcending our ego identities towards the pursuit of an ego-less world. A book for the person desiring to become closer to his or her spiritual self.

\*\*\* *The Purpose Driven Life* (2002) by Rick Warren. Philadelphia, PA: Running.

The period of 40 days has spiritual meaning in the Bible in that many significant events occurred over that time span. This book offers a 40-day journey to the reader, who is asked to read a chapter containing a spiritual message each day and to think about one's purpose beyond the self, others, and goals for one's own life. The striving to know purpose and God is the promise of this popular religious book.

\*\*\* *Flow: The Psychology of Optimal Experience* (1990) by Mihaly Csikszentmihalyi. New York: Harper Collins.

As outlined above in our review of *Finding Flow,* flow is a state of enjoyable concentration in which a person becomes absorbed while engaging in an activity. We can develop flow by setting challenges for ourselves, by stretching ourselves to the limit, by developing competent coping skills, and by combining life's many experiences into a meaningful pattern. Flow can be found in many different experiences and walks of life. Rock climbers can become so absorbed that they feel at one with the cliff face. Chess masters play in a trancelike state. Artists dab paint on a canvas for hour after hour in a state of immersed concentration. Csikszentmihalyi maintains that people can cultivate flow experiences. This 3-star resource documents that the path to happiness does not lie in mindless hedonism but rather in mindful challenges. It is a serious, thoroughly documented, and well-researched book, but our mental health experts preferred his newer book, *Finding Flow.*

\*\*\* *Illuminata: Thoughts, Prayers, Rites of Passage* (1994) by Marianne Williamson. New York: Random House.

A number 1 bestseller, this book attempts to bring prayer into our daily life. Williamson provides prayers designed to heal our souls, hearts, body, and country. The prayers are designed for people of all ages and traverse the human experience—prayers to release anger, find forgiveness, discover great love, and achieve intimacy. Another section includes rites of passage, ceremonies for the signal events in our lives, blessing of the newborn, coming of age, marriage, and death. The author concludes that through prayer, we find what we cannot find elsewhere: a peace that is not of this world. A book for the young and old who find prayer an essential part of their lives. Barely made the Recommended list in this category, probably because of its overemphasis on prayer to the neglect of other means toward spiritual growth.

**Diamonds in the Rough**

- ◆ *Sacred Contracts: Awakening Your Divine Potential* (2001) by Caroline Myss. New York: Harmony.

This book addresses the question, Why are we here? Myss guides readers in finding their divine potential by various methods, one being to pray for guidance and another being to identify the underlying patterns of thought that color memories. The author writes that, after many thousands of readings, "I came to the conclusion that an organizing principle even greater than the interplay of the chakras is shaping the energy within each of us—and shaping our lives as it does so." Highly but rarely rated in our national studies, this book that will probably appeal to the spiritually inclined.

- ◆ *The American Paradox: Spiritual Hunger in an Age of Plenty* (2000) by David G. Myers. New Haven, CT: Yale University.

Psychologist Myers reflects on the paradox that although the United States is the richest country in the world, so many of our citizens are growing less content with their lives. He notes that since the 1960s, divorce rates have doubled, teen suicide has tripled, violent crime has quadrupled, and prison populations have quintupled. He believes the explanations for the paradox are individualism, the commercial culture, and normalizing of the worst of human behavior. Myers argues for a return to moral education; he states that "Religion is good for us." Less a self-help book than a cultural critique, it is nonetheless rich in reflective observations and cogent criticisms of individual and societal responsibility. A book for all to read and ponder.

**Not Recommended**

- ★★ *Become a Better You* (2007) by Joel Osteen. Philadelphia: Running Press.
- ★★ *The Celestine Prophecy: An Adventure* (1993) by James Redfield. New York: Warner.
- ★ *The Be (Happy) Attitudes* (1985) by Robert Schuller. Waco, TX: Word.
- ★ *It's Your Time* (2009) by Joel Osteen. New York: Free Press.

**Strongly Not Recommended**

- † *The Way of the Wizard: Twenty Spiritual Lessons in Creating the Life You Want* (1995) by Deepak Chopra. New York: Harmony.
- † *Clear Body, Clear Mind* (1990) by L. Ron Hubbard. Los Angeles: Bridge.
- † *Dianetics: The Modern Science of Mental Health* (1950, reissued 2002) by L. Ron Hubbard. Los Angeles: The Church of Scientology of California.
- † *Scientology: The Fundamentals of Thought* (1988) by L. Ron Hubbard. Los Angeles: Bridge.

## ■ INTERNET RESOURCES

★★★★★ *Beliefnet* www.beliefnet.com

This commercial site is designed to help people find their spiritual path in life, no matter what that path may be. Sections include "Faiths & Prayer," "Inspiration," "Love & Family," and more. It also hosts dozens of blogs on all things dealing with religion and spirituality, with an active community that nicely supplements all of the informational materials on the site. You could spend hours exploring topics of spirituality here.

★★★★ *Spirituality & Practice* www.spiritualityandpractice.com

This website serves as a "resource for spiritual journeys" by offering a wealth of articles and related resources on spirituality. The Spirituality Practices component allows people to practice specific exercises related to a specific spiritual or life concern. It's an interesting site that also has a lot of book, audio, film, and DVD recommendations.

★★★★ *The Question of God* www.pbs.org/wgbh/questionofgod

This 4-hour miniseries produced by PBS in 2004 remains an interesting and thought-provoking look at life's central questions: What is happiness? How do we find meaning and purpose in our lives? How do we reconcile conflicting claims of love and sexuality? How do we cope with the problem of suffering and the inevitability of death? You can also search for the documentary's name on YouTube to watch the original documentary online.

★★★ *Spirituality & Health* www.spiritualityhealth.com

The website of the print magazine of the same name offers a nice set of articles and resources, including practices (similar to above), and an active blog. You'll also find select articles from the magazine republished on the website at no charge.

★★★ *Psychology of Religion Pages* psychwww.com/psyrelig/index.htm

This website acts as a nice, broad general introduction to the psychology of religion, discussing how religious beliefs affect people's lives. This may be useful for people who are struggling with social and psychological (but not spiritual) aspects of their faith. While there are dozens of articles here, they are undated, which makes it difficult to determine how current the site is.

★★★ *The Existential Primer* www.tameri.com/csw/exist

If you want an in-depth overview of the subject of existentialism, this is a good place to start. Written for people with or without a background in philosophy, the primer is surprisingly detailed and lengthy; click on "Introduction" to get started. If you want something simpler, try: www.allaboutphilosophy.org/existentialism.htm

★★★ *John Templeton Foundation* www.templeton.org

After having made millions in international investing, Sir John Templeton set up a foundation to fund research on the question of human purpose, such as evolution, forgiveness, optimism, spirituality, free will, and health.

# CHAPTER 37

# STRESS MANAGEMENT AND RELAXATION

We live in a stress-filled world. According to the American Psychological Association's Stress in America survey, 22% of us report extreme stress. According to the American Academy of Family Physicians, almost two thirds of all office visits to family doctors are for stress-related symptoms. Stress is also a major contributor to coronary disease, accidental injuries, cirrhosis of the liver, and suicide—four of the leading causes of death in the United States. Several of the bestselling drugs in the United States are antianxiety medications (alprazolam [Xanax], lorazepam [Ativan], clonazepam [Klonopin]).

There are many ways to cope effectively with stress, just as there are many ways to cope ineffectively with stress. Converging research suggests that the most effective approach is to employ a variety of strategies instead of relying on a single method. For example, people who have had heart attacks are usually advised to change more than one aspect of their lives. The advice might go something like this: Practice relaxation; learn mindfulness; confide in good friends; quit smoking; exercise several times a week; reduce your anger; and enjoy life and vacations on a regular basis. One of these alone may not turn the tide against stress, but a combination will maximize success.

In this chapter, we evaluate self-help books and websites that deal directly with relaxation and stress management (Box 37.1). Many other self-help resources reviewed in this book also provide advice on coping with stress; consult in particular Chapters 6 (Anger), 7 (Anxiety Disorders), 8 (Assertiveness), 17 (Communication and People Skills), and 34 (Self-Management). In addition, for stress stemming from a particular source, such as career problems, the death of a loved one, or divorce, the recommended resources in those chapters may prove helpful.

## ■ SELF-HELP BOOKS

### Strongly Recommended

★★★★★   *The Relaxation and Stress Reduction Workbook* (2008, 6th ed.) by Martha Davis, Elizabeth Robbins Eshelman, and Matthew McKay. Oakland, CA: New Harbinger.

This 5-star workbook proves a valuable resource to learn how to relax and manage stress in a number of environments. Now in its sixth edition with almost a million copies sold, the book provides straightforward instructions on a variety of stress-management techniques.

---

**BOX 37.1**
**RECOMMENDATION HIGHLIGHTS**

---

**SELF-HELP BOOKS**

- For comprehensive strategies to reduce stress:
  - ★★★★★ *The Relaxation and Stress Reduction Workbook* by Martha Davis et al.
  - ★★★★★ *The Stress and Relaxation Handbook* by James Madders
- For learning meditation and mindfulness:
  - ★★★★★ *Wherever You Go, There You Are* by Jon Kabat-Zinn
  - ★★★★★ *Beginning Mindfulness* by Andrew Weiss
  - ★★★★ *A Mindfulness-Based Stress Reduction Workbook* by Bob Stahl and Elisha Goldstein
- For a mind–body, behavioral medicine approach to combating stress:
  - ★★★★★ *The Wellness Book* by Herbert Benson and Eileen M. Stuart
  - ★★★★ *Why Zebras Don't Get Ulcers* by Robert M. Sapolsky
- For learning relaxation:
  - ★★★★★ *The Relaxation Response* by Herbert Benson
  - ★★★★ *Beyond the Relaxation Response* by Herbert Benson
  - ★★★ *Learn to Relax* by C. Eugene Walker
- For daily spiritually oriented meditations:
  - ★★★★ *Each Day a New Beginning* by the Hazelden Foundation
  - ★★★ *Touchstones* by the Hazelden Foundation

**INTERNET RESOURCES**

- For guidance on stress management:
  - ★★★★★ *Stress Management* stress.about.com
  - ★★★★ *Stress Management Resources* www.mindtools.com/smpage.html

---

The first two chapters are designed to examine personal reactions to stress and understand the dynamics of stress and stressors. The book is easy to read and is accompanied by pictures of proper body positioning for specific techniques. The highest-rated book in this category and among the most favorably evaluated in all our national studies, it is useful for laypersons who want to reduce stress and for professionals as a reference when assigning homework for their clients. A very popular and apparently effective resource.

★★★★★ *Wherever You Go, There You Are* (1994) by Jon Kabat-Zinn. New York: Hyperion.

This book is a practical guide to meditation—in essence, about mindfulness/wakefulness. Psychologist Kabat-Zinn repeatedly reminds us that the moment is all we really have to work with. To allow ourselves to be in the moment, we have to pause in our experience long enough to let the present moment sink in. Meditation is simply about being oneself and knowing something about who that is. Mindfulness has to do, above all, with attention and awareness. This engaging 5-star resource will be of value to both the beginning and the experienced practitioner of meditation.

★★★★★ *The Stress and Relaxation Handbook: A Practical Guide to Self-Help Techniques* (1997) by James Madders. London, UK: Vermilion.

Fully illustrated throughout, this handbook contains relaxation exercises to apply throughout the day. There are techniques designed for children, adults, and older adults. Some exercises are designed to manage the pain and tension found in such problems as migraine, insomnia, digestive disorders, and the menstrual cycle. The message here is that we all suffer emotionally and physically from the strain of life, but our reactions can be modified and controlled by training. Chapters begin with factual information about stress, our reactions to stress, and how we can reduce the negative effect of stress with proper relaxation techniques. Rated favorably in our national studies, earning a 5-star rating.

★★★★★ *The Relaxation Response* (1975) by Herbert Benson. New York: Morrow.

This early and influential book presents a particular strategy for reducing stress—learning how to relax. Benson believes that the relaxation response can improve a person's ability to cope with stressful circumstances and can reduce the likelihood of a number of diseases, especially heart attacks and strokes. He points out that the relaxation response has been used for centuries in the context of religious teachings, usually in Eastern cultures, where it often is practiced on a daily basis. Benson developed a simple method of attaining the relaxation response and explains how to incorporate it into daily life. The relaxation response consists of four essential elements: (1) locating a quiet context; (2) developing a mental device, such as a word or phrase (e.g., *om*) that is repeated in a precise way over and over again; (3) adopting a passive attitude, which involves letting go of thoughts and distractions; and (4) assuming a comfortable position. Practicing the relaxation response 15 to 20 minutes once or twice a day improves well-being, according to the research. This important 5-star book was published at a time when Americans were skeptical about the spiritual and psychological practices of Eastern cultures. Many mental health professionals recommend Benson's approach to their clients because they have found that it works. The relaxation response is a simple, effective, self-healing technique for reducing stress.

★★★★★ *The Wellness Book: A Comprehensive Guide to Maintaining Health and Treating Stress Related Illness* (1992) by Herbert Benson and Eileen M. Stuart. New York: Fireside.

Co-written by Benson of *The Relaxation Response* fame (reviewed above), this comprehensive guide applies behavioral medicine to life and to treating stress-related diseases. Behavioral medicine combines the talents of mind and body and uses psychological approaches to prevent illness and improve health. This book covers numerous wellness topics, principally the relaxation response, nutrition, exercise, body awareness, cognitive restructuring, stress management, coping, problem solving, and humor. This 5-star book was highly rated by the experts in our national studies as an excellent and practical guide to mind–body interaction, but many advised that people should undertake major lifestyle changes under the supervision of a health-care professional. The book provides sound advice for preventing disease and improving health and is especially good at describing the powerful role of relaxation in reducing the chances of incurring life-threatening diseases.

★★★★★  *Beginning Mindfulness* (2004) by Andrew Weiss. Navato, CA: New World
Library.

Many of the mindfulness books do not begin at the beginning and present the fundamentals on how to sit and walk while practicing mindfulness and meditation. This book
is intended just for that purpose. Written in plain and humorous language, these practical
applications present a 10-week program of mindfulness through body, feelings, thinking,
objects of the mind, and kindness and compassion. This program is useful for stress reduction and pain management but also for finding one's true self. Having its roots in Buddhism
does not require a spiritual or religion stance; in fact, the author emphasizes that his being
Jewish is quite compatible with these practices. A valued self-help resource for those at the
beginning.

★★★★  *Beyond the Relaxation Response* (1984) by Herbert Benson. New York: Times
Books.

This is Herbert Benson's sequel to *The Relaxation Response* (reviewed above). A decade
after Benson coined the term *relaxation response,* he concluded that combining it with
another strategy is even more powerful in combating stress. The other strategy is faith in a
healing power either inside or outside the self. Benson arrived at this conclusion because of
his own clinical studies of Tibetan monks in the Himalayas, which are described in detail
in this book. The healing power can be belief in a certain dogma or a traditional religious
system, or it can be faith in oneself, in the state attained while exercising, or in the relaxation response itself. Benson explains how to harness the power of faith in a number of
different situations—while jogging, walking, swimming, lying in bed, or praying. *Beyond
the Relaxation Response* is a 4-star book that clearly conveys the power of mental strategies
in influencing health and the healing process.

★★★★  *Minding the Body, Mending the Mind* (1987) by Joan Borysenko. New York:
Bantam.

This book focuses on the positive effects of relaxation on the mind and body. The author
discusses how deep relaxation and meditation can shift disease-promoting physiological
mechanisms into a healing mode. The exercises are designed to reduce anxiety and develop
greater control over one's life. The book also serves as a guide for conditioning the mind to
function as a healer and health enhancer. The general public can use this book as a guide to
coping with stress and disease more effectively. For those interested in the mind–body relationship to healing, this will be an informative resource. A solid book and a solid message.

★★★★  *Why Zebras Don't Get Ulcers: A Guide to Stress, Stress-Related Diseases and Coping*
(2004, 3rd ed.) by Robert M. Sapolsky. New York: Freeman.

Drawing on current scientific research, this book is provocative and often amusing as it
looks at the interconnections between emotion and physical well-being. Sapolsky discusses
the interactions between the body and the mind and the ways in which emotions affect
the health of virtually every cell in the body. Stress and our vulnerability to disease are best
understood in the context of the person who is suffering from that disease. Links are made
between stress and increased risk for certain diseases, with specific chapters on the circula-
tory system, energy storage, growth, reproduction, the immune system, depression, and

the aging process. The newest edition features information on addiction, spirituality, and personality disorders; the last chapter describes how to manage stress. For the interested reader or professional working with stressed clients, this is a very informative 4-star book. It is a scientific book for the nonscientist.

**** *Don't Sweat the Small Stuff … and It's All Small Stuff* (1995) by Richard J. Carlson. New York: Hyperion.

Carlson offers 100 meditations designed to help people keep their lives in perspective, giving priority to the important things. The book consists of 100 very brief, themed chapters that provide inspirational advice for individuals and help them understand why they shouldn't worry so much about life's minor irritations. A brief and focused bestseller. (Also reviewed in Chapter 34 on Self-Management and Self-Enhancement.)

**** *Each Day a New Beginning: Daily Meditations for Women* (1982, reissued 1996) by Karen Casey. Minneapolis: Hazelden Foundation.

This book of daily meditations for women follows the same format of *One Day at a Time in Al-Anon* and *A Day at a Time*, the daily meditative books described in Chapter 3 on Addictions. Each page of the book is devoted to one day—from January 1 through December 31—and contains three elements: a beginning quotation, a daily thought or meditation, and an ending self-affirmation. The book is a spiritually oriented approach for women coping with a wide array of stressors, not only addictions. Each day is perceived as a new opportunity for growth and successful coping. *Each Day a New Beginning* is well conceived and presents thought-provoking ideas in a warm, personal tone. The book is especially appealing to women with a spiritual orientation.

**** *A Mindfulness-Based Stress Reduction Workbook* (2010) by Bob Stahl and Elisha Goldstein. Oakland, CA: New Harbinger.

This mindfulness workbook is intended for stress reduction. Topics include transforming fear through love and kindness, interpersonal mindfulness, and health practices regarding nutrition, exercise, and sleep. The program promotes the development of a nonjudgmental stance from which one experiences daily encounters and which in itself relieves anxiety about anticipation of performance and expected outcome. Each chapter includes journaling, mindful exploration, daily activities, scheduling practices, FAQs, and resources. This program also includes CDs that can facilitate its implementation. A well-regarded workbook for mindfulness and beyond.

### Recommended

*** *Learn to Relax* (2001, 3rd ed.) by C. Eugene Walker. New York: Wiley.

This book provides multiple methods for learning how to relax, including cognitive therapy, life structuring, realistic goal setting, relaxation exercises, assertion, nutrition, exercise, communication, friendships, self-hypnosis, and professional help. The book's subtitle—*Proven Techniques for Reducing Stress, Tension, Anxiety, and Promoting Peak Performance*—says it all. Psychologist Walker cleverly covers most of the relaxation territory with a minimum of jargon.

★★★   *Touchstones* (1986, reissued 1996) by the Hazelden Foundation. New York:
        HarperCollins.

This is the male counterpart of *Each Day a New Beginning* (reviewed above). It is a
spiritual approach to coping with stress for men, with each page devoted to a day of the
year—from January 1 through December 31—and containing a quotation, a meditative
commentary, and a self-affirming statement. The breadth of the quotations is extensive,
ranging from comments by former New York Yankees baseball manager Billy Martin to passages from D. H. Lawrence and poems by Emily Dickinson. The meditative thoughts also
are broad, from awareness of one's problems, to letting go, to confession. The meditative
commentary is warm and supportive, and the self-affirmations are motivating. This book
will especially appeal to men with a spiritual orientation who are having difficulty coping
with life's stress.

★★★   *Exuberance: The Passion for Life* (2005) by Kay Redfield Jamison. New York:
        Vintage.

Exuberance, termed the energetic relative of joy, is fully explored for the vital core and
positive role it plays in loving life. Exuberance, joy, happiness, and other positive traits
have suffered "benign neglect" by psychologists in recent years. "Joy widens the view of
the world and expands imaginative thought," states psychologist Jamison, well known for
her autobiographical accounts of bipolar disorder and suicide attempts. Joy is contagious
and dispels tension. The passion for life abounds in many successful folks, such as Teddy
Roosevelt and John Muir. These and other individuals are portrayed as making the choice
to live joyfully and on the side of life that psychologists rarely investigate. Slim on self-help
guidance but heavy on interesting science and fascinating biographies.

★★★   *The Male Stress Syndrome* (1986) by Georgia Witkin-Lanoil. New York: Berkley.

This self-help resource was written by a woman for men and presents strategies for helping men cope with stress. Combining the results of a survey administered to more than
500 men and the women closest to them with examples from her own clinical practice,
Witkin-Lanoil isolates the key stressors common to most men. She also provides suggestions on how to recognize these factors and manage them. Relaxation exercises are among
the suggested strategies for men. Some stress-reduction strategies are tailored to specific
male problems, such as sex therapy for sex-related problems. This 3-star book is becoming
a bit dated but continues to provide a good understanding of male-related stress and ways
to reduce it.

★★★   *Heal Yourself with Qigong* (2009) by Suzanne B. Friedman. Oakland, CA:
        New Harbinger.

Qigong is said to cultivate the vital life-force energy in the body. Its purpose is to engage
a fuller and healthier life. The essential features of Qigong are physical movement or posture, meditation, and positive breathing. This book includes 100 exercises that can be done
in 5 minutes and can be selected from the book's four areas: energy boosters, restoration
of physical vitality, emotion balanced techniques, and practices for calming the spirit. For
those who find mind–body exercises and movement helpful in reducing stress, this book
provides basic and clear instructions on the Qigong method.

**Diamond in the Rough**

- *Inner and Outer Peace Through Meditation* (2007 updated) by Rajinder Singh. San Antonio, TX: Radiance.

The author has codified simple exercises, coupled with spiritual guidance and his own meditation experience, to help people achieve freedom from fear and achieve contentment. In plain and uncomplicated language, Singh explains how peace can be created by meditation and inner reflection. He connects the workings of inner (self) and outer (world) peace, and the Dalai Lama offers the Foreword. The key to genuine world peace is inner peace founded on interpersonal respect and love. To create inner peace, it is necessary to calm the mind; hence the need to meditate. Highly but infrequently rated, thus earning Diamond in the Rough classification. This is a book for those who are already meditating or seeking to learn the art of meditation.

- *Minding the Body Workbook* (2008) by Jason M. Satterfield. New York: Oxford University Press.

This workbook presents a cognitive-behavioral approach to reducing various types of stress. The program is composed of modules that include exercises, questions, and techniques for change. The module themes encompass (1) stress and coping, (2) mood management, (3) social support, and (4) quality of life. The workbook is structured to be implemented in conjunction with a professional or facilitator.

## ■ INTERNET RESOURCES

**Psychoeducational Materials**

**★★★★** *Stress Management* helpguide.org/mental/stress_management_relief_coping. htm

This single-page article from the nonprofit HelpGuide provides information about stress and offers some simple management strategies that include much common wisdom and familiar advice.

**★★★★★** *Stress Management* stress.about.com

This About.com site led by Elizabeth Scott, MS, offers a wealth of information about stress, including its causes and effects, and many articles about stress-management techniques.

**★★★★** *Stress Management* psychcentral.com/stress

This section of Psych Central offers a wealth of information and tips on stress basics, what it does to the body, stress-management strategies and techniques, as well as specific guides to learning deep breathing and imagery exercises to help relieve stress.

**★★★** *The Excedrin Headache Resource Center* www.excedrin.com

Although you cannot avoid the commercial aspects of this site, there are many educational materials on the types, causes, nonmedical treatment, and effects of headaches. Look in the "Headache Center" and "Migraine Center" sections.

**** *Stress Management Resources* www.mindtools.com/smpage.html

This helpful section from the Mind Tools website provides dozens of articles about stress, from understanding and building defenses against it, to helping with stressful people and situations at work. While primarily focused on workplace stress, the articles are general enough to apply to many different aspects of your life.

*** *Basic Guided Relaxation: Advanced Technique* www.dstress.com/articles/ guided_relaxation.html

A detailed guided relaxation exercise that provides a powerful stress-management technique when practiced regularly; by L. John Mason, PhD.

*** *Progressive Muscle Relaxation* www.guidetopsychology.com/pmr.htm

Progressive muscle relaxation is another reliable stress-relief method. This article provides a step-by-step guide on how to do it; by R. Richmond, PhD.

*** *The Systematic Desensitization Procedure* www.guidetopsychology.com/sysden. htm

A very good presentation of the rationale and methods behind systematic desensitization; by R. Richmond, PhD.

*** *Diaphragmatic Breathing* cmhc.utexas.edu/stressrecess/Level_Two/breathing. html

A helpful video that demonstrates this relaxation technique, which is often useful with anxiety and panic attacks. It is contained within a larger stress-reduction self-help free online course.

*** *Relieve Stress* www.fi.edu/learn/brain/relieve.html

This resource from the Franklin Institute offers some quick stress-relief tips and techniques, mentally, physically, through your senses, and in other ways.

*** *Stress Management* www.counselingcenter.illinois.edu/?page_id=194

A simple and short article about stress management from the University of Illinois at Urbana-Champaign.

** *Stress* www.intelihealth.com/IH/ihtIH/WSIHW000/24602/24602.html

At the commercial Intellihealth.com site, the "Stress Center" provides a number of help overviews and basic information about stress and stress management.

**See also** Anxiety Disorders (Chapter 7), Communication and People Skills (Chapter 17), and Self-Management and Self-Enhancement (Chapter 34).

# CHAPTER 38

# SUBSTANCE ABUSE

The Western world has taken the motto "better living through chemistry" to heart. Many of us ingest substances to wake up, to fall asleep, to stay alert, to mellow out, to feel more, to feel less. Taken to extreme, these substances graduate into addictions and wreck lives.

Most self-help authorities, as well as psychotherapists, realize the immense difficulty of recovering from substance abuse. Virtually all authors of self-help books, autobiographies, and Internet sites recognize that some form of treatment and ongoing self-help is needed for recovery. Therefore, reading a self-help book or watching a film is unlikely, by itself, to conquer or control an alcohol or drug abuse. However, good self-help materials can assist in the identification of substance abuse, can direct a person to the optimal treatment, can serve as an effective adjunct to psychotherapy, and can support the family and friends of a substance abuser.

In this chapter, we focus on alcohol and drug abuse. Addiction to gambling, sex, pornography, and the Internet are covered in a separate chapter (Chapter 3). Here we present the experts' consensual ratings on self-help books, autobiographies, films, online self-help, and Internet resources on substance abuse in its multiple manifestations (Box 38.1). The multiple films in this category are probably the best for self-help purposes than in any other chapter. The titles and contact information for prominent self-help organizations are included as well.

## ■ SELF-HELP BOOKS

### Strongly Recommended

★★★★ *Alcoholics Anonymous* (4th ed., 2001). New York: Alcoholics Anonymous World Services.

In our national studies, this and the Cermak book (listed below) emerged as the highest-rated self-help books for alcoholism. Revised three times since the first edition was published in 1939, the book is the basic text for Alcoholics Anonymous (AA) groups. AA principles have been revised and adapted by a number of self-help groups, such as Narcotics Anonymous, Gamblers Anonymous, and Al-Anon (for people with a variety of addictions and their families). Called the "Big Book" by AA, *Alcoholics Anonymous* is divided into two parts. The first part describes the AA recovery program, which relies heavily on

## BOX 38.1
## RECOMMENDATION HIGHLIGHTS

### SELF-HELP BOOKS

■ On Alcoholics Anonymous and recovery:

**** *Alcoholics Anonymous* by Alcoholics Anonymous

**** *Twelve Steps and Twelve Traditions* by Alcoholics Anonymous

■ On maintaining sobriety with or without AA:

*** *The Addiction Workbook* by Patrick Fanning and John O'Neill

*** *Controlling Your Drinking* by William R. Miller and Ricardo Munoz

*** *When AA Doesn't Work for You* by Albert Ellis and Emmett Velton

■ On adult children of alcoholics:

**** *A Time to Heal* by Timmen Cermak

*** *It Will Never Happen to Me* by Claudia Black

■ On women, couples, and drinking:

♦ *A Woman's Addiction Workbook* by Lisa Najavits

♦ *Overcoming Alcohol Problems* by Barbara S. McCrady and Elizabeth E. Epstein

### AUTOBIOGRAPHIES

■ On the descent into alcohol abuse and recovery:

**** *A Drinking Life* by Pete Hamill

**** *Getting Better* by Nan Robertson

■ On a teenager's polydrug abuse:

**** *Go Ask Alice* by Anonymous

*** *Beautiful Boy* by David Sheff

■ On the intersection of drug abuse, alcoholism, and mental disorders:

*** *Wishful Drinking* by Carrie Fisher

■ On the challenges of fetal alcohol syndrome:

**** *The Broken Cord* by Michael Dorris

### FILMS

■ On the depressing descent into alcoholism:

***** *The Lost Weekend*

***** *Days of Wine and Roses*

**** *Ironweed*

■ On the ravages of multiple addictions:

***** *Requiem for a Dream*

■ On inspiring recovery and the founding of AA:

**** *My Name Is Bill W*

■ On surrendering and recovering from addiction:

***** *The Fighter*

**** *Clean and Sober*

**** *21 Grams*

- On substance abuse in families:
  - ★★★★ *Rachel Getting Married*
  - ★★★★ *Traffic*
  - ★★★★ *When a Man Loves a Woman*

## ONLINE SELF-HELP

- For self-assessment and guided treatment of alcohol abuse:
  - ★★★★★ *Moderate Drinking* www.moderatedrinking.com
  - ★★★★ *Drinker's Check-up* www.drinkerscheckup.com
- For self-assessment and guided treatment of smoking:
  - ★★★★ *QuitNet* www.quitnet.com/qnhomepage.aspx
  - ★★★★ *Stop Smoking Center* www.stopsmokingcenter.net
  - ★★★ *Freedom From Smoking* www.ffsonline.org
- For self-assessment and guided treatment of marijuana abuse:
  - ★★★ *Check Your Cannabis* www.checkyourcannabis.net
  - ★★★ *Marijuana 101*
    www.3rdmilclassrooms.com/website/FRMJintervention.aspx

## INTERNET RESOURCES

- On all addictions:
  - ★★★★★ *Substance Abuse and Mental Health Services Administration* www.samhsa.gov
- On recovery or rehabilitation programs:
  - ★★★★ *Addiction Resource Guide* www.addictionresourceguide.com

confession, group support, and spiritual commitment to help individuals cope with alcoholism. Extensive personal testimonies by AA members from different walks of life make up the latter two thirds of the book. Successive editions of the book have expanded the case histories to include examples of alcoholics from a variety of backgrounds in the hope that alcoholics who read the book can identify with at least one of them. Brief appendixes include the Twelve AA Steps and Traditions and several testimonials to AA by ministers and physicians. The book also explains how to join AA and attend meetings.

★★★★ *Twelve Steps and Twelve Traditions* (pocket ed., 1995). New York: Alcoholics Anonymous World Services.

This book is devoted to detailed discussions of the Twelve Steps and Twelve Traditions used in AA. The Steps and Traditions represent the heart of AA's principles, providing a guide for members to use in recovery. The strong religious nature of the Twelve Steps and Traditions is apparent in the first five steps: (1) We admitted we were powerless over alcohol…that our lives had become unmanageable; (2) We came to believe that a Power greater than ourselves could restore us to sanity; (3) We made a decision to turn our will and our lives over to the care of God as we understood Him; (4) We made a searching and fearless moral inventory of ourselves; (5) We admitted to God, to ourselves, and to another human being the exact nature of our wrongs.

Almost 200 pages are devoted to elaborating the basic principles of the Twelve Steps. Like its sister book, *Alcoholics Anonymous, Twelve Steps and Twelve Traditions* earned a 4-star rating in the national studies.

Because the 12 steps have become so widely used, mental health experts have carefully analyzed them. Criticisms focus mainly on their spiritual basis. Unhappy with the strong religious flavor, some mental health experts have recast the steps in nonreligious terms to appeal to a wider range of people. Before his death, the famous behaviorist B. F. Skinner put together a psychological alternative to AA's Twelve Steps. Here are the first five: (1) We accept the fact that all our efforts to stop drinking have failed; (2) We believe that we must turn elsewhere for help; (3) We turn to our fellow men and women, particularly those who have struggled with the same problem; (4) We have made a list of the situations in which we are most likely to drink; (5) We ask our friends to help us avoid those situations.

**★★★★** *A Time to Heal: The Road to Recovery for Adult Children of Alcoholics* (1988) by Timmen L. Cermak. Los Angeles: Jeremy P. Tarcher.

This book carries the promise of hope. With a time to heal will come a time to belong. Each chapter addresses a specific time along the path of healing: a time to heal, to see, to remember, to feel, to separate, to be honest, to trust, and to belong, and a time for courage. Included are case histories of the trauma and emotional pain adult children of alcoholics (ACOAs) lived with as kids and currently as adults. Two important points made are that healing begins with honesty and that the flaws of an ACOA's lifestyle can be dissolved only by making the discipline of recovery a part of daily life. This is a helpful book for ACOAs, especially with their current relationships, and for the professionals who work with ACOAs.

**Recommended**

**★★★** *It Will Never Happen to Me* (reissued 1991) by Claudia Black. New York: Ballantine.

Unlike the AA books that are directed at alcoholics themselves, Black's book was written to help children—as youngsters, adolescents, and adults—cope with the problem of having an alcoholic parent. Black has counseled many alcoholic clients who were raised in alcoholic families, as well as spouses of alcoholics. She comments that virtually every one of them said, "It will never happen to me"; hence the title of her book. Black believes that when people grow up in alcoholic homes, they learn to not talk, not trust, and not feel, whether they drink or not. This book received an impressive rating, but by only a small number of people who were familiar with it, which is why it has a 3-star rating. Black's book is a superb self-help book for children and spouses of alcoholics. Black does a good job of describing the alcoholic cycle, paints a vivid picture of the pitfalls faced by those related to alcoholics, and is upbeat in giving them hope for recovery and positive living. In the final chapter, Black tells readers about a number of resources for relatives of alcoholics.

**★★★** *Controlling Your Drinking* (2004) by William R. Miller and Ricardo Munoz. New York: Guilford.

Psychologists Miller and Munoz point out that society has labeled those who drink alcohol as either alcoholics or not alcoholics. This labeling overlooks the critical problem of overdrinking and the critical question not of one's label, but of drinking too much for good health. Likewise, the term "problem drinker" can prove stigmatizing and can get in the way of facing the problem. The authors suggest the term "harmful drinking" because the problem is actually "the person drinking enough to harm his/her health." This valuable self-help book focuses on what bad things happen when a person drinks and how particular people, situations, and places trigger drinking. A sensible, research-based alternative for those drinking too much for their own good. Had *Controlling Your Drinking* been more frequently rated, it would have emerged as a definite 4- or 5-star resource in our studies.

★★★ *The Addiction Workbook: A Step-By-Step Guide to Quitting Alcohol and Drugs* (1997) by Patrick Fanning and John O'Neill. New York: Fine.

Prolific self-change author Fanning and drug counselor O'Neill collaborate on this comprehensive workbook for quitting alcohol and drugs. It is, as the subtitle declares, a step-by-step self-change manual, starting from "Do You Have a Problem?" in Chapter 2 and ending with "Relapse Prevention" in Chapter 12. In between there are an assortment of awareness and actions methods, including treatment possibilities, nutrition, relaxation, spirituality, emotional expression, communication, and making amends. *The Addiction Workbook* is ecumenical, compatible with 12-step programs, medications, cognitive-behavioral treatments, and the evolving sciences of addictions. Several experts in our national studies praised it for its balanced and integrative approach; in fact, had it been known by more professionals, it would have achieved a 4-star designation.

★★★ *One Day at a Time in Al-Anon* (1988). New York: Al-Anon Family Group Headquarters.

Originated by a group of women with alcoholic husbands, Al-Anon is a support group for relatives and friends of alcoholics. Like a number of self-help groups for alcoholics and their relatives, Al-Anon members follow AA's Twelve Steps of recovery. This book reflects an important principle of Al-Anon: Focus on one day at a time when living with an alcoholic. Each day is viewed as a fresh opportunity for self-realization and growth rather than for dwelling on past problems and disappointments. Like the other AA books, *One Day at a Time in Al-Anon* has a strong spiritual emphasis. Each page is devoted to one day—from January 1 to December 31—and consists of two parts: a message and a daily reminder. Religious quotations are used frequently throughout the book.

★★★ *Sober and Free: Making Your Recovery Work for You* (1996) by Guy Kettelhack. New York: Simon & Schuster.

This book focuses on maintaining sobriety, with tips on managing slips and on relearning to create significant relationships. The author stresses the importance of finding one's own way of maintaining sobriety, with help from support groups, psychotherapy, medication, family, and friends. For those in conventional programs who are looking for more, or for those who do not believe that conventional programs are working for them, this book could be a helpful resource.

★★★ *The Recovery Book* (1992) by Al J. Mooney, Arlene Eisenberg, and Howard Eisenberg. New York: Workman.

This book is designed like a road map from active addiction to recovery and then to relapse prevention. Topics covered are understanding recovery, deciding to quit, picking the right treatments, knowing the facts about treatment and support groups, maintaining sobriety dealing with temptations, recreating healthy relationships (families and social life), grappling with financial concerns, and preventing relapse. A section is devoted to dependency as a family disease. This book is a blend of medical knowledge and practical wisdom. It is also a comprehensive source for patients, families, and professionals dealing with the recovery process.

★★★  *A Day at a Time* (1976). Minneapolis: CompCare.

A book of daily reflections, prayers, and catchy phrases intended to offer inspiration and hope to recovering alcoholics. The book is based on the spiritual aspects of AA, especially the Twelve Steps and Twelve Traditions. Like Al-Anon's *One Day at a Time in Al-Anon*, each page is devoted to a day—from January 1 through December 31. Each page is divided into three parts: Reflection for the Day, Today I Pray, and Today I Will Remember. The brief daily messages come from poets, philosophers, scholars, psychologists, and AA members.

★★★  *When AA Doesn't Work for You: Rational Steps to Quitting Alcohol* (1992) by Albert Ellis and Emmett Velton. Fort Lee, NJ: Barricade.

The authors acknowledge that AA works for many people but not for everyone. The beginning chapters help readers determine whether they have a drinking problem and introduces rational-emotive therapy as the best strategy for recovery. A number of helpful step-by-step methods, including the use of a daily journal and homework assignments, are provided in later chapters. The authors focus on maladaptive thought patterns and specific ways to replace them with more adaptive ones. Unlike many of the books in the addiction category, Ellis and Velton's book does not include spiritual commitment in the recovery process; in fact, they believe that AA's notion of the alcoholic's powerlessness is an irrational idea. Rational Recovery (RR), one of an increasing number of nonreligious self-help groups for recovering alcoholics formed in recent years, traces its roots directly to the ideas of Albert Ellis and his rational-emotive therapy. RR teaches that what leads to persistent drinking is a person's belief that he or she is powerless and incompetent. Using Ellis's approach, a moderator (usually a recovered RR member) helps guide group discussion and gets members to think more rationally and act more responsibly. While AA stresses that alcoholics can never fully recover, RR tells members that recovery is not only possible but can happen in a year or so.

★★★  *Adult Children of Alcoholics* (expanded ed., 1990) by Janet Woititz. Deerfield Beach, FL: Health Communications.

Janet Woititz, the "mother" of the adult children of alcoholics (ACOA) movement, describes basic problems and vulnerabilities of ACOAs. Woititz says that reading her book can be the first step to recovery, along with Al-Anon and its Twelve Step program. The key to recovery is learning the principle of detachment. In her view, because ACOAs received inconsistent nurturing as children, as adults they hunger for nurture and are too emotionally dependent on their parents. They have to separate themselves from their parents in the least stressful way possible. Although this book was on the *New York Times* bestseller list for more than 45 weeks and sold more than 2 million copies, the ratings by the mental health experts in our studies were mixed.

**Diamonds in the Rough**

♦ *Sober for Good: New Solutions for Drinking Problems* (2001) by A. M. Fletcher. New York: Houghton Mifflin.

There is no one way to achieve sobriety. Recommendations are often for AA, yet we know that formal programs are not successful for everyone. For some, moderate drinking is a reasonable goal; for others, abstinence is best. Some do better on their own with no assistance; others succeed with support. The primary message here is permission to seek out one's best choice based on the many personal factors involved. The author interviewed 222 individuals from different walks of life and with different experiences, families, and backgrounds, all of whom had overcome their excessive drinking. Topics include the history and resolution of each person's drinking problem, one doesn't have to hit bottom to start working on the problem, how to decide whether one can have another drink, and how to stay motivated.

♦ *Overcoming Your Alcohol or Drug Problem* (2006) by Dennis C. Daley and G. Alan Marlatt. New York: Oxford University Press.

This research-supported program does not promote a particular treatment but rather assists readers in asking the right questions and in seeking the right information to choose the treatment that fits them. Depending on the individual's pattern of drinking or drug use, a variety of treatments may be selected. Intended to be used in conjunction with a professional, this book explores cognitive-behavioral therapy, tailored coping skills, the 12-step program, and relapse prevention. The goal is to maximize treatment benefits by motivating readers to develop a change plan and to learn coping strategies. Readers are encouraged to understand the process of recovery and to use skills to reduce the risk of relapse, as one of the co-authors (Marlatt) is a founder of relapse prevention. Had it been rated by a few more experts in our national studies, this splendid guide would surely have received a more enthusiastic recommendation.

♦ *A Woman's Addiction Workbook* (2002) by Lisa Najavits. Oakland, CA: New Harbinger.

The chair of the Harvard Medical School's Division of Addictions Women's Initiatives offers this holistic, step-by-step program for women. The workbook can be used as an adjunct to professional services or as a self-help tool. We are reminded that there are as many roads to recovery as there are roads to addiction; therefore, women will need to find and create a treatment plan that works for them. The book considers how women are different from men in addiction, how life patterns relate to addictions, how to understand co-occurring conditions, and how to heal. These and other topics are explored with the purpose of stopping the downward spiral.

♦ *Overcoming Alcohol Problems: A Couple-Focused Program Workbook* (2008) by Barbara S. McCrady and Elizabeth E. Epstein. New York: Oxford University Press.

Psychologists McCrady and Epstein assist couples in identifying high-risk situations that contribute to drinking and then in combating that drinking. Some situations are triggered by people, places, or things and some by thoughts, feelings, or relationships. Each session/chapter introduces a new skill or method for dealing with the drinking problem. A commitment to the program and to working with a psychotherapist on out-of-session activities is expected weekly. Exercises include conducting a functional analysis, rearranging behavioral consequences, engaging the partner in drink refusal, and preventing relapse. Based on decades of grant-funded research that involves partners to improve the success rates of problem drinkers.

### Not Recommended

★★   *The Alcoholic Man* (1990) by Sylvia Carey. Los Angeles: Lowell House.

### Strongly Not Recommended

† *The Miracle Method: A Radically New Approach to Problem Drinking* (1995) by Scott D. Miller and Insoo Kim Berg. New York: Norton.
† *Healing the Addictive Mind* (1991) by Lee Jampolsky. Berkeley, CA: Celestial Arts.

## ■ AUTOBIOGRAPHIES

### Strongly Recommended

★★★★   *The Broken Cord: A Family's Ongoing Struggle with Fetal Alcohol Syndrome* (1990) by Michael Dorris. New York: Harper Collins.

This book first brought fetal alcohol syndrome (FAS) to public attention. The author was in graduate school working on his dissertation when he decided to adopt Adam, a 3-year-old Native American child. He was aware Adam was developmentally disabled but did not know why. After the child showed a succession of serious health, behavioral, and learning problems, Adam was diagnosed with FAS. Dorris, by this time a successful author and professor, made FAS into a research project. He traveled across the nation collecting stories of Native American children with FAS (Adam's natural mother had died from drinking antifreeze) and interviewing FAS experts. The tone of the book varies among love, compassion, and rage directed at women who drink during pregnancy. There are sections by Dorris's wife, writer Louise Erdrich, and by Adam, then 20 years old. The ending is tragic, with Adam run over by a car and Dorris committing suicide. A very good book about FAS, the risks of adoption, and the urgent need for substance abuse education in Native American communities.

★★★★   *Getting Better: Inside Alcoholics Anonymous* (1988) by Nan Robertson. New York: William Morrow.

The author chronicles the growth of AA, describes meetings, and recounts her own struggle with alcoholism. This is one of the best accounts of the founding and evolution of AA, still one of the most successful and probably one of the most spiritual self-help programs. A movement history as well as a compelling autobiography.

★★★★   *Go Ask Alice* (1995) by Anonymous, edited by Beatrice M. Sparks. New York: Aladdin.

Bestselling reprinted edition of a diary kept by a 15-year-old girl, starting from her introduction to LSD at a party, the following week's experimentation with marijuana and methamphetamine, and subsequent struggles to bring her drug use and her life under control. Stark realism strips the glamour and romance from drugs as the author becomes a liar, thief, runaway, dealer, rape victim, and street person. Although partly fictional, this is a great book for teens wondering about the effects of drugs, not simply on their mood tonight but on their lives. Good book for parents, too.

**★★★★** *A Drinking Life: A Memoir* (1995) by Pete Hamill. Boston: Little, Brown.

A gritty description of growing up in a tough New York neighborhood and becoming a tough guy, brawler, drunk, rebel, and finally a writer. Noted journalist and novelist Hamill, now sober for two decades, discusses without sentimentality the critical role alcohol played in his life. Drinking was a crucial part of his early life and wrecked his first marriage. He argues that alcohol is not necessary to stimulate literary creativity. This is the book that inspired Caroline Knapp, author of *Drinking: A Love Story* (listed below), to sober up. An excellent resource for showing the effects of family and neighborhood on alcohol use and how a determined person can stop drinking on his or her own.

### Recommended

**★★★** *Note Found in a Bottle: My Life as a Drinker* (1998) by Susan Cheever. New York: Simon & Schuster.

Daughter of a famous writer with serious drinking problems, Susan Cheever discusses the role that alcohol played in her own life and in her three failed marriages. She started early in life identifying cocktails with sophistication and sociability, but soon alcohol controlled her life. Now in recovery, Cheever reflects on social aspects of alcohol use in our society. A particularly good book for a person crossing the line from social drinking to addiction. Highly rated by our mental health professionals but not widely known, thus accounting for its 3 stars.

**★★★** *Terry: My Daughter's Life-and-Death Struggle with Alcoholism* (1997) by George S. McGovern. New York: Dutton.

In the winter of 1994, police found the body of Teresa McGovern, daughter of presidential candidate and senator George McGovern, frozen in a snowbank following an evening of drinking. This is the heartbreaking account of Terry's descent into oblivion. The book draws heavily from her diary and from personal recollections of family members. Terry was genetically vulnerable, with alcoholism on her father's side and depression on her mother's. She started drinking alcohol at age 13, took marijuana and LSD in high school, spent time on the locked ward of a psychiatric hospital, almost went to jail, and tried suicide. There was a brief respite of sobriety in her 30s, with marriage and two daughters, but the marriage ended and the daughters went to live with their father. After that, she was in and out of detox and treatment programs. The diary makes it clear she knew what happening to her but was unable to prevent it. The family blames itself for not doing more, yet the reader can see from the journals that little could be done when Terry blew off all attempts at treatment. This is not a hopeful book since we know the tragic ending from the start, but it is a gripping account of a family's continued efforts to battle a daughter's addiction. Especially recommended for parents of young alcoholics and for teens who deny the ravages of alcohol addiction. The mental health professionals in our studies highly but infrequently rated this book, accounting for its 3-star rating.

★★★  *Drinking: A Love Story* (1997) by Carolyn Knapp. New York: Delta.

Daughter of a psychoanalyst, the author grew up in a well-to-do family. She graduated *magna cum laude* from Brown University before becoming a reporter and later an editor. She was an anorexic and a high-functioning alcoholic who kept her addiction hidden from her associates. She bottomed out, checked into a rehab center, joined AA, and started on the slow path to recovery. Knapp had been inspired to quit drinking by Pete Hamill's book (see above). She describes in stylish prose her complex relationship to alcohol, her self-destructive behaviors, and her early powerlessness. A book especially suitable for female alcohol abusers.

★★★  *Beautiful Boy: A Father's Journey Through his Son's Addiction* (2009) by David Sheff. Boston: Houghton Mifflin.

The author's son, Nic, was hooked on crystal meth by age 17 and went downhill from there, a journey described in the son's account *Tweak: Growing Up on Amphetamines.* The son's book complements his father's book but is no more optimistic about the likelihood of recovery, which is a continuing, even a lifetime, struggle. *Beautiful Boy* is a sobering story of a father's attempts to cope with his son's addiction and the lying and stealing to support a destructive near-fatal habit. Sheff went through the typical parental cycle of guilt, fear, and regret, "I torment myself with the same unanswerable questions: `Did I spoil him? Was I too lenient? Did I give him too little attention? Too much?'" In the end the father comes to the realization that Nic's life is his own, and that as a father he should be supportive but Nic's recovery is beyond his father's control. This is a realistic book for parents, including those whose children have not started abusing drugs: the drug epidemic is all around us and no one is immune from its effects.

★★★  *Wishful Drinking* (2009) by Carrie Fisher. New York: Simon & Schuster.

If you like celebrity memoirs, you'll like *Wishful Drinking,* which is the written script of the author's one-woman show that opened on Broadway in 2009. Carrie Fisher, the daughter of Debbie Reynolds and Eddie Fisher, achieved fame as Princess Leia in the *Star Wars* trilogy. Along with life in Tinseltown's fast lane (including a chart showing her parents' various marriages), Fisher mentions her own drug abuse, alcoholism, and bipolar disorder but without much detail. This short, easy-to-read book is witty, self-depreciating, and sarcastic, although somewhat scattered—which might be explained by the memory loss from electroconvulsive therapy she received for her bipolar disorder, discussed more fully in her subsequent memoir *Shockaholic.*

★★★  *Now You Know* (1990) by Kitty Dukakis with J. Scovell. New York: Simon & Schuster.

The wife of a former governor of Massachusetts and presidential candidate discusses her bouts with bipolar disorder and her addiction to alcohol and pills. The book is a good account of the author's two-decade battle with substance abuse and bipolar disorder.

## ■ FILMS

### Strongly Recommended

★★★★★ *The Lost Weekend* (1945) directed by Billy Wilder. Not rated. 101 minutes.

A timeless film starring Ray Milland as a writer and chronic alcoholic struggling to overcome his addiction. He goes on multiday benders and literally looses weekends. In a classic line, the bartender chides Milland: "One's too many and a hundred's not enough." He engages in typical addictive behaviors, including hiding his stash, according alcohol first priority, and rationalizing his slips. He refuses help from significant others and draws his girlfriend into his massive denial. Eventually, he accepts responsibility and treatment for his drinking. Several scenes were filmed at Bellevue Hospital in New York City, and the withdrawal symptoms are convincing indeed. The treatment methods are dated—and clients should be reassured that they will not suffer the severe delirium tremens pictured in the movie—but the addictive process and results are timeless. Widely considered one of the best films ever made about alcoholism.

★★★★★ *Days of Wine and Roses* (1962) directed by Blake Edwards. Not rated. 108 minutes.

This classic film is a portrait of a successful middle-class couple's agonizing struggles with progressive alcoholism in the 1950s. The husband recovers with AA, but the wife cannot, and he must leave her. The movie is depressing, with its depiction of job loss, repeated lapses, descent into ugliness, and the eventual dissolution of the marriage. Particularly useful as a warning and illustration of the patterns of alcoholic couples.

★★★★★ *Requiem for a Dream* (2000) directed by Darren Aronofsky. Unrated. 102 minutes.

Four addicts, four lives, four failures. Set in Brooklyn, this disturbing film portrays the descent of four substance abusers into the ugly underworld of addicts. Eye-opening consequences of chronic addiction are in full bloom, including crime, prostitution, amputation, hospitalization, poverty, incarceration, and psychosis. At the conclusion of the movie, all four characters are shown curling up in a fetal position, an apt metaphor for their regression and wasted lives. Brutally descriptive and not for the faint-hearted.

★★★★★ *The Fighter* (2010) directed by David O. Russell. R rating. 116 minutes.

A drama based on "Irish" Micky Ward's improbable road to the world welterweight boxing championship. Early in his career, he was trained by his older half-brother, who is a crack addict and the subject of an HBO documentary, and managed by his mother, who is a domineering and selfish force. The brother, Dicky, is the quintessential addict: lying, stealing, forever reliving his own boxing triumphs and disappointing everyone but the crack dealers. Micky Ward eventually splits with his brother and mother, incurring their wrath, but finds himself moving up the ranks in boxing and in self-development. Dicky gets clean and proudly helps his brother win the boxing title. Profound in showing the ravages of crack addiction, the potency of codependency, and the redemptive power of family love.

★★★★  *My Name Is Bill W* (1989) directed by Daniel Petrie. Not rated. 100 minutes.

This superbly acted television movie is the true story of the founder of AA, Bill W, a successful financial manager who gradually lost his job, friends, self-respect, and all he valued to alcoholism. Finally, he met Dr. Bob, and they kept each other sober and invented AA. Nothing is held back, and their success is highly inspirational.

★★★★  *Clean and Sober* (1988) directed by Glenn Gordon Caron. R rating. 124 minutes.

To escape the police for a murder he did not commit and a large theft from his employer, a young cocaine-addicted real estate salesman enters a drug rehabilitation program. He is in massive denial, but despite valiant attempts, he cannot escape the insights, confrontations, and caring of the counselors. The process of surrender and recovery by an ordinary and less-than-perfect client is well illustrated and believable.

★★★★  *Rachel Getting Married* (2008) directed by Jonathan Demme. R rating. 113 minutes.

Kym (Anne Hathaway) is released from rehab for a few days so that she can attend her sister Rachel's wedding. Like many polysubstance-dependent individuals early in sobriety, Kym displays her "dry drunk" immaturity, impulsivity, and narcissism with her extended family, which is naturally hypervigilant and tense. Kym maintains her sobriety throughout the wedding weekend, but after a fight with her mother, she intentionally drives her car off the road into a giant rock in an apparent suicide attempt. So much to recommend in this film for self-help purposes, among them the addict's endearing yet frustrating relationships with loved ones; the family dynamics of an addict returning from rehab; the genuine support of 12-step groups; the healing nature of family connections even when deeply conflicted; and the addict's begrudging acceptance of responsibility for past transgressions.

★★★★  *Traffic* (2000) directed by Steven Soderbergh. R rating. 140 minutes.

Three riveting, intertwined stories about drug abuse: two DEA agents in pursuit of drug kingpins; a crooked constable south of the border in pursuit of his integrity; and a U.S. drug czar in pursuit of his heroin-addicted daughter. The film accurately shows the complexity of drug trafficking—from its origins in foreign countries to its terminals in city streets—and the victimization of the young and weak. *Traffic* delves into the dark and personal corners of drug abuse, particularly the privileged daughter's descent into hopeless addiction. One of the most realistic portrayals of drugs' collective ravages on American families.

★★★★  *When a Man Loves a Woman* (1994) directed by Luis Mandoki. R rating. 124 minutes.

A film about alcoholism and families that is not overly simple, stereotyped, or designed with a happy ending. After extensive drinking and denial, the wife enters treatment and recovery, and that is when her loving and accepting husband, a born enabler, must also change. He must give up handling all the responsibilities and making the decisions. His world is thus shaken up, too. No quick or final fixes are offered, but the movie portrays treatment adequately and recovery from denial with rare realism.

★★★★    *21 Grams* (2003) directed by Alejandro González Iñárritu. R rating. 124 minutes.

Naomi Watt's character loses her husband and daughter in a hit-and-run accident and then loses her emotional bearings. She turns toward drugs and drink and turns away from people, sitting at home alone staring dully at the world. Told in scenes that are out of order, the fractured chronology leads to a confusing plot but the juxtapositions convey the alienating self-medication and the intense suffering that is both a cause and a result of the drugs. Relationships develop among the main characters, but for our purposes, Watt's portrait is the terrifying focus. The film also demonstrates in the end that identity and humanity can survive even the worst losses and drugs.

★★★★    *Walk the Line* (2005) directed by James Mangold. PG-13 rating. 136 minutes.

A popular biopic of Johnny Cash that traces his life and addictions. Born during the Great Depression in Arkansas, Cash suffered the early loss of a brother and then the loss of his father's affection. We witness his first marriage, first recording, first fame, first divorce, first reliance on booze and amphetamines, and then June Carter nursing him back to health. In the end, June accepts his marriage proposal, lifts John out of his ring of fire, and watches him triumph at a Folsom Prison concert. Although trite, the self-help message is that the love of a good woman can save a man from addiction.

★★★★    *House of Sand and Fog* (2003) directed by Vadim Perelman. R rating. 126 minutes.

An emotionally unstable woman, Kathy (Jennifer Connelly), loses her house for unpaid taxes mistakenly charged to her. A proud Iranian immigrant family takes possession of the house but is harassed by Kathy and her boyfriend attempting to reclaim her former home. Kathy's emotions spiral out of control, she relapses back into alcohol dependence, and her actions spark a tragic end that leaves no resident unscathed in the House of Sand and Fog. The film commendably shows the synergism between stress and substance abuse as well as the steps toward relapse.

★★★★    *Ironweed* (1987) directed by Hector Babenco. R rating. 143 minutes.

Meryl Streep and Jack Nicholson are compelling as homeless alcoholics during the Depression. A difficult film to watch: the two have hit rock bottom, struggle daily to survive on the streets, and trade their self-esteem and bodies for food and alcohol. The film's cold and depressing photography adds to the ambience. Although a lengthy and brutal film, it unforgettably presents the harsh realities of alcohol-consumed, homeless existence.

### Recommended

★★★    *Cat on a Hot Tin Roof* (1958) directed by Richard Brooks. 108 minutes.

Brick (Paul Newman), an alcoholic ex-football player, drinks his days away and resists the affections of his wife, Maggie (Elizabeth Taylor). A superb writer's portrayal of the greedy family of a dying Southern patriarch. The family members all try to please him for their selfish benefits, except for the guilt-ridden ex-jock son and his sexually frustrated wife. The film is a classic story of family conflict, confrontation, and escapist alcoholism.

★★★  *Ray* (2004) directed by Taylor Hackford. PG-13 rating. 152 minutes.

A splendid biopic of Ray Charles' meteoric rise from humble origins to his international triumphs in the music and sighted world. As his fame grew, so did his addictions, threatening to bring him down. Jamie Foxx doesn't sugarcoat the heroin addiction and its devastating effects on marriage, career, and self. Ray Charles ultimately overcame blindness, racism, and addiction, inspiring others far less burdened than him.

★★★  *The Prize Winner of Defiance, Ohio* (2005) directed by Jane Anderson. PG-13 rating. 99 minutes.

One of the saddest portrayals of abject alcoholism ever placed on film: Kelly Ryan (Woody Harrelson) is the father of 10 children and a chronic alcoholic who spends his paycheck on a nightly six-pack of beer and a pint of whiskey. The family faces starvation and foreclosure, but Kelly continues to drink away his life, enabled in the 1950s by a community that offers no judgment and no treatment. In fact, in one scene a priest blames Kelly's wife, Evelyn, telling her that she must try harder to provide a better home. Evelyn (Julianne Moore) deals with their poverty in Ohio by entering jingle contests and wins multiple prizes, but it's not enough to right the doomed family.

★★★  *Bright Lights, Big City* (1988) directed by James Bridges. R rating. 110 minutes.

Michael J. Fox's character suffers the death of his mother, gets dumped by his wife, and resorts to self-medicating with alcohol, cocaine, and promiscuous sex in the Big Apple. Based on Jay McInerney's acclaimed novel of New York's sex and drug scene, the film shows Fox hitting rock bottom and confronting his inner demons before they destroy him. An exceptional soundtrack and grainy photography add to the chilling effect, but many viewers will have difficulty in accepting the usually cuddly Fox as a desperate coke-snorter. Particularly applicable for younger clients who are into the party scene of urban life.

★★★  *Mask* (1986) directed by Peter Bogdanovich. PG-13 rating. 120 minutes.

A teenager, horribly disfigured by a rare disease, remains unbowed in the face of cruelties with the love and help of his gutsy albeit addicted mother (played by Cher). He succeeds at school, begins a relationship with a blind girl, relates normally to his mother's boyfriend, and lectures his mother on drug abuse. She protects and cherishes him so intensely that you believe he will somehow survive his fatal condition. The film makes the love between an addicted mother and a disfigured son palpable and inspirational.

★★★  *Leaving Las Vegas* (1995) directed by Mike Figgis. R rating. 112 minutes.

A poignant film about doomed losers. He is irretrievably dedicated to drinking himself to death, and she is a prostitute, abused and misused daily. He has no choices left, but she chooses to stay with him and care for him because he is her redemption. The film illustrates her unselfish love, charity, and gentleness despite the hardness of their lives and the weaknesses of their characters.

★★★   *Blow* (2001) directed by Ted Demme. R rating. 124 minutes.

Johnny Depp stars in the true story of George Jung, an insider in the Colombian cocaine cartel and one of the largest cocaine traffickers in the early 1970s. He makes bushels of money and becomes the target of a federal investigation. For all of his fabulous wealth, the true costs of his own addiction and treacherous occupation are visited on him and his family. More of a cautionary historical tale than a self-help film per se.

★★★   *Hustle and Flow* (2005) directed by Craig Brewer. R rating. 116 minutes.

This 3-star resource chronicles the daily life of Memphis pimp and crack dealer Djay (Terrence Howard) as he tries to make it in the hip-hop music world and as he begins to question what sort of person he wants to become. At some point, Djay looks deep inside of himself and decides that he needs to change and that rapping can be his way out from the deep hole. Beautifully acted and realistically scripted, the film reveals the transformative abilities of humans and art.

★★★   *Half Nelson* (2006) directed by Ryan Fleck. R rating. 106 minutes.

Eighth-grade history teacher and basketball coach (Ryan Gosling) is a hit with his inner-city students, but his personal life lies in shambles. He rampantly snorts cocaine and smokes crack but believes rehab is not for him. The predictable fallout is displayed in the form of failed relationships, estranged family ties, mistreated women, and self-loathing. The film concentrates on the teacher's relationship with one of his 13-year-old charges, who caught him smoking crack in the school bathroom. The ending brings to mind the truism that we are frequently better at saving each other than saving ourselves.

★★★   *Drugstore Cowboy* (1989) directed by Gus Van Sant, Jr. R rating. 100 minutes.

A junkie and his four-person "family" rob drugstores to support their habits, which consume their empty lives. The excitement of drugs and the staged robberies alternate with the ennui of their highs and the routines of moving around the country. They are all sick and try ineffectively to help each other. After the death of a member of the family and a meeting with a haunted and haunting old addict, the junkie plans to get into treatment. His wife cannot understand a world without drugs and tries to pull him back. Utterly realistic, even to its junkie logic, and wonderfully acted, this movie might help clients see what the road ahead looks like and the possibility of difficult change.

★★★   *28 Days* (2000) directed by Betty Thomas. PG-13 rating. 103 minutes.

A single woman in her late 20s, played by Sandra Bullock, involuntarily enters a 28-day, inpatient rehabilitation program for her alcohol and painkiller addictions. She passes through classic denial and withdrawal symptoms and into recovery. The movie realistically illustrates the disease concept and 12-step treatment, including group therapy, family confrontation, and eventual reevaluation of her relationships. An entertaining and moving film.

★★★   *Crazy Heart* (2009) directed by Scott Cooper. R rating. 112 minutes.

The story is a cliché—an alcoholic country singer loses multiple marriages, career successes, and love relationships, and then enters rehab. But broken-down Jeff Bridges as

Bad Blake is outstanding, and his mixed success following rehab is realistic. Less syrupy than most in the genre, and recommended for those in recovery and the women who love them.

★★★  *Postcards from the Edge* (1991) directed by Mike Nichols. R rating. 101 minutes.

A drug-addicted young actress is falling apart, barely surviving at work, sleeping around with strangers, misplacing her days, and awaiting her next fix. Her mother is a famous actress and is addicted more acceptably to alcohol. The daughter enters rehab. Her mother visits her but responds only to the attentions of her fans. Mother–daughter rivalry is dramatized, and the ladies have many parallels. Well written and acted, the film drifts and does not reveal much about recovery. It might illustrate a not uncommon mother–daughter relationship for some clients.

★★★  *MacArthur Park* (2001) directed by Billy Wirth. R rating. 86 minutes.

MacArthur is a grim park in Los Angeles that is home to addicts, criminals, and hustlers. Cody is a drug casualty and musician whose abandoned son reaches out to him. This independent film depicts the stark world of crack addiction and the various efforts to leave it behind over a 2-day interval.

★★★  *Gia* (1998) directed by Michael Cristofer. R rating. 120 minutes.

Angelina Jolie stars in this movie based on the life of supermodel Gia Marie Carangi. Originally shown on HBO, the film follows her life from a rebel working in her father's diner at age 17 to her death from AIDS at age 26. In between, Gia's life traced a downward spiral of drug abuse and failed relationships. For the purposes of self-help, the film spends excessive time on Gia's modeling and bisexuality, but if viewers can focus on her problems with drugs, it contains several important lessons about the short, drug-infested lives of the young and famous.

## ■ ONLINE SELF-HELP

★★★★★  *Moderate Drinking* www.moderatedrinking.com

This website is connected to the www.Moderation.org website, which promotes a moderation model of drinking. The moderate drinking program is interactive and based on the user's responses. The program provides feedback and recommendations tailored to each user. Users set goals for either abstinence or moderate drinking, and the program allows them to track their progress. The program provides feedback about drinking triggers and patterns and helps users develop strategies and alternatives to drinking. Users can view their alcohol use patterns in terms of amount and blood alcohol content (BAC) graphed for the past 6 months. Registered users can purchase the program monthly for $19.95/month or a 12-month subscription for $59.

★★★★  *Drinker's Check-up* www.drinkerscheckup.com

This free Web-based program is designed to help registered users identify drinking-related problems and then make a decision about changing their behavior. The program is based on the principles of Motivational Interviewing and has been shown to reduce the amount of drinking. Users complete several tests to identify their current drinking patterns, consequences of drinking, and level of motivation to change. Users are provided with feedback based on the results of completed tests. In the final section, users input personal information and integrate the previous sections into a decision. If users make a decision to cut back or stop drinking, they are directed to other programs designed for those purposes.

★★★★   *OnTrack Depression Program* www.ontrack.org.au

This free site is currently designed for users in Australia, but the developers plan to open up the site to international users soon. The site contains self-directed interactive modules in several areas, including alcohol abuse as well depression. Users can take a self-directed quiz to identify which program might be useful or select one based on a professional's recommendation. Users can use the tracking tools to track their mood and progress and keep a diary of their experiences. Along the way, interactive tools help users identify their drinking patterns, set goals, and develop plans to make changes.

★★★★   *QuitNet* www.quitnet.com/qnhomepage.aspx

This free online smoking cessation program creates an individualized quitting guide and provides information based on input from the user. The website provides a calculator where users learn how much "life" and money they save by quitting. The site contains an internal e-mail system, chat rooms, and an "ask-the-expert" e-mail option.

★★★★   *Stop Smoking Center* www.stopsmokingcenter.net

This website is a free one-visit resource that provides users with educational materials based on their answers to a smoking questionnaire. The site also contains a blog, discussion forums, and mentorship connections to other users committed to quitting.

★★★   *24/7 Help Yourself* www.247helpyourself.com

Users of this free website have the option of using the site independently or in a guided format. The guided mode consists of a four-step (4-week) program that includes an assessment of current drinking and drinking-related consequences, decision tools, and change tools. The website provides users with educational materials and an online forum to communicate with other members.

★★★   *Alcohol 101 Plus* www.alcohol101plus.org/home.html

This free online website and program was developed primarily for college age students. The self-directed program allows users to navigate through a virtual campus. At each stop, users view short multimedia vignettes and interact with the program to make decisions about drinking. Users are immediately provided feedback about how their decisions might impact their functioning. The virtual bar allows users to calculate their blood alcohol content (BAC) by selecting drinks in different combinations and at different time intervals. The website also contains accurate alcohol related information and an option for users to quiz their alcohol knowledge.

★★★ *Alcohol Help Center* www.alcoholhelpcenter.net

This free resource allows users to sign on anonymously to assess their current drinking and develop an individual plan to reduce or stop drinking. The program provides personalized information based on each user's current drinking and goals. Users can keep track of their use in a personal online diary, connect with coaches, or visit the moderated support group.

★★★ *Check Your Cannabis* www.checkyourcannabis.net

This is a free online self-directed test of cannabis use. Users can privately complete an online test to determine their risk of cannabis-related problems. Users are provided with feedback on their score in comparison with others in their same demographic group. The report also contains probable life consequences based on the user's identified level of risk.

★★★ *Check Your Drinking—University* www.checkyourdrinkingu.net

This free online self-directed test allows users to privately evaluate their drinking. It is designed for college students. After free registration, users complete an online test of their drinking behaviors. The program produces a report comparing the user's drinking with a similar group and providing a calculation of the impact on finances and physical health. Users receive recommendations for sensible drinking and reducing their risks.

★★★ *Freedom From Smoking* www.ffsonline.org

This American Lung Association program offers seven modules for smoking cessation. Users move at their own pace, but it is recommended that they progress at a rate of one module per week (10 to 15 minutes per module). In addition to readings, users complete related assignments. An upgrade to the FFS Online Premium is available for $15 for 3 months or $40 for one year. Premium users have access to additional features, including message boards, downloadable relaxation exercises, and social networking capabilities.

★★★ *Marijuana 101* www.3rdmilclassrooms.com/website/FRMJintervention.aspx

This site offers six self-guided modules on reducing marijuana use. It is primarily designed for use in educational settings with multiple individual users, such as a fraternity that has been sanctioned due to marijuana use. The modules address personal decisions, health information about marijuana, consequences of use, and the law. It also contains self-directed assessments and information on reducing or stopping use. It is based on motivational interviewing techniques. Pricing information is not currently available.

★★★ *Rethinking Drinking* www.rethinkingdrinking.niaaa.nih.gov

This free interactive site allows users to identify and rate their drinking behavior. Individualized feedback and information are given based on the user's responses. Online worksheets allow users to rate their behavior, plan their changes, and keep track of their progress. Users can complete self-directed modules to build skills in order to resist urges and identify triggers.

## ■ INTERNET RESOURCES

### General Websites

★★★★★ *Substance Abuse and Mental Health Services Administration* www.samhsa.gov

This website is the home of SAMHSA, a U.S. government agency under the Department of Health and Human Services, and offers a wealth of information regarding substance abuse and mental health issues. The public information is found under "Publications," and while it's a storefront, everything is also available for immediate free download.

★★★★★ *National Institute on Drug Abuse* drugabuse.gov

This government website from the National Institutes of Health is a great starting point to learn more about drug and alcohol addiction and how to get help for them.

★★★★ *Addictions and Recovery.org* www.addictionsandrecovery.org

An updated and well-written website detailing the basics of addiction from Dr. Steven Melemis.

★★★ *Web of Addictions* www.well.com/user/woa

A fairly reliable source of accurate information on addictions, but hasn't been updated in many years. The lack of updates means that, unfortunately, a lot of the links on the website pointing to valuable information about alcohol and substance abuse are no longer working.

★★ *Hazelden* www.hazelden.org

Hazelden, a company that runs treatment centers for addiction, really should offer a more helpful resource to consumers looking for information. It's a bit of a mess, with little in the way of informational articles that aren't pushing one of its treatment programs.

### Psychoeducational Materials

★★★★ *Drug Abuse and Addiction* helpguide.org/mental/drug_substance_abuse_
addiction_signs_Effects_treatment.htm

This single page from the nonprofit HelpGuide offers a general overview of drug abuse and addiction, warning signs, and advice for getting help. Also gives advice for when a loved one or teen has a drug abuse problem, as well as links to a handful of other online resources.

### *Codependency*

★★★ *The Issues of Codependency* www.soulselfhelp.on.ca/coda.html

This site includes essays on boundaries, the codependent personality, and similar topics.

★★★ *Codependency—Minding Your Mental Health* mentalhealth.tulane.edu/codependency.htm

A helpful page about codependency, recognizing it in yourself or others, and self-help strategies to employ.

### Alcohol

★★★★ *Secular Organization for Sobriety/Save Our Selves* www.cfiwest.org/sos

If you desire a nonreligious approach to sobriety, this page offers several fine long pieces for patients using the SOS model, the empirical evidence, and links to groups.

★★★★ *SMART: Self-Management And Recovery Training* www.smartrecovery.org

Based on Ellis's rational-emotive behavior therapy, this approach eschews war stories, sponsors, and meetings for life for structured meetings run by trained advisors. Their Four-Point Program comprises (1) building and maintaining motivation to abstain; (2) coping with urges; (3) managing thoughts, feelings, and behavior; and (4) balancing momentary and enduring satisfactions.

★★★★ *Moderation Management* www.moderation.org

Moderation Management is focused on helping people live with alcohol in their lives by emphasizing moderation, self-management, balance, and personal responsibility. Their website has information about this alternative to AA.

★★★ *Alcohol Dependence* www.mentalhealth.com/dis/p20-sb01.html

Although designed for professionals, this website from Internet Mental Health offers an interesting set of resources on this concern. Not regularly updated, however.

★★★ *Adult Children of Alcoholics* www.adultchildren.org

The website of this 12-step organization may be helpful for those who grew up in a household with an alcoholic and are looking for support in their recovery.

★★★ *Growing Up with Drinking or Substance Abuse* www.counselingcenter.illinois.edu/?page_id=144

A helpful article on adult children for college students. See also *Children of Alcoholics* www.aacap.org/cs/root/facts_for_families/children_of_alcoholics

★★★ *Alcoholism* www.mayoclinic.com/health/alcoholism/DS00340

A very well-written and comprehensive set of overview articles from the venerable Mayo Clinic.

★★★ *Al-Anon and Alateen* www.al-anon.alateen.org

This website offers the usual AA literature in a dozen languages and may serve as a good introduction for family members and teens who need support in dealing with a family member with alcoholism. You can also find AA online at www.aa.org

### Drug Abuse

★★★★ *Overcoming Drug Addiction: Drug Abuse Treatment, Recovery and Help* www.helpguide.org/mental/drug_abuse_addiction_rehab_treatment.htm

A single page of helpful information about drug addiction and ways to get help and support for it from the nonprofit HelpGuide.

★★★ *The Do It Now Foundation* www.doitnow.org/pages/pubhub.html

This website offers dozens of brochures about smoking, drugs, alcohol, street drugs, and more. Written for a teen and young adult audience, the brochures are available as PDFs or as articles you can read on the website.

★★★ *Commonly Abused Drugs: Street Names for Drugs of Abuse* www.drugabuse.gov/DrugPages/DrugsofAbuse.html

This handy chart from the National Institute on Drug Abuse features drugs' common names, street names, and commercial names; how they are administered; their DEA schedule classification; and their effects and health risks.

### Other Resources

★★★★ *National Inhalant Prevention Coalition* www.inhalants.org

This website offers articles and information about inhalant abuse, a rising problem among teens and young adults. The site also offers FAQs and information about the nonprofit organization.

★★★★ *Addiction Resource Guide* www.addictionresourceguide.com

To assist with choosing a rehabilitation or recovery program, this excellent and informative guide has descriptions of hundreds of inpatient programs across the United States, as well as a few internationally. The guide provides detailed information that is hard to find elsewhere, including the number of beds in each facility, statistics on admissions, the focus of the facility and the people it treats, and the self-pay cost per day to stay in the facility.

## ■ SUPPORT GROUPS

### Adult Children of Alcoholics World Services Organization

Phone: 562-595-7831
www.adultchildren.org
A 12-step program of recovery for adults raised in a dysfunctional environment that included alcohol abuse.

### Alateen and Al-Anon Family Groups

Phone: 757-563-1600 or 888-425-2666
www.alateen.org

A fellowship of young persons whose lives have been affected by someone else's drinking.

**Alcoholics Anonymous**

Phone: 212-870-3400
www.aa org

**American Council on Alcoholism**

Hotline: 800-527-5344
Referrals to treatment centers and DWI classes.

**Chemically Dependent Anonymous**

Phone: 1-888-232-4673
www.cdaweb.org
Twelve-step program for friends and relatives of people who are chemically dependent.

**Cocaine Anonymous**

Phone: 1-800-347-8999 or 310-559-5833
www.ca.org

**Crystal Meth Anonymous**

Phone: 213-488-4455
www.crystalmeth.org

**Dual Recovery Anonymous**

Phone: 913-991-2703
www.draonline.org

**Heroin Anonymous**

heroin-anonymous.org/haws/index.html

**LifeRing Secular Recovery**

Phone: 1-800-811-4142 or 510-763-0779
www.lifering.org

**Marijuana Anonymous World Services**

Phone: 1-800-766-6779
www.marijuana-anonymous.org

## Methadone Anonymous

Phone: 888-638-4786
www.methadone-anonymous.org

## Mothers Against Drunk Driving

Phone: 800-438-6233
www.madd.org
This large organization provides support though local chapters, education, political activism, and victim assistance.

## Moderation Management (MM)

Phone: 212-871-0974
www.moderation.org
Emphasizes self-management and moderation of alcohol abuse. Intended for early-stage problem drinkers, not those severely dependent on alcohol.

## Narcotics Anonymous

Phone: 818-773-9999
www.na.org

## Nar-Anon World Wide Service

Phone: 310-534-8188 or 800-477-6291
www.nar-anon.org
Twelve-step program of recovery for families and friends of addicts.

## National Institute on Alcohol Abuse and Alcoholism

Phone: 301-443-3860
www.niaaa.nih.gov

## Rational Recovery (RR)

www.rational.org
Phone: 530-621-2667 or 530-621-4374
Founded 1986. Abstinence-based.

## Secular Organization for Sobriety/Save Our Selves

Phone: 323-666-4295
www.sossobriety.org

### Self Management and Recovery Training (SMART)

Phone: 866-951-5357
www.smartrecovery.org
An abstinence-based, cognitive-behavioral approach.

### Women for Sobriety

Phone: 215-536-8026
www.womenforsobriety.org

**See also** Addictions (Chapter 3).

# CHAPTER 39

# SUICIDE

Suicide is a real and rising crisis. In the United States, suicide represents the tenth leading cause of death overall and the third leading cause of death among adolescents. Literally millions of people are struggling with thoughts of hurting themselves and battling the impulse to kill themselves. And it only takes one "successful" attempt to be a fatality.

Individuals contemplating or committing suicide are not the only people affected. Families, friends, and psychotherapists are continually worried about suicide contemplators. Those who commit suicide leave behind numerous friends and family members who may struggle all their lives to understand and accept the loss. The survivors may feel guilty and responsible, intensifying their grief.

In this chapter, we review mental health professionals' ratings on self-help resources that address (a) how to prevent suicides, (b) how to help people contemplating suicide, and (c) how to survive a loss due to suicide. Following our recommendation highlights (Box 39.1), we present self-help books, autobiographies, films, and Internet resources on this real and rising crisis.

## SELF-HELP BOOKS

### Recommended

★★★  *Choosing To Live* (1996) by Thomas Ellis and Cory F. Newman. Oakland, CA: New Harbinger.

A sensitive and persuasive case is made for choosing to live when confronted with suicidal impulses. This self-help book is one of the few cognitive therapy books that focuses on suicidal risk. The message is written in the first person, directly to the reader, yet it is clear that the authors intend for the book to be used as an adjunct to psychotherapy. An appendix includes excellent guidelines for concerned family and friends on the warning signs, what to do, and what to do if the person refuses help. An early self-assessment asks readers to explore the probable risk of suicide. Ellis and Newman present two profiles of suicide risk: the depressed and hopeless person who needs restoration of hope and reduction of negative thinking; and the person with control concerns and communication problems who needs reduction of conflict and problem-solving skills. The book offers a clear and well-developed series of steps on what the reader can do now: surviving the crisis, understanding his or her feelings and thoughts, implementing the cognitive treatment plan, looking forward to feeling better through coping, and solving one's problems without dying. *Choosing to Live* is an excellent choice for those

## BOX 39.1
## RECOMMENDATION HIGHLIGHTS

### SELF-HELP BOOKS

■ For individuals at risk for suicide and their families:

   ★★★ *Choosing To Live* by Thomas Ellis and Cory F. Newman

■ For partners and families of those who have committed suicide:

   ★★★ *Myths about Suicide* by Thomas E. Joiner

    ♦ *Touched by Suicide* by Michael F. Myers and Carla Fine

    ♦ *Living When a Young Friend Commits Suicide* by Earl A. Grollman and Max Malikow

### AUTOBIOGRAPHIES

■ For a personal look at suicide by an authority and a survivor:

   ★★★★★ *Night Falls Fast* by Kay R. Jamison

■ For surviving a loved one's suicide:

    ♦ *No Time to Say Goodbye* by Carla Fine

### FILMS

On healing with psychotherapy after a suicide attempt:

   ★★★★★ *Ordinary People*

On the trauma of girls who commit suicide:

   ★★★★ *'Night, Mother*

   ★★★★ *The Virgin Suicides*

On vulnerabilities and stressors leading to suicide:

   ★★★★ *House of Sand and Fog*

   ★★★★ *The Hours*

   ★★★★ *The Hospital*

### INTERNET RESOURCES

■ On understanding suicide:

   ★★★★★ *American Society of Suicidology* www.suicidology.org

■ On surviving a suicide crisis:

   ★★★★★ *If You Are Thinking about Suicide ... Read This First* www.metanoia.org/suicide

   ★★★★ *CrisisChat* www.crisischat.org

at risk and their families. One of the most favorably rated self-help resources in our national studies, but not rated frequently enough to receive a 5-star designation.

   ★★★  *Myths About Suicide* (2010) by Thomas E. Joiner. Cambridge, MA: Harvard University Press.

Clinical cases, scientific studies, and research sources are compiled to identify and dismantle the myths about suicide. For example, it is thought that those who try to commit suicide will try again. This can, of course, happen, but it is not the typical pattern. Loved ones who are left behind have unanswered questions about the suicide: Why did they make the decision to kill themselves; could we have known in advance; what was the intention in the act; and was it a message. All of these and other questions torment those left to deal with the death. This book cannot speak to individual cases; however, distinguishing the facts from the myths about suicide can help process the loss.

### Diamonds in the Rough

All three of the following self-help books were positively evaluated by mental health professionals in our national studies, but none received enough ratings to fit into the Recommended section. Sadly, books on suicide are simply not as well known as books on other mental health problems.

- *Touched by Suicide* (2006) by Michael F. Myers and Carla Fine. New York: Penguin.

The authors are a physician and a survivor of a loved one's suicide; together they share their experiences with suicide both from a professional and a personal perspective. Many first-person accounts converge on the realization that each suicide is unique but also universal in the experience of the loved ones. This book conveys that those left are not alone and share many life-altering feelings. The aftermath includes searching for reasons, wondering what they can do, asking how they can protect the family and children, and questioning how they can go on. The authors advocate breaking the silence and rightfully perceiving suicide as a public health problem.

- *Living When a Young Friend Commits Suicide* (1999) by Earl A. Grollman and Max Malikow. Boston, MA: Beacon.

This book was written to help those who have lost friends or family members to suicide by answering questions often asked and some not so often asked. Adolescent and young adult suicide is implied by the title as its focus; however, the book can be equally helpful in other relationships. The chapters are clustered into themes of coming to grips with the reality of the suicide, needing to cope with the experience, and continuing with one's life. The authors sensitively consider decisions about participating in the immediate grieving, such as attending the funeral, returning to school, and visiting the family. An informative section addresses the misconceptions about suicide, such as "attempts are gestures of looking for attention," "it runs in the family," "the friend had everything going for him." A fine self-help resource but not frequently known by the experts in our national studies.

- *Why People Die From Suicide* (2007) by Thomas Joiner. Cambridge, MA: Harvard University Press.

Suicide is discussed from both the clinical perspective of professionals and the personal perspective of survivors in this valuable book. More academic than most self-help books, it takes an investigative path into scientific study and health data regarding what we know and don't know about suicide, theories about suicide, and discussion about working with suicide (e.g., alarmist stance versus dismissive stance). The roles of genetics and coexisting mental disorders are also explored. Psychologist Joiner shares the poignant story of his father's suicide, the impact on the family, and the lifelong effect on himself. The book is a balanced blend of personal experiences and scientific studies that further our understanding.

## ■ AUTOBIOGRAPHIES

### Strongly Recommended

★★★★★ *Night Falls Fast: Understanding Suicide* (2001) by Kay Redfield Jamison. New York: Vintage.

Not an easy topic to write about, but Kay Jamison brings to the task impressive credentials in this comprehensive yet personal book. Psychologist Jamison is one of the foremost authorities on mood disorders, in which suicide is a serious risk. She had a lifelong struggle with bipolar disorder, planned for her own suicide at 17, and made her first attempt at age 28. She considers suicide, especially in young people, to be a preventable public health problem. She describes groups most at risk, the psychology of suicide notes, methods used to take one's life (including popular locations such as San Francisco's Golden Gate Bridge), effects of suicide on families, and the underlying genetic, biological, psychological, and cultural forces. This is a rational discussion of an action that appears irrational to others but seems the only rational solution to someone unable to cope. A well-researched, well-written book on a topic most people don't want to think about. Essential reading for anyone who works with young people.

### Diamonds in the Rough

♦ *No Time to Say Goodbye: Surviving the Suicide of a Loved One* (1999) by Carla Fine. New York: Crown.

Most books about suicide focus on the people who have taken their lives. This book looks at those left behind, the survivors, the families and friends of the deceased who suffer debilitating grief and often shoulder raw feelings of guilt and shame. Typically they are offered less support but more questions than those who lose loved ones to other causes. A support group for suicide survivors is highly recommended as one means of self-healing. This candid and readable book, based on the author's personal loss, will reassure survivors that others have walked the journey through grief and confusion and there is life afterward.

♦ *His Bright Light: The Story of Nick Traina* (2000) by Danielle Steel. New York: Dell.

Novelist Steel sensitively depicts her son's brief life, his struggle with bipolar disorder, and his tragic suicide at age 19. A brilliant and talented child, Nick was a good-looking, charming teenager who played in a rock band and experimented with drugs. His mother made repeated but unsuccessful attempts to find help for him. This was a time when it was unusual to diagnose a child with bipolar disorder, and Steel could not persuade mental health providers that her son had a serious disorder with a high risk of suicide. Nick's mental anguish is seen in his poems, songs, and diary notes included in the book. While this is a sad account of parental grief at the death of a child, it is also compassionate and respectful of Nick and his roller-coaster ride of a life. Also reviewed in Chapter 11 on Bipolar Disorder.

## ■ FILMS

**Strongly Recommended**

★★★★★   *Ordinary People* (1980) directed by Robert Redford. R rating. 124 minutes

Mary Tyler Moore and Donald Sutherland lead an apparently happy family whose older son dies in a boating accident. Their other son, Timothy Hutton, is so wracked by misplaced guilt and unshared grief that he attempts suicide and enters psychotherapy. The movie admirably demonstrates the emotional dynamics of the family, the denial and false coping, the feelings of shame and failure a suicide evokes in the survivors, and the fears of feeling deeply. We also adore the honest portrayal of talk psychotherapy. One of the highest-rated films in all of our national studies; a 5-star resource and an Academy Award winner. (Also reviewed in Chapter 18 on Death and Grieving.)

★★★★   *House of Sand and Fog* (2003) directed by Vadim Perelman. R rating. 126 minutes.

Kathy, a depressed recovering alcoholic, is mistakenly evicted from her home and is assisted in reclaiming it by a lustful but sympathetic deputy, Lester. After legal recourse fails to resolve the matter, Kathy makes a personal plea to the new owner, begging him to sell her the house back. However, he refuses, and a distraught Kathy attempts suicide in front of the house. Her attempt is thwarted when the new owner finds her and brings her inside to recuperate. While inside she makes a second attempt to take her life but is saved by the new owner's wife. The situation deteriorates to the point where the new owner kills his wife and then takes his own life. A compelling, magnificently acted film that accurately captures depression and alcoholism as underlying vulnerabilities to suicide, as well as loss and loneliness as immediate precipitants of suicide. (Also reviewed in Chapter 38 on Substance Abuse.)

★★★★   *Dead Poets Society* (1990) directed by Peter Weir. PG rating. 129 minutes.

The message of this coming-of-age movie is to "seize the day." Teacher Robin Williams inspires his teenage students to live to the fullest. The evidence for this quest, at least in the movie, is rather simple-minded opposition to conventions. A student opposes his father's command and then, unable to maintain his defiance, kills himself. Williams is scapegoated for the suicide and made to leave the boarding school. The suicide is not directly explored, but the feelings of adolescent desperation and alienation are clearly expressed. This movie is probably better suited to examining the experiences of teenagers and is also reviewed in Chapter 40 on Teenagers and Parenting.

★★★★   *'Night, Mother* (1987) directed by Tom Moore. PG-13 rating. 96 minutes.

A daughter announces to her mother that she is going to commit suicide. The mother tries to dissuade her as they stay up late together laughing and reminiscing. Then the daughter does in fact take her life. The daughter's painful struggle is revealed through their storytelling that night, and we see that she is living with a lifetime of challenges with which she can no longer cope. The compelling message is to deal with life's problems when they are still manageable rather than turning away and allowing the heartache to accumulate and triumph. Suicide is the daughter's desperate way of taking charge after years of being dominated by others and being devalued as a person. The film is an adaptation of a Broadway play that received a Pulitzer Prize.

**★★★★** *The Hours* (2002) directed by Stephen Daldry. PG-13 rating. 114 minutes.

Aside from the first and final scenes of the film, which depict the 1941 suicide of Virginia Woolf, the action takes place on the same day but in three different years. In 1923, Woolf begins writing *Mrs. Dalloway*, while in 1951 a depressed housewife, Laura Brown, reads *Mrs. Dalloway* to escape from her humdrum life, and in 2001 Clarissa Vaughan is the embodiment of the novel's main character, Mrs. Dalloway. Woolf has suffered several nervous breakdowns and bouts of depression. She feels trapped at home by the servants and her husband, who lives in constant fear that she will take her own life. However, Virginia asserts that if she is to live she has just as much right as anyone else to decide how she will live. Laura seems to be living the American dream but is deeply unhappy. She checks into a hotel where she plans to commit suicide. She brings along several bottles of pills and a copy of *Mrs. Dalloway*. As she reads, she slowly drifts off to sleep but awakens with a change of heart. Clarissa is throwing a party in honor of her friend and former lover. However, her lover's depression overwhelms him and he ingests many pills. He tells Clarissa he has stayed alive all this time only for her sake before he throws himself out of a window to his death. With an exemplary cast and haunting music, the film illustrates the tragedy of suicide in so many ways: the genesis, the process, the desperation, the people left behind. (Also reviewed in Chapter 20 on Depression.)

**★★★★** *The Virgin Suicides* (2000) directed by Sofia Coppola. R rating. 97 minutes.

All the teenage boys in one suburban town loved and lusted after the Lisbon sisters in their typically gawky and insecure ways. Josh Harnett has an ideal sexual moment with Kristen Dunst, abandons her, and goes on to a life of compromises and reality. This theme is worth more exploration, and perhaps sensitive adolescents and their parents might do so. A second theme is that Kristen and her sisters kill themselves, and the movie explores why. Their mother is hysterical over the girls' blooming sexuality and the father is a nonentity, but these are not really explanations. We never understand why, and that may be the best point of the suicide theme.

**★★★★** *The Hospital* (1971) directed by Arthur Hiller. PG rating. 103 minutes.

Although a farce and "black comedy" from the 1970s, the scene of George C. Scott's suicide contemplation is superb. His wife and kids have left him, he is impotent, and someone is killing the patients in his hospital. He is rescued by a "hippie chick," Diana Rigg, whose wisdom and beauty revive him through love. If you can ignore the trite Hollywood ending, the stresses leading to Scott's suicide are beautifully shown.

## Recommended

**★★★** *The Slender Thread* (1965) directed by Sydney Pollack. 98 minutes.

This film is based on the true story of a college student working on a crisis hotline who finds himself on the phone with a woman who has taken an overdose of sleeping pills and doesn't know where she is. She has reached the point of despair because her husband has discovered that he is not the father of their son; she is deeply depressed and does not have the strength to go on. His frantic attempts to keep her on the phone while the police track her location is a story of caring about the life of a stranger and the desperate state that people reach before they reach out.

### Not Recommended

* ★ *Last Tango in Paris* (1972) directed by Bernardo Bertolucci. X rating. 129 minutes.

## ▨ INTERNET RESOURCES

### General Websites

★★★★★ *American Society of Suicidology* www.suicidology.org

This professional association is focused on helping clinicians and researchers better understand and reduce the prevalence of suicide, but also offers helpful public resources in the categories of Thinking About Suicide?, Suicide Loss Survivors, and Suicide Attempt Survivors.

★★★ *IMAlive* www.imalive.org

IMAlive is a nationwide online crisis network that is staffed by certified volunteers designed to help people who need suicide counseling. Despite the organization's good intent, however, the chat is only available a few hours per week at this time, meaning the service is unavailable most of the week. Let's hope its resources will meet the actual need of 24/7 services soon.

★★★★ *International Suicide Prevention Wiki* suicideprevention.wikia.com

The International Suicide Prevention Wiki is an international directory of suicide helpline, hotlines, and related resources.

### Psychoeducational Materials

★★★★★ *If You Are Thinking about Suicide…Read This First* www.metanoia.org/suicide

This helpful article written by Martha Ainsworth remains one of the Internet's leading passive crisis interventions. The article is engaging and helps people to stop and think before acting irrationally.

★★★★ *CrisisChat* www.crisischat.org

CrisisChat is a not-for-profit collaboration overseen by CONTACT USA that offers online immediate chat services for people in crisis or who are suicidal. Simply log onto the website and start chatting with a trained crisis counselor.

★★★ *Common Hotline Phone Numbers* psychcentral.com/lib/2007/common-hotline-phone-numbers

An updated list of hotline, helpline, and warm line telephone numbers for a wide range of concerns for U.S. citizens.

★★★★ *SA/VE—Suicide Awareness/Voices of Education* www.save.org

The site offers, besides support, a dozen well-written and helpful brochures on thoughts of suicide, talking to children about suicide, misconceptions about suicide, and more.

★★★★ *Befrienders International* www.befrienders.org

This charity organization's website offers a wealth of resources and articles for those feeling suicidal and those worried about a loved one's suicidality. This site also offers materials on homosexuality, bullying, and self-harm and help and support, all available in many languages.

★★★ *Now Is Not Forever: A Survival Guide* by J. Kent Griffiths, DSW    drkentgriffiths.com/information/survival_vs_suicide_h.html

A well-written article about helping a person make the decision to live.

### Self-Injury
★★★★ *Self-Injury: You Are Not the Only One* users.palace.net/~llama/selfinjury

This is a high-quality, rich site that sadly hasn't been updated in years. The Quick Primer is very educational, as is Self-Help. There are a questionnaire, quotes, references, chat, and more. Much of it can be used with Linehan's dialectical behavior therapy.

## ■ SUPPORT GROUPS

### American Foundation for Suicide Prevention

Phone: 888-333-AFSP or 212-363-3500
www.afsp.org

### Emotions Anonymous

Phone: 651-647-9712
www.emotionsanonymous.org
A 12-step organization for people struggling with emotional difficulties.

### Friends for Survival

Phone: 916-392-0664; 800-646-7322
www.friendsforsurvival.org
For family, friends, and professionals after a suicide death.

## Heartbeat

heartbeatsurvivorsaftersuicide.org/index.shtml
Provides mutual support for those who have lost a loved one through suicide.

## National Suicide Hotline

Phone: 800-784-2433

## National Suicide Prevention Lifeline Network

Phone: 1-800-273-8255

## Suicide Awareness/Voices of Education (SA/VE)

Phone: 952-946-7998
www.save.org

## The Trevor Project

Phone: 866-488-7386
www.thetrevorproject.org
Committed to end suicide among LGBTQ youth by providing resources such as a 24/7
crisis intervention lifeline, digital community, and advocacy/educational programs.

## Yellow Ribbon Suicide Prevention Program

Phone: 303-429-3530
www.yellowribbon.org

**See also** Bipolar Disorder (Chapter 11) and Depression (Chapter 20).

# CHAPTER 40

# TEENAGERS AND PARENTING

Growing up has never been easy. It wasn't easy for the parents of today's adolescents when they were teenagers. It isn't easy for today's youth. What will become of this younger generation? It will grow up and start worrying about the next generation.

In matters of taste and manners, the youth of every generation seem radical, unnerving, and opposed to adults—different in their behavior, music, hairstyles, clothing, and activities. Acting out and boundary testing are time-honored ways in which teenagers move toward accepting, rather than rejecting, parental values. But parents want to know why their adolescents talk back to them and challenge their rules and values. They want to know if they should be authoritarian or permissive. They want to know why adolescents have such mercurial moods—happy one moment, sad the next. And they want to keep their adolescents from drinking alcohol, taking drugs, dropping out of school, becoming depressed, hanging out with the wrong peer group, and becoming sexually permissive.

As parents worry about these treacherous roads, adolescents have their own concerns. For them, the transition from childhood to adulthood is a time of evaluation, of commitment, and of carving out a place in the world. They try on one face after another, trying to find an identity of their own. They want to discover who they are, what they are all about, and where they are going in life. They move through a seemingly endless preparation for life. They want their parents to understand them but often feel they don't. And in the end, there are two paradoxical gifts they hope parents will give them—one is roots, the other is wings.

Self-help resources on teenagers and parenting fall into three main categories: resources written to help adolescents navigate the muddle of the middle years; those that provide parenting recommendations; and those that focus exclusively on parent–adolescent relationships. Let us now consider self-help books, films, and websites for adolescents and their worried parents (Box 40.1).

## ■ SELF-HELP BOOKS

### Strongly Recommended

★★★★★ *Get Out of My Life but First Could You Drive Me and Cheryl to the Mall?* (2002) by Anthony E. Wolf. New York: Farrar, Straus, and Giroux.

First and most importantly, the author reminds parents of teenagers, for whom this book is written, that adolescence is a stage; it's not forever. The world in which teenagers

## BOX 40.1
## RECOMMENDATION HIGHLIGHTS

**SELF-HELP BOOKS**

■ For improving parent–adolescent relationships:

★★★★★ *Get Out of My Life but First Could You Drive Me and Cheryl to the Mall?* by Anthony E. Wolf.

★★★★★ *Between Parent and Teenager* by Haim Ginott

★★★ *Positive Parenting Your Teens* by Karen Joslin and Mary Decher

■ For adolescent girls and their parents:

★★★★★ *Reviving Ophelia* by Mary Pipher

■ For teenagers:

★★★★ *All Grown Up and No Place to Go* by David Elkind

★★★ *When Living Hurts* by Sol Gordon

♦ *Bringing Up Parents* by Alex J. Packer

♦ *Yes, Your Parents Are Crazy* by Michael J. Bradley

**FILMS**

■ On friendship, coming of age, and the adolescent passage:

★★★★★ *Stand by Me*

★★★★ *The Breakfast Club*

★★★★ *Circle of Friends*

★★★★ *Little Women*

■ On identity development, peer influence, and authority conflicts:

★★★★ *Dead Poets Society*

★★★★ *A Bronx Tale*

★★★★ *Thirteen*

■ On struggling with giftedness and buried child abuse:

★★★★ *Good Will Hunting*

**INTERNET RESOURCES**

■ On the social, emotional, and sexual development of adolescents:

★★★★★ *A Parent's Guide to Surviving the Teen Years*
kidshealth.org/parent/growth/growing/adolescence.html

★★★★★ *TeensHealth* www.teenshealth.org

★★★★ *Parenting Teens* parentingteens.about.com

live now is much different from even a few years ago. No longer can they just grow up, get a job, get a family, and settle in for life. They grow up and then see what happens. Wolf offers many suggestions about dealing with these significant changes by explaining why teenagers do what they do, translating behavior into less complicated meaning, and revealing what teens mean when they say what they say. The author adds much-needed humor to the discussion, which is both refreshing and honest; for example, parents as an embarrassment, they don't listen to anything I say, and teenagers' traps for parents. Topics not always discussed are included, such as sex, drinking and drugs, gay and lesbian teens, and the impact of the Internet. A marvelous source of comfort and guidance for baffled parents.

★★★★★ *Reviving Ophelia: Saving the Selves of Adolescent Girls* (1994) by Mary Pipher. New York: Grosset/Putnam.

This is a sensitive, insightful journey into the torn lives of adolescent girls who as children were eager, confident, and curious but who upon the arrival of adolescence lose their way and their selves. Psychologist Pipher observes the dark turn of culture in which adolescent girls are pressured to conform, compete, and be superficially physically attractive. She tells moving stories of many adolescent clients and her experiences with them in psychotherapy. Chapters on families, mothers, fathers, divorce, depression, and other forces that touch adolescent girls present ways parents can support their daughters and also identify ways parents become agents of culture and unknowingly steer girls toward self-doubt. Pipher discusses healthy directions that she takes in psychotherapy, including teaching skills on centering, separating thinking and feeling, making conscious choices, holding boundaries, managing pain, modulating emotions, and enjoying altruism. *Reviving Ophelia* received high marks from mental health professionals and is a very popular book for adolescent girls.

★★★★★ *Between Parent and Teenager* (1969) by Haim Ginott. New York: Avon.

Although this valuable book is well past adolescence itself (it was published more than 40 years ago), it continues to be one of the most widely read and recommended books for parents who want to communicate more effectively with their teenagers. It has sold several million copies. Ginott describes a number of commonsense solutions for parents who have difficulty understanding and communicating with their teenagers. At the same time parents are trying to shape up their teenagers, the teenagers are fighting to be the masters of their own destiny. For Ginott, parents' greatest challenge is to let go when they want to hold on; only by letting go can parents reach a peaceful and meaningful coexistence with teenagers. Throughout, Ginott connects with parents through catchy phrases such as "Don't collect thorns"; "Don't talk in chapters" (that is, don't lecture, but rather be a good listener); "Accept teenagers' restlessness and discontent" (which reminds parents that normal adolescents experience a great deal of uncertainty); and "Don't put down their wishes and fantasies" (which underscores that normal adolescents are idealists). Ginott's nontechnical, easy-to-read writing style and many examples of interchanges between parents and adolescents give parents a sense of what to say (and how and when to say it). His strategies can make the life of parents and teenagers a kinder, gentler world.

★★★★ *All Grown Up and No Place to Go: Teenagers in Crisis* (revised ed., 1997) by David Elkind. Reading, MA: Addison-Wesley.

Psychologist Elkind believes that raising teenagers is more difficult than ever. He argues that today's teens are expected to confront adult challenges too early in their development, which is also a theme in his child development book, *The Hurried Child*. By being pressured into adult roles too soon, they are all grown up with no place to go—hence the title of his book. The book is divided into three parts. Part I, Needed: A Time to Grow, describes today's teenagers as in the midst of a crisis, informs parents about how adolescents think, outlines the perils of puberty, and provides details about peer shock. Part II, Given: A Premature Adulthood, analyzes American society and explains that adolescents don't have any rites of passage to guide them, discusses how the hodgepodge of American family structures has made adolescence a difficult transition, and outlines how bad secondary schools really are. Part III, Results: Stress and Its Aftermath, examines the effects of these family and societal problems on teenagers' identity and ability to cope with stress and other problems. A helpful appendix provides a list of services for troubled teenagers. This 4-star book provides important recommendations for how parents, teachers, and other adults could communicate and interact more effectively with teenagers. Elkind does an especially good job of showing how adolescents develop and how our society has neglected their needs.

### Recommended

★★★ *You and Your Adolescent: A Parent's Guide for Ages 10–20* (2nd ed., 1997) by Laurence Steinberg and Ann Levine. New York: HarperCollins.

This self-help resource presents an excellent overview of adolescent development and mixes in wise parenting strategies along the way. Steinberg and Levine tackle the dual tasks of giving parents a solid understanding of adolescent development and prescribing parenting strategies. Part I, The Basics, paints a picture of what makes a good parent, the nature of family communication, and what today's families are like. Part II, The Preteens: From 10 to 13, discusses the nature of physical health and development (puberty, sexual awakening, drugs), psychological health and development, and the social world of the young adolescent (peers, dating, middle school and junior high, achievement). Part III, The Teens: From 14 to 17, focuses on sex and the high-school student, drug and alcohol use in high school, the search for identity, a number of problem behaviors such as delinquency and running away, friends and social life, school, and work. Part IV, Toward Adulthood: From 18 to 20, explores the transition from adolescence to adulthood and how parents can ease this transition for themselves and their offspring. Two aspects of Steinberg and Levine's book set it apart from other self-help books in this genre. First, the authors accurately tell readers that some of the horror stories they have heard about adolescence are false. Second, Steinberg and Levine's book is organized developmentally: experts on adolescence increasingly recognize that the 12-year-old is different in many ways from the 17-year-old. Our mental health experts noted that *You and Your Adolescent* presents a good balance between educating parents about the nature of adolescence and giving parenting recommendations.

★★★ *Positive Parenting Your Teens* (1997) by Karen Renshaw Joslin and Mary Bunting Decher. New York: Fawcett Columbine.

The organizational style of this book is unique, as it is intended to be a sequel to *Positive Discipline A–Z* (reviewed in Chapter 15 on Child Development). Several short sections describe how to create an atmosphere of cooperation and responsibility and how to have discussions, engender trust, and accomplish follow-through. The major focus of the book is teaching how to solve the 100 common concerns that parents and teens have. For each concern, the authors offer an example, explain how to understand the situation, tell what to say and do, suggest preventive measures, and explain how to know when to seek help. The list is thorough (e.g., rebelliousness, friends, depression, clothes, swearing), and the authors effectively address each concern. Our mental health experts consistently rated this book very favorably, but not enough rated it to move it to the 4-star or 5-star category.

★★★ *When Living Hurts: For Teenagers and Young Adults* (revised ed., 1994) by Sol Gordon. New York: Union of American Hebrew Congregations.

The table of contents of this book is labeled "A table of wisdom, worry, and what to do," which conveys a sense of the book's style, sincerity, and good old-fashioned advice. The topics are timely (e.g., suicide, depression, sex, religion, parents, purpose of life). More important, however, is the person-to-person approach and the format, which includes thoughts for the day, slogans, advice, short writings of teenagers, funny poems, photos, and brief narratives, such as "What's a mensch?" This book reads as if the teenager is having a confidential conversation with a favorite uncle. It is written for teenagers, but it is applicable for parents, and those of all faiths. Highly regarded but not particularly well known by the psychologists in our national studies.

★★★ *Chicken Soup for the Teenage Soul on Tough Stuff: Stories of Tough Times and Lessons Learned* (1997) by Jack Canfield, Mark Hansen, and Kimberly Kirberger. Deerfield Beach, FL: Health Communications.

Adolescents from around the world express their opinions and share their stories about coping with adolescence. More inspiration than self-help per se.

★★★ *Queen Bees and Wannabes: A Parent's Guide to Helping Your Daughter Survive Cliques, Gossip, Boyfriends, and Other Realities of Adolescence* (2002) by Rosalind Wiseman. New York: Crown.

Wiseman describes the problems that teenage girls might experience during the gossipy and clique-filled world of adolescence. The "Queen Bee" is the teenage girl who dictates rules, such as who wears what and who dates whom; the "Wannabe" is the teenage girl who strives to get into a clique or who is the target of a clique's wrath. Wiseman offers parents of teenage daughters advice on how to help their daughters understand and cope with this world.

★★★ *Toughlove* (reissue ed., 1997) by Phyllis York, David York, and Ted Wachtel. New York: Bantam.

This controversial book squarely places the blame for adolescents' problems on the adolescents, not the parents. The book communicates that many parents are victimized by the guilt caused by their teenagers' behavior. According to the authors, many parents are too hard on themselves instead of on the teenager and the peer group when their adolescent takes drugs, fails at school, engages in promiscuous sex, or commits delinquent acts. *Toughlove* teaches parents how to face crises, take stands, demand cooperation, and meet challenges by getting tough with teenagers. Although tough love may in the short run widen the gulf between parents and teenagers, in the long run it is the only way the teenager will develop maturity, according to tough love advocates. Most experts, however, preferred the gentler, more balanced approaches advocated by Wolf, Pipher, Ginott, and Elkind to the harsh approach of *Toughlove*. Its problem, in addition to its punitive approach, is that controlled research has not been conducted on the method; it may lead parents to exaggerate their teenagers' problems; and it may inadvertently blame individual adolescents for societal or family problems.

**Diamonds in the Rough**

♦ *Yes, Your Parents Are Crazy: A Teen Survival Guide* (2004) by Michael J. Bradley. Gig Harbor, WA: Harbor.

Addressed directly to teenagers, this book is meant to help them make sense of and navigate the new world they are entering after childhood. The book targets the challenging world of adolescents with the expected topics of parents, family, friends, and school but also focuses on the difficult topics of blended families, Internet insanity, bullying, sexual abuse, racism, and pregnancy. Bradley offers many stories of teens with whom he has worked, their challenges, and the importance of support. Affirming passages recount the importance of friends and the value of confiding in some adult, anyone whom the teen feels is trustworthy. Teens will identify themselves and feel affirmed in the narratives.

♦ *Parents' Guide to Building Resilience in Children and Teens: Giving Your Child Roots and Wings* (2006) by Kenneth R. Ginsburg. Grove Village, IL: American Academy of Pediatrics.

This book promotes resilience and is intended for parents seeking ways to be a positive force in their children's development. Many parents see their children's vulnerabilities and try to protect them from hurt or failure, but the authors believe the most valuable tool we can teach our children is resilience. Parents are encouraged to think in terms of protective factors to buffer their children from what went wrong rather than focusing on what went wrong. The chapters are organized around the seven C's of critical qualities: Confidence, Competence, Connection, Character, Contribution, Coping, and Control. Well regarded but not widely known.

♦ *Bringing Up Parents: The Teenager's Handbook* (1992) by Alex J. Packer. Minneapolis: Free Spirit.

This humorous book proffers advice to teenagers, and Packer's informal, matter-of-fact, and collaborative style is consistent with that aim. The book targets 12- to 17-year-old readers and is not written from an "us-against-them" perspective but rather as "how to take the first step in making the relationship better." Chapter titles include "Taking Charge of the Fight Brigade," "Tricks and Treats," and "Close Encounters of the Worst Kind." Packer focuses on the perennial conflicts and developmental tensions between parents and teenagers. Parents will not feel ganged up on by this book but would agree with the author on the identified problems and solutions. The strong albeit infrequent ratings and interesting slant of this text give it Diamond in the Rough status.

**Not Recommended**

★★ *Preparing for Adolescence* (1978) by James Dobson. Santa Ana, CA: Vision House.

## ▮ FILMS

**Strongly Recommended**

★★★★★ *Stand by Me* (1987) directed by Rob Reiner. R rating. 89 minutes.

An excellent film about the rites of passage of four adolescents who grow toward manhood through a series of events ignited by the accidental death of a young boy. The boys learn the importance of friendship and loyalty. During their two-day journey, they encounter a number of adventures that further clarify for each what kind of a person he is becoming. As their journey progresses, each boy is put to the test, and each responds with a mixture of childish fear or grief within his evolving person. One of the highest-rated movies in our national studies.

★★★★ *Dead Poets Society* (1990) directed by Peter Weir. PG rating. 129 minutes.

An English teacher struggles to fit into a conservative prep school. His passion for poetry and his charismatic personality help establish a strong bond with his male students. Several of the boys revive a secret society. Conflict ensues between the boys and adults, with tragedy befalling one of the boys as his father tries to pull him out of the theater society. The teacher's inspirational motto is "seize the day." A powerful and uneasy movie that received several Academy Award nominations. (Also reviewed in Chapter 39 on Suicide.)

★★★★ *A Bronx Tale* (1993) directed by Robert De Niro. R rating. 121 minutes.

A boy is offered disparate models of manhood by two men who care about him. His hardworking father says a man becomes a hero by working hard, providing for his family, and living honestly. But a Mafioso advises him to live a fancier life, be loyal, and live by his own values. In another relevant plot, at 17 the boy falls in love with a Black girl and, since this is forbidden in 1968 among both the Italians and Blacks in the Bronx, he seeks the men's advice. He is told that he must do what he thinks is best and face the consequences. In a different subplot, he finds himself, because of peer pressure, about to do a terrible thing that would affect his whole future. The themes are universal in adolescence even if the circumstances are not. This film offers teenagers much to ponder and discuss.

★★★★ *The Breakfast Club* (1985) directed by John Hughes. R rating. 95 minutes.

Five high-school students from different walks of life in suburban Chicago serve Saturday detention together. As the day progresses, they delve into each other's private worlds and struggle to be honest with themselves and one another. The realistic diversity and the separation of roles among the students are likely to resonate with many adolescents. A valuable lesson on how misleading first impressions and preconceived ideas often get in the way of nurturing relationships.

★★★★ *Thirteen* (2003) directed by Catherine Hardwicke. R rating. 100 minutes.

*Thirteen* tells the chilling tale of Tracy, a good girl who makes the wrong decisions. Tracy is an honor-roll student who enjoys a healthy relationship with her mother but proves unpopular in school. She desperately wants to become friends with the most popular girl, Evie, and so she steals a purse and hands the money over to Evie. This moment marks the beginning of a downward spiral for Tracy as she embarks on a path of drugs, crime, and unwanted pregnancies led by Evie. The relationship between Tracy and her mother deteriorates as she continues to self-destruct. The film ends with the mother holding her daughter and crying over Tracy's and her uncertain futures. Tracy's unsettling story can serve as an example of how strong and destructive peer influences can be and the need for close parenting during the teenage years.

★★★★ *Circle of Friends* (1995) directed by Pat O'Connor. PG-13 rating. 112 minutes.

This roommate comedy set in Ireland in 1957 is a good old-fashioned coming-of-age story about three friends who confront their changing lives in unique ways. The combined and complex forces of church, economics, social class, and sex weigh heavily on their choices.

★★★★ *Little Women* (1933) directed by George Cukor. Unrated. 117 minutes.

From the timeless classic by Louise May Alcott, this movie about transition to adulthood during the Civil War era details the ups and downs of four sisters. A humorous story of how they learn moral lessons and grow from childish pleasures to adult joys. Received many Academy Award nominations.

★★★★ *Good Will Hunting* (1997) directed by Gus Van Sant. R rating. 126 minutes.

Will Hunting, a brilliant 20-year-old man, is acting out his conflicts through oppositional behavior, which lands him in a life-altering relationship with a psychologist played by Robin Williams. Will is a college janitor who is discovered to be a mathematical genius and is mentored by a math professor who sees a great future for Will. There is no future, however, until Will can resolve several dilemmas in his turbulent psychotherapy. He must accept that his intellectual gift will lead him away from his blue-collar culture and friends; he must heal his rage and shame from unacknowledged childhood abuse; and he must recognize that his intellect and his secret have squelched his ability to feel. This is a powerful story that illuminates class struggle, the responsibility of giftedness, and the centrality of human connection. This film won an Academy Award for Best Original Screenplay in 1997, and Robin Williams won the Best Supporting Actor award.

## Recommended

★★★ *My Bodyguard* (1980) directed by Michael Hayes. PG rating. 96 minutes.

The son of a hotel manager finds himself the target of a school bully, then employs a school outcast, the biggest kid in class, to be his bodyguard. The adolescents struggle with communication and conflict resolution, friends and support systems, and parent–child relationships. Filmed in and around Chicago, this comedy/drama is entertainment with an enduring message. (Also reviewed in Chapter 13 on Bullying.)

★★★ *Splendor in the Grass* (1961) directed by Elia Kazan. Not rated. 124 minutes.

This is the story of a blue-collar girl and a rich boy who fall in love in the 1920s. They are young, passionate, and conflicted about where their relationship is leading. The girl, played by Natalie Wood, attempts suicide and is placed in a psychiatric institution. In the meantime, the devil-may-care boy, played by Warren Beatty, continues with his free-spirited, fast-paced lifestyle. The film presents the moral conflicts and gender differences characteristic of the 1920s. The moral of the story, however, is how Natalie Wood's character awakens and matures to see the shallowness and limitations of her boyfriend.

★★★   *Powder* (1995) directed by Victor Salva. PG-13 rating. 111 minutes.

On her way to the delivery room, a mother is struck by lightning and dies. Her child is born an albino, and the distraught father calls him Powder because of his white skin. Left to be raised by his grandparents, Powder lives in a basement. He possesses a photographic memory, an exceptionally high IQ, and telepathic powers. All of these qualities provide him with his greatest ability: compassion. A well-meaning film that goes to supernatural heights to demonstrate acceptance and rejection, love and hate, and identity development.

★★★   *Pretty in Pink* (1986) directed by Howard Deutch. PG-13 rating. 96 minutes.

A high-school girl lives with her loving father who must budget their money wisely. Accompanied by her insecure best friend, she feels threatened when a wealthy and well-meaning boy asks her out on a date. An entertaining and sensitive movie about growing pains and the meaning of money.

★★★   *Sixteen Candles* (1984) directed by John Hughes. PG rating. 93 minutes.

A fresh comedy about a 16th birthday that turns out to be anything but sweet when a girl's parents forget about her birthday while preparing for her sister's wedding. The story focuses on the feelings of a 16-year-old girl who dreams of finding Mr. Right, who already has his eye on her.

**Not Recommended**

★★   *St. Elmo's Fire* (1986) directed by Joel Schumacher. R rating. 110 minutes.

## ■ INTERNET RESOURCES

**General Websites**

★★★★★   *A Parent's Guide to Surviving the Teen Years* kidshealth.org/parent/growth/grow-ing/adolescence.html

This guide from the Nemours Foundation is a solid, excellent resource to help parents better understand the changes their teenager is going through, and to help them along the way.

★★★★★   *TeensHealth* www.teenshealth.org

This excellent resource from the Nemours Foundation is directed toward a teen audience and offers hundreds of articles on topics including body, mind, sexual health, food, fitness, drugs, health conditions, infections, schools, and jobs, among many others. Articles are well written, engaging, and just the right length. Regularly updated with new information.

★★★★   *Parenting Teens* parentingteens.about.com

This resource from About.com guide Denise Witmer offers a lot of regularly updated tips, advice, and solid information on helping to raise a well-balanced adolescent, with special sections on high school and troubled teens.

★★★   *Active Minds* www.activeminds.org

Active Minds is a nonprofit organization working to "utilize the student voice to change the conversation about mental health on college campuses." It has over 150 chapters on local college campuses, and its website acts primarily as an organizational tool for these chapters and people looking to get more involved with this group. The site provides useful links to many mental health resources, as well as the many programs it has developed to help spread the message about positive mental health.

## Psychoeducational Materials

★★★★★   *Teen Center* www.wholefamily.com/parent-center/window-into-your-teen-s-world

A helpful resource from WholeFamily.com.

★★★★★   *Info for Teens* www.plannedparenthood.org/info-for-teens

This large, high-quality, and rich site, as would be expected from Planned Parenthood, offers information written for adolescents on relationships, sexuality, LGBTQ, ask the experts, and pregnancy.

★★★★   *The Teenager's Guide to the Real World* www.bygpub.com/books/tg2rw/tg2rw-toc.htm

Sections from the book of the same name include essays on dating and relationships, sexuality, studying, volunteering, jobs, cars, college, and others.

★★★★   *Self-Help Brochures* www.counselingcenter.illinois.edu/?page_id=7

The University of Illinois at Urbana-Champaign's counseling center has posted dozens of helpful online brochures for their students, which address issues many teens deal with. Well written and generally brief, they are targeted toward young adults and teenagers.

★★★★   *Information Sheets for Teens* teenadvice.about.com/od/factsheetsforteens/Fact_Sheets_for_Teens.htm

On this website you'll find two dozen fact sheets that are well written and could be useful for opening discussions of topics such as date rape, oral sex, marijuana, lying, and many more. Part of the larger About.com Teen Advice website, which is a great resource for teens to learn more about dating and sex, their bodies, and school and money topics.

★★★   *Friends First* www.friendsfirst.org

A nonprofit and nonsectarian organization dedicated to helping teens make informed decisions about their sexual behavior with a focus on abstinence, as well as alcohol, tobacco, and drug use. The website doesn't appear to be updated too often.

## ■ SUPPORT GROUPS

### Boys Town

Phone: 800-448-3000
www.boystown.org/home.htm
They provide crisis intervention, information, and referrals for the general public. Free, confidential crisis intervention. They work with children and families.

### Covenant House

Phone: 800-999-9999
Nineline is a nationwide crisis/suicide hotline. Referrals are made for youths who are having trouble with drugs, domestic violence, homelessness, runaways, and so on. They offer message relays, report abuse, and help parents with problems with their kids.

### Families Anonymous

Phone: 800-736-9805
www.familiesanonymous.org
A 12-step fellowship for relatives and friends concerned about substance abuse and behavioral problems.

### KidsPeace

Phone: 800-543-7283
www.kidspeace.org
They offer information and referrals to public and private services for children and adolescents in crisis.

### Parents Anonymous

Phone: 909-621-6184
www.parentsanonymous.org
Professionally facilitated peer-led group for parents who are having difficulty and would like to learn more effective ways of raising their children.

### Parents Without Partners

Phone: 800-637-7974 or 561-391-8833
www.parentswithoutpartners.org
Brings teens from single-parent homes together to share ideas and problems, develop leadership skills, and plan fun activities.

### S.A.D.D. (Students Against Drunk Driving)

Phone: 1-877-SADD-Inc or 508-481-3568
www.sadd.org

**See also** Child Development and Parenting (Chapter 15), Families and Stepfamilies (Chapter 23), and Violent Youth (Chapter 41).

# VIOLENT YOUTH

$V$iolent acts committed by children and adolescents have become shockingly public in recent years. The Sandy Hook, Columbine, and Virginia Tech shootings sensitized us and confronted us with the increasing prevalence of violent youth. The number of offenders under age 18 admitted to American prisons more than doubled from 1985 to 1997 (U.S. Department of Justice Bureau of Statistics, 2002). We are beginning to realize that violent youth is a reality that cannot be ignored. Families, clinicians, educators, and community members alike are searching for effective ways to prevent violence and to treat violent children.

For our purposes, the topic of violent youth includes school violence, criminal behavior, and the formal diagnoses of oppositional defiant disorder (ODD) and conduct disorder. These disorders are defined as persistent patterns in which children behave aggressively, violate the basic rights of others, and repeatedly defy social rules. The major difference between the two is severity: ODD is less severe than conduct disorder. Both disorders are more common among boys than girls.

In this chapter, we showcase self-help books, films, autobiographies, and websites about violent youth (Box 41.1). In each case, the resources are divided between those written for the troubled youths themselves and those written for the people with the task of caring for them.

## ■ SELF-HELP BOOKS

In our national studies, only 10 of 27 listed self-help books on violent children were rated by more than five experts. Unfortunately, the self-help books in this area are not yet widely known among the mental health community.

### Strongly Recommended

★★★★★ *Your Defiant Child* (1998) by Russell A. Barkley and Christine M. Benton. New York: Guilford.

This thorough self-help book offers an eight-step plan for families struggling with a combative child. Psychologist Barkley, famous for his books on ADHD (Chapter 9), emphasizes consistency and cooperation, promoting changes through a system of praise, rewards, and mild punishment. The book clearly details what causes defiance, when it becomes a problem, and how it can be resolved. It also offers assessment tools to help evaluate a situation. This practical book is filled with charts, questionnaires, and checklists. An excellent,

---

## BOX 41.1
## RECOMMENDATION HIGHLIGHTS

### SELF-HELP BOOKS

- On reducing oppositional and defiant behavior:

  ★★★★★ *Your Defiant Child* by Russell Barkley and Christine Benton

  ★★★★ *The Explosive Child* by Ross Greene

  ★★★ *The Defiant Child* by Douglas Riley

  ★★★ *The Kazdin Method for Parenting the Defiant Child* by Alan E. Kazdin

- On understanding and intervening with violent youth:

  ★★★ *Lost Boys* by James Garbarino

- On rescuing boys from the destructive myths of boyhood:

  ★★★ *Raising Cain* by Dan Kindlon and Michael Thompson

  ★★★ *Real Boys* by William Pollack

### AUTOBIOGRAPHIES

- On running with a street gang in violent neighborhoods:

  ◆ *Monster by* Sanyika Shakur

  ◆ *Always Running* by Luis J. Rodriguez

- On growing up in tough surroundings and juvenile homes:

  ★★★ *All Souls* by Michael Patrick MacDonald

### FILMS

- On school violence in the United States:

  ★★★★ *Bowling for Columbine*

  ★★★ *Elephant*

- On surviving a violent stepfather and a passive mother:

  ★★★ *This Boy's Life*

### INTERNET RESOURCES

- On youth violence in general:

  ★★★★ *Striving To Reduce Youth Violence Everywhere* www.safeyouth.org

  ★★★★ *Youth Violence* www.cdc.gov/violenceprevention/youthviolence

- On preventing youth violence:

  ★★★★ *Committee for Children* www.cfchildren.org

---

research-based resource for families and clinicians alike, *Your Defiant Child* tops the list of self-help books in this area according to the experts in our national studies.

★★★★    *The Explosive Child* (1999) by Ross Greene. New York: Harper Collins.

Green attempts to explicate the dynamics of violent behavior in children. In a compassionate style, the author helps readers to reduce the child's meltdowns and the parents' frustration. The text is long and serious, covering an enormous amount of ground. Excerpts from actual sessions with parents and children will help psychotherapists, families, and identified patients understand the origins of these violent acts and how a treatment plan can be developed. The book addresses the education, psychotherapy, and medication of violent children. A splendid albeit lengthy resource.

**Recommended**

★★★ *The Defiant Child: A Parent's Guide to Oppositional Defiant Disorder* (2002) by Douglas A. Riley. Dallas: Taylor.

Riley explains the mindset of ODD children and teaches parents how to recognize the signs and modify the child's oppositional behavior. He helps parents remain in control when their children are acting out. The book is written like a behavioral treatment plan for parents, filled with practical interventions, case examples, and family therapy techniques. This well-written, easy-to-read book is a perfect fit for parents who hunger for information about ODD. If it had been rated by a few more experts in our national studies, this book would have received at least a 4-star rating.

★★★ *Raising Cain: Protecting the Emotional Life of Boys* (2000) by Daniel J. Kindlon and Michael Thompson. New York: Ballantine.

Two psychologists examine the "culture of cruelty" boys live in, the "tyranny of toughness," the disadvantages of being a boy in elementary school, the systematic squelching of boys' emotional lives, and the corrective actions that society can take without turning "boys into girls." The authors assert that boys need to become more "emotionally literate." They advance seven things that boys need to protect their emotional lives. Topics covered include harsh discipline, the distance between father and sons, the connection between mother and sons, depression and suicide, the role of drugs and alcohol in attempting to fill the emotional void, relationships with girls, and anger/violence. For parents, teachers, and anyone working with violent children.

★★★ *The Kazdin Method for Parenting the Defiant Child* (2009) by Alan E. Kazdin. New York: First Mariner.

Kazdin, a leading psychologist on treating conduct disorder, argues that parents often discipline their children in probably instinctive but ineffective ways. When parents nag, lecture, and explain, they forget to praise and reinforce. Punishing rarely changes anything more than the current behavior, and nagging makes the desirable behavior less likely to occur. Kazdin applies his extensively researched methods to children of differing ages and includes troubleshooting, special situations, and parental stress. He notes the commonsense but important actions that parents often forget to take, such as instruct calmly, listen to your child, encourage social interaction, always know where your child is, and develop rituals and routines with the child. An excellent, research-guided method for harried parents of defiant children.

★★★ *Lost Boys: Why Our Sons Turn Violent and How We Can Save Them* (2000) by James Garbarino. New York: Anchor.

This author looks at violence in boys and explores the etiology and treatment of violent behavior. Garbarino delves into the social, psychological, and moral factors that lead boys into violence. He offers a clear and broad-spectrum approach to reclaiming these lost boys. He blends statistics, personal experiences, and clinical suggestions with compassion and reality.

★★★ *Real Boys: Rescuing Our Sons from the Myths of Boyhood* (1998) by William Pollack. New York: Henry Holt.

The author explores boys' feelings of sadness, loneliness, and confusion while they try to appear tough, cheerful, and confident. Pollack discusses how to let real boys be real men by revising the "Boys' Code" and still feeling connected. He writes about what boys are like, how to help them, and what happens if they aren't helped. Adults working with violent boys will probably find this book valuable. Also reviewed in Chapter 29, Men's Issues, where it received a higher, 4-star rating.

### Diamond in the Rough

♦ *High Risk: Children Without a Conscience* (1990) by Ken Magid and Carole A. McKelvey. New York: Bantam.

Children without a conscience are growing in number and are increasingly at risk for becoming "trust bandits," conmen, dance-away lovers, backstabbers, and even sociopathic killers. Magid and McKelvey discuss what attachment is and what happens when that bond does not occur in people's lives. On the book jacket, the authors ask, "Who are these children without a conscience?" They answer, "They are children who cannot trust, children who cannot love, and children who will not be loved." Highly but rarely rated in our national studies, leading to a Diamond in the Rough designation. A book for parents and professionals alike.

## ■ AUTOBIOGRAPHIES

### Recommended

★★★ *Sleepers* (1996) by Lorenzo Carcaterra. New York: Ballantine.

As a young man growing up in a tough neighborhood, the author and his friends engaged in crime. When they were caught, the four teenagers were sent to a juvenile home, where they were assaulted and raped by guards. Years later, one is now a lawyer, another is a journalist (Carcaterra), and the other two are murderers, and they take revenge against their tormentors. A fast-paced emotional tale that has been made into a movie, with names, dates, and places changed "to protect the innocent and the guilty." Questions have been raised about the authenticity of the story, but whether it is a true story or the invention of its journalist-author, the book describes brutal conditions of confinement and the vicious cycle of violence. Also reviewed in Chapter 2 on Abuse.

★★★ *All Souls: A Family History from Southie* (2000) by Michael Patrick MacDonald. New York: Ballantine.

Gripping, gritty story of growing up in South Boston's poor Irish Catholic housing projects. The author was the seventh of nine children born to a single mom who worked hard to provide for her family. Describes neighborhood and family loyalty in the face of grinding poverty, rampant corruption (everyone who could, hustles or is on the take), violent youth terrorizing the residents, unwanted pregnancies, and drug dealing. MacDonald lost half his siblings to violence or suicide. A story of resilience, survival, and redemption. The author is a neighborhood activist working on social programs in South Boston. A good book for understanding the scars, both visible and invisible, left by growing up in a brutal neighborhood.

### Diamonds in the Rough

◆ *Monster: The Autobiography of an L.A. Gang Member* (2004) by Sanyika Shakur. New York: Grove.

Shooting several rival gang members without remorse brought 11-year-old Kody Scott initiation into the Eight Tray Crips, one of Los Angeles' most notorious street gangs. His ruthlessness and brutality as a street soldier earned him the nickname "Monster." While confined in a maximum security cell during one of his many prison terms, he took on a new persona, becoming Sanyika Shakur, a Black nationalist and activist campaigner against the causes of inner-city violence and poverty. This is a hard-hitting, graphic account, full of "hood slang" and of gang warfare in the projects, on inner-city streets, and in prison, where violence is often a way of life. The book provides insight into a parallel and disturbing reality.

◆ *Always Running: La Vida Loca: Gang Days in L.A.* (2005) by Luis J. Rodriguez. New York: Touchstone.

The autobiography is a disturbing account of the author's crazy life (*la vida loca*) as a member of the East Los Angeles street gang he joined when he was 11. He adapted at an early age to a world in which beatings, murder, maiming, robbery, rape, drug use, and extortion were rampant. He started inhaling an aerosol spray, which almost killed him, and experimented with heroin. To join another gang, Rodriguez was required to shoot a man. He was sentenced to prison where, like the author of *Monster*, who describes Black "gangsta" life, he underwent a personal transformation. The violent deaths of so many friends finally sank in, and he decides to start a new life as a poet, journalist, community organizer, and peacemaker warning young people of the dangers of gangbanging. Writing about his experiences assisted in his transformation. He believed he had put the crazy years behind him until his son Ramiro joined a Chicago street gang and got into trouble with the law. Rodriguez subsequently opened a cultural center in Sylmar, California, aimed at helping Latino youth find alternatives through art and literature to the senseless violence plaguing *barrio* life.

## ■ FILMS

### Strongly Recommended

★★★★ *Bowling for Columbine* (2002) directed by Michael Moore. MA rating. 120 minutes.

Inspired by the devastating shootings at Columbine, this documentary explores the excessive violence in our society and its effects on our youth. Moore juxtaposes the violence in the United States with Canada, a country with far fewer cases of violence. He does this while showing past school shootings and thus providing a frame of reference for the Columbine tragedy. The film powerfully reminds viewers of the prevalence of violent youth and of the urgent need for change.

### Recommended

⋆⋆⋆  *This Boy's Life* (1993) directed by Michael Caton-Jones. R rating. 114 minutes.

After her divorce, a mother takes her son, played by Leonard DeCaprio, and heads west. She settles in Concrete (Washington) and for a vicious but colorful man, Robert DeNiro, who makes DeCaprio's life miserable with his pretensions, bullying, lying, and violence. The mother, desperate for the paycheck DeNiro provides, remains neutral. As a consequence, DeCaprio is forced to accept the abuse and to grow up faster and more independent. Based on a true story, the film is a realistic tale of a child surviving an abusive stepfather and a passive mother. Had this film been more frequently known by the mental health professionals in our studies, it would have probably garnered a 4- or 5-star rating.

⋆⋆⋆  *Elephant* (2003) directed by Gus Van Sant. R rating. 81 minutes.

This film reenacts the shootings at a high school similar to Columbine. The day unfolds as students and teachers interact with the shooters before the violence ensues. Several students are killed while others escape. We are not given a reason why certain people survive while others die or even why the shooting happened. This unique film offers no explanations or insights into the incident, but forces viewers to think long and hard about the origins of youth violence after the credits end. No thematic tricks or neat closure here; just in-your-face honesty about a societal plague.

⋆⋆⋆  *Holes* (2002) directed by Andrew Davis. PG rating. 117 minutes.

After being wrongfully convicted of stealing a pair of baseball shoes, Stanley is sent to Camp Green Lake, a juvenile work camp, to serve his punishment. The camp is located in a dried-up lake in the middle of the desert, where the boys are forced to dig a hole 5 feet deep and 5 feet wide each day. The warden claims it will build character but is secretly trying to find buried treasure. Stanley becomes friends with another delinquent, Zero, who escapes from the camp. A worried Stanley follows, and not only do they find each other but they also unearth the curse that has plagued Stanley's family for generations—as well as the buried treasure. Though the film has elements of mystery and fantasy, it delves into the lives of several troubled youths. It depicts the boys' troubles that have led them to the camp.

⋆⋆⋆  *The United States of Leland* (2004) directed by Matthew Ryan Hoge. R rating. 108 minutes.

This psychological drama revolves around the imprisoned Leland, who has been convicted of murdering a disabled boy. The film depicts the troubled home life of Leland while also attempting to unravel the motivations behind the murder. The prison's writing teacher, Mr. Madison, takes a special interest in Leland's case with the intent to write a book. Through his investigation he discovers several details of the murder and its impact on those involved. Throughout, Leland comes to accept that "nothing can make what happened unhappen."

★★★ *The Good Son* (1993) directed by Joseph Ruben. R rating. 87 minutes.

Macaulay Culkin plays an evil boy of about 10 who commits crimes, enjoys torture, kills his baby brother, and performs assorted psychopathic acts. His evil is unrecognized by the adults, including a psychiatrist, but it is seen by Elijah Wood, who suffers from it as well. It is not a suitable film for children; its only redeeming value is the frightening presentation of unfettered violence.

### Not Recommended

★★ *City of God* (2003) directed by Fernando Meirelles and Katia Lund. R rating. 130 minutes.

## ■ INTERNET RESOURCES

Bullying resources are included in Chapter 13.

### General Websites

★★★★ *Striving To Reduce Youth Violence Everywhere* www.cdc.gov/violenceprevention/stryve/index.html

STRYVE, a website sponsored by the Centers for Disease Control & Prevention, tries to prevent youth violence. It's primarily meant for educators and policymakers and offers a wealth of resources, including online training.

★★★★ *Youth Violence* www.cdc.gov/violenceprevention/youthviolence

This resource from the U.S. Centers for Disease Control & Prevention covers a wide range of topics related to youth violence, including links to the Surgeon General's report on youth violence and other government policy documents. Additional topics covered are bullying, prevention strategies, school violence, aggression online, and more.

### Psychoeducational Materials

★★★★ *The Warning Signs of Youth Violence* www.apa.org/helpcenter/warning-signs.aspx

This set of articles from the American Psychological Association offers a handy set of information about recognizing youth violence, understanding the reasons behind it, and what we can do about it.

★★★★ *Early Warning, Timely Response: A Guide to Safe Schools* www2.ed.gov/about/offices/list/osers/osep/gtss.html

This guide from the U.S. Department of Education offers research-based practices designed to assist school communities identify warning signs early and develop prevention, intervention, and crisis response plans.

★★★★  *Committee for Children* www.cfchildren.org

This nonprofit organization is working to prevent bullying, violence, and child abuse and offers information about their programs on this website, which is primarily intended for educators and policymakers.

★★★  *National Association of School Psychologists* www.nasponline.org

The National Association of School Psychologists has a section devoted to Families that offers helpful information about bullying and school violence.

### Statistics and Data
★★★★  *Youth Violence* www.ncjrs.gov/yviolence

The National Criminal Justice Reference Service provides this site to offer easy access to statistics on youth violence, youth gangs, and school violence; articles about gun violence and prevention; as well as a regularly updated list on the latest research in this area and more.

**See also** Anger (Chapter 6), Bullying (Chapter 13), Child Development and Parenting (Chapter 15), and Teenagers and Parenting (Chapter 40).

# CHAPTER 42

# WOMEN'S ISSUES

The mental health professions have historically portrayed human behavior using male-dominant themes. While much progress has been made in recent decades, sexism is still evident in society, and women continue to be discriminated against in the workplace, in politics, at home, and perhaps in self-help resources.

Critics argue that self-help materials have perpetuated many stereotypes and myths harmful to women. What are these stereotypes? We can journey through the chapters of this *Self-Help That Works* and find resources that condemn women for dysfunctional personalities, that treat codependency as a woman's disease, that consider eating disorders as uniquely female problems, and that blame mothers for most of their children's problems. We find books that overdramatize sex differences and that favor the male "difference" (women are described as overly invested in romantic love, dependent on others, and incapable of controlling their emotions). Few authors have historically written about the positive features of being female, and fewer still give credence to many of the daily responsibilities women have traditionally performed and continue to manage.

The best self-help resources on women's issues address such concerns and help women become aware that what have been labeled as character defects in the past are actually strengths that should be nurtured, rewarded, and cherished. Of course, many resources in other categories address women's issues and provide self-help advice for women. In other chapters, we recommend a number of excellent self-help books on specific aspects of women's lives, such as assertion, communication, parenting, intimacy, pregnancy, and sexuality.In this chapter, we describe and evaluate self-help resources—books, autobiographies, films, and websites—that address quintessentially women's issues (Box 42.1). These include work roles, gender stereotypes, sex differences, feminist concerns, and women's health.

## ■ SELF-HELP BOOKS

### Strongly Recommended

★★★★★   *Our Bodies, Ourselves: A New Edition for a New Era* (2005) by the Boston Women's Health Book Collective. New York: Touchstone.

Hailed by *Time* magazine as one of the most influential nonfiction books of the 20th century, this classic updates earlier editions with new information on nutrition, exercise, sexual health, older women, birth control methods, and disorders that primarily affect women, to name just a few topics. The newer editions keep women updated on physical

## BOX 42.1
## RECOMMENDATION HIGHLIGHTS

**SELF-HELP BOOKS**
- On women's health and well-being:
  - ★★★★★ *Our Bodies, Ourselves* by the Boston Women's Health Book Collective
  - ★★★ *The Wisdom of Menopause* by Christiane Northrup
  - ◆ *Half the Sky* by Nicholas D. Kristof and Sheryl WuDunn
- On women's work and parenting roles:
  - ★★★★ *The Second Shift* by Arlie Hochschild
- On women's life stages and transitions:
  - ★★★★ *The Seasons of a Woman's Life* by Daniel J. Levinson and Judy D. Levinson
  - ★★★ *Life Preservers* by Harriet Lerner
- On inspiring and nurturing women:
  - ★★★★ *Chicken Soup for the Woman's Soul* by Jack Canfield et al.
- On gender stereotypes and self-image traps:
  - ★★★★ *The Mismeasure of Woman* by Carol Tavris
  - ★★★ *Body Traps* by Judith Rodin

**AUTOBIOGRAPHIES**
- On the remarkable lives and searches of multitalented woman:
  - ★★★★★ *Heart of a Woman* by Maya Angelou
  - ★★★ *Reason for Hope* by Jane Goodall
- On a personal look at the women's movement:
  - ★★★ *Deborah, Golda, and Me* by Letty Cottin Pogrebin
  - ◆ *In Our Time* by Susan Brownmiller
  - ◆ *Life So Far* by Betty Friedan
- On influential women and mothering experiences:
  - ◆ *Mothers* by Alexandra Stoddard

**FILMS**
- On women bonding on the baseball field and thriving without men:
  - ★★★★ *A League of Their Own*
- On the interdependence of women and the ability to change:
  - ★★★★ *Fried Green Tomatoes*
  - ★★★★ *How to Make an American Quilt*
- On the balance between family and career and midlife reevaluations:
  - ★★★★ *The Turning Point*
- On the history of women's rights and suffrage:
  - ★★★ *Iron Jawed Angels*

**INTERNET RESOURCES**

- On general women's issues:
  - ★★★★★ *Women's Issues* womensissues.about.com
  - ★★★★ *Huffington Post: Women* www.huffingtonpost.com/women
- On women's medical concerns:
  - ★★★★★ *Womenshealth.gov* www.womenshealth.gov
  - ★★★★★ *North American Menopause Society* www.menopause.org
- On employment discrimination:
  - ★★★★★ *Equal Employment Opportunity Commission* www.eeoc.gov

and mental health, along with legal, political, and social organizational realities of women's identities. A mission for the authors is to encourage women to get together—to meet, talk to, and listen to each other. Women interested in women's passions and potentials will thoroughly enjoy this resource. This 5-star book will probably leave women feeling, to use one of the most overused words of past decade, empowered. With more than 4 million copies sold, this is one of the most highly regarded self-help resources in any of our national studies, and deservedly so.

★★★★  *The Second Shift* (1989) by Arlie Hochschild. New York: Viking.

This self-help resource focuses on the inequality of gender roles in two-career couples with children. Hochschild conducted extensive interviews and home observations of 50 two-career couples with children under the age of 6 to discover how they allotted their time and responsibility to careers, child rearing, and household chores. Not surprisingly, she found that women handled the bulk of child care and housework in addition to holding down full-time jobs outside the home. Hochschild categorizes married couples as traditional (the husband works and the wife stays at home), transitional (both work, and he does less than she thinks he should around the house), or egalitarian (both spend equal time on work and home responsibilities). In her study, all the families were in the last two categories, and the majority were transitional. Hochschild believes that men and women use gender strategies that are based on deep-seated emotional beliefs about manhood and womanhood as they try to define how to juggle jobs and child-rearing and household responsibilities. A central goal in *The Second Shift* is to bring these gender strategies into the open so that married couples can discuss and benefit from them. Multiple solutions—from the personal to the societal—are presented to rectify the inequalities. What separates *The Second Shift* from standard feminist fare is the texture of the reporting and the subtlety of the insights. A valuable, if disconcerting, book.

★★★★  *The Mismeasure of Woman* (1992) by Carol Tavris. New York: Simon & Schuster.

This book explores the stereotyping of women and comparative characteristics with men. Topics include the question of women's inferiority or superiority to men; premenstrual syndrome; postmenstrual syndrome; the diagnostic bias that women get sick and men have problems; and fables of female sexuality. Tavris hypothesizes that no matter how hard women try, discrimination determines that they can't measure up. They are criticized for being too feminine or not feminine enough and are judged by how well they fit into a male world. The book contains a review of research that documents how women continue to be ignored, misrepresented, and even harmed by male-dominated health professions. Tavris believes that more evidence exists for similarities between the sexes that for differences between them. She explores how society pathologizes women through psychiatric diagnoses, sexist divorce rulings, and images of women as moody, self-defeating, and unstable. This is an excellent analysis of gender stereotyping and how women should be measured by their own standards. Although getting dated, *The Mismeasure of Woman* is well documented and captivating, presenting a witty feminist portrayal of women's dilemmas and what can be done about them.

★★★★   *The Seasons of a Woman's Life* (1996) by Daniel J. Levinson and Judy D. Levinson. New York: Knopf.

This book, the counterpart to Daniel Levinson's *Seasons of a Man's Life* (reviewed in Chapter 4 on Adult Development), traces the developmental stages of women's adulthood. It is based on lengthy interviews conducted in the 1980s of 55 randomly selected women from various professions and at various stages in their lives. This study confirms that in every woman's life, there is a mixture of joy and sorrow, success and failure, and self-fulfillment and self-defeat. This 4-star book is favorably regarded and compellingly addresses women's development throughout the life cycle.

★★★★   *Chicken Soup for the Woman's Soul* (1996) by Jack Canfield, Mark Victor Hansen, Jennifer Read Hawthorne, and Marci Shimoff. Deerfield Beach, FL: Health Communication.

These best-selling *Chicken Soup* authors have written another inspiring book, this time for women. The book is designed to reinforce the bonds between women via 101 stories describing the unique and the common life experiences of girls and women. Some of the experiences shared in this book address goals, relationships, giving birth, job responsibilities, family, and friendships. This is a book you can pick up for 2 minutes or 2 hours that will probably make you feel moved and guided.

**Recommended**

★★★   *Too Good for Her Own Good: Breaking Free from the Burden of Female Responsibility* (1990) by Claudia Bepko and Jo-Ann Krestan. New York: Harper & Row.

The authors sensitively examine how low self-esteem in women results from feeling that they are not good enough. The "Goodness Code" requires women to be attractive, ladylike, unselfish, altruistic, and competent—all without complaining. The authors argue that goodness comes to most women almost instinctively; they feel they must be competent in virtually everything they do while remaining responsible for the happiness of others. Yet no matter how hard women work to please others, they often feel inadequate, because part of being good is knowing that they are never good enough. The result is that far too many women suffer from low esteem and feel insecure. The authors then discuss how to break free by changing the balance of various factors. A number of case histories buttress the authors' points. The book's enthusiasts said that many women with low self-esteem who have lived their lives in the service of others' needs will find themselves described on almost every page of this book.

★★★ *Body Traps* (1992) by Judith Rodin. New York: Morrow.

Society has constructed a destructive perception of female bodies, and this book shows how women can free themselves from this trap. Psychologist Rodin argues that good looks, appearance, and fitness have become the measures women use to evaluate their self-worth. A number of the traps discussed by Rodin are the variety trap, the shame trap, the competition trap, the food trap, the dieting rituals trap, the fitness trap, and the success trap. Mental health experts in our studies consistently rated the book favorably, but it was not frequently rated. The book is a thoughtful, penetrating look at society's preoccupation with women's appearance and the unrealistic expectations and harmful effects the preoccupation has produced. *Body Traps* is informative and well written, and it is a helpful guide to what women's bodies mean to them.

★★★ *The Wisdom of Menopause* (2012 revised ed.) by Christiane Northrup. New York: Bantam.

From her perspective as an obstetrician-gynecologist and from her own menopausal journey, Northrup movingly traces women's changes through the menopausal experience. Initial chapters chronicle her movement toward authenticity, self-fulfillment, and an excitement for life that is unleashed as a result of menopausal changes. The author argues that women's ease in showing anger, intolerance for disrespect, and rejection of diminished roles at perimenopause are not the negative result of raging hormones, but rather the beginning of clarity in self-perception and a confrontation with the cultural prescription of women as relational caretakers. Many topics will hit home with women of a wide age range, such as cultural ambivalence about the meaning of money, the decision about hormone replacement, and understanding the physiological effects of menopause, including hot flashes, mental fuzziness, headaches, and mood swings. Valuable information is offered regarding mammograms, brain functioning, skin changes, bone density and osteoporosis, cardiac protection, and sex after the age of 50. A splendid and bestselling self-help resource grounded in both medical science and feminist analysis.

★★★ *Life Preservers: Good Advice When You Need It Most* (1996) by Harriet Lerner. New York: Harper Collins.

*Life Preservers* compiles the questions and answers published in the author's monthly *New Woman* magazine column, "Harriet Lerner's Good Advice." Some of the questions are frequently asked ones; others are rarely voiced. Topics include work and creativity, anger and intimacy, friendship and marriage, children and parents, loss and betrayal, and sexuality and health. The questions are diverse, poignant, and candid, questions many would want to ask but do not. Lerner's answers are thoughtful and straightforward and offer well-developed directions that walk the reader through a decision-making process, identifying as she goes the possible consequences of taking action. Her writing style is colorful and humorous yet compatible with the seriousness of her work.

★★★ *The Silent Passage* (2010 updated ed.) by Gail Sheehy. New York: Random House.

As reviewed in Chapter 4 on Adult Development, this bestseller addresses menopause. Sheehy's objectives are to erase the stigma of menopause, normalize the process, and direct women to medical and psychological resources they may need. An engaging and easy read on a neglected topic.

★★★ *Women Who Run with the Wolves: Myths and Stories of the Wild Woman Archetype* (1992) by Clarissa Pinkola Estes. New York: Ballantine.

Estes's work as a Jungian analyst influences her "psychoarcheological" portrait of the female archetype. She draws a parallel between healthy wolves and healthy women in two ways: (1) They share certain psychic characteristics, keen sensing, a playful spirit, and a heightened capacity for devotion and (2) both have been hounded, harassed, and falsely accused of being devouring, devious, and overly aggressive by their detractors. Estes maintains that once women reassert their relationship with their wild nature, they will be gifted with a permanent and internal watcher, a visionary, who will guide them. In this book, *wild* means to live a natural life, one in which a creature has innate integrity and healthy boundaries. On the positive side, this 3-star (almost 4-star) resource can be deeply inspiring and insightful. On the negative side, some mental health experts contend that it can be easily misinterpreted and misapplied and complain that the Jungian orientation has little scientific support.

★★★ *Backlash: The Undeclared War Against American Women* (1991) by Susan Faludi. New York: Crown.

Faludi uncovers a growing backlash against women and feminism in the United States. This backlash has hurt women in at least two ways: first, by convincing women that their feelings of dissatisfaction are the result of too much feminism and independence; and second, by simultaneously undermining the minimal progress that women have made at work, in politics, and in their own minds. She cites the (in)famous Harvard–Yale study, which in 1988 reported that a single, college-educated woman over the age of 30 has only a 20% chance of ever getting married, and that by the time she is 40, she will have only a 1.3% chance. Faludi says that the "man shortage" is only one of the myths propagated by the media (another is the infertility epidemic) and finds evidence of other antifeminist orientations in movies, television, and fashion advertising. The result is that feminism declined in the 1980s and early 1990s. *Backlash* received a 3-star rating, and although a bestseller when published, it has received mixed reviews. Some of the book's supporters say that it makes a brilliantly argued case for feminist backlash in the media. However, several critics argue that it is another 1980s-type bashing book that, while scholarly, makes stick-figure stereotypes of relationships between women and men. Clearly, it is a controversial book about which people rarely feel neutral.

★★★ *We Are Our Mother's Daughters* (1998) by Cokie Roberts. New York: Morrow.

This chief congressional analyst for ABC News discusses the pressing concerns facing women. She explores the diverse roles women have assumed throughout American history. Each essay introduces several fascinating women the author has encountered during her career. This book celebrates the diversity of choices and perspectives available to women today. Roberts' position is that women are connected throughout time and, in turn, are their mother's daughters. A 3-star book that helps women experience the great conversation all women have shared throughout history, but doesn't offer much direct self-help guidance.

★★★ *My Mother/Myself* (1977, reissued 1987) by Nancy Friday. New York: Delacorte.

Friday has written a number of bestselling books on women's sexuality, including this one and *My Secret Garden*, about women's sexual fantasies. *My Mother/Myself* was based on more than 200 interviews with women (most were mothers and, of course, all were daughters) as well as consultations with a number of mental health experts. Its basic premise is psychoanalytic in nature: Daughters identify with their mothers while becoming their mothers' rivals, and the influence of this complex relationship is felt throughout a daughter's life. Friday also describes the conflicting messages daughters receive from their mothers about their body and sexuality, as well as unconscious introjection of the mothers' bad qualities. She describes the mother–daughter relationship in early childhood, then moves through a number of women's milestones, such as loss of virginity and menopause. One of her themes is that society's denial of women's sexuality often conflicts with their role as mothers. This book was easily the most widely rated book in the Women's Issues category, evaluated by 187 psychologists. The book's supporters said that it broke new ground when it was published in the late 1970s by providing a probing, insightful analysis of mother–daughter relationships and society's negative portrayal of women's sexuality. However, critics argued that Friday overdramatizes and stereotypes the body inferiority and sexual difficulties of women. All told, an interesting if dated resource on women's sexuality.

### Diamonds in the Rough

♦ *Half the Sky: Turning Oppression into Opportunity for Women Worldwide* (2010) by Nicholas D. Kristof and Sheryl WuDunn. New York: Vintage.

The authors of this important and moving chronicle, journalists at the *New York Times*, have dedicated their careers to traveling the world reporting on the oppression, violence, sex slavery, and other horrific maltreatments of women. This book is not about victimization, although there are many examples of such, but rather of empowerment and the efforts by growing numbers of humanitarian organizations and governments to end violence against women around the globe. Kristof and WuDunn reveal many stories of despair but also of bravery, protection of children, and hope for eventual safe and fulfilling lives. The book also offers information about the organizations and individuals making a difference, one person at a time.

♦ *I Am My Mother's Daughter: Making Peace with Mom Before It's Too Late* (2006) by Iris Krasnow. New York: Basic.

A self-help book about reconciliation with the past and finding a way to connect with aging mothers of Baby Boomer daughters before it is too late. Women are living much longer, into their nineties, as the author reminds us, so there is still time, but daughters are encouraged not to delay. Over 100 women were interviewed by the author/journalist regarding "how they related to their mothers, then and now." Women told moving, sad, joyous, painful, and authentic stories about their relationships with their mothers. The book's focus, however, is what to do now and how to reconnect or change the quality of our maternal relationships. "Guilt, Grief, and Moving On" is the title of one chapter and communicates the purpose of these stories.

> ♦ *Finding Your Voice: A Woman's Guide to Using Self Talk for Fulfilling Relationships, Work, and Life* (2004) by Dorothy Cantor, Carol Goodheart, et al. Hoboken, NJ: Wiley.

Women may possess more freedom today, but freedom doesn't make life easier; in fact, women may feel more frightened than empowered and more confused than self-directed. The authors recount that Albert Einstein said if he had an hour to solve a problem he would spend 55 minutes thinking of questions that define the problem and 5 minutes solving the problem. Seven psychologists teach women to engage in "self talk" in order to define the problems and then to solve them. Each chapter identifies an expectation that we likely hold for ourselves now that we can do everything. Each chapter then suggests questions to ask and self talk to answer. Barely known among mental health experts in our latest study, but we think highly of the authors (many of them friends) and their self-help guidance.

### Strongly Not Recommended

> † *Secrets About Men Every Woman Should Know* (1990) by Barbara DeAngelis. New York: Delacorte.

## ■ AUTOBIOGRAPHIES

### Highly Recommended

> ★★★★★ *Heart of a Woman* (1982) by Maya Angelou. New York: Bantam.

Angelou continues to chronicle the remarkable trajectory of her life in this fourth volume of her bestselling autobiography. She overcame many obstacles to become a premier poet, film writer, director, and activist. In this book, she has a young son and is working as a nightclub singer in Los Angeles when she decides to become part of the vibrant art scene in New York City. She joins the Harlem Writers Guild, becomes northern coordinator for the Southern Christian Leadership Conference, marries an African freedom fighter, travels to Africa as a journalist, and after the marriage dissolves returns to the United States to resume her extraordinary life and career. Throughout all the excitement and turbulence, she remained close to her young son. Candid account of being a Black single mom in New York City with an amazing life and talent. Inspiring story for anyone, especially for young women.

### Recommended

> ★★★ *Reason for Hope: A Spiritual Journey* (2000) by Jane Goodall. New York: Warner.

A *National Geographic* cover story and PBS special brought to public attention Jane Goodall's groundbreaking research with chimpanzees in the Gombe Reserve. In this spiritual autobiography, she recounts the inner life that sustained her. Goodall had been a young waitress in England when she went to Africa, became secretary to paleontologist Louis Leakey, and without formal training or academic degrees undertook her pioneering studies of chimpanzees. She tells the joys and frustrations of building a research institute, arduous fundraising and public speaking to gain support, the opposition she had to overcome, and the personal tragedies in her life. Throughout it all, her faith in the sacredness of all life and belief in the moral evolution of humanity remained strong. This autobiography shows how determination and intelligence, without formal credentials, can lead to a successful career and how the inner and outer worlds are connected. A very favorably rated autobiography in our national studies, but unfortunately not yet widely known.

★★★   *Deborah, Golda, and Me: Being Female and Jewish in America* (1992) by Letty Cottin Pogrebin. New York: Doubleday.

A founding member of *Ms.* magazine and a noted feminist thinker, Pogrebin uses this book to reconcile her Jewish faith, which she rejected for much of her life, with her feminism. The book touches on a variety of related issues, including anti-Semitism within the women's movement and the sometimes strained relations between Blacks and Jews. Especially helpful book for those who want to integrate their Judaism and feminism.

### Diamonds in the Rough

♦   *Life So Far: A Memoir* (2006) by Betty Friedan. New York: Simon and Schuster.

A key figure in the women's liberation movement, Friedan was a co-founder of NOW and several organizations devoted to women's reproductive and political rights and is best known for her 1963 book, *The Feminine Mystique.* In frank terms, this autobiography looks at what was accomplished in the women's movement, how it was done, and at what cost—fortunately not in lives, as was the case in the parallel civil rights movement, but in the many personal conflicts, ideological arguments, and name-calling of the feminist movement. Friedan also describes her own remarkable life, her belief in "Jewish existential conscience," which obliges her to make the world a better place, and her 22-year marriage, which ended in physical abuse and a messy divorce.

♦   *Mothers: A Celebration* (1997) by Alexandra Stoddard. New York: Avon.

In this color-illustrated book, the popular author Alexandra Stoddard (*Grace Notes, Living a Beautiful Life, Living in Love*) recounts her experiences as a mother and step-mother and writes about the women who influenced her life. Many poignant anecdotes and stirring personal recollections about what it means to be a mother. Favorably evaluated by just a few respondents in our national studies, thus earning a Diamond in the Rough designation.

♦   *In Our Time: Memoir of a Revolution* (2000) by Susan Brownmiller. New York: Random House.

Demonstrating that the political is personal, Brownmiller describes her experiences as an activist in the sixties and seventies, times when feminism began to see itself as a civil rights movement. These were heady and dramatic days for the emerging women's liberation movement, and Brownmiller knew all the key players. She recounts the effects of this involvement on her life. Among her other achievements, she wrote *Against Our Will*, which redefined rape in American society. In fast-paced prose that remains balanced and analytical, *In Our Time* documents the coming together, the debates, the schisms, the disorganization, and the personality conflicts that developed and how she rode the waves in the eye of the storm.

## ■ FILMS

### Strongly Recommended

★★★★ *Fried Green Tomatoes* (1992) directed by Jon Avnet. PG-13 rating. 130 minutes.

Kathy Bates is dowdy, unhappily married, and generally trapped. On a visit to a nursing home she meets a spunky elderly lady, Jessica Tandy, who tells her an old story of rural life filled with memorable characters, racial bigotry, a mysterious murder, and, most importantly, how a varied group of women helped each other thrive. Though the story and the modeling, Ms. Bates's character gathers courage, stops overeating, confronts her slovenly husband, and recaptures her life. An inspiring tale for women on two levels: the interdependence of women in the past and the ability to change in the present.

★★★★ *A League of Their Own* (1993) directed by Penny Marshall. PG rating. 124 minutes.

An excellent film depicting the formation of the All American Girls Professional Baseball League. The film starts in the 1990s at the Baseball Hall of Fame and then flashes backs to the 1943 season, a time the female players cherish forever. This feminist film shows team sports building character and binding women together. It also effectively demonstrates women's societal struggles during World War II and the attendant changes in gender roles. Widely known and favorably evaluated in our national studies.

★★★★ *The Turning Point* (1977) directed by Herbert Ross. PG rating. 119 minutes.

Two former friends and rivals meet years after following different paths, one to pursue a single life of a professional ballerina and the other to raise a family. Both envy the other's path, wondering about roads not taken. Their earlier rivalry is reignited when the ballerina mentors the other's daughter. A dated film, but one that poignantly illustrates women's life choices (and losses), midlife reevaluations, and the balance between career and family.

★★★★ *How to Make an American Quilt* (1995) directed by Jocelyn Moorhouse. PG-13 rating. 116 minutes.

A gathering of women to make a wedding quilt turns into a social support network. The quilt serves as a metaphor for their varied experiences with life and love. Although not an uplifting film, it refreshingly shows strong women alive and doing well. It deservedly received a bevy of awards.

★★★★ *Eating* (1990) directed by Henry Jaglom. R rating. 110 minutes.

A group of women attending a birthday party sit and talk about food and life. Their conversations are realistic, fascinating, and often hilarious. Not as well known as other movies in this category, but a valuable and entertaining flick. (Also reviewed in Chapter 22 on Eating Disorders.)

### Recommended

★★★ *Iron Jawed Angels* (2004) directed by Katja von Garnier. Unrated. 125 minutes.

This film demonstrates the struggle of feminists, lead by the historic Alice Paul, as they fight to gain citizenship and the right to vote. The women endure countless hardships, including physical violence, alienation from family and friends, and unjust imprisonment. They become known as "iron-jawed angels" after they undertake a hunger strike. The film ends on an uplifting note with the passage of the 19th Amendment to the Constitution, the fulfillment of the suffrage movement. The film's vivid depictions of the violence and animosity directed at the movement will likely be unsettling to the viewer, but its honesty warrants the numerous award nominations it received.

★★★    *The Piano* (1993) directed by Jane Campion. R rating. 121 minutes.

This complex film is, among other things, a Gothic romance dressed in Victorian clothes. A mute mother with modern and unconventional sensibilities travels with her daughter to New Zealand, where the mother meets her new husband. The bond among mother, daughter, and music (the piano) provides them with a mutual security and vehicle for expression during some dark times, which include physical abuse. A beautiful and haunting picture nominated for multiple Academy Awards, *The Piano* effectively demonstrates women's struggles for emotional and physical survival.

★★★    *My Breast* (1994) directed by Betty Thomas and Michael Scott. Not rated. 90 minutes.

A New York journalist has an unsatisfying relationship with her boyfriend. The diagnosis of breast cancer leads her to dramatically change her life. This television movie received modest and mixed reviews by our mental health experts, but it is one of the few that addresses breast cancer forthrightly.

★★★    *Working Girl* (1988) directed by Mike Nichols. R rating. 116 minutes.

Melanie Griffith has fabulous ideas but is a secretary and is too working class to move up to management. She gets a new female boss who has the right voice, clothes, and hair for her managerial job. When Griffith finds that her boss plans to steal her great idea, she pretends to be an executive, finds a guy at another firm who can make this happen, and unfortunately sleeps with him. Both a comedy and a thriller, this film fully illustrates some of the difficulties women face in the workplace and in relationships. In the end, authenticity and initiative pay off.

★★★    *Thelma and Louise* (1992) directed by Ridley Scott. R rating. 129 minutes.

Two women find each other when all seems hopeless in their lives. This controversial movie follows their cross-country jaunt. Searching for freedom and fighting for survival, the women ride into a tragic ending. The movie is unsettling, with easy justification of murder, rape, and escape. It is bound to precipitate heated discussions about women's power and choices.

## ■ INTERNET RESOURCES

### General Websites

★★★★★    *Women's Issues* womensissues.about.com

This section on About.com is overseen by guide Linda Lowen and offers a wide range of ever-changing topics on issues of relevance to women, including gender bias, workplace issues, reproductive rights, resources for teens and young women, protecting yourself from cyber stalking, and learning to balance work and child rearing. This is a large section that is constantly updated.

★★★★  *Huffington Post: Women* www.huffingtonpost.com/women

This mainstream, popular commercial site offers an eclectic mix of new articles every day on topics such as love and sex, careers and money, book reviews, women's health, and more. Although the articles aren't always thought-provoking, they're often entertaining and engaging.

## Psychoeducational Materials

### Health
★★★★★  *Womenshealth.gov* www.womenshealth.gov

This well-designed website provided by the U.S. Office on Women's Health offers a comprehensive resource to learn more about virtually any women's health concern, ranging from body image, breast cancer, and heart health, to menopause, mental health, and pregnancy. Though the articles are often short and no-nonsense, they link to more in-depth government resources.

★★★★  *Women's Health* www.cdc.gov/women

This resource from the U.S. Centers for Disease Control & Prevention offers a nice, succinct guide to government women's health resources. Its design may be easier to navigate for some than the above womenshealth.gov, and it does seem to offer more from a scientific and research perspective.

★★★★  *LifeScript.com* www.lifescript.com

This attractive, mainstream commercial website offers sections on health, diet, food, life, and soul, offering healthy living resources for women. Includes an ask-the-experts feature, daily news, quizzes, and more. Some advertising was intrusive, however.

★★★★  *Women's Health Issues* www.acog.org/For_Patients

This website from the American College of Obstetricians and Gynecologists offers dozens of women's health articles that are regularly updated.

### Feminism
★★★★  *Viva la Feminista* www.vivalafeminista.com

This blog covers all topics on the intersection between motherhood and feminism. Engaging to read, it's actively updated multiple times most weeks.

★★★★  *Ms. Blog* msmagazine.com/blog

This blog, a part of the larger *Ms.* magazine website, offers an active, sometimes funny and insightful look into women's issues, updated multiple times each week. Categories include arts, global, health, justice, life, media, national, and work.

### *Menopause*
★★★★★  *North American Menopause Society* www.menopause.org

This website from the nonprofit North American Menopause Society offers a wealth of information and resources for women interested in learning more about menopause. The consumer-oriented information is fittingly placed in the section "For Consumers."

### *Workplace Rights*
★★★★★  *Equal Employment Opportunity Commission* www.eeoc.gov

If you have concerns about employment discrimination, this is the place to start. Click on "Employees & Applicants" to get started.

★★★  *Employment Discrimination: An Overview* www.law.cornell.edu/wex/ Employment_discrimination

The site offers links to all the important documents and decisions. It is likely to be of use to sophisticated readers who need legal support before contacting a lawyer.

★★★  *National Committee on Pay Equity* www.pay-equity.org

Lots of information on the wage gap between the sexes and what to do about it. See also *Working Women: Equal Pay* from the AFL-CIO at www.aflcio.org/issues/jobseconomy/women.

## ▪ SUPPORT GROUPS

### Business and Professional Women

Phone: 202-293-1100
www.bpwfoundation.org
Organization composed of working women to promote workplace equity and provide networking opportunities.

### National Black Women's Health Project

Phone: 202-548-4000
www.blackwomenshealth.org
Committed to the empowerment of all women through wellness.

**National Organization for Women**

Phone: 202-628-8669
www.now.org/index.html

**Women Employed**

Phone: 312-782-3902
www.womenemployed.org

**See also** Abuse (Chapter 2), Eating Disorders (Chapter 22), Pregnancy (Chapter 32), and Sexuality (Chapter 35).

# CHAPTER 43

# FOR CONSUMERS: EVALUATING AND SELECTING SELF-HELP RESOURCES

A massive and systemic revolution is occurring in mental health: self-help without professional treatment (Druss & Rosencheck, 2000). This year more Americans will seek mental health information from the Internet or attend a self-help group than will consult all mental health professionals combined (Kessler, Mickelson, & Zhao, 1997). In fact, some experts claim that self-help will become the nation's *de facto* treatment of choice for many behavioral disorders and life predicaments by the year 2020 (Goodman & Jacobs, 1994).

Self-help is big business. Americans spend an estimated $10 billion each year on self-improvement products (Marketresearch.com, 2011). We buy almost $600 million in self-help books each year and surf more than 25,000 websites devoted to mental health (Paul, 2001).

While self-help is big business, it is, alas, not always a scientific business. As the volume and accessibility of self-help information soar, the question of quality becomes urgent. Of the thousands of websites launched yearly and of the estimated 5,000 self-help books published annually, the vast majority are published without any controlled research documenting their accuracy or effectiveness as self-help. The Internet, in particular, is awash in snake oil. Many self-help companies are eager to separate you from your money.

When you evaluate or select self-help materials, you obviously want those that are the most relevant and effective, and in the preceding chapters we have tried to provide just that. The expert ratings and descriptions of self-help books, autobiographies, films, online programs, and Internet resources are designed so that you can select the mental health resources that will benefit you the most.

There is no magic key to the self-help kingdom, but several strategies can help you select the best resources and avoid the clunkers. Following are 12 strategies for selecting an effective self-help resource.

## ■ 1. DON'T CHOOSE A SELF-HELP RESOURCE BECAUSE OF ITS COVER, TITLE, OR ADVERTISING

The old saying, "You can't tell a book by its cover," probably applies to self-help books more than to any other type of book. Publishers spend huge sums of money to create splashy covers with sensational titles and develop attention-grabbing advertising campaigns. They describe each year's new crop of self-help books as "phenomenal breakthroughs" and "scientific revolutions" in understanding life's problems. Some good self-help books have fancy covers and catchy titles, but so do some bad ones. The same is true with expensive advertisements—the bad books are just as likely to have huge advertising outlays as the good books.

One category with especially flashy titles that makes good fodder for talk shows is love and marriage. Several of our Not Recommended books were bestsellers with catchy titles and huge advertising campaigns. Based on what you hear and see on talk shows, book covers, and advertising, there isn't any way people can sort through titles in this category and tell which books are good self-help books.

Publishers and bookstores influence self-help book purchases by the number of books they display and where the books are located. However, this year's top-selling book, the one that's stacked from floor to ceiling, often finds its way into next year's wastebasket. Or something worse happens: Lavish advertising and support by book chains enable some bad self-help books to sell extremely well. Without guidelines, consumers don't know that these books will probably prove unhelpful. When one area of self-help becomes popular, many authors jump on the bandwagon and quickly pump out books in rapid succession, hoping to exploit the latest "in" topic or movement. In the 1990s, codependency, the inner child, and dieting were especially hot topics, and authors whipped out books about them at an astonishing pace. In the 2000s, spirituality and finance were in the ascendancy. Yet many of the books in these hot categories were not rated favorably by mental health experts.

In sum, become an intelligent consumer of psychological knowledge by going beyond the glitzy cover, the celebrity testimonials, the fancy ads, and the bookstore's elaborate display. Instead, make your choices based on the next 11 strategies.

## ■ 2. SELECT A RESOURCE THAT MAKES REALISTIC RATHER THAN GRANDIOSE CLAIMS

If you have a problem, you want to cope with it as effectively and painlessly as possible. The quicker you can fix the problem, the better. Unfortunately, the self-help resources that make extravagant claims are the most alluring and thus sell better than books that are more realistic. Most problems do not arise overnight, and most can't be solved overnight. Avoid books that promise wondrous insights that can immediately solve problems.

When a self-help claim appears too good to be true, it probably is not true. If a resource states that a "miraculous" new diet guarantees you will lose one pound a day and keep the weight off permanently, don't buy it. More reasonable books are not as eye-catching and not as sensational, but they present a more balanced approach to weight loss—and tend not to sell as well, even though they are far better self-help books.

Try to make a realistic judgment about the book's claims. Be skeptical of anything that sounds easy, magical, and wondrous. Overcoming depression, improving relationships, and becoming more self-fulfilled are not easy tasks. Coping effectively with any of life's important tasks or problems—anxiety, parenting, divorce, addiction, or career development—is a continuing project.

## ■ 3. EXAMINE THE RESEARCH EVIDENCE REPORTED IN THE SELF-HELP RESOURCE

Many self-help resources are not based on reliable scientific evidence but rather on the author's anecdotal experiences or clients' testimonials. In some instances, evidence is gleaned from interviews with a narrow range of people or a few clients seen in psychotherapy. Too much of what you read in the self-help literature is based on speculative intuition.

Most of the self-help resources highly rated by the mental health professionals are based on reliable research. The cognitive therapy of depression advocated by Aaron Beck, Albert Ellis, and David Burns (Chapter 20) has undergone careful scrutiny by the clinical and research community. Likewise, the online self-help programs sprinkled throughout the book have been subjected to years of controlled scientific research and found to be effective for most people. The same is true for *Learned Optimism* by Martin Seligman (Chapter 25), *Changing for Good* by James Prochaska and associates (Chapter 34), and the strongly recommended resources on relaxation, stress management, and mindfulness (Chapter 37). These books are not based on the subjective opinions of the authors or the testimonials of others; they are based on years of sound research and clinical results.

Hardly any self-help resource contains elaborate research citations. This is by design because lengthy citations make them difficult to read. However, authors of the most effective resources typically summarize the research evidence, the clinical evidence, or both and list research sources in an appendix or endnotes.

## ■ 4. FAVOR SELF-HELP THAT HAS BEEN TESTED AS SELF-HELP

Yes, that does sound crazy, doesn't it? But many crafty marketers have realized that consumers are becoming more informed and sophisticated, looking for some indication that the self-help product has been subjected to research. But the research they advertise is more likely than not based on the methods being applied by a mental health professional, not as standalone self-help. Therefore, "research proven" and "clinically tested" usually mean that the methods work in the hands of a psychotherapist, but we have no way of knowing whether those same methods are feasible and effective as self-help.

More than three quarters of laypersons cannot, according to the research (Rosen, Glasgow, & Moore, 2003), successfully self-administer a toilet training program, a sexual dysfunction method, or an antianxiety procedure on their own. Sure, the self-help materials will proudly proclaim that they have been "clinically tested at a major university." And they have: as provided in a clinic by a trained professional, not at home by a self-changer. If you, like us, have tried to toilet train your child in a single day using one of the popular self-help books claiming that it can be done in 24 hours, then you have probably experienced a similar humbling fate as us.

The strategy, then, is to look for evidence that the self-help works as, well, self-help! The online self-help programs listed in this book have already passed that test. To make it into our book, they have demonstrated in controlled research that laypeople on their own can benefit from them.

## ■ 5. SELECT SELF-HELP MATERIALS THAT RECOGNIZE PROBLEMS ARE CAUSED BY A NUMBER OF FACTORS AND HAVE MULTIPLE SOLUTIONS

It's not just your imagination. You are a complex human living in a complex world. Your problems are not so simple that they have a simple cause and a single solution. Yet the human mind is biased toward simple answers to complex problems. After all, solving a problem is easier if there is a single cure than if you have to modify a number of factors in your life.

Consider stress and anxiety. Thinking positively may well help you cope more effectively with stress, but self-help resources that deal only with positive thinking often oversimplify the change process. Stress and anxiety reduction can be facilitated by thinking optimistically, rearranging your life, practicing relaxation, exercising regularly, meditating, eating healthfully, learning assertion skills, training your breathing, knowing your personality, and cultivating more interpersonal support.

Counter the "single trick" mentality by selecting self-help that offers multiple causes and multiple sources of assistance. A variety of self-change methods in your repertoire will assuredly be more useful than a solitary technique. In that way, self-help can be tailored to your unique needs and preferences as a complex human.

## ■ 6. SEEK SELF-HELP THAT FOCUSES ON A PARTICULAR PROBLEM RATHER THAN THOSE THAT CLAIM TO BE A GENERAL SOLUTION FOR ALL OF YOUR PROBLEMS

Effective self-help tends to concentrate on a specific problem rather than promising to cure all of life's ills. Materials that try to solve all problems are shallow and lack the precise assessments and detailed recommendations needed to improve a particular problem. When authors claim that their methods will solve all of your problems and will help everybody, don't buy it, figuratively and literally.

The more authors can convince the public that their products are for everyone, the greater their chances of selling millions of copies. That is exactly what far too many self-help developers try to do—producing materials that are so broad in scope that they will appeal to a huge audience. The concept of codependency (Chapter 3), for example, initially applied to the specific problems of people married to alcoholics, especially women married to male alcoholics. But the concept spread rapidly to a host of other circumstances, and codependency authors now claim that codependency occurs in every relationship. That is far too broad and all-encompassing to be useful.

Most of the leading self-help resources canvassed in our studies tackle specific disorders. Certainly all of the online self-help programs featured in this book focus on a particular problem. One of the highest-rated books, Davis and associates' *The Relaxation and Stress Reduction Workbook,* provides a perfect illustration. As the title indicates, it is specific and detailed; it does not promise to be a panacea for all conditions. The many excellent resources on infant development and parenting (Chapter 26) deal with a specific age—from birth to 2 years of age—and how parents should respond to infants with different temperaments. These books don't try to reel everyone in and don't pretend to be all things to all people.

## ■ 7. CHOOSE SELF-HELP THAT CLEARLY EXPLAINS ITS LIMITATIONS AND CONTRAINDICATIONS

A single self-help resource is applicable for only a limited range of behavioral disorders and life challenges. We do not expect for, say, a self-help book on pregnancy or an Internet site on trauma to help with career development. It sounds so obvious, but many self-help resources do not delineate the boundaries of their applicability. In an effort to reach millions of people and sell more copies, marketers push products for everything that ails you.

Effective self-help materials clearly state their limits. Good books and sites explain which individuals should not use them and describe when their use is, in fact, contraindicated.

Meritorious self-help informs you about the potential downside of using the resource on your own and will provide guidance for seeking professional treatment. Self-help materials that are not forthcoming about their limits are simply dishonest.

## ■ 8. DON'T BE CONNED BY PSYCHOBABBLE AND SLICK WRITING

In 1977, R. D. Rosen wrote *Psychobabble*, a sizzling attack on the psychological jargon that fills the space between the covers of some self-help resources. Unfortunately, 35 years later psychobabble is still alive and well. Psychobabble is a hip and vague language that will not improve your ability to cope with a problem. Too many self-help authors write in psychobabble, saying things like "You've got to get in touch with your feelings"; "Get with the program"; "You've got to get it"; "The real you"; "To solve your problem you need some high-energy experiences"; "You are sending off the wrong vibes"; and on and on. In a number of chapters, we specifically criticized several books for too much psychobabble and praised others for being free of it.

Psychobabble is not the only semantic problem of poor self-help materials. Some disguise their inadequacies with slick writing that is so friendly that it seems as if the author is personally talking to you. After you have read only a few pages of the book or website, you say to yourself, "Wow! This sounds just like me. It can really help me." All too often such slick books offer little more than one or two basic ideas that could be communicated in a few pages. The rest of the book is filled with personal anecdotes and case examples that provide little additional knowledge. Such books lack the detailed recommendations and sound strategies that you need to cope more effectively with life's problems.

Mind you: we are not opposed to personal and fluid writing. However, it takes a lot more than an author's slick language to assist you. Select self-help materials that are clearly written in language you can understand and that include detailed recommendations for how to change.

## ■ 9. SEARCH FOR SELF-HELP THAT WILL TAKE YOU THROUGH THE ENTIRE CHANGE PROCESS

Self-help characterized by psychobabble frequently resorts to motivational cheerleading and inspirational sermons. These pump you up to confront a problem but then let you down by giving you no specific skills. After a few weeks, the buzz wears off because the author's recommendations lack depth. Examples of bestsellers characterized by this approach are Zig Ziglar's *Steps to the Top* (in contrast to Steven Covey's *The 7 Habits of Highly Effective People*, which offers detailed strategies; Chapter 34) and Leo Buscaglia's *Loving Each Other* (in contrast to several recommended books that examine the complexity of love and its many avenues; Chapter 27).

A pet peeve of many self-help consumers is exactly this narrow focus on only one part of the change process. Imagine if someone promised to help you do your taxes but only motivated you to begin collecting the paperwork. Or gave you advice on how to organize your receipts and nothing else. The rest of the process remains unfinished. Well, that aptly describes much of self-help: incomplete and futile.

Instead, select self-help resources that walk you through the entire change process. This will probably entail, in order, gaining knowledge, taking a self-assessment, becoming motivated, preparing to change your behavior, learning skills, practicing those skills, persevering through slips, and maintaining those changes for the long haul. That's a number of steps across time for making permanent lifestyle changes.

## ■ 10. CHECK OUT THE AUTHOR'S EDUCATIONAL AND PROFESSIONAL CREDENTIALS

Not all self-help authors are mental health professionals who have gone through rigorous educational training at respected universities and spent years rendering professional treatment or researching effective self-help. Just about anyone can get their self-help ideas onto the Web if they have a modicum of computer skills, and most can get those ideas into print if they have the resources to self-publish or can convince a publisher that they will make money. Indeed, the author of the recent blockbuster (and largely discredited) *The Secret* is a former television producer. But most of the best self-help books and Internet sites (excluding autobiographies) are written by mental health professionals, not writers or media producers.

In our national studies, the authors of 80% to 90% of the top self-help books are PhDs or MDs and have conducted extensive research or have undergone clinical training. Psychologists David Barlow, Edna Foa, Martin Antony, and Edmund Bourne, all authors of excellent resources for anxiety and obsessive-compulsive disorders, are world-renowned researchers in their areas. Psychiatrists Aaron Beck, George Vaillant, and David Burns, the authors of excellent books on depression, relationships, and aging, are respected medical school professors. T. Berry Brazelton, author of highly touted books, is an esteemed pediatrician who has decades of experience working with parents and babies; Margaret Caudill, author of a highly regarded chronic pain book, is an expert in pain management and health care improvement. Both are affiliated with the Harvard Medical School. Drs. Harriet Lerner (*The Dance of Anger, The Dance of Intimacy*), Mary Pipher (*Reviving Ophelia, The Shelter of Each Other*), and Kay Redfield Jamison (*An Unquiet Mind, Night Falls Fast*) are all distinguished psychologists. Independent evaluations of self-help books regularly find that the most scientifically grounded and highly regarded books are those written by mental health professionals holding doctoral degrees (Redding et al., 2008, Herbert, Forman, & Gaudiano, 2008).

Of course, the reverse can also happen: having a PhD or an MD degree does not guarantee a wonderful self-help resource. The consensus of the mental health experts in our national studies was that Phil McGraw, Joyce Brothers, John Gray, James Dobson, and Wayne Dyer, all of whom have PhDs, have each written self-help books that are not recommended.

## ■ 11. BE WARY OF AUTHORS WHO REJECT THE CONVENTIONAL KNOWLEDGE OF HEALTH PROFESSIONALS

Some self-help authors attack the mental health professions as being too conservative and overly concerned with scientific evidence. Consider such attacks a red flag, and avoid these authors. These anti-establishment, anti-science mavericks avow that their ideas are way ahead of their time and that it will take years for mental health professionals to catch up with their avant-garde thinking. Many New Age and Scientology authors, such as L. Ron Hubbard, fall into this category.

There is nothing wrong with new ideas, of course, but there is something seriously wrong with new ideas uncritically hyped in the absence of reliable evidence of their effectiveness and safety. In our experience, the materials of self-help authors who condemn the mental health establishment will not meaningfully assist you for the most part. Health care has come to demand scientific evidence, and self-help should be seconding that demand.

## ■ 12. DISTINGUISH BETWEEN BALANCED INFORMATION AND SUBTLE ADVERTISING

The Internet offers a wealth of information, but it is virtually uncontrolled. The traditional firewalls between reliable information on the one hand, and advertising on the other, are often blurred on the Web. Frequently, conflicts of interest are not disclosed, financial sponsors are hidden, and advertisements are not labeled as such.

Many health and consumer groups, including Consumer Union, have launched programs to develop disclosure standards for the Internet and to report on the business practices of websites. But in the meantime, cast a critical eye upon Internet sites and realize that some sites charge for listings or are actually lengthy advertisements for drug companies and for-profit clinics, to take two common examples. Check the "Who Are We?" and the "Privacy Notice" sections of the websites; if these are sketchy or absent, let that be notice that the materials may be quite biased.

Even armed with these dozen strategies for selecting an effective self-help resource, you may still have initial difficulty in sorting through the morass and picking the worthy ones. With practice in using the strategies, you will become a more knowledgeable and critical consumer.

For us, the most trustworthy strategy for selecting effective self-help and avoiding the lemons is accessing the knowledge of the most highly trained mental health professionals in the United States. We have compiled and shared their knowledge in this book. As explained in the Preface and Chapter 1, our 12 national studies have involved nearly 5,000 psychologists in evaluating self-help books, autobiographies, and films. Their evaluative ratings can educate individuals and their caregivers about effective, affordable, and accessible self-help resources. Professional consensus is no guarantee, but it proves superior to individual judgments, random selection, and bestseller lists.

We trust the scientific research and the collective expertise of thousands of mental health professionals. Use their knowledge, the research, and *Self-Help That Works* to pick effective self-help materials.

# CHAPTER 44

# FOR PRACTITIONERS: INTEGRATING SELF-HELP INTO TREATMENT*

Health professionals routinely recommend self-help to their clients, but many desire guidance on the optimal methods and resources for doing so. In this chapter, we offer practical suggestions for integrating self-help into formal treatment. By your behavior as a health professional, you can enhance the effectiveness of self-help within the treatment context.

The statistics on professionally untreated mental disorders are compelling. Approximately 85% of Americans will not receive health-care treatment for their diagnosable mental or substance abuse disorder within a year (WHO World Mental Health Survey Consortium, 2004). In fact, more than 70% of them will never receive specialized mental health care (Kessler et al., 1997).

By contrast, Americans do regularly turn to self-help. Five percent to 7% of American adults attended a self-help group in the past year (Eisenberg et al., 1998; Kessler et al., 1997), and up to 18% have done so at some point in their lifetime (Kessler et al., 1999). Approximately 80% of all Internet users have sought health-care information there (pewinternet.org/Reports/2010), with mental health disorders and relationship problems leading the list. Self-help books appear at the estimated rate of 5,000 per year (Bogart, 2011).

To be sure, most mental health professionals around the globe already recommend self-help to their patients. In Canada, nearly 70% of mental health practitioners prescribe self-help books to clients (Adams & Pitre, 2000). A total of 93% of clinical psychologists in Norway recommend self-help materials to clients, and approximately half (55%) receive requests from their clients for such materials (Nordgreen & Havik, 2011). The vast majority of school psychologists in the United States use self-help with their clients: 43% said they employ self-help materials with 20% or fewer of their clients, 36% employ self-help materials with 20% to 50% of their clients, and 21% with half or more (O'Conner & Kratochwill, 1999).

Table 44.1 displays the percentages of U.S. psychologists in our 2011 studies recommending self-help to their clients. As seen there, 85% recommended self-help books, 79%

---

* Portions of this chapter are reprinted with permission from Norcross, J. C. (2006). Integrating self-help into psychotherapy: 16 practical suggestions. *Professional Psychology: Research & Practice, 37,* 683–693. Copyright of the American Psychological Association.

**TABLE 44.1 Frequency of Psychologists Recommending Self-Help Resources to Their Patients in the Last 12 Months**

| | % Recommending | | % of Patients Recommended to | |
|---|---|---|---|---|
| Resource | 2002 | 2011 | 2011 M | 2011 Mdn |
| Self-help/ support group | 82 | 79 | 15.9 | 10 |
| Self-help book | 85 | 85 | 27.6 | 20 |
| Autobiography | 24 | 28 | 3.6 | 0 |
| Film | 46 | 54 | 10.5 | 5 |
| Internet site | 34 | 78 | 22.8 | 15 |
| Online program | – | 23 | 3.8 | 0 |

*N* = 1,229 in 2002  *N* = 1,306 in 2011

support groups, 78% Internet sites, 28% autobiographies, and 23% online self-help programs in the past year. These percentages have modestly increased over the past decade, with the exception of huge leaps in the number of psychologists recommending Internet sites and online self-help.

At the same time, practitioners frequently ask how they can be more effective and systematic in integrating self-help into their professional work: more frequent use of self-help, more types of self-help resources, more creative synthesis into our practices, and more use of research-supported and peer-consensus resources. As also shown in Table 44.1, the actual percentage of clients receiving self-help prescriptions is still small.

We attribute these small numbers to multiple factors, but principally a paucity of training. Most professionals receive only on-the-job training in using self-help resources as part of treatment; few of us received such training in our graduate programs. At least two studies (Adams & Pitre, 2000; Norcross et al., 2000) found that experienced practitioners are more likely to use bibliotherapy with their clients than their less-experienced colleagues. This difference suggests a deficiency in graduate training, a paucity of continuing education on the topic, and/or growth in self-help knowledge and skill over years of practice.

In this chapter, we offer a medley of 17 suggestions, culled from both the research literature and clinical experience, to integrate self-help into formal treatment. The literature and experience demonstrate that clinicians, by their behavior, can significantly enhance the effectiveness of self-help—with or without professional treatment (Kelly, 2003). Along the way, we present several caveats and cautions to the wholesale incorporation of self-help into the psychotherapeutic enterprise.

Before doing so, a few words on words. *Self-help* ordinarily refers to endeavors occurring outside of formal treatment or psychotherapy. How, then, can self-help be integrated into psychotherapy? And does it remain self-help once addressed or incorporated into treatment? As we use the phrase throughout this chapter, *integrating self-help* refers to resources initially developed as standalone self-help materials—bibliotherapy, films, Internet sites, computer programs, and so on—that are recommended, addressed, or used in the course of treatment to increase efficiency, efficacy, and applicability. We might think of self-help in treatment as "the materials formerly known as self-help."

## ■ 1. ENLARGE OUR CONCEPTUALIZATION OF CHANGE MECHANISMS

Psychotherapy is one indisputably effective pathway toward behavior change. Although it is the process that most of us professionals have favored in our practice and our own lives, it is hardly the only effective pathway. We can begin by broadening our conception of how people change; as psychotherapists, we need to avoid hardening of our categories, too.

Humans change through many routes, but the predominant pathway is self-change or self-help. Approximately 75% of the people who change behavioral and addictive disorders do so on their own (Klingemann et al., 2001; Swindle et al., 2000). Self-help has the added benefits of being the least restrictive, least intrusive, and least costly option. One of the key challenges for future research is to reliably predict who is likely to benefit from self-help and who is likely to require more intensive assistance (Baillie & Rapee, 2004).

Professionals can frame self-help participation in treatment as experimenting with alternatives so that the client can find the best combination for himself or herself. This frame will generate less resistance than pressuring a client to seek help only from a particular resource or a specific group (Klaw & Humphreys, 2005). In the same way we incorporate conjoint sessions or pharmacotherapy into ongoing treatment, we can integrate self-help naturally into the process. Self-help is thus seen as a seamless part of behavior change and growth.

## ■ 2. RECOGNIZE THE EFFECTIVENESS OF SELF-HELP

Decades of empirical research and dozens of meta-analyses have underscored the effectiveness of self-help programs in mental health. The meta-analyses consistently indicate that improvement by clients using self-help substantially exceeds that of wait-list and no-treatment controls (e.g., Den Boer, Wiersma, & Van Den Bosch, 2004; Klingemann et al., 2001; Menchola, Arkowitz, & Burke, 2007; Mains & Scogin, 2003). The mean effect sizes ($d$) of self-help versus control conditions are typically .70 to .80 at posttreatment and .50 to .70 at follow-up (Den Boer et al., 2004). The effect sizes for self-help versus formal treatment typically show that they are not as effective as therapist-assisted interventions within the same studies.

These positive evaluations also pertain to the effectiveness of bibliotherapy—using self-help books. Meta-analyses have found that bibliotherapy for depression and anxiety is superior to no treatment and slightly less effective than therapist-administered treatments (e.g., Den Boer et al., 2004; Menchola et al., 2007). A meta-analysis of 29 outcome studies of cognitive bibliotherapy for depression, for example, reported an effect size of .77 (Gregory, Canning, Lee, & Wise, 2004). That best estimate of effect size compares favorably with outcomes from individual psychotherapy. A meta-analysis of 12 controlled studies of bibliotherapy for sexual dysfunctions demonstrated a mean effect size of .68 compared with a control group (van Lankveld, 1998). For a final example, a meta-analysis of 22 studies evaluating bibliotherapy for alcohol problems found modest support for decreasing at-risk and harmful drinking (Apodaca & Miller, 2003). The accumulating findings provide support for the cost-effective use of bibliotherapy with many clients (Watkins & Clum, 2008).

The research on self-help groups is similarly encouraging. Sophisticated meta-analyses (Kownacki & Shadish, 1999; Tonigan, Toscoova, & Miller, 1995) have found that participation in Alcoholics Anonymous (AA) is positively related to reductions in drinking. Three large, well-controlled evaluations of 12-step programs for addictive disorders have shown that they typically perform as effectively as professional treatment (Morgenstern, Labouvie, McCrady, Kahler, & Frey, 1997; Ouimette, Finney, & Moos, 1997; Project MATCH Research

Group, 1997). Research on other self-help groups concludes that participation is generally beneficial (Kyrouz, Humphreys, & Loomis, 2002); practitioners can be confident that many of their patients will derive at least some benefit from participating in a self-help group (Barlow, Burlingame, Nebeker, & Anderson, 1999). In addition, participants frequently evaluate self-help groups as being as helpful as psychotherapy (Seligman, 1995).

Of course, meta-analyses can only aggregate the results of existing studies. The sad fact is that the vast majority of self-help materials have not been empirically evaluated, a point addressed throughout this book. Further, defining and controlling the self-help independent variable in empirical research is more dauntingly complex than commonly anticipated. Suffice it to say that it is a painstaking task to attempt to isolate self-administered treatments from minimal therapist contact and those from psychotherapy with self-help recommendations. That is part of this chapter's *leitmotif*: the continuity and synergy of behavior change.

Self-help resources are no more a panacea than psychotherapy, but this brief review of the research on the efficacy of self-help is intended to help practitioners embrace its palliative and occasionally curative power. As we shall see, holding favorable views toward self-help involvement is associated with increased goal attainment for patients (Hodges & Segal, 2002; Kelly, 2003).

## ■ 3. CEASE DEVALUING SELF-HELP

In our experience, many mental health professionals maintain an ambivalent, hostile-dependent relationship with self-help: we recommend it but still mistrust it. Effective self-help is invisible to many mental health practitioners (Beck, 1976). In part, we do not see because we literally do not believe it. Professionals seldom encounter people who recover on their own (Klingemann et al., 2001). We act as though psychotherapists' self-esteem and economic survival are contingent on our distinctive ability to help people change (Norcross, 2000). The net result is that, for some of us, the evidence for the efficacy of self-change is threatening and frequently dismissed (Prochaska, Norcross, & DiClemente, 1995).

All of this is to say that we must be aware of professional-centrism, the belief that professional services and expertise are the primary components of mental health care for the populace (Salzer, Rappaport, & Segre, 2001). Such prejudices may reduce appreciation of self-help and may decrease the frequency of professionals recommending or referring clients to self-help resources.

## ■ 4. BROADEN THE DEFINITION OF SELF-HELP

What immediately comes to your mind when you hear *self-help*? Like other mental health professionals, you probably think of self-help books and 12-step groups. However, self-help is much more. If we are to incorporate self-help into treatment, then we should be aware of and potentially employ multiple self-help routes.

Here are eight major self-help pathways at your disposal—and your patient's. Six of these have been featured throughout *Self-Help That Works,* but let us comment on a couple more.

- Self-help books
- Commercial films
- Computer programs
- Expressive writing and journaling
- Autobiographies
- Websites
- Self-help and support groups
- Structured workbooks

Expressive writing and structured workbooks represent active self-help resources that emphasize a person's communicative and interactive output (Harwood & L'Abate, 2010). They have been subjected to considerable research and have been helpfully compiled in a series of books by Dr. Lu L'Abate (e.g., L'Abate, 2000, 2004, 2010).

While broadening the definition of self-help, let us be careful not to open it so far that research evidence is ignored or that patient care is compromised. A Cochrane Collaboration review (Murray et al., 2004, Burns, See Tai, Lai, & Nazareth, 2004) provides a sage warning that indiscriminate use of health-related Internet materials can prove deleterious. The review of 28 studies and 4,042 people with chronic medical disorders found that those who used the Internet to locate information on their disorders reported (a) more feelings of social support and (b) more knowledge about their disorders and treatments. However, those same Internet users had worse health outcomes. Why? In part, because people with worse outcomes surfed the net for alternatives, and also in part because the patients obtained so much information that they made their own decisions and ignored professional advice. Such studies, not yet conducted on most mental disorders, remind us of the importance of our collaborative function in guiding self-help.

## ■ 5. CAPITALIZE ON THE DIVERSITY OF SELF-HELP BENEFITS

Self-help is not restricted to delivering change methods. Among the most frequent purposes for which psychologists recommend self-help are to educate clients about diagnosis and treatment, encourage them and improve motivation, empower them, offer them a sense of universality ("I am not alone"), reinforce specific points or strategies worked on in a session, provide support and knowledge for family members, and provide social support (Campbell & Smith, 2003). In other words, we can conceptualize and recommend self-help for multiple benefits.

Consider the case of Ms. Andrews, a 60-year-old married woman suffering from bouts of clinical depression, the latest precipitated by learning that her husband had been diagnosed with mid-stage Alzheimer's disease. On her own, she had purchased and read the highly rated self-help book *The 36-Hour Day* (Mace & Rabins, 1999), which she found "quite helpful" in providing information and rendering practical advice. She did, however, find it lacking in emotional resonance and interpersonal support. One of us recommended John Bayley's (1999) autobiography *Elegy for Iris* (later adapted into the film *Iris*). In our next session, Ms. Andrews related that she had "consumed" the book in 2 days and found it a sensitive tale of loss, grieving, and remembrance of times past with her husband. She stated that the autobiography "was exactly what I needed—someone who understands what I am feeling." Ms. Andrews later joined a local Alzheimer's support group while continuing individual psychotherapy and antidepressant medication.

## ■ 6. FAMILIARIZE YOURSELF WITH SELF-HELP

Mental health professionals can routinely familiarize themselves with self-help resources. This might entail visiting a self-help meeting, reading a self-help book on a topic of interest, investigating the newer online programs for a specific disorder, perusing an autobiography of a mental health client, and surfing the Web on a particular mental health topic. Educate yourself about the nature of self-help resources in general and specialized resources in particular. This will facilitate informed, I-have-been-there referrals. This is especially the case for clients struggling with addictions, who are often wary of professionals who have no personal experience with addiction (Schencker, 2009).

One of the advantages of familiarizing yourself with self-help books and Internet sites is that you will probably detect the interpersonal presence and support of the author(s). Effective self-help is typically embedded within a therapeutic relationship, even if the author/therapist is not physically present. David Burns' (1999) *Feeling Good*, one of the bestselling self-help books in history, is warm and supportive. The author generously self-discloses and presents his own foibles. Kay Jamison's autobiographies, *An Unquiet Mind* (1997) and *Night Falls Fast* (2000), sensitively offer mental health professionals support when they confront their own demons. The point is that a supportive relationship is built into some of the best self-help materials.

We routinely encourage our colleagues and students to attend a meeting of a self-help group and to read an autobiography of a mental health patient. When students anonymously rate the experience of attending an open AA or Narcotics Anonymous meeting, they are enthusiastic in their responses. Their initial skepticism and devaluation of self-help groups as harmful or antiprofessional quickly give way to their impressions of solidarity, support, and sincerity. Likewise, when students rate the value of their reading autobiographies in the Abnormal Psychology course, their responses were favorable indeed: across three evaluations, over 95% rated the assignment positively (Norcross, Sommer, & Clifford, 2001).

Being familiar with the self-help materials that clients may be using or that you may be recommending also decreases the probability of misplaced advice. Probably more than the other self-help genres, films require certain warnings and preparation. Viewers are asked to suspend belief and to enter a fantasy world, but not to overidentify or overgeneralize from a single cinematic episode. The young and the squeamish should be directed away from stark, frightening portrayals. People suffering from debilitating psychological disorders should be forewarned of possible negative consequences of dramatic films, and those who recently suffered from trauma depicted in films should be careful not to be retraumatized.

## ■ 7. ASSESS CLIENTS' SELF-HELP EXPERIENCES

Seasoned professionals have learned to thoughtfully assess what patients have done and are doing in the way of self-help. They avoid recommending what clients have already tried and found wanting, and they build on what previously succeeded. It takes but a moment in an early session to assess previous self-help experiences.

When you inquire about the client's history of psychotherapy and psychotropic medications, also inquire about use of self-help books, groups, autobiographies, computer programs, and the Web. You are likely to be quite surprised by the prevalence and variety of clients' self-help attempts in the recent past. The four patients one of us saw in a representative afternoon tried, in toto, Anthony Robbins' audiotapes ordered from an infomercial, kava acquired over the counter, a self-help group, three self-help books, sexual enrichment videotapes ordered from a *New York Times* advertisement, and lots of prayer (Norcross, 2000). These were the self-help resources used by physicians and mental health professionals; imagine what less-informed patients have used and what they have not yet shared with you!

A survey of 262 psychotherapy clients found that only 34% reported that they had discussed their use of alternative therapies with their psychotherapist (Elkins, Marcus, Rajab, & Durgam, 2005). Of interest, in those cases in which use of alternative therapies was discussed in session, the topic was brought up by the client about half of the time. Patients' responses about their self-help histories will assist in case formulation and treatment selection. For example, some patients will say that they understand the concepts of self-help resources but need assistance with compliance. Other patients will say that cognitive-behavioral methods helped them, but they think the wound goes deeper or their goals are more spiritual. Still other patients say that they need more than inspiration and support from a self-help group; they need concrete and specific direction.

## ■ 8. HELP ADMINISTER DIFFICULT SELF-HELP PROGRAMS

Many patients enter treatment following one or more "failures" with self-help resources. More than three quarters of laypersons cannot, according to research reviews (Rosen, Glasgow, & Moore, 2003), successfully self-administer a toilet training protocol, a sexual dysfunction treatment, or a desensitization procedure. Just because a resource is labeled as *self-help* does not mean that most laypersons can understand or perform the methods on their own: many clients will require therapist-guided self-help (Andersson et al., 2008).

The results of several studies remind us to individualize our self-help recommendations and ministrations. One controlled study (Haeffel, 2010) investigated whether ruminators might actually get worse using self-help programs for depression. By focusing on their negative or unrealistic thoughts, such programs could provide more fodder for ruminative tendencies. That's what happened: students prone to rumination deteriorated after recording their realistic and unrealistic thoughts in workbooks. The upshot is to avoid recommending certain types of self-help for ruminating clients. Another study (Febbraro et al., 1999) cast doubt on the efficacy of bibliotherapy and self-monitoring for panic attacks when used independent from a professional.

Ineffective self-help is problematic in many ways. Most immediately, it leaves consumers/clients feeling frustrated, deflated, and probably incapable. More generally, ineffective self-help may be harmful; it may be innocuous but deprive individuals of time and resources, it may erode public credibility in the mental health professions, and it may reduce the scientific foundation of our profession and science (Lilienfeld, Lynn, & Lohr, 2003).

Professionals can render personal assistance with difficult self-help programs. Assuming that the self-help resource is applicable, we can assist clients in implementing the program and then later with its maintenance. We can also reassure patients that they should not feel miserable or resort to self-blame if the self-help materials are difficult to apply or not effective when applied (Rosen et al., 2003). We have found it useful to remind our patients that there is no legal or professional regulation of self-help claims; just because a self-help resource advertises itself as "clinically tested," "proven effective," and "in a single day" does not necessarily make it so as standalone self-help.

## ■ 9. OFFER TANGIBLE SUPPORT WHEN LINKING CLIENTS WITH SELF-HELP

Professionals can take specific steps to increase client immersion in self-help activities to supplement the work of treatment. These include:

- Holding favorable views toward self-help involvement, as favorable views are associated with increased goal attainment for patients (e.g., Hodges & Segal, 2002)
- Identifying local chapters of self-help and support groups, as opposed to wondering aloud in the session whether there are such groups available (two valuable national clearinghouses can be found at mentalhelp.net/selfhelp/ and www.mhselfhelp.org/)
- Connecting with self-help groups during the session and arranging for someone to accompany the client to a meeting (100% of clients in one study attended at least

one self-help meeting when these two steps were accomplished, versus virtually 0% attendance when a self-help meeting was simply suggested in the course of treatment; Sisson & Mallams, 1981).

■ Encouraging patients to attend 12-step groups, secure a sponsor, and engage in other AA-related behaviors, which increases involvement in self-help groups during and after treatment (Mankowski, Humphreys, & Moos, 2001)

■ Distributing copies of popular self-help books and autobiographies to clients during the session or making them available in the waiting room. (Expect most of them to never reappear in your office; console yourself with the realization that the professional expense incurred has furthered their growth.)

■ Giving patients specific Internet site URLs and titles of movies, as opposed to a general suggestion

In other words, practitioners' attitudes and behaviors in session translate concretely into patient involvement in self-help.

## ■ 10. RECOMMEND RESEARCH-SUPPORTED SELF-HELP

Dozens of self-help books and computer-based treatments have proven effective in controlled studies as standalone self-help. These include all of the online self-help programs sprinkled throughout this book and a growing number of self-help books. Among the latter are Burns' *Feeling Good*, Ellis and Harper's *A Guide to Rational Living*, Lewinsohn, Munoz, Youngren, and Zeiss's *Control Your Depression*, Linehan's *Skills Training Manual for Treating Borderline Personality Disorder*, Clum's *Coping with Panic*, Gordon's *Parent Effectiveness Training*, Fairburn's *Overcoming Binge Eating*, Heiman and LoPiccolo's *Becoming Orgasmic*, Craske and Barlow's *Mastery of Your Anxiety and Panic*, several forms of parent management training (Elger & McGrath, 2003), and sleep stimulus control instructions (Morin et al., 1999). The *Handbook of Self-Help Therapies* (Watkins & Clum, 2008) contains helpful research reviews on their effectiveness for ten disorders.

Of course, hundreds of additional self-help books are based on demonstrably effective treatments conducted by psychotherapists; however, we do not yet reliably know whether they can be practically and effectively implemented with little or no therapist contact. In the words of Rosen and colleagues (2003):

> The only way to know the effectiveness of well-intentioned instructional materials, when they are entirely self-administered, is to test those specific materials in the specific context of their intended usage. Psychologists who write self-help materials based on methods they find effective in office settings have no assurance that the public can successfully apply these procedures on their own. (p. 410, italics in original)

Pity the well-intentioned client valiantly trying to identify a meritorious self-help book or Internet site on his or her own. Literally thousands of such resources are competing for attention and sales. Gleaning trustworthy information on the Internet is like taking a 2-year-old on a walk: the toddler picks up a few pretty pebbles but also lots of garbage and dirt (Skow, 1999). Professionals may know when a beguiling irrelevancy can be dismissed with a click of the mouse, but the average person rarely does.

The take-home strategy is, whenever possible, to leverage the scientific research and advance those self-help materials that are supported as stand-alone interventions.

## ■ 11. RELY ON PROFESSIONAL CONSENSUS IN THE ABSENCE OF THE RESEARCH

The need to apply and recommend self-help far exceeds the controlled studies on their effectiveness. We estimate that less than 5% of commercial self-help books and websites possess any research evidence on their effectiveness or safety. Where does this leave the practitioner? We desire to be empirically informed, but so little self-help has been subjected to scrutiny as self-administered treatments. We cannot read 5,000 self-help books per year or surf the more than 25,000 websites devoted to mental health.

How might we proceed? By conducting more research, of course, and by developing demonstrably effective self-help. In the meantime, we can proceed in the tradition of evidence-based practice by integrating the best available research with clinical expertise in the context of patient characteristics, culture, and preferences (APA Task Force on Evidence-Based Practice, 2006). That is what we have tried to do over the past two decades with our 12 national studies and multiple editions of this book.

Professional consensus is just that: majority opinion as opposed to unanimity. Case in point is *The Courage to Heal* (Bass & Davis, 1994), a bestselling self-help book that received high ratings from scores of psychologists for its sensitive portrayal of adults who were sexually abused as children. The book has been criticized in many circles for, first, advancing research-unsubstantiated signs of sexual abuse and, second, inadvertently encouraging erroneous memories or false accusations of sexual abuse. Its supporters contend that the book fosters an acceptance and trust toward women whose abuse was probably denied by others. Few consensual picks are as controversial, but, in either case, the contention surrounding this book underscores practitioners' dual obligations to be familiar with the self-help resources they recommend and, whenever possible, to process clients' understanding and application of those resources.

The clinical expertise of the nearly 5,000 mental health professionals can guide your recommendations to clients. Although professional consensus is no guarantee and is inferior to controlled research, it is probably superior to consumer choice, random selection, or bestseller lists. We would, of course, prefer to rely on lists of self-help resources that have been subjected to controlled research and found to be demonstrably effective and safe. But until that time, we can rely on the collective knowledge of thousands of peers to navigate the bewildering self-help maze.

## ■ 12. TAILOR THE RECOMMENDATION TO THE PERSON, NOT ONLY THE DISORDER

The traditional means of matching a patient with self-help is by the clinical disorder or presenting problem being addressed in treatment—depression, addiction, relationship distress, anxiety, and so on. The sophisticated referral will be to the disorder AND to the person. That is, we should try to tailor the self-help recommendation to multiple transdiagnostic qualities of the patient: gender, age, religion, sexual orientation, ethnicity, occupation, and so on. As Sir William Osler, father of modern medicine, said: "It is sometimes much more important to know what sort of a patient has a disease than what sort of disease a patient has."

Two of our self-help recommendations of late were particularly well accepted and enacted because the recommendations were individualized. One of us located a specialty AA meeting for a lesbian client and recommended Comer and Poussaint's (1992) *Raising Black Children* to an African-American father. The clients had complained that the available resources were too "straight" and "vanilla," respectively, to apply to their unique situations.

However, it is sometimes difficult to identify self-help on a particular topic or disorder for clients who are members of racial/ethnic and sexual orientation minorities. Support groups for marginalized clients may not be available in the local community, and self-help books may not be available for a specific cultural population; we recently searched in vain for a culture-specific resource for an immigrant Vietnamese family struggling with bipolar disorder, for instance. More culture-specific resources are sorely needed.

When tailoring the self-help to the individual patient and his or her unique situation, also consider three treatment adaptation methods that have received considerable research support: patient preferences, stage of change, and theory of cause/cure (Norcross, 2011). Some patients struggle with reading, some do not own computers, some will not attend a movie by themselves, and still others (particularly adolescents) will refuse to consult anything *not* on a computer screen. Match their preferences and cultivate their strengths in recommending self-help.

With regard to stage of change, some self-help materials are indicated for the precontemplation and contemplation stages, whereas others are written for the action stage. For addictions, the AA *Big Book* and Pete Hamill's autobiography *A Drinking Life* are particularly indicated for contemplators because these books focus on recognizing the disorder and identifying the person's defenses, but they are short on specific action plans and thus not indicated for the action stage.

Self-help resources can similarly be matched to clients' (or clinicians') favored theory of cause and cure. Following with the addictions example, clients (and clinicians) favoring a disease model and abstinence only will be more disposed toward the AA *Big Book* and *Twelve Steps and Twelve Traditions*, whereas those more inclined to ecumenical treatments and the possibility of moderation will respond better to *Controlling Your Drinking* by Miller and Munoz, *When AA Doesn't Work for You* by Ellis and Velton, *The Addiction Workbook* by Fanning and O'Neil, and other such resources (see Chapter 38).

Mental health professionals would be wise to avoid the error of the outdated medical model that identifies clients by pathology alone. By adapting self-help to the transdiagnostic individuality of the client, we can enhance its applicability and efficacy.

## ▓ 13. RECOMMEND SELF-HELP FOR LIFE TRANSITIONS (AS WELL AS DISORDERS)

Our patients confront more than their disorders; they confront life with all of its vicissitudes. While addressing the most pressing disorders in treatment, clients can be simultaneously using self-help for life transitions. Leading the list are pregnancy, child development, parenting, adolescence, career changes, marriage, divorce, grieving, retirement, aging, and death, to name a few. There are some excellent self-help resources as well for growth and actualization: assertion, love, communication, happiness, self-management, relaxation, and spirituality, to name a few. The point is that self-help resources can be used for patient concerns not targeted in treatment and for their stressful life transitions.

## ▓ 14. EMPLOY SELF-HELP DURING WAITING PERIODS AND MAINTENANCE

Self-help in its varied guises—12-step groups, self-help books, computer programs, and Internet sites—can be a powerful intervention for wait-list patients, enabling natural recovery for some individuals and increasing motivation for those in need of professional treatment. On the other end, self-help can facilitate maintenance and generalization of treatment gains that will help sustain patients after professional services have ended (Klaw & Humphreys, 2005). In this sense, self-help should be considered not only as part of active treatment but also as wait-list and maintenance interventions.

## ■ 15. ADDRESS COMMON CONCERNS

Many patients and practitioners hold legitimate reservations about select aspects of self-help. In practice with clients and in workshops with colleagues, we have repeatedly encountered a triad of heartfelt concerns about incorporating self-help into treatment. Below we address these concerns with research findings and clinical experiences.

■ *Self-help discourages treatment and medication.* It is true that a few self-help books, Internet sites, and more than a few 12-step programs might direct patients away from professional treatment and medications. In years past, AA members would occasionally report that fellow members would accuse them of not being sober or abstinent if they were taking psychotropic medications. However, the incidence seems to be decreasing and the empirical evidence for this cited barrier is scarce (Kelly, 2003). In fact, the vast majority of AA members surveyed believe that the use of psychotropic medications intended to reduce relapse risk is a "good idea" and reported that they had not been pressured to stop taking medications (Rychtarik, Connors, Dermen, & Stasiewicz, 2000). Most self-help resources explicitly recommend treatment, and many now invite professionals to serve on their advisory boards. Put differently, this concern seems to be dated and fading.

■ *Incompatibility with treatment philosophy.* This concern typically relates to 12-step theistic groups. In our practices, we find that the vast majority of patients can relate profitably to 12-step, AA-model groups, either because they accept the teachings or reinterpret the language into spiritual concepts more compatible with their own beliefs. A study of 3,018 substance abusers indicated that theists and non-theists were equally likely to follow through on and benefit from referrals to AA (Winzelberg & Humphreys, 1999). Patients high in religious involvement have not been found to attend 12-step groups any more frequently (Brown et al., 2001) or to respond any better to them (Connors et al., 2001). Thus, consider referring both religious and nonreligious clients to 12-step groups and materials.

For the minority of clients who remain opposed to AA philosophy or who have experienced unsatisfactory connections, refer to non–12-step groups. There are alternatives for every addictive disorder, as listed in the respective chapters in this book.

■ *Possibility of harm.* The third reservation is that self-help actually harms patients. However, both psychotherapist reports and meta-analyses of self-help research attest to a low deterioration effect. As summarized in Table 1.1, psychologists in our national studies estimated that only 3% to 7% of their patients experienced any harm from self-help resources they recommended. This iatrogenic or deterioration rate is lower than that associated with professional treatment. At the same time, it is possible that psychologists using self-help interventions may be attending to only positive results (Rosen, 1993). Across five self-help studies, Scogin and colleagues (1996) found a low rate of negative outcomes for self-help, similar to or lower than that associated with professional treatment. Unfortunately, we do not know the magnitude of selection bias in the self-help materials chosen for empirical scrutiny;

one can safely conjecture that highly implausible self-help may be less likely to be put to controlled tests than more conventional self-help resources. We can confidently say that the possibility of harm is quite low for scientifically tested self-help materials and is yet unknown for nontested self-help materials. Negative outcomes are more of a concern with purely self-administered treatments than with self-help integrated into ongoing treatment (Scogin, 2003).

## ▪ 16. MONITOR PATIENT PROGRESS WITH SELF-HELP

It's often not enough to simply recommend self-help resources and then leave it to the patient to actually read the book, visit the website, or join the support group. The research suggests that self-help resources work best when guided or reinforced by a professional—or at least when a professional occasionally checks in with the patient about such use.

Regular monitoring of the use of self-help—such as progress with a 12-step group or an online program—also provides an opportunity for the patient to ask questions, clarify concerns, and correct misunderstandings. It can also end the patient's relationship with an unhelpful resource earlier on, before serious damage or harm has come to the patient (for instance, a support group that is causing more harm than good). Last, monitoring can reinforce the benefits of self-help and remind clients that you're interested in their progress in all aspects of their life—not just what is done in treatment.

When one self-help resource has been completed by a patient, the professional can then help summarize its positive role in the patient's recovery. If the patient needs guidance or assistance in finding another resource, the therapist will be well prepared and equipped to do so.

## ▪ 17. COLLABORATE WITH SELF-HELP ORGANIZATIONS

Studies suggest that cooperative relationships between self-help organizations and mental health professionals are characterized by frequent contact and cross-participation (Kurtz, 1984). Self-help groups seek collaboration with and resources from professionals. Consider generating referrals and providing meeting space and publicity (Klaw & Humphreys, 2005). Consider providing presentations to local chapters of self-help groups. Also consider disseminating self-help brochures, sample books, and meeting notices in your waiting room.

If you have the proficiencies, you can provide advanced training and technical assistance to self-help organizations. A study by the Substance Abuse and Mental Health Services Administration of 13 federally funded consumer service programs found that 70% of them desired such training in organizational and staff development (Van Tosh & del Vecchio, 2000).

When working with self-help organizations, enter into a collaborative relationship. Avoid the professional temptation to control the process, restructure the organization, or think of the self-help organization as the patient. If asked, agree to serve as a volunteer professional sponsor, who serves, not controls, the organization. In two articles, Jason and associates (1985, 1988) provided compelling examples of how professionals can collaborate with self-help organizations. In the first, Jason (1985) gave self-help groups radio time for one hour a week. A mental health professional acted as moderator, informed the audience of appropriate referrals, and facilitated the self-help process in the studio. Several group members demonstrated the self-help group process on the air and then took calls from the listening audience. In the second example, Jason et al. (1988) consulted with clergy members on behalf of various self-help groups. As a result, self-help activity increased dramatically—the number of referrals, group publicity, and new self-help groups all increased. In both examples, the mental health professionals acted as community gatekeepers who collaborated with self-help organizations to everyone's benefit.

## ■ IN CLOSING

The rise of self-help is part and parcel of the transformation of health care toward consumer-driven care. More companies and insurers are turning to consumer-directed health plans, which transfer control (and some of the costs) to the insured. The New Freedom Commission on Mental Health (govinfo.library.unt.edu/mentalhealthcommission/) highlighted as its second goal, "Mental health care is consumer and family driven." In an ideal program, consumers will actively participate in designing and developing the care in which they are involved.

Professional guidance on the selection and administration of self-help materials and minimal therapist contact when using them increase the probability of success (Scogin, 2003). We can direct our clients toward effective resources and away from ineffective remedies.

As two early American Psychological Association task forces on self-help therapies proclaimed, self-help offers tremendous potential to the public, but untested programs also pose risks to the consumers (Rosen, 2004). Giving psychology away is aimed not only at disseminating evidence-based methods and relationships but also at countering what has not been tested or not been supported (Norcross, 2000). Popular psychology need not be nonscientific psychology (Lilienfeld, 1998). This entails a process of sharing, as opposed to imposing, the fruits of our scientific enterprise and its demonstrably effective applications.

We mental health professionals can harness and incorporate self-help into treatment for the benefit of our patients and the populace. We, by our behavior, can significantly enhance the effectiveness of self-help.

# THE 12 NATIONAL STUDIES

Over the past 20 years, we have conducted a series of national studies to determine the most useful and most frequently recommended self-help resources for diverse problems and life challenges. The resources we evaluated were self-help books, autobiographies, and films. In each case, the methodology and the samples were very similar: a lengthy survey mailed to clinical and counseling psychologists residing in the United States. The responding psychologists rated self-help resources with which they were sufficiently familiar on the same 5-point scale:

| +2 | Extremely good | Outstanding; highly recommended book, best or among best in category |
| +1 | Moderately good | Provides good advice, can be helpful; worth purchasing |
| 0 | Average | An average self-help book |
| −1 | Moderately bad | Not a good self-help book; may provide misleading or inaccurate information |
| −2 | Extremely bad | This book exemplifies the worst of the self-help books; worst, or among worst in its category |

The precise wording was slightly altered, of course, for ratings of autobiographies and films. For example, the wording read "An average autobiographical account," "Outstanding; highly recommended film," and so on.

As authors of this book and lead researchers on the dozen studies, we strove to avoid theoretical bias. Our theoretical orientations are explicitly integrative; that is, we believe that a number of treatment approaches can be used to help people overcome disorders and cope effectively with life transitions. Something of value can be found among the dizzying diversity of treatments ranging from A to Z—analytical, behavioral, cognitive, all the way to Zen Buddhism.

Overall, the mental health experts were far more likely to rate the self-help resources positively than negatively. The stars (1 to 5) and the dagger assigned to the various resources were based primarily on the average rating of the resource and secondarily on its frequency of rating. After extensive discussions and data analyses, we selected the cutoff points for 1 to 5 stars described in Chapter 1 and presented below:

★★★★★ Average rating of 1.25 or higher; the resource was rated by 30 or more psychologists

★★★★  Average rating of 1.00 or higher; rated by 20 or more psychologists
★★★  Average rating of 0.50 through 0.99; rated 10 or more times
★★  Average rating of 0.25 through 0.49; rated 10 or more times
★  Average rating of 0.00 through 0.24; rated 10 or more times
† Average negative rating; rated by 10 or more mental health professionals

The sole exception to this rating system was the autobiographies. There, we used a cut-off of 8 or more ratings, as opposed to 10, simply because fewer psychologists were sufficiently familiar with autobiographies than with self-help books or movies and because in one of our investigations (Study 2) we had previously used 8 as the minimum number of raters. Thus, the rating system for autobiographies was:

★★★★★  Average rating of 1.25 or higher; rated by 24 or more psychologists
★★★★  Average rating of 1.00 or higher; rated by 16 or more mental health professionals
★★★  Average rating of 0.50 through 0.99; rated 8 or more times
★★  Average rating of 0.25 through 0.49; rated 8 or more times
★  Average rating of 0.00 through 0.24; rated 8 or more times
† Average negative rating; rated by 8 or more mental health professionals

Our recommendations in each chapter are guided by the collective expertise of the mental health experts in our studies. The Strongly Recommended self-help resources are those receiving 5 or 4 stars. The 3-star resources receive the more modest designation of Recommended. Although the 1-star and 2-star books were in the positive range, they were low positive and received a large number of 0 and even some negative ratings. Thus, we opted not to recommend them. And, as described in Chapter 1, the worst rating—the dagger (†)—was reserved for books, autobiographies, and films receiving a negative rating. This rating, it should be noted, was given to only about 5% of all the self-help resources in our studies.

The individual ratings for all the self-help resources canvassed in our 12 studies are detailed in Appendix B (self-help books), Appendix C (autobiographies), and Appendix D (films). Across the studies, nearly 5,000 psychologists contributed their expertise and judgment to evaluate self-help resources. Below we briefly review the survey methodology and sample composition of each study.

## ■ STUDY 1: SELF-HELP BOOKS

The first study entailed mailing a questionnaire to 4,000 members of the clinical and counseling psychology divisions of the American Psychological Association (APA). Almost 800 psychologists returned the questionnaires, but full ratings of the books were completed by just under 600. Some of the members had died, and their spouses returned the unanswered questionnaires with a note; more than 100 respondents filled out the first part of the questionnaire (demographic information and general items about self-help books) but did not rate individual books; and some respondents returned the forms unanswered. In many such studies, a follow-up mailing is conducted to increase the sample size. We considered this alternative but did not exercise it for a simple reason: inadequate funds. The results of the first national study formed the basis for *The Authoritative Guide to Self-Help Books* by John W. Santrock, Ann M. Minnett, and Barbara D. Campbell (1994).

The responding mental health professionals all held doctorates. They lived in every state and represented a broad cross-section of clinical and counseling psychologists in the United States. While the respondents were members of the clinical and counseling psychology divisions of the APA, their evaluations of self-help books in the study and in this book are not in any way endorsed by the APA itself.

## ■ STUDY 2: AUTOBIOGRAPHIES

A few years later, we expanded our focus to embrace autobiographies of people with a behavioral or mental disorder. Our inclusion criteria were that they be first-person narrative accounts that dealt primarily or substantially with the author's disorder or treatment in book-length works. Excluded were fictional and second-person accounts. Brief articles, poetry collections, and film accounts were also excluded. Our aim was to obtain solid, national data on the published autobiographies that psychologists recommend to their clients.

We mailed a cover letter, a four-page questionnaire, and a stamped return envelope to 1,000 randomly selected members of the APA's Division of Psychotherapy living in the United States. Of these, 379 questionnaires (38%) were returned; however, 17 were not usable because the psychologists were retired or did not wish to participate. The final sample consisted of 362 psychologists who demographically and geographically represented the entire Division of Psychotherapy membership. Thirty-five percent of the psychologists were women, and 94% were Caucasian. Primary employment settings were private practice (66% of sample), universities (10%), hospitals (5%), and outpatient clinics (5%). Portions of these results were reported in a *Professional Psychology* article authored by Jennifer S. Clifford, John C. Norcross, and Robert Sommer (1999).

## ■ STUDY 3: SELF-HELP BOOKS

Study 3 canvassed self-help books that had been published since Study 1 was performed and included self-help books on three additional disorders: schizophrenia, attention-deficit/hyperactivity disorder (ADHD), and dementia/Alzheimer's disease. Two separate surveys were mailed to a total of 3,000 randomly selected members of the APA's clinical and counseling psychology divisions. The first questionnaire was sent to 1,500 psychologists soliciting quality ratings on self-help books for 14 problem areas; the second questionnaire was sent to another 1,500 psychologists requesting ratings on self-help books on a different set of 15 problems. The first questionnaire was returned by 336 psychologists, and full ratings of the books were completed by 324. The total response rate was 22%. The second questionnaire was completed and returned by 376 psychologists; of these, 357 provided usable data. This yielded a total response rate of 25%. The psychologists returning the questionnaires were demographically, professionally, and geographically representative of the APA divisions of clinical and counseling psychology (Bechtoldt, Norcross, Wyckoff, Pokrywa, & Campbell, 2001).

## ■ STUDY 4: AUTOBIOGRAPHIES

Study 4 assessed psychologists' knowledge and evaluations of autobiographies not covered in our earlier study. A lengthy questionnaire was mailed to 1,500 members of APA's clinical psychology and counseling psychology divisions seeking their ratings on the value of autobiographies concerning 13 different problems. Of these, 328 were returned, but 21 were incomplete, leaving 307 usable questionnaires. As in the other studies, the primary reasons for returning an incomplete questionnaire were that the psychologists were not in clinical practice or had recently retired. The response rate for this study was 22%.

## ■ STUDY 5: FILMS

In Study 5 we entered new territory: psychologists' evaluations of commercial films as self-help resources. We sent a questionnaire concerning the value of specific movies to 1,500 members of the APA's clinical and counseling psychology divisions. Psychologists were asked to rate the quality of listed movies with which they were sufficiently familiar for 20 problem areas. A total of 417 surveys were returned, with usable data provided by 401 of the respondents, a 28% total response rate. As in the previous studies, the participating mental health experts were all doctoral-level psychologists of various genders, ethnicities, theoretical orientations, and work settings.

## ■ STUDY 6: SELF-HELP BOOKS

In preparation for the last edition, we conducted three additional studies covering self-help books, autobiographies, and films. For Study 6, we mailed an extensive questionnaire requesting evaluations of self-help books for 15 behavioral disorders and life challenges to 1,666 members of the APA clinical and counseling psychology divisions. A total of 257 questionnaires were retuned, with ratings of the books completed by 237.

The responding psychologists constituted a broad sample of mental health experts. Hailing from every state in the union, they all held doctoral degrees and averaged 19 years of postdoctoral experience. The psychologists represented diverse theoretical orientations, with integrative (37%), cognitive (24%), and psychodynamic (12%) leading the pack, and a variety of employment sites, largely private practice and academia.

## ■ STUDY 7: SELF-HELP BOOKS

The rapid proliferation of self-help books required yet another questionnaire on self-help books, simply to canvass the remaining behavioral disorders and life challenges we cover. Together, Study 6 and Study 7 collected evaluative data on books in 36 areas, including the new chapters in that edition devoted to trauma, obsessive-compulsive disorder, violent youth, borderline and narcissistic personality disorders, bipolar disorder, and suicide.

Specifically, we compiled a questionnaire on recent self-help books for 21 problem areas and mailed it to another 1,666 psychologists who belonged to the APA clinical and counseling psychology divisions. A total of 292 psychologists participated, but 31 of them returned the questionnaire incomplete for various reasons. The respondents were nearly evenly divided in terms of gender (53% men, 47% women) and were employed in a variety of settings, with independent practices, university departments, and outpatient clinics the most frequent.

## ■ STUDY 8: FILMS AND AUTOBIOGRAPHIES

Our eighth study again involved a lengthy questionnaire, this one concerning the value of particular films and autobiographies for particular disorders. Paralleling all of our previous studies, we mailed the questionnaire to a large sample of American psychologists who were members of APA's division of clinical or counseling psychology. We sent 1,666 questionnaires and received 338 returns, for a total response rate of 20%. Three hundred sixteen of the returned questionnaires were usable, for a usable return rate of 19%.

## ■ STUDIES 9 AND 10: SELF-HELP BOOKS

In preparation for this edition of the book, in 2011 we conducted four new studies: two devoted to self-help books, one on autobiographies, and the other on films. In addition to the behavioral disorders and life challenges covered in our earlier studies, we added autism and Asperger's, bullying, chronic pain, GLB issues, and happiness. Again, lengthy questionnaires were constructed and psychologists were again asked to rate those self-help resources with which they were sufficiently familiar; however, for these most recent studies, we dispensed with the expensive mailing method and instead e-mailed psychologists the link to online surveys. This procedure was more efficient and less costly, but, as expected, did result in lower response rates.

The survey links were emailed to 9,184 doctoral-level psychologists belonging to the National Register of Health Service Providers in Psychology. One fourth received the link to the self-help book survey, one fourth to the second self-help survey, another fourth to self-help films, and the final fourth to autobiographies. Across the four surveys, 279 of the e-mails were returned as undeliverable, and after several reminder e-mails, 15.7% of the remaining psychologists participated. That percentage translated into 330 psychologists completing the Study 9 questionnaire and 368 psychologists completing the Study 10 questionnaire, both dedicated to self-help books published since our previous studies.

Table A1 summarizes the demographic and professional characteristics of the psychologists participating in Study 9 and Study 10 as well as Study 11 and 12 (described below). Approximately 80% of the National Register psychologists were also members of the APA, providing good reason to believe that the participants from Studies 1 through 8 were indeed reasonably comparable to those from these latest four studies.

## ■ STUDY 11: AUTOBIOGRAPHIES

A separate survey was required to canvass psychologists' expertise on the proliferating number of memoirs published in the past decade on behavioral disorders. Study 11 did just that, asking psychologists to evaluate the approximately 200 autobiographies with which they were sufficiently familiar. In all, 303 professionals participated.

As shown in Table A1, the psychologists were equally distributed in terms of gender, but ethnic/racial backgrounds were largely Caucasian/white (90%). Across the four latest studies, the theoretical orientations were prototypically eclectic/integrative (32%), cognitive (26%), and psychodynamic (13%). They were predominantly employed in private practice (61%).

## ■ STUDY 12: FILMS

Our final study gathered evaluative judgments on the self-help value of commercial films (and a few documentaries) for the behavioral disorders and life challenges. We compiled the films by examining movie guides (e.g., Hesley & Hesley, 2001; Wedding et al., 2010), reviewing lists of top-grossing films (e.g., www.imdb.com), and consulting colleagues. The questionnaire was completed by 305 psychologists (see Table A1), a return rate of 13.7%.

**TABLE A1. Descriptive Summary of Responding Psychologists in the Four Latest Studies**

| Characteristic | Study 9 (N = 330) | Study 10 (N = 368) | Study 11 (N = 303) | Study 12 (N = 305) |
|---|---|---|---|---|
| | % | % | % | % |
| Gender | | | | |
| Male | 48 | 42 | 49 | 50 |
| Female | 52 | 58 | 51 | 50 |
| Ethnic/racial background | | | | |
| Native American | 2 | 1 | 1 | 2 |
| African American/Black | 2 | 1 | 2 | 2 |
| Caucasian/White | 91 | 93 | 90 | 91 |
| Hispanic/Latino | 2 | 1 | 3 | 3 |
| Asian American | 2 | 2 | 2 | 1 |
| Multiple/Other | 1 | 2 | 2 | 1 |
| Theoretical orientation | | | | |
| Behavioral | 7 | 7 | 6 | 7 |
| Cognitive | 25 | 26 | 25 | 27 |
| Eclectic/integrative | 33 | 37 | 29 | 29 |
| Humanistic/existential | 4 | 3 | 5 | 5 |
| Interpersonal | 7 | 3 | 4 | 5 |
| Psychodynamic/analytic | 12 | 10 | 15 | 14 |
| Systems/family systems | 3 | 4 | 4 | 4 |
| Other | 9 | 10 | 12 | 9 |
| Employment setting | | | | |
| Private practice | 64 | 63 | 55 | 56 |
| General hospital | 5 | 5 | 6 | 5 |
| Outpatient clinic & HMO | 8 | 7 | 6 | 5 |
| Psychiatric hospital | 3 | 2 | 5 | 5 |
| University | 4 | 7 | 10 | 8 |
| Medical school | 3 | 4 | 3 | 4 |
| Other/None | 13 | 12 | 15 | 17 |

In summary, by the numbers, our national studies have spanned two decades, entailed 12 surveys, and involved 4,829 psychologists from across the United States. Their collective wisdom and combined expertise have been aggregated in Appendices B, C, and D and have informed the entire book.

# RATINGS OF SELF-HELP BOOKS
# IN THE NATIONAL STUDIES

Only those self-help books rated five or more times in our national studies are included in this list. Some books appear on this list but were not included in the text because they were rated by fewer than 10 mental health experts. Please consult Appendix A for details on the methodology of the national studies and the meaning of the guide ratings.

| Category and Title | Author(s) | Study # | Avg. Rating | # of Raters | Guide Rating |
|---|---|---|---|---|---|
| **Abuse** | | | | | |
| *Abused No More* | Ackerman & Pickering | 1 | 0.48 | 57 | ★★ |
| *Allies in Healing* | Davis | 3 | 1.24 | 33 | ★★★★ |
| *Battered Wives* | Martin | 1 | 0.85 | 56 | ★★★ |
| *Battered Woman, The* | Walker | 1 | 1.22 | 121 | ★★★★ |
| *Beginning to Heal* | Bass & Davis | 3 | 0.84 | 43 | ★★★ |
| *Breaking the Cycle of Abuse* | Engel | 9 | 0.85 | 27 | ★★★ |
| *Breaking Violence in a Relationship* | Blue | 3 | 1.00 | 6 | — |
| *Courage to Heal, The* | Bass & Davis | 1 | 1.53 | 244 | ★★★★★ |
| *Facing the Shadow* | Carnes | 6 | 1.17 | 6 | — |
| *From Child Sexual Abuse to Adult Sexual Risk* | Koenig et. al. | 9 | 0.27 | 15 | ★★ |
| *Getting Free* | NiCarthy | 1 | 1.00 | 38 | ★★★★ |
| *Healing the Incest Wound* | Courtois | 6 | 1.31 | 54 | ★★★★★ |
| *Healing the Shame That Binds You* | Bradshaw | 1 | 0.56 | 192 | ★★★ |
| *Healing the Trauma of Abuse* | Copeland & Harris | 6 | 1.25 | 12 | ★★★ |
| *Hush* | Bradley | 9 | 0.40 | 15 | ★★ |
| *I Never Called It Rape* | Warshaw | 3 | 1.53 | 17 | ★★★ |
| *Invisible Wounds* | Douglas | 6 | 0.80 | 5 | — |
| *It's My Life Now* | Dugan & Hock | 9 | 0.20 | 10 | ★ |
| *Me Nobody Knows, The* | Bean & Bennett | 6 | 1.13 | 8 | — |
| *Reclaiming the Inner Child* | Abrams | 1 | 0.20 | 97 | ★ |

| Category and Title | Author(s) | Study # | Avg. Rating | # of Raters | Guide Rating |
|---|---|---|---|---|---|
| Secret of Overcoming Verbal Abuse | Ellis & Grad-Powers | 6 | 0.81 | 16 | ★★★ |
| Secret Trauma, The | Russell | 6 | 1.30 | 10 | ★★★ |
| Sexual Healing Journey, The | Maltz | 6 | 1.44 | 18 | ★★★ |
| Toxic Parents | Forward | 1 | 0.47 | 119 | ★★ |
| Victims No Longer | Lew | 3 | 1.19 | 21 | ★★★★ |
| Verbally Abusive Relationship, The | Evans | 3 | 1.61 | 13 | ★★★ |
| Waking the Tiger | Levine & Frederick | 3 | 0.83 | 6 | — |
| When Your Child Has Been Molested | Hagans & Case | 6 | 1.30 | 10 | ★★★ |
| Wounded Boys, Heroic Men | Sonkin | 3 | 0.80 | 10 | ★★★ |
| Wounded Heart, The | Allender & Crabb | 6 | 0.86 | 7 | — |
| Why Does He Do That? | Bancroft | 9 | 0.36 | 14 | ★★ |
| You Are Not Alone | Rouse | 6 | 1.40 | 5 | ◆ |
| You Can't Say That to Me! | Elgin | 3 | 1.00 | 9 | — |
| **Addictions (not Drugs and Alcohol)** | | | | | |
| Addiction and Grace | May | 1 | 0.67 | 26 | ★★★ |
| Beyond Codependency | Beattie | 3 | 0.90 | 61 | ★★★ |
| Co-Dependence | Whitfield | 1 | 0.04 | 52 | ★ |
| Digital Diet, The | Sieburg | 9 | −0.67 | 6 | — |
| Facebook Addiction | Osuagwu | 9 | 0.00 | 7 | — |
| Healing the Wounds of Sexual Addiction | Laaser | 9 | 0.52 | 23 | ★★★ |
| How to Break Your Addiction to a Person | Halpern | 1 | 0.49 | 72 | ★★ |
| Infidelity Online Workshop, The | Young | 9 | −0.22 | 9 | — |
| Infidelity Online Workshop, The | Young | 9 | −0.022 | 9 | — |
| In the Shadows of the Net | Carnes et al. | 9 | 0.73 | 15 | ★★★ |
| Love Is a Choice | Helmfelt et al. | 1 | 0.05 | 41 | ★ |
| Overcoming Your Pathological Gambling | Ladouceur & Lachance | 9 | 0.09 | 11 | ★ |
| Out of the Shadows | Carnes | 3 | 0.67 | 39 | ★★★ |
| Real Solutions for Overcoming Internet Addictions | Watters | 9 | 0.42 | 12 | ★★ |
| Overcoming Your Pathological Gambling | Ladouceur & Lachance | 9 | 0.09 | 11 | ★ |
| Real Solutions for Overcoming Internet Addictions | Watters | 9 | 0.42 | 12 | ★★ |
| Resisting 12-Step Coercion | Peele et al. | 3 | 0.17 | 6 | — |
| Sex Addiction Workbook, The | Sbraga et. al. | 9 | 0.44 | 16 | ★★ |
| Truth about Addiction and Recovery, The | Peele et al. | 3 | 0.73 | 11 | ★★★ |
| **Adult Development** | | | | | |
| 50+ Wellness Program, The | McIlwain et al. | 1 | 0.24 | 17 | ★ |
| Bad Childhood—Good Life | Schlessinger | 9 | −0.78 | 27 | † |

| Category and Title | Author(s) | Study # | Avg. Rating | # of Raters | Guide Rating |
|---|---|---|---|---|---|
| *Becoming a Life Change Artist* | Mandell & Jordan | 9 | 0.37 | 8 | — |
| *Fly Fishing Through the Midlife Crisis* | Raines | 3 | 1.00 | 5 | — |
| *How to Deal with Your Parents* | Osterkamp | 1 | 0.50 | 24 | ★★★ |
| *Making Peace with Your Parents* | Bloomfield | 1 | 0.99 | 69 | ★★★ |
| *Necessary Losses* | Viorst | 1 | 1.10 | 182 | ★★★★ |
| *Old Folks Going Strong* | York | 1 | 0.61 | 7 | — |
| *Passages* | Sheehy | 1 | 0.72 | 356 | ★★★ |
| *Retire Smart, Retire Happy* | Schlossberg | 9 | 0.89 | 27 | ★★★ |
| *Seasons of a Man's Life* | Levinson | 1 | 1.05 | 222 | ★★★★ |
| *Second Blooming for Women* | Logan & Smith | 9 | 0.22 | 9 | — |
| *Silent Passage, The* | Sheehy | 3 | 0.81 | 73 | ★★★ |
| *Social Animal, The* | Brooks | 9 | 0.85 | 26 | ★★★ |
| *What Do You Want to Do When You Grow Up* | Cantor & Thompson | 6 | 0.57 | 7 | — |
| *When You and Your Mother Can't Be Friends* | Secunda | 1 | 0.60 | 30 | ★★★ |
| **Aging** | | | | | |
| *20 Years Younger* | Green et. al. | 9 | 0.46 | 13 | ★★ |
| *Ageless Body, Timeless Mind* | Chopra | 3 | 0.77 | 43 | ★★★ |
| *Aging Well* | Vaillant | 6 | 1.29 | 14 | ★★★ |
| *Aging Well* | Fries | 1 | 0.84 | 16 | ★★★ |
| *Another Country* | Pipher | 6 | 1.36 | 11 | ★★★ |
| *Chicken Soup for the Golden Soul* | Canfield | 6 | 0.25 | 9 | — |
| *Complete Guide to Health and Well-being After 50* | Weiss & Subak-Sharpe | 1 | 0.88 | 24 | ★★★ |
| *Emotional Survival Guide for Caregivers, The* | Jacobs | 9 | 1.11 | 19 | ★★★ |
| *Enjoy Old Age* | Skinner & Vaughan | 6 | 1.00 | 15 | ★★★ |
| *Fountain of Age, The* | Friedan | 3 | 0.69 | 16 | ★★★ |
| *Gift of Years* | Chittister | 9 | 0.79 | 19 | ★★★ |
| *Healthy Aging* | Weil | 9 | 1.29 | 34 | ★★★★★ |
| *How to Live Longer and Feel Better* | Pauling | 1 | 0.53 | 46 | ★★★ |
| *It's Better to be Over the Hill than Under It* | LeShan | 3 | 1.18 | 11 | ★★★ |
| *Mature Mind* | Cohen | 9 | 0.67 | 9 | — |
| *My Time* | Trafford | 9 | 0.25 | 8 | — |
| *Not Dead Yet …* | Fanning | 9 | 0.14 | 7 | — |
| *What's Age Got to Do with It?* | McGraw | 9 | 0.50 | 10 | ★★★ |
| *You: Staying Young* | Roizen & Oz | 9 | 1.16 | 25 | ★★★★ |
| *Your Renaissance Years* | Veninga | 3 | 1.00 | 5 | ♦ |

| Category and Title | Author(s) | Study # | Avg. Rating | # of Raters | Guide Rating |
|---|---|---|---|---|---|
| **Anger** | | | | | |
| *Act on Life, Not on Anger* | Eifert et al. | 9 | 1.00 | 22 | ★★★★ |
| *Anger at Work* | Weisinger | 3 | 1.33 | 6 | — |
| *Anger Control Workbook, The* | McKay & Rogers | 6 | 1.41 | 37 | ★★★★★ |
| *Anger: Deal with It, Heal with It* | DeFoore | 1 | 0.38 | 24 | ★★ |
| *Anger: The Misunderstood Emotion* | Tavris | 1 | 1.18 | 83 | ★★★★ |
| *Anger Free* | Gentry | 6 | 1.14 | 7 | — |
| *Anger Kills* | Williams & Williams | 3 | 1.44 | 9 | ◆ |
| *Anger Workbook, The* | Bilodeau | 3 | 1.13 | 31 | ★★★★ |
| *Angry All the Time* | Potter-Efron | 3 | 1.21 | 14 | ★★★ |
| *Angry Book, The* | Rubin | 1 | 0.52 | 95 | ★★★ |
| *Anger Management for Everyone* | Tafrate & Kassinove | 9 | 0.94 | 17 | ★★★ |
| *Anger Workbook for Teens, The* | Lohmann | 9 | 0.72 | 18 | ★★★ |
| *Anger Workbook for Women, The* | Petracek | 9 | 0.46 | 13 | ★★ |
| *Angry Men and the Women Who Love Them* | Hegstrom | 3 | 0.71 | 7 | — |
| *Angry Self, The* | Gottlieb | 6 | 1.33 | 9 | ◆ |
| *Beyond Anger* | Harbin | 6 | 1.14 | 7 | — |
| *Dance of Anger, The* | Lerner | 1 | 1.39 | 211 | ★★★★★ |
| *Freeing the Angry Mind* | Bankart | 9 | 0.12 | 8 | — |
| *Gift of Anger, The* | Cannon | 9 | 0.57 | 14 | ★★★ |
| *Healthy Anger* | Golden | 9 | 0.67 | 9 | — |
| *How to Control Your Anger Before It Controls You* | Ellis & Tafrate | 3 | 1.14 | 35 | ★★★★ |
| *Letting Go of Anger* | Potter-Efron & Potter-Efron | 3 | 1.30 | 23 | ★★★★ |
| *Overcoming Anger in Your Relationship* | Nay | 9 | 0.33 | 6 | — |
| *Prisoners of Hate* | Beck | 6 | 1.58 | 12 | ★★★ |
| *Rage* | Potter-Efron | 9 | 0.80 | 15 | ★★★ |
| *Transforming Anger* | Childre & Rozman | 9 | 0.33 | 6 | — |
| *Volcano in My Tummy, A* | Whitehouse & Pudney | 3 | 1.33 | 6 | ◆ |
| *What to Do When Your Temper Flares* | Huebner | 9 | 0.43 | 14 | ★★ |
| *When Anger Hurts* | McKay et al. | 1 | 0.92 | 36 | ★★★ |
| *When Anger Scares You* | McCarthy & McCarthy | 9 | −0.17 | 6 | — |
| *When Chicken Soup Isn't Enough* | Barris | 6 | 0.57 | 7 | — |
| **Anxiety Disorders** | | | | | |
| *Anxiety and Panic Attacks* | Handly | 1 | 0.81 | 27 | ★★★ |
| *Anxiety and Phobia Workbook, The* | Bourne | 3 | 1.58 | 117 | ★★★★★ |

| Category and Title | Author(s) | Study # | Avg. Rating | # of Raters | Guide Rating |
|---|---|---|---|---|---|
| *Anxiety Disease, The* | Sheehan | 1 | 0.64 | 59 | ★★★ |
| *Anxiety Disorders and Phobias* | Beck & Emery | 1 | 1.18 | 172 | ★★★★ |
| *Anxiety Workbook for Teens, The* | Schab | 9 | 0.73 | 15 | ★★★ |
| *Beyond Anxiety and Phobia* | Bourne | 6 | 1.33 | 21 | ★★★★ |
| *Dance of Fear, The* | Lerner | 9 | 1.26 | 62 | ★★★★★ |
| *Don't Panic* | Wilson | 1 | 1.04 | 82 | ★★★★ |
| *End to Panic, An* | Zuercher-White | 3 | 1.42 | 12 | ★★★ |
| *Feel the Fear and Do it Anyway* | Jeffers | 3 | 1.15 | 34 | ★★★★ |
| *Good News about Panic, Anxiety, and Phobias, The* | Gold | 1 | 0.59 | 45 | ★★★ |
| *Healing Fear* | Bourne | 6 | 1.00 | 5 | — |
| *How to Control Your Anxiety before It Controls You* | Ellis | 3 | 0.95 | 59 | ★★★ |
| *I Bet I Won't Fret* | Sisemore | 9 | 0.71 | 7 | — |
| *I Don't Want to Go to School* | Pando & Voerg | 9 | 0.73 | 11 | ★★★ |
| *Life without Fear* | Wolpe & Wolpe | 3 | 0.85 | 33 | ★★★ |
| *Managing Social Anxiety Workbook* | Hope et al. | 9 | 0.15 | 26 | ★ |
| *Mastery of Your Anxiety and Panic III* | Craske & Barlow | 3 | 1.53 | 58 | ★★★★★ |
| *Mastering Your Fears and Phobias Workbook* | Antony et al. | 9 | 1.45 | 47 | ★★★★★ |
| *My Anxious Mind* | Tompkins & Martinez | 9 | 0.83 | 6 | — |
| *Overcoming Anxiety* | Kennerley | 6 | 0.88 | 9 | — |
| *Overcoming Anxiety for Dummies* | Elliott & Smith | 9 | 0.75 | 12 | ★★★ |
| *Overcoming Generalized Anxiety Disorder* | White | 6 | 1.14 | 7 | ◆ |
| *Overcoming Shyness and Social Phobia* | Rapee | 6 | 1.46 | 13 | ★★★ |
| *Overcoming Social Anxiety and Shyness* | Butler | 9 | 0.83 | 12 | ★★★ |
| *Panic and Anxiety Disorder* | Manassee-Buell | 6 | 1.00 | 6 | — |
| *Panic Disorder* | Rachman & de Silva | 3 | 0.93 | 29 | ★★★ |
| *Peace from Nervous Suffering* | Weekes | 1 | 0.88 | 57 | ★★★ |
| *Perfect Madness* | Warner | 9 | 0.67 | 6 | — |
| *Shyness and Social Anxiety Workbook* | Anthony & Swinson | 6 | 1.21 | 24 | ★★★★ |
| *Sky Is Falling, The* | Dumont | 3 | 1.33 | 9 | ◆ |
| *Stopping Anxiety Medication* | Otto et al. | 9 | 1.00 | 15 | ★★★ |
| *When Perfect Isn't Good Enough* | Antony & Swinson | 9 | 1.17 | 23 | ★★★★ |
| *When Panic Attacks* | Burns | 9 | 1.16 | 38 | ★★★★ |
| *Why Does Everything Have to Be Perfect?* | Shackerman | 6 | 1.00 | 6 | — |
| *Women Who Worry Too Much* | Haxlett-Stevens | 9 | 0.55 | 11 | ★★★ |
| *Worry* | Hallowell | 6 | 1.40 | 10 | ★★★ |
| *Worry Cure, The* | Leahy | 9 | 0.15 | 20 | ★ |

| Category and Title | Author(s) | Study # | Avg. Rating | # of Raters | Guide Rating |
|---|---|---|---|---|---|
| *Worry Trap, The* | LeJeune | 9 | 0.40 | 5 | — |
| **Assertiveness** | | | | | |
| *Assert Yourself* | Lendenfield | 6 | 1.13 | 8 | — |
| *Asserting Yourself* | Bower & Bower | 3 | 1.10 | 20 | ★★★★ |
| *Assertive Woman, The* | Phelps & Austin | 3 | 1.35 | 43 | ★★★★★ |
| *Assertiveness Workbook, The* | Peterson | 6 | 1.17 | 18 | ★★★ |
| *Civilized Assertiveness for Women* | McClure | 9 | −0.11 | 9 | — |
| *Control Freaks* | Piaget | 1 | 0.00 | 11 | ★ |
| *Cool, Calm, and Confident* | Schab | 9 | 0.55 | 11 | ★★★ |
| *Creative Aggression* | Bach & Goldberg | 1 | 0.43 | 72 | ★★ |
| *Don't Say Yes When You Want to Say No* | Fensterheim & Baer | 1 | 0.91 | 150 | ★★★ |
| *Gentle Art of Verbal Self-Defense* | Elgin | 1 | 0.66 | 61 | ★★★ |
| *Good-Bye to Guilt* | Jampolsky | 1 | 0.77 | 31 | ★★★ |
| *How to Be a Bitch with Style* | Ashley | 6 | −0.20 | 5 | — |
| *How to Grow a Backbone* | Marshall | 9 | −0.25 | 8 | — |
| *My Answer is No ... If that's Okay with You* | Gartrell | 9 | 0.00 | 8 | — |
| *Looking Out for Number One* | Ringer | 1 | −0.73 | 67 | † |
| *Pulling Your Own Strings* | Dyer | 1 | 0.19 | 148 | ★ |
| *Stand Up, Speak Out, Talk Back* | Alberti & Emmons | 1 | 1.11 | 75 | ★★★★ |
| *Stick Up for Yourself* | Kaufman & Raphael | 3 | 0.67 | 3 | ♦ |
| *When I Say No, I Feel Guilty* | Smith | 1 | 1.00 | 223 | ★★★★ |
| *Winning Through Intimidation* | Ringer | 1 | −1.11 | 83 | † |
| *Your Perfect Right* | Alberti & Emmons | 1 | 1.37 | 283 | ★★★★★ |
| **Attention-Deficit/Hyperactivity Disorder** | | | | | |
| *ADD and the College Student* | Quinn | 6 | 0.89 | 9 | — |
| *ADHD and Teens* | Alexander-Roberts | 3 | 1.17 | 12 | ★★★ |
| *ADHD Workbook for Kids, The* | Shapiro | 9 | 0.95 | 22 | ★★★ |
| *ADHD Workbook for Teens, The* | Honos-Webb | 9 | 0.00 | 9 | — |
| *Adventures in Fast Forward* | Nadeau | 6 | 1.30 | 9 | ♦ |
| *All About Attention Deficit Disorder* | Phelan | 6 | 1.00 | 8 | — |
| *Answers to Distraction* | Hallowell & Ratey | 6 | 1.25 | 12 | ★★★ |
| *Distant Drums, Different Drummers* | Ingersoll | 3 | 1.00 | 8 | — |
| *Driven to Distraction* | Hallowell & Ratey | 3 | 1.26 | 73 | ★★★★★ |
| *Gift of Adult ADD, The* | Honos-Webb | 9 | 0.53 | 12 | ★★★ |
| *Is It You, Me, or Adult ADD?* | Pera | 9 | 0.25 | 8 | — |
| *Learning to Slow Down and Pay Attention* | Nadeau & Dixon | 3 | 1.13 | 15 | ★★★ |
| *Living with ADD* | Roberts & Jansen | 6 | 1.40 | 5 | — |

| Category and Title | Author(s) | Study # | Avg. Rating | # of Raters | Guide Rating |
|---|---|---|---|---|---|
| Living with ADHD Children | Buntman | 3 | 1.00 | 13 | ★★★ |
| Making the System Work for Your Child with ADHD | Jensen | 9 | 0.83 | 6 | — |
| Mastering Your Adult ADHD | Safren et al. | 9 | 1.00 | 15 | ★★★ |
| Overcoming ADHD | Greenspan | 9 | 0.84 | 19 | ★★★ |
| Putting on the Brakes | Quinn & Stern | 6 | 1.31 | 29 | ★★★★ |
| Ritalin Is Not the Answer | Stein | 6 | 0.00 | 7 | — |
| Ritalin Nation | DeGrandpre | 3 | 0.00 | 6 | — |
| Running on Ritalin | Diller | 3 | 0.60 | 5 | — |
| Taking Charge of ADHD | Barkley | 3 | 1.41 | 65 | ★★★★★ |
| Taking Charge of Adult ADHD | Barkley | 9 | 1.65 | 55 | ★★★★★ |
| Teenagers with ADD | Zeigler Dendy | 6 | 1.20 | 5 | ◆ |
| **Autism and Asperger's** | | | | | |
| Autism Sourcebook, The | Exkorn | 9 | 1.11 | 9 | ◆ |
| Complete Guide to Asperger's Syndrome, The | Attwood | 9 | 1.33 | 43 | ★★★★★ |
| Engaging Autism | Greenspan & Wieder | 9 | 0.45 | 11 | ★★ |
| Helping a Child with Nonverbal Learning Disorder or Asperger's Disorder | Stewart | 9 | 0.43 | 7 | — |
| Helping Your Child with Autism Spectrum Disorder | Lockshin et al. | 9 | 0.60 | 5 | — |
| Mind Apart, A | Szatmari | 9 | 0.29 | 7 | — |
| 1001 Great Ideas for Teaching and Raising Children with Autism or Asperger's | Notbohm & Zysk | 9 | 0.30 | 10 | ★★ |
| Parent's Guide to Asperger Syndrome and High Functioning Autism, A | Ozonoff et al. | 9 | 1.00 | 16 | ★★★ |
| Social Skills Picture Book Teaching Play, Emotion, and Communication with Autism, The | Baker | 9 | 0.75 | 12 | ★★★ |
| Ten Things Every Child with Autism Wishes You Knew | Notbohm | 9 | 0.56 | 9 | — |
| **Bipolar Disorder** | | | | | |
| Bipolar 101 | White & Preston | 9 | 0.62 | 8 | — |
| Bipolar Child, The | Papolos & Papolos | 7 | 0.88 | 26 | ★★★ |
| Bipolar Disorder | Mondimore | 7 | 0.45 | 11 | ★★ |
| Bipolar Disorder for Dummies | Fink & Kraynak | 9 | 0.40 | 10 | ★★ |
| Bipolar Kids | Greenberg | 9 | −0.33 | 6 | — |
| Bipolar Disorder Survival Guide, The | Miklowitz | 7 | 1.18 | 11 | ★★★ |
| Bipolar Teen, The | Miklowitz & George | 9 | 0.82 | 11 | ★★★ |
| Bipolar Workbook, The | Basco | 9 | 0.92 | 13 | ★★★ |
| Depression Workbook, The | Copeland | 7 | 0.93 | 42 | ★★★ |

| Category and Title | Author(s) | Study # | Avg. Rating | # of Raters | Guide Rating |
|---|---|---|---|---|---|
| *Dialectical Behavior Therapy Skills Workbook for Bipolar Disorder, The* | Van Dijk | 9 | 1.00 | 20 | ★★★★ |
| *Facing Bipolar* | Federman & Thomson | 9 | 0.00 | 5 | — |
| *Loving Someone with Bipolar Disorder* | Fast & Preston | 9 | 1.00 | 10 | ★★★ |
| *New Hope for People with Bipolar Disorder* | Fawcett | 7 | 1.00 | 5 | — |
| *Overcoming Depression and ManicDepression* | Wider | 7 | 0.88 | 8 | — |
| *When Someone You Love Is Bipolar* | Last | 9 | 0.73 | 11 | ★★★ |
| **Borderline & Narcissistic Personality Disorders** | | | | | |
| *Borderline Personality Disorder Survival Guide, The* | Chapman & Gratz | 9 | 0.91 | 11 | ★★★ |
| *Children of the Self-Absorbed* | Brown | 6 | 1.40 | 5 | — |
| *Culture of Narcissism* | Lasch | 6 | 1.00 | 16 | ★★★ |
| *Disarming the Narcissist* | Behary | 9 | 1.10 | 10 | ★★★ |
| *Drama of the Gifted Child, The* | Miller | 6 | 1.41 | 58 | ★★★★★ |
| *Humanizing the Narcissistic Style* | Johnson | 6 | 1.00 | 7 | — |
| *I Hate You—Don't Leave Me* | Kriesman | 6 | 0.95 | 37 | ★★★ |
| *Loving the Self-Absorbed* | Brown | 9 | 0.37 | 8 | — |
| *Narcissism* | Lowen | 6 | 0.83 | 6 | — |
| *New Hope for People with Borderline Personality Disorder* | Bockian et al. | 9 | 0.71 | 7 | — |
| *Overcoming Borderline Personality Disorder* | Porr | 9 | 0.71 | 7 | — |
| *Shame* | Morrison | 6 | 1.17 | 6 | — |
| *Skills Training Manual for Treating Borderline Personality Disorder* | Linehan | 6 | 1.70 | 53 | ★★★★★ |
| *Sometimes I Act Crazy* | Kreisman & Straus | 9 | 0.80 | 10 | ★★★ |
| *Stop Walking on Eggshells* | Mason & Kreger | 6 | 0.80 | 10 | ★★★ |
| *Surviving a Borderline Parent* | Roth | 9 | 1.15 | 13 | ★★★ |
| *Trapped in the Mirror* | Golomb | 6 | 1.40 | 5 | ◆ |
| **Bullying** | | | | | |
| *Bullies and Victims* | Fried & Fried | 7 | 1.20 | 5 | ◆ |
| *Bullies to Buddies* | Kalman | 9 | 1.33 | 15 | ★★★ |
| *Bullying Beyond the Schoolyard* | Hinduja & Patchin | 9 | 0.62 | 8 | — |
| *Bullyproof Your Child for Life* | Haber & Glatzer | 9 | 0.71 | 7 | ◆ |
| *Don't Pick on Me* | Green | 9 | 0.89 | 9 | ◆ |
| *Little Girls Can Be Mean* | Anthony & Lindert | 9 | 0.20 | 5 | — |
| *Say Something* | Moss | 9 | 0.33 | 6 | — |
| **Career Development** | | | | | |
| *Best Advice I Ever Got, The* | Couric | 9 | 0.39 | 18 | ★★ |
| *Career Anchors* | Schein | 3 | 1.20 | 5 | — |

| Category and Title | Author(s) | Study # | Avg. Rating | # of Raters | Guide Rating |
|---|---|---|---|---|---|
| *Career Mastery* | Levinson | 3 | 0.80 | 5 | ♦ |
| *Diversity and Women's Career Development* | Farmer et al. | 3 | 1.28 | 7 | — |
| *Do What You Love, the Money Will Follow* | Sinetar | 1 | 0.57 | 38 | ★★★ |
| *Go Put Your Strengths to Work* | Buckingham | 9 | 1.00 | 5 | ♦ |
| *Knock 'Em Dead* | Yate | 1 | 0.74 | 15 | ★★★ |
| *Let Your Life Speak* | Palmer | 9 | 1.46 | 13 | ★★★ |
| *Life Choices* | Sharf | 6 | 1.17 | 6 | — |
| *100 Best Companies to Work for in America, The* | Levering & Moskowitz | 1 | 0.27 | 33 | ★★ |
| *Portable MBA, The* | Collins & Devanna | 1 | 0.40 | 15 | ★★ |
| *Shifting Gears* | Hyatt | 1 | 0.85 | 20 | ★★★ |
| *Staying the Course* | Weiss | 1 | 1.06 | 33 | ★★★★ |
| *Upward Nobility* | Edwards | 1 | 0.00 | 6 | — |
| *What Color Is Your Parachute?* | Bolles | 1 | 1.32 | 324 | ★★★★★ |
| *Win—Win Negotiating* | Jandt | 1 | 1.02 | 47 | ★★★★ |
| **Child Development and Parenting** | | | | | |
| *Battle Hymn of the Tiger Mother* | Chua | 9 | −0.70 | 30 | † |
| *Between Parent and Child* | Ginott | 1 | 1.30 | 261 | ★★★★★ |
| *Blessing of a Skinned Knee* | Mogel | 9 | 1.44 | 16 | ★★★ |
| *Boys Into Men* | Boyd-Franklin et al. | 6 | 1.38 | 8 | — |
| *Child Psychology & Development for Dummies* | Smith & Elliott | 9 | 0.33 | 6 | — |
| *Childhood* | Konner | 1 | 0.67 | 9 | — |
| *Children* | Dreikurs | 1 | 1.27 | 126 | ★★★★★ |
| *Cinderella Ate my Daughter* | Orenstein | 9 | 0.67 | 6 | — |
| *Common Sense Parenting* | Burke & Herron | 3 | 1.43 | 7 | ♦ |
| *Difficult Child, The* | Turecki | 6 | 1.21 | 28 | ★★★★ |
| *Drama of the Gifted Child, The* | Miller | 1 | 1.90 | 5 | — |
| *Dr. Spock on Parenting* | Spock | 1 | 1.05 | 114 | ★★★★ |
| *Essential 55* | Clark | 9 | 0.40 | 5 | — |
| *Everyday Blessings* | Kabat-Zinn & Kabat-Zinn | 6 | 1.14 | 7 | — |
| *Helping the Child Who Doesn't Fit In* | Nowicki & Duke | 3 | 1.00 | 7 | — |
| *How to Behave So Your Children Will Too* | Severe | 6 | 1.43 | 7 | — |
| *How to Discipline Your 6- to 12-Year-Old without Losing Your Mind* | Wyckoff & Unell | 1 | 0.57 | 22 | ★★★ |
| *How to Raise a Child with a High EQ* | Shapiro | 6 | 1.43 | 7 | — |
| *How to Talk So Kids Will Listen and Listen So Kids Will Talk* | Faber & Mazlish | 3 | 1.35 | 63 | ★★★★★ |
| *Hurried Child, The* | Elkind | 1 | 1.17 | 114 | ★★★★ |

| Category and Title | Author(s) | Study # | Avg. Rating | # of Raters | Guide Rating |
|---|---|---|---|---|---|
| *In Praise of Stay at Home Moms* | Schlessinger | 9 | −1.00 | 18 | † |
| *Living with Children* | Patterson | 1 | 1.83 | 11 | ★★★ |
| *Mind at a Time, A* | Levine | 9 | 1.00 | 21 | ★★★★ |
| *Mother Dance, The* | Lerner | 6 | 1.00 | 11 | ★★★ |
| *Nutureshock* | Bronson & Merrymen | 9 | 0.87 | 8 | — |
| *1–2-3 Magic* | Phelan | 3 | 1.27 | 33 | ★★★★★ |
| *Over-Scheduled Child* | Rosenfeld et al. | 6 | 0.60 | 5 | — |
| *Parent Effectiveness Training* | Gordon | 1 | 1.15 | 259 | ★★★★ |
| *Parenthood by Proxy* | Schlessinger | 6 | −2.00 | 7 | — |
| *Parenting the Strong-Willed Child* | Forehand & Long | 3 | 1.45 | 20 | ★★★★ |
| *Parenting Young Children* | Dinkmeyer & McKay | 1 | 1.96 | 8 | ◆ |
| *Parent Power!* | Rosemond | 3 | 0.27 | 11 | ★★ |
| *Perfect Madness* | Warner | 9 | 1.00 | 6 | ◆ |
| *Positive Discipline A–Z* | Nelson et al. | 3 | 0.94 | 16 | ★★★ |
| *Supernanny* | Frost | 9 | 0.58 | 12 | ★★★ |
| *Raising Resilient Children* | Brooks & Goldstein | 6 | 1.31 | 13 | ★★★ |
| *Tips for Toddlers* | Beebe | 1 | 0.71 | 7 | — |
| *Toddlers and Parents* | Brazelton | 1 | 1.37 | 101 | ★★★★★ |
| *To Listen to a Child* | Brazelton | 1 | 1.41 | 89 | ★★★★★ |
| *Touchpoints Three to Six* | Brazelton & Sparrow | 6 | 1.38 | 16 | ★★★ |
| *Your Defiant Child* | Barkley & Benton | 6 | 1.55 | 38 | ★★★★★ |
| **Chronic Pain** | | | | | |
| *Arthritis Helpbook, The* | Lorig & Fries | 9 | 0.87 | 8 | — |
| *Coping with Chronic Illness* | Wright & Ellis | 9 | 0.82 | 11 | ★★★ |
| *Healing Yoga for Neck & Shoulder Pain* | Krucoff | 9 | 0.50 | 6 | — |
| *Managing Chronic Pain* | Otis | 9 | 0.82 | 11 | ★★★ |
| *Managing Pain before It Manages You* | Caudill & Benson | 9 | 1.52 | 33 | ★★★★★ |
| *Mindfulness Solution to Pain, The* | Gardner-Nix & Costin-Hall | 9 | 1.00 | 10 | ★★★ |
| *Pain Survival Guide, The* | Turk & Winter | 9 | 1.35 | 23 | ★★★★ |
| *Sick and Tired of Being Sick and Tired* | Donoghue & Siegel | 9 | 0.73 | 15 | ★★ |
| *You Don't Look Sick!* | Selak & Overman | 9 | 0.40 | 5 | — |
| **Communication and People Skills** | | | | | |
| *Are You the One for Me?* | DeAngelis | 3 | 0.11 | 18 | ★ |
| *Body Language* | Fast | 1 | 0.20 | 113 | ★ |

| Category and Title | Author(s) | Study # | Avg. Rating | # of Raters | Guide Rating |
|---|---|---|---|---|---|
| Boundaries | Cloud & Townsend | 3 | 1.44 | 23 | ★★★★ |
| Coping with Difficult People | Bramson | 1 | 0.87 | 62 | ★★★ |
| Dance of Connection, The | Lerner | 6 | 1.24 | 25 | ★★★★ |
| Difficult Conversations | Stone et al. | 6 | 1.40 | 5 | — |
| Difficult People | Cava | 3 | 0.91 | 22 | ★★★ |
| Games People Play | Berne | 1 | 0.62 | 350 | ★★★ |
| Getting to Yes | Fisher & Ury | 1 | 1.03 | 69 | ★★★★ |
| How to Argue and Win Every Time | Spence | 3 | 0.29 | 14 | ★★ |
| How to Communicate | McKay et al. | 3 | 1.17 | 23 | ★★★★ |
| How to Start a Conversation and Make Friends | Gabor | 1 | 0.42 | 12 | ★★ |
| How to Win Friends and Influence People | Carnegie | 1 | 0.24 | 161 | ★ |
| Intimate Connections | Burns | 1 | 1.08 | 46 | ★★★★ |
| Intimate Strangers | Rubin | 1 | 1.18 | 82 | ★★★★ |
| Just Friends | Rubin | 1 | 1.07 | 31 | ★★★★ |
| Mars and Venus on a Date | Gray | 3 | −0.31 | 32 | † |
| Men Are from Mars, Women Are from Venus | Gray | 3 | 0.32 | 167 | ★★ |
| Messages Workbook | Davis et al. | 9 | 0.58 | 12 | ★★★ |
| New Peoplemaking, The | Satir | 6 | 1.17 | 59 | ★★★★ |
| Opening Up | Pennebaker | 1 | 0.91 | 18 | ★★★ |
| People Skills | Bolton | 1 | 1.03 | 32 | ★★★★ |
| Shyness | Zimbardo | 1 | 1.14 | 164 | ★★★★ |
| Stop! You're Driving Me Crazy | Bach & Deutsch | 1 | 0.50 | 46 | ★★★ |
| Talk Book, The | Goodman & Esterly | 3 | 1.11 | 9 | ♦ |
| That's Not What I Meant! | Tannen | 1 | 0.99 | 61 | ★★★ |
| You Just Don't Understand | Tannen | 1 | 1.24 | 148 | ★★★★ |
| Why Men Don't Listen and Women Can't Read Maps | Pease & Pease | 6 | −0.57 | 7 | — |
| Win | Luntz | 9 | 0.20 | 5 | — |
| Women Can't Hear What Men Don't Say | Farrell | 6 | 0.60 | 5 | — |
| Yes | Goldstein et al. | 9 | 0.00 | 5 | — |
| **Death and Grieving** | | | | | |
| Ambiguous Loss | Boss | 6 | 1.80 | 5 | ♦ |
| Being with Dying | Halifax & Byock | 9 | 0.80 | 5 | — |
| Bereaved Parent, The | Schiff | 1 | 2.00 | 5 | — |
| Coming Back | Stern | 1 | 0.78 | 9 | — |
| End-of-Life Handbook, The | Feldman et al. | 9 | 0.33 | 6 | — |
| Final Exit | Humphrey | 1 | −0.33 | 61 | † |

| Category and Title | Author(s) | Study # | Avg. Rating | # of Raters | Guide Rating |
|---|---|---|---|---|---|
| *Gentle Willow* | Mills | 9 | 0.80 | 10 | ★★★ |
| *Grief Recovery Handbook, The* | James & Cherry | 3 | 1.46 | 26 | ★★★★ |
| *Grieving As Well As Possible* | Horowitz | 9 | 1.11 | 9 | ♦ |
| *Healing Journey Through Grief* | Rich | 6 | 1.50 | 6 | — |
| *Helping Children Grieve* | Huntley | 1 | 1.08 | 25 | ★★★★ |
| *How to Go on Living When Someone You Love Dies* | Rando | 1 | 1.25 | 31 | ★★★★★ |
| *How to Survive the Loss of a Love* | Colgrove et al. | 1 | 1.41 | 100 | ★★★★★ |
| *How We Die* | Nuland | 3 | 0.58 | 19 | ★★★ |
| *Learning to Say Good-By* | LeShan | 1 | 1.22 | 52 | ★★★★ |
| *Life After Loss* | Volkan & Zintl | 3 | 0.78 | 9 | — |
| *Life Lessons* | Kübler-Ross & Kessler | 6 | 1.45 | 22 | ★★★★ |
| *Living through Personal Crisis* | Stearns | 1 | 1.06 | 18 | ★★★ |
| *Needs of the Dying* | Kessler | 9 | 1.13 | 8 | ♦ |
| *On Children and Death* | Kübler-Ross | 3 | 1.28 | 61 | ★★★★★ |
| *On Death and Dying* | Kübler-Ross | 1 | 0.99 | 355 | ★★★ |
| *Recovering from the Loss of a Child* | Donnelly | 1 | 1.15 | 27 | ★★★★ |
| *Samantha Jane's Missing Smile* | Kaplow & Pincus | 9 | 0.14 | 7 | — |
| *Saying Goodbye to the Pet You Love* | Greene & Landis | 9 | 0.77 | 13 | ★★★ |
| *Staring at the Sun* | Yalom | 9 | 1.05 | 22 | ★★★★ |
| *Sudden Infant Death* | DeFrain et al. | 1 | 1.00 | 16 | ★★★ |
| *Talking about Death* | Grollman | 1 | 1.23 | 40 | ★★★★ |
| *Time to Say Good-bye, A* | Goulding | 3 | 1.20 | 10 | ★★★ |
| *When Bad Things Happen to Good People* | Kushner | 3 | 1.29 | 150 | ★★★★★ |
| *When Children Grieve* | James & Friedman | 6 | 1.14 | 7 | ♦ |
| *Why Did You Die? Activities to Help Children Cope* | Leeuwenburgh & Goldring | 9 | 0.40 | 5 | — |
| *Widowed* | Brothers | 1 | -0.02 | 34 | † |
| *Widow's Handbook, The* | Foehner & Cozart | 1 | 0.54 | 13 | ★★★ |
| *Working It Through* | Kübler-Ross | 3 | 1.19 | 36 | ★★★★ |
| **Dementia/Alzheimer's** | | | | | |
| *Alzheimer's Caregiver, The* | Hodgson | 3 | 1.14 | 14 | ★★★ |
| *Caregiver's Guide to Alzheimer's Disease, A* | Callone et al. | 9 | 0.78 | 9 | ♦ |
| *Hidden Victims of Alzheimer's Disease* | Zarit et al. | 3 | 1.18 | 11 | ★★★ |
| *Learning to Speak Alzheimer's* | Coste | 9 | 0.71 | 7 | ♦ |
| *Living Your Best with Early Stage Alzheimer's* | Snyder | 9 | -0.17 | 6 | — |
| *100 Simple Things You Can Do to Prevent Alzheimer's and Age-Related Memory Loss* | Carper | 9 | 0.20 | 5 | — |

| Category and Title | Author(s) | Study # | Avg. Rating | # of Raters | Guide Rating |
|---|---|---|---|---|---|
| *36-Hour Day, The* | Mace & Rabins | 3 | 1.55 | 49 | ★★★★★ |
| *What's Happening to Grandpa?* | Shriver | 9 | 0.56 | 9 | — |
| *When Your Loved One Has Alzheimer's* | Carroll | 3 | 0.86 | 7 | ◆ |
| **Depression** | | | | | |
| *Against Depression* | Kramer | 9 | 0.22 | 9 | — |
| *Breaking the Patterns of Depression* | Yapko | 7 | 0.69 | 13 | ★★★ |
| *Cognitive Behavioral Workbook for Depression, The* | Knaus | 9 | 1.00 | 25 | ★★★★ |
| *Cognitive Therapy and the Emotional Disorders* | Beck | 1 | 1.16 | 198 | ★★★★★ |
| *Complete Idiot's Guide to Beating the Blues* | McGrath & Kogan | 7 | 0.13 | 8 | — |
| *Control Your Depression* | Lewinsohn et al. | 3 | 1.28 | 36 | ★★★★★ |
| *Depression Cure, The* | Ilardi | 9 | 0.78 | 9 | — |
| *Depression for Dummies* | Smith & Elliott | 9 | 0.60 | 5 | — |
| *Feeling Good* | Burns | 1 | 1.51 | 254 | ★★★★★ |
| *Feeling Good Handbook, The* | Burns | 1 | 1.38 | 116 | ★★★★★ |
| *Getting Over the Blues* | Vernick | 9 | 0.60 | 5 | — |
| *Getting Your Life Back* | Wright & Basco | 7 | 0.50 | 6 | — |
| *Getting Un-Depressed* | Emery | 1 | 0.93 | 42 | ★★★ |
| *Good News About Depression, The* | Gold | 1 | 0.01 | 50 | ★ |
| *Hand Me Down Blues* | Yapko | 7 | 0.80 | 10 | ★★★ |
| *How to Cope with Depression* | DePaulo & Ablow | 1 | 0.65 | 20 | ★★★ |
| *How to Stubbornly Refuse to Make Yourself Miserable about Anything* | Ellis | 3 | 0.84 | 31 | ★★★ |
| *I Don't Want to Talk About It* | Real | 7 | 0.90 | 20 | ★★★ |
| *Listening to Prozac* | Kramer | 3 | 0.57 | 83 | ★★★ |
| *Mind over Mood* | Greenberger & Padesky | 3 | 1.43 | 61 | ★★★★★ |
| *Mindful Way Through Depression, The* | Williams et al. | 9 | 1.59 | 46 | ★★★★★ |
| *Overcoming Depression* | Gilson & Freeman | 7 | 0.77 | 13 | ★★★ |
| *Overcoming Depression One Step at a Time* | Addis & Martell | 9 | 1.00 | 9 | ◆ |
| *Overcoming Teen Depression* | Kaufman | 7 | 1.33 | 6 | ◆ |
| *Raising a Moody Child* | Fristad & Arnold | 9 | 0.56 | 9 | — |
| *Rescuing Your Teenager from Depression* | Berlinger | 9 | 0.20 | 5 | — |
| *Self-Coaching* | Luciani | 7 | 0.33 | 6 | — |
| *Self-Help Guide to Managing Depression, A* | Baker | 3 | 1.13 | 8 | — |
| *Stop Depression Now* | Brown et al. | 7 | −0.80 | 5 | — |
| *Understanding and Overcoming Depression* | Bates | 7 | 0.58 | 12 | ★★★ |
| *Undoing Depression* | O'Connor | 9 | 0.40 | 5 | — |
| *When Feeling Bad Is Good* | McGrath | 3 | 1.04 | 27 | ★★★★ |

| Category and Title | Author(s) | Study # | Avg. Rating | # of Raters | Guide Rating |
|---|---|---|---|---|---|
| *When Living Hurts* | Yapko | 3 | 1.15 | 27 | ★★★★ |
| *When the Blues Won't Go Away* | Hirschfield | 1 | 0.62 | 13 | ★★★ |
| *Winter Blues* | Rosenthal | 7 | 1.06 | 16 | ★★★ |
| *You Can Beat Depression* | Preston | 3 | 1.23 | 13 | ★★★ |
| *You Mean I Don't Have to Feel This Way?* | Dowling | 1 | 0.44 | 16 | ★★ |
| *Zoloft, Paxil, Luvox, & Prozac* | Sullivan | 3 | 0.17 | 6 | — |
| **Divorce** | | | | | |
| *Boys and Girls Book about Divorce, The* | Gardner | 1 | 1.39 | 212 | ★★★★★ |
| *Chicken Soup for the Soul: Divorce* | Canfield et al. | 9 | 0.60 | 20 | ★★★ |
| *Coping with Divorce, Single Parenting, and Remarriage* | Heatherington | 7 | 1.05 | 20 | ★★★★ |
| *Crazy Time* | Trafford | 3 | 1.44 | 16 | ★★★ |
| *Creative Divorce* | Krantzler | 1 | 0.66 | 88 | ★★★ |
| *Custody Revolution, The* | Warshak | 3 | 0.60 | 5 | — |
| *Dinosaurs Divorce* | Brown & Brown | 1 | 1.42 | 44 | ★★★★★ |
| *Divorce* | Wemhoff | 3 | 1.33 | 6 | — |
| *Divorce Book, The* | McKay et al. | 7 | 0.90 | 10 | ★★★ |
| *Divorce Poison* | Warshak | 7 | 0.57 | 7 | — |
| *Does Wednesday Mean Mom's House or Dad's* | Ackerman | 7 | 0.57 | 7 | — |
| *Don't Divorce Us! Kids' Advice to Divorcing Parents* | Sommers-Flannigan et al. | 7 | 1.00 | 6 | — |
| *For Better or For Worse* | Heatherington & Kelly | 7 | 1.00 | 12 | ★★★ |
| *Forgive Your Parents, Heal Yourself* | Grosskopf | 7 | 0.80 | 5 | — |
| *Good Divorce, The* | Ahrons | 7 | 1.19 | 16 | ★★★ |
| *Growing Up with Divorce* | Kalter | 1 | 1.00 | 33 | ★★★★ |
| *Helping Children Cope with Divorce* | Teyber | 7 | 1.25 | 12 | ★★★ |
| *Helping Your Kids Cope with Divorce* | Neuman & Romanowski | 3 | 1.05 | 18 | ★★★ |
| *How It Feels When Parents Divorce* | Krementz | 1 | 1.09 | 70 | ★★★★ |
| *Mars and Venus Starting Over* | Gray | 3 | 0.09 | 22 | ★ |
| *My Parents Are Divorced Too* | Blackstone-Ford et al. | 7 | 0.71 | 7 | — |
| *Parents Book About Divorce, The* | Gardner | 7 | 0.87 | 52 | ★★★ |
| *Second Chances* | Wallerstein & Blakeslee | 1 | 0.99 | 102 | ★★★ |
| *Surviving the Breakup* | Wallerstein & Kelly | 7 | 1.03 | 38 | ★★★★ |
| *Truth About Children and Divorce, The* | Emery | 9 | 1.00 | 10 | ★★★ |
| *Two Homes* | Masurel & Denton | 9 | 0.83 | 12 | ★★★ |
| *Unexpected Legacy of Divorce, The* | Wallertein et al. | 7 | 1.08 | 37 | ★★★★ |

| Category and Title | Author(s) | Study # | Avg. Rating | # of Raters | Guide Rating |
|---|---|---|---|---|---|
| *Way We Were, The* | Foster | 9 | 0.14 | 7 | — |
| *What Can I Do? A Book for Children of Divorce* | Lowry | 7 | 1.17 | 6 | — |
| **Eating Disorders** | | | | | |
| *Anatomy of Anorexia* | Levenkron | 7 | 0.88 | 8 | ♦ |
| *Anorexia Workshop, The* | Hefner & Eifert | 10 | 0.89 | 19 | ★★★ |
| *Binge No More* | Nash | 7 | 0.00 | 7 | — |
| *Body Betrayed, The* | Zerbe | 3 | 1.11 | 9 | — |
| *Brave Girl Eating* | Brown | 10 | 0.20 | 15 | ★ |
| *Bulimia* | Sherman & Thompson | 7 | 1.00 | 5 | — |
| *Bulimia/Anorexia* | Boskind-White & White | 7 | 0.92 | 12 | ★★★ |
| *Dying to Be Thin* | Sacker & Zimmer | 3 | 1.24 | 21 | ★★★★ |
| *Eat, Drink, and Be Mindful* | Albers | 10 | 0.88 | 24 | ★★★ |
| *Emotional Eating* | Abramson | 7 | 0.56 | 9 | — |
| *Fat Is a Family Affair* | Hollis | 1 | 0.88 | 41 | ★★★ |
| *Feeling Good About the Way You Look* | Wilhelm | 10 | 0.50 | 14 | ★★★ |
| *Food for Thought* | Hazelden Foundation | 1 | 0.66 | 32 | ★★★ |
| *Golden Cage, The* | Bruch | 7 | 0.92 | 36 | ★★★ |
| *Good Enough* | Bitter | 7 | 0.57 | 7 | — |
| *Healing the Hungry Self* | Price | 3 | 1.10 | 10 | ★★★ |
| *Helping Your Teenager Beat an Eating Disorder* | Lock & LeGrange | 10 | 0.83 | 18 | ★★★ |
| *Hunger Within, The* | Migliore & Ross | 3 | 1.36 | 11 | ★★★ |
| *Just a Little Too Thin* | Strober & Schneider | 10 | 0.08 | 12 | ★ |
| *Love Hunger* | Minirth et al. | 1 | 0.13 | 31 | ★ |
| *Love-Powered Diet, The* | Moran | 1 | −0.91 | 11 | † |
| *Overcoming Binge Eating* | Fairburn | 3 | 1.06 | 18 | ★★★ |
| *Twelve Steps & Twelve Traditions of Inner Eating* | Billigmeier | 1 | 0.22 | 9 | — |
| *Twelve-Steps and 12 Traditions of Overeaters Anonymous, The* | Overeaters Anonymous | 3 | 1.00 | 14 | ★★★ |
| *Weight Watchers Stop Stuffing Yourself* | Weight Watchers | 7 | 0.40 | 10 | ★★ |
| *When Food is Love* | Roth | 1 | 0.66 | 32 | ★★★ |
| *When Your Child Has an Eating Disorder* | Natenshon | 7 | 0.33 | 6 | — |
| *Why Weight?* | Roth | 1 | 0.68 | 22 | ★★★ |
| *You Can't Quit Eating Until You Know What's Eating You* | LeBlanc | 1 | 0.47 | 17 | ★★ |
| **Families and Stepfamilies** | | | | | |
| *Adult Children* | Friel & Friel | 1 | 0.52 | 49 | ★★★ |

| Category and Title | Author(s) | Study # | Avg. Rating | # of Raters | Guide Rating |
|---|---|---|---|---|---|
| *Back to the Family* | Guarendi | 1 | 0.91 | 11 | ★★★ |
| *Blending Families* | Shimberg | 3 | 1.08 | 13 | ★★★ |
| *Bradshaw on the Family* | Bradshaw | 1 | 0.34 | 129 | ★★ |
| *Families* | Patterson | 1 | 1.78 | 12 | ★★★ |
| *Family First* | McGraw | 10 | 0.11 | 9 | — |
| *Family Crucible, The* | Napier & Whitaker | 1 | 1.04 | 108 | ★★★★ |
| *Love in the Blended Family* | Clubb | 1 | 1.23 | 13 | ★★★ |
| *Mom's House, Dad's House* | Ricci | 7 | 1.35 | 17 | ★★★ |
| *Old Loyalties, New Ties* | Visher & Visher | 1 | 1.28 | 42 | ★★★★★ |
| *Second Time Around, The* | Janda & MacCormack | 1 | 1.20 | 10 | ★★★ |
| *Shelter of Each Other, The* | Pipher | 3 | 1.43 | 14 | ★★★ |
| *Smart Stepfamily* | Deal | 10 | 0.46 | 13 | ★★ |
| *Step by Step-Parenting* | Eckler | 1 | 1.30 | 20 | ★★★★ |
| *Stepfamilies* | Bray & Kelly | 7 | 1.00 | 11 | ★★★ |
| *Step-Fathering* | Rosin | 1 | 1.10 | 21 | ★★★★ |
| *Strengthening Your Stepfamily* | Einstein & Albert | 1 | 1.10 | 10 | ★★★ |
| **Gay, Lesbian, and Bisexual Issues** | | | | | |
| *Always My Child* | Jennings & Shapiro | 10 | 0.58 | 12 | ★★★ |
| *Coming Out, Coming Home* | Lasala | 10 | 0.69 | 13 | ★★★ |
| *Friendship, Dating, and Relationships* | Payment | 10 | 0.00 | 8 | — |
| *Gay and Lesbian Parents* | Fields | 10 | 0.12 | 8 | — |
| *GLBT Teens and Society* | Nagle | 10 | 0.00 | 8 | — |
| *GLBTQ* | Huegel | 10 | 0.45 | 11 | ★★ |
| *How It Feels to Have a Gay or Lesbian Parent* | Snow | 10 | −0.17 | 6 | — |
| *Invisible Families* | Stewart | 10 | 0.22 | 9 | — |
| *Permanent Partners* | Berzon | 7 | 1.11 | 9 | ♦ |
| *Smashing the Stereotypes* | Seba | 10 | 0.25 | 8 | — |
| *Velvet Rage* | Downs | 10 | 0.44 | 9 | — |
| **Happiness** | | | | | |
| *4:8 Principle, The* | Newberry | 10 | 0.29 | 7 | — |
| *Art of Happiness, The* | Dalai Lama & Cutler | 7 | 0.96 | 23 | ★★★ |
| *How to Live 365 Days a Year* | Schindler | 1 | 0.58 | 12 | ★★★ |
| *Learned Optimism* | Seligman | 1 | 1.27 | 89 | ★★★★★ |
| *Mojo* | Goldsmith | 10 | −0.63 | 8 | — |
| *Positive Illusions* | Taylor | 1 | 1.23 | 13 | ★★★ |
| *Power of Now* | Toll | 10 | 0.94 | 34 | ★★★ |
| *Power of Optimism, The* | McGinnis | 1 | 0.27 | 11 | ★★ |
| *Power of Positive Thinking, The* | Peale | 1 | 0.22 | 153 | ★ |

| Category and Title | Author(s) | Study # | Avg. Rating | # of Raters | Guide Rating |
|---|---|---|---|---|---|
| Present, The | Johnson | 10 | 0.55 | 11 | ★★★ |
| A Short Guide to a Happy Life | Quindlen | 7 | 0.80 | 15 | ★★★ |
| Stumbling on Happiness | Gilbert | 10 | 1.21 | 34 | ★★★★ |
| What's Right with You | Duncan | 10 | 0.58 | 12 | ★★★ |
| **Infant Development and Parenting** | | | | | |
| Baby 411 | Fields & Brown | 10 | 1.30 | 10 | ★★★ |
| Baby Book, The | Sears & Sears | 7 | 1.13 | 16 | ★★★ |
| Becoming a Calm Mom | Ledley | 10 | 0.80 | 10 | ★★★ |
| Brain Rules for Baby | Medina | 10 | 0.80 | 5 | — |
| Dr. Spock's Baby and Child Care | Spock & Parker | 1 | 1.43 | 187 | ★★★★★ |
| Father's Almanac, The | Sullivan | 1 | 0.90 | 16 | ★★★ |
| First Three Years of Life, The | White | 1 | 1.34 | 102 | ★★★★★ |
| First Twelve Months of Life, The | Caplan | 1 | 1.33 | 60 | ★★★★★ |
| Happiest Baby on the Block, The | Karp | 10 | 1.00 | 22 | ★★★★ |
| Infants and Mothers | Brazelton | 1 | 1.47 | 114 | ★★★★★ |
| My Family, My Family | Francesca & Ghahren | 10 | 0.78 | 9 | — |
| Secrets of the Baby Whisperer | Hogg & Blau | 7 | 0.13 | 8 | — |
| What Every Baby Knows | Brazelton | 1 | 1.44 | 105 | ★★★★★ |
| What to Expect the First Year | Eisenberg et al. | 1 | 1.44 | 37 | ★★★★★ |
| What to Expect the Toddler Years | Eisenberg et al. | 7 | 1.49 | 35 | ★★★★★ |
| Your Baby and Child | Leach | 1 | 1.32 | 32 | ★★★★★ |
| **Love and Intimacy** | | | | | |
| Art of Loving, The | Fromm | 1 | 1.05 | 257 | ★★★★ |
| Conversation, The | Harper | 10 | 0.67 | 9 | — |
| Couples | Dym & Glenn | 3 | 0.86 | 7 | — |
| Creating Love | Bradshaw | 3 | 0.74 | 35 | ★★★ |
| Dance of Connection, The | Lerner | 7 | 1.21 | 43 | ★★★★ |
| Dance of Intimacy, The | Lerner | 1 | 1.23 | 145 | ★★★★ |
| Day I Shot Cupid, The | Hewitt | 10 | -0.29 | 7 | — |
| Do I Have to Give Up Me to Be Loved by You? | Paul & Paul | 1 | 0.83 | 56 | ★★★ |
| Fear of Intimacy | Firetone & Catlett | 7 | 1.17 | 12 | ★★★ |
| 5 Love Languages | Chapman | 10 | 1.30 | 90 | ★★★★★ |
| Going the Distance | Barbach & Geisinger | 1 | 0.67 | 33 | ★★★ |
| I Only Say This Because I Love You | Tannen | 7 | 1.04 | 25 | ★★★★ |
| In the Meantime | Vanzant | 3 | 1.50 | 8 | ♦ |
| Keeping the Love You Find | Hendrix | 7 | 1.15 | 33 | ★★★★ |
| Love Cycle | Cutler | 1 | 0.60 | 5 | — |
| Love Dare, The | Kendrix & Kendrix | 10 | 0.69 | 13 | ★★★ |

| Category and Title | Author(s) | Study # | Avg. Rating | # of Raters | Guide Rating |
|---|---|---|---|---|---|
| *Love Is Never Enough* | Beck | 3 | 1.36 | 67 | ★★★★★ |
| *Love the Way You Want It* | Sternberg | 3 | 0.67 | 6 | — |
| *Loving Each Other* | Buscaglia | 1 | 0.31 | 94 | ★★ |
| *Mars and Venus in the Bedroom* | Gray | 3 | −0.16 | 38 | † |
| *Men Who Can't Love* | Carter | 1 | 0.27 | 141 | ★★ |
| *Men Who Hate Women and the Women Who Love Them* | Forward | 1 | 0.29 | 141 | ★★ |
| *Obsessive Love* | Forward & Buck | 1 | 0.94 | 18 | ★★★ |
| *Relationship Cure, The* | Gottman & DeClaire | 7 | 1.25 | 24 | ★★★★ |
| *Relationship Rescue* | McGraw | 7 | 0.43 | 14 | ★★ |
| *Return to Love, A* | Williamson | 3 | 0.60 | 15 | ★★★ |
| *Soul Mates* | Moore | 3 | 0.72 | 39 | ★★★ |
| *Straight Talk, No Chaser* | Harvey | 10 | −0.08 | 12 | † |
| *Triangle of Love, The* | Sternberg | 1 | 1.00 | 23 | ★★★★ |
| *Vixen Manual* | Steffans | 6 | −0.67 | 6 | — |
| *What Every Woman Should Know About Men* | Brothers | 1 | −0.94 | 48 | † |
| *What Smart Women Know* | Carter & Sokol | 1 | 0.09 | 11 | ★ |
| *When Someone You Love Is Someone You Hate* | Arterburn & Stoop | 1 | 0.10 | 10 | ★ |
| *Women Men Love, Women Men Leave* | Cowan & Kinder | 1 | −0.17 | 29 | † |
| *Women Who Love Too Much* | Norwood | 1 | 0.64 | 194 | ★★★ |
| **Marriage** | | | | | |
| *All You Need Is Love and Other Lies About Marriage* | Jacobs | 10 | 0.50 | 10 | ★★★ |
| *Conversation, The* | Harper | 10 | 0.75 | 8 | — |
| *Couple's Survival Workbook, The* | Olsen & Stephens | 7 | 1.25 | 8 | — |
| *Divorce Busting* | Weiner-Davis | 3 | 1.04 | 24 | ★★★★ |
| *Do I Stay or Do I Go* | Occhetti et al. | 7 | 0.60 | 5 | — |
| *Essential Manners for Couples* | Post | 10 | 0.13 | 8 | — |
| *Fighting for Your Marriage* | Markman et al. | 7 | 1.00 | 18 | ★★★ |
| *Getting it Right the First Time* | McCarthy & McCarthy | 10 | 0.85 | 13 | ★★★ |
| *Getting It Right This Time* | McCarthy & McCarthy | 10 | 0.57 | 7 | — |
| *Getting the Love You Want* | Hendrix | 3 | 1.05 | 63 | ★★★★ |
| *Getting Together and Staying Together* | Glasser & Glasser | 7 | 0.50 | 12 | ★★★ |
| *Hard Questions, The* | Piver | 10 | 1.08 | 12 | ★★★ |
| *Husbands and Wives* | Kinder & Cowan | 1 | 0.55 | 10 | ★★★ |
| *I Love You, Let's Work It Out* | Viscott | 3 | 0.90 | 10 | ★★★ |
| *Intimacy, The* | Mellody & Freundlich | 10 | 0.60 | 5 | — |

| Category and Title | Author(s) | Study # | Avg. Rating | # of Raters | Guide Rating |
|---|---|---|---|---|---|
| *Intimate Partners* | Scarf | 1 | 1.06 | 87 | ★★★★ |
| *Love for a Lifetime* | Dobson | 3 | 1.14 | 7 | ♦ |
| *Power of Two, The* | Heitler & Singer | 7 | 0.60 | 5 | — |
| *Power of Two Workbook, The* | Heitler & Hirsch | 10 | 0.90 | 10 | ★★★ |
| *Proper Care and Feeding of Husbands, The* | Schlessinger | 10 | −0.96 | 24 | † |
| *Reconcilable Differences* | Christensen & Jacobson | 7 | 1.00 | 10 | ★★★ |
| *Seven Principles for Making Marriages Work, The* | Gottman & Silver | 7 | 1.51 | 53 | ★★★★★ |
| *Sticking Together in a World that Pulls Us Apart* | Doherty | 10 | 0.86 | 7 | — |
| *10 Stupid Things Couples Do to Mess Up Their Relationships* | Schlessinger | 7 | −0.88 | 32 | † |
| *Too Good to Leave, Too Bad to Stay* | Kirshenbaum | 7 | 1.00 | 9 | — |
| *We Love Each Other but ...* | Wachtel | 3 | 1.40 | 5 | ♦ |
| *Why Marriages Succeed or Fail* | Gottman | 3 | 1.59 | 34 | ★★★★★ |
| **Men's Issues** | | | | | |
| *Act Like a Lady, Think Like a Man* | Harvey | 10 | 0.71 | 17 | ★★★ |
| *Adonis Complex, The* | Pope et al. | 7 | 0.40 | 5 | — |
| *Being a Man* | Fanning & McKay | 3 | 1.56 | 16 | ★★★ |
| *Chicken Soup for the Father's Soul* | Canfield et al. | 7 | 0.64 | 14 | ★★★ |
| *Every Man's Battle: One Victory at a Time* | Arterburn et al. | 10 | 0.86 | 7 | — |
| *Fatherloss* | Chethik | 7 | 1.00 | 5 | ♦ |
| *Fire in the Belly* | Keen | 1 | 0.61 | 86 | ★★★ |
| *Hazards of Being Male, The* | Goldberg | 1 | 0.81 | 63 | ★★★ |
| *Iron John* | Bly | 1 | 0.30 | 158 | ★★ |
| *Man Enough* | Pittman | 3 | 1.00 | 14 | ★★★ |
| *Masculinity Reconstructed* | Levant & Kopecky | 7 | 0.75 | 16 | ★★★ |
| *Measure of a Man, The* | Shapiro | 3 | 0.67 | 6 | — |
| *New Male, The* | Goldberg | 1 | 0.67 | 39 | ★★★ |
| *Real Boys* | Pollack | 7 | 1.37 | 27 | ★★★★ |
| *Seasons of a Man's Life* | Levinson | 1 | 1.05 | 222 | ★★★★ |
| *Straight Talk to Men* | Dobson | 7 | 0.45 | 11 | ★★ |
| *Ten Stupid Things Men Do to Mess Up Their Lives* | Schlessinger | 3 | −0.50 | 22 | † |
| *What Men Really Want* | Bakos | 1 | −0.12 | 25 | † |
| *Why Men Don't Get Enough Sex and Women Don't Get Enough Love* | Kramer & Dunaway | 1 | 0.10 | 20 | ★ |
| *Victims No Longer* | Lew | 10 | 1.13 | 15 | ★★★★ |
| **Obsessive-Compulsive Disorder** | | | | | |
| *Brain Lock* | Schwartz & Beyette | 6 | 1.40 | 15 | ★★★ |

| Category and Title | Author(s) | Study # | Avg. Rating | # of Raters | Guide Rating |
|---|---|---|---|---|---|
| *Coping with OCD* | Hyman & DuFrene | 10 | 1.07 | 14 | ★★★ |
| *Freedom from Obsessive-Compulsive Disorder* | Grayson | 10 | 1.07 | 15 | ★★★ |
| *From Thoughts to Obsessions* | Thomsen | 10 | 0.33 | 9 | — |
| *Getting over OCD* | Abramowitz | 10 | 1.08 | 26 | ★★★★ |
| *The Hair–Pulling Problem* | Penzel | 10 | 0.92 | 12 | ★★★ |
| *It's Only a False Alarm* | Piacentini et al. | 10 | 0.67 | 6 | — |
| *Loving Someone with OCD* | Landsman et al. | 10 | 0.75 | 8 | — |
| *Mastery of Obsessive-Compulsive Disorder* | Kozak & Foa | 10 | 1.39 | 23 | ★★★★ |
| *Obsessive-Compulsive Disorder* | De Silva & Rachman | 6 | 1.20 | 5 | ◆ |
| *Obsessive–Compulsive Disorders* | Penzel | 6 | 1.50 | 6 | ◆ |
| *Obsessive-Compulsive Disorders* | Levenkron | 1 | 1.00 | 31 | ★★★★ |
| *Obsessive-Compulsive Disorder for Dummies* | Elliott & Smith | 10 | 1.70 | 9 | ◆ |
| *OCD Workbook, The* | Hyman & Pedrick | 10 | 1.32 | 47 | ★★★★★ |
| *Overcoming Compulsive Checking* | Munford | 10 | 0.83 | 6 | — |
| *Overcoming Obsessive-Compulsive Disorder* | Steketee | 6 | 1.32 | 22 | ★★★★ |
| *Overcoming Obsessive Thoughts* | Purdon & Clark | 10 | 0.12 | 8 | — |
| *S.T.O.P. Obsessing* | Foa & Wilson | 3 | 1.36 | 50 | ★★★★★ |
| *What to Do When Your Brain Gets Stuck* | Huebner | 10 | 1.26 | 27 | ★★★★ |
| **Posttraumatic Stress Disorder** | | | | | |
| *After the Storm* | Johnson | 10 | 1.06 | 16 | ★★★ |
| *Coping with Trauma* | Allen | 7 | 1.00 | 5 | — |
| *Do-It-Yourself Eye Movement Technique for Emotional Health* | Friedberg | 10 | −0.22 | 9 | — |
| *Energy Tapping for Trauma* | Gallo | 10 | 0.43 | 14 | ★★ |
| *Healing the Hurt Within* | Sutton | 7 | 0.86 | 7 | — |
| *Healing Together* | Phillips & Kane | 10 | 1.00 | 9 | ◆ |
| *I Can't Get Over It* | Matsakis | 7 | 1.27 | 26 | ★★★★ |
| *Life After Trauma* | Rosenbloom et al. | 7 | 1.18 | 11 | ★★★ |
| *Moving On After Trauma* | Scott | 10 | 0.44 | 9 | — |
| *Overcoming the Trauma of Your Motor Vehicle Accident* | Blanchard & Hickling | 10 | 0.91 | 11 | ★★★ |
| *Post-Traumatic Stress Disorder Sourcebook* | Schiraldi | 7 | 0.78 | 9 | — |
| *Prolonged Exposure Therapy for PTSD Teen Workbook* | Chrestman et al. | 10 | 0.92 | 13 | ★★★ |
| *PTSD Workbook, The* | Williams & Poijula | 7 | 1.33 | 12 | ★★★ |
| *Rebuilding Shattered Lives* | Chu | 7 | 1.50 | 8 | — |
| *Reclaiming Your Life After Rape* | Rothbaum & Foa | 7 | 1.53 | 15 | ★★★ |
| *Reclaiming Your Life from a Traumatic Experience* | Rothbaum et al. | 10 | 1.16 | 19 | ★★★ |

| Category and Title | Author(s) | Study # | Avg. Rating | # of Raters | Guide Rating |
|---|---|---|---|---|---|
| Scared Child, The | Brooks & Siegel | 7 | 0.50 | 6 | — |
| Survivor Guilt | Matsakis | 7 | 1.20 | 5 | ♦ |
| Trauma and Recovery | Herman | 7 | 1.42 | 50 | ★★★★★ |
| Victims No Longer | Lew | 10 | 0.90 | 20 | ★★★ |
| Waking the Tiger | Levine & Frederick | 7 | 0.75 | 8 | — |
| Writing to Heal | Pennebaker | 10 | 1.00 | 17 | ★★★ |
| Your Surviving Spirit | Miller | 10 | 0.20 | 5 | — |
| **Pregnancy** | | | | | |
| Complete Book of Pregnancy and Childbirth, The | Kitzinger | 1 | 1.41 | 39 | ★★★★★ |
| Expectant Father, The | Brott & Ash | 3 | 1.40 | 5 | ♦ |
| From Here to Maternity | Marshall | 1 | 0.80 | 10 | ★★★ |
| Girlfriend's Guide to Pregnancy, The | Iovine | 7 | 1.14 | 7 | ♦ |
| Holistic Baby Guide | Neustaedter | 10 | 0.67 | 6 | — |
| Pregnancy After 35 | McCauley | 1 | 0.90 | 20 | ★★★ |
| Pregnancy, Childbirth, and the Newborn | Simkin | 1 | 0.83 | 6 | — |
| Pregnancy Countdown Book, The | McGee & Nakisbendi | 10 | 0.20 | 5 | — |
| Pregnancy & Postpartum Anxiety Workbook | Wiegartz & Gyoerkoe | 10 | 0.33 | 5 | — |
| Well Pregnancy Book, The | Samuels & Samuels | 1 | 0.87 | 15 | ★★★ |
| What to Eat When You're Expecting | Eisenberg et al. | 1 | 1.00 | 16 | ★★★ |
| What to Expect When You're Expecting | Eisenberg et al. | 3 | 1.56 | 43 | ★★★★★ |
| Will It Hurt the Baby? | Abrams | 1 | 1.00 | 5 | — |
| Working Woman's Pregnancy Book, The | Greenfield | 10 | 1.00 | 6 | ♦ |
| **Schizophrenia** | | | | | |
| Complete Family Guide to Schizophrenia, The | Mueser & Gingerich | 10 | 1.25 | 12 | ★★★ |
| Coping with Schizophrenia | Mueser & Gingerich | 7 | 1.33 | 12 | ★★★ |
| Helping Someone with Mental Illness | Carter & Golant | 7 | 0.87 | 15 | ★★★ |
| How to Cope with Mental Illness in Your Family | Marsh & Dickens | 3 | 1.08 | 12 | ★★★ |
| Recovered, Not Cured | McLean | 10 | 0.56 | 9 | — |
| Schizophrenia for Dummies | Levine & Levine | 10 | 0.50 | 6 | — |
| Surviving Schizophrenia | Torrey | 3 | 1.25 | 40 | ★★★★★ |
| Understanding Schizophrenia | Keefe & Harvey | 7 | 1.50 | 6 | ♦ |
| **Self-Management and Self-Enhancement** | | | | | |
| All I Really Needed to Know I Learned in Kindergarten | Fulghum | 3 | 0.78 | 89 | ★★★ |
| Awaken the Giant Within | Robbins | 3 | 0.00 | 14 | ★ |
| Be a Better You | Osteen | 10 | 0.23 | 22 | ★ |
| Change Your Brain, Change Your Body | Amen | 10 | 0.77 | 60 | ★★★ |
| Change Your Thoughts—Change Your Life | Dyer | 10 | 0.74 | 47 | ★★★ |
| Changing for Good | Prochaska et al. | 3 | 1.17 | 23 | ★★★★ |

| Category and Title | Author(s) | Study # | Avg. Rating | # of Raters | Guide Rating |
|---|---|---|---|---|---|
| Chicken Soup for the Soul | Canfield & Hansen | 3 | 0.72 | 100 | ★★★ |
| Do It! Let's Get Off Our Butts | McWilliams | 1 | −0.06 | 9 | — |
| Don't Blame Mother | Caplan | 1 | 1.00 | 20 | ★★★★ |
| Don't Sweat the Small Stuff … and It's All Small Stuff | Carlson | 3 | 1.06 | 95 | ★★★★ |
| Drive | Pink | 10 | 1.00 | 10 | ★★★ |
| Emotional Intelligence | Goleman | 3 | 0.97 | 118 | ★★★ |
| Excuses Be Gone | Dyer | 10 | 0.53 | 17 | ★★★ |
| Feel the Fear and Do It Anyway | Jeffers | 1 | 1.24 | 25 | ★★★★ |
| Get Out of Your Mind and Into Your Life | Hayes & Smith | 10 | 1.41 | 44 | ★★★★★ |
| How to Stop Worrying and Start Living | Carnegie | 1 | 0.15 | 65 | ★ |
| I'm O.K, You're O.K | Harris | 1 | 0.60 | 318 | ★★★ |
| Infinite Possibilities | Dooley | 10 | 0.62 | 8 | — |
| Just Who Will You Be? | Shriver | 10 | 0.09 | 11 | ★ |
| Last Lecture, The | Pausch & Zaslow | 10 | 1.31 | 72 | ★★★★★ |
| Life's Little Instruction Book | Brown | 3 | 0.82 | 33 | ★★★ |
| Life Strategies | McGraw | 7 | 0.83 | 24 | ★★★ |
| Magnificent Mind at Any Age | Amen | 10 | 0.35 | 20 | ★★ |
| New Guide to Rational Living, A | Ellis & Harper | 1 | 1.12 | 238 | ★★★★ |
| One Month to Live | Shook & Shook | 10 | 0.17 | 20 | ★ |
| Opening Up | Pennebaker | 7 | 1.33 | 15 | ★★★ |
| Overcoming Procrastination | Ellis & Knaus | 1 | 1.00 | 69 | ★★★★ |
| Positive Addiction | Glasser | 1 | 0.82 | 89 | ★★★ |
| Power of Full Engagement, The | Loehr & Schwartz | 10 | 0.87 | 8 | — |
| Power Thoughts | Meyer | 10 | 0.00 | 8 | — |
| Secret, The | Byrne | 10 | −0.14 | 51 | † |
| Self-Directed Behavior | Watson & Tharp | 7 | 1.15 | 13 | ★★★ |
| Self Matters | McGraw | 7 | 0.43 | 14 | ★★ |
| 7 Habits of Highly Effective People, The | Covey | 1 | 1.28 | 67 | ★★★★★ |
| Simple Abundance | Breathnach | 7 | 0.72 | 29 | ★★★ |
| 60-Second Shrink, The | Lazarus & Lazarus | 3 | 0.97 | 30 | ★★★ |
| Soul Mind Body Medicine | Sha | 10 | 0.00 | 6 | — |
| Soul Wisdom | Sha | 10 | 0.44 | 9 | — |
| Spontaneous Healing | Weil | 3 | 1.10 | 41 | ★★★★ |
| Steps to the Top | Zigler | 1 | 0.13 | 23 | ★ |
| Stop Whining, Start Living | Schlessinger | 10 | −1.22 | 27 | † |
| Success Is a Choice | Pitino & Reynolds | 3 | 1.33 | 9 | ♦ |
| Switch | Heath & Heath | 10 | 0.43 | 7 | — |
| Take Time for Your Life | Richardson | 7 | 0.43 | 7 | — |
| Talking to Yourself | Butler | 1 | 0.80 | 18 | ★★★ |

| Category and Title | Author(s) | Study # | Avg. Rating | # of Raters | Guide Rating |
|---|---|---|---|---|---|
| *Ten Days to Self-Esteem* | Burns | 7 | 1.16 | 45 | ★★★★ |
| *Tough Times Never Last but Tough People Do* | Schuller | 1 | 0.41 | 42 | ★★ |
| *Unlimited Power* | Robbins | 1 | 0.54 | 14 | ★★★ |
| *What to Say When You Talk to Yourself* | Helmstetter | 1 | 1.10 | 21 | ★★★★ |
| *What You Can Change and What You Can't* | Seligman | 3 | 1.27 | 59 | ★★★★★ |
| *Who Moved My Cheese?* | Johnson | 7 | 0.77 | 60 | ★★★ |
| *Winner Within, The* | Riley | 3 | 0.43 | 7 | — |
| *You Can Heal Your Life* | Hay | 10 | 0.81 | 37 | ★★★ |
| *You Can't Afford the Luxury of a Negative Thought* | John-Rogers & McWilliams | 1 | 0.44 | 6 | — |
| *Your Erroneous Zones* | Dyer | 1 | 0.37 | 169 | ★★ |
| *Your Maximum Mind* | Benson | 1 | 0.47 | 25 | ★★ |
| **Sexuality** | | | | | |
| *Becoming Orgasmic* | Heiman & LoPiccolo | 7 | 1.69 | 32 | ★★★★★ |
| *Dr. Ruth's Guide to Erotic and Sensuous Pleasures* | Westheimer & Lieberman | 1 | −0.42 | 47 | † |
| *Dr. Ruth's Guide to Good Sex* | Westheimer | 1 | −0.66 | 65 | † |
| *Enhancing Sexuality* | Wincze | 10 | 0.50 | 8 | — |
| *Family Book About Sexuality, The* | Calderone & Johnson | 3 | 1.60 | 5 | ◆ |
| *For Each Other* | Barbach | 3 | 1.69 | 29 | ★★★★ |
| *For Women Only* | Berman & Berman | 7 | 1.00 | 11 | ★★★ |
| *For Yourself* | Barbach | 1 | 1.87 | 17 | ★★★ |
| *Illustrated Manual of Sexual Therapy* | Kaplan | 3 | 1.19 | 41 | ★★★★ |
| *New Love and Sex After 60, The* | Butler & Lewis | 10 | 0.62 | 13 | ★★★ |
| *Making Love* | White | 1 | 0.81 | 27 | ★★★ |
| *Making Love* | Davis | 1 | 0.77 | 26 | ★★★ |
| *Male Sexual Awareness* | McCarthy & McCarthy | 7 | 1.13 | 8 | ◆ |
| *New Joy of Sex, The* | Comfort | 1 | 0.99 | 173 | ★★★ |
| *New Male Sexuality, The* | Zilbergeld | 1 | 1.89 | 18 | ★★★ |
| *Rekindling Desire* | Barry & McCarthy | 10 | 1.13 | 23 | ★★★★ |
| *Seven Weeks to Better Sex* | Renshaw | 3 | 1.00 | 8 | — |
| *Sex Matters for Women* | Foley et al. | 10 | 0.00 | 5 | — |
| *Sex Smart* | Zolbrod | 10 | 0.29 | 7 | — |
| *Sexual Awareness* | McCarthy & McCarthy | 3 | 1.67 | 12 | ★★★ |
| *Short Book About Lasting Longer, A* | Birch | 10 | 0.00 | 6 | — |
| *Soul of Sex, The* | Moore | 3 | 0.80 | 10 | ★★★ |
| *Tired Woman's Guide to Passionate Sex, A* | Mintz | 10 | 0.43 | 7 | — |

| Category and Title | Author(s) | Study # | Avg. Rating | # of Raters | Guide Rating |
|---|---|---|---|---|---|
| *What Really Happens in Bed* | Carter & Coopersmith | 1 | 0.80 | 15 | ★★★ |
| **Spiritual and Existential Concerns** | | | | | |
| *American Paradox, The* | Myers | 7 | 1.80 | 5 | ♦ |
| *Become a Better You* | Osteen | 10 | 0.41 | 22 | ★★ |
| *Be (Happy) Attitudes, The* | Schuller | 1 | 0.23 | 21 | ★ |
| *Care of the Soul* | Moore | 3 | 0.87 | 62 | ★★★ |
| *Celestine Prophecy, The* | Redfield | 3 | 0.28 | 76 | ★★ |
| *Clear Body, Clear Mind* | Hubbard | 1 | −1.62 | 62 | † |
| *Decoding Potential* | Flower | 10 | 0.33 | 3 | — |
| *Dianetics* | Hubbard | 1 | −1.77 | 187 | † |
| *Finding Flow* | Csikszentmihalyi | 3 | 1.32 | 25 | ★★★★ |
| *Flow* | Csikszentmihalyi | 1 | 0.57 | 43 | ★★★ |
| *From Beginning to End* | Fulghum | 3 | 0.60 | 5 | — |
| *Further Along the Road Less Traveled* | Peck | 3 | 0.93 | 61 | ★★★ |
| *Illuminata* | Williamson | 7 | 0.55 | 11 | ★★★ |
| *It's Your Time* | Osteen | 10 | 0.22 | 18 | ★ |
| *Loving What Is* | Katie & Mitchell | 7 | 0.60 | 5 | — |
| *Man's Search for Meaning* | Frankl | 1 | 1.27 | 260 | ★★★★★ |
| *One Thousand Gifts* | Voskamp | 10 | 0.40 | 5 | — |
| *Peace, Love, and Healing* | Siegel | 1 | 1.13 | 66 | ★★★★ |
| *Power of Now, The* | Tolle | 7 | 1.08 | 12 | ★★★ |
| *Purpose Driven Life, The* | Warren | 10 | 0.58 | 62 | ★★★ |
| *Radical* | Platt | 10 | 0.80 | 5 | — |
| *Road Less Traveled, The* | Peck | 1 | 1.03 | 285 | ★★★★ |
| *Sacred Contracts* | Myss | 7 | 1.38 | 8 | ♦ |
| *Scientology* | Hubbard | 1 | −1.88 | 173 | † |
| *Search for Significance, The* | McGee | 3 | 1.11 | 9 | — |
| *Seven Spiritual Laws of Success, The* | Chopra | 3 | 0.63 | 32 | ★★★ |
| *Spiritual Healing* | Grayson | 3 | 1.20 | 5 | — |
| *Third Jesus, The* | Chopra | 10 | 0.69 | 16 | ★★★ |
| *Way of the Wizard, The* | Chopra | 3 | −0.20 | 10 | † |
| *When All You Ever Wanted Isn't Enough* | Kushner | 1 | 1.20 | 72 | ★★★★ |
| *Your Sacred Self* | Dyer | 7 | 0.62 | 13 | ★★★ |
| **Stress Management and Relaxation** | | | | | |
| *Beginning Mindfulness* | Weiss | 10 | 1.09 | 33 | ★★★★★ |
| *Beyond Chaos* | West | 1 | 0.83 | 6 | — |
| *Beyond the Relaxation Response* | Benson | 1 | 1.22 | 135 | ★★★★ |
| *Cool Cats, Calm Kids* | Willliams & Burke | 3 | 0.83 | 6 | — |

| Category and Title | Author(s) | Study # | Avg. Rating | # of Raters | Guide Rating |
|---|---|---|---|---|---|
| *Don't Sweat the Small Stuff... and It's All Small Stuff* | Carlson | 7 | 1.05 | 43 | ★★★★ |
| *Each Day a New Beginning* | Casey | 1 | 1.05 | 34 | ★★★★ |
| *Exuberance* | Jamison | 10 | 0.77 | 13 | ★★★ |
| *Heal Yourself with Qigong* | Friedman | 10 | 0.64 | 11 | ★★★ |
| *Inner and Outer Peace Through Meditation* | Singh | 3 | 1.60 | 5 | ♦ |
| *Learn to Relax* | Walker | 7 | 0.92 | 13 | ★★★ |
| *Male Stress Syndrome, The* | Witkin-Lanoil | 1 | 0.68 | 22 | ★★★ |
| *Mindfulness-Based Stress Reduction Workbook, A* | Stahl & Goldstein | 10 | 1.00 | 33 | ★★★★ |
| *Minding the Body, Mending the Mind* | Borysenko | 3 | 1.21 | 48 | ★★★★ |
| *Minding the Body Workbook* | Satterfield | 10 | 1.00 | 9 | ♦ |
| *No Gimmick Guide to Managing Stress* | Neidhart | 1 | 0.88 | 8 | — |
| *Relaxation and Stress Reduction Workbook, The* | Davis et al. | 3 | 1.52 | 81 | ★★★★★ |
| *Relaxation Response, The* | Benson | 1 | 1.28 | 212 | ★★★★★ |
| *Staying on Top When Your World Is Upside Down* | Cramer | 1 | 1.50 | 8 | — |
| *Stress and Relaxation Handbook, The* | Madders | 3 | 1.36 | 47 | ★★★★★ |
| *Stresses* | Curran | 1 | 0.89 | 9 | — |
| *Touchstones* | Hazelden Foundation | 1 | 0.90 | 30 | ★★★ |
| *Wellness Book, The* | Benson & Stuart | 3 | 1.26 | 38 | ★★★★★ |
| *Wherever You Go, There You Are* | Kabat-Zinn | 3 | 1.45 | 53 | ★★★★★ |
| *Why Zebras Don't Get Ulcers* | Sapolsky | 3 | 1.19 | 21 | ★★★★ |
| *Write Your Own Prescription for Stress* | Matheny & McCarthy | 7 | 0.67 | 6 | — |

**Substance Abuse (also see Addictive Disorders)**

| | | | | | |
|---|---|---|---|---|---|
| *Addiction Workbook, The* | Fanning & O'Neill | 6 | 1.20 | 10 | ★★★ |
| *Adult Children of Alcoholics* | Woititz | 1 | 0.52 | 220 | ★★★ |
| *Alcoholic Man, The* | Carey | 1 | 0.35 | 17 | ★★ |
| *Alcoholics Anonymous* | Alcoholics Anonymous | 1 | 1.13 | 179 | ★★★★ |
| *Controlling Your Drinking* | Miller & Munoz | 10 | 1.37 | 16 | ★★★ |
| *Day at a Time, A* | CompCare | 1 | 0.72 | 52 | ★★★ |
| *Drugs & Your Kid* | Rogers | 10 | 0.20 | 5 | — |
| *Healing the Addictive Mind* | Jampolsky | 1 | −1.05 | 20 | † |
| *It Will Never Happen to Me* | Black | 1 | 1.61 | 14 | ★★★ |
| *Miracle Method, The* | Miller & Berg | 3 | −0.08 | 12 | † |
| *One Day at a Time in Al-Anon* | Al-Anon Family Group | 1 | 0.93 | 110 | ★★★ |
| *Overcoming Alcohol Problems* | McCrady & Epstein | 10 | 1.00 | 5 | ♦ |
| *Overcoming Alcohol Use Problems* | Epstein | 10 | 0.50 | 6 | — |

| Category and Title | Author(s) | Study # | Avg. Rating | # of Raters | Guide Rating |
|---|---|---|---|---|---|
| *Overcoming Your Alcohol or Drug Problem* | Daley & Marlatt | 10 | 1.33 | 9 | ♦ |
| *Recovery Book, The* | Mooney et al. | 3 | 0.86 | 21 | ★★★ |
| *Responsible Drinking* | Rotgers et al. | 10 | 1.29 | 7 | — |
| *Sober and Free* | Kettelhack | 3 | 0.86 | 14 | ★★★ |
| *Sober for Good* | Fletcher | 10 | 1.37 | 8 | ♦ |
| *Time to Heal, A* | Cermak | 3 | 1.14 | 22 | ★★★★ |
| *Twelve Steps and Twelve Traditions* | Alcoholics Anonymous | 1 | 1.02 | 180 | ★★★★ |
| *When AA Doesn't Work for You* | Ellis & Velton | 3 | 0.88 | 33 | ★★★ |
| *Woman's Addiction Workbook, A* | Najavits | 10 | 1.17 | 7 | ♦ |
| **Suicide** | | | | | |
| *After a Parent's Suicide* | Requarth | 10 | 0.60 | 5 | — |
| *Aftershock* | Arrington & Cox | 10 | 0.40 | 5 | — |
| *Choosing to Live* | Ellis & Newman | 7 | 1.70 | 10 | ★★★ |
| *Dying to Be Free* | Beverly & Larch | 10 | 0.60 | 5 | — |
| *Living When a Young Friend Commits Suicide* | Grollman & Malikow | 7 | 0.86 | 7 | ♦ |
| *Myths about Suicide* | Joiner | 10 | 1.09 | 11 | ★★★ |
| *Silent Grief* | Lukas & Seiden | 10 | 0.40 | 5 | — |
| *Touched by Suicide* | Myers & Fine | 10 | 0.87 | 8 | ♦ |
| *Why People Die by Suicide* | Joiner | 10 | 0.67 | 6 | ♦ |
| **Teenagers and Parenting** | | | | | |
| *All Grown Up and No Place to Go* | Elkind | 1 | 1.20 | 49 | ★★★★ |
| *Available Parent* | Duffy | 10 | 0.80 | 5 | — |
| *Between Parent and Teenager* | Ginott | 1 | 1.34 | 181 | ★★★★★ |
| *Bringing Up Parents* | Packer | 3 | 1.25 | 8 | ♦ |
| *Chicken Soup for the Teenage Soul on Tough Stuff* | Canfield et al. | 7 | 0.86 | 14 | ★★★ |
| *Get Out of My Life but First Could You Drive Me and Cheryl to the Mall?* | Wolf | 10 | 1.44 | 34 | ★★★★★ |
| *Good Enough Teen, The* | Sachs | 10 | 0.86 | 7 | — |
| *Insider Story on Teenage Girls, The* | Zager | 10 | 0.50 | 6 | — |
| *Overcoming Teenage Depression* | Kaufman | 7 | 0.83 | 6 | — |
| *Parent's Guide to Building Resilience in Teens* | Ginsburg | 10 | 1.00 | 8 | ♦ |
| *Positive Parenting Your Teens* | Joslin & Decher | 3 | 1.54 | 11 | ★★★ |
| *Preparing for Adolescence* | Dobson | 3 | 0.36 | 11 | ★★ |
| *Queen Bees and Wannabes* | Wiseman | 7 | 0.73 | 11 | ★★★ |
| *Reviving Ophelia* | Pipher | 3 | 1.42 | 87 | ★★★★★ |
| *Surviving Adolescence* | Dumont | 1 | 0.95 | 21 | ★★★ |
| *Toughlove* | York et al. | 1 | 0.54 | 124 | ★★★ |

| Category and Title | Author(s) | Study # | Avg. Rating | # of Raters | Guide Rating |
|---|---|---|---|---|---|
| *What Teenagers Want to Know About Sex* | Children's Hospital et al. | 3 | 1.00 | 6 | — |
| *When Living Hurts* | Gordon | 3 | 1.25 | 12 | ★★★ |
| *You and Your Adolescent* | Steinberg & Levine | 3 | 1.00 | 11 | ★★★ |
| *Yes, Your Parents Are Crazy* | Bradley | 10 | 1.20 | 5 | ◆ |
| *Yes, Your Teen is Crazy* | Bradley | 10 | 0.60 | 5 | — |
| **Violent Youth** | | | | | |
| *Coping Power* | Wells et al. | 10 | 0.50 | 6 | — |
| *Defiant Child, The* | Riley | 7 | 1.44 | 16 | ★★★ |
| *Explosive Child, The* | Greene | 7 | 1.50 | 20 | ★★★★ |
| *High Risk* | Magid & McKelvey | 7 | 1.40 | 5 | ◆ |
| *How Children Become Violent* | Seifert | 10 | 0.67 | 6 | — |
| *Kazdin Method for Parenting the Defiant Child, The* | Kazdin | 10 | 1.06 | 18 | ★★★ |
| *Lost Boys* | Garbarino | 7 | 0.86 | 14 | ★★★ |
| *Raising Cain* | Kindlon & Thompson | 7 | 1.08 | 13 | ★★★ |
| *Real Boys* | Pollack | 7 | 1.11 | 18 | ★★★ |
| *Savage Spawn* | Kellerman | 7 | 1.00 | 9 | — |
| *Why Do They Act That Way?* | Walsh | 10 | 0.00 | 5 | — |
| *Your Defiant Child* | Barkley & Benton | 7 | 1.32 | 44 | ★★★★★ |
| **Women's Issues** | | | | | |
| *Backlash* | Faludi | 1 | 0.87 | 47 | ★★★ |
| *Before the Change* | Gittleman | 10 | 0.80 | 5 | — |
| *Body Traps* | Rodin | 3 | 1.18 | 17 | ★★★ |
| *Captivating* | Eldredge & Eldredge | 10 | 0.60 | 5 | — |
| *Chicken Soup for the Woman's Soul* | Canfield et al. | 3 | 1.00 | 25 | ★★★★ |
| *Half the Sky* | Kristof & WuDunn | 10 | 1.43 | 7 | ◆ |
| *I Am My Mother's Daughter* | Krasnow | 10 | 1.14 | 7 | ◆ |
| *Juggling* | Crosby | 1 | 0.75 | 8 | — |
| *Life Preservers* | Lerner | 7 | 1.08 | 12 | ★★★ |
| *Making It Work* | Houston | 1 | 1.00 | 6 | — |
| *Menopause and the Mind* | Warga | 7 | 0.60 | 5 | — |
| *Mismeasure of Woman, The* | Tavris | 7 | 1.25 | 20 | ★★★★ |
| *My Mother/Myself* | Friday | 1 | 0.59 | 187 | ★★★ |
| *Our Bodies, Ourselves, The* | Boston Women's Collective | 3 | 1.54 | 81 | ★★★★★ |
| *Seasons of a Woman's Life, The* | Levinson & Levinson | 3 | 1.20 | 25 | ★★★★ |

| Category and Title | Author(s) | Study # | Avg. Rating | # of Raters | Guide Rating |
|---|---|---|---|---|---|
| *Second Shift, The* | Hochschild | 1 | 1.39 | 28 | ★★★★ |
| *Secrets about Men Every WomanShould Know* | DeAngelis | 1 | -0.42 | 19 | † |
| *Silent Passage, The* | Sheehy | 3 | 0.96 | 67 | ★★★ |
| *Too Good for Her Own Good* | Bepko & Krestan | 1 | 1.26 | 16 | ★★★ |
| *We Are Our Mother's Daughters* | Roberts | 3 | 0.81 | 26 | ★★★ |
| *Wisdom of Menopause* | Northrup | 7 | 1.14 | 14 | ★★★ |
| *Women on Top* | Friday | 3 | 0.25 | 8 | — |
| *Women Who Run with the Wolves* | Estes | 3 | 0.95 | 58 | ★★★ |

# RATINGS OF AUTOBIOGRAPHIES
# IN THE NATIONAL STUDIES

Only those autobiographies rated five or more times in our national studies are included in this list. Some books appear on this list but were not included in the text because they were rated by fewer than eight mental health experts. Please consult Appendix A for details on the methodology of the national studies and the meaning of the guide ratings.

| Category and Title | Author(s) | Study # | Avg. Rating | # of Raters | Guide Rating |
|---|---|---|---|---|---|
| **Abuse** | | | | | |
| *All That Is Bitter & Sweet* | Judd et al. | 11 | 0.67 | 9 | ★★★ |
| *Beyond the Tears* | Tolson | 11 | 0.75 | 8 | ★★★ |
| *Call Me Crazy* | Heche | 8 | −1.29 | 7 | — |
| *Child Called "It," A* | Pelzer | 4 | 1.00 | 9 | ★★★ |
| *Crazy Love* | Steiner | 11 | 0.56 | 9 | ★★★ |
| *Daddy's Girl* | Allen | 4 | 0.92 | 25 | ★★★ |
| *Invisible Tears* | Lawrence | 11 | 0.71 | 7 | — |
| *Lost Boy, The* | Pelzer | 8 | 1.40 | 20 | ★★★★ |
| *Lucky: A Memoir* | Sebold | 11 | 0.50 | 14 | ★★★ |
| *Man Named Dave, A* | Pelzer | 8 | 1.41 | 22 | ★★★★ |
| *Piece of Cake, A* | Brown | 11 | 0.43 | 7 | — |
| *Redemption* | Lannert & Kemp | 11 | 0.71 | 7 | — |
| *Secret Life* | Ryan | 2 | 0.54 | 13 | ★★★ |
| *Sleepers* | Carcaterra | 4 | 0.78 | 9 | ★★★ |
| *Surviving Domestic Violence* | Weiss & Magill | 8 | 0.83 | 6 | — |
| *Tiger, Tiger* | Fragoso | 11 | 0.67 | 6 | ♦ |
| *Triumph Over Darkness* | Wood | 4 | 0.60 | 5 | — |
| *Why Me?* | Burleton | 11 | 0.43 | 7 | — |

| Category and Title | Author(s) | Study # | Avg. Rating | # of Raters | Guide Rating |
|---|---|---|---|---|---|
| **Addictions (also see Substance Abuse)** | | | | | |
| *Born to Lose* | Lee | 11 | 0.56 | 9 | ★★★ |
| *Codependent No More* | Beattie | 2 | 1.00 | 142 | ★★★★ |
| *Cyber Junkie* | Roberts | 11 | 0.63 | 8 | ★★★ |
| *Gripped by Gambling* | Lancelot | 11 | 0.60 | 5 | — |
| *Love Sick* | Silverman | 11 | 0.78 | 9 | ★★★ |
| *She Bets Her Life* | Sojourner | 11 | 0.67 | 6 | — |
| *Unplugged* | Van Cleave & Griffiths | 11 | 0.67 | 6 | — |
| **Adult Development** | | | | | |
| *Fly Fishing Through the Midlife Crisis* | Raines | 8 | 0.80 | 10 | ★★★ |
| *Forward From Here* | Lindbergh | 11 | 0.63 | 8 | ★★★ |
| *My Life in the Middle Ages* | Atlas | 11 | 0.67 | 6 | — |
| *No Paltry Thing* | Meyer | 11 | 0.43 | 7 | — |
| *Tuesdays with Morrie* | Albom | 4 | 1.58 | 59 | ★★★★★ |
| *Whatever!* | Mahone | 11 | 0.71 | 7 | ♦ |
| *Winging It* | Goldhammer | 11 | 0.83 | 6 | — |
| **Aging** | | | | | |
| *Bittersweet Season, A* | Gross | 11 | 1.00 | 7 | ♦ |
| *Changing Places* | Kramer | 8 | 1.11 | 9 | ★★★ |
| *Fountain of Age, The* | Friedan | 4 | 0.96 | 23 | ★★★ |
| *Getting Over Getting Older* | Pogrebin | 11 | 0.92 | 12 | ★★★ |
| *I'm Not as Old as I Used to Be* | Weaver | 11 | 0.60 | 10 | ★★★ |
| *Last Gift of Life, The* | Heilbrun | 8 | 1.00 | 9 | ★★★ |
| *No More Words* | Lindbergh | 8 | 1.00 | 5 | — |
| *Tales of Graceful Aging from the Planet Denial* | Hollander | 11 | 0.86 | 7 | — |
| *Virtues of Aging, The* | Carter | 4 | 1.24 | 17 | ★★★★ |
| **Anxiety Disorders** | | | | | |
| *Afraid of Everything* | Woods | 2 | 0.89 | 9 | ★★★ |
| *Anxiety Expert, The* | Raskin | 11 | 0.86 | 7 | ♦ |
| *Brief History of Anxiety, A* | Pearson | 11 | 0.80 | 5 | — |
| *Earl Campbell Story* | Campbell | 8 | 1.33 | 6 | ♦ |
| *Flock, The* | Casey & Wilson | 4 | 0.71 | 7 | — |
| *Hell of Social Phobia, The* | Cunningham | 11 | 0.80 | 5 | — |
| *If I Can Do It, You Can Too!* | Miller | 11 | 0.80 | 5 | — |
| *Memoirs of an Amnesiac* | Levant | 2 | 0.93 | 14 | ★★★ |
| *Mind of My Own, A* | Sizemore | 2 | 1.00 | 8 | ★★★★ |

| Category and Title | Author(s) | Study # | Avg. Rating | # of Raters | Guide Rating |
|---|---|---|---|---|---|
| *Panic Attack Recovery Book, The* | Swede & Jaffe | 4 | 1.25 | 12 | ★★★ |
| *Phantom Illness* | Cantor & Fallon | 2 | 0.89 | 9 | ★★★ |
| *Rae* | Swigget | 11 | 0.80 | 5 | — |
| *Sybil* | Schreiber | 4 | 0.32 | 91 | ★★ |
| *When Rabbit Howls* | Chase | 2 | 0.48 | 48 | ★★ |
| *Wish I Could Be There* | Shawn | 11 | 0.80 | 5 | ◆ |
| **Attention-Deficit/ Hyperactivity Disorder** | | | | | |
| *ADHD: An Autobiography of Survival* | Kuendig | 11 | 1.00 | 6 | — |
| *ADHD & Me* | Taylor | 11 | 0.83 | 6 | ◆ |
| *ADHD Handbook for Families* | Weingartner | 4 | 1.15 | 13 | ★★★ |
| *Little Monster, The* | Jergen | 11 | 1.09 | 11 | ★★★ |
| *Maybe You Know My Kid* | Fowler | 4 | 1.14 | 7 | ◆ |
| *One Boy's Struggle* | Hutchinson | 11 | 0.83 | 6 | — |
| *Parenting a Child with ADHD* | Boyles &Contadino | 4 | 1.06 | 16 | ★★★★ |
| *What Makes Ryan Tick* | Hughes | 8 | 0.67 | 6 | — |
| **Autism & Asperger's** | | | | | |
| *All I Can Handle* | Staglliano & McCarthy | 11 | -0.75 | 8 | † |
| *Atypical* | Saperstein | 11 | 0.62 | 8 | ★★★ |
| *Born On A Blue Day* | Tammet | 11 | 1.08 | 48 | ★★★★ |
| *Emergence* | Grandin & Scariano | 11 | 1.53 | 15 | ★★★ |
| *Look Me in the Eye* | Robison | 11 | 0.73 | 15 | ★★★ |
| *Making Peace with Autism* | Senator | 11 | 0.73 | 3 | — |
| *Mind Tree, The* | Mukhopadhyay | 11 | 0.83 | 6 | — |
| *Parallel Play* | Page | 11 | 0.80 | 5 | — |
| *Raising Blaze* | Ginsberg | 11 | 0.40 | 5 | — |
| **Bipolar Disorder** | | | | | |
| *Bipolar Advantage, The* | Wootton | 11 | 1.14 | 7 | — |
| *Breakdown* | Sutherland | 2 | 0.62 | 8 | ★★★ |
| *Brilliant Madness, A* | Duke & Hochman | 2 | 1.08 | 48 | ★★★★ |
| *Call Me Anna* | Duke | 2 | 0.85 | 39 | ★★★ |
| *Burn* | Feldman | 11 | 0.83 | 6 | — |
| *Daughter of the Queen of Sheba* | Lyden | 11 | 1.00 | 9 | ★★★ |
| *His Bright Light* | Steel | 11 | 0.50 | 8 | ★★★ |
| *Loony-Bin Trip, The* | Millett | 2 | 0.07 | 13 | ★ |
| *Madness* | Hornbacher | 11 | 1.00 | 7 | — |
| *Manic* | Cheney | 11 | 0.67 | 6 | — |

| Category and Title | Author(s) | Study # | Avg. Rating | # of Raters | Guide Rating |
|---|---|---|---|---|---|
| *Pain* | Anderson | 2 | 0.93 | 14 | ★★★ |
| *Scattershot* | Lovelace | 11 | 0.60 | 5 | — |
| *Skywriting* | Pauley | 11 | 1.10 | 10 | ★★★ |
| *Unquiet Mind, An* | Jamison | 2 | 1.39 | 49 | ★★★★★ |
| **Borderline & Narcissistic Personality Disorders** | | | | | |
| *Boomerang Love* | Melville | 11 | 0.67 | 6 | — |
| *The Buddha & The Borderline* | Van Gelder | 11 | 1.11 | 9 | ★★★ |
| *Get Me Out of Here* | Reiland | 11 | 1.25 | 8 | ★★★ |
| *Girl, Interrupted* | Kaysen | 2 | 1.22 | 41 | ★★★★ |
| *Girl in Need of a Tourniquet* | Johnson | 11 | 0.60 | 5 | — |
| *Skin Game* | Kettlewell | 11 | 0.83 | 6 | — |
| *Web of Lies* | Tate | 11 | 0.50 | 6 | — |
| *Welcome to My Country* | Slater | 11 | 0.88 | 8 | ★★★ |
| **Bullying** | | | | | |
| *Please Stop Laughing at Me* | Blanco | 11 | 0.80 | 5 | ♦ |
| **Death and Grieving** | | | | | |
| *After the Death of a Child* | Finkbeiner | 4 | 1.30 | 10 | ★★★ |
| *Death Be Not Proud* | Gunther | 8 | 1.52 | 50 | ★★★★★ |
| *Epilogue* | Roiphe | 11 | 0.60 | 5 | — |
| *Eric* | Lund | 8 | 1.43 | 7 | ♦ |
| *Grief Observed, A* | Lewis | 4 | 1.58 | 36 | ★★★★★ |
| *Hannah's Gift* | Housden | 8 | 1.43 | 7 | ♦ |
| *Lament for a Son* | Wolterstorff | 11 | 0.89 | 9 | ★★★ |
| *Letting Go* | Schwartz | 8 | 1.64 | 55 | ★★★★★ |
| *Long Goodbye, The* | O'Rourke | 11 | 1.00 | 7 | — |
| *Motherless Daughter* | Edleman | 4 | 1.35 | 23 | ★★★★ |
| *Widow's Story, A* | Oates | 11 | 0.81 | 16 | ★★★ |
| *Wheel of Life, The* | Kübler-Ross & Gold | 8 | 1.37 | 19 | ★★★★ |
| *Year of Magical Thinking, The* | Didion | 11 | 1.39 | 44 | ★★★★★ |
| **Dementia/Alzheimer's** | | | | | |
| *Alzheimer's, A Love Story* | Davidson | 8 | 1.71 | 7 | ♦ |
| *Alzheimer's From the Inside Out* | Taylor | 11 | 1.00 | 6 | ♦ |
| *Death in Slow Motion* | Cooney | 11 | 0.71 | 7 | — |
| *Diminished Mind, The* | Tyler & Anifantakis | 1 | 0.87 | 23 | ★★★ |
| *Elegy for Iris* | Bayley | 8 | 1.53 | 17 | ★★★★ |
| *French Fries, Ice Cream, & Cucumber Sandwiches* | Dale | 11 | 0.40 | 5 | — |
| *Keeper* | Gillies | 11 | 0.40 | 5 | — |
| *Last of His Mind, The* | Thorndike | 11 | 0.60 | 5 | — |

| Category and Title | Author(s) | Study # | Avg. Rating | # of Raters | Guide Rating |
|---|---|---|---|---|---|
| *Long Hello, The* | Borrie | 11 | 0.40 | 5 | — |
| *Story of My Father, The* | Miller | 11 | 0.71 | 7 | — |
| **Depression** | | | | | |
| *Beast, The* | Thompson | 8 | 1.50 | 8 | ★★★ |
| *Bell Jar, The* | Plath | 4 | 0.86 | 87 | ★★★ |
| *Behind the Smile* | Osmond et al. | 11 | 0.75 | 8 | ★★★ |
| *Darkness Visible* | Styron | 2 | 1.34 | 71 | ★★★★★ |
| *Down Came the Rain* | Shields | 11 | 1.00 | 10 | ★★★ |
| *Hide & Seek* | Aron | 11 | 0.83 | 6 | — |
| *Holiday of Darkness* | Endler | 8 | 1.17 | 6 | — |
| *My Depression* | Swados | 11 | 0.88 | 8 | ★★★ |
| *Noonday Demon, The* | Solomon | 8 | 1.31 | 13 | ★★★ |
| *On the Edge of Darkness* | Cronkite | 8 | 1.07 | 14 | ★★★ |
| *Prozac Nation* | Wurtzel | 2 | 0.49 | 37 | ★★ |
| *Rage Against the Meshugenah* | Evans | 11 | 0 | 6 | — |
| *Shoot the Damn Dog* | Brampton | 11 | 0.60 | 5 | — |
| *Undercurrents* | Manning | 2 | 1.11 | 25 | ★★★★ |
| **Eating Disorders** | | | | | |
| *Am I Still Visible?* | Heater | 2 | 1.09 | 11 | ★★★ |
| *Born Round* | Bruni | 11 | 0.67 | 6 | — |
| *Breaking Free from Compulsive Eating* | Roth | 4 | 1.59 | 22 | ★★★★ |
| *Feeding the Hungry Heart* | Roth | 4 | 1.35 | 37 | ★★★★★ |
| *Gaining* | Liu | 11 | 0.80 | 5 | ◆ |
| *Good Enough* | Bitter | 4 | 0.86 | 7 | ◆ |
| *Holy Hunger* | Bullitt-Jonas | 8 | 1.20 | 5 | — |
| *Inner Hunger* | Apostolides | 4 | 0.60 | 5 | — |
| *My Life So Far* | Fonda | 11 | 0.89 | 9 | ★★★ |
| *Purge* | Johns | 11 | 0.40 | 5 | — |
| *Starving for Attention* | O'Neill | 2 | 0.91 | 22 | ★★★ |
| *Unbearable Lightness* | De Rossi | 2 | 0.14 | 7 | — |
| *Wasted* | Hornbacher | 11 | 0.91 | 11 | ★★★ |
| **Gay, Lesbian, and Bisexual Issues** | | | | | |
| *Family Heart, The* | Dew | 11 | 1.00 | 5 | ◆ |
| **Happiness** | | | | | |
| *Eat, Pray, Love* | Gilbert | 11 | 0.45 | 66 | ★★ |
| *Happiness Project, The* | Rubin | 11 | 1.10 | 10 | ★★★ |
| *How Starbucks Saved My Life* | Gill | 11 | 0.67 | 6 | — |
| *Tao of Willie, The* | Nelson & Pipkin | 11 | 1.00 | 5 | ◆ |

| Category and Title | Author(s) | Study # | Avg. Rating | # of Raters | Guide Rating |
|---|---|---|---|---|---|
| *This Is Not The Story You Think It Is* | Munson | 11 | 0.43 | 7 | — |
| **Obsessive-Compulsive Disorder** | | | | | |
| *Amen, Amen, Amen* | Sher | 11 | 0.50 | 6 | — |
| *Boy Who Finally Stopped Washing, The* | B. | 11 | 0.86 | 7 | ♦ |
| *Devil in the Details* | Traig | 11 | 0.50 | 6 | — |
| *"It'll Be Okay"* | Shy | 11 | 0.60 | 5 | — |
| *Memoirs of an Amnesiac* | Levant | 2 | 0.93 | 14 | ★★★ |
| *Passing for Normal* | Bell | 11 | 0.40 | 5 | — |
| *Rewind, Replay, Repeat* | Bell | 11 | 1.40 | 5 | ♦ |
| *Saving Sammy* | Maloney | 11 | 0.17 | 6 | — |
| **PTSD** | | | | | |
| *I Am the Central Park Jogger* | Meili | 11 | 1.00 | 7 | ♦ |
| *I Can Still Hear Their Cries, Even in My Sleep* | McFall | 11 | 1.00 | 5 | ♦ |
| *Making and Un-making of a Marine, The* | Winters | 11 | 0.40 | 5 | — |
| *River of Forgetting, The* | Rowan | 11 | 0 | 5 | — |
| *Soft Spots* | Van Winkle | 11 | 0.80 | 5 | — |
| *Telling* | Francisco | 11 | 0.90 | 6 | ♦ |
| **Schizophrenia** | | | | | |
| *Angel at My Table, An* | Frame | 2 | 0.70 | 10 | ★★★ |
| *Autobiography of a Schizophrenic Girl* | Sechehaye | 4 | 0.67 | 9 | ★★★ |
| *Center Cannot Hold, The* | Saks | 11 | 1.40 | 16 | ★★★★ |
| *Day the Voices Stopped, The* | Steele | 8 | 1.20 | 5 | — |
| *Divided Minds* | Spiro & Wagner | 11 | 1.00 | 6 | — |
| *Eden Express, The* | Vonnegut | 2 | 0.89 | 53 | ★★★ |
| *Father, Have I Kept My Promise?* | Weisskopf-Joelson | 2 | 0.88 | 8 | ★★★ |
| *I Never Promised You a Rose Garden* | Greenberg | 8 | 1.33 | 156 | ★★★★★ |
| *Memoirs of My Nervous Illness* | Shreber | 8 | 0.83 | 6 | — |
| *Nobody's Child* | Balter & Katz | 2 | 0.90 | 29 | ★★★ |
| *Out of the Depths* | Boisen | 2 | 1.27 | 22 | ★★★★ |
| *Quiet Room, The* | Schiller & Bennett | 4 | 0.64 | 11 | ★★★ |
| *Rescuing Patty Hearst* | Holman | 11 | 1.00 | 5 | — |
| *Soloist, The* | Lopez | 11 | 1.38 | 13 | ★★★ |
| *Too Much Anger, Too Many Tears* | Gotkin & Gotkin | 2 | 1.12 | 16 | ★★★★ |
| *When the Music's Over* | Gates & Hammond | 2 | 0.88 | 8 | ★★★ |

| Category and Title | Author(s) | Study # | Avg. Rating | # of Raters | Guide Rating |
|---|---|---|---|---|---|
| **Substance Abuse (also see Addictive Disorders)** | | | | | |
| *Beautiful Boy* | Sheff | 11 | 1.20 | 10 | ★★★ |
| *Both Sides of Recovery* | Harrison & Harrison | 4 | 1.00 | 5 | — |
| *Broken* | Moyers & Ketcham | 11 | 1.00 | 5 | — |
| *Broken Cord, The* | Dorris | 8 | 1.40 | 20 | ★★★★ |
| *Drinking: A Love Story* | Knapp | 2 | 1.00 | 16 | ★★★ |
| *Drinking Life, A* | Hamill | 2 | 1.07 | 29 | ★★★★ |
| *Getting Better: Inside AA* | Robertson | 2 | 1.10 | 28 | ★★★★ |
| *Go Ask Alice* | Anonymous | 8 | 1.06 | 33 | ★★★★ |
| *Lit* | Karr | 11 | 1.14 | 7 | — |
| *Note Found in a Bottle* | Cheever | 8 | 1.38 | 8 | ★★★ |
| *Now You Know* | Dukakis | 2 | 0.60 | 32 | ★★★ |
| *Portraits of Recovery* | Gaynor | 4 | 1.00 | 6 | — |
| *Smashed* | Zailckas | 11 | 0.60 | 5 | — |
| *Terry* | McGovern | 8 | 1.33 | 9 | ★★★ |
| *Wishful Drinking* | Fisher | 11 | 0.87 | 15 | ★★★ |
| **Suicide** | | | | | |
| *Grieving the Unexpected* | Leblanc | 11 | 0.50 | 6 | — |
| *His Bright Light* | Steel | 8 | 0.50 | 6 | ♦ |
| *Night Falls Fast* | Jamison | 8 | 1.52 | 33 | ★★★★★ |
| *No Time to Say Goodbye* | Fine | 11 | 0.80 | 5 | ♦ |
| **Violent Youth** | | | | | |
| *All Souls* | MacDonald | 11 | 0.78 | 9 | ★★★ |
| *Always Running* | Rodriguez | 11 | 1.00 | 5 | ♦ |
| *Monster* | Shakur | 11 | 1.33 | 6 | ♦ |
| *Sleepers* | Carcaterra | 4 | 0.78 | 9 | ★★★ |
| *Tornado Warning* | Waldal | 11 | 0.80 | 5 | — |
| **Women's Issues** | | | | | |
| *Deborah, Golda, and Me* | Pogrebin | 4 | 1.09 | 11 | ★★★ |
| *Heart of a Woman* | Angelou | 8 | 1.38 | 24 | ★★★★★ |
| *In Our Time* | Brownmiller | 11 | 1.00 | 6 | ♦ |
| *Insecure at Last* | Ensler | 11 | 0.60 | 5 | — |
| *Life So Far* | Friedan | 11 | 1.42 | 7 | ♦ |
| *Mothers: A Celebration* | Stoddard | 4 | 1.00 | 5 | ♦ |
| *Reason for Hope* | Goodall | 8 | 1.63 | 8 | ★★★ |

# RATINGS OF FILMS IN THE NATIONAL STUDIES

Only those films rated five or more times in our national studies are included in this list. Some films appear on this list but were not included in the text because they were rated by fewer than 10 mental health experts. Please consult Appendix A for details on the methodology of the national studies and the meaning of the guide ratings.

| Category and Title | Study # | Avg. Rating | # of Raters | Guide Rating |
|---|---|---|---|---|
| **Abuse** | | | | |
| Accused, The | 12 | 1.09 | 65 | ★★★★ |
| Antwone Fisher | 12 | 1.04 | 49 | ★★★★ |
| Apostle, The | 8 | 0.78 | 59 | ★★★ |
| Boyhood Shadows | 12 | 0.50 | 6 | — |
| Capturing the Friedmans | 12 | 0.92 | 25 | ★★★ |
| Color Purple, The | 5 | 1.24 | 245 | ★★★★ |
| Dolores Claiborne | 8 | 0.93 | 58 | ★★★ |
| Enough | 8 | −0.17 | 6 | — |
| Magdalene Sisters, The | 12 | 1.13 | 23 | ★★★★ |
| Matilda | 8 | 0.31 | 29 | ★★ |
| Mommie Dearest | 5 | 0.34 | 149 | ★★ |
| Monster | 12 | 0.87 | 61 | ★★★ |
| Mysterious Skin | 12 | 0.78 | 9 | — |
| Mystic River | 12 | 1.13 | 102 | ★★★★ |
| Personal Velocity | 12 | 0.13 | 8 | — |
| Prince of Tides, The | 5 | −0.02 | 245 | † |
| Radio Flyer | 5 | 1.00 | 41 | ★★★★ |
| Sleeping with the Enemy | 5 | 0.60 | 134 | ★★★ |
| Slumdog Millionaire | 12 | 1.00 | 139 | ★★★★ |
| Thelma and Louise | 5 | 0.40 | 229 | ★★ |
| This Boy's Life | 5 | 1.14 | 49 | ★★★★ |

| Category and Title | Study # | Avg. Rating | # of Raters | Guide Rating |
|---|---|---|---|---|
| *Thousand Acres, A* | 8 | 1.00 | 37 | ★★★★ |
| *What's Love Got to Do with It?* | 5 | 0.88 | 83 | ★★★ |
| **Addictions (see also Substance Abuse)** | | | | |
| *Choke* | 12 | 0.82 | 11 | ★★★ |
| *Gambler, The* | 12 | 0.88 | 26 | ★★★ |
| *I Am a Sex Addict* | 12 | 0.33 | 6 | — |
| *Love Sick* | 12 | 0.71 | 7 | ◆ |
| *On-line* | 12 | 0.29 | 7 | — |
| *Owning Mahowny* | 12 | 0.67 | 9 | ◆ |
| *Rounders* | 12 | 0.80 | 20 | ★★★ |
| **Adult Development** | | | | |
| *17 Again* | 12 | 0.34 | 38 | ★★ |
| *Christmas Carol, A* | 5 | 0.89 | 170 | ★★★ |
| *Doctor, The* | 5 | 1.28 | 88 | ★★★★★ |
| *Field of Dreams* | 5 | 0.96 | 252 | ★★★ |
| *It's a Wonderful Life* | 5 | 1.22 | 246 | ★★★★ |
| *Mr. Holland's Opus* | 8 | 1.14 | 184 | ★★★★ |
| *Trip to Bountiful, The* | 5 | 1.42 | 124 | ★★★★★ |
| **Aging** | | | | |
| *About Schmidt* | 12 | 1.04 | 79 | ★★★★ |
| *Cocoon* | 5 | 0.92 | 247 | ★★★ |
| *Curious Case of Benjamin Button, The* | 12 | 0.64 | 121 | ★★★ |
| *Grumpy Old Men* | 8 | 0.32 | 179 | ★★ |
| *On Golden Pond* | 5 | 1.47 | 307 | ★★★★★ |
| *Space Cowboys* | 8 | 0.44 | 91 | ★★ |
| *Wrestling Ernest Hemingway* | 8 | 1.00 | 16 | ★★★ |
| **Anxiety Disorders** | | | | |
| *Adaptation* | 12 | 0.16 | 44 | ★ |
| *Black Swan* | 12 | 0.78 | 92 | ★★★ |
| *Cracks* | 12 | 0.14 | 7 | — |
| *High Anxiety* | 5 | −0.03 | 127 | † |
| *In Broken English* | 12 | −0.17 | 6 | — |
| *Panic* | 12 | 0.38 | 13 | ★★ |
| *Panic Room* | 12 | 0.21 | 82 | ★ |
| *Sybil* | 5 | 0.79 | 159 | ★★★ |
| *What About Bob?* | 5 | 0.15 | 244 | ★ |
| **Autism & Asperger's** | | | | |
| *Black Balloon, The* | 12 | 0.13 | 8 | — |
| *Boy Who Could Fly, The* | 12 | 0.90 | 21 | ★★★ |

| Category and Title | Study # | Avg. Rating | # of Raters | Guide Rating |
|---|---|---|---|---|
| *Breaking and Entering* | 12 | 0.40 | 5 | — |
| *Marathon* | 12 | 0.86 | 7 | — |
| *Mozart & the Whale* | 12 | 1.84 | 19 | ★★★★ |
| *Rain Man* | 12 | 1.28 | 210 | ★★★★★ |
| *Silent Fall* | 12 | 0.33 | 6 | — |
| *Temple Grandin* | 12 | 1.68 | 75 | ★★★★★ |
| *What's Eating Gilbert Grape?* | 12 | 1.22 | 95 | ★★★★ |
| *Wizard, The* | 12 | 0.17 | 6 | — |
| **Bipolar Disorder** | | | | |
| *Blue Sky* | 12 | 1.00 | 18 | ★★★ |
| *Call Me Anna* | 12 | 0.25 | 8 | — |
| *Garden State* | 12 | 0.80 | 50 | ★★★ |
| *Michael Clayton* | 12 | 0.81 | 73 | ★★★ |
| *Mr. Jones* | 12 | 0.06 | 17 | ★ |
| *Limitless* | 12 | 0.71 | 21 | ★★★ |
| *Respiro* | 12 | 0.50 | 6 | — |
| **Borderline & Narcissistic Personality Disorders** | | | | |
| *After Hours* | 8 | 0.00 | 11 | ★ |
| *Alone* | 12 | 0.67 | 6 | — |
| *Black Snake Moan* | 12 | 0.47 | 15 | ★★ |
| *Fatal Attraction* | 8 | 0.84 | 188 | ★★★ |
| *Girl, Interrupted* | 8 | 1.07 | 103 | ★★★★ |
| *Great Santini, The* | 8 | 1.23 | 115 | ★★★★ |
| *Groundhog Day* | 8 | 0.21 | 164 | ★ |
| *In the Company of Men* | 8 | 0.28 | 18 | ★★ |
| *Like Water for Chocolate* | 8 | 1.00 | 109 | ★★★★ |
| *Lovelife* | 12 | 0.50 | 6 | — |
| *Margot at the Wedding* | 12 | 0.91 | 33 | ★★★ |
| *Misery* | 8 | 0.89 | 76 | ★★★ |
| *Murder by Numbers* | 8 | −0.25 | 12 | † |
| *Notes on a Scandal* | 12 | 0.95 | 22 | ★★★ |
| *Phone Booth* | 12 | 0.16 | 25 | ★ |
| *Prozac Nation* | 12 | 0.81 | 21 | ★★★ |
| *Roger Dodger* | 12 | 0.73 | 11 | ★★★ |
| *Sunset Boulevard* | 8 | 1.20 | 60 | ★★★★ |
| *White Oleander* | 12 | 0.76 | 29 | ★★★ |
| *Vicky Cristina Barcelona* | 12 | 0.75 | 64 | ★★★ |
| **Bullying** | | | | |
| *Karate Kid* | 12 | 1.01 | 162 | ★★★★ |

| Category and Title | Study # | Avg. Rating | # of Raters | Guide Rating |
|---|---|---|---|---|
| Knockout | 12 | 0.50 | 10 | ★★★ |
| My Bodyguard | 12 | 1.03 | 65 | ★★★★ |
| Odd Girl Out | 12 | 0.60 | 10 | ★★★ |
| Revenge of the Nerds | 12 | 0.13 | 71 | ★ |
| **Child Development and Parenting** | | | | |
| Baby Boom | 8 | 0.32 | 41 | ★★ |
| Big | 5 | 0.71 | 192 | ★★★ |
| I am Sam | 8 | 1.00 | 38 | ★★★★ |
| Little Man Tate | 5 | 1.02 | 94 | ★★★★ |
| Parenthood | 5 | 0.69 | 115 | ★★★ |
| Searching for Bobby Fischer | 5 | 1.19 | 108 | ★★★★ |
| **Communication and People Skills** | | | | |
| Children of a Lesser God | 5 | 1.26 | 182 | ★★★★★ |
| Dead Poets Society | 5 | 1.11 | 284 | ★★★★ |
| He Said, She Said | 5 | 0.44 | 57 | ★★ |
| **Death and Grieving** | | | | |
| Accidental Tourist, The | 5 | 0.84 | 146 | ★★★ |
| Bucket List, The | 12 | 1.21 | 133 | ★★★★ |
| Corrina, Corrina | 8 | 1.32 | 41 | ★★★★★ |
| Ghost | 5 | 0.37 | 209 | ★★ |
| In the Bedroom | 8 | 1.15 | 47 | ★★★★ |
| Lion King, The | 5 | 0.62 | 176 | ★★★ |
| Message in a Bottle | 8 | 0.44 | 75 | ★★ |
| Moonlight Mile | 12 | 0.57 | 7 | ♦ |
| My Girl | 5 | 0.50 | 30 | ★★★ |
| My Life | 5 | 0.93 | 40 | ★★★ |
| Ordinary People | 5 | 1.49 | 281 | ★★★★★ |
| Rabbit Hole | 12 | 0.86 | 29 | ★★★ |
| River Runs through It, A | 5 | 1.15 | 214 | ★★★★ |
| Steel Magnolias | 5 | 1.18 | 220 | ★★★★ |
| Summer of '42, The | 5 | 0.77 | 170 | ★★★ |
| Truly, Madly, Deeply | 8 | 1.14 | 28 | ★★★★ |
| Unstrung Heroes | 8 | 1.08 | 12 | ★★★ |
| **Dementia/Alzheimer's** | | | | |
| Away from Her | 12 | 1.43 | 40 | ★★★★★ |
| Forgetting, The | 12 | 0.43 | 7 | — |
| Do You Remember Love? | 5 | 1.20 | 10 | ★★★ |
| Iris | 8 | 1.62 | 40 | ★★★★★ |

| Category and Title | Study # | Avg. Rating | # of Raters | Guide Rating |
|---|---|---|---|---|
| *Memories of Me* | 5 | 0.90 | 10 | ★★★ |
| *Notebook, The* | 12 | 1.37 | 94 | ★★★★★ |
| **Depression** | | | | |
| *American Splendor* | 12 | 0.97 | 34 | ★★★ |
| *Beaver, The* | 12 | 0.44 | 9 | — |
| *Call Me Anna* | 8 | 1.00 | 7 | — |
| *Hours, The* | 12 | 1.07 | 57 | ★★★★ |
| *Mind the Gap* | 12 | 0.20 | 5 | — |
| *My First Mister* | 12 | 0.44 | 9 | — |
| *Prozac Nation* | 12 | 0.95 | 21 | ★★★ |
| *Woman Under the Influence, A* | 8 | 1.24 | 34 | ★★★★ |
| **Divorce** | | | | |
| *Bye Bye Love* | 5 | 0.53 | 17 | ★★★ |
| *First Wives' Club* | 5 | 0.19 | 196 | ★ |
| *Four Seasons, The* | 5 | 0.93 | 115 | ★★★ |
| *Good Mother, The* | 5 | 0.88 | 40 | ★★★ |
| *Husbands & Wives* | 8 | 0.76 | 21 | ★★★ |
| *Kramer vs. Kramer* | 5 | 1.24 | 280 | ★★★★ |
| *Mrs. Doubtfire* | 5 | 0.57 | 266 | ★★★ |
| *Squid and the Whale, The* | 12 | 1.42 | 57 | ★★★★★ |
| *Starting Over* | 8 | 0.68 | 37 | ★★★ |
| *Unmarried Woman, An* | 5 | 1.02 | 94 | ★★★★ |
| *War of the Roses, The* | 5 | −0.05 | 203 | † |
| **Eating Disorders** | | | | |
| *Best Little Girl in the World* | 5 | 1.19 | 31 | ★★★★ |
| *Center Stage* | 12 | 0.60 | 15 | ★★★ |
| *Eating* | 5 | 1.00 | 25 | ★★★★ |
| *For the Love of Nancy* | 5 | 0.64 | 11 | ★★★ |
| *Karen Carpenter Story, The* | 5 | 1.25 | 76 | ★★★★★ |
| *Thin* | 12 | 0.40 | 15 | ★★ |
| **Families and Stepfamilies** | | | | |
| *Family Man, The* | 8 | 1.24 | 35 | ★★★★ |
| *Father of the Bride, The* | 5 | 0.67 | 169 | ★★★ |
| *Fly Away Home* | 5 | 1.15 | 62 | ★★★★ |
| *Joy Luck Club, The* | 5 | 1.43 | 196 | ★★★★★ |
| *Life as a House* | 8 | 1.35 | 46 | ★★★★★ |
| *Pieces of April* | 12 | 1.12 | 26 | ★★★★ |
| *Radio Flyer* | 5 | 1.02 | 43 | ★★★★ |

| Category and Title | Study # | Avg. Rating | # of Raters | Guide Rating |
|---|---|---|---|---|
| *Rain Man* | 5 | 1.15 | 274 | ★★★★ |
| *Rhapsody in Bloom* | 12 | −0.20 | 5 | — |
| *Stepmom* | 8 | 1.06 | 65 | ★★★★ |
| *Terms of Endearment* | 5 | 1.19 | 256 | ★★★★ |
| *What's Eating Gilbert Grape?* | 5 | 1.14 | 133 | ★★★★ |
| **Gay, Lesbian, and Bisexual Issues** | | | | |
| *Angels in America* | 12 | 1.37 | 49 | ★★★★★ |
| *Beautiful Thing* | 12 | 1.00 | 11 | ★★★ |
| *Big Eden* | 12 | 0.82 | 11 | ★★★ |
| *Boys in the Band, The* | 5 | 0.77 | 107 | ★★★ |
| *Brokeback Mountain* | 12 | 1.23 | 140 | ★★★★ |
| *I Now Pronounce You Chuck & Larry* | 12 | −0.61 | 44 | † |
| *In & Out* | 12 | 0.79 | 28 | ★★★ |
| *Imagine Me & You* | 12 | 0.63 | 8 | — |
| *Kissing Jessica Stein* | 12 | 0.89 | 37 | ★★★ |
| *Milk* | 12 | 1.52 | 93 | ★★★★★ |
| *Out of the Silence* | 12 | 0.00 | 5 | — |
| *Prayers for Bobby* | 12 | 0.55 | 11 | ★★★ |
| *Paris Is Burning* | 5 | 0.80 | 46 | ★★★ |
| *Torch Song Trilogy* | 5 | 1.22 | 81 | ★★★★ |
| **Love and Intimacy** | | | | |
| *Four Seasons, The* | 5 | 0.97 | 116 | ★★★ |
| *9± Weeks* | 5 | −0.67 | 127 | † |
| *Pretty in Pink* | 5 | 0.36 | 103 | ★★ |
| *Serendipity* | 8 | 0.03 | 35 | ★ |
| *Sleepless in Seattle* | 5 | 0.55 | 259 | ★★★ |
| *Story of Us, The* | 8 | 0.61 | 31 | ★★★ |
| *Way We Were, The* | 5 | 0.73 | 174 | ★★★ |
| *When Harry Met Sally* | 5 | 0.94 | 289 | ★★★ |
| **Marriage** | 12 | 1.18 | 95 | ★★★★ |
| *The Kids are All Right* | 12 | 1.06 | 63 | ★★★★ |
| *Revolutionary Road* | | | | |
| **Men's Issues** | | | | |
| *American Beauty* | 8 | 0.68 | 196 | ★★★ |
| *Antwone Fisher* | 12 | 0.98 | 45 | ★★★ |
| *Billy Elliot* | 8 | 1.46 | 104 | ★★★★★ |
| *City Slickers* | 5 | 0.67 | 208 | ★★★ |
| *Disney's The Kid* | 8 | 0.83 | 23 | ★★★ |
| *Fields of Dreams* | 5 | 1.11 | 245 | ★★★★ |

| Category and Title | Study # | Avg. Rating | # of Raters | Guide Rating |
|---|---|---|---|---|
| Glengarry Glen Ross | 8 | 0.96 | 82 | ★★★ |
| I Never Sang for My Father | 5 | 1.48 | 80 | ★★★★★ |
| Nothing in Common | 5 | 0.90 | 40 | ★★★ |
| October Sky | 5 | 1.31 | 48 | ★★★★★ |
| Rape of Richard Beck, The | 5 | 0.50 | 20 | ★★★ |
| Tootsie | 5 | 0.66 | 246 | ★★★ |
| Up in the Air | 12 | 1.06 | 84 | ★★★★ |
| **Obsessive-Compulsive Disorder** | | | | |
| As Good as It Gets | 5 | 1.16 | 267 | ★★★★ |
| Aviator, The | 12 | 0.99 | 102 | ★★★ |
| Matchstick Men | 12 | 0.77 | 35 | ★★★ |
| Waiting for Ronald | 12 | 0.00 | 6 | — |
| **Posttraumatic Stress Disorder** | | | | |
| Accused, The | 8 | 1.20 | 45 | ★★★★ |
| Angel Eyes | 8 | 0.23 | 13 | ★ |
| Beloved | 8 | 0.42 | 45 | ★★ |
| Born on the Fourth of July | 5 | 0.97 | 148 | ★★★ |
| Brothers | 12 | 0.95 | 21 | ★★★ |
| Client, The | 8 | 0.69 | 91 | ★★★ |
| Deer Hunter, The | 5 | 0.76 | 175 | ★★★ |
| Dry Land, The | 12 | 0.17 | 6 | — |
| Fearless | 8 | 1.17 | 12 | ★★★ |
| Fisher King, The | 8 | 0.97 | 100 | ★★★ |
| Full Metal Jacket | 5 | 0.52 | 103 | ★★★ |
| Ground Truth, The | 12 | 0.40 | 5 | — |
| Hurt Locker, The | 12 | 0.31 | 111 | ★★ |
| In the Valley of Elah | 12 | 1.41 | 37 | ★★★★★ |
| Legend of Bagger Vance, The | 8 | 0.37 | 86 | ★★ |
| Messenger, The | 12 | 1.21 | 19 | ★★★ |
| Reign Over Me | 12 | 0.86 | 14 | ★★★ |
| War at Home, The | 12 | 0.57 | 7 | — |
| **Pregnancy** | | | | |
| Baby M. | 5 | 0.00 | 13 | ★ |
| Father of the Bride II | 5 | 0.12 | 92 | ★ |
| Juno | 12 | 1.16 | 146 | ★★★★ |
| Knocked Up | 12 | 0.10 | 96 | ★ |
| Next Best Thing, The | 8 | −0.56 | 9 | — |
| Nine Months | 5 | 0.02 | 41 | ★ |
| Steel Magnolias | 5 | 0.77 | 168 | ★★★ |

| Category and Title | Study # | Avg. Rating | # of Raters | Guide Rating |
|---|---|---|---|---|
| *Where the Heart Is* | 8 | 0.92 | 12 | ★★★ |
| **Schizophrenia** | | | | |
| *Beautiful Mind, A* | 8 | 1.29 | 214 | ★★★★★ |
| *Benny and Joon* | 5 | 0.97 | 93 | ★★★ |
| *Birdy* | 5 | 1.18 | 66 | ★★★★ |
| *Canvas* | 12 | 0.17 | 6 | — |
| *Fisher King, The* | 5 | 1.02 | 150 | ★★★★ |
| *Mad Love* | 5 | 0.06 | 17 | ★ |
| *Proof* | 12 | 1.04 | 23 | ★★★★ |
| *Shine* | 5 | 1.14 | 149 | ★★★★ |
| *Spider* | 12 | 0.50 | 10 | ★★★ |
| *Soloist, The* | 12 | 1.41 | 82 | ★★★★★ |
| **Substance Abuse (also see Addictive Disorders)** | | | | |
| *21 Grams* | 12 | 1.03 | 30 | ★★★★ |
| *28 Days* | 8 | 0.73 | 55 | ★★★ |
| *Blow* | 8 | 0.88 | 49 | ★★★ |
| *Bright Lights, Big City* | 8 | 0.90 | 10 | ★★★ |
| *Cat on a Hot Tin Roof* | 5 | 0.99 | 171 | ★★★ |
| *Clean and Sober* | 5 | 1.19 | 90 | ★★★★ |
| *Crazy Heart* | 12 | 0.73 | 11 | ★★★ |
| *Days of Wine and Roses* | 5 | 1.37 | 167 | ★★★★★ |
| *Down to the Bone* | 12 | −0.14 | 7 | — |
| *Drugstore Cowboy* | 5 | 0.75 | 76 | ★★★ |
| *Fighter, The* | 12 | 1.25 | 64 | ★★★★★ |
| *Gia* | 8 | 0.60 | 10 | ★★★ |
| *Half Nelson* | 12 | 0.79 | 14 | ★★★ |
| *House of Sand and Fog* | 12 | 1.02 | 47 | ★★★★ |
| *Hustle and Flow* | 12 | 0.86 | 21 | ★★★ |
| *Ironweed* | 8 | 1.00 | 26 | ★★★★ |
| *Leaving Las Vegas* | 5 | 0.88 | 154 | ★★★ |
| *Lost Weekend, The* | 8 | 1.38 | 77 | ★★★★★ |
| *Love Lisa* | 12 | 0.29 | 7 | — |
| *MacArthur Park* | 12 | 0.62 | 13 | ★★★ |
| *Mask* | 5 | 0.89 | 121 | ★★★ |
| *My Name is Bill W* | 5 | 1.22 | 54 | ★★★★ |
| *Postcards from the Edge* | 5 | 0.68 | 108 | ★★★ |
| *Prize Winner of Defiance, Ohio, The* | 12 | 0.92 | 12 | ★★★ |
| *Rachel Getting Married* | 12 | 1.16 | 43 | ★★★★ |
| *Ray* | 12 | 0.93 | 55 | ★★★ |

| Category and Title | Study # | Avg. Rating | # of Raters | Guide Rating |
|---|---|---|---|---|
| Requiem for a Dream | 12 | 1.35 | 34 | ★★★★★ |
| Spun | 12 | 0.40 | 5 | — |
| Traffic | 8 | 1.03 | 121 | ★★★★ |
| Walk the Line | 12 | 1.02 | 84 | ★★★★ |
| When a Man Loves a Woman | 5 | 1.03 | 80 | ★★★★ |
| When Love Is Not Enough | 12 | 0.50 | 8 | — |
| **Suicide** | | | | |
| Dead Poets Society | 8 | 1.14 | 218 | ★★★★ |
| Eternal High | 12 | 0.00 | 6 | — |
| Field, The | 8 | 1.20 | 5 | — |
| Hospital, The | 8 | 1.00 | 21 | ★★★★ |
| Hours, The | 12 | 1.08 | 50 | ★★★★ |
| House of Sand and Fog | 12 | 1.17 | 48 | ★★★★ |
| Inside Moves | 12 | 0.44 | 9 | — |
| Last Tango in Paris | 8 | 0.15 | 92 | ★ |
| Love Lisa | 12 | 0.57 | 7 | — |
| 'Night, Mother | 5 | 1.10 | 42 | ★★★★ |
| Ordinary People | 8 | 1.56 | 229 | ★★★★★ |
| Self-Made Man, The | 12 | 0.20 | 5 | — |
| Slender Thread, The | 5 | 0.94 | 16 | ★★★ |
| Virgin Suicides, The | 8 | 1.00 | 23 | ★★★★ |
| **Teenagers and Parenting** | | | | |
| Breakfast Club, The | 5 | 1.16 | 198 | ★★★★ |
| Bronx Tale, A | 8 | 1.17 | 29 | ★★★★ |
| Circle of Friends | 5 | 1.11 | 71 | ★★★★ |
| Dead Poets Society | 5 | 1.23 | 275 | ★★★★ |
| Good Will Hunting | 5 | 1.03 | 275 | ★★★★ |
| Little Women | 5 | 1.10 | 156 | ★★★★ |
| My Bodyguard | 5 | 0.83 | 93 | ★★★ |
| Pretty in Pink | 5 | 0.63 | 102 | ★★★ |
| Powder | 5 | 0.66 | 47 | ★★★ |
| St. Elmo's Fire | 5 | 0.49 | 121 | ★★ |
| Sixteen Candles | 5 | 0.62 | 97 | ★★★ |
| Splendor in the Grass | 5 | 0.71 | 82 | ★★★ |
| Stand by Me | 5 | 1.35 | 185 | ★★★★★ |
| Thirteen | 12 | 1.13 | 31 | ★★★★ |
| **Violent Youth** | | | | |
| Bowling for Columbine | 12 | 1.13 | 78 | ★★★★ |
| City of God | 12 | 0.25 | 28 | ★★ |

| Category and Title | Study # | Avg. Rating | # of Raters | Guide Rating |
|---|---|---|---|---|
| Elephant | 12 | 0.92 | 13 | ★★★ |
| Good Son, The | 8 | 0.50 | 16 | ★★★ |
| Holes | 12 | 0.69 | 32 | ★★★ |
| This Boy's Life | 8 | 1.15 | 13 | ★★★ |
| United States of Leland, The | 12 | 0.60 | 10 | ★★★ |
| **Women's Issues** | | | | |
| Eating | 5 | 1.00 | 26 | ★★★★ |
| Fried Green Tomatoes | 8 | 1.19 | 223 | ★★★★ |
| How to Make an American Quilt | 5 | 1.02 | 102 | ★★★★ |
| Iron Jawed Angels | 12 | 0.92 | 12 | ★★★ |
| League of Their Own, A | 5 | 1.18 | 190 | ★★★★ |
| My Breast | 5 | 0.70 | 10 | ★★★ |
| Piano, The | 5 | 0.88 | 235 | ★★★ |
| Thelma and Louise | 5 | 0.63 | 244 | ★★★ |
| Turning Point, The | 8 | 1.16 | 97 | ★★★★ |
| Working Girl | 8 | 0.69 | 126 | ★★★ |

# REFERENCES

Ackerson, J., Scogin, F., McKendree-Smith, N., & Lyman, R. D. (1998). Cognitive bibliotherapy for mild and moderate adolescent depressive symptomatology. *Journal of Consulting and Clinical Psychology, 66,* 685–690.

Adams, S. J., & Pitre, N. (2000). Who uses bibliotherapy and why? A survey from an underserviced area. *Canadian Journal of Psychiatry, 45,* 645–649.

Albom, M. (1997). *Tuesdays with Morrie.* New York: Doubleday.

Andersson, G., Carlbring, P., & Grimlund, A. (2008). Predicting treatment outcome in internet versus face to face treatment of panic disorder. *Computers in Human Behavior, 24,* 1790–1801.

Andersson, G., & Cuijpers, P. (2009). Internet-based and other computerized psychological treatments for adult depression: A meta-analysis. *Cognitive and Behavior Therapy, 38,* 196–205.

APA (American Psychological Association) Task Force on Evidence-Based Practice. (2006). Evidence-based practice in psychology. *American Psychologist, 61,* 271–285.

Apodaca, T. R., & Miller, W. R. (2003). A meta-analysis of the effectiveness of bibliotherapy for alcohol problems. *Journal of Clinical Psychology, 59,* 289–304.

Baillie, A. J., & Rapee, R. M. (2004). Predicting who benefits from psychoeducation and self help for panic attacks. *Behaviour Research & Therapy, 42,* 513–527.

Barak, A., Hen, L., Boniel-Nissim, M., & Shapira, N. (2008). A comprehensive review and meta-analysis of the effectiveness of Internet-based psychotherapeutic interventions. *Journal of Technology in Human Services, 26,* 109–160.

Barlow, S. H., Burlingame, G. M., Nebeker, R. S., & Anderson, E. (1999). Meta-analysis of medical self-help groups. *International Journal of Group Psychotherapy, 50,* 53–69.

Bass, E., & Davis, L. (1994). *The courage to heal* (3rd ed.). New York: Harper Perennial.

Bayley, J. (1999). *Elegy for Iris.* New York: St. Martin.

Bechtoldt, H., Norcross, J. C., Wyckoff, L. A., Pokrywa, M. L., & Campbell, L. F. (2001). Theoretical orientations and employment settings of clinical and counseling psychologists: A comparative study. *The Clinical Psychologist, 54*(1), 3–6.

Beck, A. T. (1976). *Cognitive therapy and the emotional disorders.* New York: International Universities Press.

Bogart, D. (2011). *Library and book trade almanac.* Medford, NJ: Information Today.

Brown, B. S., O'Grady, K. E., Farrell, E. V., Flechner, I. S., & Nurco, D. N. (2001). Factors associated with frequency of 12-step attendance by drug abuse clients. *American Journal of Drug and Alcohol Abuse, 27,* 147–160.

Burns, D. (1999). *Feeling good: The new mood therapy.* New York: Avon.

Campbell, L. F., & Smith, T. P. (2003). Integrating self-help books into psychotherapy. *Journal of Clinical Psychology: In Session, 59,* 177–186.

Carlbring, P., Westling, B. E., & Andersson, G. (2000). A review of published self-help books for panic disorder. *Scandinavian Journal of Behaviour Therapy, 29,* 5–13.

Centers for Disease Control. (2011). *Understanding bullying.* Factsheet available at www.cdc.gov/ViolencePrevention/pub/understanding_bullying.html

Clifford, J. S., Norcross, J. C., & Sommer, R. (1999). Autobiographies of mental health clients: Psychologists' uses and recommendations. *Professional Psychology: Research and Practice, 30,* 56–59.

Clum, G. A. (1990). *Coping with panic.* Pacific Grove, CA: Brooks/Cole.

Comer, J. P., & Poussaint, A. E. (1992). *Raising Black children.* New York: Plume.

Connors, G. J., Tonigan, S., & Miller, W. R. (2001). *Religiosity and responsiveness to alcoholism treatments.* Bethesda, MD: Department of Health and Human Services.

Craske, M. G., & Barlow, D. H. (2000). *Mastery of your anxiety and panic III.* Albany, NY: Graywind.

Cuijpers, P. (1997). Bibliotherapy in unipolar depression: A meta-analysis. *Journal of Behavior Therapy and Experimental Psychiatry, 28,* 139–147.

Cuijpers, P. (1998). A psychoeducational approach to the treatment of depression: A meta-analysis of Lewinsohn's "Coping with Depression" course. *Behavior Therapy, 29,* 521–533.

Cuijpers, P., Donker, T., van Straten, A., & Andersson, G. (2010). Is guided self-help as effective as face-to-face psychotherapy for depression and anxiety disorders? A systematic review and meta-analysis of comparative studies. *Psychological Medicine, 40,* 1943–1957.

Davis, R., & Miller, L. (1999, July 15). Millions comb the web for medical information. *USA Today.*

Den Boer, P. C. A. M., Wiersma, D., & Van Den Bosch, R. J. (2004). Why is self-help neglected in the treatment of emotional disorders? A meta-analysis. *Psychological Medicine, 34,* 959–971.

DeVoe, J. F., & Kaffenberger, S. (2005). Student reports of bullying: results from the 2001 school crime supplement to the national crime victimization survey (NCES 2005–310). U.S. Department of Education, National Center for Education Statistics. Washington, DC: U.S. Government Printing Office.

Druss, B. G., & Rosencheck, R. A. (2000). Use of practitioner-based complementary therapies by persons reporting mental conditions in the United States. *Archives of General Psychiatry, 57,* 708–714.

Eisenberg, D. M., Davis, R. B., Ettner, S. L., Appel, S., Wilkey, S., Rompay, M. V., & Kessler, R. C. (1998). Trends in alternative medicine use in the United States, 1990–1997. *Journal of the American Medical Association, 280,* 1575–1589.

Elger, F. J., & McGrath, P. J. (2003). Self-administered psychosocial treatments for children and families. *Journal of Clinical Psychology, 59,* 321–339.

Elkins, G., Marcus, J., Rajab, M. H., & Durgam, S. (2005). Complementary and alternative therapy use by psychotherapy clients. *Psychotherapy, 42,* 232–235.

Ellis, A., & Velton, E. (1992). *When AA doesn't work for you: Rational steps to quitting alcohol.* Fort Lee, NJ: Barricade.

Fairburn, C. G. (1995). *Overcoming binge eating.* New York: Guilford.

Fanning, P., & O'Neill, J. (1997). *The addiction workbook: A step-by-step guide to quitting alcohol and drugs.* New York: Fine.

Febbraro, G. A. R., Clum, G. A., Roodman, A. A., & Wright, J. H. (1999). The limits of bibliotherapy: A study of the differential effectiveness of self-administered interventions in individuals with panic attacks. *Behavior Therapy, 30,* 209–222.

Fleming, L. M., & Tobin, D. J. (2005). Popular child-rearing books: Where is Daddy? *Psychology of Men & Masculinity, 6,* 18–24.

Fried, S. B., & Schultis, G. A. (1995). *The best self-help and self-awareness books.* Chicago: American Library Association.

Gabbard, G. O., & Gabbard, K. (1999). *Psychiatry and the cinema* (2nd ed.). Washington, DC: American Psychiatric Press.

Gallego, J. M., & Emmelkamp, P. M. G. (2011). Effectiveness of Internet psychological treatments for mental health disorders. In L. L'Abate & D. A. Kaiser (Eds.), *Handbook of technology in psychology, psychiatry, and neurology.* New York: Nova Science.

Gatz, M. (2007). Genetics, dementia, and the elderly. *Current Directions in Psychological Science, 16,* 123–130.

Gergen, K. (1991). *The saturated self.* New York: Basic Books.

Goodman, G., & Jacobs, M. (1994). The self-help, mutual support group. In A. Fuhriman & G. Burlingame (Eds.), *Handbook of group psychotherapy* (pp. 489–526). New York: Wiley.

Gordon, T. (1975). *Parent effectiveness training.* New York: Random House.

Gould, R. A., & Clum, G. A. (1993). A meta-analysis of self-help treatment approaches. *Clinical Psychology Review, 13,* 169–186.

Gregory, R. J., Canning, S. S., Lee, T. W., & Wise, J. C. (2004). Cognitive bibiliotherapy for depression: A meta-analysis. *Professional Psychology: Research and Practice, 35,* 275–280.

Grohol, J. M. (1999) *The insider's guide to mental health resources online.* New York: Guilford Press.

Haeffel, G. J. (2010). When self-help is no help: Traditional cognitive skills training does not prevent depressive symptoms in people who ruminate. *Behaviour Research and Therapy, 48,* 152–157.

Hamill, P. (1995). *A drinking life: A memoir.* Boston: Little, Brown.

Harwood, T. M., & L'Abate, L. (2010). *Self-help in mental health.* New York: Springer.

Heiman, J., & LoPiccolo, J. (1988). *Becoming orgasmic: A sexual growth program for women* (Rev. ed.). New York: Prentice-Hall.

Hesley, J. W., & Hesley, J. G. (2001). *Rent two films and let's talk in the morning: Using popular movies in psychotherapy* (2nd ed.). New York: Wiley.

Hodges, J. Q., & Segal, S. P. (2002). Goal advancement among mental health self-help agency members. *Psychiatric Rehabilitation Journal, 26,* 78–85.

Jamison, K. R. (1999). *An unquiet mind.* New York: Random House.

Jamison, K. R. (2000). *Night falls fast.* New York: Random House.

Jason, L. A. (1985). Using the media to foster self-help groups. *Professional Psychology: Research and Practice, 16,* 455–464.

Jason, L. A., Tabon, D., Tait, E., Iacono, G., Goodman, D., Watkins- Farrell, P., & Huggins, G. (1988). The emergence of the inner city self-help center. *Journal of Community Psychology, 16,* 287–295.

Joshua, J. M., & DiMenna, D. (2000). *Read two books and let's talk next week.* New York: Wiley.

Kazdin, A. E., & Blasé, S. L. (2011). Rebooting psychotherapy research and practice to reduce the burden of mental illness. *Perspectives on Psychological Science, 6,* 21–37.

Kelly, J. F. (2003). Self-help for substance abuse disorders: History, effectiveness, knowledge gaps, and research opportunities. *Clinical Psychology Review, 23,* 639–663.

Kessler, R. C., Ustun, T. B., et al. (2004). Prevalence, severity, and unmet need for treatment of mental disorders in the World Health Organization world mental health surveys. *Journal of the American Medical Association, 291,* 2581–2590.

Kessler, R. C., Mickelson, K. D., & Zhao, S. (1997). Patterns and correlates of self-help group membership in the United States. *Social Policy, 27,* 27–46.

Kessler, R. C., Zhao, S., et al. (1999). Past-year use of outpatient services for psychiatric problems in the National Comorbidity Survey. *American Journal of Psychiatry, 156,* 115–123.

Klaw, E., & Humphreys, K. (2005). Facilitating client involvement in self-help groups. In G. P. Koocher, J. C. Norcross, & S. S. Hill (Eds.), *Psychologists' desk reference* (2nd ed.; pp. 502–506). New York: Oxford University Press.

Klingemann, H., Sobell, L., Barker, J., Blomqvist, J., Cloud, W., Ellinstad, T., Finfgeld, D., Granfield, R., Hodgings, D., Hunt, G., Junker, C., Moggi, F., Peele, S., Smart, R., Sobell, M., & Tucker, J. (2001). *Promoting self-change from problem substance abuse.* Boston: Kluwer.

Kownacki, R. J., & Shadish, W. R. (1999). Does Alcoholics Anonymous work? The results from a meta-analysis of controlled experiments. *Substance Use and Misuse, 34,* 1897–1916.

Kurtz, L. F. (1984). Linking treatment centers with Alcoholics Anonymous. *Social Work in Health Care, 9,* 85–95.

Kurtz, L. F. (1997). *Self-help and support groups.* Thousand Oaks, CA: Sage.

Kurtzweil, P. L., Scogin, F., & Rosen, G. M. (1996). A test of the fail-safe N for self-help programs. *Professional Psychology: Research and Practice, 27,* 629–630.

Kyrouz, E. M., Humphreys, K., & Loomis, C. (2002). A review of research on the effectiveness of self-help mutual aid groups. In B. J. White & E. J. Madara, *The self-help sourcebook: Your guide to community and online support groups* (6th ed., pp. 71–85). Cedar Knolls, NJ: American Self-Help Clearinghouse.

L'Abate, L. (Ed.). (2000). *Distance writing and computer-assisted interventions in psychiatry and mental health.* Westport, CT: Praeger.

L'Abate, L. (Ed.). (2004). *Using workbooks in mental health.* New York: Routledge.

L'Abate, L. (2010). *Low-cost approaches to promote physical and mental health: Theory, research, and practice.* New York: Springer.

Lampropoulos, G. K., Kazantzis, N., & Deane, F. P. (2004). Psychologists' use of motion pictures in clinical practice. *Professional Psychology: Research and Practice, 35,* 535–541.

Lawrence, S., & Giles, C. L. (1999). Accessibility of information on the web. *Nature, 400,* 107–109.

Lazarus, R. S. (2003). Does the positive psychology movement have legs? *Psychological Inquiry, 14,* 93–109.

Leon, K., & Angst, E. (2005). Portrayals of stepfamilies in film: Using media images in remarriage education. *Family Relations, 54,* 3–23.

Lewinsohn, P., Munoz, R., Youngren, M. A., & Zeiss, A. (1996). *Control your depression.* Englewood Cliffs, NJ: Prentice-Hall.

Lezak, M. D. (1995). *Neuropsychological assessment.* New York: Oxford University Press.

Lilienfeld, S. O. (1998). Pseudoscience in contemporary clinical psychology: What it is and what we can do about it. *The Clinical Psychologist, 51*(4), 3–9.

Lilienfeld, S. O., Lynn, S. J., & Lohr, J. M. (Eds.). (2003). *Science and pseudoscience in clinical psychology.* New York: Guilford.

Lissman, T. L., & Boehnlein, J. K. (2001). A critical review of Internet information about depression. *Psychiatric Services, 52,* 1046–1050.

Mace, N., & Rabins, P. (1999). *The 36-hour day: A family guide to caring for persons with Alzheimer's disease, related dementing illness and memory loss in later life* (3rd ed.). Baltimore: Johns Hopkins University.

Mains, J. A., & Scogin, F. R. (2003). The effectiveness of self-administered treatments: A practice-friendly review of the research. *Journal of Clinical Psychology, 59,* 237–246.

Mankowski, E. S., Humphreys, K., & Moos, R. H. (2001). Individual and contextual predictors of involvement in twelve-step self-help groups after substance abuse treatment. *American Journal of Community Psychology, 29,* 537–563.

MarketResearch.com. (2011). The US market for self-improvement products & services. Marketdata Enterprises Inc. Accessed 11/18/11. www.marketresearch.com

Marks, I. M., Cavanagh, K., & Gega, L. (2007). *Hands-on help: Computer-aided psychotherapy.* New York: Psychology Press.

Marrs, R. W. (1995). A meta-analysis of bibliotherapy studies. *American Journal of Community Psychology, 23,* 843–870.

Menchola, M., Arkowitz, H. S., & Burke, B. L. (2007). Efficacy of self-administered treatments for depression and anxiety. *Professional Psychology, 38,* 421–429.

Morgenstern, J., Labouvie, E., McCrady, B. S., Kahler, C. W., & Frey, R. M. (1997). Affiliation with Alcoholics Anonymous after treatment: A study of its therapeutic effects and mechanisms of action. *Journal of Consulting and Clinical Psychology, 65,* 768–777.

Morin, C. M., Hauri, P. J., Espie, C. A., Spielman, A. J., Buysee, D. J., & Bootzin, R. R. (1999). Nonpharmacologic treatment of chronic insomnia: An American Academy of Sleep Medicine review. *Sleep, 22*(8), 134–1156.

Murray, E., Burns, J., See Tai, S., Lai, R., & Nazareth, I. (2004). Interactive health communication applications for people with chronic disease. *The Cochrane Database of Systematic Reviews, 4,* Article No.: CD004274. pub2. DOI: 10.1002/14651858.CD004274.pub2.

Nathan, D. (2011). *Sybil exposed: The extraordinary story behind the famous multiple personality case.* New York: Free Press.

Newman, M. G. (Ed.). (2004). Technology in psychotherapy [Special issue]. *Journal of Clinical Psychology: In Session, 60*(2).

Norcross, J. C. (2000). Here comes the self-help revolution in mental health. *Psychotherapy, 37,* 370–377.

Norcross, J. C. (2006). Integrating self-help into psychotherapy: 16 practical suggestions. *Professional Psychology: Research & Practice, 37,* 683–693.

Norcross, J. C. (Ed.). (2011). *Psychotherapy relationships that work: Evidence-based responsiveness* (2nd ed.). New York: Oxford University Press.

Norcross, J. C., Hedges, M., & Prochaska, J. O. (2002). The face of 2010: A Delphi poll on the future of psychotherapy. *Professional Psychology: Research and Practice, 33,* 316–322.

Norcross, J. C., Hogan, T. P., & Koocher, G. P. (2008). *Clinician's guide to evidence-based practices: Mental health and the addictions.* New York: Oxford University Press.

Norcross, J. C., Santrock, J. W., Campbell, L. F., Smith, T. S., Sommer, R., & Zuckerman, E. L. (2000). *Authoritative guide to self-help resources in mental health.* New York: Guilford.

Norcross, J. C., Santrock, J. W., Campbell, L. F., Smith, T. S., Sommer, R., & Zuckerman, E. L. (2003). *Authoritative guide to self-help resources in mental health* (2nd ed.). New York: Guilford.

Norcross, J. C., Sommer, R., & Clifford, J. S. (2001). Incorporating published autobiographies into the abnormal psychology course. *Teaching of Psychology, 28,* 125–128.

Nordgreen, T., & Havik, O. E. (2011). Use of self-help materials for anxiety and depression in mental health services: A national survey of psychologists in Norway. *Professional Psychology, 42,* 185–191.

O'Conner, E. P., & Kratochwill, T. R. (1999). Self-help interventions: The reported practices of school psychologists. *Professional Psychology: Research and Practice, 30,* 147–153.

Ouimette, P. C., Finney, J. W., & Moos, R. H. (1997). Twelve-step and cognitive-behavioral treatment for substance abuse: A comparison of treatment effectiveness. *Journal of Consulting and Clinical Psychology, 65,* 230–240.

Paul, A. M. (2001, March/April). Self-help: Shattering the myths. *Psychology Today,* 58–68.

Pew Internet and American Life Project. (2010). *Internet Health Resources.* www.pewinternet.org/reports/toc.asp?Report=95

Pizzo, P. A., & Clark, N. M. (2012). Alleviating Suffering 101: Pain relief in the United States. *New England Journal of Medicine, 366,* 97–199.

Prochaska, J. O., Norcross, J. C., & DiClemente, C. C. (1995). *Changing for good.* New York: Avon.

Project MATCH Research Group. (1997). Matching alcoholism treatments to client heterogeneity: Project MATCH posttreatment drinking outcomes. *Journal of Studies on Alcohol, 58,* 7–29.

Rains, S. A., & Young, V. (2009). A meta-analysis of research on formal computer-mediated support groups: Examining group characteristics and health outcomes. *Human Communication Research, 35,* 311–330.

Reavley, N. J., & Jorm, A. F. (2011). The quality of mental disorder information websites: A review. *Patient Education and Counseling, 85,* e16–e25.

Redding, R. E., Herbert, J. D., Forman, E. M., & Gaudiano, B.A. (2008). Popular self-help books for anxiety, depression, and trauma: How scientifically grounded and useful are they? *Professional Psychology, 39,* 537–545.

Richards, D., & Richardson, T. (2012). Computer-based psychological treatments for depression: A systematic review and meta-analysis. *Clinical Psychology Review, 32,* 329–342.

Riessman, F., & Carrol, D. (1995). *Redefining self-help: Policy and practice.* San Francisco, CA: Jossey-Bass.

Riper, H., Spek, V., Boon, B., Conijn, B., Kramer, J., Martin-Abello, K., & Smit, F. (2011). Effectiveness of e-self-help interventions for curbing adult problem drinking: A meta-analysis. *Journal of Medical Internet Research, 13,* e42.

Rosen, G. M. (1987). Self-help treatment books and the commercialization of psychotherapy. *American Psychologist, 42,* 46–51.

Rosen, G. M. (1993). Self-help or hype? Comments on psychology's failure to advance self-care. *Professional Psychology: Research and Practice, 24,* 340–345.

Rosen, G. M. (2004). Remembering the 1978 and 1990 task forces on self-help therapies. *Journal of Clinical Psychology, 60*, 111–113.

Rosen, G. M., Glasgow, R. E., & Moore, T. E. (2003). Self-help therapy: The science and business of giving psychology away. In S. O. Lilienfeld, S. J. Lynn, & J. M. Lohr (Eds.), *Science and pseudoscience in clinical psychology* (pp. 399–424). New York: Guilford.

Rosen, R. D. (1977). *Psychobabble*. New York: Atheneum.

Rychtarik, R. G., Connors, G. J., Dermen, K. H., & Stasiewicz, P. R. (2000). Alcoholics Anonymous and the use of medications to prevent relapse: An anonymous survey of member attitudes. *Journal of Studies on Alcohol, 61*, 134–138.

Salzer, M. S., Rappaport, J., & Segre, L. (2001). Mental health professionals' support of self-help groups. *Journal of Community and Applied Social Psychology, 11*, 1–10.

Santrock, J. W., Minnett, A. M., & Campbell, B. D. (1994). *The authoritative guide to self-help books*. New York: Guilford Press.

Schencker, M. (2009). *A clinician's guide to 12-step recovery*. New York: Norton.

Scogin, F. (1998). Bibliotherapy: A nontraditional intervention for depression. In P. E. Hartman-Stein et al. (Eds.), *Innovative behavioral healthcare for older adults: A guidebook for changing times* (pp. 129–144). San Francisco: Jossey-Bass.

Scogin, F., Floyd, M., Jamison, C., Ackerson, J., Landreville, P., & Bissonnette, L. (1996). Negative outcomes: What is the evidence on self-administered treatments? *Journal of Consulting and Clinical Psychology, 64*, 1086–1089.

Scogin, F. R. (Ed.). (2003). Special section: The status of self-administered treatments. *Journal of Clinical Psychology, 59*, 247–349.

Seligman, M. E. P. (1995). The effectiveness of psychotherapy. *American Psychologist, 50*, 965–974.

Sisson, R. W., & Mallams, J. H. (1981). The use of systematic encouragement and community access procedures to increase attendance at Alcoholics Anonymous and Al-Anon meetings. *American Journal of Drug and Alcohol Abuse, 8*, 371–376.

Skow, J. (1999). Lost in cyberspace. *Time*, p. 61.

Solomon, G. (1995). *The motion picture prescription*. Santa Rosa, CA: Aslan.

Sommer, R., Clifford, J. S., & Norcross, J. C. (1998). A bibliography of mental patients' autobiographies: An update and classification system. *American Journal of Psychiatry, 155*, 1261–1264.

Swanson, S. A., Crow, S. J., LeGrange, D., Swendsen, J., & Merikangas, K. R. (2011). Prevalence and correlates of eating disorders in adolescents: Results from the National Comorbidity Survey Replication Adolescent Supplement. *Archives of General Psychiatry, 68*, 714–723.

Swindle, R., Heller, K., Pescosolido, B., & Kikuzawa, S. (2000). Responses to nervous breakdowns in America over a 40-year period. *American Psychologist, 55*, 740–749.

Tonigan, J. S., Toscoova, R., & Miller, W. R. (1995). Meta-analysis of the literature on Alcoholics Anonymous: Sample and study characteristics moderate findings. *Journal of Studies on Alcohol, 57*, 65–72.

*Twelve Steps and Twelve Traditions*. (1995). New York: Alcoholics Anonymous World Services.

U.S. Department of Justice Bureau of Statistics: Profile of State Prisoners Under Age 18, 1985–97 [On-line]. (June 16, 2002) Available at: www.ojp.usdoj.gov/bjs/abstract/pspa1897.htm

van Lankveld, J. J. D. M. (1998). Bibliotherapy in the treatment of sexual dysfunctions: A meta-analysis. *Journal of Consulting and Clinical Psychology, 66*, 702–708.

Van Tosh, L., & del Vecchio, P. (2000). *Consumer-operated self-help programs: A technical report*. Rockville, MD: U.S. Center for Mental Health Services.

Walters, G. D. (2000). Behavioral self-control training for problem drinkers: A meta-analysis of randomized clinical studies. *Behavior Therapy, 31*, 135–149.

Watkins, P. L., & Clum, G. A. (Eds.). (2008). *Handbook of self-help therapies*. New York: Routledge.

Wedding, D., & Boyd, M. A. (1999). *Movies and mental illness: Using films to understand psychopathology*. New York: McGraw-Hill.

Wedding, D., Boyd, M. A., & Niemiec, R. M. (2010). *Movies and mental illness* (3rd ed.). Cambridge, MA: Hogrefe.

Weekes, C. (1996). Bibliotherapy. In C. G. Lindemann (Ed.), *Handbook of the treatment of the anxiety disorders* (2nd ed., pp. 375–384). Northvale, NJ: Jason Aronson.

White, B. J., & Madara, E. J. (1995). *The self-help sourcebook* (5th ed.). Denville, NJ: American Self-Help Clearinghouse.

WHO World Mental Health Survey Consortium. (2004). Prevalence, severity, and unmet need for treatment of mental disorders in the World Health Organization world mental health surveys. *Journal of the American Medical Association, 291,* 2581–2590.

Williams, D. R. (2003). The health of men: Structured inequalities and opportunities. *American Journal of Public Health, 93,* 724–731.

Winzelberg, A., & Humphreys, K. (1999). Should patients' religious beliefs and practices influence clinicians' referral to 12-step self-help groups? Evidence from a study of 3,018 male substance abuse patients. *Journal of Consulting and Clinical Psychology, 67,* 790–794.

Zaccaria, J. S., & Moses, H. A. (1968). *Facilitating human development through reading.* Champaign, IL: Stipes.

# INDEX